RESEARCH HANDBOOK OF COMPARATIVE EMPLOYMENT RELATIONS

NEW HORIZONS IN MANAGEMENT

Series Editor: Cary L. Cooper, CBE, *Distinguished Professor of Organizational Psychology and Health, Lancaster University, UK*

This important series makes a significant contribution to the development of management thought. This field has expanded dramatically in recent years and the series provides an invaluable forum for the publication of high-quality work in management science, human resource management, organizational behaviour, marketing, management information systems, operations management, business ethics, strategic management and international management.

The main emphasis of the series is on the development and application of new original ideas. International in its approach, it will include some of the best theoretical and empirical work from both well-established researchers and the new generation of scholars.

Titles in the series include:

Research Handbook of Comparative Employment Relations

Edited by

Michael Barry

Griffith University, Australia

Adrian Wilkinson

Griffith University, Australia

NEW HORIZONS IN MANAGEMENT

Edward Elgar
Cheltenham, UK • Northampton, MA, USA

Published by
Edward Elgar Publishing Limited
The Lypiatts
15 Lansdown Road
Cheltenham
Glos GL50 2JA
UK

Edward Elgar Publishing, Inc.
William Pratt House
9 Dewey Court
Northampton
Massachusetts 01060
USA

Paperback edition 2013
Paperback edition reprinted 2016

A catalogue record for this book
is available from the British Library

Library of Congress Control Number: 2011922861

ISBN   978 1 84720 889 7 (cased)
        978 1 78100 044 1 (paperback)

Typeset by Servis Filmsetting Ltd, Stockport, Cheshire
Printed and bound in Great Britain by the CPI Group (UK) Ltd

Contents

Contributors

Maurizio Atzeni, Lecturer, Labour and Industrial Relations, School of Business and Economics, Loughborough University, UK

Lucio Baccaro, Professor, Département de Sociologie, Université de Genève, Switzerland

Michael Barry, Associate Professor and Head of Department, Employment Relations and Human Resources, Griffith Business School, Griffith University, Australia

David G. Collings, Senior Lecturer, International Management, Department of Management, J.E. Cairnes School of Business and Economics, NUI Galway, Ireland

Fang Lee Cooke, Professor, Human Resource Management and Chinese Studies, Department of Management, Monash University, Melbourne, Australia

Sean Cooney, Associate Professor, Associate Director (Taiwan), Asian Law Centre, Melbourne Law School, The University of Melbourne, Australia

Tony Dundon, Senior Lecturer, Employment Relations and Human Resource Management, Department of Management, J.E. Cairnes School of Business and Economics, NUI Galway, Ireland

Fernando Durán-Palma, Senior Lecturer, Department of Human Resource Management, University of Westminster, UK

Ingo Forstenlechner, Assistant Professor, Human Resources Management, Department of Business Administration, Arab Emirates University College of Business and Economics, United Arab Emirates

Peter Gahan, Associate Professor, Human Resource Management, Department of Management, Monash University, Melbourne, Australia

Pablo Ghigliani, Professor of Social History, Universidad Nacional de la Plata, Argentina

Patrick Gunnigle, Professor, Business Studies, Department of Personnel and Employment Relations, Kemmy Business School, University of Limerick, Ireland

Hester Houwing, Expertise Advisor, Employee Insurance Services (Uitvoeringsinstituut Werknemersverzekeringen UWV), Amsterdam, the Netherlands

Richard W. Hurd, Professor, Industrial and Labor Relations, Cornell University, ILR School, New York, USA

Terence Jackson, Professor of Cross Cultural Management, Middlesex University Business School, UK

EeHwan Jung, Professor, Sociology, Seoul National University of Technology, Korea

Bruce E. Kaufman, Professor of Economics, Andrew Young School of Policy Studies, Georgia State University, USA; Senior Research Fellow, Centre for Work, Organization, and Wellbeing, Griffith University, Australia; and Principal Research Fellow, Work and Employment Research Unit, University of Hertfordshire, UK

John Kelly, Professor, Employment Relations, Department of Management, Birkbeck, University of London, UK

Maarten Keune, Professor, University of Amsterdam, the Netherlands

Jonathan Lavelle, IRCHSS Post-doctoral Fellow, Department of Personnel and Employment Relations, Kemmy Business School, University of Limerick, Ireland

Kamel Mellahi, Professor of Strategic Management, The University of Warwick Business School and University of Sheffield, UK

Richard Mitchell, Professor, Department of Business Law and Taxation, Monash University, Melbourne, Australia

Philippe Pochet, General Director, European Trade Union Institute, Belgium

Tony Royle, Lecturer, Department of Management, J.E. Cairnes School of Business and Economics, NUI Galway, Ireland

Sara Slinn, Associate Professor, Osgoode Hall Law School, York University, Toronto, Canada

Kurt Vandaele, Senior Researcher, European Trade Union Institute, Belgium

Nick Wailes, Associate Professor, Work and Organisational Studies, The University of Sydney, Australia

Adrian Wilkinson, Professor and Director, Centre for Work, Organisation and Wellbeing, Griffith University, Australia

Geoffrey Wood, Professor, Human Resource Management, School of Management, University of Sheffield, UK

Stefan Zagelmeyer, Professor, Economics and Human Resource Management, International University of Applied Sciences Bad Honnef-Bonn, Germany

PART 1

INTRODUCTION

1 Re-examining comparative employment relations

Michael Barry and Adrian Wilkinson

INTRODUCTION

Our starting point for this project is the belief that the field of comparative employment relations is underdeveloped and lacks integration. Our intention in producing this book is to provide a comprehensive volume of studies that examines the regulation of the employment relationship across a range of issues, in a wide variety of settings. In addition we want to show how a range of different intellectual perspectives can be usefully employed to help us understand this field.

As Bean (1985) noted, the two dominant employment relations comparative approaches are either the selection of a number of countries or of a number of employment relations themes. There are a number of texts that compare employment relations themes across different countries (e.g., Bean, 1985; Eaton, 2000). However, the extent of comparison in some of these texts is patchy or underdeveloped. Some thematic comparative texts deliberately focus on a single (or small selection of) issues(s). Notable among these are editions that examine the comparative fortunes of trade unions, and efforts to revive unions in different national contexts (Fairbrother and Yates, 2003; Frege and Kelly, 2004; Verma and Kochan, 2004; Frege, 2007).

Another common theme of comparative studies can be referred to as 'learning from abroad'. Studies included in this approach have focused on the employment components of so-called high performance work systems, in countries such as Japan and Germany (Eaton, 2000; Jacoby, 2005). The possibility that certain employment practices could be transplanted from one system to another to achieve similar levels of performance has generated considerable interest in learning from abroad. Perhaps most notably, researchers at MIT heralded the system of 'lean production' in the Japanese auto industry as the prototype of a high performance work system (Womack et al., 1990).

Claims such as this have led to attempts to benchmark 'best practice' and have created pressure on actors to adopt changes to existing practices (Delbridge et al., 1995). Although managerial support for benchmarking

3

best practice has attained a normative status that makes resistance difficult, proponents of learning from abroad have been subject to criticism for discounting the cultural and institutional impediments to transplantation (e.g., Berggren, 1993).

The alternative approach to comparing employment relations themes is to select a number of countries as comparators. Country-based studies often canvass a number of employment issues, but may lack systematic comparison of these issues across the selected countries. In effect, this type of approach makes these single country collections more international employment relations texts rather than comparative employment relations texts (e.g., Bamber et al., 2010). There are also texts that cover a number of countries but only within a particular region, such as Europe (Hyman and Ferner, 1994) or Asia and the South Pacific (Bamber et al., 2000).

OUR APPROACH

One of the limitations of the field of employment relations is said to be that it lacks a theoretical core. As Dunlop (1958) famously observed of the study of industrial relations, 'facts have outrun theory', or as Coase (1984, p. 230) claimed, 'without a theory they had nothing to pass on except a mass of descriptive material waiting for a theory or a fire'. We believe that any attempt to claim a theoretical core is inherently problematic because employment relations can properly be approached from a range of different perspectives. We note that a number of important contributions to the comparative employment relations literature come from scholars who are not designated as employment relations specialists but, rather, are interested in examining issues of 'labour' and 'employment' from related disciplinary fields such as political economy, labour law, institutional economics, comparative politics, and so on.

We have attempted to highlight what we consider to be the dominant perspectives informing the study of comparative employment relations. Perspectives are discussed in Part 2 of the book. Our contention is that each perspective offers valuable insights, and that the multi-disciplinary nature of the subject should be seen as a strength, rather than the difficulties of determining a common theoretical core being viewed as an endemic weakness of the field.

Part 2 includes perspectives that have been or could be important frames of reference for contributors to comparative employment relations and are summarized below. The bulk of the comparative research in the discipline of industrial/employment relations falls under an institutional perspective. Originating in the studies of authors such as John Commons in the

US and the Webbs in the UK, the continuing emphasis in this field is on the role of rule-making to mediate divergences of interest between capital and labour. Patterns of institutional employment relations that attract considerable attention include developments in employee (and to a lesser extent employer) representation, and the role of the state in creating and recreating institutional regulatory architecture. Here, the classic approach to comparison has been to examine the extent to which observable changes in patterns of employment relations can be seen as providing evidence of a common convergence in national employment relations systems. What commonly emerges is a mixed picture of convergence (see, for example, Wailes et al., 2008).

In *Converging Divergences*, Katz and Darbishire (2000) found that within very distinct national systems there was a considerable degree of convergence in both union decline and income inequality. Thus, neo-institutionalists in industrial relations and in comparative politics/political economy assert that while numerous studies have demonstrated convergence, there are also examples of persistent variations at the national level to this common pattern (including, the maintenance of very high levels of unionization in parts of Scandinavia). There are also variations in the extent to which convergence patterns actually affect how the employment relationship is regulated. To take unionization as an example, it is arguable that the capacity of French unions to mobilize at very low levels of unionization is greater than that of other union movements to do so in nations with higher levels of union density. This points to a problem with descriptive comparisons of differences in institutional arrangements across nations. Such description cannot explain the capacity of labour market actors to shape the contested 'regulatory space' within which they operate because this capacity reflects not only institutional measures, such as union density and collective bargaining coverage, but also broader socioeconomic and cultural factors, as well as patterns of historical development, which themselves mediate the processes of institutional change (Hancher and Moran, 1989; Thelen, 2009).

Intuitionalists and neo-institutionalists have constructed overarching categorizations of regulatory systems to help guide comparative analysis of similarities and differences in work and employment relations across countries. Albert (1993) identified key differences between an Anglo-Saxon model of employment relations and a Rhineland model, arguing, for example, that because Germany could not follow a path of competitive price adjustment it needs to develop a high-quality approach built on a particular structure of regulation. More recently, the varieties of capitalism (VoC) literature has come as an important advance in comparative business systems analysis, and has sparked, from a neo-institutionalist perspective, renewed interest in understanding the basis for national diversity. In developing the VoC framework, Hall and Soskice (2001) saw firms as crucial regulatory agents, however, they also noted that the key regulatory systems operate largely at the level of the nation state. The starting point for these scholars is that nations can be categorized into different varieties of capitalism according to how they resolve fundamental coordination problems in the areas of vocational training and education, corporate governance and employment/industrial relations.

VoC groups countries under two distinct varieties of capitalism, the liberal market economy (LME) and coordinated market economy (CME) models. VoC defines LMEs as countries with strong market relations, where employment relations systems are defined by high levels of flexibility with regard to matters pertaining to hiring and firing and payment systems. In CME countries, industry associations act as strong non-market forms of regulation, preventing such high levels of labour flexibility. In these countries, the wide coverage of collective agreements across firms provides for greater standardization, which lessens wages competition, and limits labour poaching. These non-competitive behaviours are reinforced by greater guarantees of employment security in CME countries that (as noted elsewhere) also encourage firms and employees to invest in specific skills (see Mares, 2003). Thus, whereas in LME countries markets resolve coordination problems, in CME nations interlocking systems of industrial relations, training and education and corporate governance (that provide board-level representation for labour) prevent the types of employment relations opportunism that are typical of LME countries. In LME countries, employment relations opportunism is a function of the greater capacity of the system of labour market regulation to generate flexibility. Flexibility is itself essential because the ability of firms to raise capital is dependent on current profitability, which in turn requires greater capacity for labour adjustment.

Following publication of the Hall and Soskice volume, there has been a burgeoning literature on varieties of capitalism. A number of contributions to this literature have criticized the capacity of VoC as an analytical tool. Some have charged that by proffering two distinct models, VoC creates a polar diversity that is overly deterministic, and that this might lead to the mis-classification of some countries that exist along, rather than at either end of, the LME–CME spectrum. A related criticism is that VoC does not allow for processes of institutional change that might cause countries to transition between these ideal types. In this sense the model is static in as much as it characterizes economies at one point in time without having the capacity to explain how in the case of some countries, dramatic processes of change over relatively short periods might lead to diverging views about the status of an economy as either an LME or CME proxy (e.g., Lane, 2005 on Germany and Briggs, 2006 on Australia). Yet another criticism is that the model is focused too heavily on institutional structures and does not account for the role that underlying interests play in shaping institutional structures and outcomes (Wailes et al., 2008).

The focus on the role institutions (within national systems of regulation) play in retarding the common convergence pressures associated with globalization has also led to a tendency to downplay the significance of regional patterns of employment relations (ER) variation. According to Hyman (2004), employment relations is ethnocentric, which enables the development of 'theories in' but not 'theories of' employment relations. For Hyman, any attempt to develop theory within the field of ER needs to take account of the regional diversity (or context) of ER systems, and through comparison, it is then possible to discern patterns of difference and similarity across relevant issues leading to the testing of hypotheses.

In assessing the contribution of the institutional and neo-institutional perspective, Bruce Kaufman, in Chapter 2, throws the net wide in offering a review of a process of theory development that Hyman described, provocatively, as 'neither possible nor desirable'. Kaufman's analysis suggests that while theory in comparative ER may be difficult, it is not damned to eternal confusion. He crisply draws out the key controversies and questions, providing a big picture summary of the field from a historical perspective. Amongst his critical contributions are a suggestion that three views of the key dependent variable in comparative economic relations have emerged: one that he calls the institutional architecture of systems (such as the degree of centralization of wage determination), second, outcomes or behaviour from an employment relations perspective, such as union density, and third, macro-performance-related variables, such as GDP or unemployment. He also distinguishes usefully between comparative employment relations and international employment relations. Kaufman suggests that the proper domain of comparative employment relations is the comparison of two or more distinct employment systems across two or more countries, with the intent to delineate differences and similarities and generate theoretical outcomes. International employment relations studies on a case-by-case basis employment systems in different countries, with less of an emphasis on comparisons and more on description. Kaufman tartly remarks that while employment relations internationally may or may not be converging, theory undoubtedly is. 'Nearly all participants agree that an explanation of cross-national variation . . . is crucial', he notes, and equally, there is considerable consensus on the critical variables in explaining employment relations diversity.

John Kelly, in Chapter 3, assesses developments in employment relations from a political economy perspective. In doing so he poses an 'intellectual challenge' to scholars within employment relations: how to theoretically capture the shift in power of the last 50 years, a shift that has seen a dramatic decline in the power of unions and a concurrent incline in the power of multinational corporations, along with a shift in economic muscle away from the US and Europe. Kelly discusses three broad theoretical lenses, namely market forces, institutions and actors' strategic choices, to illuminate these changes. There is no overarching theory capable of explaining the inter-relations between market forces, institutions and actor strategies, Kelly argues, so at best, comparative employment relations consists of 'attempts to specify the strengths and weaknesses, the insights and limitations of different perspectives'. Kelly calls for a tightening up of the discipline's theory – adding discipline to the discipline so to speak – as an urgent next step. 'Nobody disputes that market forces are powerful, that institutions can both attenuate and amplify such forces and that actors usually have some strategic choices, however limited', he notes. 'Perhaps one of the major challenges facing comparative researchers is to think through how we can specify more precisely the conditions under which each of these sets of "variables" is more or less effective'. One of the strong points of Kelly's chapter is that he clearly chalks out questions that need answering, and by doing so, provides a rich source of guidance for future researchers.

While employment relations scholars have been interested observers of processes of change to the structures of employment relations regulation, legal scholars have similarly observed important changes to legal rights governing the employment relationship. In this realm neoliberal statutes have altered the balance between traditional collective rights (which have been eroded) and individual employment rights (which have been enhanced by systematic state intervention). Clearly, the balance between collective and individual rights (as well as the respective roles of employees, employers and the state) varies across different national contexts. These differences have prompted those interested in comparative labour law to categorize different types of legal systems. Thus, according to the legal origins thesis, countries can be divided according to their history as common law or civil law systems. Interestingly, like with the categorization of LME countries under VoC, common law systems rely on market/outsider regulation while civil law systems, which are typically CME contexts, rely on insider/relational systems of regulation.

Sean Cooney, Peter Gahan and Richard Mitchell provide, in Chapter 4, a review of legal origins theory, a relatively new theory that has taken a leap into the real world of business, through such extensions as the World Bank's 'Doing Business' scales, which evaluate the regulatory frameworks of countries from the perspective of business-friendliness. Indeed, legal origins theory is having a disproportionate effect on policy, considering its relative novelty. Politics has long dominated the debate over the shaping of employment relations, and until recently, the notion that the German, French, Scandinavian or English ancestry of a country's laws, rather than the politics, could be the skeleton underneath the body of employment relations would have been dismissed. One of the strengths of this chapter is Cooney et al.'s extraction of the underlying data of difference from Botero et al. (2004), which does provide some substantial backing to legal origins theory, helping to explain international variance in use of fixed-term contracts and maximum pre-overtime working hours, for example. As the authors suggest, in its relatively brief life, legal origins theory has proved sufficiently fruitful so as to suggest a long, 'illuminating and controversial' future.

Terence Jackson, in Chapter 5, rounds out Part 2 by outlining the importance of cross-cultural studies for comparative employment relations. Jackson goes back to one of the thickest roots of comparative employment relations, Geert Hofstede's 1984 volume, *Cultures Consequences*, and assembles a cohort of influences that moved with Hofstede through the 1980s–90s until now. His argument is that, despite the continuing value of Hofstede's work in framing and stimulating the debate, Hofstede offers simplistic and 'rather blunt tools' to explore multicultural management and ER issues, and Jackson similarly tackles the post-Hofstede work of Trompenaars vigorously. Instead, he proposes that a cultural 'interfaces' approach, which in a sense is what this volume espouses, is more likely to illuminate cross-cultural dynamics as they relate to employment relations. He points to studies, for example, of countries connected or disconnected by history, such as West and East Germany, who retained parallel values during the Iron Curtain years. 'When a Hofstede . . . or a Trompenaars . . . or a Schwarz . . . or a House . . . comes along with their questionnaire to ask questions about the values of a representative of the "culture" of (for example) South Africa, they are in trouble', Jackson says. Each individual, he argues, is not a representative of a culture, but an amalgam of cultural interfaces that 'can only be accessed through the agency of individuals' cultural identity'. Everything is culturally bounded: there is no 'view from nowhere'. Jackson reminds us that institutions are inseparable from their host culture, and globalization is merely succeeding in making disentangling culture from institutions more fraught.

Paired Country Comparisons

As mentioned, one of the key debates in comparative employment relations is whether institutional structures, once firmly established, remain resilient to change, and therefore become path-dependent (Deeg and Jackson, 2008). By selecting for comparison cases of countries with similar embedded institutional arrangements, we can usefully interrogate whether the forces of path dependence (i.e., endogenous interests) that might determine institutional continuity continue to outweigh the opposing forces that might promote institutional change (i.e., exogenous shocks). Thus, we are interested to learn whether institutional changes that become a point of divergence for once similar national systems have arisen as a result of issues associated with globalization, or reflect a changing alignment of dominant political/industrial/societal interests that have been shaped more obviously by domestic considerations. As Henke and Goyer (2005, pp. 53–4) have argued in proffering a qualified view of institutional path-dependence, similar institutional frameworks may produce different economic outcomes because frameworks offer actors different adjustment paths and therefore how actors operate within institutional frameworks matters.

It is also important to note, as we take countries as our basis for comparison, and as we are interested in questions of convergence and diversity, that nation states are integrated into the global economy rather than existing separately from the processes and pressures of globalization. As Morgan et al. (2005, pp. 4–5) note, viewing nations as separate and self-contained entities may create a false impression that the dominant questions for comparative analysis are about convergence and divergence rather than the degree of integration and fit, and the capacity of actors at the firm level to make *choices* about regulatory approaches within the sets of constraints imposed by institutions, history and international/environmental context. In short, there may be 'alternative paths' from which actors can make choices at critical junctures.

In choosing to compare countries we are mindful that a key enduring debate in employment relations is whether the forces of internationalization and globalization have promoted convergence across previously distinct *national* patterns of employment relations. This convergence proposition was first articulated by Kerr et al. (1960) in relation to impact of technological development on employment relations. The so-called logic of industrialization was said to promote convergence in employment relations. How national models of employment relations have 'refracted' convergence pressures to retain their distinctiveness (at least in some measure) remains a key question for comparative employment relations and one that is at the heart of the 'new institutionalist' contribution to the employment relations and comparative politics literatures.

Our approach in Part 3 of the book is to provide a selection of paired country comparisons from each of the main trading regions: North

America, South America, Europe, Asia and the South Pacific and the Middle East. We believe that this approach to coverage is important to overcome one of the identified limitations of the extant literature in the field. Thus, a common trend in international and comparative volumes is to select what might be referred to as 'the usual suspects'. These are typically a range of European countries, generally including the likes of Germany, Sweden, Italy/France and the United Kingdom; a sample of North America (either the US and/or Canada); and one or two Asian countries (usually Japan and/or South Korea). One example of this tendency is the VoC literature, which postulates a distinction between LME and CME countries, but is limited in its heuristic capacity because it is based on a number of countries that are primarily located in either Europe or North America. In this sense, as Hay (2005) has pointed out, the comparison is of varieties of (two) regional capitalisms rather than varieties of world capitalism.

Another limitation of comparative employment relations is that there are few studies of rapidly emerging/industrializing nations in spite of their importance to the global economy. In this volume we include a paired comparison of China and India, in recent years the two fastest developing countries in world. The volume also includes chapters of countries and regions that both receive scant treatment in major texts in the field. For example, we include paired comparisons from South America, of Chile and Argentina; from Africa, of Mozambique and South Africa; and from the Middle East, of Oman and the UAE.

We have chosen countries that we regard as 'relatively' close comparators. Where countries begin from a common employment relations base, we seek to understand emerging differences in processes, structures and outcomes of labour market regulation. In some cases our comparators are countries that have shared common and unique structures of labour market regulation – such as the development of compulsory arbitration systems of Australia and New Zealand, and their more recent decline (Wailes, Chapter 12 this volume). In other cases, such as Argentina and Chile, we have comparisons of countries that share similar traditions in terms of their cultural, economic and political systems, and their patterns of industrialization.

Beginning with Argentina and Chile, in Chapter 6, we note there is a paucity of comparative employment relations analyses, which is surprising, considering, as Maurizio Atzeni, Fernando Durán-Palma and Pablo Ghigliani point out, these countries share a language and cultural heritage, the world's third-longest international border and parallel and highly politicized patterns of socioeconomic development. The team describe their chapter as a 'modest introduction', but in fact their study goes a long way to bridging this gap, showing that despite the common ground, there are a number of country-specific differences between Chile and Argentina. While they share an industrial history driven by import substitution, and a political context that has taken a relatively heavy-handed role in employment relations issues, historians of the two nations have taken very different approaches to tracking and explaining changes in their domestic contexts. Atzeni, Durán-Palma and Ghigliani give a fascinating insight into the South American brand of neoliberal restructuring, and the means by which what they term 'concrete national realities' have played a fundamental role in giving the Argentinian and Chilean cases a unique character. Readers from a non-South American perspective will find new insights into their domestic issues from the authors' discussion of the trend towards recommodification of labour, the rise of informal work practices and the battle to stem the erosion of organized labour.

The second largest country in the world, Canada, is in many senses the forgotten partner of its southern neighbour, the United States, and Sara Slinn and Richard Hurd illuminate this so-close-yet-so-far-apart relationship from an employment relations perspective in Chapter 7. Two factors, the authors point out, make the Canadian situation essentially more complex: the fact that its politics, through its social democratic tradition, is much more closely entwined with organized labour than in the US; and the fact that in the US, federal power reigns over state rights to a much greater degree than in Canada. In Canada, as a result, the ER theorist deals with a multiplicity of models, which nevertheless add up to a much more supportive climate for collectivity. The US has complexities of its own, not the least caused by its sheer economic power, and greater degree of income inequality. With union density in Canada more than double that in the US, developments in the US, such as the Wagner Act, have exerted significant influence over the expression of Canadian union–employer relations. The influence goes the other way as well, with US unions seeking to transplant Canadian reforms south of the border. Against this backdrop of two-way influence is the reality of an increasingly close trading relationship between Canada and the US, which, Slinn and Hurd argue, will force the junior of the two in terms of economic power, Canada, to bend to the American way.

Relatively newly minted powerhouses of the new world economic order, India and China make a particularly important comparison study on any grounds, and while geopolitical, economic and sociocultural studies abound, there have been relatively few detailed studies contrasting the employment relations status of these two Asian neighbours. Fang Lee Cooke, in Chapter 8, acknowledges the limitations of applying largely Western templates of employment relations on Asian systems of 'doing' business and 'doing' labour, and sidesteps these problems by instead focusing on the 'unique historical, cultural, economic and political cir- cumstances' of India and China, and how these circumstances have been imbued into the labour relations, both organized (more commonly) and disorganized, of the pair. If, as Cooke points out, the Chinese and Indian cases are often discussed in Western academic circles in abstract and simplistic terms, her valuable overview points out how much more com- plicated reality on the ground can be. In China, for example, a national minimum wage has not yet been enacted in practice: in theory, a national standard was only set in 1993. Both nations are headed down a path of pri- vatization, and both are in the ascendant. Cooke's study provides a vital insight for scholars needing to keep an eye on the shifting sands of two of the key players on the world stage.

The Republic of Ireland and the United Kingdom are united by language, history, culture and even share the common umbrella of the European Union. In Chapter 9, Tony Dundon and David Collings offer an overview of post-war employment relations of two countries unified by a shared heritage, but divided by very different trajectories. The influ- ence of unions in post-Thatcherist Britain continues to decline despite years of Labour influence, while in Ireland, despite its engagement with the European Union, union power has been buttressed by national pay agreements. In the wake of the global financial crisis, and its puncturing of the Irish 'miracle', the power of organized labour is under greater threat than ever in Ireland, with Dundon and Collings pointing to the court win by one of Ireland's most anti-union employers, airline Ryanair, as proof of the temper of the times. While both Ireland and the UK have followed the voluntarist path, in Britain there has been a revival in individualistic values, while in Ireland collectivism tinged with corporatism has predomi- nated. The authors point out that the Europeanization of employment relations is likely to see the two neighbours begin to converge in approach.

Japan's post-war democratic tradition – albeit one dominated by a single party – contrasts sharply with Korea's last 60 years, dominated by a chain of authoritarian regimes. Despite the firm grip of dictatorships, however, it is Korea, rather than Japan, whose industrial relations history has been dominated by adversarial battles. While acknowledging that it was only when observed through a long lens that Japanese and Korean employ- ment relations history bore any resemblance to each other, EeHwan Jung notes, in Chapter 10, that more than geographical proximity is beginning to unite the pair. After all, respect for seniority is a cultural norm that has penetrated both nations' employment relations fabric, and both countries manifest enterprise-based unions – ironically developed in Japan's case, as Jung notes, by the occupying Americans seeking to promote democracy.

In Korea's case, free labour unions emerged with democratization, in the late 1980s, and have only even more recently shifted away from the enterprise union model. Even more recently, Jung points out, the casualization of the workforce – Japan and Korea share the dubious honour of having two of the highest rates of 'non-regular' workers in the OECD – has become a unifying force. Jung points out that the Japan–Korea comparison suggests that the field needs an East Asian model – one focused on 'strong firm internal labor markets and labor market segmentation'.

'Less a scientific than a loose multi-dimensional concept', flexicurity is, according to the team composed of Hester Houwing, Maarten Keune, Philippe Pochet and Kurt Vandaele in Chapter 11, hard to pin down. Houwing and her coauthors take the case of the Netherlands, often singled out as a premier example of the concept outside its birthplace of Denmark, and its close cousin Belgium, as a proving ground for a concept borne (interestingly, in Dutch academic circles) of frustration at an increasingly complex European labour market. Like most of the other pairs explored in this volume, Belgium and the Netherlands are geographically close, and have a language and cultural overlap. They share a belief in social partnerships that have expressed themselves in the employment relations field through corporatist institutions and a strong welfare state. Both, however, have seen political shifts to the right in recent years, with an increasingly volatile electorate and restive workforce propelling the creation of new social contracts. However, Belgium's status as the oldest industrialized nation in continental Europe, and the apparent affinity of the Netherlands to the Scandinavian revolution in employment relations adds spice to the comparison. The flexicurity question is of more than academic interest in a comparative employment relations context, with the European Commission clearly seeking to explore the apparent employment advantage flexicurity has given to Denmark and the Netherlands (even during the economic crisis) as a template for other European nations. However, Houwing et al. do more than simply relate the glories of flexicurity, pointing out that on full-time-equivalent rates, Belgium is in some instances ahead of the Netherlands, and certainly not as far behind in employment rates as a bare look at the figures suggests. The authors in fact highlight this 'apples with apples' argument as one of the key insights offered by their Belgium–Netherlands case, highlighting the 'pitfalls of an excessively stylized comparison'.

Australia and New Zealand are a perfect pigeon pair, Nick Wailes suggests in Chapter 12, when it comes to providing a comparison: both have a similar colonial heritage, language and are geographical neighbours, and both developed a unique form of labour regulation, compulsory conciliation and arbitration. They are, as Wailes puts it, 'almost perfect real world examples of . . . similar countries', heavily influenced by British social liberalism. However, the last handful of decades have seen a divergence, as New Zealand led the way in searching for greater market flexibility. A strong literature exists comparing these two relatively minor players in the world economic scene, but Wailes highlights the role played by material interests in differentiating what otherwise might have been matching historic pathways. The differing degree to which labour, on the one hand, and employers, on the other, were unified, help make the way Australia and New Zealand transited through the 1980s an interesting natural experiment. The two countries' employment relations systems have, in more recent times, converged, and Wailes suggests the convergence raises 'questions about the overwhelming emphasis that this literature placed on organizational and institutional factors', and he suggests that, instead, the greater economic crisis faced by New Zealand in the 1980s may have had stronger impact than commentators have previously accepted.

In his comparison of Mozambique and South Africa in Chapter 13, Geoffrey Wood is offering a guidebook to exotic territory for most employment relations scholars. His comparison doesn't just explore relatively new geographical territory – studies on Mozambique are few and far between – but tackles a pair that despite their geographical proximity, have trod divergent paths since they were first colonized, one by the Portuguese, the other by Britain. Their legal and political systems are different, and, as Wood points out, there are practical impediments: researchers working in English will find few resources in Mozambique, but plenty in South Africa. In this chapter, Wood also gives an insight into factors playing a role in employment relations in the developing world. Nowhere in US employment relations history, for example, does the breaking of a drought feature prominently. In the case of apartheid, Wood has access to a particularly well-known example of a macro-sociopolitical mechanism of employment relations change. His chapter provides a longer view of both South African and Mozambican development than many theorists choose to make, in the case of Mozambique tracing back its trading history to ancient times, when the landscape was beset with foreign intervention and slavery. With a shared modern employment history undoubtedly bloodier than many other comparisons, and a shared prominence of the informal sector, the Mozambique and South African example makes for a sobering counterbalance to analyses focused on the developed world.

In Chapter 14, Stefan Zagelmeyer considers France and Germany as a prism through which to examine the convergence-versus-divergence hypotheses. The chapter does provide a compact overview of a sprawling literature, although Zagelmeyer focuses mainly on private sector developments, and in the case of Germany, mainly on the territory west of the old Berlin wall. What makes the study of Germany and France important as well as interesting is the fact that the two former enemies now control the engine room of the European economy, and have leadership influence beyond their GDP. Historically, as Zagelmeyer points out, France has been of particular interest to employment theorists due to the unique role played in society as well as the economy of trade unions (despite the fact, as he points out, France now has the lowest level of union density in any OECD country) and its state-influenced *dirigiste* political economy. Germany's role in a climate of international economic uncertainty, despite the economic trauma wrought by unification, is a stabilizing and conservative one. Its role is also undoubtedly expanding. As to the future in these two powerhouses, Zagelmeyer suggests that France and Germany, despite their integration into the EU and close economic and political relations, and despite both featuring employment relations determined by pronounced constitutional genetics, retain 'distinct features and characteristics'. France, despite a right-of-centre government, is still living in an era of government intervention in employment, and Germany's employment relations tableau, despite the tensions of the times, remains marked by heavy corporate fingerprints.

In Chapter 15, Kamel Mellahi and Ingo Forstenlechner tap what has been, for traditional employment relations researchers, very much a backwater in the field: the oil-rich Gulf countries. Their chapter offers a fascinating insight into a region with some highly distinctive characteristics, including a heavy dependence on expatriate labour and a correspondingly low employment participation rate for the domestic population, a blend of traditional and modern institutional structures, and a disinterest in issues, such as employee voice and reducing staff turnover, that are standard in other parts of the world. The Gulf region is undergoing a significant employment revolution, with many nations in the region moving to recognize collective labour, and promote indigenous workforces, but despite efforts at reform, Gulf workforces are dominated at the lower levels and in the private sector by expatriates, and at the public sector by nationals. The determination to nationalize labour, currently not matched by success, is proving a highly distorting force in employment relations, with the authors, for example, pointing to a recent 70 per cent increase in salaries for public sector workers in the country with the highest percentage of expatriate workers, the UAE. Such distortions are, Mellahi and Forstenlechner point out, part of a social contract quite distinct from those that readers would be more familiar with. They are aimed, squarely, at distributing oil wealth. Apart from exploring the fascinating and unique public/private sector divide in many Gulf countries, the authors provide an insight into a parallel world with which readers may well be very familiar: academia.

Academia has traditionally operated within much greater constraints, with traditional autocratic lines of command, but, like the rest of employment relations within the Gulf region, gradually, the sands are shifting.

Broader Comparative Influences

We are interested in understanding interlinkages between national, international and supranational regulation. Part 4 of the volume situates national comparative employment relations within a broader context. Here our contributors identify key contextual forces such as global labour standards, the role of multinational corporations and regional regulatory contexts. Institutions that operate beyond the nation state can be considered both agents of globalization and constraints inhibiting globalization. In considering the role of multinationals, for example, an obvious question that arises is, to what extent are MNCs able to transplant source nation practices into host nation operations? The ability, or inability, of MNCs to do so goes directly to questions of whether regulatory systems embedded in nation states can resist the pressures of convergence associated with instruments (such as MNCs) of globalization.

Context matters for comparative employment relations in other ways as well. Context both leaves open and closes down certain employment relations options. An example is how the regulatory context for employee representation operates in different regions. For example, while union decline is a common theme of comparative employment relations, in Europe employees retain the formal ability to access 'voice' because there are both national and regional regulations (statutes and European directives) that provide for an alternative channel of representation through works councils. Outside Europe there is no established culture, nor any institutional guarantees, of such voice arrangements. Meanwhile, employer efforts to embed their own voice arrangements through HRM may also act as an inhibitor to the development of employee-inspired voice structures, particularly in the more liberal Anglo-Saxon countries. Additionally, as is often observed, a common distinction between European and other jurisdictions is the ability in Europe for collective bargaining outcomes to be 'extended' by statute to non-union employees. This again mitigates the impact of union density by making collective bargaining coverage less dependent on unionization than it is in other, more decentralized, jurisdictions (see, for example, Freeman and Rogers, 1999). Taken together, these regional considerations will have an important impact on the extent to which common changes to the prevailing pattern of interaction actually produce divergent outcomes in terms of wages and conditions, as well as a crucial influence on options for employee representation in different jurisdictions.

Lucio Baccaro's work in Chapter 16 unites a curious couple, Italy and Ireland, a pair that have, on the surface, the least in common of all the comparisons in this volume, but he uses the volatile examples of these two nations' recent histories of corporatism to advance a compelling hypothesis: that the 'demise' of corporatist bargaining was an illusion created by a series of unusual and 'highly symbolic' events, such as the collapse of centralized bargaining in Sweden. While corporatism lives on, in a somewhat softer guise, it has begun to make way for neoliberalism, not as a partner in reform, but as a channel for neoliberalism. Gone are the tendencies towards redistribution of what Baccaro calls the corporatist golden age. Rather than seeing a convergence of employment relations models towards the Anglo-Saxon model of decentralized bargaining, corporatism is back. Baccaro's study offers a broad canvas to consider the changes of the last two decades not just in Italy and Ireland, two countries where the corporatist revival was perhaps the most visible and, as Baccaro points out, surprising (both having been previously identified by scholars as being intrinsically resistant to its charms) but across Europe.

Multinational enterprises (MNEs) have a special role in comparative employment relations from an international perspective, and are particularly worthy of a systematic scholarly focus, considering that half the top 150 economic entities in the world are nations and the other half are MNEs. What complicates the picture is that MNEs 'do not operate in isolation from the environment around them but rather must organize their activities in the context of the multiple institutional environments in which they operate' – environments that are essentially intra-national. MNEs are influenced by their hosts, but go on to spread that influence beyond national borders, potentially promoting or inhibiting change in nations far beyond their 'parent' nation. In Chapter 17, David Collings, Jonathan Lavelle and Patrick Gunnigle position MNEs as key ingredients of revitalization and innovation on a global scale and introduce the notions of 'adaptive innovation', those defined as where the MNEs display a 'healthy regard' for their host nations' traditions and contrast such innovation with 'disruptive innovation', an 'against-the-grain' approach such as those famously deployed by US multinationals Walmart and McDonald's. Collings et al. present both the 'Bleak House' and the more optimistic – and relatively European – vision of the challenge posed to diversity and nation states by MNEs. They also focus on two major counterbalances against MNE power: trade unions, with their growing international unity, and international organizations such as the OECD and ILO.

In Chapter 18, Tony Royle examines the power of international labour standards in protecting against the further erosions of national labour standards. Royle's review considers challenges posed by global capital to workers' rights and conditions on the shop floor, as well as the role played by the International Labour Organization in developing a set of core pillars in resisting the MNC tide, and the MNC response in terms of voluntary private initiatives. Royle digs beneath the theory to provide a summary of how MNC power is working on the ground in countries such as China and India, depressing wages, shaping legislation and impacting on human rights. The chapter also serves as a useful overview of the history and power parameters of the ILO, and how the emergence of the World Trade Organization further delimited that power. A new era of private codes of conduct and corporate–NGO agreements appears to be upon us, and Royle provides a fascinating insight into the revelations (for example, in relation to Nike) of the 'spotlight phenomenon'; a form of diffuse power reliant on media attention and consumer trends. This contribution highlights that contemporary analysis requires a broader definition of regulation – moving beyond traditional regulatory instruments such as rules – to focus on informal regulatory tools, such as embarrassment, shaming and moral suasion, and indeed that a broader definition of institutions is perhaps required that sees institutions as incentive systems rather than particular organizational structures (North, 1991). In fact, consumer activism, expressed through global purchasing power, is, Royle suggests, becoming a significant player in guiding corporate behaviour in employment matters.

CONCLUSION

This introduction has advanced the proposition that comparative analysis in employment relations requires development and integration. The contributors to this volume take up this challenge by exploring a number of interrelated issues. These include: how learning from abroad takes place, the mechanisms by which this can occur, and how practices associated with particular regimes can be transplanted to other nations; what forces are prompting change and how certain actors mobilize to achieve such change and others mobilize against it; and how institutions evolve, and what this means for fundamental issues such as disparity of pay and conditions of employment, employee engagement and voice, and equity, fairness and democracy in the workplace.

Framing each of these issues is the broader question of the extent to which the common forces associated with globalization are placing pressure on once-distinct national systems to become more similar. Similarities and differences are explored in this volume through the selection of case comparisons of paired countries that have similar histories, cultures, laws and institutions. While the greater proportion of this volume is dedicated to these paired country comparisons of common issues and developments, we also examine wider issues and debates.

Thus, overall, this volume seeks to be comprehensive in its analysis of comparative employment relations. It sets out to do so by (in Part 2) moving beyond traditional intellectual frameworks to understand key phenomena, then (in Part 3) selecting a wide number of cases, from all regions of the globe, to explore important employment issues in both developed and developing economies, and finally (in Part 4) not only looking both within and across selected cases, but also beyond these cases at issues and developments that are relevant to all developed and emerging economies.

REFERENCES

Albert M. (1993), *Capitalism vs. Capitalism*, New York: Four Walls Eight Windows.
Bamber, G.J., Lansbury, R.D. and Wailes, N. (eds) (2010), *International and Comparative Employment Relations: Globalisation and Change*, 5th edition, Sydney: Sage; London: Allen and Unwin.
Bamber, G.J., Park, F., Lee, C., Ross, P.K. and Broadbent, K. (eds) (2000), *Employment Relations in the Asia-Pacific: Changing Approaches*, St Leonards: Allen and Unwin.
Bean, R. (1985), *Comparative Employment Relations*, London: Croom Helm.
Berggren, C. (1993), *The Volvo Experience: Alternatives to Lean Production in the Swedish Auto Industry*, Basingstoke: Macmillan.
Botero, J.C., Djankov, S., La Porta, R., Lopez-de-Silanes, F. and Schleifer, A. (2004), 'The regulation of labour', *The Quarterly Journal of Economics*, 119(4), 1339–82.
Briggs, C. (2006), 'The return of lockouts down under in comparative perspective: Globalisation, the state, and employer militancy', *Comparative Political Studies*, 39(7), 855–79.
Coase, R.H. (1984) 'The new institutional economics', *Journal of Institutional and Theoretical Economics*, 140(1), 229–31.
Deeg, R. and Jackson, G. (2008), 'How many varieties of capitalism? From institutional diversity to the politics of change', *Review of International Political Economy*, 15(4), 679–708.
Delbridge, R., Lowe, J. and Oliver, N. (1995), 'The process of benchmarking: A study from the automotive industry', *International Journal of Operations and Production Management*, 5(4), 50–62.
Dunlop, J.T. (1958), *Industrial Relations Systems*, New York: Holt.
Eaton, J. (2000), *Comparative Employment Relations: An Introduction*, London: Polity.
Fairbrother, P. and Yates, C. (eds) (2003), *Trade Unions in Renewal: A Comparative Study*, London: Routledge.
Freeman, R. and Rogers, J. (1999), *What Workers Want*, New York: Cornell University Press.
Frege, C. (2007), *Employment Research and State Traditions: A Comparative History of Britain, Germany and the United States*, Oxford: Oxford University Press.
Frege, C. and Kelly, J. (eds) (2004), *Varieties of Unionism: Comparative Strategies for Union Renewal*, Oxford: Oxford University Press.
Hall, P.A. and Soskice, D.W. (2001), *Varieties of Capitalism: The Institutional Foundations of Comparative Advantage*, New York: Oxford University Press.

Hancher, L. and Moran, M. (1989), 'Organizing regulatory space', in L. Hancher and M. Moran (eds), *Capitalism, Culture, and Economic Regulation*, Clarendon Press: Oxford.

Hay, C. (2005), 'Two can play at that game. . . . Or can they? Varieties of capitalism, varieties of institutionalism', in D. Coates (ed.), *Varieties of Capitalism, Varieties of Approaches*, Basingstoke, UK and New York: Palgrave Macmillan.

Henke, B. and Goyer, M. (2005), 'Degrees of freedom', in G. Morgan, R. Whitley and E. Moen (eds), *Changing Capitalisms? Institutional Change and Systems of Economic Organization*, Oxford: Oxford University Press.

Hofstede, G. (1984), *Culture's Consequences: International Differences in Work-related Values*, California: Sage Publications.

Hyman, R. (2004), 'Is industrial relations theory always ethnocentric?', in B.E. Kaufman (ed.), *Theoretical Perspectives on Work and the Employment Relationship*, Madison, WI: IRRA.

Hyman, R. and Ferner, A. (eds) (1994), *New Frontiers in European Industrial Relations*, Oxford: Blackwell.

Jacoby, S. (2005), *The Embedded Corporation: Corporate Governance and Employment Relations in Japan and the United States*, Princeton: Princeton University Press.

Katz, H. and Darbishire, O. (2000), *Converging Divergences: Worldwide Changes in Employment Systems*, New York: Cornell University Press.

Kerr, C. (1960), *Industrialism and Industrial Man: The Future of Industrialized Societies*, Cambridge, MA: Harvard University Press.

Lane, C. (2005), 'Institutional transformation and system change: Changes in the corporate governance of German corporations', in G. Morgan, R. Whitley and E. Moen (eds), *Changing Capitalisms? Complementarities, Contradictions and Capability Development in an International Context*, Oxford: Oxford University Press, pp. 78–109.

Mares, I. (2003), *The Politics of Social Risk: Business and Welfare State Development*, New York: Cambridge University Press.

Morgan, G., Whitley, R. and Moen, E. (eds) (2005), *Changing Capitalisms? Institutional Change and Systems of Economic Organization*, Oxford: Oxford University Press.

North, D. (1991), 'Institutions', *Journal of Economic Perspectives*, **5**(1), 97–112.

Thelen, K. (2009), 'Institutional change in advanced political economies', *British Journal of Industrial Relations*, **47**(3), 471–98.

Verma, A. and Kochan, T.A. (eds) (2004), *Unions in the 21st Century*, Houndmills: Palgrave MacMillan.

Wailes, N., Kitay, J. and Lansbury, R. (2008), 'Varieties of capitalism, corporate governance and employment relations under globalization', in S. Marshall, R. Mitchell and I. Ramsay (eds), *Varieties of Capitalism, Corporate Governance and Employees*, Melbourne, AUS: Melbourne University Press, pp. 19–38.

Womack, J.P., Jones, D.T. and Roos, D. (1990), *The Machine that Changed the World: The Story of Lean Production – Toyota's Secret Weapon in the Car Wars that is now Revolutionizing World Industry*, New York: Rawson Associates.

PART 2

PERSPECTIVES

2 Comparative employment relations: institutional and neo-institutional theories
Bruce E. Kaufman

INTRODUCTION

Comparative employment relations (CER) has enjoyed a resurgence of interest and scholarly research in recent years. A significant reason is the rising tide of globalization and its present and future impact on employment relations institutions and practices. Rather quickly the furthest corners of the earth have become interconnected in an international division of labor and system of market exchange, inevitably raising questions about the nature and extent of change in national employment relations (ER) systems and the degree to which they are converging to a similar model.

As all participants know, CER is an incredibly large and complex undertaking because of the huge diversity in employment relations systems (ERSs) across nations and the large complications introduced by differences in languages, cultures, institutions and legal systems. This has made theorizing in CER particularly difficult and challenging. Illustratively, international/comparative textbooks typically have at best a modest discussion of theory and for the most part consist of a chapter by chapter descriptive review of major labor institutions and laws across countries (e.g., Bean, 1994; Van Ruysseveldt et al., 1995; Bamber et al., 2004). Also indicative of the underdeveloped and challenged nature of CER theory are these comments by well-recognized people. Jack Barbash begins the volume *Theories and Concepts in Comparative Industrial Relations* (Barbash and Barbash, 1989, p. 3) with the statement, 'If we are not bound by one theory it is just possible that common values inform our work', while in the mid-1990s Richard Locke et al. (1995, pp. 15–16, emphasis added) assert, 'The last major attempt to develop a comprehensive framework for thinking about national differences in industrial relations was the Ford Foundation's interuniversity study, a project initiated *in the late 1950s*'. Still more recently, Richard Hyman (2004) asserts that in the early twenty-first century not only does the ER field still lack a common theoretical corpus but that attempts to develop one for cross-national comparative work are 'neither possible nor desirable' (p. 267) because cultural and institutional diversities are so large they effectively preclude useful and reliable generalization.

Part of the scholarly mission is to advance scientific knowledge and nothing is more essential to this task than theory. One must ask, therefore, whether things on the theory front in CER are really as dark as these quotations suggest. As this review demonstrates, the answer is No and, indeed, a steady stream of theoretical models and insights has appeared in the CER field over a several-decade period. On the other hand, this review also affirms that theorizing in CER is indeed a challenging exercise and certainly to this date no consensus theory or paradigm has emerged. Rather, what we have are diverse frameworks, theories and models that highlight key actors, institutions and forces that shape ERSs at a point in time and cause them to change over time. These frameworks, theories and models have come from several different disciplines and schools of thought, including radical/Marxist sociology, neoclassical economics and international human resource management (HRM).

Situated more or less in the middle of this literature and occupying the largest space are theories and models that are broadly known as 'institutional' and 'neo-institutional' (INI). The institutional perspective in CER was large in the immediate post-World War II period, went into eclipse in the 1970s–80s and has rebounded as neo-institutionalism (or 'new institutionalism') during the last 20 years. The center of gravity was originally in economics and the US; since the early 1990s it has shifted to Europe and sociology and political science.

The INI literature on comparative employment relations, because it crosses disparate disciplines and different countries, has to date existed in a rather fragmented and non-integrated state. To help remedy this situation, and also to provide easier access to this field of study for people coming to it for the first time, I undertake in this chapter a review and synthesis of the institutional-oriented literature on CER. Other useful if somewhat differently focused reviews are provided by Strauss (1998), Godard (2004), Martin and Bamber (2004), Hamann and Kelly (2008) and Hall and Wailes (2010). The review here is limited to issues of theory and to the English language portion of the field.

DEFINITION, BOUNDARY AND SPECIFICATION ISSUES IN CER

The first issue a person faces in exploring comparative employment relations is the question: what is CER? This question is worth asking because there is evident diversity of opinion on this matter and it introduces a similar diversity into CER theorizing and dialogue (Strauss, 1998).

Other chapters in this volume, and particularly the introductory chapter by the volume editors, consider in some depth the domain and major subject areas in CER so I only broach certain key issues here as they bear on theorizing. These issues fall into five categories.

The first is the subject area that CER covers and that a theory therefore needs to explain. One sees in the literature both a broad and narrow conception of CER's subject territory (Crouch, 1993; Budd, 2004; Kaufman, 2008). The narrow conception focuses on *collective* aspects of employment relationships and, in particular, differences across countries in union density, union structure, collective bargaining practices and outcomes, and union-related labor laws and institutions. The second and broader conception focuses on employment relationships of *all types* and, in particular, variation across countries in employment institutions and outcomes such as the occupational and industrial distribution of employment, wage structures and inequalities, extent of female employment and child labor, degree of state regulation of employment conditions and the various union-related topics already mentioned.

A second issue concerns the difference between comparative ER and international ER. Sometimes the terms are used more or less interchangeably; experts in the field (e.g., Poole, 1986; Bamber et al., 2004), however, often treat them as separate if substantially overlapping. The domain of international ER is the study of employment systems in different countries, with an emphasis on description and case-by-case analysis (e.g., Blum, 1981; Doeringer, 1981; Ferner and Hyman, 1992). Comparative ER, on the other hand, involves an explicit comparison of ER systems across two or more countries with the intent to identify common patterns and theoretical generalizations.

A third issue is the nature of the dependent variable in CER theorizing. A review of the literature reveals that studies have used three different specifications. The first dependent variable is a measure of the institutional architecture of an employment relations system, such as the degree of centralization in wage determination. A second dependent variable is an employment relations behavior or outcome, such as cross-national variation in union density or income inequality. A third dependent variable measures some aspect of employment relations performance, such as national GDP or employment growth.

A fourth issue concerns the level of analysis in CER theorizing. Differences in employment relations architectures, outcomes and performance can be examined at a firm, industry, regional, national, or international level. Most CER studies use the national level and look at variation in employment relations institutions and outcomes across nation states. However, many nations exhibit distinct variation in employment relations across firms, industries and regions (e.g., services versus manufacturing; Northern versus Southern Italy) and quite possibly this within-country variation is as interesting and revealing as the across-country variation (Katz and Darbishire, 2000; Crouch, 2005). Methodologically, one can also argue that a macro-theory of cross-national differences in employment relations needs to be built on a consistent micro-version developed at the firm level.

A fifth issue concerns the range of countries included in CER theorizing. Conceptually one would think all countries are included; for theoretical, practical and ethnocentric reasons, however, most researchers limit the list and exclude or greatly minimize countries classified as less developed (LDCs), micro-states, or socialist (e.g., Zimbabwe; Luxembourg, Cuba). Regarding LDCs, a theoretical reason is that a large portion of jobs in LDCs are either in agriculture or the informal sector and thus these countries have neither the labor movements nor conventional employment relationships that are the traditional objects of analysis in CER; similarly, in socialist countries the ER systems may well be non-comparable with those in capitalist countries. A practical reason is that data on employment structures and outcomes are often not available or the sample size is too small for LDCs, micro-states and socialist countries. Also entering the picture is ethnocentrism, as one finds that most writers come from a small number of advanced Western countries and their attention tends to focus on these countries, with the US, Britain and Germany leading the list.

SETTING THE STAGE: EMPLOYMENT RELATIONS THEORY

As now viewed by the majority of researchers, the field of ER deals with the subjects of work; the structure, management and regulation of the employment relationship and the quality of work life (Edwards, 2003; Kaufman, 2004a). This field was until recently called industrial relations (IR) and, indeed, the two names coexist and are used more or less interchangeably.

The ER/IR field (hereafter EIR) typically looks at employment relations in the context of a particular country and thus the nation state becomes the standard unit of analysis. Further, the most common theoretical approach in EIR is to look at a nation's employment relations as a *system* (described more below). Thus, it is common to talk about the US EIR system, the French EIR system, and so on.

The task undertaken by CER is to broaden the focus of analysis from the individual nation state to a cross-country comparison of EIR systems. In particular, a principal goal of CER is to understand and explain the differential structure, function and performance of alternative EIR systems. To the degree possible, one would like a theory, model or at least conceptual framework to help guide and illuminate this investigation. But where should one look?

Perhaps the most obvious answer is to search among existing EIR theories that pertain to the individual nation state and then see if they can be broadened/expanded to explain cross-national variation. The subject of international economics, for example, is largely an application of demand/supply theory developed for individual goods and countries to issues of global finance and trade; in similar fashion one could well think that what is called for is *not* an entirely new and novel theory of CER but, rather, an application of existing EIR models, theories and frameworks to cross-country comparison.

A number of books and articles have been written on EIR theory so no comprehensive review need be undertaken here (see Adams and Meltz, 1993; Edwards, 2003; Blyton and Turnbull, 2004; Kaufman, 2004b; Müller-Jentsch, 2004). Certain salient points and important studies deserve highlighting, however.

It must first be admitted that development of a formal theory of EIR has made only modest and incomplete progress. The first self-claimed attempt to develop a 'general theory' of industrial relations is by John Dunlop in his book *Industrial Relations Systems* (1958). His model will be reviewed below so I postpone detailed description of it. What merit comment here are two aspects. The first is that the system idea is Dunlop's most influential conceptual contribution to EIR theory; the second is that in most people's eyes Dunlop's model is a useful conceptual framework but is not a theory of employment relations per se – at least if the desideratum of a theory is a testable hypothesis.

A second relevant point about EIR theory is that authors build their models around different core features of the employment relationship. Flanders (1965), for example, theorizes IR as a model of 'job regulation'; Barbash's (1984) model explains workplace conflict as the collision of management's drive for efficiency and low cost and employees' desire for good pay, conditions and security; Kochan, Katz and McKersie (1986) select strategic choice as the key variable explaining different EIR configurations; Begin (1991) derives alternative ERSs based on different organizational architectures; Hills (1995) portrays ERSs as built around different systems of workplace control; Marsden (1999) derives alternative ERSs as an outcome of EIR practices that constrain opportunism and free-riding by employers and employees; Budd (2004) makes the central focus of EIR the balanced attainment of efficiency, equity and voice; while Kaufman (2010) argues that the core concept in EIR theory is the human nature of labor. Some of these models are similar to Dunlop's in that they largely serve as useful taxonomical guides and frameworks; several, however, go further and yield testable hypotheses. A particular hypothesis of importance concerns complementarity and, in particular, the idea that EIR components are not put together randomly or by 'mix and match' but rather are consciously chosen so they fit together as an integrated and synergistic whole.

Third, a large portion of recent theorizing on EIR systems is not taking place in the EIR field itself but rather in contiguous fields such as economic sociology, political economy and strategic human resource management. North America was the locus of most EIR theorizing up until the late 1980s; after that the EIR field (particularly in the US) started on a long and cumulatively substantial decline and interest in EIR theory went with it (with certain exceptions, as given by citations above). Other fields picked up the EIR systems idea, albeit typically under different names and labels, and continued to develop it. In strategic HRM, for example, authors have developed different models of employment systems and 'HRM architectures' (Lepak and Snell, 1999; Toh et al., 2008); likewise, researchers in the Marxist/radical-oriented labor process field have developed alternative EIR systems built around the concept of 'regimes of control' (Edwards, 1979). Of particular relevance to this chapter is the work on EIR systems in economic sociology and political economy, particularly in Europe. Best known under the rubric 'varieties of capitalism' (VoC), this literature seeks to theorize the determinants of economic structure, organization and performance within and across nation states. This theory encompasses all dimensions of an economy but a central part in most studies is the EIR system.

Fourth, and finally, the dominant theoretical wellspring of EIR theories is what is loosely called 'institutionalism'. The field of industrial relations began as a formal entity in the United States around 1920, was positioned as the labor subfield of the institutional approach to economics and was led by John Commons and other members of the Wisconsin School who were proponents of the institutional approach (Kaufman, 1993, 2004a). Institutionalism in the US had strong links to both the discipline of sociology and European-style historical/social economics. In the US later generations of industrial relationists followed in the institutional and neo-institutional tradition, exemplified by Dunlop, Kochan, Budd and others. The field of EIR was slow to develop in continental Europe and still today has only a modest organized presence (Kaufman, 2004a); hence, this lacuna is mostly filled by sociology and, in particular, economic sociology (aka, socioeconomics). One of the fathers of sociology, Emile Durkheim ([1895]1938), identified the subject matter of the discipline as the 'study of institutions' and, not surprisingly, institutionalism is a particularly strong theoretical tradition in VoC and similar EIR-related work among European sociologists, political scientists and business theorists.

INSTITUTIONALISM: A BRIEF SURVEY

Institutionalism has diverse roots going back a century and more (Hodgson, 1998; Hollingsworth, 2002; Kaufman, 2004a). Its original source was late nineteenth-century German historical/social economics (HSE). HSE was a reaction against two other economic doctrines. One is the English classical and neoclassical economics that largely models economies as a mechanical working-out of commodity exchanges among a mass of unconnected individuals in a highly competitive marketplace where government, culture, social groups and legal institutions have little or no role to play. The chief architect of this type of 'non-institutional' economics is Leon Walras and his style of general equilibrium economics ruled orthodox economics for much of the 20th century. The second economic doctrine that spurred the development of HSE was Marxist economics and, in particular, Marx's brand of economic determinism that forecast the replacement of capitalism and representative government with socialism and a dictatorship of the proletariat.

From a neoclassical perspective, differences in employment relations institutions across countries arise from either competitive market forces or the interference of government and other collective actors – a view first enunciated by Adam Smith ([1776]1937). To the degree it is the former, institutions are created by economic agents to facilitate production and exchange and exist as long as they serve this objective. From this functional perspective, institutions do not have independent explanatory power but are creatures of market forces and neutrally transmit these forces (Hodgson, 2002). To the degree institutions arise from the interference of government and other collective actors, they serve mostly as agents of redistribution and rent-seeking and, in all but exceptional cases of market failure, interfere with the efficient functioning of the economy. A prominent line of thought in neoclassical economics, and also among 'universalistic' theorists in strategic human resource management (Boxall and Purcell, 2008), holds that over the long run, globalization, market forces and profit-seeking will erode and eliminate non-competitive institutions and, hence, economies should converge to some form of competitive market system along neoliberal lines with a universalistic set of 'best practice' HRM methods.

The neoclassical perspective has two large implications for the field of CER. The first is to largely dismiss it as an interesting line of inquiry on the grounds that EIR institutions are substantively unimportant, mostly anti-market, and/or transitory from a long-run perspective. The second is to suggest that if one wants to explain cross-national differences in EIR institutions then the place to start is cross-national levels of economic development – given the presumption that the configuration of EIR institutions functionally serves economic efficiency and that different configurations are therefore called for at different stages of economic development. The implication is that one should look to neoclassical growth theory to explain cross-national variation in development level and, as illustrated by modern treatises on this subject (e.g., Acemoglu, 2009), institutions play a distinctly secondary role and most of the action comes from differences in economic variables such as capital investment, labor force growth, human capital accumulation and technological change.

On the opposite end of the spectrum is Marxist economics. Where neoclassical economics suggests that a market economy leads to harmony, efficiency, growth and a reasonably equitable income distribution, Marxism predicts just the opposite. Capitalism survives and reproduces by exploiting labor to obtain surplus value that is then funneled into further capital investment. Expanded capital investment, however, leads to a falling rate of profit and concentration of industry (i.e., growing monopoly) – both of which lead to a decline in the economy's growth rate and eventual emergence of stagnation. To prop up profits, employers seek to expand markets through imperialism, colonialism and foreign wars while at the same time they work to reduce production cost by further squeezing labor through speed-ups, longer hours and hiring of women and child labor. Thus, control and exploitation become the imperatives for employers under capitalism while protection and resistance are the mirror image imperatives for workers (Hyman, 1975; Thompson and Hartley, 2007). Over time, class conflict, strikes and socioeconomic polarization grow until a proletarian revolution replaces capitalism with socialism and a workers' state.

Marxism also has implications for the study of CER. Like neoclassical economics, it also predicts a convergence over time in the nature/shape of national economies and, hence, in EIR institutions and practices. Also like neoclassical economics, it downplays the independent role that institutions play in economic growth. That is, while in neoclassical economics, institutions are largely a 'veil' for market forces, in Marxism institutions are also largely a veil but in this case for requirements of the production system. That is, in the Marxist schema the 'forces of production' largely determine the 'relations of production' (i.e., social, economic, political institutions). In one respect, however, Marxism leads to the opposite conclusion of neoclassicism with regard to cross-national variation in EIR institutions. A neoclassical perspective predicts that over time competitive market forces and globalization should gradually erode and eventually eliminate trade unions and other non-competitive labor market institutions; a Marxist perspective predicts, however, that trade unions, strikes and other institutions of worker protectionism should increase as capitalists intensify their drive for surplus value in the face of mounting economic stagnation and crises.

Institutionalism carves out a middle space between the neoclassical and Marxist paradigms. It combines elements of both but at the same time amends certain key assumptions and introduces new concepts. The end result is that in this paradigm institutions play a central role in structuring and shaping national economies, their growth trajectories and configuration of EIR practices and outcomes (Hollingsworth and Boyer, 1998; Budd, 2004; North, 2005).

The first key modification in the institutional paradigm is to move away from economic determinism à la Walras and Marx. To do so, institutional theory starts with a more realistic model of the human agent (Commons, 1934; Coase, 1992). People are modeled as purposive, largely self-interested and intelligent but nonetheless also endowed with significant cognitive constraints, perceptual biases, powerful emotional states and social orientations. The external environment to the agent is also modified so domains of fundamental uncertainty exist in economic life that cannot be reasonably captured in theory by an assumed probability distribution.

The next key modification is to drop the neoclassical assumption that a stable society, well-functioning government, well-enforced regime of contract law and a competitive market system are somehow exogenously provided. Rather, in institutional theory the major challenge facing every country is to create, structure and maintain an institutional order that provides these things (Coase, 1992). That is, people have to collectively create a government, maintain law and social order, decide the kind of economy they want and the objectives it should serve and create mechanisms that solve market failures and maintain social peace (Aoki, 2000; North, 2005).

The foundation of the institutional paradigm, therefore, is boundedly rational people who must cooperate in constructing and maintaining an institutional order when they face substantial uncertainty and come to the situation with selfish motives, partially non-rational and destructive emotions, diverse and perhaps divisive cultural/religious/political allegiances and asymmetric information and objectives. To make progress in constructing an institutional order, these people create organizations called governments vested with sovereign authority to maintain law and order, create a legal code, enforce contracts and establish the infrastructure needed for a functioning economy. These governments define the modern nation state and it is these nation states that become the basic unit of analysis in institutional CER.

In the institutional paradigm there are few 'universals' of human behavior, given that human behavior is always embedded in and therefore shaped by diverse cultural, social and historical contexts (Polanyi, 1944; Hollingsworth and Boyer, 1998; Jessop, 2002). Given this, the government and all subsidiary institutions in a nation state are to a large degree context-specific and develop along path-dependent historical trajectories (Deeg and Jackson, 2007). As in the neoclassical and Marxist paradigms, CER systems across countries reflect stages of economic development; unlike in these paradigms, however, the collectivities of people and ruling elites in each nation determine through a constructed institutional order what kind of economy they have, how it operates, whose interests and objectives it serves and how problems and disputes are solved. The result is a huge diversity in societies, economies and CER systems, considerable persistence and stability in CER institutions and therefore outside of crisis situations mostly incremental change and only weak-to-modest forces leading to convergence through either market competition or universal requirements of production.

The core proposition of institutionalism is 'institutions matter' in predicting an economy's architecture and performance. However, no one theory of institutionalism commands universal agreement; indeed, Strycker (2002, p. 53) speaks of a 'variety of institutionalisms'. What can be said, however, is that institutionalism in economics, after a 30–40-year downturn following World War II and the neoclassical resurgence, has re-emerged since the early 1990s – sometimes under the labels 'neo-institutionalism' and 'new institutionalism' – as a popular and growing area of research. In the US, economists such as Coase, North and Williamson are prominent names in new institutionalism; in Europe a mix of sociologists, political economists and political scientists have spearheaded the neo-institutional movement. Important names include Amable, Boyer, Hall, Soskice, Streeck and Thelen.

ANGLO-AMERICAN INI THEORIES

The CER theoretical literature can usefully be divided into two parts. The first is in employment and industrial relations proper (the EIR field) and comes largely from authors in Anglo-American countries. The second is largely centered in European sociology and gives emphasis to theories such as varieties of capitalism. I focus on the Anglo-American set of INI theories in this section and move to those from European sociology in the next.

Micro-theories of EIR Systems

As discussed earlier, the central organizing concept in CER is the notion of an EIR *system*. As also earlier discussed, on methodological grounds one can make a good argument that 'macro'-theories of cross-national variation in CERs should be built on consistent 'micro'-theories as developed for individual firms, industries and nations. Toward this end, I start here with a brief review of several micro-theories of employment relations systems and then move to macro-theories. Included in the former section is discussion of Dunlop's notion of an industrial relations system.

ERS models

John Commons, the academic co-founder of the IR field and US branch of institutional economics, is also the originator of ERS typologies. In his book *Industrial Goodwill* (1919) Commons identifies five alternative 'theories of labor' – commodity (demand/supply), machinery (scientific management), goodwill (commitment), public utility (a publicly protected resource) and citizenship (industrial autocracy/democracy) – and discusses how each theory leads to a different model of people management and associated practices. Commons's explanation of these systems is discursive but one finds sprinkled here and there factors that he points to as determinative. The commodity model, for example, is a good fit for low-skill jobs where the work is standardized and easily monitored; the goodwill model, on the other hand, is a good fit where jobs require higher-level and more intangible-type skills and where cooperation and good citizenship behavior have particular value.

For the next major ERS contributions in industrial relations we now fast-forward to the 1950s. One comes from economist Clark Kerr and the other from John Dunlop.

Kerr (1950, 1954) first divides labor markets into 'structured' and 'unstructured'. The latter is equivalent to Commons's 'commodity model' where undifferentiated labor is traded back and forth, turnover is high, demand and supply determine wages and other terms and conditions of employment and employer HRM practices are very bare-bones. The former correspond to what Kerr calls 'institutional' labor markets that are structured by various rules, norms and organizational features created by employers, unions and/or government. He divides structured labor markets into two generic ERS types: 'communal ownership' and 'private property'. The former is exemplified by an occupational labor market or industry organized by a craft union where jobs require well-recognized skills but the skills are general and therefore portable (e.g., in nursing, construction); the latter is exemplified by a factory or company organized by an industrial union where job access is regulated by seniority and skills tend to be company-specific (e.g., in an auto plant). Of the two, the private property model has the more extensively developed internal labor market (ILM) and HRM system since the longevity of the employment relationship makes all aspects of HRM more important to organizational performance.

Dunlop's contribution to the ERS literature is the concept of an 'industrial relations system'. In his well-known book *Industrial Relations Systems* (1958), Dunlop defines an IR system as 'the complex of interrelations among managers, workers, and the agencies of government' where 'the parts and elements are interdependent and each may affect other elements and outcomes of the system as a whole' (p. 13). He identified three main actors in an ERS – employers and their representatives, employees and their representatives and government and its agencies; four main structural components – budget constraints, technology, power relations and statuses of the actors and labor management ideology; and made the central explanatory task of the model 'why particular rules are established in particular industrial-relations systems and how and why they change' (p. 9). In practice, Dunlop gave most attention to unions and collective bargaining as determinants of the rules of the ERS. Although the influence of Dunlop's book has faded in recent years, for several decades it was paradigmatic, per the observation of Cochrane (1979, p. 97), 'The book continues to be the basis for a large portion of industrial relations research around the world'.

EIR theorizing on employment systems next moves to the 1970s and 1980s and two more contributions. The first is Doeringer and Piore (1971). Their contribution is to delineate four factors that create ILMs: skill specificity, on-the-job training, unions and customary law. Higher levels of these four factors promote more internalization of labor coordination and, hence, a more HRM-intensive ERS. The second study is by Osterman (1987). He identifies four dominant employment systems (ESs): industrial, salaried, craft and secondary. The nature of these different ESs is evident from their names; what distinguishes Osterman's paper is that he then links different ES models to different configurations of four HRM practice areas – job classification, deployment (staffing), security and wage rules – and identifies five factors as the chief determinants of ERS selection – goals of the firm (cost minimization, flexibility, predictability), production technology, social technology, labor force characteristics and government policies.

Our review of the EIR stream ends with recent contributions from the 1990s to date. Three contributions merit brief mention (also see Appelbaum et al., 2000; Orlitzky and Frenkel, 2005). First is Arthur (1992). His article is noteworthy because it integrates the IR system idea; the role that strategy plays in shaping ERSs; and the 'high performance' model of work organization. He looks at steel minimills, differentiates between 'cost minimization' and 'product differentiation' business strategies and then examines if they map into a 'command and control' or 'high commitment' HRM/IR system. Cluster analysis reveals that the ERSs in the minimills sort into distinct types in line with the two strategies.

The second contribution is Marsden's *A Theory of Employment Systems* (1999). The book is almost entirely a work of theory and is based on ideas from institutional economics (IE, the 'mother paradigm' of IR) and, in particular, works by Coase (1937), Simon (1951) and Williamson (1975). Marsden identifies the constraints on behavior that are necessary for the employment relationship to be a viable economic proposition for both employers and workers; from these constraints he identifies four permutations of job design and skill development in firms' production systems, and in the last section of the book examines specific HRM practices that go with each production system. His theory indicates that ILMs and 'transformed' HRM systems develop when transaction costs are high and knowledge requirements are high and firm-specific – conditions created in turn by factors such as interdependent job tasks, tacit knowledge, learning on the job and difficulty of monitoring job performance.

A third contribution is Kaufman's (2004c, 2010) ERS model. It is similar to Marsden in that it uses IE and, in particular, the transaction cost (TC) concept. He demonstrates that in a world of very low TC, organizations disagglomerate into small units and HRM systems are 'externalized' and 'simple'; in a world of very high TC, organizations agglomerate into very large units and employment systems become 'internalized' and 'HRM-intensive'. Variation of five variables, in turn, causes different ERS permutations between these polar opposites: the degree of bounded decision-making, interdependence in utility functions, interdependence in production functions, indivisibilities and gaps in property rights and legal restrictions on trade by the sovereign.

Summary

EIR micro-theories of employment systems suggest several things for macro-theory construction. First, these models suggest that factors external and internal to firms cause employers to configure EIR practices in a relatively small number of discrete configurations. Second, these models suggest that at the most fundamental level ERSs divide into two polar opposites. On one end is a largely market-driven employment system where labor is treated as a commodity (a 'hired hand'); the firm's strategy focuses on cost minimization; EIR practices and internal labor markets are sparse and porous; workers are likely to feel low commitment and trust; and the employment relationship tends to be viewed by both sides as a zero-sum game. On the other end of the spectrum is a human capital/commitment employment model where labor is viewed as an asset (a 'human resource'); the firm's strategy seeks competitive advantage through superior employee motivation, skills and behaviors; considerable investment is made in EIR practices, job security and internal labor markets; employees feel considerable loyalty and dedication to the organization; and the employment relationship is viewed by both sides as a positive-sum game. Third, these micro-ERS-theories suggest that a finer analysis reveals that employment systems sort not just into two opposite ideal types but, rather, into a small number of distinct but complementary systems. Although authors give different names to these employment systems, in generic form they sort into models centered on, respectively, market forces, the technology of production, organizational structure characteristics, occupational norms and skills and employee motivation and firm-specific skill development – in some cases reinforced by the forces of trade unionism and labor law. Fourth, these theories also pinpoint specific variables that influence firms' choice of ERS systems: for example, the firm-specific nature of skills, the degree to which technology can control and monitor the quantity and quality of work, the importance of human capital in production, firms' positioning strategy for competitive advantage, economic conditions in product and labor markets (e.g., degree of competition, extent of surplus labor supply), and the relative importance for production of discretionary employee work effort and citizenship behavior.

Macro-theories of EIR Systems

We now come to EIR theories and models that explicitly address cross-national variation in employment relations practices and outcomes. I winnow the literature and present a synopsis of studies that represent significant contributions and explicit theoretical generalizations, presented in chronological order of publication. Studies with more general but less testable classifications, frameworks and implications (e.g., Dore, 1973; Adams, 1995; Locke et al., 1995; Martin and Bamber, 2004) are perforce omitted due to space constraints, although they also offer valuable insights. The same is true for comparative studies limited to specific EIR topic areas, such as unions and collective bargaining (e.g., Hyman, 2001) and multinational corporations (Briscoe et al., 2009). As before, the focus is on studies broadly in the institutional and neo-institutional tradition.

The place to start has to be the book *Industrialism and Industrial Man* by Kerr et al. (1960). This book is without doubt the most ambitious and large-scale study ever done in CER; furthermore, the project secured large-sized funding from the Ford Foundation and sponsored a wave of additional comparative EIR work by scholars from across the world that over a two-decade period produced more than 40 additional books. The 1950s and 1960s were a 'golden age' for the pioneers of CER research; furthermore, the work of Kerr et al. and collaborators greatly helped spread the industrial relations field beyond its narrow Anglo-American base. Representative titles produced include *Human Resources for Egyptian Enterprises* (Harbison and Ibrahim, 1958), *Industrial Relations in India* (Myers and Kannappan, 1970) and *Human Resources in Japanese Industrial Development* (Levine and Kawada, 1980). Other scholars from a variety of countries were also attracted into the CER field, such as Hugh Clegg, Everett Kassalow, Frederick Meyers, James Morris, Ben Roberts and Adolf Sturmthal.

Kerr et al. spent seven years visiting numerous countries around the world assembling evidence for the book. Remarkably, while hailed as a great work at the time it has since largely faded into anonymity or become a standard reference for critics of the 'convergence thesis'. *Industrialism and Industrial Man* takes Dunlop's earlier IR systems model and extends it to a cross-country comparison; further, while Dunlop's IR systems model is largely static, Kerr et al. endeavor to put a dynamic element into it (via the industrialization process). Their thesis is that CER exhibits both unity and diversity. The unity comes from the inexorable process of industrialization – a process well advanced in some countries and only beginning in others – which poses through technological and organizational constraints a significant degree of conformity in broad EIR practices and outcomes (e.g., all industrialized countries have large firms, bureaucratic employment systems and labor movements). The diversity in EIR comes from a variety of factors that are country- or region-specific: examples include the different industrialization strategies of the ruling elites, diverse cultural and social conditions and different political and management-labor ideologies. Kerr et al. predict a 'first order' trend toward convergence among nations in the 'web of rules' that define national EIR systems as at some point all countries are seen as getting on the industrialization bandwagon; nonetheless, they also predict continued 'second order' diversity in the EIR web of rules due to long-lasting cross-national differences in cultural, social and political factors.

Theorizing in CER entered a relatively inactive period during the 1970s and early 1980s. The ice was broken, however, with publication of *Industrial Relations: Origins and Patterns of National Diversity* by Michael Poole (1986). Similar to the 'micro'-EIR model of Barbash (1984), Poole defines EIR broadly as 'all aspects of the employment relationship' (p. 4) but then designates employer–employee conflict as the central dependent variable of interest (p. 6). Poole also follows Dunlop (1958) in making employers, employees and the state as the three principal actors. He argues that divergent interests between employers and employees characterize the employment relationship in both the spheres of production and distribution; hence, the task of CER theory is to identify the variables that generate conflictive interests and the institutions and practices designed by the three actors to ameliorate and resolve these conflicts. Poole allows that, 'at the current state of our knowledge, attempts to establish a general inclusive comparative industrial relations theory are likely to prove fruitless' (p. 198). Nonetheless, he believes it is possible to identify principal variables and causal pathways. In this spirit, Poole identifies the state of economic development, the strategies of the actors, cultural values and ideologies, the nation's politico-economic structure, the power of the actors and the institutional structure of firms and EIR organizations as principal explanatory variables.

The third CER model examined here is by Colin Crouch in his book *Industrial Relations and European State Traditions* (1993). It is an example of the genre of CER that focuses primarily on the collective dimension of employment relations; in addition, it represents a precursor to important ideas in the VoC literature surveyed in the next section.

As is true for many other authors, Crouch is critical of many specific aspects of Dunlop's IR systems model but, nonetheless, utilizes the basic systems idea. His focus is on European countries and the central 'dependent variable' is the degree of centralization and coordination of industrial relations between organized capital (Capital) and organized labor (Labor). In this respect, Crouch exemplifies a European tendency to define EIR narrowly as 'collective employment relations'. High coordination and centralization is representative of 'neo-corporatist' EIR systems, such as Germany and Scandinavia; low coordination and decentralization is representative of 'pluralist' or 'conflictive' EIR systems, such as France and Britain. His thesis is that the pluralist/conflict EIR model is the zero-sum (or even negative sum) 'default' option, much as in a Prisoner's Dilemma game, while the cooperative neo-corporatist model creates positive-sum outcomes. Both systems exist in modern Europe; hence, the issue for theory is to identify the variables that cause countries to gravitate toward one or the other. Crouch argues that three factors are crucial. First, Labor must be powerful and be able to threaten Capital with large losses, hence motivating Capital to seek accommodation and partnership. Second, Capital and Labor must cover a significant part of the workforce and have centralized organizational structures so they can incorporate diverse constituencies, demands and effects. And, third, both Capital and Labor 'peak organizations' must be able to police their members and maintain intra-organizational unity. If these three factors are met, Capital and Labor develop dense interactions and interdependencies, a culture of trust and cooperation and a problem-solving communication approach that collectively allows them to move from the conflictive/pluralist zero-sum outcome to the neo-corporatist/cooperative positive-sum outcome.

Next is the book *Dynamic Human Resource Systems: Cross-national Comparisons* by James Begin (1997). Begin, a professor of industrial relations, describes his model as a blend of ideas and concepts from the neo-institutionalist and strategic human resource management literatures. Begin develops a CER theory and then applies it to an explanation of the EIR systems in six nations: Germany, Japan, Singapore, Sweden, United Kingdom and United States. His model is ambitious because he endeavors to explain not only differences in EIR architectures and practices but also cross-national differences in four outcomes: degree of employee competence and commitment; the degree of organizational flexibility; the degree of organizational integration; and level of organizational performance. Unlike Crouch, Begin assumes EIR applies to both union and non-union employment relations.

Begin follows Dunlop and theorizes CER in terms of discrete systems; further, he takes the rules of the workplace as an intermediate variable in the causal chain that links external and internal explanatory variables to differences in EIR architectures, practices and performance. EIR systems are decomposed into six subsystems: work/job design, employee development, staffing, workforce governance, rewards and EIR management structure. According to Begin, one driver of differences in EIR systems across nations is differences in competitive strategies on the part of business firms. Given different resource endowments, levels of technology and other contextual factors, each nation comes to the global marketplace with different competitive advantages. Government policies, national cultures and business strategies adapt to align with and exploit these competitive niches. Thus, the competitive advantage of the United States is mass production of consumption goods, Germany's is quality production of differentiated durables and investment goods, and Japan's is technological innovation and high-quality manufacturing. Differences in these production regimes lead to predictable differences in EIR systems. Differences in production regimes then interact in a complementary way with other external and internal factors to further differentiate EIR systems. One example in Begin's model is the external state-supported education system and the internal firm-created employee training system. Japan's and Germany's strategy of quality production, for example, is partly conditioned on a state school system that produces large numbers of graduates with top-end reading, math and science skills and well-developed in-firm training systems where workers get life-long training and skill development in ILMs. The US, by way of contrast, gravitates toward a mass production EIR system in part because the education system also 'mass produces' low-to-medium-quality secondary-level graduates and firms rely less on in-firm training systems for needed employee skills than hiring from external labor markets.

A fifth study providing CER theory with INI roots is *Converging Divergences* by Harry Katz and Owen Darbishire (2000). It raises an interesting empirical finding vis-à-vis the Crouch study (just reviewed) and the VoC studies coming up. Crouch argues that a centralized neo-corporatist EIR system maximizes national performance; perhaps ominously, Katz and Darbishire observe that in seven major European, North American and Asian economies the late twentieth-century trend in EIR systems is the other way – that is, toward decentralization and deunionization. This common trend in each country provides the 'converging' theme for the book. Within and across countries, however, they observe growing dispersion and variety in EIR practices and outcomes and movement toward a larger number of discrete ESs in countries (e.g., Germany) where centralized bargaining institutions once covered most of the field. This increased ES variation provides the 'divergences' theme for the book.

Based on their seven country comparisons, Katz and Darbishire identify four discrete employment systems that represent the major options in each nation. They label them: Low Wage, HRM, Japanese-oriented, and Joint-team-based. The convergence trend toward decentralization and deunionization, they argue, arises in broad outline from certain common economic forces (globalization, deregulation) and organizational/technological factors (flatter hierarchies, flexible manufacturing techniques). The rapidity and extent of decentralization and deunionization across countries, however, is principally determined by the starting point of each country in terms of the breadth and depth of institutional coordination and regulation of the EIR system; that is, in more coordinated/regulated EIR systems the pace of decentralization and deunionization is slower. In a complementary way, Katz and Darbishire also find that the growth of within-country dispersion in EIR practices varies inversely with the pre-existing level of institutional coordination and regulation.

A sixth CER study of note is by Jill Rubery and Damian Grimshaw (2003). Reflecting more a neo-Marxist and labor process (or 'materialist') orientation, they argue that central to any theory of CER must be the nature of the production system in each country. Their work falls in the INI tradition, however, because they do not posit a one-way causal arrow from the forces of production to the relations of production, as in classic Marxist theory, but rather two-way interactive arrows where the institutions of the economy also influence the production system. Based on a number of features of production systems, they sort OECD countries into four types: Japanese lean production, German diversified quality production, Italian flexible specialization and Swedish socio-technical. They then identify the major competitive strategy that accompanies each and the derivative EIR system. For example, the Japanese system features high work intensity, long-term employment security and enterprise unions; the German system features a highly skilled workforce, extensive training and strong unions and industry-wide bargaining; the Italian system features small workshops with skilled labor, informal training and weak and fragmented unions; and the Swedish system features extensive team working, social welfare provisions and nationwide collaboration between employers' associations and trade union federations.

The final Anglo-American CER model considered here is by John Budd in his book *Employment with a Human Face* (2004). Budd argues that every EIR system is built around three fundamental structural constraints and desired behavioral outcomes: attainment of efficiency, equity and voice. Attainment of these three outcomes leads to convergence among national EIR systems along certain important dimensions. For example, efficiency dictates that manufacturing firms in a given product line (e.g., autos) adopt EIR systems with certain common job skills, training methods and horizontal and vertical lines of job mobility; likewise, maintenance of internal and external equity dictates that these same firms link pay to individual job performance and provide some formal method for dispute resolution. But diversity in EIR systems is made possible because to some significant degree, companies, industries and nations put different weights on efficiency, equity and voice and choose different methods to achieve them. This allows Budd to develop a 'geometry' of CER (see his Figure 7.1) where national EIRs sort into different efficiency, equity and voice combinations. A Social Partnership (neo-corporatist) form of EIR system, for example, scores relatively high on formal employee voice, low-to-medium on efficiency and middle-high on equity; a Weak Voluntarist system, on the other hand, adopts EIR architectures and practices that score high on promoting efficiency, flexibility and low cost but score relatively low on both equity and voice.

EUROPEAN-BASED INI THEORIES

A largely separate but complementary CER theoretical literature has developed with roots mostly (but not exclusively) in continental Europe. As noted earlier, the field of industrial relations was a relative latecomer to Europe (a term hereafter used to mean continental Europe) and never established a significant institutional/organizational home-base in its universities. Further, European sociology has taken within its borders many aspects of the employment relationship, a fact that has also reduced the opportunities for EIR in Europe to develop the same degree of autonomy and presence as it has in Anglo-American countries.

Nonetheless, the same forces of globalization that over the last several decades have stirred renewed interest in CER among Anglo-American scholars have also done so among their European counterparts, leading to a parallel resurgence in scholarship in this area. Both literatures have a substantial base in institutionalism but the European branch, being more influenced by sociology and political science than economics and human resource management – as well as distinctive European intellectual and ideological traditions, has developed a distinctive theoretical discourse and set of ideas that distinguishes it from Anglo-American theorizing in CER. The differences, however, are often more of emphasis and idiom; further, several Anglo-American authors have made substantive contributions to developing this European-based literature (e.g., Piore and Sabel, 1984; Hollingsworth in Hollingsworth and Boyer, 1998) and in recent years a number of Anglo-American authors have further extended it, particularly with respect to employment relations and CER (e.g., Godard, 2004; Wailes et al., 2008).

EIR-related research in Europe (hereafter 'Euro-EIR') spans disciplines but has its center of gravity in economic sociology, albeit with significant cross-disciplinary contributions from political science and other fields. While Anglo-American EIR traces its roots to founders such as the Webbs, Commons and Perlman, economic sociology looks to people such as Durkheim, Weber, Polanyi and Marx for foundational ideas. Like neoclassical economists, for example, Durkheim makes the division of labor a central organizing concept for sociology; the difference is that he insists the division of labor is coordinated by more than competitive market forces – for example, power, authority, social norms, custom and law – and functions within a network of constraining and enabling formal and informal institutions. From this heritage grows two themes that are at the center of institutionalism in modern economic sociology: the social embeddedness of economic life and the coordination role played by institutions (Polanyi, 1944; Hall and Soskice, 2001). Added to these are other concepts, probably the most important and oft-cited are institutional complementarity and institutional comparative advantage.

Euro-EIR parallels Dunlop in one important respect but then quickly diverges on another. The common element is that both portray EIR practices and outcomes as an interconnected system; the divergent element is that Dunlop argues the EIR system can be treated for purposes of analysis as largely a separate self-contained subsystem of the national economy and society while Euro-EIR argues (reflecting, in part, the stronger influence of Marxism) that the EIR system cannot be divorced from or taken out of the larger economic and social system in which it is embedded. This premise immediately leads to what is perhaps the most distinctive – certainly the most cited – conceptual part of Euro-EIR: the notion that advanced industrial nations sort into varieties of capitalism and, thus, by principles of complementarity and coherence into varieties of EIR systems.

Many writers (e.g., Crouch, 2005) attribute the initial inspiration for the VoC idea to the book *Capitalism vs. Capitalism* by Michel Albert (1993); by all accounts, however, its most influential and oft-cited source is the edited volume *Varieties of Capitalism* by Hall and Soskice (2001) and, in particular, the editor's introductory chapter. Behind these scholarly works, it should also be noted, are important real world events, such as the fall of the Berlin Wall and the end of socialism as a seemingly viable economic alternative to capitalism. The subtitle of Albert's book gives a flavor of the argument; it also accurately indicates that the main line of this literature is to some degree critical of a US-style neoliberal market economy and favorable toward a Northern European-type 'social market' economy. The subtitle reads: *How America's Obsession with Individual Achievement and Short-term Profit Has Led it to the Brink of Collapse.* This subtitle also reveals, although less directly, another feature of the VoC literature, which bears on its utility as a basis for comparative work in EIR. That is, the concept and focus of VoC potentially omits a large number of the world's countries from analysis – that is, all those lacking relatively modern and mature capitalist economies. Indeed, as a number of commentators have noted, in VoC the attention tends to be on two countries as the archetypes – Germany and the US or, somewhat more broadly, Germany/Japan and the US/UK (Streeck and Yamamura, 2001). In recent years some authors have endeavored to broaden the reach of VoC by distinguishing one or more other models, such as an Asian variety of capitalism (Yeung, 2000) and a Mediterranean variety of capitalism (Amable, 2003), although these remain somewhat peripheral to the literature and still effectively leave out many other regions. I should further note that the comparisons in VoC between Germany/Japan and the US/UK are not entirely novel as an earlier 1980s' literature on corporatism focused on many of the same differences in the respective economic systems (Goldthorpe, 1984).

Given these points of context, two different approaches – a deductive (theory-driven) and an inductive (data-driven) method – have been taken to identify different models of capitalism. I start with the deductive approach. It seeks to develop distinct models of capitalism based on a focal theoretical concept; this concept is then used to deduce alternative ideal types (Deeg and Jackson, 2007). Three major focal concepts have been used, respectfully: institutional means of economic coordination, corporate governance systems and national business systems. To a significant degree, the models that emerge are overlapping, complementary and nested one in the other.

The first approach distinguishes VoC on the basis of differences in the mechanism that coordinates market economies (Hall and Soskice, 2001). On one end of the spectrum is reliance on relatively unfettered markets and competitive market forces of demand and supply; in effect, coordination is performed by the 'invisible hand' of the market. On the other end is reliance on highly structured and regulated markets where market forces get a large degree of coordination and guidance from the 'visible hand' of the state and lower-tier organizations, such as employers' associations and trade unions. The former is typically referred to as a liberal market economy (LME) and the latter as a coordinated market economy (CME) (Streeck and Yamamura, 2001). Corollary features of an LME are a more individualistic cultural ethos, lower union density, a less interventionist government and a smaller and more porous social safety net; features of a CME are largely the opposite.

The second deductive approach distinguishes VoC based on different forms of corporate governance (Dore, 2000; Gospel and Pendleton, 2005). On one end of the spectrum is the shareholder model of capitalism; on the other is the stakeholder model. In shareholder countries public policy treats corporations as the creatures and servants of their shareholder owners; that is, corporations exist for only one purpose – to serve the interests of the shareholders – and the shareholders' interests in turn are focused on maximizing the value of the stock shares. Corporate governance, therefore, is structured so that the capital owners exercise dominant if not sole authority in running the company, restrictions on capital investment decisions and mergers/acquisitions are minimized, and financial markets are well developed, highly competitive and emphasize raising capital through stock and bond markets. Typically, managers operate with a shorter time horizon in shareholder countries.

In stakeholder countries, the situation is much the reverse. Corporations are created by the state and while they must operate to earn profits for shareholders they must also serve broader social objectives – with the idea that maximum profit may subtract from accomplishment of certain social goals (e.g., a cleaner environment) and fail to achieve others (a reduction in the length of the work week). Hence, corporate governance is diffused among different stakeholders so each has a say in the goals and operation of the company, such as intended with the German model of codetermination. In stakeholder countries, corporations are more highly regulated, are embedded in a thicker institutional network of trade unions, employers' associations and government agencies, and obtain capital relatively more from banks and governments. Hence, these companies have 'patient capital' so executives can make business decisions with a longer-term payback period; likewise, the limits on takeovers and mergers and acquisitions to some degree insulates executives from short-term pressure to raise the stock price and cut operating costs so they can better balance the interests and needs of not only shareholders but also workers and communities.

The third deductive approach makes use of a concept called 'national business systems' and makes the focal theoretical construct alternative state strategies for growth and development (Whitley, 1999, 2005). Of all institutions in an economy, the state is the most consequential because it sets the constitutional rules that determine the legal framework of the economy and, therefore, the shape of private organizations, the goals and constraints of individual agents and the nature of the coordination mechanisms used to bind together transactors. States choose different growth and development strategies depending on various factors, including the composition and objectives of the national elites, the nation's culture and history, sources of comparative advantage and exposure to international trade. Based on these factors, Whitley (2005) derives four state-created models of capitalism: Arm's Length, Dominant Developmental, Business Corporatist and Inclusive Corporatist. In Arm's Length countries (e.g., the US), the state's growth strategy emphasizes competitive markets and modest-to-little government intervention and encouragement of organized interest groups (e.g., unions, industry associations). Nations using the Dominant Developmental strategy (e.g., South Korea) give the state a large and active role in guiding the economy; further, the state dominates or represses intermediary organized interest groups. A variant is the Business Corporatist model where the state (e.g., Japan) again plays a dominant role but gives more space to intermediary interest groups with employer associations given high-level access to state policy-makers and labor groups tolerated but given less access. The Inclusive Corporatist model (e.g., Sweden) is similar except that both organized labor and business groups are given high-level access and important coordinating roles.

These deductive models of VoC have been criticized on various grounds

(Crouch, 2005; Streeck and Thelen, 2005; Hancké et al., 2007; Kesting and Nielsen, 2008); for example, for being overly static, deterministic, firm-centered and downplaying conflict and the cross-country role of multinational corporations. Another criticism is that they impose arbitrary and sometimes ill-fitting distinctions upon countries. An opposite approach, therefore, is empirical and inductive where VoC categories are formed by using statistical techniques (e.g., cluster analysis) to sort countries into similar patterns. A good example is Amable (2003). He examines 21 OECD economies. Based on a large number of statistical indicators, he finds these countries sort into five relatively distinct models of capitalism. He calls these, respectively, Market-based, Social Democratic, Asian, Mediterranean and Continental European.

Described to this point are various VoC models and associated theories. For them to be relevant to CER, these models must be used to generate predictions about the architectures and outcomes of EIR systems (Brewster et al., 2006). Here enters the core concept of institutional complementarity. What all of these VoC models have in common is that they generate differences in national business systems from non-labor attributes of societies – that is, factors such as state development strategies and different forms of corporate governance. Thus, the challenge is to then derive the EIR system that matches the core VoC attribute. Toward this end, INI writers go back to the 'systems' idea and posit that the pieces of a national business system are adjusted by economic agents until they (approximately) fit together and interact in a (more or less) functionally coherent and perhaps synergistic manner. This notion of 'pieces fitting together' encapsulates the idea of complementarity, also found in the human resource management literature in the form of the 'configurational' hypothesis (Boxall and Purcell, 2008). More formally, INI writers state that two institutions are complementary when, 'the presence (or efficiency) of one increases the returns from (or efficiency of) the other' (Hall and Soskice, 2001, p. 17).

It is useful before going further to remind the reader that in most of the European-based VoC literature (e.g., Hall and Soskice, 2001) the term 'industrial relations' is defined narrowly to include only (or mostly) collective employment relations and, in particular, the institutions, laws and practices pertaining to unions, employers associations and other aspects of collective bargaining and voice. In what follows, however, I follow contemporary Anglo-American convention and define IR broadly to include all types of employment relationships, all types of employment practices (including HRM) and all types of social welfare regimes.

The most popular and oft-cited typology in VoC is between LMEs and CMEs (Hancké et al., 2007; Kesting and Nielsen, 2008). VoC writers hypothesize that each form of capitalism should utilize a distinctly different

EIR system (Hall and Soskice. 2001; Godard, 2004; Wailes et al., 2008). LMEs, for example, favor competitive market coordinating mechanisms, arm's-length and non-interventionist governments, shareholder governance systems and low levels of organized interest group involvement. These characteristics are hypothesized, via the principle of institutional complementarity, to lead to predictable patterns in the associated LME employment system. In particular, the EIR system in an LME should feature more labor market volatility and employment in-flows and out-flows, greater dispersion in employment outcomes (e.g., inter-industry wages, income inequality), more porous and truncated ILMs, low levels of institutionalized employment security, greater labor flexibility for firms, greater emphasis on competitive advantage through low-cost production and frame-breaking product innovation, more reliance on buying skills in the market rather than in-house development, a relatively porous and thinly developed net of social insurance programs, relatively weak protective labor laws, low union density and decentralized collective bargaining. As indicated previously, the archetype of an LME employment system is the US – with recognition that within the US is a considerable degree of diversity in EIR systems that gets glossed over at this high level of abstraction.

The features of the EIR system in a CME are much the opposite. Union density is relatively high, collective bargaining is centralized and plays a large role in wage determination, the state actively consults and coordinates with employers' associations and union federations, both labor markets and firms feature a substantial degree of stability and standardization in wages and other economic terms of employment, ILMs are well developed and widespread and employers spend considerable resources on skill development and training, state- and union-mandated employment protection is high, managements have much less flexibility in hiring, pay and termination practices, workers enjoy a wide and generous social safety net of social insurance programs and workers are given voice through a variety of institutional channels besides unions (e.g., works councils). Germany is the archetypical example of a CME.

VoC thus generates a fairly detailed set of hypotheses for CER analysis – at least for the advanced industrial capitalist countries it largely applies to. It goes further, however, and also generates predictions about which type of economy and EIR system yield higher performance (Hall and Soskice, 2001; Streeck and Thelen, 2005). LMEs and CMEs both have performance advantages and disadvantages. The LME, for example, tends to favor radical innovation, gives firms greater flexibility and lower cost, requires lower tax rates and less government bureaucracy and regulation, and benefits from the spur of 'do or die' competition. These factors promote economic performance. Working against performance, however, are a mediocre educated and trained workforce, an employee relations climate characterized by more adversarialism, distrust and free-riding, a short-term 'stock market' approach to workforce investment and management, socially corrosive levels of inequality and insecurity and more boom and bust.

The CME also has performance advantages and disadvantages. On the plus side, for example, are hypothesized factors such as a higher-educated and skilled workforce, an employment relationship with greater trust, cooperation and commitment, more stable and non-inflationary wage settlements, continuous if incremental innovation and quality improvement and greater equality and social solidarity. On the downside, the EIR system in a CME is relatively rigid and inflexible, entails higher costs on firms, can make it difficult to terminate employees for poor performance or in economic downturns and can discourage new business formation and in-country capital investment.

Is there a clear prediction about which variety of capitalism is preferable? Most VoC writers tend to favor the CME model (Streeck, 1998; Hall and Soskice, 2001). On economic grounds, they believe that in the long run a CME outperforms an LME because the former emphasizes a 'high road' strategy of growth and development based on skills, cooperation and trust while the LME emphasizes a 'low road' strategy of cost cutting, Taylorist work practices (deskilling, narrow training) and an adversarial/low-trust climate. In effect, VoC theorists look at the employment relationship as a form of Prisoner's Dilemma game and predict that LMEs gravitate toward the low-performance 'lose–lose' option while CMEs are able to move to the high-performance 'win–win' outcome because their EIR systems generate better communication, trust and cooperation among the social partners. Further, they argue that different national business systems develop an institutional comparative advantage and path-dependent trajectory and moving from one system to another (e.g., from a CME to LME) can therefore lead to very suboptimal performance (Deeg and Jackson, 2007).

Since this chapter is focused on theory I will not review the extensive empirical literature and accompanying debates on these issues. Suffice it to say, however, the evidence is quite mixed. If attention is focused only on rates of GDP and employment growth, the LMEs appear to win. If a broader set of objectives is considered, including social outcomes such as employment security and income equality, then performance shifts toward CMEs. What this perhaps indicates is again the importance of institutions. Certain countries, such as in the Anglo-American sphere, for historical and cultural reasons favor a more market-oriented and individualized EIR system and use political institutions to create rules of the game that favor this type of system and the high GDP growth/high inequality outcomes it produces; other countries, such as in continental Europe, favor a more regulated and collective form of capitalism and use political institutions that set rules of the game that trade off lower GDP growth for greater security for workers and equality for all parts of society.

CONCLUSION

Comparative employment relations has been an active area of research for more than a half-century. Whether nations are converging to a common EIR system remains a hotly debated question. What can safely be said, however, is that some convergence has taken place in theorizing about the origins of cross-national differences in EIR systems. Nearly all participants agree that an explanation of cross-national variation in EIR institutional architectures is crucial to a viable CER theory. There is also a wide degree of consensus on the types of variables that are important to explaining this diversity in EIR institutions. Following Marxist models, attention must be focused on the nature of national production systems; following neoclassical models attention must also be focused on characteristics of national market systems and the stage of economic development; following human resource management, attention must also be given to national differences in EIR strategies among the actors; and following sociology and anthropology, attention must be given to cross-national cultural/social traditions and values. EIR also brings its own unique perspective and contribution to CER theorizing, however. It does so partly by melding and synthesizing these other perspectives into an integrated model; it also does so through its own unique concepts and ideas. Central to CER, for example, is the concept of an employment relations system, different models and typologies of ERSs, identification of key variables and constraints that form ERSs and the role of institutional complementarities. All of this represents a promising beginning; much more, however, awaits to be done – particularly with respect to greater analytical development.

REFERENCES

Acemoglu, D. (2009), *Introduction to Modern Economic Growth*, Princeton, NJ: Princeton University Press.

Adams, R. (1995), *Industrial Relations Under Liberal Democracy*, Columbia, SC: University of South Carolina Press.

Adams, R. and Meltz, N. (1993), *Industrial Relations Theory: Its Nature and Pedagogy*, Metuchen, NJ: Scarecrow Press.

Albert, M. (1993), *Capitalism vs. Capitalism*, New York: Four Walls Eight Windows.

Amable, B. (2003), *The Diversity of Modern Capitalism*, Oxford: Oxford University Press.

Aoki, M. (2000), *Information, Corporate Governance, and Institutional Diversity*, Oxford: Oxford University Press.

Appelbaum, E., Bailey, T., Berg, P. and Kalleberg, A. (2000), *Manufacturing Advantage: Why High-performance Work Systems Pay Off*, Ithaca, NY: Cornell University Press.

Arthur, J. (1992), 'The link between business strategy and industrial relations systems in American steel minimills', *Industrial and Labor Relations Review*, **45**(3), 488–506.

Bamber, G., Lansbury, R. and Wailes, N. (2004), *International and Comparative Employment Relations*, 4th edition, New York: Sage.

Barbash, J. (1984), *The Elements of Industrial Relations*, Madison, WI: University of Wisconsin Press.

Barbash, J. and Barbash, K. (1989), *Theories and Concepts in Comparative Industrial Relations*, Columbia, SC: University of South Carolina Press.

Bean, R. (1994), *Comparative Industrial Relations*, 2nd edition, New York: Routledge.

Begin, J. (1991), *Strategic Employment Policy: An Organizational Systems Perspective*, Englewood Cliffs, NJ: Prentice-Hall.

Begin, J. (1997), *Dynamic Human Resource Systems: Cross-national Comparisons*, New York: De Gruyter.

Blum, A. (1981), *International Handbook of Industrial Relations*, Westport, CT: Greenwood Press.

Blyton, P. and Turnbull, P. (2004), *The Dynamics of Employee Relations*, 3rd edition, London: Palgrave Macmillan.

Boxall, P. and Purcell, J. (2008), *Strategy and Human Resource Management*, 2nd edition, New York: Palgrave Macmillan.

Brewster, C., Wood, G. and Brookes, M. (2006), 'Varieties of capitalism and varieties of firms', in G. Wood and P. James (eds), *Institutions, Production, and Working Life*, Oxford: Oxford University Press, pp. 217–34.

Briscoe, D., Schuler, R. and Claus, L. (2009), *International Human Resource Management: Policies and Practices for Multinational Corporations*, 3rd edition, New York: Routledge.

Budd, J. (2004), *Employment with a Human Face: Balancing Efficiency, Equity, and Voice*, Ithaca, NY: Cornell University Press.

Coase, R. (1937), 'The nature of the firm', *Economica*, **4**(16), 386–405.

Coase, R. (1992), 'The institutional structure of production', *American Economic Review*, **82**(4), 713–19.

Cochrane, J. (1979), *Industrialism and Industrial Man in Retrospect*, Ann Arbor, MI: University of Michigan Press.

Commons, J. (1919), *Industrial Goodwill*, New York: McGraw Hill.

Commons, J. (1934), *Institutional Economics: Its Place in Political Economy*, New York: Macmillan.

Crouch, C. (1993), *Industrial Relations and European State Traditions*, Oxford: Clarendon Press.

Crouch, C. (2005), *Capitalist Diversity and Change*, Oxford: Oxford University Press.

Deeg, R. and Jackson, G. (2007), 'Toward a more dynamic theory of capitalist development', *Socio-Economic Review*, **5**(1), 149–79.

Doeringer, P. (1981), *Industrial Relations in International Perspective*, New York: Holmes and Meier.

Doeringer, P. and Piore, M. (1971), *Internal Labor Markets and Manpower Analysis*, Lexington: Lexington Books.

Dore, R. (1973), *British Factory, Japanese Factory: The Origins of National Diversity in Industrial Relations*, Berkeley, CA: University of California Press.

Dore, R. (2000), *Stock Market Capitalism: Welfare Capitalism*, Oxford: Oxford University Press.

Dunlop, J. (1958), *Industrial Relations Systems*, New York: Holt.

Durkheim, E. ([1895]1938), *Rules of the Sociological Method*, 8th edition, Glencoe, IL: Free Press.

Edwards, P. (2003), 'The employment relationship and the field of industrial relations', in P. Edwards (ed.), *Industrial Relations: Theory and Practice*, 2nd edition, London: Blackwell, pp. 1–36.

Edwards, R. (1979), *Contested Terrain: The Transformation of the Workplace in the Twentieth Century*, New York: Basic Books.

Ferner, A. and Hyman, R. (1992), *Industrial Relations in the New Europe*, London: Blackwell.

Flanders, A. (1965), *Industrial Relations: What's Wrong With the System? An Essay on its Theory and Future*, London: Faber and Faber.

Godard, J. (2004), 'The new institutionalism, capitalist diversity, and industrial relations', in B. Kaufman (ed.), *Theoretical Perspectives on Work and the Employment Relationship*, Champaign, IL: Industrial Relations Research Association, pp. 229–64.

Goldthorpe, J. (1984), *Order and Conflict in Contemporary Capitalism*, Oxford: Oxford University Press.

Gospel, H. and Pendleton, P. (2005), *Corporate Governance and Labour Management*, Oxford: Oxford University Press.

Hall, P. and Soskice, D. (2001), *Varieties of Capitalism: The Institutional Foundations of Comparative Advantage*, Oxford: Oxford University Press.

Hall, R. and Wailes, N. (2010), 'International and comparative human resource management', in A. Wilkinson, N. Bacon, T. Redman and S. Snell (eds), *The Sage Handbook of Human Resource Management*, New York: Sage, pp. 115–32.

Hamann, K. and Kelly, J. (2008), 'Varieties of capitalism and industrial relations', in P. Blyton, N. Bacon, J. Fiorito and E. Heery (eds), *The Sage Handbook of Industrial Relations*, New York: Sage, pp. 129–48.

Hancké, B., Rhodes, M. and Thatcher, M. (2007), 'Introduction: Beyond varieties of capitalism', in B. Hancké, M. Rhodes and M. Thatcher (eds), *Beyond Varieties of Capitalism*, Oxford University Press, pp. 3–38.

Harbison, F. and Ibrahim, I. (1958), *Human Resources in Egyptian Enterprises*, New York: McGraw-Hill.

Hills, S. (1995), *Employment Relations and the Social Sciences*, Columbia, SC: University of South Carolina Press.

Hodgson, G. (1998), *Foundations of Evolutionary Economics, 1890–1973*, Cheltenham, UK and Lyme, NH, USA: Edward Elgar.

Hodgson, G. (2002), 'Institutional blindness in modern economics', in J. Hollingsworth, K. Müller and E. Hollingsworth (eds), *Advancing Socio-Economics: An Institutionalist Perspective*, Boston: Rowman and Littlefield, pp. 147–70.

Hollingsworth, J. (2002), 'On institutions', in J. Hollingsworth, K. Müller and E. Hollingsworth (eds), *Advancing Socio-Economics*, London: Rowman and Littlefield, pp. 83–7.

Hollingsworth, J. and Boyer, R. (1998), *Contemporary Capitalism: The Embeddedness of Institutions*, Cambridge: Cambridge University Press.

Hyman, R. (1975), *Industrial Relations: A Marxist Introduction*, London: Macmillan.

Hyman, R. (2001), *European Trade Unionism: Between Market, Class and Society*, London: Sage.

Hyman, R. (2004), 'Is industrial relations theory always ethnocentric?', in B. Kaufman (ed.), *Theoretical Perspectives on Work and the Employment Relationship*, Champaign, IL: Industrial Relations Research Association, pp. 265–92.

Jessop, B. (2002), 'The social embeddedness of the economy and its implications for economic governance', in F. Adaman and P. Devine (eds), *Economy and Society: Money, Capitalism and Transition*, New York: Black Rose Books, pp. 192–224.

Katz, H. and Darbishire, O. (2000), *Converging Divergences: Worldwide Changes in Employment Systems*, Ithaca, NY: Cornell University Press.

Kaufman, B. (1993), *The Origin and Evolution of the Field of Industrial Relations in the United States*, Ithaca, NY: ILR Press.

Kaufman, B. (2004a), *The Global Evolution of Industrial Relations: Events, Ideas, and the IIRA*, Geneva: ILO.

Kaufman, B. (2004b), *Theoretical Perspectives on Work and the Employment Relationship*, Champaign, IL: Industrial Relations Research Association.

Kaufman, B. (2004c), 'Employment relations and the employment relations system: A guide to theorizing', in B. Kaufman (ed.), *Theoretical Perspectives on Work and the Employment Relationship*, Champaign, IL: Industrial Relations Research Association, pp. 41–75.

Kaufman, B. (2008), 'Paradigms in industrial relations: Original, modern, and versions in-between', *British Journal of Industrial Relations*, **46**(2), 314–39.

Kaufman, B. (2010), 'The theoretical foundation of industrial relations and its implications for labor economics and human resource management', *Industrial and Labor Relations Review*, **64**(1), 74–108.

Kerr, C. (1950), 'Labor markets: Their character and consequences', *American Economic Review*, **40**(2), 278–91.

Kerr, C. (1954), 'The Balkanization of labor markets', in E. Bakke (ed.), *Labor Mobility and Economic Opportunity*, Cambridge, MA: MIT Press, pp. 92–110.

Kerr, C., Dunlop, J.T., Harbison, F.H. and Myers, C.A. (1960), *Industrialism and Industrial Man*, Cambridge, MA: Harvard University Press.

Kesting, S. and Nielsen, K. (2008), 'Varieties of capitalism: Theoretical critique and empirical observation', in W. Elsner and H. Hanappi (eds), *Varieties of Capitalism and New Institutional Deals*, Cheltenham, UK and Northampton, MA: Edward Elgar, pp. 23–52.

Kochan, T., Katz, H. and McKersie, R. (1986), *The Transformation of American Industrial Relations*, New York: Basic Books.

Lepak, D. and Snell, S. (1999), 'The human resource architecture: Toward a theory of human capital allocation and development', *Academy of Management Review*, **24**(1), 31–48.

Levine, S. and Kawada, H. (1980), *Human Resources in Japanese Industrial Development*, Princeton, NJ: Princeton University Press.

Locke, R., Kochan, T. and Piore, M. (1995), *Employment Relations in a Changing World Economy*, Cambridge, MA: MIT Press.

Marsden, D. (1999), *A Theory of Employment Systems: Micro Foundations of Societal Diversity*, Oxford: Oxford University Press.

Martin, R. and Bamber, G. (2004), 'International comparative employment relations theory: Developing the political economy perspective', in B. Kaufman (ed.), *Theoretical Perspectives on Work and the Employment Relationship*, Champaign, IL: Industrial Relations Research Association, pp. 293–321.

Müller-Jentsch, W. (2004), 'Theoretical approaches to industrial relations', in B. Kaufman (ed.), *Theoretical Perspectives on Work and the Employment Relationship*, Champaign, IL: Industrial Relations Research Association, pp. 1–40.

Myers, C. and Kannappan, S. (1970), *Industrial Relations in India*, New York: Asia Publishing House.

North, D. (2005), *Understanding the Process of Economic Growth*, Princeton, NJ: Princeton University Press.

Orlitzky, M. and Frenkel, S. (2005), 'Alternative pathways to high performance workplaces', *International Journal of Human Resource Management*, **16**(8), 1325–48.

Osterman, P. (1987), 'Choice of employment systems in internal labor markets', *Industrial Relations*, **26**(1), 46–67.

Piore, M. and Sabel, C. (1984), *The Second Industrial Divide: Possibilities for Prosperity*, New York: Basic Books.

Polanyi, K. (1944), *The Great Transformation*, New York: Farrar and Rinehart.

Poole, M. (1986), *Industrial Relations: Origins and Patterns of National Diversity*, London: Routledge and Kegan.

Rubery, J. and Grimshaw, D. (2003), *The Organization of Employment: An International Perspective*, London: Palgrave Macmillan.

Simon, H. (1951), 'A formal theory of the employment relationship', *Econometrica*, **19**(3), 293–305.

Smith, A. ([1776]1937), *An Inquiry into the Nature and Causes of the Wealth of Nations*, New York: Modern Library.

Strauss, G. (1998), 'Comparative international industrial relations', in K. Whitfield and G. Strauss (eds), *Researching the World of Work*, Ithaca, NY: Cornell University Press, pp. 175–92.

Streeck, W. (1998), 'Beneficial constraints: On the economic limits of rational voluntarism', in J. Hollingsworth and R. Boyer (eds), *Contemporary Capitalism: The Embeddedness of Institutions*, Cambridge: Cambridge University Press, pp. 197–219.

Streeck, W. and Thelen, K. (2005), *Beyond Continuity: Institutional Change in Advanced Political Economies*, Oxford: Oxford University Press.

Streeck, W. and Yamamura, K. (2001), *The Origins of Nonliberal Capitalism: Germany and Japan in Comparison*, Ithaca, NY: Cornell University Press.

Stryker, R. (2002), 'The future of socio-economics and of the society for the advancement of socio-economics', in J. Hollingsworth, K. Müller and E. Hollingsworth (eds), *Advancing Socio-Economics: An Institutionalist Perspective*, Boston: Rowman and Littlefield, pp. 51–8.

Thompson, P. and Hartley, B. (2007), 'HRM and the worker: Labor process perspectives', in P. Boxall, J. Purcell and P. Wright (eds), *Oxford International Handbook of Human Resource Management*, Oxford: Oxford University Press, pp. 147–65.

Toh, S., Morgeson, F. and Campion, M. (2008), 'Human resource configurations: Investigating fit with the organizational context', *Journal of Applied Psychology*, **93**(4), 864–82.

Van Ruysseveldt, J., Huiskamp, R. and van Hoof, J. (1995), *Comparative Industrial and Employment Relations*, London: Sage.

Wailes, N., Kitay, J. and Lansbury, R. (2008), 'Varieties of capitalism, corporate governance and employment relations under globalization', in S. Marshall, R. Mitchell and I. Ramsay (eds), *Varieties of Capitalism, Corporate Governance and Employees*, Melbourne, AU: Melbourne University Press, pp. 19–38.

Whitley, R. (1999), *Divergent Capitalisms*, Oxford: Oxford University Press.

Whitley, R. (2005), 'How national are business systems? The role of states and complementary institutions in standardizing systems of economic coordination and control at the national level', in G. Morgan, R. Whitley and E. Moen (eds), *Changing Capitalisms? Internationalization, Institutional Change, and Systems of Economic Organization*, Oxford: Oxford University Press, pp. 190–231.

Williamson, O. (1975), *Markets and Hierarchies*, New York: Free Press.

Yeung, H. (2000), 'The dynamics of Asian business systems in a globalizing era', *Review of International Political Economy*, **7**(3), 399–433.

3 The political economy of comparative employment relations
John Kelly

INTRODUCTION

The 'Golden Age of Capitalism', from the late 1940s until the mid-1970s, was characterized by unprecedented rates of economic growth, dramatic rises in consumption and levels of unemployment lower than at any time before or since (Marglin and Schor, 1990). It also represented the high water mark of trade union power and militancy and of 'political exchange', as governments sought to curb rising inflation and unemployment by negotiating wage restraint with organized labour (Pizzorno, 1978). The intervening years have witnessed a far-reaching and fundamental transformation of employment relations, both in the advanced capitalist world as well as in the major, new economic powers represented by the BRIC countries: Brazil, Russia, India and China (Dicken, 2007). Trade union membership and strike activity have declined in many countries (Phelan, 2007; van der Velden et al., 2008); both authoritarian *and* human resource management approaches to employment relations have become more widespread (cf. Katz and Darbishire, 2000); multinational corporations have become increasingly influential in shaping the labour policies of governments around the globe (Sklair, 2002, pp. 59–83); manufacturing employment has declined in Western Europe and North America but expanded in the Southern Hemisphere (Dicken, 2007); and governments have become more interventionist, not only in wage bargaining but in welfare systems and in labour market policy (Hamann and Kelly, 2010). Although two of the core institutions of employment relations – high collective bargaining coverage and works councils – have remained largely intact in most of Western Europe as of 2010, collective regulation of employment relations has been significantly eroded in the 'liberal market economies' such as the UK and the US (Hall and Soskice, 2001a). The economic background to this transformation has often been encapsulated under the umbrella term 'globalization', whose hallmarks are an escalation of the intensity and geographical scale of both product and labour market competition and a ubiquitous upheaval of the organization of work through the impact of micro-computer technologies (Dicken, 2007).

The intellectual challenge for employment relations scholars has been, and remains, how best to think about these ongoing changes in the forms and outcomes of the regulation of the employment relationship. In this chapter I propose to look in turn at three broad theoretical approaches that emphasize market forces, institutions and actors' strategic choices respectively. The impact of labour and product market competition on wage bargaining outcomes and on levels of union membership are familiar themes in employment relations research and the globalization of competition appears to have lent added force to the analytical power of the economic 'lens' (cf. Brown, 2008). Yet one of the staple propositions of recent comparative political economy is that 'institutions matter'. For despite the immense economic pressures brought to bear on European welfare states, wage bargaining systems and labour markets in recent years, it is clear they continue to display substantial cross-national variations (see, for instance, Katz and Darbishire 2000; Hall and Soskice, 2001a; Swank, 2002). If the properties of economic and other institutions provide one alternative approach to that of market economics, a third approach lays more emphasis on actor strategies. In mainstream employment relations the role of strategic choice was emphasized many years ago by Kochan et al. (1986) in their study of the US, and more recently it has been deployed by Chris Howell (2005) in his seminal historical analysis of the transformations of British industrial relations since the late 1880s.

If we think about each of these approaches as embodying a dominant set of variables and underlying assumptions, it is a truism that almost all writers in employment relations will accord some importance to each of these clusters of variables (e.g., Katz and Darbishire, 2000; Kelly and Frege, 2004). Yet it can also be argued that writers vary in the relative importance they assign to market forces, institutions and actor strategies. We do not have a widely accepted, overarching theory that can specify the inter-relations between these variables so at present theoretical progress in the field consists of attempts to specify the strengths and weaknesses, the insights and limitations of different perspectives in relation to different phenomena. In this chapter I will look in turn at each of these approaches and for each of them will set out their core propositions; the type of evidence normally deployed to support the approach; and the conceptual, theoretical and empirical problems with the approach.

EMPLOYMENT RELATIONS IN A GLOBAL ECONOMY: THE ROLE OF MARKETS

> At the end of April 2008, the Nokia management and works council signed a social plan for the workers of the company's site in Bochum in Western Germany which is to close by the end of June 2008. . . . Nokia has announced the plant's closure and relocation of production lines to Hungary and Romania . . . the Chair of Nokia's Board of Directors, Olli-Pekka Kallasvuo . . . stated that labour costs at the Bochum site were too high, particularly in view of the declining prices for mobile phones. According to Mr Kallasvuo, the level of labour costs was also deterring closely affiliated suppliers from choosing Bochum as a location so that the competitiveness of Nokia's Bochum site had been increasingly impaired. (EIRO, 2008, p. 1)

This short quote encapsulates three of the main themes in the growing literature on globalization and employment relations: the driving role of international product market competition; the priority assigned by companies to the reduction of labour costs; and the capacity of mobile capital to exploit dramatic international variations in labour markets, a tendency that has become especially pronounced since the accession to the EU of a number of low-wage East European states. Product market competition has also led to the transfer of manufacturing jobs from the United States to low-cost locations around the world, particularly in Asia. In the clothing sector, for example, Levi Strauss used to employ 28 000 of its 40 000 global labour force in 35 US factories. Successive closures and relocations steadily cut the workforce and in 2003 the company closed its remaining four US factories (Dicken, 2007, pp. 265–6). In automobiles, the big US firms Ford and General Motors have shut more and more facilities in the US and expanded in China, Mexico and other low wage countries so that by 2005 car production in Mexico was almost 25 per cent of the US level (ibid., p. 309). China, once a predominantly agricultural economy, has been transformed beyond recognition and by 2005 had become the world's fourth largest manufacturing producer and exporter (ibid., pp. 54, 57). The incorporation into the capitalist world economy of parts of Latin America, Asia, particularly China and India, as well as the former communist countries of Eastern Europe has created an enormous expansion of cheap labour reserves and new markets for Western multinational companies (MNCs).

To these three points about global market forces, labour costs and capital mobility, we can add two additional points, about institutions and strategic choice. One implication of what Held et al. (1999) refer to as the 'hyper-globalist' perspective is that industrial relations institutions that are ill-adapted to the market will either be forced to adjust or they will impose a competitive disadvantage on the firms that are regulated by them. There are three major industrial relations developments that appear consistent with this approach. First, there is the almost ubiquitous decentralization of collective bargaining structures since the early 1980s throughout Western Europe (Flanagan, 2008, p. 414). Second, there has been a widespread (though not universal) decline of trade union membership and density both in Europe and other parts of the advanced capitalist world over the same time period (Hamann and Kelly, 2008, p. 138). Finally, the declining coverage of collective bargaining and works councils in Germany, the classical 'coordinated market economy', could be taken as evidence in support of the corrosive power of markets over institutions (Hassel, 2007). One corollary of this type of evidence is that institutional design that cuts against the grain of market forces may no longer be feasible; in other words, the strategic choices open to the industrial relations actors are strictly limited.

Whilst 'hyper-globalist' writers agree on the over-riding power of market forces they disagree profoundly on the implications for workers' terms and conditions (Held et al., 1999, pp. 3–5). Marx and Engels' 1848 *Manifesto of the Communist Party*, arguably the first analysis of global capitalism, predicted a long-run 'immiseration' of the working class as successive reserves of labour around the globe became available and were used to depress wages (Marx and Engels, 1976). In John Gray's (1998) more recent, non-Marxist account, the expansion of the global economy engenders a global 'race to the bottom' because companies seek to drive labour costs ever lower. As MNCs seek out low-wage production sites around the globe, their 'regime shopping' compels governments to offer tax and other incentives to attract foreign direct investment and to retain existing firms. Average corporation tax in the OECD countries was 40 per cent in 1981 but had fallen to 29 per cent by 2001 (Glyn, 2006, p. 165). Turning to the newly industrializing countries (NICs), writers such as Naomi Klein (2000) have documented the long hours, low wages and dangerous working conditions prevailing in many foreign-owned factories within the export processing zones of the NICs of Asia and Central America.

Yet this type of evidence on the negative labour consequences of global market forces has also been challenged from a variety of perspectives. One group of critics has drawn attention to the uneven impact of globalization, noting that average earnings have increased in the advanced capitalist world and in many NICs between 1980 and the late 1990s, although there are groups of workers who have experienced real wage declines, especially in Brazil and India, for example (Ghose, 2003, pp. 62–3). It is also clear that whilst substantial numbers of employees in India and China have been lifted out of poverty within the space of a generation, the economic fruits of globalization have been very unequally distributed in the NICs. In many of the largest cities of the Southern Hemisphere fabulous wealth coexists with the most extreme poverty (Glyn, 2006, pp. 93–5; Dicken, 2007, pp. 514–15). From a different perspective, Silver (2003) has argued that low wages and poor working conditions characterize only the early stages of industrial relations in foreign-owned plants in the NICs. Before too long, workers begin to organize in unions and take collective action, thus forcing employers to concede substantial wage increases, as in US and Japanese car plants in Brazil, South Africa and South Korea in the 1980s.

The picture within the advanced capitalist world is also more complex than figures on average earnings growth appear to suggest. Income inequality within the OECD, measured by the 90:10 post-tax income ratio, rose significantly from 3.4 in 1980 to 3.7 in 2001, with particularly sharp increases in the UK and the US (Glyn, 2006, p. 169). At the bottom end of the labour market, young, unskilled workers often experience long periods of unemployment whilst unskilled women and migrant workers often fill minimum wage service sector jobs (Goos and Manning, 2003). Whether globalization has also been associated with increases in inter-country income inequalities is less clear and the subject of considerable debate (Milanovic, 2007).

Second, writers coming from a more conventional neoclassical economic perspective have argued that the wage effects of globalization are generally more positive than critics suggest and that any observed wage stagnation in the advanced capitalist world is due to other factors such as technological change (Bhagwati, 2004, pp. 123–7). The same author notes, contrary to Gray (1998) and Klein (2000), that the location decisions of MNCs are influenced by product market as well as labour market advantages, a point that explains why 88 per cent of the 2004 world stock of foreign direct investment was in the high wage countries of Europe and North America (Dicken, 2007, p. 40). Such writers therefore challenge the notion that MNCs seek to maximize profit by locating wherever possible to countries where wages are low and trade unions weak. Finally, there are writers whose work provides a bridge between the analysts of market forces and those who stress the role of institutions. Brown (2008), for example, notes that governments in the past have been able to encourage or facilitate the creation of regulatory institutions – industry-wide collective bargaining, for example – that can partially protect workers from the vicissitudes of market forces. But he then proceeds to argue that global product market competition has dramatically eroded the capacity of governments to insulate national product markets from global competition: hence the decline of union density and collective bargaining in the UK.

HOW DO MARKETS WORK?

Despite radically differing assessments of the benign or destructive power of market forces, these different writers are located within a set of theoretical frameworks, whether neoclassical, institutional or Marxist economics, that assigns analytical priority to product and labour market competition and its impact on profit-maximizing firms, governments, workers and trade unions. Some of these writers work within an economic perspective in which markets transmit 'signals' to rational actors, who are likely to vary in their access to such information, but this is a thin account of market mechanisms. Political scientists and sociologists in particular have considerably enriched our understanding of the modus operandi of markets by focusing on three other ways in which market competition secures its effects: through institutions, through discourse and rhetoric and through the exercise of power. One body of work, described by Peters (1999) as 'empirical institutionalism', has explored the impact on industrial relations actors of two major pro-market institutions: an independent central bank and the Maastricht Treaty on European Monetary Union. Franzese Jr and Hall's (1999) comparative and time series evidence suggests that national, central bank independence tends to raise the rate of unemployment, which in turn moderates wage settlements and lowers the rate of inflation. More recent work by Johnston and Hancké (2009) suggests that the wage-moderating effect of an independent central bank is especially acute in the sector of the economy exposed to global competition but much weaker in the 'sheltered' sector, such as public and some private services.

Other literature has taken a more critical stance towards pro-market institutions, such as the Organisation for Economic Co-operation and Development (OECD) and the International Monetary Fund (IMF). The OECD's influential *Jobs Study* (1994) argued that the over-regulation of European labour markets threatened the competitive success of European firms by hindering their capacity to respond quickly and effectively to market 'signals'. The report therefore called for greater wage and work time flexibility, reduced worker protection against dismissal and redundancy and reductions in unemployment benefit levels, duration and/or eligibility. A number of studies offered highly critical, empirical appraisals of this popular and widely disseminated rationale for reducing worker and trade union rights and enhancing employer freedoms. A number of essays in Esping-Andersen and Regini (2000) and David Howell (2005) found no systematic and robust link between employment protection legislation (EPL) and overall levels of unemployment. Countries with equally high levels of EPL recorded radically different rates of unemployment in the

1990s, for example, Spain and Portugal, whilst countries with equally low unemployment in the late 1990s, such as the UK and the Netherlands, recorded very different EPL scores. In relation to the IMF, the economist and former IMF employee Joseph Stiglitz (2002) has sharply criticized the pro-market, deflationary policies pursued by the Fund over many years. In similar vein Sklair (2001) has argued that the 'Washington Consensus' in favour of low corporation tax, wage restraint, labour flexibility and welfare retrenchment 'does not just happen. It is thought out, organized, managed, promoted and defended against its opponents by identifiable groups of people working in identifiable organizations. These people make up the transnational capitalist class' (p. x).

One of the ways in which governments and employers seek popular support for pro-market policies is through the deployment of 'rhetorics of globalization', arguments designed to portray the requirements of the global economy or of European integration as external constraints that governments are powerless to challenge. There is no single, overarching 'discourse' used by political actors, but considerable variation in the content, coherence and effectiveness of pro-market arguments between countries and between party families (Social Democrat compared with Conservative) within countries (Hay and Rosamond, 2002; Schmidt, 2002, pp. 257–302). Finally, political economists have explored the links between patterns of industrial conflict and economic outcomes and performance. The now classical article by Cameron (1984) showed that countries with higher levels of strike activity (days lost per 1000 workers) between 1965 and 1982 (the UK, Ireland, Italy, for example) recorded faster increases in nominal earnings but higher levels of unemployment. More recently Glyn (2006, pp. 6–7) has shown that the rise and fall in industrial militancy in 16 OECD countries between the late 1960s and 2000 has been highly correlated with a fall and subsequent rise in the manufacturing profit share (as a percentage of value-added). In other words the distribution of national income is not only influenced by 'market forces' but by market power and patterns of class struggle.

EVALUATING THE ROLE OF MARKETS

Critical appraisals of the role of markets have set out three types of argument and evidence. First, there is a normative critique that challenges the 'mutual gains' narrative associated with neoclassical economics and identifies significant groups of workers who bear the costs of labour market and wage flexibility (see above). Second, a number of critics have disputed the implicit claim that industrial relations institutions that are no longer well adapted to global market forces, such as centralized collective bargaining, must be radically reformed. For example, despite the market pressures on German industry, collective bargaining and works council coverage both remain high even by European standards (and see below). Third, critics of the hyper-globalist perspective have argued that governments (and other industrial relations actors) can, and do, exercise strategic choice about how to compete in the global economy. Some firms and some governments have elected the 'high road' to competitive success, based on investment in skills, high wages and high productivity; others in contrast have opted for the 'low road', based on cheap and flexible labour. In food retailing Walmart is a good example of a 'low-road' employer whose low-price business strategy entails low wages and poor fringe benefits whilst Marks & Spencer is a niche, high-road employer, offering above-average wages and benefits (Blyton and Turnbull, 2004, pp. 278–86; Rosen, 2006). Within the airline industry there is evidence of increased diversity of employment relations practices, even within the same broad product market, as some carriers drive down labour costs and avoid unions in order to compete on price whilst others continue to recognize unions and compete on quality of service (e.g., Ryanair and Aer Lingus respectively in Ireland: see Bamber et al., 2009). Finally, whilst many researchers would agree that changes in product and labour markets have played a significant role in reducing the level of strike action, especially in those parts of the private sector exposed to international competition, does this mean that trade union power and influence in society as a whole has declined? Recent research on general strikes in Western Europe has found this type of collective action, directed against government rather than employers, has proved remarkably resilient between 1980 and 2008. Moreover, analysis of the outcomes of such strikes, on issues such as welfare, pension and labour market reform, has found a wide range of outcomes, indicating that under certain conditions the general strike has elicited significant concessions from government (Kelly and Hamann, 2009). By broadening our conceptualization of industrial relations to encompass the political sphere as well as the economy, we can begin to discover that the trajectory of trade union power is more complex than purely economic models might suggest. These types of points, to be elaborated below, have informed two related literatures, critical of the market perspective: one is based on the core proposition that 'institutions matter' whilst the other asserts that even within a given institutional environment, actors' strategic choices matter.

INDUSTRIAL RELATIONS INSTITUTIONS AND VARIETIES OF CAPITALISM[1]

The 'varieties of capitalism' (VoC) literature does not represent the only approach to comparative institutional analysis (see Rubery and Grimshaw, 2003 on the societal effect theory) but within the field of comparative political economy it is now the dominant approach. It is grounded in two key empirical observations: first, that there are significant and enduring differences in the way capitalist economies and their industrial relations institutions and welfare states are organized; second, that there is no systematic tendency for any particular variety of capitalism to outperform any other over the long run because very different sets of institutions are compatible with strong and sustained economic performance and social welfare. The most influential framework for understanding the varieties of capitalism is that of Hall and Soskice (2001b). In a context of economic globalization and restructuring, firms act as 'key agents of adjustment' and therefore constitute the centrepiece of the analysis (Hall and Soskice, 2001a, p. 5). All firms face coordination issues in five spheres: industrial relations, vocational training and education, corporate governance, inter-firm relations and employees. The different institutions in these spheres are not isolated, but interconnected, producing what Hall and Soskice (ibid., p. 9) call 'institutional complementarities', where different institutions reinforce and complement each other. One implication of this view is that institutions possess a remarkable degree of resilience even in the face of powerful market pressures and that institutional changes that do occur are likely to be incremental, revealing a strong degree of 'path dependency'. For example, collective bargaining coverage across Western Europe has remained extremely high since 1980 despite calls from some employers for more local bargaining and wage flexibility (Hamann and Kelly, 2008). These interlocking and mutually reinforcing institutions are thought to co-vary systematically, yielding two ideal types of capitalist political economy, liberal market economies (LMEs) and coordinated market economies (CMEs), and a possible third type, the Mediterranean economy (ME), which has only recently become the subject of systematic discussion (e.g., Molina and Rhodes, 2007). In LMEs 'firms coordinate their activities primarily via hierarchies and competitive market arrangements' whereas in CMEs, by contrast, firms' coordination activities depend more heavily on non-market relationships (Hall and Soskice, 2001a, p. 8).

Contrary to the OECD view of labour market institutions as fetters on economic performance, the VoC literature conceptualizes institutions as 'beneficial constraints' on company strategy. For example, a legal minimum wage makes it harder for firms to compete primarily on low labour cost and pushes them to compete more on product quality or productivity. Whilst LMEs and CMEs show comparable levels of long-term economic performance, they differ significantly in terms of income inequality: the compressed earnings distributions of the CMEs contrast with the much higher levels of inequality typically found in the LMEs (ibid., p. 21). This difference is related to a striking divergence in industrial relations institutions between the two main varieties of capitalism: LMEs typically have lower union density, lower collective bargaining coverage and more poorly organized employer associations compared with CMEs (Hamann and Kelly, 2008). Within this literature the paradigmatic LMEs are Britain and the US whilst the typical CME is Germany (see, for instance, the chapters by Casper, Culpepper, Hall and Soskice, Thelen, Vitols and Wood in Hall and Soskice, 2001b and the chapters by Börsch and Goyer in Hancké et al., 2007).

The performance of labour market institutions, especially labour force participation rates and the volume, duration and composition of unemployment, is itself influenced by the structure and generosity of welfare state regimes, such as rules on unemployment benefit. In his seminal book *The Three Worlds of Welfare Capitalism*, Esping-Andersen (1990) identifies three distinct types of welfare state: liberal, conservative and social-democratic. The liberal model emphasizes welfare measures that are means-tested and provides only modest universal transfers and social insurance plans and is found predominantly in the LMEs such as the US, Canada and Australia. The conservative regime is present in highly corporatist countries (mostly CMEs) such as Austria and Germany and emphasizes status differences with few redistributive policies. The social-democratic regime emphasizes universalism and 'de-commodification' of social rights to the working and the middle classes and is found primarily in Scandinavia. Subsequent literature has modified both capitalist and welfare regime classifications. Several authors have added a third variety of capitalism in which the state plays a far more interventionist role in regulating the economy compared with the LMEs and CMEs, for example, France, Italy, Spain (Schmidt, 2002; Molina and Rhodes, 2007), whilst some writers have argued for a social-democratic variant of capitalism, in line with the welfare state literature (e.g., Amable, 2003; Hamann and Kelly, 2008).

Two kinds of evidence have generally been presented in support of the VoC perspective: there are case studies involving two or three country comparisons, for example, Germany, France and the UK, taken to be representative of the different varieties of capitalism; and there are VoC comparisons based around pooled time-series analysis of large datasets, for example Pontusson's (2005) comparison of 'Social Europe vs. liberal America'. Whilst some studies have looked at wage bargaining institutions (e.g., Hancké and Herrmann, 2007), the VoC approach covers a wide range of institutions dealing with issues such as inter-firm coordination and corporate governance and has examined many economic outcomes one step removed from industrial relations, such as patterns of innovation. Nonetheless the approach is consistent with a longstanding body of work in comparative industrial relations that has identified national variations in the structures, processes and outcomes of union–management relations (e.g., Crouch, 1993; Hyman and Ferner, 1994; Rubery and Grimshaw, 2003).

EVALUATING THE ROLE OF INSTITUTIONS

One of the truisms of comparative political economy is that despite the pressures of global market forces, 'institutions matter'. Economies can perform successfully with high or low bargaining coverage, high or low trade union density and with tightly or weakly regulated labour markets (see above). But four questions remain unclear: first, how much do institutions matter compared with other factors? Second, do institutions always matter or can they decay and become 'hollow shells'? Third, how do institutions change? The concept of 'institutional complementarities' could imply that disturbances in one part of the capitalist system, let's say inter-firm relations, will trigger counteracting forces that return the system to equilibrium. In that case how does radical change come about? And finally to what extent are cross-national differences or within-country changes in industrial relations the product of VoC-type institutional variables as compared with the roles of market forces or actors' strategic choices?

Another way of phrasing the first question is to ask whether institutions simply provide different ways in which economies adapt to market pressures or to what extent they permit national economies to challenge these pressures. Take the case of the statutory national minimum wage in the UK, introduced in 1998. The neoclassical claim was that by raising the price of labour this institution would artificially depress labour demand and significantly raise unemployment. In fact the available evidence suggests there was no discernible impact on unemployment (Metcalf, 2009). The 'beneficial constraint' of the minimum wage appears to have forced many employers to find ways of recouping higher labour costs without laying off workers, such as raising productivity, putting up prices or reducing worker hours, that is, it forced them to move away from a low wage–low productivity policy.

The actual regulatory effect of institutions is another important issue on which further research is required. Numerous studies have shown a strong, negative correlation between the degree of coordination of collective bargaining within a national economy and the level of income inequality (Hamann and Kelly, 2008, pp. 139–41). Yet we know from British experience in the 1950s and 1960s that the impact of highly coordinated industrywide bargaining on gross earnings was rapidly diminishing over time because of the continuing decentralization of collective bargaining to company and workplace level (Flanders, 1970).

The mechanisms by which institutions change have recently become a major issue, partly because of the recent far-reaching labour market and welfare reforms in Germany and partly because of a growing recognition of the salience of this issue by major VoC theorists in response to criticism (cf. Crouch, 2005). Hall and Thelen (2009, pp. 18–20) have argued that substantial change can occur even in the midst of apparent institutional stability and they cite the case of German collective bargaining. Whilst noting that sectoral wage bargaining continues to dominate the economy, they also point out that in metalworking a growing number of small firms has defected from the employers' organization and from bargaining coverage. In addition some large employers have begun to reinterpret the meaning of key terms in recent collective agreements in order to facilitate the pursuit of local job security–wage trade-offs (see also Thelen, 2009). Whilst it is clear that VoC theorists are beginning to develop some precise concepts for helping us think about institutional change, this line of research opens the way to another problem. How far can institutional change proceed before we argue that an entire variety of capitalism has been eroded and transformed into a different variety? Hassel (2007), for instance, notes the recent, dramatic decline of German trade union density, the reduced regulatory power of trade unions and the emergence of a large, secondary labour market characterized by low wages and job insecurity. Yet she concludes that Germany remains a coordinated market economy despite the emergence of labour market features more reminiscent of an LME. The interesting conceptual issue is what would need to change, and beyond what point, before we could announce the death of the German coordinated model? Finally, in relation to mechanisms of change, Chris Howell's (2005) important study of the evolution of British industrial relations in the twentieth century links to the role of strategic choices by governments. At a few key historical periods, marked by economic restructuring and heightened industrial conflict, he argues it became possible for the executive to initiate a radical overhaul of the existing industrial relations institutions.

STRATEGIC CHOICE

Howell's (2005) study belongs to a growing body of comparative research that has argued that whilst markets and institutions generate constraints and opportunities for the different industrial relations actors, and shape their actions to varying degrees, there always remains some degree of latitude within which the actors can make significant policy choices (see also Boxall, 2008). Apart from the expositions by Kochan et al. (1984, 1986) and Boxall (2008) this mode of analysis remains theoretically underdeveloped, although potentially powerful. For example, it is clear that the incidence of human resource management practices varies significantly even among firms in the same sector of the economy (Wood and Bryson, 2010). Assuming they are exposed to similar degrees of product market competition, such variation in managerial policy is suggestive of strategic choices. As Bacon (2008) has argued, however, it remains unclear how much choice and over what issues is available to employers in different institutional and market environments. Nonetheless, three types of evidence can be adduced to support the importance of strategic choices in shaping industrial relations structures, processes and outcomes. First, the speed of industrial relations change in certain economies suggests that institutional arrangements, often thought of as resilient or 'sticky', are unlikely to shed much light on such developments. For instance, the British Conservative government legislated a series of major restrictions on trade union collective action between 1980 and 1984; faced down a number of major strikes, especially in the steel and coalmining industries; and effectively abandoned tripartite consultation with the trade unions (Howell, 2005). In conjunction with a sharp rise in unemployment, the result of these government measures was that trade union membership and strike activity all began to fall swiftly from 1980 and continued to decline until the 2000s. Likewise in New Zealand the Conservative government elected in 1990 enacted legislation the following year (the Employment Contracts Act) that abolished centralized arbitration and conciliation and facilitated the break-up of collective bargaining structures. Within five years trade union density had plummeted from 41.5 per cent to less than 20 per cent as bargaining coverage rapidly contracted (Harbridge et al., 2002).

The second type of evidence draws on comparative research and uses similar national cases to control for economic, institutional and other variables, arguing that residual differences in either actor policies or industrial relations and economic outcomes must therefore reflect actors' strategic choices. For example, both Irish and British governments in the 1970s responded to union militancy and rising inflation by trying to secure union support for incomes policy. These corporatist experiments enjoyed only short-lived success at best. From the late 1980s, however, government policy in the two countries radically diverged: Conservative governments continue to pursue a policy of union exclusion from policy formation and steadily abolished a number of tripartite institutions. Although unions were not entirely excluded from policy-making in the Labour governments from 1997, their influence over government and the Labour Party was deliberately minimized by a party leadership convinced that close relations with unions were an electoral liability. In Ireland by contrast, despite a similar history of corporatism and similar industrial relations institutions and economic problems, successive governments pursued a radically different policy between 1987 and 2009, based on tripartite social pacts negotiated with trade unions and employers (Hamann and Kelly, 2010). In both countries governments responded to electoral pressures, and to economic problems, with very different policy choices (see also Chapter 9 by Dundon and Collings in this volume).

The third type of evidence that can be adduced in favour of strategic choice consists of studies showing substantial intra-organization debate around different policies. Insofar as the outcomes of such debates are hard to predict then the existence of such debate is consistent with the claim that government, employer or trade union policies are not simply constrained by external forces but are open to some degree of choice. For example, the British Conservative Party in the 1970s was divided between a union-exclusionist, neoliberal wing (led by Margaret Thatcher) and a union-inclusionist, corporatist wing (led by James Prior); British Labour in the late 1980s was divided between a centre-left group committed to union inclusion and a centre-right group willing to distance the party and government from unions in order to secure electoral success (Howell, 2005; Hamann and Kelly, 2010). The victories for the union exclusionists were not inevitable since all of the intra-party groupings could, and did, mobilize substantial levels of support for their respective platforms. In principle these debates could have yielded different outcomes and led the respective governments to make different choices.

EVALUATING STRATEGIC CHOICE

Some of this evidence is sufficiently ambiguous that it does not decisively confirm the value of strategic choice because although institutions may not change rapidly, markets do. Between 1979 when the Conservatives were elected to office, and 1983 (when they were re-elected), unemployment in Britain rose from 1.3 to 3.1 million, suggesting that product and labour market pressures are surely part of the explanation for the precipitate decline of British trade unionism in the early 1980s. However, there are other sudden changes in government industrial relations policy that cannot be so readily accounted for by reference to market forces. For example, between 1990 and 1993, Italian governments agreed a series of far-reaching tripartite social pacts with unions and employers on the reform of wage indexation, collective bargaining structures and pensions. In summer 1994 the newly-elected Conservative government led by Silvio Berlusconi announced its intention to reform pensions without union consultation. Although eventually forced into negotiations by a general strike in November 1994, the government's temporary abandonment of tripartism was a strategic choice that could not be accounted for by any sudden change in economic pressures. The new Conservative government believed its electoral success was due to the popularity of its repudiation of the 'old politics' of tripartite agreements with the major interest groups. It was therefore determined to use its majority in the legislature to act in accordance with its manifesto pledge (Hamann and Kelly, 2010).

It is also possible to provide an institutional account of some of the actor choices we have already described. For example, it could be noted that the type of decisive, legislative action pursued by the Thatcher government in the 1980s was made possible by key features of the British institutional environment: a majoritarian electoral system, a weak upper chamber, a strong executive and an unwritten Constitution. In Germany by contrast the Christian Democrat government of Helmut Kohl (1982–98) would have found it much harder to pursue a 'Thatcherite' programme because of the country's closer approximation to the 'consensus' as opposed to the 'Westminster' model of democracy in which government action is more constrained by a strong upper chamber and a written Constitution (Lijphart, 1999, pp. 10–21). In relation to trade union strategies, Kelly and Frege (2004, pp. 183–5) have argued that the strategic choice by British and US unions to commit substantial resources to union organizing, compared with unions in Germany, Spain and Italy, was in part a reflection of the different institutional opportunities and constraints prevailing in the respective countries. In particular the low levels of bargaining coverage and the weak legal supports for centralized collective bargaining in the UK and the US increased the incentives to recruit new union members and stem the erosion of union density.

CONCLUSION

Most comparative industrial relations researchers would agree that almost any phenomenon of interest, whether it is patterns of income inequality or trends in trade union membership, is likely to be influenced by a range of variables, including markets, institutions and actors' strategies. On the other hand to assert that markets, institutions and actor strategic choices all matter is to say very little because nobody would disagree. Nobody disputes that market forces are powerful, that institutions can both attenuate and amplify such forces and that actors usually have some strategic choices, however limited. Perhaps one of the major challenges facing comparative researchers is to think through how we can specify more precisely the conditions under which each of these sets of 'variables' is more or less effective. The types of questions we should be asking include the following: under what conditions can governments radically change institutions? To what extent can downward market pressures on wages be effectively resisted by unions or government? Is the impact of global product markets significantly greater on unions organizing in the 'exposed' sectors of the economy but far weaker in the sheltered sector, especially in essential public services? To what extent will the institutional arrangements of the different varieties of capitalism continue to differ or are we likely to witness some convergence towards the liberal market model of capitalism?

NOTE

1. Some of the material in this section is taken from Hamann and Kelly (2008).

REFERENCES

Amable, Bruno (2003), *The Diversity of Modern Capitalism*, Oxford: Oxford University Press.
Bacon, Nicolas (2008), 'Management strategy and industrial relations', in Paul Blyton, Nicolas Bacon, Jack Fiorito and Edmund Heery (eds), *The Sage Handbook of Industrial Relations*, London: Sage, pp. 241–57.
Bamber, Greg, Gittel, Jody H., Kochan, Thomas A. and von Nordenflycht, Andrew (2009), *Up in the Air: How Airlines Can Improve Performance by Engaging Their Employees*, Ithaca, NY: ILR Press.
Bhagwati, Jagdish (2004), *In Defense of Globalization*, New York: Oxford University Press.
Blyton, Paul and Turnbull, Peter (2004), *The Dynamics of Employee Relations*, 3rd edition, London: Macmillan.
Boxall, Peter (2008), 'Trade union strategy', in Paul Blyton, Nicolas Bacon, Jack Fiorito and Edmund Heery (eds), *The Sage Handbook of Industrial Relations*, London: Sage, pp. 209–24.
Brown, William (2008), 'The influence of product markets on industrial relations', in Paul Blyton, Nicolas Bacon, Jack Fiorito and Edmund Heery (eds), *The Sage Handbook of Industrial Relations*, London: Sage, pp. 113–28.
Cameron, David R. (1984), 'Social democracy, corporatism, labour quiescence, and the representation of economic interest in advanced capitalist society', in John H. Goldthorpe

(ed.), *Order and Conflict in Contemporary Capitalism: Studies in the Political Economy of Western European Nations*, Oxford: Clarendon Press, pp. 143–78.

Crouch, Colin (1993), *Industrial Relations and European State Traditions*, Oxford: Clarendon Press.

Crouch, Colin (2005), *Capitalist Diversity and Change: Recombinant Governance and Institutional Entrepreneurs*, Oxford: Oxford University Press.

Dicken, Peter (2007), *Global Shift: Mapping the Changing Contours of the World Economy*, 5th edition, London: Sage.

EIRO (2008), 'Social plan for redundant workers agreed at Nokia plant in Bochum', EIRO Observatory, available at http://www.eurofound.europa.eu/eiro/2008/05/articles/de0805019i.htm; accessed 05 January 2011.

Esping-Andersen, Gøsta (1990), *The Three Worlds of Welfare Capitalism*, Princeton, NJ: Princeton University Press.

Esping Andersen, Gøsta and Regini, Marino (eds) (2000), *Why Deregulate Labour Markets?*, Oxford: Oxford University Press.

Flanagan, Robert J. (2008), 'The changing structure of collective bargaining', in Paul Blyton, Nicolas Bacon, Jack Fiorito and Edmund Heery (eds), *The Sage Handbook of Industrial Relations*, London: Sage, pp. 406–19.

Flanders, Allan (1970), *Management and Unions: The Theory and Reform of Industrial Relations*, London: Faber and Faber.

Franzese Jr, Robert J. and Hall, Peter A. (1999), 'Institutional dimensions of coordinating wage bargaining and monetary policy', in Torben Iversen, Jonas Pontusson and David Soskice (eds), *Unions, Employers, and Central Banks: Macroeconomic Coordination and Institutional Change in Social Market Economies*, New York: Cambridge University Press, pp. 173–204.

Ghose, Ajit K. (2003), *Jobs and Incomes in a Globalizing World*, Geneva: International Labour Office.

Glyn, Andrew (2006), *Capitalism Unleashed: Finance, Globalization, and Welfare*, Oxford: Oxford University Press.

Goos, Maarten and Manning, Alan (2003), 'McJobs and MacJobs: The growing polarisation of jobs in the UK', in Richard Dicken, Paul Gregg and Jonathan Wadsworth (eds), *The Labour Market Under New Labour*, Basingstoke: Palgrave Macmillan, pp. 70–85.

Gray, John (1998), *False Dawn: The Delusions of Global Capitalism*, London: Granta Books.

Hall, Peter A. and Soskice, David (2001a), 'An introduction to varieties of capitalism', in Peter A. Hall and David Soskice (eds), *Varieties of Capitalism: The Institutional Foundations of Comparative Advantage*, Oxford: Oxford University Press, pp. 1–68.

Hall, Peter A. and Soskice, David (eds) (2001b), *Varieties of Capitalism: The Institutional Foundations of Comparative Advantage*, Oxford: Oxford University Press.

Hall, Peter A. and Thelen, Kathleen (2009), 'Institutional change in varieties of capitalism', *Socio-Economic Review*, **7**(1), 7–34.

Hamann, Kerstin and Kelly, John (2008), 'Varieties of capitalism and industrial relations', in Paul Blyton, Nicolas Bacon, Jack Fiorito and Edmund Heery (eds), *The Sage Handbook of Industrial Relations*, London: Sage, pp. 129–48.

Hamann, Kerstin and Kelly, John (2010), *Parties, Elections, and Policy Reforms in Western Europe: Voting for Social Pacts*, London: Routledge.

Hancké, Bob and Herrmann, Andrea Monika (2007), 'Wage bargaining and comparative advantage in EMU', in Bob Hancké, Martin Rhodes and Mark Thatcher (eds), *Beyond Varieties of Capitalism: Conflict, Contradictions, and Complementarities in the European Economy*, Oxford: Oxford University Press, pp. 122–44.

Hancké, Bob, Rhodes, Martin and Thatcher, Mark (eds) (2007), *Beyond Varieties of Capitalism: Conflict, Contradictions, and Complementarities in The European Economy*, Oxford: Oxford University Press.

Harbridge, Raymond, Crawford, Aaron and Hince, Kevin (2002), 'Unions in New Zealand: What the law giveth. . .', in Peter Fairbrother and Gerard Griffin (eds), *Changing*

Prospects for Trade Unionism: Comparisons Between Six Countries, London: Continuum, pp. 177–99.

Hassel, Anke (2007), 'What does business want? Labour market reforms in CMEs and its problems', in Bob Hancké, Martin Rhodes and Mark Thatcher (eds), *Beyond Varieties of Capitalism: Conflict, Contradictions, and Complementarities in the European Economy*, Oxford: Oxford University Press, pp. 253–77.

Hay, Colin and Rosamond, Ben (2002), 'Globalisation, European integration and the discursive construction of economic imperatives', *Journal of European Public Policy*, 9(2), 147–67.

Held, David, McGrew, Anthony, Goldblatt, David and Perraton, Jonathan (1999), *Global Transformations: Politics, Economics and Culture*, Cambridge: Polity Press.

Howell, Chris (2005), *Trade Unions and the State: The Construction of Industrial Relations Institutions in Britain, 1890–2000*, Princeton, NJ: Princeton University Press.

Howell, David (ed.) (2005), *Fighting Unemployment: The Limits of Free Market Orthodoxy*, New York: Oxford University Press.

Hyman, Richard and Ferner, Anthony (eds) (1994), *New Frontiers in European Industrial Relations*, Oxford: Blackwell.

Johnston, A. and Hancké, Bob (2009), 'Wage inflation and labour unions in EMU', *Journal of European Public Policy*, 16(4), 601–22.

Katz, Harry C. and Darbishire, Owen (2000), *Converging Divergences: Worldwide Changes in Employment Systems*, Ithaca, NY: ILR Press.

Kelly, John and Frege, Carola (2004), 'Conclusions: Varieties of unionism', in Carola Frege and John Kelly (eds), *Varieties of Unionism: Strategies for Union Revitalization in a Globalizing Economy*, Oxford: Oxford University Press, pp. 181–95.

Kelly, John and Hamann, Kerstin (2009), 'General strikes in Western Europe 1980–2008', Paper to Juan March Institute, Madrid, October.

Klein, Naomi (2000), *No Logo*, London: Flamingo.

Kochan, Thomas A., Katz, Harry C. and McKersie, Robert B. (1984), 'Strategic choice and industrial relations theory', *Industrial Relations*, 23(1), 16–39.

Kochan, Thomas A., Katz, Harry C. and McKersie, Robert B. (1986), *The Transformation of American Industrial Relations*, New York: Basic Books.

Lijphart, Arend (1999), *Patterns of Democracy: Government Forms and Performance in Thirty-Six Countries*, New Haven, CN: Yale University Press.

Marglin, Stephen A. and Schor, Juliet B. (eds) (1990), *The Golden Age of Capitalism*, Oxford: Clarendon Press.

Marx, Karl and Engels, Frederick (1976), *Collected Works*, Vol. 6, London: Lawrence and Wishart.

Metcalf, David (2009), 'Why has the British National Minimum Wage had little or no impact on employment?', *Journal of Industrial Relations*, 50(3), 489–512.

Milanovic, Branko (2007), 'Globalization and inequality', in David Held and Kaya Ayse (eds), *Global Inequality*, Cambridge: Polity Press, pp. 26–49.

Molina, Oscar and Rhodes, Martin (2007), 'The political economy of adjustment in mixed market economies: A study of Spain and Italy', in Bob Hancké, Martin Rhodes and Mark Thatcher (eds), *Beyond Varieties of Capitalism: Conflict, Contradictions, and Complementarities in the European Economy*, Oxford: Oxford University Press, pp. 223–51.

OECD (1994), *Jobs Study*, Paris: Organisation for Economic Co-operation and Development.

Peters, B. Guy (1999), *Institutional Theory in Political Science: The 'New Institutionalism'*, London: Pinter.

Phelan, Craig (2007), 'Worldwide trends and prospects for trade union revitalisation', in Craig Phelan (ed.), *Trade Union Revitalisation: Trends and Prospects in 34 Countries*, Bern: Peter Lang, pp. 11–38.

Pizzorno, Alessandro (1978), 'Political exchange and collective identity in industrial conflict', in Colin Crouch and Alessandro Pizzorno (eds), *The Resurgence of Class Conflict in Western Europe Since 1968*, Vol. 2, London: Macmillan, pp. 277–98.

Pontusson, Jonas (2005), *Inequality and Prosperity: Social Europe vs. Liberal America*, Ithaca, NY: Cornell University Press.

Rosen, Ellen I. (2006), 'How to squeeze more out of a penny', in Nelson Lichtenstein (ed.), *Wal-Mart: The Face of Twenty-first-century Capitalism*, New York: The New Press, pp. 243–59.

Rubery, Jill and Grimshaw, Damian (2003), *The Organization of Employment: An International Perspective*, Basingstoke: Palgrave Macmillan.

Schmidt, Vivien (2002), *The Futures of European Capitalism*, New York: Oxford University Press.

Silver, Beverly (2003), *Forces of Labor: Workers' Movements and Globalization Since 1870*, New York: Cambridge University Press.

Sklair, Leslie (2001), *The Transnational Capitalist Class*, Oxford: Blackwell.

Sklair, Leslie (2002), *Globalization: Capitalism and its Alternatives*, 3rd edition, Oxford: Oxford University Press.

Stiglitz, Joseph (2002), *Globalization and its Discontents*, London: Penguin.

Swank, Duane (2002), *Global Capital, Political Institutions, and Policy Change in Developed Welfare States*, New York: Cambridge University Press.

Thelen, Kathleen (2009), 'Institutional change in advanced political economies', *British Journal of Industrial Relations*, **47**(3), 471–98.

van der Velden, Sjaak, Dribbusch, Heiner, Lyddon, Dave and Vandaele, Kurt (eds) (2008), *Strikes Around the World, 1968–2005: Case-studies of 15 Countries*, Amsterdam: Aksant.

Wood, Stephen and Bryson, Alex (2010), 'High involvement management', in William Brown, Alex Bryson, John Forth and Keith Whitfield (eds), *The Evolution of the Modern Workplace*, Cambridge: Cambridge University Press, pp. 151–75.

4 Legal origins, labour law and the regulation of employment relations
Sean Cooney, Peter Gahan and Richard Mitchell

INTRODUCTION

The proposition that a country's legal institutions and regulatory approach are likely to condition the operation of labour markets and employment relations has been a continuing theme in the social sciences. Even in a period in which it was often presumed that globalization would undermine the distinctive institutional features that distinguish one national system from another (Mills et al., 2008), the idea that countries could be classified into different 'families', 'types' or 'varieties' has persisted. Indeed, over the course of the last decade, it has again emerged as one of the most important questions among economists, political scientists, sociologists and other scholars, including those in the field of employment relations. This renewed interest in comparing national institutions is not merely a response to globalization; it is also a consequence of the transition of former socialist economies in Eastern Europe and Asia to market economies, and the rapid growth of the developing economies of South-East and East Asia.

Legal origins theory is without doubt the most influential approach to classifying and analysing national institutions to emerge in the 1990s. The theory is grounded in the work of a group of economists located principally at Harvard and Yale Universities and at the World Bank (Rafael La Porta, Florencio Lopez-de-Silanes, Andrei Shleifer and Robert Vishny – collectively referred to as LLSV). In a series of highly influential articles, these authors argued that there is a strong empirical correlation between a nation's *regulatory style* and the origin of its legal system.[1] This approach has been particularly prominent in comparative law and comparative economics,[2] and the core journal articles authored by LLSV have been among the most widely cited research in business and economics over the past decade.[3]

The influence of legal origins theory has not been limited to academic debates. The research it spawned has formed the basis of ranking systems, such as that deployed in the World Bank's *Doing Business*[4] reports (2004–10), which evaluate the extent to which countries adopt 'business-friendly' regulatory frameworks. Countries that fail to do so, for example by passing laws ostensibly protecting labour, come in for regular criticism. Given the World Bank's role in promoting economic reforms in developing countries, the agency's adoption of the legal origins approach in several of its operations demonstrates that legal origins theory has clear and practical policy impacts.

The rapidly expanding legal origins literature has brought comparative law from relative obscurity to the forefront of international debates about business and labour market regulation. It has also resuscitated a taxonomy of legal systems that has long been controversial. Until recently, whether the ancestry of a country's laws could be traced to English common law or French civil codes did not seem to be especially relevant to the operation of its labour laws, let alone economic resource allocation. Now, influential economists claim that that legal ancestry is not only a relevant but also a dominant factor in determining a country's approach to regulation and, consequently, its economic performance. Many social scientists will view this claim with surprise. Is not political context, for example, more important in shaping a country's labour institutions than the early history of its legal system? However, the influence of legal origins theory on international agencies and the large number of publications citing or critiquing the approach compels scholars and policy-makers to take its claims very seriously.

This pervasive influence suggests that legal origins theory deserves examination in a book on comparative employment relations. The aim of this chapter is, therefore, to provide a critical overview of the theory of legal origins, both in general terms and as it relates specifically to comparative labour law and industrial relations. The chapter begins by explaining what is meant by 'legal origins' and how it has been deployed to compare and assess regulatory arrangements in different countries. We then look at some of the main criticisms of the legal origins approach, both conceptual and methodological. We conclude by considering, in brief, some of the implications that arise from an application of legal origins theory to employment relations institutions and outcomes.

COMPARATIVE LAW AND THE THEORY OF LEGAL ORIGINS

The Concept of Legal Families

Comparative lawyers have long sought to categorize legal systems, although there is much disagreement about the usefulness of the various taxonomies that have been devised (Biddulph and Nicholson, 2008). One basis of classification is to trace the historical source of a country's key legal concepts and institutions – its legal origins.[5] This approach has led many comparative lawyers to group countries together in 'legal families'.

One of the best-known attempts to classify countries in this way, one that has been particularly influential in the writing of the main progenitors of the legal origins literature, is by German scholars Zweigert and Kötz (1998). They claim that each family has its own 'legal style' (ibid., pp. 63–73). Legal style is determined by five factors: a legal system's historical development; its distinctive mode of legal reasoning; its legal institutions; its sources of law; and its ideology. This concept of 'legal style' (and the closely related term 'regulatory style') assumes central importance for legal origins scholars (see Djankov et al., 2003; La Porta et al., 2008).

In the third edition of their major work published in 1998, Zweigert and Kötz, identify four 'great legal systems of the world', all derived from Europe. Among these four great systems, one, the 'Nordic' legal family, is confined to Scandinavia. This means that the large majority of the world's countries are grouped into the remaining three families.

One of these legal families consists of those jurisdictions whose legal style is said to derive from England. This is the 'Anglo-American' or 'common law' legal family. This family is largely co-extensive with former parts of the British Empire and includes most of the United Kingdom, the United States and Canada, as well as many jurisdictions in the Asia-Pacific, Africa and the Caribbean (including Australia, India, Malaysia, Kenya, Hong Kong, and so on). Characteristic of this family is the prominent role of the judge and of decisions of courts in creating the central principles of private law.

Even more numerous are jurisdictions that are classified as part of the French or 'Romanistic' legal family. One of the main characteristics of this group is the fact that the fundamental doctrines of private law (contract, property, inheritance and so on) are to be found in codes, rather than in the decisions of courts. This means that judges in the French civil law family have, at first glance, less capacity to mould the law than those in common law countries. With the French conquest of much of Europe, the codes spread through that continent to countries including Spain and the Netherlands, and subsequently into European colonies in Latin America, Africa and to parts of Asia, such as Indonesia (Zweigert and Kötz, 1998, pp. 98–118).

German law, like French law, makes extensive use of codes to proclaim central private law doctrines. Both jurisdictions (sometimes together with the sui generis Nordic legal systems) are therefore described as being part of the broad 'civil law tradition' in contrast to the common law. However, while influenced by French law, the modern German legal system was constructed almost a century later, when the country was in an advanced stage of industrialization (Deakin, 2009, p. 50). It has a sufficiently different 'legal style' in the minds of many comparative lawyers to warrant the creation of a separate legal family. This style includes a prominent role for academic jurists, the influence of distinctive philosophical concepts such as the *Rechtsstaat* ('state of law') and a more expansive role for judges and judgments than in the French system. Many jurisdictions share features derived from German law or from related systems such as those of Switzerland and Austria. This is largely as a result of voluntary adoption rather than (as is the case with the other two families) colonization. Thus, several Eastern European states have many features derived from German and Swiss law. German and/or Swiss law has also provided a model for parts of legal systems in East Asia, including those of Japan, South Korea and Taiwan and, more recently, China.[6]

From Legal Families to Legal Origins

The taxonomy of legal families long remained the preserve of comparative lawyers. That has now fundamentally changed. Beginning with two ground-breaking studies in 1997 and 1998, legal origins economists have been the leading proponents of the contention that a country's legal origin has significant impacts on its economic performance (La Porta et al., 1997 and 1998).

As these scholars were economists, not comparative lawyers, their methodology was quite different from those who had developed the concept of legal families. Instead of providing detailed descriptive accounts of rules and institutions – the preferred methodology of comparative lawyers – they employed a 'leximetric' approach (see Siems, 2005 and Lele and Siems, 2007). This approach involves the quantitative measurement of the economic effects of legal rules on businesses and other economic actors.

In the ensuing years, LLSV and their collaborators, and other scholars adopting a similar methodology, applied the analysis to many areas of business law, producing three general categories of research findings relating to: (1) investor protection, (2) government regulation of economic activity (including labour market regulation) and (3) the judiciary and judicial enforcement of contractual and property rights. These findings were reviewed in a survey of the legal origins literature published by three of the original authors, La Porta, Lopez-de-Silanes and Shleifer (2008). They concluded that:

> In all these spheres [of law], civil law is associated with a heavier hand of government ownership and regulation than common law. Many of these indicators

of government ownership and regulation are associated with adverse impacts on markets, such as greater corruption, larger unofficial economy, and higher unemployment. . . In still other studies, we have found that common law is associated with lower formalism of judicial procedures and greater judicial independence than civil law. These indicators are in turn associated with better contract enforcement and greater security of property rights. (La Porta et al., 2008, p. 286)[7]

Drawing on Zweigert and Kötz's concept of legal style, the legal origins scholars observed that when a legal system is transplanted (say from France to Spain, Germany to Korea, or from England to New Zealand), it is not only 'black letter' laws that are conveyed but also the underlying features and values of the originating system, such as its distinct institutional structures and ideological perspectives. LLSV argue that, historically, the common law, being fearful of abusive state control, tended to limit governmental interference in markets and permit more assertive and independent judges, whereas the civil law states, being fearful of disorder, supported stronger government intervention and a weak role for judges. These differing ideologies, which have been transmitted around the globe through colonization and adoption, continue to exert a powerful impact today, outweighing political influences (such as whether a country has a social democratic or neoliberal government), national culture or historically significant events (La Porta et al., 2008, p. 287).

Legal origins scholars point to at least two possible mechanisms through which legal origins continue to have an impact on economic outcomes. One is that civil law systems are prone to greater political 'interference' because their alleged preference for statutory law over judge-made law exposes them to the attempts of legislators to mandate solutions to social problems. These solutions may be market-restricting, especially in the event of rent-seeking by interests supporting a legislative measure.[8] The common law, given its claimed predilection for judge-made law, is said to be less vulnerable to these pressures, and less market-distorting. A second claimed advantage of common law systems is their adaptability. As judge-made law develops incrementally, and in response to specific cases, it is said that it gradually improves over time, in the sense that it becomes more responsive to changing business needs.

CRITIQUES OF LEGAL ORIGINS THEORY

Unsurprisingly, given its generally negative view of civil law jurisdictions and of government intervention, the legal origins literature has come under intense scrutiny. Despite the increasingly sophisticated methodology of its proponents, central contentions of legal origins seem startling. For example, is it really the case that France, Germany, Japan, China, Sweden and Switzerland have greater in-built legal impediments to efficient resource allocation than the United States, India, Australia or Ireland? Is the fact that a country has a predominantly social-democratic political history, as opposed to a conservative one, really less significant for its labour law than the ancestry of its private law? Critiques have come from a variety of directions, not least from labour law and labour market scholars.[9]

Classification and Hybridity

One line of criticism maintains that the principal legal origins scholars (being financial economists, not lawyers) misclassify the legal systems that they are attempting to study. It is argued that their division of world legal systems into (largely) the common law and French and German civil law traditions is overly simplistic, failing to take seriously enough the extensive comparative law literature demonstrating the limitations of the legal families concept.

Most comparative lawyers treat the taxonomy of legal families with considerable caution, and sometimes scepticism. A major difficulty is that many jurisdictions do not readily fit into the legal family framework; there are very many *hybrid* systems (Orücü, 2004 and Siems, 2007a). Even in the 'core' common law countries of the United States, the United Kingdom and Canada, the legal systems of Scotland, Louisiana and Quebec operate with many civil law elements. Moreover, in discrete areas of law, such as capital markets and corporate governance, internationalization and international conventions have been associated with varying degrees of hybridization, rather than convergence, of legal systems (Clift, 1997). But entire countries defy easy classification. For example, Sri Lanka, Israel, South Africa, the Philippines and Thailand have mixed common and civil law legacies. Brazil, Turkey and Greece have both French and German features. In many countries, indigenous or religious legal traditions remain highly significant and are a source of legal rules even in commercial settings. Islamic societies are the most obvious examples of this (see, for example, Lindsey, 2007). Indeed, the multiplicity of influences on the laws of South-East Asian countries has led Andrew Harding (2002, p. 49) to assert that, in this region, the concept of legal families 'makes no sense whatsoever'.

Again, countries in transition from socialist legal systems, such as China and Russia, do not fit comfortably into the legal origins classification of legal families (Partlett, 2008). China was classified by legal origins scholars as a socialist legal system in 2004 (Botero et al., 2004), but as a member of the German civil law family in the 2008 review by the same group of authors (La Porta et al., 2008, p. 288). This revision apparently resulted from the claim that German law has been the major influence on Chinese commercial law. However, as Mathias Siems (2007a, p. 66) has pointed out, China's commercial law has multiple influences and, unlike Germany, it does not (yet) have a civil code.[10]

Further, the areas of central concern to the legal origins scholars are mostly governed by statute in *both* common law and civil law countries. Thus, as LLSV acknowledge, labour and financial markets (Roe, 2006) are extensively regulated by legislation in both common and civil law countries (Braithwaite and Drahos, 2000). While the legal origins scholars contend that common law statute-making is heavily imbued with judicially inspired concepts, Deakin has challenged this view, suggesting that most of the business law innovations, even in the nineteenth century, were in fact statutory (Deakin, 2009, p. 51). For example, many of the distinctive doctrines of labour law developed in common law countries were located in longstanding master and servant acts, even well into the twentieth century (Hay and Craven, 2004).

The Importance of History and Politics

LLSV respond to these critiques by acknowledging hybridity and the role of statutes in common law countries, but assert that 'generally a particular legal tradition dominates in each country' (La Porta et al., 2008, pp. 288 and 306–9) and that despite changes in specific legal rules, the underlying style of the originating legal system persists:

> [s]uccessive generations of judges, lawyers, and politicians all learn the same broad ideas of how the law and the state should work . . . it is [this] incorporation of beliefs and ideologies into the legal and political infrastructure that enables legal origins to have such persistent consequences for rules, regulation, and economic outcomes. (Ibid., pp. 307–8)

This idea of an underlying disposition transmitted through time and space and influencing social and economic outcomes is plausible. Even some of the sharpest critics of LLSV note that the orientation of business rules (such as the extent of mandatory requirements) can differ according to a country's legal family (Deakin, 2009, p. 42). However, these critics contend that the existence of such a disposition does not obviate the need for close analysis of how strongly and in what respects a disposition manifests itself in modern legal systems. In any one country, other influences may be at least as significant. Thus, Pistor and her collaborators have found that, in relation to corporate regulation, while membership of a legal family is an important factor in accounting for the style of corporate regulation in *originating* countries (England, France), in *transplant* countries corporate law evolved quite differently from the original model – with several cases of both stagnation and erratic changes (Pistor et al., 2003). Similarly, a number of researchers have highlighted the potential role of related factors such as colonization and language (Acemoglu et al., 2001; Siems, 2007b).

Other critics have stressed the relevance of politics. For example, Roe, writing about corporate regulation, has argued that it is not so much legal origins that prevents a country from adopting market-friendly regulation, but political history (Roe, 2006). Thus, European governments sought to restrain capital markets and protect labour, as their populations, devastated by World War II, did not support pro-market policies. This was not simply a consequence of the greater 'political interference' in the law permissible in civil law societies (according to LLSV), but because of specific exogenous historical events. LLSV contend that Roe misinterprets the empirical evidence, and that their data and regressions demonstrate that political variables, while significant, are not as important in explaining variation in legal rules as legal origins (La Porta et al., 2008, p. 321).

The Leximetric Problem

Another line of critique is directed at the theory's leximetric methodology and argues that the leading legal origins exponents have made multiple methodological errors. Deakin and Siems and their collaborators claim to have identified, and sought to correct, many of these (Ahlering and Deakin, 2007; Siems and Deakin, 2010).

First, they maintain that legal origins researchers have tended to compare formal legal rules rather than 'functional equivalents'.[11] While the concept of functional equivalents is not uncontroversial in comparative law (Legrand and Munday, 2003), it has the merit of directing attention, when comparisons are made, not simply to the formal law but to wider forms of regulation that interact with those formal rules. Thus, in many countries, labour markets are not merely regulated by statute, but by collective agreements and/or industry awards. If these are excluded from consideration, a misleading impression will be created as to the rules in place and a country will be incorrectly coded. Similarly, failure to deal adequately with the distinction between the 'law on the books' and the 'law in action' (that is, whether it is actually implemented and enforced in practice) can generate error.

Second, in coding countries, the legal origins scholars weigh each variable equally, and they are simply aggregated, even though they may not be equally important. For example, it is not self-evident that the variable in Botero et al.'s (2004) study of labour market regulation concerning termination rights should be treated equivalently to that relating to whether there is a right to establish a works council. Deakin et al. (2007) also highlight the fact that different rules may have differential impacts across sectors and, consequently, may need to be weighted accordingly in different national settings.

Third, most empirical research testing the claims of legal origins research is cross-sectional, not longitudinal. Thus, it fails to capture developments *within* legal systems over time. As the work of Pistor et al. and more recently Deakin et al. has illustrated, legal systems can change markedly, even radically, over time and a static analysis will ignore this. Deakin and collaborators have constructed time-series data on shareholder, creditor and worker protection for the period 1970 to 2005 for five countries: the originating jurisdictions of England, France, Germany and the two major 'transplant' countries of the United States and India (Amour et al., 2009). They find that each of these areas of protection show diverse patterns of change, with only the area of labour law showing some evidence of a clear legal origin effect. To this extent, the more detailed, historically nuanced, approach of Deakin and his colleagues suggests that the differences between legal families, and their effects, are not as dominant as legal origins scholars have proposed. They describe this as evidence of distinctive legal cultures, rather than differences in the source of legal rules. These different legal cultures, they suggest, are manifest in different 'legal ground rules',[12] which 'allocate responsibility for the control of economic relationships differently in the common law and civil law . . . Thus in civil law, the tendency is for freedom of contract to be socially conditioned when, in common law systems, it is formally constrained' (Ahlering and Deakin, 2007, p. 901).

LEGAL ORIGINS AND THE REGULATION OF LABOUR

While international comparisons between employment relations and labour law jurisdictions are common in academic writing,[13] until recently little emphasis had been placed on the concepts of legal family and legal origin. Consequently, in seeking to account for differences between labour law regimes, scholars have focused on factors such as political context or the difficulties associated with transplanting a foreign legal model (Teubner, 1998; Cooney et al., 2002).

The widespread interest in legal origins as a mode of analysing differences between labour law systems is thus a very recent phenomenon. Legal origins scholars turned their attention to labour market regulation in 2004 with the publication of 'The regulation of labor' (Botero et al., 2004). Continuing with their leximetric methodology, Botero et al. evaluated labour and social security law across more than 60 dimensions in 85 countries by scoring each jurisdiction in relation to a number of variables based on specific legal rules purporting to protect employees.

The authors found that there was a strong relationship between high aggregate scores on these indices and legal origin, much stronger even than the relationship between labour laws and the political orientation of the enacting government. Consistent with their earlier studies, the authors found that the civil law countries, and especially those in the French civil law family, were, overall, more protective of labour (or, from the authors' point of view, *less* protective of business investors) than those of common law origin.[14] The authors went on to consider correlations between these aggregate variables and several indicators relating to the health of a country's labour market (including size of the unofficial economy, workforce participation and employment rates). They found that the more protective labour regulation associated with the civil law countries had generally 'no benefits, and some costs' (ibid., p. 1375). These costs included a larger informal sector, higher unemployment (especially youth unemployment) and lower male workforce participation.[15]

The analysis in the Botero et al. (2004) study of labour market regulation was soon taken up by the World Bank in its *Doing Business* project. Its 'Employing Workers Index', which is based on the employment law variables in Botero et al. (2004) ranks countries according to the degree to which their labour laws allegedly impede business. Countries are accordingly praised for making working hours more flexible, reducing compensation for dismissal and reducing restrictions on non-standard work (World Bank, 2009).

Qualifications, Extensions and Challenges

Beyond the landmark study conducted by Botero et al. (2004), a number of more recent studies have now been published that examine the interaction between legal origins, labour law and its consequences.[16] Some of these were concerned principally with critically reviewing the application of the leximetric approach to the study of labour law, whilst others have been concerned with qualifying and extending it.

One of the most wide-ranging *methodological* critiques is provided by Pozen (2007). He concludes that the 'methodological weaknesses' of Botero et al. (2004) 'severely undermine its putative contributions' (p. 44). His critique highlights three main problems with the way Botero et al. have measured and assessed the relationship between legal origins and labour market regulation: measurement and coding issues; omitted variables; and ahistoricity. All three parallel to a degree the critiques that have been directed at legal origins research more generally. Scholars at the International Labour Organization have also drawn attention to the unrepresentative nature of the model 'business' and 'employee' used in the Botero research; they are atypical in developing countries, in particular (Berg and Cazes, 2007; Lee et al., 2008).

The most significant group of studies that attempt to rework the leximetric approach has been those conducted by Deakin and his colleagues (Ahlering and Deakin, 2007; Deakin et al., 2007; Deakin, 2008 and 2009; Amour et al., 2009; Deakin and Sarkar, 2009). These authors accept that there are 'significant differences in regulatory style between the common law and civil law', and that these may 'hamper the flow of ideas from one system to another' and, conversely, that they may 'facilitate the exchange of legal models *within* the main legal families' (Deakin et al., 2009, p. 137; emphasis in original). 'To that extent, a legal origin effect could be expected to arise from the division of systems into different legal families' (ibid.). As we have noted above, however, the legal origins arguments have been criticized as overstating, or mis-stating, the role of legal origins in legal evolution. Deakin et al. (2007) stress, in particular, that the strength of a legal origins effect 'would differ from one context to another', and that it cannot be assumed a priori. Thus, the impact of legal origins is a matter for empirical analysis (ibid., pp. 137–41; Jones and Mitchell, 2008). Important issues to be taken into account include the extent to which foreign legal rules may be adapted to local economic, cultural and political conditions (endogenization), the strength of 'opposing tendencies for the convergence of legal rules' deriving from various harmonizing and transnationalizing influences, and particularly the timing and nature of legal innovations in relation to the process of industrialization. Rather than a strong 'functionalist' legal origins effect, the force of legal origin depends on 'context': this is a 'weak' legal origins effect (Deakin et al., 2007, p. 141).

Deakin et al. (2007) illustrate the importance of the timing of industrialization by reference to the evolution of British labour law. When the process of industrialization commenced in Britain, the old forms of labour regulation based on master and servant laws and feudal obligations of service were still extant, whereas in Europe the codified private law of contract was already in place at the time of major-scale industrialization (Deakin, 2008). In Britain the old forms of regulation persisted into the late nineteenth century (and in its colonies, for much longer), continuing the tradition of strong managerial prerogative through ownership, and employment as service, enforced through criminal sanctions. In regulating labour markets it was these ideas, in the form of different variants of master and servant legislation, that were passed on to the British colonies rather than the idea of the 'efficiency' of free contracting between the autonomous parties to industrial relationships (Hay and Craven, 2004). The contract of employment as it is now understood in the common law world did not fully emerge in Britain until the 1920s–30s (Deakin, 1998, 2009).

The Deakin studies can also be distinguished from the Botero et al. (2004) study of labour market regulation in terms of how labour law is measured. Although the Deakin studies have adopted a leximetric approach to investigating cross-national differences in labour law, the authors have discarded some of the variables used in the Botero et al. index,[17] and have adopted a longitudinal index, charting labour law regulation from 1970 to 2005, thus allowing for investigation of legal evolution over time rather than at a fixed historical point. In compiling their index the authors have also accounted for the role of self-regulating mechanisms (such as collective agreements), and the extent to which laws were mandatory or capable of modification by the parties (default rules). Unlike the Botero et al. study, Deakin et al. (2007, p. 44, footnote 9) also cite specific sources for each of their variables.

Together with our colleagues Shelley Marshall and Andrew Stewart, we have applied an approach similar to Deakin's and completed a longitudinal coding of Australian labour law (Cooney et al., 2009). This coding suggests that 'the timing of stages of economic development, perhaps the type of labour market and industry structure, and changes in the political environment, may be more important for explaining the direction of legal evolution than legal origins' (ibid., p. 37). There is nonetheless, some evidence of a weak legal origins effect; that is, the protective strength of Australian labour law tends to resemble other common law jurisdictions (such as the US and UK, much less so India) more than it does civil law jurisdictions (Germany and France), but with significant variation over time.[18]

Other labour law researchers engaging in legal origin debates have questioned the implicit normative commitments associated with legal origins measures. For example, Lee et al. have argued strongly that the negative evaluation of working time regulation in Botero et al. (2004) and the World Bank's *Doing Business* reports conflict with International Labour Office (ILO) Conventions (Lee et al., 2008). They maintain that there is a fundamental failure to appreciate the potential benefits of labour regulation, such as the positive health impact of limiting excessive working hours or restrictions on arbitrary and discriminatory dismissal (ibid., pp. 421–2).

Lee et al. (2008) also question the claimed link between 'deregulated' jurisdictions and prosperity. They point out that the Botero et al. methodology as applied in *Doing Business* leads to highly questionable evaluations, when specific countries are considered. Thus, employment flexibility in Haiti, Afghanistan and New Guinea is ranked more favourably than for Finland, the Netherlands and Sweden, despite the manifestly superior employment and productivity performance of the latter group.[19] As a result of these and other concerns, the World Bank Group decided to revise the Employing Workers Indicator in 2009 and suspended its use for policy purposes.[20]

CONSEQUENCES OF LEGAL ORIGINS FOR EMPLOYMENT RELATIONS

Although considerable disagreement remains over the *extent* to which legal origins effects are evident, even the fiercest critics of the legal origins research accept that a country's legal origin has significant consequences for the form and extent of labour market regulation. There are also obvious implications for employment relations and labour market practices, which we illustrate here with two brief examples.

Globalization and the Consequences of Legal Origins

This issue is particularly salient given the question of how the changing economic environment and globalization have undermined cross-national differences in labour market regulation and patterns of employment relations. A key concern has been the extent to which labour standards and labour law have converged across national settings, particularly as globalization has created pressures on countries to adjust regulatory settings to promote competition and direct foreign investment (see Drezner, 2001, for a review of this literature). While the precise meaning of the term convergence in this context is somewhat ambiguous, it has been asserted that a process of convergence may reflect a number of forces (Drezner, 2005). Perhaps the most prominent view has been that economic forces of globalization and competition have made it increasingly difficult for national governments to maintain distinctive systems of labour market regulation. From this perspective, it is generally argued that competition among countries to attract direct foreign investment is associated with a 'race to the bottom' – a tendency to reduce the protective strength of labour law to a common low standard (Braithwaite and Drahos, 2000). While there is substantial case study evidence of multinational corporations shifting production and jobs to low-cost countries (Tonelson, 2000), the evidence of a 'race to the bottom' effect on labour standards is at best mixed (OECD, 1996; van Beers, 1998). Legal scholars have suggested globalization may nonetheless induce a level of convergence in legal systems towards a single model through the influence of international institutions (such as the World Bank) or via the influence of major economic powers. These influences may arise due to the perceived potential economic benefits associated with transnational harmonization of legal rules, or as a direct consequence of the diffusion of more efficient rule-making procedures among countries with diverse legal systems. Researchers using this argument suggest that globalization is associated with a process of convergence towards a particular regulatory type, notably some variation of a common law model, which provides greater flexibility and a reduction in employment security (Kelemen and Sibbitt, 2004).

While these arguments have been used to support the proposition that convergence is towards a *single* model, other scholars have hypothesized that convergence may involve a 'bipolar convergence' around two competing styles (Drezner, 2005). This may occur, for example, where rivalry between economic powers, 'combined with increasing returns to scale of regulatory harmonization', leads countries 'to attract as many allies as possible' (ibid., p. 856). In the context of legal origins theory, this argument has been associated with the view that colonization resulted in the transplant of legal systems from Europe to other countries, which were subsequently 'locked-in' and have remained divergent (Glaeser and Shleifer, 2003).

A third possible variation would suggest that there may be a degree of convergence between countries of different legal origins and legal cultures, without specifying the model to which those countries are converging. This type of argument would tend to indicate that other factors, such as economic and/or political unification, will ultimately be more powerful than legal origins in driving convergence. Significantly, this process would potentially result in the creation of 'hybrid' legal systems that do not necessarily conform to the predictions of legal origins theory. For example, Deakin et al. (2007, pp. 152–3) suggest that, notwithstanding their different legal origins, the degree of convergence observed in the UK towards France and Germany reflects its openness to European Union influences.

As most of the data collected by legal origins scholars is cross-sectional, it is not possible to make any assessment of any of these alternative convergence hypotheses from that source. However, longitudinal data on the protective strength of labour market regulation in a considerably smaller sample of countries has been collected by Deakin et al. (2007) and, more

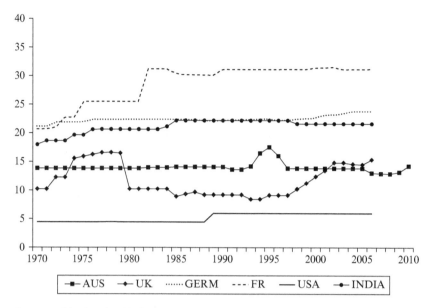

Sources: The data for this figure are based on Deakin et al. (2007) and Cooney et al. (2009). For a full description of the Labour Market Regulation Index, see Deakin et al. (2007).

Figure 4.1   *Aggregate Labour Market Regulation Index, international comparisons*

recently, supplemented by Cooney et al. (2009). Figure 4.1 shows the value of the Labour Market Regulation Index over the period 1970 to 2005 for six countries for which data is available (Australia, France, Germany, India, United Kingdom and the United States). Although the small number of countries makes it difficult to draw strong conclusions, the data illustrate a persistent general legal origins effect on the protective strength of labour law.

But to what extent do the data indicate *convergence* in the protective strength of labour law over time? Whilst the data do show that the level of labour market protection in many countries has ebbed and flowed over the period for which the data are available, it is difficult to conclude from Figure 4.1 that there has been convergence to any great degree. There is no evidence of a regulatory 'race to bottom' or convergence on a variant of the common law model of labour market regulation. Nor does the evidence support a 'bipolar convergence' around common law and civil law models of labour market regulation.

Employment Relations Outcomes

The Botero et al. (2004) data provide a broad indication of the way legal origins can influence a range of employment relations outcomes. In order to illustrate the connection between legal origins and employment relations outcomes we have extracted from their data some indicative differences in labour market regulation across some legal families (see Table 4.1).[21] Table 4.1 reports on variables that relate to three core sets of employment relations outcomes: the protection of worker entitlements, limits on managerial prerogative and forms of employee voice. Here the mean value for each variable is given for all countries (Column 1), and then for groups of countries in each legal family in subsequent columns. Statistically significant differences in the mean value between groups are reported for each variable, with common law countries as the base group.[22]

Across most variables, it will be seen that common law countries have a weaker level of protection than other legal families. This is particularly evident in relation to the level of protection afforded to most worker entitlements. Moreover, common law countries are typically less likely than each of the civil law groups of countries to provide universal coverage of entitlements, notably through the extension of collective agreements to non-union workers. Compared with countries from other legal families, common law countries are, on average, significantly less likely to place limits on managerial prerogatives through, for example, restrictions on the use of fixed-term contracts or requirements to notify a third party (such as a government agency or union) of intentions to make workers redundant. With the exception of legal provisions providing for worker or union representation on company boards, however, legal protection for employee voice was not significantly different from that in other countries. Interestingly, with the exception of countries from the Scandinavian civil law family, there were no statistically significant differences in union density rates across common and civil law countries. As noted earlier in this chapter, there are several reasons to be cautious in accepting the validity of this data, but it does serve the purpose of indicating the importance of the issue.

CONCLUSION

The application of legal origins theory to the study of labour law and employment relations is an emergent area of research that is generating both extensive scholarship and policy recommendations. As we have seen,

Table 4.1   Differences in labour market regulation, by legal family

	(1) All Countries	(2) Comm on Law (n = 24)	(3) French Civil Law (n = 32)	(4) German Civil Law (n = 6)	(5) Scandi- navian Civil Law (n = 4)
Protection of worker entitlements					
Overtime premium	1.4	1.4	1.4	1.4	1.5
	(0.25)	(0.25)	(0.05)	(0.05)	(0.00)
Annual leave	18.9	13.0***	21.7***	22.8***	25.8***
entitlement	(7.37)	(0.06)	(1.00)	(2.30)	(1.89)
Redundancy notice	4.7	4.4	4.5	4.6	8.1*
period	(3.23)	(1.36)	(0.60)	(0.90)	(0.55)
Redundancy	7.07	4.3**	10.2***	5.7	0.0
payment	(0.60)	(0.74)	(1.40)	(2.63)	(0.00)
Extension of	0.5	0.3**	0.6**	0.7*	0.8*
collective agreements	(0.50)	(0.10)	(0.10)	(0.21)	(0.25)
Limits on managerial prerogatives					
Limits on use of	0.4	0.1***	0.5***	0.4*	0.4*
fixed-term contracts	(0.35)	(0.06)	(0.05)	(0.14)	(0.15)
Limits on use of	0.9	0.8	0.9	0.9	0.9
part-time contracts	(0.28)	(0.07)	(0.04)	(0.08)	(0.13)
Max. working hours	2088.5	2171.6***	2063.6**	2060.6	1831.0***
(annual) before overtime is paid	(189.97)	(33.84)	(32.78)	(77.89)	(30.0)
Requirement to	0.5	0.3**	0.6***	0.3	0.8*
notify third parties of dismissals	(0.50)	(0.10)	(0.09)	(0.21)	(0.25)
Requirement to gain	0.2	0.2	0.2	0.0	0.0
approval from a third party to make dismissal	(0.39)	(0.09)	(0.07)	(0.00)	(0.00)
Limits on capacity to	0.8	0.7	0.9	0.8	0.8
dismiss striking workers	(0.40)	(0.10)	(0.06)	(0.17)	(0.25)
Employee voice					
Right to join a union	0.8	0.7	0.9	0.8	0.8
	(0.40)	(0.95)	(0.06)	(0.17)	(0.25)

Table 4.1   (continued)

Representation on	0.1	0.0**	0.0	0.3***	0.8***
company boards	(0.29)	(0.00)	(0.03)	(0.21)	(0.25)
Mandatory works	0.4	0.3	0.3	0.7	0.8
council	(0.49)	(0.10)	(0.08)	(0.21)	(0.25)
Union density	0.3	0.2	0.2	0.3	0.8***
	(0.22)	(0.04)	(0.03)	(0.05)	(0.02)

Notes:
See Botero et al. (2004) for full variable definitions. The table shows the mean value for each variable. Standard errors are in parentheses.
Statistical significance: *** p<0.01, ** p<0.05, * p<0.1. For common law countries, the test is for a statistically different mean for each variable from all other groups; for all other groups, the test is for statistically significant difference in mean value of each variable compared with the mean value for common law countries.

Source: Data are taken from Botero et al. (2004).

the theory has been subject to vigorous criticism, not least because it has been invoked to attack labour standards.

There are clearly many shortcomings in the approach taken by the original legal origins scholars to labour regulation. Despite its flaws, however, it does not follow that the attempt to find relationships between legal rules at particular points in time and socioeconomic circumstances is uninteresting or unimportant. Certainly, any attempts will be beset with methodological difficulties and be provisional. Nonetheless, in suggesting that such relationships may exist (albeit not necessarily the ones they find) the legal origins scholars have opened up intriguing possibilities for research. Are there, for example, correlations between particular legal *rules* (such as those regulating the labour market) and/or particular legal *styles* and social indicators, such as those relating to poverty? Do reforms to particular legal rules really have much effect on resource allocation and economic performance if the nature of the legal system as a whole remains unchanged? How do laws protecting workers interact with those protecting shareholders and creditors? What is the relationship between legal rules and legal style and the ordering of employment relations *within* the business enterprise? What are the points of similarity and difference with alternative theories of business operations in market economies? Work on these questions is just beginning, and we can expect a proliferation of illuminating and controversial findings in the near future.

NOTES

1. See La Porta et al. (1997, 1998, 1999, 2000, 2006, 2007, 2008); Johnson et al. (2000); Glaeser and Shleifer (2002, 2003); Djankov et al. (2003); Botero et al. (2004); Djankov and La Porta et al. (2008).
2. Legal origins theory shares some common ideas with a number of alternative approaches, most particularly the 'varieties of capitalism' literature and business systems theory, both of which are dealt with elsewhere in this volume. The distinction between liberal and coordinated market economies, which is central to the varieties of capitalism approach pioneered by Hall and Soskice (2001), has a great deal in common with legal origins theory. Liberal market economies are typically aligned to common law countries, while coordinated market economies typically include civil law countries. There are, however, a number of important differences. Whitley's (1992, 1999, 2005) business systems theory similarly draws connections between the regulatory approach, corporate governance and employment systems. For a discussion of the common-alities and differences between these alternative theories of comparative capitalism, see Jackson and Deeg (2006).
3. Thomson's ISI rankings shows that Shleifer, La Porta and Lopez-de-Silanes are the three most cited scholars in related fields of business and economics. La Porta et al. (1999) is the third most cited paper in business and economics over the last ten years. See ISI Web of Knowledge at www.isiwebofknowledge.com (accessed 9 January 2011).
4. See www.doingbusiness.org for details of the annual reports (accessed 9 January 2011).
5. Note that this is different from examining *how* the rules were introduced (e.g., coloniza-tion, voluntary adoption), which is also of interest to many comparative lawyers.
6. See below, note 10.
7. While these authors contrast civil law and common law in this and many other pas-sages, it is clear from their studies overall that the principal contrast is between Anglo-American law and French law. In several of the regression studies, the German and Nordic jurisdictions (in aggregate) are much less associated with adverse market impacts that the French legal systems.
8. For a more detailed discussion of the benefits and pitfalls of political interventions in a legal origins framework, see Glaeser and Shleifer (2002) and Djankov et al. (2003).
9. For critiques focusing on labour law/labour market economics perspective, see the very helpful literature review by Lee et al. (2008).
10. China has been quite eclectic in choosing models for its reconstructed legal system. US influence, for example, has been extensive. For overviews of its legal system see Peerenboom (2002) and Chen (2008). China has a uniform Contract Law and General Principles of the Civil Law. However, these two laws do not constitute a code in the same way as the French and German models do.
11. Although other methods are used, see, for example, Djankov and Hart et al. (2008).
12. The term 'legal ground rules' derives from the work of Pistor, who along with Deakin has been one most forceful critics of legal origins theory; see Pistor (2006).
13. A longstanding well-known example is Kahn-Freund (1974).
14. The authors contrast New Zealand and Portugal.
15. These findings are similar to the recent labour market analyses, which (without invok-ing the concept of legal origins) claim negative effects for many forms of regulation intended to protect labour; see, for example, Haltiwanger et al. (2006).
16. These include: Siebert (2005); Chor and Freeman (2005); Pozen (2007); Lee et al. (2008); Djankov and Ramalho (2009) and Cooney et al. (2009).
17. The index of labour market regulation developed by Botero et al. includes measures of social security. Neither these measures, nor any equivalent measures of social security provisions, are included in the index constructed by Deakin et al. (2007).
18. Details of the data used in this study and a full report are available from: www.buseco. monash.edu.au/mgt/research/acrew (accessed 9 January 2011).
19. In 2009, for instance, Azerbaijan and Burkino Faso were complimented for easing

restrictions on fixed-term contracting and removing dismissal requirements. On the other hand, China was criticized for making dismissal more difficult (because of its landmark Labour Contract Law), the United Kingdom for increasing paid annual leave, and Sweden and Korea for increasing restrictions on fixed-term employment.

20.   See: www.doingbusiness.org/documents/EWI_guidance_note.pdf (accessed 9 January 2011).
21.   Countries designated as belonging to the socialist legal family are excluded.
22.   For common law countries, the test is for a statistically significantly difference in the mean value for each variable for common law countries as a group, compared with the mean value for each variable for all other groups combined. For all other groups, the test for statistical significance is between each group and the group of common law countries.

REFERENCES

Acemoglu, Daron, Johnston, Simon and Robinson, James A. (2001), 'Colonial origins of comparative development: An empirical investigation', *American Economic Review*, **91**(5), 1369–401.
Ahlering, Beth and Deakin, Simon (2007), 'Labour regulation, corporate governance and legal origin: A case of institutional complementarity?', *Law and Society Review*, **41**(4), 865–908.
Armour, John, Deakin, Simon, Lele, Priya and Siems, Mathias (2009), 'How do legal rules evolve? Evidence from a cross-country comparison of shareholder, creditor and worker protection', *American Journal of Comparative Law*, **57**, 579–629.
Berg, Janine and Cazes, Sandrine (2007), 'The *Doing Business Indicators*: Measurement issues and political implications', Economic and Labour Market Paper No. 2007/6, Geneva, ILO: Employment Analysis and Research Unit, Economic and Labour Market Analysis Department.
Biddulph, Sarah and Nicholson, Penelope (Pip) (2008), 'Expanding the circle: Comparative legal studies in transition', in Pip Nicholson and Sarah Biddulph (eds), *Examining Practice, Interrogating Theory: Comparative Legal Studies in Asia*, Leiden: Martinus Nijhoff Publishers, pp. 9–24.
Botero, Juan, Djankov, Simeon, La Porta, Rafael, Lopez-de-Silanes, Florencio and Shleifer, Andrei (2004), 'The regulation of labor', *Quarterly Journal of Economics*, **119**(1), 1339–82.
Braithwaite, John and Drahos, Peter (2000), *Global Business Regulation*, Cambridge: Cambridge University Press.
Chen, Jianfu (2008), *Chinese Law: Context and Transformation*, Leiden: Martinus Nijhoff.
Chor, David and Freeman, Richard B. (2005), 'The 2004 Global Labor Survey: Workplace institutions around the world', NBER Working Paper No. 11598, Cambridge, MA: National Bureau of Economic Research.
Clift, Ben (1997), 'French corporate governance in the new global economy: Mechanisms of change and hybridization within models of capitalism', *Political Studies*, **55**(3), 546–67.
Cooney, Sean, Lindsey, Tim, Mitchell, Richard and Zhu, Ying (2002), 'Labour law and labour market regulation in East Asian states: Problems and issues for comparative inquiry', in Sean Cooney, Tim Lindsey, Richard Mitchell and Ying Zhu (eds), *Law and Labour Market Regulation in East Asia*, London: Routledge, pp. 1–26.
Cooney, Sean, Gahan, Peter, Marshall, Shelley, Mitchell, Richard and Stewart, Andrew (2009), 'Legal origins and the evolution of Australian Labour Law, 1970–2010', unpublished Research Report, Monash University, available at: http://www.buseco.monash.edu.au/blt/wclrg/reports.html; accessed 9 January 2011.
Deakin, Simon (1998), 'The evolution of the contract of employment, 1900–1950', in Noel Whiteside and Robert Salais (eds), *Governance, Industry and Labour Markets in Britain and France*, London: Routledge, pp. 212–30.

Deakin, Simon (2008), 'Timing is everything: Industrialization, legal origin and the evolution of the contract of employment in Britain and Continental Europe', in Brian Bercusson and Cynthia Estlund (eds), *Regulating Labour in the Wake of Globalization: New Challenges, New Institutions*, Oxford: Hart, pp. 67–87.
Deakin, Simon (2009), 'Legal origin, juridical form and industrialization in historical perspective: The case of the employment relation and the joint stock company', *Socio-Economic Review*, 7(1), 35–65.
Deakin, Simon and Sarkar, Prabirjit (2009), 'Assessing the long-run economic impact of labour law systems: A theoretical reappraisal and analysis of new time series data', *Industrial Relations Journal*, 39(6), 453–87.
Deakin, Simon, Lele, Priya and Siems, Mathias (2007), 'The evolution of labour law: Calibrating and comparing regulatory regimes', *International Labour Review*, 146(3–4), 133–62.
Djankov, Simeon and Ramalho, Rita (2008), 'Employment laws in developing countries', Centre for Economic Policy Research (CEPR) Discussion Paper No. DP7097, available at SSRN: http://ssrn.com/abstract=1344676; accessed 9 January 2011.
Djankov, Simeon, Hart, Oliver, McLiesh, Carlee and Shleifer, Andrei (2008), 'Debt enforcement around the world', *Journal of Political Economy*, 116(6), 1105–49.
Djankov, Simeon, La Porta, Rafael, Lopez-de-Silanes, Florencio and Shleifer, Andrei (2008), 'The law and economics of self-dealing', *Journal of Financial Economics*, 88(3), 430–65.
Djankov, Simeon, Glaeser, Edward, La Porta, Rafael, Lopez-de-Silanes, Florencio and Shleifer, Andrei (2003), 'The new comparative economics', *Journal of Comparative Economics*, 31(4), 595–619.
Drezner, Daniel W. (2001), 'Globalization and policy convergence', *International Studies Review*, 3(1), 53–78.
Drezner, Daniel W. (2005), 'Globalization, harmonization and competition: The different pathways to policy convergence', *Journal of European Public Policy*, 12(5), 841–59.
Glaeser, Edward and Shleifer, Andrei (2002), 'Legal origins', *Quarterly Journal of Economics*, 117(4), 1193–1229.
Glaeser, Edward and Shleifer, Andrei (2003), 'The rise of the regulatory state', *Journal of Economic Literature*, 41(2), 401–25.
Hall, Peter A. and Soskice, David (eds) (2001), *Varieties of Capitalism*, Oxford: Oxford University Press.
Haltiwanger, John, Scarpetta, Stephano and Schweiger, Helena (2006), 'Assessing job flows across countries: The role of industry, firm size, and regulations', World Bank Policy Research Working Paper No. 4070.
Harding, Andrew (2002), 'Global doctrine and local knowledge: Law in South East Asia', *International and Comparative Law Quarterly*, 51(1), 35–53.
Hay, Douglas and Craven, Paul (eds) (2004), *Masters, Servants and Magistrates in Britain and the Empire, 1562–1955*, Chapel Hill, NC: University of North Carolina Press.
Jackson, Gregory and Deeg, Richard (2006), 'How many varieties of capitalism? Comparing the comparative institutional analyses of capitalist diversity', MPIfG Discussion Paper No. 06/02, Cologne: Max Planck Institute for the Study of Societies.
Johnson, Simon, La Porta, Rafael, Lopez-de-Silanes, Florencio and Shleifer, Andrei (2000), 'Tunnelling', *American Economic Review*, 90(2), 22–7.
Jones, Meredith and Mitchell, Richard (2008), 'Legal origins, legal families and the regulation of labour in Australia', in Shelley Marshall, Richard Mitchell and Ian Ramsay (eds), *Varieties of Capitalism, Corporate Governance and Employees*, Melbourne: Melbourne University Publishing, pp. 60–94.
Kahn-Freund, Otto (1974), 'The uses and misuses of comparative law', *Modern Law Review*, 37(1), 1–27.
Kelemen, R. Daniel and Sibbitt, Eric C. (2004), 'The globalization of American law', *International Organization*, 58(1), 103–36.
La Porta, Rafael, Lopez-de-Silanes, Florencio and Shleifer, Andrei (1999), 'Corporate ownership around the world', *Journal of Finance*, 54(2), 471–517.

La Porta, Rafael, Lopez-de-Silanes, Florencio and Shleifer, Andrei (2006), 'What works in securities laws?', *Journal of Finance*, **61**(1), 1–32.

La Porta, Rafael, Lopez-de-Silanes, Florencio and Shleifer, Andrei (2008), 'The economic consequences of legal origins', *Journal of Economic Literature*, **46**(2), 285–332.

La Porta, Rafael, Djankov, Simeon, McLiesh, Caralee and Shleifer, Andrei (2007), 'Private credit in 129 countries', *Journal of Finance*, **84**(2), 299–329.

La Porta, Rafael, Lopez-de-Silanes, Florencio, Shleifer, Andrei and Vishny, Robert (1997), 'Legal determinants of external finance', *Journal of Finance*, **52**(3), 1131–50.

La Porta, Rafael, Lopez-de-Silanes, Florencio, Shleifer, Andrei and Vishny, Robert (1998), 'Law and finance', *Journal of Political Economy*, **106**(6), 1113–55.

La Porta, Rafael, Lopez-de-Silanes, Florencio, Shleifer, Andrei and Vishny, Robert (2000), 'Agency problems and dividend policies around the world', *Journal of Finance*, **58**(1–2), 3–27.

Lee, Sangheon, McCann, Deirdre and Torm, Nina (2008), 'The World Bank's "Employing Workers" Index: Findings and critiques – a review of recent evidence', *International Labour Review*, **147**(4), 416–32.

Legrand, Pierre and Munday, Roderick (eds) (2003), *Comparative Legal Studies: Traditions and Transition*, Cambridge: Cambridge University Press.

Lele, Priya and Siems, Mathias (2007), 'Shareholder protection – a leximetric approach', *Journal of Corporate Law Studies*, **7**, 17–50.

Lindsey, Tim (ed.) (2007), *Indonesia: Law and Society*, 2nd edition, Sydney: Federation Press.

Mills, Melinda, Blossfeld, Hans-Peter, Buchholz, Sandra, Hofäcker, Dirk, Bernardi, Fabrizio, Hofmeister, Heather (2008), 'Converging divergences? An international comparison of the impact of globalization on industrial relations and employment careers', *International Sociology*, **23**(4), 561–95.

OECD (1996), *Trade, Employment and Labour Standards: A Study of Core Workers' Rights and International Trade*, Paris: Organisation for Economic Co-operation and Development.

Örücü, Esin (2004), *The Enigma of Comparative Law: Variations on a Theme for the Twenty-first Century*, Leiden: Martinus Nijhoff.

Partlett, William (2008), 'Reclassifying Russian law: Mechanisms, outcomes, and solutions for an overly politicized field', *Columbia Journal of East European Law*, **2**, 1–55.

Peerenboom, Randall (2002), *China's Long March Toward Rule of Law*, Cambridge, UK: Cambridge University Press.

Pistor, Katharina (2006), 'Legal ground rules in coordinated and in liberal market economies', in Klaus Hopt, Eddy Wymeersch, Hideki Kanda and Harald Baum (eds), *Corporate Governance in Context: Corporations, States and Markets in Europe, Japan, and the United States*, New York: Oxford University Press, pp. 249–80.

Pistor, Katharina, Keinan, Yoram, Kleinheisterkamp, Jan and West, Mark (2003), 'The evolution of corporate law: A cross-country comparison', *University of Pennsylvania Journal of International Economic Law*, **23**(4), 791–871.

Pozen, David (2007), 'The regulation of labor and the relevance of legal origin', *Comparative Labor Law and Policy Journal*, **27**(2), 43–56.

Roe, Mark (2006), 'Legal origins, politics and modern stock markets', *Harvard Law Review*, **120**(2), 460–527.

Siebert, William. S. (2005), 'Labour market regulation: Some comparative lessons', *Economic Affairs*, **25**(3), 3–10.

Siems, Mathias (2005), 'Numerical comparative law – do we need statistical evidence in order to reduce complexity?', *Cardozo Journal of International and Comparative Law*, **13**, 521–40.

Siems, Mathias (2007a), 'Legal origins: Reconciling law and finance and comparative law', *McGill Law Journal*, **52**, 55–81.

Siems, Mathias (2007b), 'The end of comparative law', *The Journal of Comparative Law*, **2**(2), 133–50.

Siems, Mathias and Simon, Deakin (2010), 'Comparative law and finance: Past, present and future research', *Journal of Institutional and Theoretical Economics*, **166**(1), 120–40.

Teubner, Gunther (1998), 'Legal irritants: Good faith in British law or how unifying law ends up in new divergences', *Modern Law Review*, **61**(1), 11–32.

Tonelson, Alan (2000), *The Race to the Bottom*, Boulder, Colorado: Westview Press.

van Beers, C. (1998), 'Labour standards and trade flows of OECD countries', *The World Economy*, **21**(1), 57–73.

Whitley, Richard (1992), *Business Systems in East Asia: Firms, Markets and Societies*, London: Sage.

Whitley, Richard (1999), *Divergent Capitalisms*, Oxford: Oxford University Press.

Whitley, Richard (2005), 'How national are business systems? The role of states and complementary institutions in standardizing systems of economic coordination and control and the national level', in Glenn Morgan, Richard Whitley and Eli Moen (eds), *Changing Capitalisms? Internationalization, Institutional Change, and Systems of Economic Organization*, Oxford: Oxford University Press, pp. 190–234.

World Bank (2009), *Doing Business in 2010*, Washington: World Bank.

Zweigert, Konrad and Hein, Kötz (1998), *An Introduction to Comparative Law*, 3rd edition, Oxford: Oxford University Press.

5 Cross-cultural studies
Terence Jackson

INTRODUCTION

The area of cross-cultural management and organization studies has been dominated by Hofstede's (1980a) seminal work on cultural values dimensions. Despite much recent criticism, and perhaps because of it, he remains the most cited author in this area. It is difficult to start any account in this field without reference to his work, and this is certainly the starting point here. This chapter first looks at the main contributions of the work of Hofstede, and others working parallel with him or subsequent to his main body of work. This includes looking at the merits of studies including the World Values Survey (WVS), Trompenaars (1993) and its subsequent reinterpretation by Peter Smith (Smith et al., 1996) and the more recent work of the GLOBE study (House et al., 2004). Yet, how useful are these and what are their shortcomings?

This chapter then goes on to argue that although contributing greatly to the development of a subdiscipline, cross-cultural management, the 'paradigm' that Hofstede (2007) claims to have created has straight-jacketed this field. Yet this is no new paradigm that he has created; it is merely that of the positivism that social scientists have critiqued over the years, and still appears to persist particularly in the field of cross-cultural psychology. The other influence that it appears to have had is in accepting, and then propagating, an artificial distinction between a 'cultural' approach and an 'institutional' approach. This is also discussed in this chapter.

The approach of comparing 'cultures' on a limited number of 'values' is fraught with dangers. Mainly, it neglects the dynamics not only of interpersonal and inter-organizational interaction, but it also ignores the important geopolitical power dynamics of globalization. This chapter goes on to argue that an approach that focuses on cultural 'interfaces' is more likely to lead to greater understanding of the cross-cultural dynamics and issues that affect employment relations. This does not just include working at an international level. Most countries are becoming more and more multicultural, with multicultural workforces. Issues such as cultural identity are becoming more complex, yet more important to understand. It is hoped that this chapter will provide a contribution to that understanding.

THE CULTURAL VALUES APPROACH

One of the most important contributions of Hofstede (1980a) and the cultural values approach to comparing nations is in providing a critique of the universal nature of management knowledge, policies and practices. Hofstede (1980b) in particular questions whether US management practices, such as participative management, are appropriate in countries that have cultural values that are quite distinct from that of the Anglo-American cultures. This will be returned to later.

Hofstede's (1980a) work, as noted above, has been extensively cited, and cross-cultural comparisons of management, organization and work values (e.g., Shackleton and Ali, 1990; Gerhart, 2008) and, less so, employment relations (e.g., Garcia et al., 2009; Posthuma, 2009) frequently refer to this work. We might ascribe the success of his concepts to their ease of understanding. His theory is very easy to teach, and this simplicity also points to one of its many weaknesses. In this first part of this chapter, the positivist paradigm within which the cultural values approach is seated is momentarily accepted. This is in order to paint a more comprehensive picture of this approach, and to extend it past a limited appreciation of the rather blunt tools of Hofstede.

Among extensive cross-national studies that focus on cultural values, it is possible to distinguish between those that relate to wider societal values (Inglehart et al., 1998; Schwartz, 1999) and those that relate more directly to organizations and management (Hofstede, 1980a; Trompenaars, 1993; Smith et al., 1996; House et al., 2004). Although the former have been used to discuss issues in people management and organization (particularly Schwartz: see, for example, Gatley et al., 1996), they may represent values at different levels: namely macro and meso/micro. For example, Jackson (2002a) pointed out that Schwartz's (1994) data on the former West and East Germanys indicate similarities of values, suggesting that the prevailing cultural values of the two Germanys were more similar and pervasive during the Iron Curtain years than is suggested by data from studies of organizational employees and managers (such as Trompenaars, 1993). There may therefore be differences (as in the case with the former two Germanys) between values in the wider communities and those in corporations. This may also be the case in former colonial countries where work organizations may not reflect the wider values of the societies within which they exist (Jackson, 2004). Yet, there are also connections between organizational values and societal values.

The worth of studies that explore wider societal values is that they provide an indication of fit with organizational values. Understanding the values of the wider (macro-) society within which organizations evolve or are imposed is important. First, Western countries such as Britain, France, the US do business abroad with a set of cultural values that often are not manifest or explicit and are assumed to be universal. As we saw above, this is one of the major quests of cross-cultural studies, and of studies of multinational enterprises (MNEs) and employment relations (ER) research, to question whether management practices used in the home country are appropriate in other countries. It is important to understand the values from which management systems, or sets of policies and implicit rules used in organizations, are derived, and how they influence the way organizations are managed in other countries.

WORLD VALUES SURVEY: A VIEW FROM OUTSIDE THE CORPORATION

Of national comparative studies of societal values, that of Ronald Inglehart and colleagues is the most extensive, and unlike other studies takes a longitudinal perspective. The World Values Survey (WVS) has its origin in a set of surveys conducted in ten Western European countries, and now known as the European Values Study. The WVS, growing out of the European study, was initiated in 1981 'to study the values and attitudes of mass publics across nations of different economic, educational, and cultural backgrounds'. Four waves of the study have been conducted: 1981–82, 1990–91, 1995–97 and 1999–2001. The most recent of these covers over 60 countries; and there will be new wave of surveys in 2010–12, which will provide a 30-year time-series for the analysis of social and political change. In general terms, the survey 'explores the hypothesis that mass belief systems are changing in ways that have important economic, political, and social consequences' (ESDS, 2011). They are based on random, stratified samples of adults in the general population. Each study contains data from interviews conducted with between 300 and 4000 respondents per nation. The areas covered include: the importance of work, family, friends, leisure time, politics and religion; attitudes towards government and religion including the frequency of participating in group activity in governmental and religious organizations; perceptions of economic, ethnic, religious and political groups and feelings of trust and closeness with these groups; assessment of relative importance of major problems facing the world and willingness to participate in solutions; assessment of self in terms of happiness and class identity.

Inglehart's (1997) main theory is that the shift of societies generally towards modernization and materialist values, emphasizing economic and physical security, is giving way to postmodern/postmaterialist values. Core elements in the modernization trend include industrialization, increased urbanization, growing occupational specialization and higher levels of formal education. A corollary of this would normally be higher levels of mass political participation, for example. Modernization might also be associated with 'cultural' changes like values conducive to economic accumulation. Postmodernization, he believes, is gradually replacing these outlooks or world views associated with modernization that have existed since the Industrial Revolution. Essentially he sees modernization as emphasizing economic efficiency, bureaucratic authority and scientific rationality; and, the move towards postmodernization as moving towards 'a more human society with more room for individual autonomy, diversity and self expression' (p. 12).

He appears to view modernization and postmodernization as stages in human or societal evolution with postmodernization representing 'a later stage of development' (p. 8). One could take a cynical view of this: less industrialized societies are gradually catching up with industrialized societies and moving towards modernization; yet industrialized societies are now moving to postmodernization, so less industrialized societies have even further to go in following the path of the more advanced countries. The move also towards greater 'individual autonomy' appears to reflect a movement towards more individuality and away from collectivism and communalism (see discussion below around Hofstede's 1980 concepts).

This may be an element that is endemic in what Human (1996) has called 'maximalist' studies of cultural values. It is certainly a feature of the critique of Hofstede's work (e.g., Human, 1996, p. 21, who states: 'the value judgements attached to the various dimensions have also rarely been explored as well as the self-fulfilling nature of the imposition of such classification on people'). Hence, to say that one society is higher in 'individualism' or 'power distance' than another, or lower in 'femininity' than another (Hofstede, 1980a) may be implying a value judgement (or at least one might be inferred) that one society is better than another. Certainly when linking such cultural dimensions to measures of economic development and prosperity as indeed, for example, Hofstede (1980a) and Ingelhart (1997) do, there does appear to be an implied value judgement in terms of a correlation between economic and social development and cultural values. The value judgement on Inglehart's part is more than implied. He contends (as co-author with Baker: Inglehart and Baker, 2001, pp. 16–17) that low-income and high-income societies differ systematically, in a polarization between traditional and secular-rational on the one hand, and between survival and self-expression values on the other. These dimensions are used by Inglehart to map the world in terms of modernization and postmodernization.

The first dimension (Inglehart, 1997), 'traditional authority vs. secular-rational authority' (later simply called 'traditional vs. secular-rational values': Inglehart and Baker, 2000 and 2001) is based on items that reflect an emphasis on obedience to traditional authority, often religious authority and adherence to family and communal obligations and norm sharing, versus items emphasizing a secular worldview where authority is legitimized by rational-legal norms and an emphasis on economic accumulation and individual achievement. Hence, items loading positively and representing the traditional pole are: God is very important in respondent's life; it is more important for a child to learn obedience and religious faith than independence and determination; abortion is never justified; respondent has a strong sense of national pride; respondent favours more respect for authority. Secular-rational emphasizes the opposite values: that is, provides negative scores on the above items. Inglehart and Baker (2000) also produce a list of a further 24 items that correlate (between 0.89 and 0.41) with this values dimension. These are mainly concerning the importance of religion, respect for parents and family including the dominance of the husband's role, importance of work and loyalty to country; with a positive correlation representing traditional values. This suggests a modernization process away from traditional values and norms, and towards industrialization and the centrality of work.

The second dimension (Inglehart, 1997) 'survival values vs. well-being values' (later termed 'survival vs. self-expression values': Inglehart and Baker, 2000 and 2001) reflects, according to Inglehart et al. (1998, pp. 14–15):

> the fact that in post-industrial society, historically unprecedented levels of wealth and the emergence of the welfare state have given rise to a shift from scarcity norms, emphasizing hard work and self-denial, to postmodern values emphasizing the quality of life, emancipation of women and sexual minorities and relatively postmaterialist priorities such as emphasis on self-expression.

Items loading on the factor 'survival' are: respondent gives priority to economic and physical security over self-expression and quality of life; respondent describes self as not very happy; respondent has not signed nor would sign a petition; homosexuality is never justifiable; you have to be very careful about trusting people. Self-expression emphasizes the opposite values: that is, provides negative scores on the above items. Inglehart and Baker (2000) also produce a list of a further 31 items that correlate (between 0.86 and 0.42) with this values dimension. These emphasize the different role of men and women, dissatisfaction with own situation, rejection of people who are different including foreigners, favouring of technology, lack of emphasis on preserving the environment, emphasis of material well-being and hard work, with a positive correlation representing survival values.

Countries classified under 'Protestant European' (e.g., Scandinavian countries, two Germanys, Netherlands and Switzerland) score high on both the secular-rational (modernist) and self-expression (postmodernist) dimensions. They also represent countries with the highest GNP per capita (Inglehart and Baker, 2000). At the opposite extreme and representing countries with the lowest GNP per capita (Inglehart and Baker, 2001), those whose scores represent traditional (pre-modern/pre-industrialized) and survival (pre-postmodern) are the countries clustered in an 'Africa' group (South Africa, Nigeria, Ghana) and 'South Asia' group (Pakistan, Bangladesh, Philippines, Turkey and India).

Bordering the self-expression end of the survival/self-expression dimension, but still representing traditional values on the traditional/ secular-rational dimension, are countries clustered in a 'Latin America' group: Peru, Venezuela, Columbia, Brazil; and bordering on the secular-rational: Mexico, Argentina, Uruguay. An 'Ex-communist/Baltic' group (Estonia, Lithuania, Latvia, Czech) is clustered high on the secular-rational end of the traditional secular-rational dimension and at the survival end of the survival/self-expression dimension.

Bordering this group, towards the self-expression side of the dimension is a 'Confucian' group (China, S. Korea, Taiwan and Japan), and towards the middle of the traditional/secular-rational dimension, but still at the survival side of the survival/self-expression dimension an 'Orthodox' group (Russia, Ukraine, Bulgaria, and others).

An 'English-speaking' cluster (US, Britain, Ireland, Australia, New Zealand, Canada) is grouped in the middle of the traditional/secular-rational dimension, and high on self-expression. In the middle of both dimensions is a 'Catholic Europe' cluster that includes Belgium, France, Italy, Spain and Austria towards the self-expression side of the survival/ self-expression dimension, and overlapping with the 'Orthodox' group towards survival are Slovenia, Croatia, Slovakia, Hungary.

Inglehart and Baker (2001) point out that the US, contrary to what some modernist commentators suppose, is not the archetypal modern/ postmodern or secular-rational and self-expression society that serves as the model for all other societies. In fact on Inglehart's (1997) cultural map of the world it is a 'deviant case'. Although high on self-expression, it is also high on traditional values with high levels of religiosity and national pride comparable to 'developing' countries.

Inglehart and Baker (2000) also look at the movement of nations on these dimensions from the original survey to the most recent survey. The trajectory generally confirms their hypothesis that countries are moving towards secular-rational and self-expression. Yet countries such as Russia, Belarus, Bulgaria, Estonia, Lithuania and Latvia appear to be moving in the opposite direction. They assert that as a result of the collapse of the economic, social and political systems of the Soviet Union, there is an increasing emphasis on survival values, and even on traditional values. The former trend is certainly confirmed in the management literature where former Soviet countries show a bigger emphasis on what Jackson (2002b) calls 'instrumental' values where there is a perceived need for a quick move towards Western prosperity by the wholesale and uncritical importing of Western management approaches to human resource management, for example.

China shows a big shift towards more traditional values between 1990 and 1995 that is not really explained by Inglehart and Baker (2000). Also not explained is the shift of South Africa, Turkey and Brazil towards more traditional values. This could in part reflect a search for traditional approaches, and melding these with Western approaches reflected in the management literature (Jackson, 2002a, 2004). It is also interesting to note that between 1981 and 1998 Britain moved more towards secular-rational and more towards survival. Perhaps this was a reflection of the Thatcher years: a time of tough economic reform, weakening trade union influence with a decline in manufacturing and increased unemployment, and growth of the service sector and increased returns in the finance sector.

SCHWARTZ'S VALUE DIMENSIONS: A VIEW FROM THE CUSTODIANS OF CULTURE

Shalom Schwartz (1999) argues that there are three basic issues that confront all societies. The first issue is the relation between the individual and the group; the second is the way it is possible to guarantee responsible behaviour to maintain the social fabric; the third is the relationship between human beings and the natural and social world within which they exist.

The way the first issue is addressed, he reminds us, is reflected in the large body of literature on individualism–collectivism. Much of this literature is contained within management and organizational studies. Schwartz (ibid.) also explains that this concept is reflected in a wider literature and described as individualism–communalism, independence–interdependence, autonomy–relatedness and separateness–interdependence (see Schwartz, ibid., for a bibliography). He suggests that inherent within this issue are two themes: the extent to which the individual's or the group's interests should take precedence; and the extent to which persons are autonomous versus their embeddedness in their group, important themes in ER. He believes that the latter is more fundamental, as the extent to which a person is embedded in their group determines the extent to which conflicts of interests are unlikely to be experienced. One pole of this dimension reflects cultural values that see a person as being embedded in the collectivity, finding meaning in life mainly through social relationships and identifying with the group through participation in a shared way of life. This set of values is encompassed in Schwartz's empirically derived value-type 'conservatism', or 'a cultural emphasis on maintenance of the status quo, propriety, and restraint of actions or inclinations that might disrupt the solidarity group or the traditional order (social order, respect for tradition, family security, wisdom)' (ibid., p. 27). The other pole reflects individual autonomy. He distinguishes between two types of autonomy. These are 'intellectual autonomy': 'A cultural emphasis on the desirability of individuals independently pursuing their ideas and intellectual directions (curiosity, broadmindedness, creativity)'; and 'affective autonomy': 'A cultural emphasis on the desirability of individuals independently pursuing affectively positive experiences (pleasure, exciting life, varied life)' (ibid.).

The second issue seeks to address the way it is possible to guarantee responsible behaviour to maintain the social fabric, and gives rise to two polar resolutions. From Schwartz's (ibid.) empirical work, one resolution involves using power differences, and the other involves voluntary responses to promoting the welfare of others. He terms the first 'hierarchy': 'A cultural emphasis on the legitimacy of an unequal distribution of power, roles and resources (social power, authority, humility, wealth)'. The second Schwartz (ibid., p. 28) terms 'egalitarianism': 'A cultural emphasis on transcendence of selfish interests in favour of voluntary commitment to promoting the welfare of others (equality, social justice, freedom, responsibility, honesty)'.

The third issue that addresses the relationship between humankind and the natural and social world is resolved again through two possible responses. The first seeks to master, change and exploit the outside world out of personal or group interests; the second seeks to fit into the natural world and to accept it as it is. From his empirical study Schwartz (ibid.) defines these two value types as 'mastery': 'A cultural emphasis on getting ahead through active self-assertion (ambition, success, daring, competence); and 'harmony': 'A cultural emphasis on fitting harmoniously into the environment (unity with nature, protecting the environment, world of beauty).[1]

So, for each of the three issues, there is a bipolar dimension that represents alternative resolutions of the issue that can be found in different cultural groups: (1) relation of individual and group (conservatism versus autonomy); (2) preservation of the social fabric (hierarchy versus egalitarianism); and (3) relation to nature (mastery versus harmony).

Schwartz's (1994) samples are from teachers and students. He argues that the former are good representatives of the cultures as they are custodians of cultures and it is they who pass this on to the next generation. The samples of university students generally corroborate results from school teachers. They reflect societal values (rather than those in corporate settings) because of the populations from which Schwartz took his samples.

There also appears to be some overlap with Inglehart and colleagues' theory concerning modernization/postmodernization trends and associated societal values, suggested in Table 5.1. Hence, we could postulate that conservatism and hierarchy may prevail in Inglehart's 'traditional' cultures (reflecting 'developing' countries) as well as in 'secular-rational'/'survival' cultures (such as in rapidly industrialized or 'emerging' countries, e.g., Eastern European countries); autonomy in 'secular-rational'/'self-expressive' cultures (such as Western European and Anglo-Saxon countries); egalitarianism in 'secular-rational'/'self-expression' cultures; mastery in 'secular-rational'/'survival' cultures (such as the Eastern European and rapidly industrialized countries); and, harmony in both 'traditional' and 'self-expression' cultures (Table 5.1).

SMITH'S REINTERPRETATION OF TROMPENAARS' WORK: A VIEW FROM WITHIN THE CORPORATION

The work of Fons Trompenaars (1993) has severe limitations in methodology and academic rigour. Yet it has been used extensively, particularly in connection with cross-cultural management development activities. Here the reanalysis of Trompenaars' extensive database led by Peter Smith (Smith et al., 1996) is discussed, as its concepts are partly related to those of Schwartz and, as we see below, to those of Hofstede.

Trompenaars' (1993) work was conceptually built on Parsons and Shils (1951) and Kluckholn and Strodtbeck's (1961) formulations of cultural differences, and other dimensions drawn from Hall (1959) and Rotter (1966). These are: regard for rules or relations (universalism–particularism), individualism–collectivism, neutral–affective expression of emotions, low and high context societies (specific–diffuse) and the way status is accorded (achievement–ascription). Trompenaars (1993) also considers attitudes to time (synchronic–sequential) and relation to nature (external–internal locus of control). His results are presented in terms of the percentage of positive (or negative) responses to each of several questions for each of some 50 different nationalities. His information was gathered through administering a questionnaire to attendees of management seminars in the various countries surveyed (Trompenaars, 1993).

Table 5.1   Conceptual associations of value dimensions with Inglehart's modernization and postmodernization trends

WVS Trends	Modernization		Postmodernization	
	Traditional	Secular-rational	Survival	Self-expression
Schwartz's issues/ values				
Individual & group: Conservatism–autonomy	Conservatism	Conservatism–autonomy	Conservatism	Autonomy
Social fabric: Hierarchy–egalitarianism	Hierarchy	Hierarchy–egalitarianism	Hierarchy	Egalitarianism
Relation to natural and social world: Mastery–harmony	Harmony	Mastery	Mastery	Harmony
Smith et al.'s broad values dimensions				
Conservatism–egalitarian commitment	Conservatism	Egalitarian commitment	Conservatism	
Utilitarian involvement–loyal involvement	Loyal involvement	Utilitarian involvement		Utilitarian involvement
Hofstede's cultural dimensions				
Power distance	High power distance	Medium to high power distance	High power distance	Low to medium power distance
Uncertainty avoidance	Low to medium uncertainty avoidance	Medium to high uncertainty avoidance	High uncertainty avoidance	Low uncertainty avoidance
Individualism–collectivism	Collectivism	Individualism	Collectivism	Individualism
Masculinity–femininity	Femininity	Masculinity	Masculinity	Femininity

Table 5.1   (continued)

WVS Trends	Modernization		Postmodernization	
	Traditional	Secular-rational	Survival	Self-expression
GLOBE dimensions				
Power distance	High power distance	Medium to high power distance	High power distance	Low to medium power distance
Uncertainty avoidance	?	?	High power distance	Low power distance
Humane orientation	?	?	?	?
Institutional collectivism	High institutional collectivism	Low institutional collectivism	Medium to high institutional collectivism	Low institutional collectivism
In-group collectivism	High in-group collectivism	Low in-group collectivism	Medium to high in-group collectivism	Low in-group collectivism
Assertiveness	Low assertiveness	High assertiveness	High assertiveness	Low assertiveness
Gender egalitarianism	High gender egalitarianism	Low gender egalitarianism	Low gender egalitarianism	High gender egalitarianism
Future orientation	?	?	?	?
Performance orientation	Possibly low performance orientation	Possibly high performance orientation	Possibly high performance orientation	Possibly low performance orientation

Source: From Jackson (2011).

Smith et al. (1996) then undertook a rigorous statistical reanalysis of Trompenaars' extensive international database. This provides two major value dimensions through multidimensional scaling, which are now discussed. It is still useful to refer back to Trompenaars' original 'dimensions' to describe these larger values dimensions that in part correlate with Schwartz's dimensions, and those of Hofstede. Smith et al.'s (1996) dimensions are as follows:

- *Conservatism*: comprises items that represent ascribed status, particularist/paternalistic employers and formalized hierarchies, and represents an external locus of control. It correlates with Hofstede's collectivism and power distance (see below) and falls just short of a significant correlation with Schwartz's conservatism.
- *Egalitarian commitment*: comprises achieved status, universalistic and non-paternalistic values, as well as functional hierarchy and internal locus of control. It correlates with Hofstede's individualism and low power distance. It also correlates with Schwartz's egalitarianism.
- *Utilitarian involvement*: comprises aspects of individualism that emphasize individual credit and responsibility. It correlates with Hofstede's individualism and low power distance.
- *Loyal involvement*: comprises aspects of collectivism that stress loyalty and obligation to the group, as well as corporate loyalty and obligation. It correlates with Hofstede's collectivism and high power distance.

Conservatism–Egalitarian Commitment

Of Trompenaars' (1993) dimensions referred to above, universalism–particularism, achievement-ascription and locus of control are the most relevant to our present discussion. In some cultures people see rules and regulations as applying universally to everyone, regardless of who they are. In cultures that are more particularist, people see relationships as more important than applying the same rules for everyone. There is an inclination to apply the rules according to friendship and kinship relations. This has implications for recruitment and promotion policies in organizations in some Asian countries, which may be at variance with practices in countries such as the United States and Britain where this might be termed 'nepotism'. Hence, it might make more sense to recruit a friend or family member, or someone from the same community where one knows the abilities of the person recruited and can have family pressure placed on them if they do not perform, rather than recruiting a complete stranger. However, there are differences in European countries. Greece, Spain and France are seen as more particularist, and Sweden, former West Germany and Britain as more universalist.

Also within the conservatism–egalitarian commitment construct is Trompenaars' concept of achievement–ascription. Status is accorded to people on the basis of what they achieve in their jobs and their lives (achievement) or who they are and where they come from such as family background, their school or some other prior factor (ascription). Quite often more traditional societies attribute status according to the latter precept. Again, this may influence recruitment and promotion policies, which may be at variance to practices in some (but not all) Western cultures, and again may raise ethical issues. On some measures Austria, Belgium, Spain and Italy are more ascription-oriented, and Denmark, Britain and Sweden more achievement-oriented.

Locus of control is another concept that is subsumed within the con-servatism–egalitarian commitment construct. People tend to believe that what happens to them in life is their own doing (internal locus of control), or they have no or little control over what happens to them (external locus of control), the causes of which are external to them. Although a connection has not been made directly to Schwartz's (1994) harmony–mastery construct (Smith et al., 1996), locus of control does raise issues about how people relate to their environment, and the level of control they believe they have over the natural world. This may have implications for the nature of interaction with the natural and social world, and raise issues about power (in the social sphere) and environment controls (in the natural sphere). It also may have implications regarding the nature of management control in organizations. For example, setting targets may be inappropriate as a form of management control in a society that culturally has an external locus of control (a hypothesis perhaps that suggests the need for further empirical research).

Paternalism is also an important concept in cross-cultural management research (Aycan, 2006) and is captured in part by Trompenaars' (1993) concept of specific–diffuse, which contains questionnaire items such as 'Should the company provide housing?' and involves the extent to which relationships at work, particularly with the boss, are carried through to other aspects of one's life. It is subsumed within the construct of conserva-tism, and may have ethical implications for the regard for interference/ protection in one's life by the corporation. Paternalism is, however, more thoroughly investigated elsewhere (see Aycan, 2006).

Utilitarian Involvement–Loyal Involvement

This dimension is most allied to Hofstede's individualism–collectivism and power distance (see below), but reflects the nature of loyalty of the individual to the group and corporation. While individuals may have a contractual relationship with the organization within the utilitarian involvement construct, members of a group or corporation have relations with the wider collective that involve obligation and reciprocity.

HOFSTEDE'S CULTURAL VALUES: A VIEW FROM WITHIN ONE CORPORATION

Geert Hofstede (1980a) was one of the first to attempt to develop a universal framework for understanding cultural differences in managers' and employees' values based on a worldwide survey within the company that employed them at the time: IBM. Hofstede's work focuses on 'value systems' of national cultures, which are represented by four dimensions:

- *Power distance*: the extent to which inequalities among people are seen as normal. This dimension stretches from equal relations being seen as normal to wide inequalities being viewed as normal. For example, the former West Germany scored (scores are nominally between 100 and 0) a relatively low 35, US a relatively low to medium 40, Britain 35 and France a relatively high 68. Brazil scored 69 and Mexico 81. China was not included in the study. Hong Kong scored 68 and Taiwan 58. Eastern European countries were also not included in the study. An all-white South African sample scored 49. Schwartz's (1994) concept of hierarchy equates with power distance.
- *Uncertainty avoidance*: refers to a preference for structured situations versus unstructured situations. This dimension runs from being comfortable with flexibility and ambiguity to a need for extreme rigidity and situations with a high degree of certainty. For example, the former West Germany scored a medium 65, France a high 86 on a level with Spain. US scored a relatively low 46, with Britain at 35. Brazil scored 76 and Mexico 82. It is difficult to infer a score for PR China, which was not included in Hofstede's (1980a) original study as Hong Kong scored 29 and Taiwan 69 – a reflection perhaps of the hybrid nature of these societies. The all-white South African sample scored 49.
- *Individualism–collectivism*: looks at whether individuals are used to acting as individuals or as part of cohesive groups, which may be based on the family (which is more the case with Chinese societies) or the corporation (as may be the case in Japan). This dimension ranges from collectivism (0) to individualism (100). US is the highest (91). France scores 71 and Britain 89. The former West Germany scored 67. Brazil scored 38 and Mexico 30 (Guatemala was the most collectivist at 6). Hong Kong scored 25, and Taiwan 17. The all-white South African sample scored 65. Schwartz's (1994) concept of conservatism–autonomy has similarities with this dimension.
- *Masculinity–femininity*: Hofstede distinguishes 'hard values' such

as assertiveness and competition, and the 'soft' or 'feminine' values of personal relations, quality of life and caring about others, where in a masculine society gender role differentiation is emphasized. The US scored a medium to high (masculinity) 62, with the former West Germany at 66. Britain scored 66 and France 43. Brazil scored 49 and Mexico 69. Taiwan scored 45 and Hong Kong 56. The all-white South African sample scored 63. Aspects of Schwartz's (1994) concept of mastery–harmony have similarities to this dimension.

Hofstede (1980a/2003, 1991) conceptually extrapolates from these dimensions derived from factor analysis of items on his questionnaire, to infer wider descriptions of the nature and implications of cultural values both within and outside the corporate setting, as follows.

Power distance is polarized into small and large power distance and comprises attitudes that people within the culture have about the acceptable inequalities between people in the society or organization. In small power distance cultures there is a belief that inequalities among people should be minimized, that parents should treat children as equals and that teachers expect student initiative in the classroom. Hierarchies in work organizations are established as a convenience only to manage inequality of roles. Decentralization is popular, subordinates expect to be consulted and privileges are frowned upon in a small power distance society. Conversely, in a large power distance culture, inequalities are expected and desired, parents teach children obedience and teachers are expected to take the initiative in the classroom. Hierarchies in organizations reflect the natural order of inequalities between the higher-ups and the lower-downs, centralization is popular and subordinates expect that they are told what to do. Privilege and status symbols are expected.

Weak uncertainty avoidance cultures accept uncertainty as a feature of everyday life, there is generally low stress and people feel comfortable in ambiguous situations. People are curious with what is different. Students are happy with open-ended learning situations, and teachers can say 'I don't know'. Rules should only be for what is necessary. People may be lazy, and work hard only when needed. Punctuality has to be learned, and people are motivated by achievement and esteem or belonging to a group.

Strong uncertainty avoidance is characterized by the threat of uncertainty that is always present but must be fought. It is characterized by high stress and a fear of ambiguous situations and unfamiliar risk. There is a feeling that what is different must be dangerous. Students are more comfortable in a structured learning situation and like to be told the right answer: teachers are supposed to know the answers. There is an emotional need for rules, even when these may not work. There is a need to be busy, and a feeling that time is money: an inner urge to work hard. Punctuality is natural, and people are motivated by security, esteem or belongingness.

In societies where individualism describes cultural values people look after themselves and the immediate nuclear family. A person's identity is based on him or her as an individual. Speaking one's mind is respected. Education is aimed at learning to learn, and academic and professional diplomas increase self-respect and potential economic worth. The employer–employee contract is assumed to be based on mutual advantage, and hiring decisions are supposed to be based on individual competence. Managers manage individuals, and tasks are more important than relationships.

In collectivistic societies people are born into and protected by extended families, to which they exchange loyalty. One's identity is based in the belongingness to a social group or network. Children are taught to think of 'we' not 'I'. Rather than speaking one's mind, harmony should be maintained and direct confrontation avoided. The purpose of education is to learn how to do, and diplomas provide an entry into higher-status groups. Rather than purely a contract, the employer–employee relationship is seen as a moral one such as a family relationship, and when hiring or firing, the employee's in-group (or, for example, familial relationship with the employer) is considered. Managers manage groups, and relationships are more important than tasks.

In a society that Hofstede (1980a) would designate as having masculinity values emphasis would be placed on material success, money and possessions. Men are expected to be assertive and ambitious, and women tender and concerned with relationships. The father deals with facts and the mother with feelings. There is sympathy for the strong and the best student is the norm: failing in school is seen as a disaster. People live in order to work. Managers are expected to be decisive and assertive, and there is a stress on competition, performance and resolution of conflict by fighting them out. Certainly with an emphasis on such 'masculine' values, there tends to be a contrast between gender roles, and this may have an impact on the way equity and gender discrimination is dealt with in the workplace (Rothwell, 1985).

In contrast, in a society that Hofstede (1980a) would designate as having femininity values there would be an emphasis on caring for others and preservation rather than progress. People and good relationships are more important than money and things, and people are expected to be modest. Both men and women are expected to be concerned with relationships, and both mother and father should deal with feelings and facts. There is sympathy for the weak, and the average student is the norm. Failing in school is a minor accident. People work in order to live. Managers use intuition and try to gain consensus. There is a stress on equality, solidarity and quality of work life. Conflicts are resolved by compromise and negotiation.

A fifth dimension was added by Hofstede to the original four. This was developed through the Chinese Cultural Connection study (CCC, 1987) and in part justified by Hofstede's warning of the dangers of developing constructs from a Western point of view. The Chinese Cultural Connection was an attempt to counter this by introducing an Eastern perspective and values. The study reinforced three out of the four dimensions in Hofstede's original study: the Chinese dimension of 'human-heartedness', which incorporates values such as kindness, courtesy and social consciousness, correlates negatively with masculinity; 'integration', which encompasses the cultivation of trust, tolerance and friendship, correlates negatively with power distance; 'moral discipline', including values of group responsiveness, moderation, adaptability and prudent behaviour, correlates negatively with individualism.

None of the new dimensions correlated with uncertainty avoidance, but rather a new dimension termed 'Confucian dynamism' and then 'long-term orientation', with values of persistence and perseverance, ordering relationships by status and observing order, thrift and having a sense of shame. Uncertainty avoidance is concerned with absolute truth, which may not be a relevant value in Chinese society and other Eastern cultures, which are more concerned with virtue. Of particular relevance is the virtue of working hard and acquiring skills, thrift, being patient and persevering: these are all values connected with this fifth dimension that may replace uncertainty avoidance as a relevant Eastern concept. On a scale from a minimum score of 0 to a maximum 118, Pakistan scores 0 and China 118. The Chinese societies of Hong Kong (96) and Taiwan (87) are towards the top of the scale with Japan (80) and South Korea (75) next. Brazil scores 65, Singapore 48 and Netherlands 44. Sweden (33), Poland (32) and the former West Germany (31) follow. The US scores a relatively low 29, with Britain at 25. Of African countries, Zimbabwe (25) scores the same as Britain (perhaps a reflection of the historic British presence in Zimbabwe and the current work institutions and management training based on Anglo-American models), and Nigeria is second from bottom with 16. This seems to bear out an assumption that the Eastern 'tiger' countries, which have done well economically are high on this dimension, with the Anglo-Saxon countries relatively low, and African countries with a short-term economic perspective scoring very low.

GLOBE CULTURE CONSTRUCTS: TRYING TO IMPROVE ON HOFSTEDE

The GLOBE project (Global Leadership and Organizational Behavior Effectiveness Research Program) is a more recent cross-national study undertaken by Robert House and a team of 170 researchers across 62 societies (House et al., 2004). Its main focus is the relationship between culture and leadership characteristics. In some ways the study is disappointing because it did little to break out of the conceptual framework of cultural dimensions set by Hofstede in the early 1980s, and it mirrors many of Hofstede's cultural dimensions. Yet this, for our current purpose, is useful as it provides a more up to date view of these cultural dimensions, and like the other studies examined above, provides a basis for considering the appropriateness of transferring management theory and practice. It also purports to investigate both 'values' (e.g., 'followers *should be* expected to obey their leaders without question') and 'practices' (e.g., 'followers *are* expected to obey their leaders without question'). The cultural value dimensions proffered by the GLOBE project are as follows (House et al., 2004, p. 30):

- *Power distance*: 'The degree to which members of a collective expect power to be distribute equally'. This ('practices' only, not 'values') correlates positively with Hofstede's power distance and Schwartz's hierarchy.
- *Uncertainty avoidance*: 'The extent to which a society, organization or group relies on social norms, rules, and procedures to alleviate unpredictability of future events'. Curiously 'values' correlates positively and 'practices' negatively with Hofstede's uncertainty avoidance. It correlates positively with Schwartz's 'embeddedness' (this is Schwartz's 1994 dimension at the individual level, and equates with conservatism at the group level).
- *Humane orientation*: 'The degree to which a collective encourages and rewards individuals for being fair, altruistic, generous, caring and kind to others'. This does not appear to correlate with Hofstede's or Schwartz's dimensions.
- *Collectivism I* (institutional collectivism): 'The degree to which organizational and societal institutional practices encourage and reward collective distribution of resources and collective action'. 'Values' correlates negatively with Hofstede's individualism, but not with any of Schwartz's dimensions.
- *Collectivism II* (in-group collectivism): 'The degree to which individuals express pride, loyalty, and cohesiveness in their organizations

or families'. 'Practices' correlates negatively with Hofstede's individualism, but not with any of Schwartz's dimensions.

- *Assertiveness*: 'The degree to which individuals are assertive, confrontational, and aggressive in their relationships with others'. 'Practices' correlates positively with Hofstede's masculinity and negatively with Schwartz's egalitarianism.
- *Gender egalitarianism*: 'The degree to which a collective minimizes gender inequalities'. This does not correlate with any of Hofstede's dimensions, but correlates positively with Schwartz's egalitarianism.
- *Future orientation*: 'The extent to which individuals engage in future-oriented behaviors such as delaying gratification, planning, and investing in the future'. This does not appear to correlate with any of Hofstede's or Schwartz's dimensions.
- *Performance orientation*: 'The degree to which a collective encourages and rewards group members for performance improvement and excellence'. Again this appears not to correlate with Hofstede's or Schwartz's dimensions.

The GLOBE project findings reflect many of the cultural dimensions proffered in earlier studies, and as such do not add conceptually to our descriptive understanding of values across cultures. They do, however, provide current information that is perhaps more rigorously validated, and covers more countries than previous studies. For example, it covers some six African countries and six post-communist countries. Yet despite these more comprehensive studies such as WVS and GLOBE, Hofstede's theory, maybe in its apparent simplicity, remains in the forefront (perhaps rekindled by his updating of his work in 2003) of the comparative cultural values studies in the positivist paradigm.

TRANSFERABILITY AND APPROPRIATENESS: CROSS-CULTURAL STUDIES AS CRITIQUE

One of Hofstede's (1980b) main contributions to management scholarship has been to introduce a cross-cultural critique of the transferability of Western (US) management principles to non-Western (non-US) countries. From this, not only should we ask if management is effective, but also we should be asking if it is appropriate within a particular cultural context. Yet for whom it should be appropriate implies relationships of power. This is a question Hofstede (ibid.) did not take up. For example, what is appropriate for foreign shareholders of a multinational corporation operating in an African country might not be appropriate for local employees or the local community within which the subsidiary is located ('effectiveness' for a Western firm operating in Africa implies that it is operating appropriately for its shareholders in making profits). Not only should power relations within international organizations be considered, however, but geopolitical issues also. This was not really taken up in the management literature until over ten years later in another landmark publication.

The Parochial Dinosaur – a Hint at Power Dynamics

This landmark article, Boyacigiller and Adler (1991), outlines the ascendancy of US management thought, principles and practices around the world due to the economic dominance of the United States after World War II. In the end these two authors ascribe this to parochialism on the part of US managers, rather than anything more sinister. They hint at power relations, yet this is not developed, and has not been taken up generally in the ensuing cross-cultural literature. Concepts of leadership and participatory management, for which Hofstede (1980b) provided the basis for a critique of transferability, have been propagated through MBA programmes and management textbooks throughout the world. This has only attracted a degree of derision among scholars working in developing country contexts. For example, a leading book on management in Africa of the 1990s states:

> Current theories of leadership . . . in the West place high value . . . on teamwork, empowerment. . . . The problem is that the amount of hype surrounding such putative features implies it is a hard sell, even in its place of origin. . . . Transformational leadership in the West . . . is more a construct of the rhetoric of management consultants than it is the reality of management practice. It seems likely that – as with Coca-Cola – the less the worth of the product to the consumer the more one needs to envelop it in a promotional mystique . . . and this helps to disguise its discordance with most of the cultures in which its tenets are applied. (Blunt and Jones, 1997, p. 1)

More recent international events have brought the same type of geopolitical forces in operation here into even sharper relief, where Western concepts of 'democracy' have been enforced through military intervention (for example, Chomsky's 2003 critique is illuminating on this subject). Normally within the confines of academia, international power relations are carried out in a far more subtle way, yet reflecting what many commentators have regarded as neo-colonialism in the practices of multinational corporations including those in the not-for-profit sector. For example, Cooke and Kothari (2002) provide a useful critique of the imposition of participatory management mainly in the NGO sector. Within the same edited volume, the following harsh critique is delivered:

> participatory discourse and practices are part of a wider attempt to obscure the relations of power and influence between elite interests and less powerful groups . . .
>
> I would argue, however, that participatory discourses are utilized in both the development and managerial contexts because they serve essentially the same purpose of giving the 'sense' and warm emotional pull of participation without its substance, and are thus an attempt to placate those without power and obscure the real levers of power inherent in the social relations of global capitalism. (Taylor, 2002, pp. 122 and 125)

Postcolonial theory has provided an elaboration and critique of these more subtle power dynamics within literary studies (Said's 1978 *Orientalism* is the landmark study), in development studies (e.g., Mohan, 2002, provides an outline) and more recently in organization studies (Prasad, 2003). Mohan (2002, p. 157) for example, puts it rather sharply when saying 'Postcolonial studies alerts us to the epistemic violence of Eurocentric discourses of the non-West and the possibilities of recovering the voices of the marginalized'. Yet he warns that 'much of this abstracts cultural processes away from material conditions and is unable to stand outside (or suggest alternatives to) the dominant epistemological frameworks against which they argue'.

It seems that this debate has largely passed by the field of cross-cultural management. Since initiating a critique of Western management hegemony in 1991, Boyacigiller and Adler's article has been much quoted, but little has been done to expand on this and to take it on board. International world events, in contributing to cross-cultural dynamics and contextualizing the study of cross-cultural management, seem also to pass us by.

Before moving on to how cross-cultural theory may be developed, there are three other important aspects in considering the limitations of Hofstede's theory, and where we go from here: crossvergence and cultural interfaces, and cultural identities.

Crossvergence and Cultural Interfaces

Hofstede's theory appears to remain firmly within the 'divergence' camp. That is, there is an assumption that country cultures remain distinct from each other. Hence, there are fundamental differences assumed between French and Italian managers, or US and Japanese managers. However, the difficulties in identifying the 'culture' of a location such as Hong Kong, at a confluence of Western and Chinese influence, suggest that things might be more complicated than supposed.

Hong Kong represents a complex interface of Western and Chinese culture, business practices and management processes. It is perhaps no accident that theories of cultural crossvergence have been developed by management academics focusing on Hong Kong (Ralston et al., 1994; Priem et al., 2000). This concept brings together opposing views of globalization, namely convergence and divergence theories.

Convergence is based on an assumption that all societies are following the same trajectory. As societies industrialize they embrace capitalism and technology and evolve towards the (Western) industrialized societies (from Kerr et al., 1960). Contained within this must also be noted the influence of television, Hollywood, the global reach of multinational companies, global brands such as Coca-Cola and McDonald's, conditional financial aid, structural adjustment programmes, US/Western management education programmes, migration, cosmopolitanization, and so on. These all influence a tendency towards cultural convergence.

Divergence argues that national cultures continue to be a primary influence on values, beliefs and attitudes despite globalizing forces and industrialization, and that culture is a long-lived rather than a transient phenomenon. Successive studies that focus on comparing national cultures have sought to demonstrate this as we have seen.

Yet both concepts, of convergence or divergence, do not appear to consider the process of what goes on during cross-cultural interactions. Rather than trying to identify the nature of a cultural entity, such as a country, it would seem more legitimate to discover the nature of inter-cultural interactions at different levels of analysis, and (to borrow from a phrase from Hofstede, 1980a/2003) their consequences.

A third perspective (Beals, 1953; Ralston et al., 1994; Priem et al., 2000), that of cultural crossvergence, suggests that culture and industrialization will interact to produce a new value system, such as in the case of Hong Kong. It is possible to go further than this in asserting, for example in relation to the way people are managed in organizations, that although there may be hegemonic influences from stronger and more successful economies such as the United States that propel transitional and emerging countries to adopt inappropriate solutions, crossvergence or the interaction of different cultural influences in cultures such as South Korea and Hong Kong has given rise to successful hybrid management systems (Jackson, 2002a).

Crossvergence theory, when stressing the importance of interaction at different levels, may well be the key to understanding not culture as a product or characteristic of a discrete cultural entity such as a nation, but as an interface between or interfaces among different cultural influences; between attitudes, beliefs and values (and institutions as cultural manifestations as argued below) and within relationships containing power dynamics.

'Interaction' as a term is normally applied at the social psychological level of interpersonal relations (Adler and Graham, 1989; Fink et al., 2006). Hence the term 'interfaces' implies a broader conceptual framework whereby geopolitical dynamics at the macro-level are considered, through to the meso-levels of inter-organizational interactions, and micro-level of interpersonal interactions; and, whereby these different levels further interact to produce diverse hybrid social forms of organization, and multiple forms of individual cultural identity. Before considering this in more detail, it is necessary to discuss the relationship (in international management and organization studies) between what is considered 'cultural' and what is considered 'institutional'. This is a particularly important issue when it comes to looking at cultural interfaces within regions of the world (at least 80 per cent of the globe) that have a postcolonial legacy.

INTERFACES AND THE CULTURAL–INSTITUTIONAL DEBATE

Within a continuing debate between 'culturists' and 'institutionalists', differences across nations are either attributed to institutional arrangements, which are seen as fundamental (e.g., Hickson and McMillan, 1981); or, differences are attributed to cultural factors or, in Hofstedian parlance, to differences in the 'software of the mind' (Hofstede, 1991). Sorge (2004) believes that the two approaches should be complementary. He cites Giddens (1986) in saying that individual behaviour and social structure are reciprocally constituted, that is, normative customs that are instituted to be binding are kept in place by acting individuals. Yet on the other hand, individuals do not make behavioural choices without regard to such norms. Sorge (2004) believes that such an integrative approach will consider both the construction of actors, that is, people with values, preferences and knowledge, and the construction of social and societal systems as reciprocally related to an extent that they cannot be separated from each other.

From this point of view the concept of culture should take in the oft quoted classic definitions of Tylor (1871) 'that complex whole which involves knowledge, beliefs, art, morals, law, customs and other capabilities and habits acquired by man as a member of society' and Herskovits (1948) the 'human-made part of the environment'. In other words, institutions as part of 'culture' are created by sentient human beings in interaction interpersonally, inter-organizationally, and internationally. Their rules reflect societal values, and the societal values reflect institutional rules.

Jack Goody (1994), a prominent British social anthropologist, points to the dichotomy in the US tradition of *cultural* anthropology between 'cultural studies' concerned with symbols and meaning, and the social (social structures, organizations etc.). He maintains that in the European tradition of *social* anthropology this dichotomy is not readily accepted, and has tended to treat these two categories as virtually synonymous. Certainly this is reflected in Tylor's classic definition (above), and, for example, Firth's (1951) view where culture is seen as the content of social relations, not as some distinct entity. Hence the institutional context both shapes meaning, and is shaped by it. Both are what can be described as culture. Institutions are cultural constructs with rules that are applied in society, and they also shape and are shaped by values, which are part of the meaning systems of society. This is different, for example, from the conceptualization of the US cultural anthropologist Geertz (1973, p. 89), who sees culture as 'an historically transmitted pattern of meaning embodied in symbols of inherited conceptions expressed in symbolic forms by means which men communicate', and distinguishes between cultural symbols as 'vehicles of thought' and social structure as 'forms of human association' with a 'reciprocal interplay' occurring between them.

Goody (1994, p. 252) therefore maintains that 'attempts to differentiate the cultural from the social, or the symbolic from other forms of human interaction, seem open to question. The terms may serve as general signposts to areas of interest within a wider field of social action'. In terms of this debate Hofstede seems to be firmly in the US camp, distinguishing 'the software of the mind' as meaning/value systems and juxtaposing himself to the institutionalists.

However, just when this debate, at least in the European tradition, appears to be redundant, things start to get complicated in 'developing' countries that have a history of colonization. Dia (1996) takes the view that institutions (including the 'firm' and public sector and civil service structures) were imposed on African societies during the colonial period. They have largely remained and evolved through the post-colonial period, and mostly are seen as still inappropriate to African societies and their context. Here, rules seem to be at odds with values; institutions appear to be at odds with symbolic culture. The split between (local) culture and 'global' or 'Western' institutions in Africa and other post-colonial countries can only be explained by geopolitical power relations.

The introduction of colonial institutions into Africa, no doubt, involved a number of elements: first, the (cultural) background of the colonizing countries; second, the interaction of colonizers with colonized societies and institutions (for example, African institutions such as chiefdoms were integrated into colonial administrations to enlist the help of local chiefs to keep law and order and to collect taxes: Gluckman, 1956); and third, the wielding of (economic, military and then ideological) power by the colonizers within the interactions with local communities. There is no doubt also that these institutions have an influence on African communities today, and that they have helped to shape modern and urban African cultures. Through interactions these institutions have also been shaped by African cultural influences that include African institutions (Ayitter, 1991).

The interaction effects among 'rules' (institutions), 'values' (culture), and 'control' (power), may therefore be the way forward in understanding culture as a dynamic, rather than a static entity. In other words, culture is created/recreated at the point of intersection – the interface. Central to this is 'power', in Foucault's (1979, p. 194) terms, for example: 'power produces, it makes reality; it produces domains of objects and rituals of truth'. He contends that power relations do not stand apart from other relations, but power is inherent in all relations and is the effect of divisions, inequalities and imbalances found in these relations, and at the same time are preconditions for these differentiations. Dominance in a power relationship has a legitimizing effect. Yet, for Foucault power also infers the possibility of resistance, and that resistance is always part of a power relationship. Hence, values (culture) come into conflict with rules (institutions).

So, in post-colonial societies 'culture' (as a concrete noun) starts to get fuzzy. When a Hofstede (1980a), or a Trompenaars (1993), or a Schwartz (1999), or a House (House et al., 2004) comes along with their questionnaire to ask questions about the values of a representative of the 'culture' of (for example) South Africa, they are in trouble. Their individual 'subject' represents not a 'culture', but the confluence of a complex and multi-layered interface that can only be accessed through the agency of individuals' cultural identity, but can only really be understood through an analysis of the cultural interfaces involved.

CONCLUSION

The positivist view of social science allows no place for value judgements. Hence the position of Hofstede, and those who have developed 'maximalist' (Human, 1996) approaches to comparing nations, would not contemplate the question 'We know that organizations in country X operate in a national culture that is higher in power distance than our own, where the boss's word is law, and cannot be questioned: what do we do about it?' However, the answer may be provided in the implicit derogation of high power distance. If a scholar, or manager, came from a country that favoured a lower power distance, it would be natural to look down on countries that favoured high power distance and felt okay about inequalities in the work place. Yet approaches such as Hofstede's express 'a view from nowhere', which Flyvbjerg (2001) reminds us is impossible in the social sciences. For scholars who focus on cross-cultural differences, and an understanding of different cultures, this is somewhat surprising. All scholarship in social science takes a 'view from somewhere', yet this is inadequately articulated in cross-cultural management studies of this sort.

As Nonaka and Toyama (2007, who also refer to Flyvbjerg) point out, the relativist view that everything is subjective with no universality is of little practical use. Indeed, they site the interactions of different subjectivities within the realm of knowledge creation: 'What is "truth" depends on who we are (values) and from where we look at it (context). And it is the differences in our values and contexts that create new knowledge' (ibid., p. 374).

The objective of studying cultural interfaces is not merely to learn about the influences (antecedents) of hybrid cultural forms. It is also about studying what knowledge is created from this and how; and, what use is this, and to whom (the appropriateness of the knowledge created to the context in which it is applied: for example, people management principles and practices that are created through interaction between powerful Western organizations and weak African/Eastern European/Latin American, and so on, organizations or individual managers, and their appropriateness to local staffs).

Bound up with this is the analysis of power within each interface: who/ what wields power in what form and how? What are the results of power in this relationship? In an abstract way each of these 'world views' within any point of analysis (interfaces) may be equal in value to any other. But as Foucault (1979) suggests, power legitimizes. This legitimization takes two forms: the legitimization of the view of the most powerful in the relationship, and the legitimization of the scholar (not forgetting that in most cases this will be undertaken from a Western perspective, with indigenous interpretations/explanations struggling for legitimization) with the relationship between researcher and researched constituting another interface, and the relationship between foreign manager and local staff another.

An important issue in cross-cultural management research is not so much that nations or cultural groups are different, and have different world views, but what we do with this information when looking at the consequences in the interface between two of those 'entities'. If Hofstede's theory suggests that it may be inappropriate to transpose participatory management from a low power culture to a high one, what do we do about it?

Clearly, cross-cultural theory, and the way it may inform employment relations, has some way to go beyond mere references to Hofstede, and indeed critiques of Hofstede. In order to explore national comparisons international employment relations should not only take cognizance of some of the more sophisticated, yet more complex value dimension studies, but also consider the conceptual difficulties in separating institutions from culture, and indeed institutional studies from cross-cultural studies. As cultural identity (of individuals and organizations) becomes a more complex issue in a globalized world, theory of cultural crossvergence and the study of cultural interfaces should come to the fore. Yet geopolitical power relations (particularly in a post-colonial world) should take centre stage, particularly in challenging a 'view from nowhere' that currently dominates cross-cultural studies.

NOTE

1. Single values in brackets that relate to each pole of each value dimension are examples from his values questionnaire that Schwartz (1999) provides in the original.

REFERENCES

Adler, N.J. and Graham, J.L. (1989), 'Cross-cultural interaction: The international comparison fallacy?', *Journal of International Business Studies*, **20**(3), 515–37.
Aycan, Z. (2006), 'Paternalism: Towards conceptual refinement and operationalization', in K.S. Yang, K.K. Hwang and U. Kim (eds), *Scientific Advances in Indigenous Psychologies: Empirical, Philosophical and Cultural Contributions*, Cambridge: Cambridge University Press, pp. 445–66.
Ayitter, G.B.N. (1991), *Indigenous African Institutions*, New York: Transnational Publishers.
Beals, R. (1953), 'Acculturation', in A.L. Kroebner (ed.), *Anthropology Today*, Chicago: University of Chicago Press.
Blunt, P. and Jones, M.L. (1997), 'Exploring the limits of Western leadership theory in East Asia and Africa', *Personnel Review*, **26**(1/2), 6–23.
Boyacigiller, N.A. and Adler, N.J. (1991), 'The parochial dinosaur: Organizational science in a global context', *Academy of Management Review*, **16**(2), 262–90.
CCC (Chinese Cultural Connection) (1987), 'Chinese values and the search for culture-free dimensions of culture', *Journal of Cross-Cultural Psychology*, **18**(2), 143–64.
Chomsky, N. (2003), *Hegemony or Survival: America's Quest for Global Dominance*, London: Penguin.
Cooke, B. and Kothari, U. (2002), *Participation: The New Tyranny?*, London: Zed Books.
Dia, M. (1996), *Africa's Management in the 1990s and Beyond*, Washington, DC: World Bank.

ESDS (2011), ESDS International: World Values Survey, available at: http://www.esds. ac.uk/international/access/wvs.asp; accessed 3 February 2011.

Fink, G., Neyer, A.K. and Kolling, M. (2006), 'Understanding cross-cultural management interaction: Research into cultural standards to complement cultural value dimensions and personality traits', *International Studies of Management. & Organization*, **36**(4), 38–60.

Firth, R. (1951), *Elements of Social Organization*, London: Watts.

Flyvbjerg, B. (2001), *Making Social Science Matter*, Cambridge: Cambridge University Press.

Foucault, M. (1979), *Discipline and Punish*, New York; Vintage Books, p. 194.

Garcia, M.F., Posthuma, R.A. and Roehling, M.V. (2009), 'Comparing preferences for employing males and nationals across countries: Extending relational models and social dominance theory', *International Journal of Human Resource Management*, **20**(12), 2471–93.

Gatley, S., Lessem, R. and Altman, Y. (1996), *Comparative Management: A Transcultural Odyssey*, London: McGraw-Hill.

Geertz, C. (1973), *The Interpretation of Cultures*, New York: Basic Books.

Gerhart, B. (2008), 'Cross-cultural management research: Assumptions, evidence, and suggested directions', *International Journal of Cross Cultural Management*, **8**(3), 259–74.

Giddens, A. (1986), *The Constitution of Society*, Berkeley, CA and Los Angeles: University of California Press.

Gluckman, M. (1956), *Custom and Conflict in Africa*, Oxford: Basil Blackwell.

Goody, J. (1994), 'Culture and its boundaries: A European perspective', in R. Borofsky (ed.), *Assessing Cultural Anthropology*, New York: McGraw-Hill, pp. 250–61.

Hall, E.T. (1959), *The Silent Language*, New York: Anchor Press/Doubleday.

Herskovits, M.J. (1948), *Man and His Works: The Science of Cultural Anthropology*, New York: Knopf.

Hickson, D.J. and McMillan, C.J. (eds) (1981), *Organization and Nation: The Aston Programme*, Aldershot: Gower.

Hofstede, G. (1980a/2003), *Cultures Consequences*, 1st edition (2nd edition 2003), Thousand Oaks: Sage.

Hofstede, G. (1980b), 'Motivation, leadership and organization: Do American theories apply abroad?', *Organizational Dynamics*, **9**(1), 42–63.

Hofstede, G. (1991), *Cultures and Organizations: Software of the Mind*, London: McGraw-Hill.

Hofstede, G. (2007), 'Hofstede after Hofstede: What should be done with my dimensions', presentation at IACCM Conference 'Crosscultural Life of Social Values', 18 May 2007, Rotterdam.

House, R., Hanges, P.J., Javidan, M. and Dorfman, P.W. (2004), *Leadership, Culture and Organizations: The GLOBE Study of 62 Societies*, Thousand Oaks, CA: Sage.

Human, L. (1996), *Contemporary Conversations*, Dakar, Senegal: The Goree Institute.

Inglehart, R. (1997), *Modernization and Postmodernization: Cultural, Economic, and Political Change in 43 Societies*, Princeton, NJ: Princeton University Press.

Inglehart, R. and Baker, W.E. (2000), 'Modernization, cultural change, and persistence of traditional values', *American Sociological Review*, **65**(1), 19–51.

Inglehart, R. and Baker, W.E. (2001), Modernization's challenge to traditional values: Who's afraid of Ronald McDonald?', *The Futurist*, March–April 2001, 16–21.

Inglehart, R., Basanez, M. and Moreno, A. (1998), *Human Values and Beliefs: A Cross-cultural Sourcebook*, Ann Arbor, MI: The University of Michigan Press.

Jackson, T. (2002a), *International HRM: A Cross-cultural Approach*, London: Sage.

Jackson, T. (2002b), 'The management of people across cultures: Valuing people differently', *Human Resource Management*, **41**(4), 455–75.

Jackson, T. (2004), *Management and Change in Africa: A Cross-cultural Perspective*, London: Routledge.

Jackson, T. (2011), *International Management Ethics: A Critical, Cross-cultural Perspective*, Cambridge: Cambridge University Press.

Kerr, C., Dunlop, J.T., Harbison, F.H. and Myers, C.A. (1960), *Industrialism and Industrial Man*, Cambridge, MA: Harvard University Press.

Kluckholn, F. and Strodtbeck, F. (1961), *Variations in Value Orientations*, Westport, CT: Greenwood Press.

Mohan, G. (2002), 'Beyond participation: Strategies for deeper empowerment', in B. Cooke and U. Kothari (eds), *Participation: The New Tyranny?*, London: Zed Books, pp. 153–67.

Nonaka, I. and Toyama, R. (2007), 'Strategic management as distributed practical wisdom (phronesis)', *Industrial and Corporate Change*, **16**(3), 371–94.

Parsons, T. and Shils, E. (1951), *Towards a General Theory of Action*, Cambridge, MA: Harvard University Press.

Posthuma, R.A. (2009), 'National culture and union membership: A cultural-cognitive perspective', *Relations Industrielles/Industrial Relations*, **6** (3), 507–29.

Prasad, A. (ed.) (2003), *Postcolonial Theory and Organizational Analysis: A Critical Reader*, London: Palgrave Macmillan.

Priem, R.L., Love, L.G. and Shaffer, M. (2000), 'Industrialization and values evolution: The case of Hong Kong and Guangzhou, China', *Asia Pacific Journal of Management*, **17**(3), 473–92.

Ralston, D.A., Gaicalone, R.A. and Terpstra, R.H. (1994), 'Ethical perceptions of organizational politics: A comparative evaluation of American and Hong Kong managers', *Journal of Business Ethics*, **13**(12), 989–99.

Rothwell, S. (1985), 'Is management a masculine role?', *Management Learning*, **16**, 79–98.

Rotter, J.B. (1966), 'General expectancies for internal versus external control of reinforcement', *Psychological Monographs*, **80**(1), 1–28.

Said, Edward (1978), *Orientalism*, London: Penguin.

Schwartz, S. (1994), 'Beyond individualism/collectivism: New cultural dimensions of values', in U. Kim, H.C. Triandis, C. Kâğitçibaşi, S.-C. Choi and G. Yoon, *Individualism and Collectivism: Theory, Method and Application*, Beverly Hills, CA: Sage, pp. 85–119.

Schwartz, S.H. (1999), 'A theory of cultural values and some implications for work', *Applied Psychology: An International Review*, **48**(1), 23–47.

Shackleton, V.J. and Ali, A.H. (1990), 'Work-related values of managers: A test of the Hofstede model', *Journal of Cross-Cultural Psychology*, **21**(1), 109–18.

Smith, P.B., Dugan, S. and Trompenaars, F. (1996), 'National culture and the values of organizational employees: A dimensional analysis across 43 nations', *Journal of Cross-Cultural Psychology*, **27**(2), 231–64.

Sorge, A. (2004), 'Cross-national differences in human resources and organization', in A.-W. Harzing and J. van Ruysseveldt (eds), *International Human Resource Management*, London: Sage, pp. 117–40.

Taylor, H. (2002), 'Insights into participation from critical management and labour process perspectives', in B. Cooke and U. Kothari (eds), *Participation: The New Tyranny?*, London: Zed Books, pp. 122–38.

Trompenaars, F. (1993), *Riding the Waves of Culture: Understanding Cultural Diversity in Business*, London: Nicholas Brealey.

Tylor, E.B. (1871), 'Primitive culture', cited in C. Levi-Strauss (1963) (trans. C. Jacobson and B.G. Schoel), *Structural Anthropology*, Harmondsworth: Penguin.

PART 3

PAIRED COUNTRY COMPARISONS

6 Employment relations in Chile and Argentina

Maurizio Atzeni, Fernando Durán-Palma and Pablo Ghigliani

INTRODUCTION

The study of employment relations in Chile and Argentina has been the outcome of research in various disciplines, particularly sociology, political science, law and history. This broadly defined scholarship has followed similar lines of analysis in both countries, reflecting their parallel socio-economic transformations and corresponding changes in employment relations actors and institutions – from the rise of import-substituting industrialization and developmentalist populist regimes in the 1930s, which provided the base upon which 'classic' employment relations systems began to take shape, to the crises and replacement of such regimes by military dictatorships and the introduction of neoliberalism in the 1970s, which redefined the relationship between capital and labour.

A review of the literature has identified two main foci of study that roughly overlap with these two socioeconomic eras. A more traditional line of enquiry has focused on the centrality of labour movements in the making of history, politics and socioeconomic development of each country and has been particularly concerned with examining the shifting relations between trade unions, the state and political parties. A more contemporary focus of study has concentrated on the imposition of neoliberalism, transitions to democracy, labour reform as well as on the implications of new managerial practices on the dynamics of employment relations.

With regard to the first focus, the literature on Chilean employment relations can be traced back to historians working from a classic Marxist tradition (Jobet, 1951; Segall, 1953; Ramírez Necochea, 1956; Barría, 1971).[1] They centred on organized workers – particularly the industrial and mining proletariat – whose social consciousness and collective action was essentially conceived of as autonomous and socio-political. Sociologists and political scientists questioned the revolutionary, conscious and trans-formative nature of Chilean workers presented by historians, and concentrated instead on explaining the relationship between trade union action and political action (Landsberger et al., 1964; Di Tella et al., 1966; Petras and Zeitlin, 1967; Angell, 1972). In parallel, a more conventional literature has kept a record of traditional 'industrial relations' data including union membership and density, collective bargaining and industrial conflict (Morris and Oyadener, 1967; Pizarro, 1986; Frías, 1993).

In Argentina, labour historians and sociologists have often concentrated on the dynamics of trade unionism analysing cases of mobilization, trade union development and organization, and the role of the state in these processes, trying to disentangle the complexity of the relations between trade union and Peronism (Torre, 1988; James, 1990; Doyon, 2006; Atzeni and Ghigliani, 2009). Political scientists have looked at the role of trade unions in shaping the government's political agenda towards forms of 'corporatism' (Drake, 1996) or 'neocorporatism' (Etchemendy and Collier, 2007), as well as their interaction with political parties (Levitsky, 2005).

In terms of the second focus, studies on the imposition and impact of neoliberal restructuring on Chilean employment relations have been extensive and covered a broad range of issues. Studies have analysed the socioeconomic transformations carried out by the Pinochet dictatorship (Collins and Lear, 1995; Silva, 1996b) and the nature and dynamics of trade unionism under military rule (Campero and Cortázar, 1985; Ruiz-Tagle, 1989). Research has also discussed the socioeconomic record of the democratic regime (Martínez and Díaz, 1996; Drake and Jaksic, 1999), labour and capital's role in the transition to democracy and the issue of social concertation (Silva, 1996a; Frank, 2004), as well as the nature of employment relations legislation and labour reform (Frank, 2002a; Haagh, 2002; López, 2004; Durán-Palma et al., 2005). During the late 1990s and 2000s, numerous studies have looked at the emergence of new categories of workers as a result of an increasingly flexible and precarious labour market (Echeverría, 1997; Winn, 2004; Soto Roy, 2008), as well as the changing nature of worker and employer collective action (Monckeberg, 2001; Arriagada, 2004; Abarzúa, 2008; Durán-Palma and López, 2009), collective bargaining (González, 1998; Montero et al., 2000), technological change and work organization (Agacino et al., 1998; De Laire, 1999).

In the case of Argentina, research includes the study of changes in labour market dynamics and the growth of the informal sector (Villanueva, 1997; Piva, 2005), trade union crisis and changes in employment relations (Fernández and Bisio, 1999; Novick, 2001), trade union resistance to privatization (Ghigliani, 2010), the introduction of flexible working at firm level (Martínez, 1994), industrial conflict (Iñigo Carrera, 2007), the organization of the unemployed movement (Dinersein, 2001), as well as inter-union alliances and competition as a result of market reforms (Murillo, 2001). More recently, and following the post-2001 economic recovery, new studies have looked at aspects of union renewal (Atzeni and Ghigliani, 2007), workers' resistance (Lenguita and Montes Cató, 2008), and grassroots democracy and workers representation (Vocos, 2010).

Despite these two potentially converging research trends, comparative studies of Chile and Argentina have been unusual. Although these two countries have occasionally featured together in edited publications at regional level (some past and contemporary examples include: Alexander, 1962; Bergquist, 1986; Falabella, 1989; Cook, 1998, 2002, 2007; Munck, 1994; Drake, 1996; Etchemendy, 2004; Marshall, 2006), direct (paired) comparison between them has been extremely rare. This is particularly surprising given that Chile and Argentina share a common historical and cultural heritage, the world's third-longest international border, and parallel patterns of socioeconomic development, but nonetheless show a number of country-specific differences and adaptations in their employment relations systems.

In this chapter we aim to provide a modest introduction to the main similarities and differences in employment relations between Chile and Argentina. The first section provides a historical account of these countries' traditional employment relations in the context of import-substituting industrialization. The second section discusses the nature and impact of the imposition of neoliberal restructuring. The third section focuses on novel worker responses to the increasing divide between formal and informal employment. A short conclusion will follow.

INDUSTRIALIZATION, TRADE UNIONS AND EMPLOYMENT RELATIONS

Argentina, Brazil, Mexico and to lesser extent Chile, became regional leaders in the process of import substituting industrialization (ISI) that characterized the 'short twentieth century' in Latin America's largest countries. In contrast to the hitherto over-reliance on laissez-faire and primary exports for the world markets, ISI aimed to 'develop industries oriented toward the domestic market by using trade restrictions such as tariffs and quotas to encourage the replacement of imported manufactures by domestic products' (Krugman and Obstfeld, 2003, p. 258). While there were strong common variables involved, national variations, particularly in terms of the origins of ISI and the nature and timing of initial labour legislation, played a significant role in shaping the character of what were to become these countries' 'traditional' models of employment relations.

In Chile, the breakdown of the laissez-faire primary-export-based pattern of accumulation led to the incremental adoption of ISI as strategy to resume growth after the Great Depression of 1929. Chile's first Labour Code was enacted in 1931 on the basis of piecemeal legislation passed in the 1920s. It was protective of the individual employee, instituted fragmented collective bargaining as the norm and subjected unions to the supervision of the state. In contrast to Chile's more stable state-building path and industrialization policy (Silva, 2007), ISI in Argentina emerged as the product of a narrow and unexpected alliance between trade unions, a small elite of army and government authorities and some domestic industrialists, and was not initially accompanied by the introduction of an organic system of employment relations. Eventually, this alliance evolved into a national political movement, Peronism, which led industrialization and built a vigorous system of collective employment relations in the 1940s and 1950s.

Strong labour movements emerged in Chile and Argentina during the ISI era. This was mutually reinforcing as ISI created a concentrated industrial labour force that was amenable to political organization, while strong trade unions provided an organized mass constituency to support ISI policies (Roberts, 2002). State–labour relations in Chile and Argentina during ISI were characterized by the incorporation of labour movements. But while Chile became an example of state incorporation with governments aiming to control the labour movement, Argentina fell in the category of political party incorporation (Collier and Collier, 1991), evidencing variants of labour mobilization by strong leftist and populist political parties respectively (Roberts, 2002). As a result, the Chilean labour movement turned into a political arena for the struggles of Communists, Socialists and Christian Democrats, and Argentina's became the ideological, financial and structural base of Peronism (*Partido Justicialista* – PJ).

Chile

The political corruption, economic laissez-faire and strictly free, unregulated labour market that characterized the period that followed the 1891 Civil War began to break down in the late 1910s, reflecting the ups and downs of Chile's overdependence on nitrate exports. The 1920s were characterized by regular economic crises, heightened levels of industrial conflict, the introduction of primitive employment relations legislation and by a succession of short-lived governments proposing radical alternatives to the breakdown of the model of 'outward-oriented' development (Salazar, 2003). The 1930s constituted a critical juncture in Chile's political economy and development of employment relations institutions, as the progressive adoption of ISI policies, the enactment of the 1925 Constitution, and the 1931 Labour Code began to shape the milieu of political, economic and social adjustments known as 'inward-oriented' development.

After becoming one of the worst casualties of the Great Depression of 1929 – with exports and imports decreasing 78 per cent and 84 per cent between 1929 and 1932 while the world economy contracted 'only' by 25 per cent (Pinto and Salazar, 2002) – consensus grew stronger on the need for the state to promote domestic industry, an incremental process that gained a definite impetus with the formal adoption of ISI by the Popular Front in 1938. Complementarily, the 1925 Constitution came into force in 1932, replacing a corrupted pseudo-parliamentary system with a presidential political system that provided for the broad and solid political framework that would later back the developmentalist state (Lucena and Covarrubias, 2006).

Chile's first Labour Code was enacted in 1931. A consolidation of early and new labour legislation, the code was protective of the individual employee and characterized by extensive and highly detailed regulations. It distinguished between blue- and white-collar workers, for whom separate social security schemes were created (Cook, 1998; Mizala and Romaguera, 2001; Walker, 2002). In line with this distinction, collective regulations instituted fragmented collective bargaining as the norm and were restrictive of labour organizations, subjecting them to the supervision of the state (Córdova, 1996). State intervention was particularly evident in the Ministry of Labour's role in collective bargaining, from which unions had to secure permission before negotiating, which supervised their finances and ran an obligatory conciliation service, which in turn sanctioned the legality or illegality of strikes. Blue- and white-collar workers were forbidden to join the same union, but had to organize in industrial and professional unions respectively. For Roddick (1989, p. 203) the fragmented character of the 1931 Labour Code 'ultimately forced most of Chile's labour movement into legally differentiated boxes, bargaining under different preconditions and with different institutional horizons'.

Socialists and Communists identified with the Popular Front and participated in government between 1938 and 1948. They committed to abide by the collective bargaining institutions of the Labour Code and to observe 'social peace' while in government. As a result, the new system of employment relations began to settle, industrial conflict decreased considerably throughout the decade, and Socialists and Communists became the dominant force within the labour movement to the expense of their anarchist rivals.

The main characteristics of Chile's 'classic' or 'legal Marxist' unionism began to crystallize after the formation of CUT (*Central Unica de*

Trabajadores) in 1953, a unification of all major confederations. Classic unionism was largely confrontational in relations with employers and favoured organization at higher levels. Channelling grievances through federations and confederations had socio-political visibility and helped to overcome weak bargaining power at company level. In this context, political parties performed an intermediary role between unions and the state in control of the employment relations system and, as a result, Chile's labour movement turned into a political arena for the struggles of Communist, Socialists and later, Christian Democrats.

The diffuse differentiation between political parties and trade unions resulted in a loss of autonomy of the latter in relation to the former. For some commentators, classic unionism represented an expression of class struggle, but limited to economic grievances and subordinated to political parties, resulting in a weak 'autonomous politicization' of the labour movement in contrast to the highly militant politicization of its leadership. For others, that labour strategy developed in this way was a mere consequence of legal restrictions, and the resulting overlapping of interests with parties of the left (Rojas and Aravena, 1999). That these and other characteristics are widely considered to represent the labour movement in this period should not obscure the fact that, as ever, the labour movement is a largely heterogeneous entity (Campero and Cortázar, 1985).

Despite legally induced fragmentation, organized labour's traditional indicators of power and participation in the polity increased throughout the period of inward-oriented development. Union density grew from 21 per cent in 1940 to its 29 per cent historical peak in 1973. Likewise, collective bargaining coverage rose to an average of 13 per cent of the occupied workforce between 1965 and 1970, decreasing slightly to 11 per cent between 1971 and 1973 (Mizala and Romaguera, 2001). Likewise, the restrictions governing strikes were no obstacle for union mobilization, as industrial conflict – albeit illegal – increased heavily during the 1960s (Pizarro, 1986). Furthermore, CUT played a decisive role in national politics, which culminated with the democratic election of Salvador Allende and the Popular Unity coalition in 1970. As socialist reforms deepened however, a coalition of landowners, middle classes, as well as US corporations in Chile began a series of destabilizing activities and an economic blockade that fuelled political polarization and social conflict ending in the coup d'état of 11 September 1973 (US Senate, 1975; US Department of State, 2000).

Argentina

The 1930s also hastened important economic and political changes in Argentina. The political unrest generated by the Great Depression ended in a military coup d'état that dramatically changed the country's political situation, and gravely affected unions as repression increased. While the military government that followed had no interest in nationalism or industrial policy (Silva, 2007), ISI emerged from a narrow and unexpected alliance between trade unions, a small elite of army and government authorities and some domestic industrialists. At this stage, ISI produced an expansion of the working class and increase in unionization, but was not accompanied by the introduction of an organic system of employment relations. Although after the peak of strikes of 1935–36 the state gradually increased its role in labour disputes through the *Departamento Nacional del Trabajo*, employment relations continued to rest on voluntarism until the rise of Peronism a decade later. Until then, the Argentinean labour movement faced a continuous combination of political exclusion and industrialization without income redistribution, which fuelled growing working class discontent.

The arrival of Colonel Perón at the *Secretaría de Trabajo y Previsión* in 1943 and his two consecutive democratic presidencies (1946–55) encouraged the political integration of the labour movement, and brought about the emergence of a system of state intervention and regulation of the capital–labour relationship. Between 1943 and 1955, both military and democratic authorities backed union recognition, enforced previous labour laws, promoted new legislation and actively intervened in labour conflicts, collective bargaining and social security. Argentina's labour movement became the ideological, financial and structural base of Peronism.[2] This development was at the expense of the previous influence of Anarchists, Socialists and Communists, as the rise of Peronism ran parallel to the growth of anti-communist policies and oligarchic tendencies within the labour movement.

From the point of view of labour, the backbone of the system was the 1945 Law Decree on trade union organization. Inter alia, it established the monopoly of labour representation in collective bargaining based on the legal recognition of the union with the greatest number of members, and consolidated the dominance of industry-wide trade unions (Marshall, 2006). The law recognized the right of workers to organize, granted the state influence on legal procedures and unions' internal activities, gave employment protection to union officials, typified anti-union practices and supported trade union initiatives in social security.

Union density reached its 48 per cent historical peak in 1954 (Lamadrid and Orsatti, 1991). Unions were able to translate workers' mobilization into advantageous labour contracts. Important union demands like the introduction of workplace structures (*comisiones internas*), the closed-shop, or financial benefits like pension schemes and health services, were originally obtained by unions in collective agreements, and only later incorporated into labour legislation.

In 1944 and 1953, first by decree and then by special legislation, the state encouraged collective bargaining, extended its coverage and secured the participation of ministerial authorities on the bargaining table. Ever since, collective agreements are valid only if approved by the Ministry of Labour and their terms extended to all workers in a particular industry or economic activity irrespective of union membership. The state was granted and still maintains a powerful role as it can refuse to validate and/ or impose changes to a collective agreement. In practice, this power is normally not used and instead parties usually seek ministerial advice and approval before negotiating on sensible issues.

It is important to note, however, that between 1953 and 1988, trade unions and employers were able to freely negotiate collective agreements during 11 years only as both military and democratic governments frequently suspended the application of bargaining legislation. Yet, these collective agreements were able to shape Argentina's employment relations because of a legal disposition by which any agreement remains valid until it is formally replaced or repealed. The resulting juridification of employment relations placed regulatory public institutions at the centre of the system, made politics pivotal to its practice and certainly contributed to the development of bureaucratic leaderships incorporated into the Peronist movement. Ultimately, this led to the Workers' General Confederation (*Confederación General del Trabajo* – CGT) and other trade union political bodies like *Las 62 Organizaciones Peronistas*, to engage in a sort of political exchange with different governments whenever the chance arose.

Nevertheless, this juridification did not reach the workplace to the same extent, because the rank and file were able to build up strong and lively workplace structures between 1946 and 1955. The *comisiones internas* became, and still are, determinant in defending workers' interests, particularly in terms of making employers observe the terms of collective agreements.

Peronist legislation also encouraged the institutionalization of union-provided health care for workers and their families, perhaps the most salient feature of Argentinean trade unions. The *obras sociales* were created in the late 1950s and early 1960s through collective agreements with employers and although both sides contribute to financing these schemes, their administration was the reserve of the unions. In 1970, employers and unions were legally obliged to create and extend *obras sociales* to non-unionized workers in the same industry. As a result, a worker was able to pay *obra social* dues without becoming a union member, strengthening union finances and protecting them against free riders in collective bargaining. The *obras sociales* have become one of the pillars of the country's health system, and as such a source of power and an axis of political exchange for the unions.

The significance of these various institutions for the strength of the Argentine labour movement is evident when considering that every single attempt to curtail trade unions' power, by both military and civil governments since 1955, has manifested in an open attack to their legal basis, the institutions of collective bargaining, the *comisiones internas*, and since 1970, the union control of the *obras sociales*.

THE CONTINUING EFFECTS OF NEOLIBERAL RESTRUCTURING ON EMPLOYMENT RELATIONS

By the mid-1970s, Chile and Argentina began to abandon ISI and impose neoliberalism under harsh military dictatorships. The military rejected ISI's high levels of state involvement in the economy, protectionism and inclusive social policies. As they brutally repressed the labour movement, authoritarian regimes imposed policies oriented to facilitate the role of the market through trade liberalization, capital market deregulation, privatization and a dismantling of labour regulations. But as Cook (2002, 2007) has extensively discussed, the nature and sequence of the 'dual transitions' that have characterized the last three decades – from ISI to neoliberalism, and from dictatorship back to democracy – have differed greatly between the two countries.

Chile experienced market reforms before democratic transition. Neoliberal restructuring and the revamp of labour legislation were largely consolidated by a dictatorship able to suppress most forms of resistance. Since 1990, the democratic governments of the *Concertación* (coalition) have maintained the majority of socioeconomic policies originally associated with Pinochet, within a largely stable political setting and expanding economy. In contrast, Argentina experienced democratic transition before consolidating market economic reforms. Although the latter were initiated by the military between 1976 and 1982, they were questioned during the democratic transition (1983–89). Indeed, the bulk of Argentinean neoliberal restructuring was introduced by the civilian government of Carlos Menem during the 1990s, in the midst of political confrontation and economic and social turmoil.

This has had significant, albeit contrasting, consequences for the direction and politics of labour law reform in both countries under their democratic regimes. While the direction of labour reform in Chile was protective, reflecting efforts to redress the legacy of the dictatorship, labour reform in Argentina was characterized by attempts to flexibilize and reverse earlier labour protections (Cook, 1998). Nevertheless, current employment relations systems have neither gained an exclusively protective nor flexible character respectively. Indeed, the nature of Chile's employment relations remains essentially flexible while Argentina's may be described as between flexibility and protection (Cook, 1998).

The consolidation of structural reforms during the 1990s was achieved through the intervention of labour-supported coalitions and political parties. In Chile, CUT supported the *Concertación* and engaged in social concertation with the state and employers, accepting and legitimizing the bulk of neoliberal model in exchange for meagre labour reforms. In Argentina, the CGT showed an ambivalent attitude to Menem's Peronist government, supporting individual reforms oriented to labour flexibility in exchange for protection for trade unions' traditional organizational and financial structures.

As a result of neoliberal restructuring, both countries now show high levels of atypical employment, precariousness, informality and inequality. In contrast, there is a significant difference between Chile and Argentina in terms of collective labour relations. In Chile, effective collective representation has become a rarity with stagnant or declining levels of unionization and collective bargaining. In Argentina, union density and coverage among unionizable workers remains high, and unions remain financially and politically powerful. Moreover, while the outcomes of bargaining tend to be modest in Chile, the opposite is currently the case in Argentina.

Chile

After a short period of policy indecision, the Pinochet regime (1973–90) began implementing neoliberal restructuring in 1975, imposing draconian stabilization programmes, privatization and the rapid, thorough liberalization of capital markets, prices and trade (Silva, 1996a). Given the perceived success of the policies, market logic began to expand into most key areas of social policy in the late 1970s, including health, pensions and the revamp of employment relations legislation.

Individual legislation was first reformed in 1978 when the regime derogated protective norms imposing in effect a 'neoliberal approach to flexibility', characterized by a downward adjustment of terms of employment, quantitatively through wage cutting and substandard contracts, and qualitatively in the restoration of managerial authority (Streeck, 1987). Collective labour relations were re-regulated in 1979 through a series of acts designed to weaken unions as bargaining agents and centred on preventing collective action from having an effect on the labour market (Valenzuela, 1989). The 1979 Labour Plan – strictly speaking a 'trade union plan' according to its author (Piñera, 1990) – re-legalized trade unionism but limited union activity exclusively to the level of the firm, set strict limits to union power, decentralized collective bargaining completely, restricted the right to strike and reduced the role of the state in employment relations.

Although the immediate result of the plan was the resurfacing of union organizations, over time it institutionalized a fragile and fragmented unionism. Nevertheless (illegal) national-level organizations were able to reorganize and played a decisive role in the plebiscite that led to the recovery of democracy in 1990. The *Concertación*, a labour-supported centre-left coalition led by Christian Democrats and Socialists, remained in power until 2010.

Deepening democracy, reforming the 'predatory, dependent, and excluding' economic model, and reforming the regime's employment relations legal framework ('no democracy without labour reform') were all in the *Concertación*'s agenda. Fearful of a conservative backlash and showing significant doses of pragmatism in an expanding economy, however, the *Concertación* quickly backed away from any plan to substantially change Chile's neoliberal socioeconomic model. Instead, the coalition pledged to reduce the social deficit accumulated under military rule and committed itself to foster 'growth with equity' within the 'protective' political framework inherited from the dictatorship (Durán-Palma et al., 2005).

In this context, compromise and moderation were argued by the government to be the most effective way to achieve concessions from militant employers and a strong opposition in reforming employment relations legislation. Aylwin's government (1990–93) sought to promote social concertation at national level among the government, CUT and the main employers' association, the CPC. In this period, broad tripartite agreements were signed and various laws passed that later consolidated into the 1994 Labour Code. By the mid-1990s, tripartism was abandoned as it had actually turned into bilateral exchanges between the government and employers (Silva, 1996a).

By the end of the Frei administration (1994–99), labour reform had become a hot political issue. Reforms were introduced and blocked in the Senate during the 1999 presidential elections, which arguably helped the coalition to stay in power. The Lagos government (2000–06) passed weakened reforms in 2001. The last *Concertación* administration (Bachelet 2006–10) was also elected in the midst of another 'hot employment relations summer' (see next section).

Social concertation and labour reform have delivered meagre results. While the 1994 and 2001 reforms reduced the repressive character of authoritarian legislation, many emblematic changes had provisions that contributed in practice to preserving the essentially flexible and restrictive character of labour legislation. This is not to say that reforms have not encouraged pluralism and improved the level of social protection for the most vulnerable, but that the enjoyment of labour rights typically associated with 'advanced' employment relations systems remains limited (Frank, 2002a; Durán-Palma et al., 2005).

Research explaining the failure of social concertation and the limitations of labour reform have highlighted several factors (Frank, 2002a, 2002b; Haagh, 2002; Durán-Palma et al., 2005). Perhaps the most evident have to do with the institutional compromises made as a result of the early transition process, the political right's recalcitrant opposition to reform and employers' lack of interest in fostering better relations with labour (Frank, 2004). More important, however, it has been the progressive identification of the *Concertación* with neoliberalism that has constrained the possibility of systemic reform inter alia in the area of employment relations because cheap and flexible labour with few rights to collective action are critical to the model, and have indeed been central to the recovery and expansion of Chilean capitalism (Taylor, 2004). But the resilience of the model has also been the result of a weakened labour movement and its strategic choices. Due to its close ties with the *Concertación*, the CUT gave priority to the consolidation of democracy over class struggle and the organizational needs of the labour movement (Frank, 2004).

As a result, 'a conspicuous tension remains in the discrepancy between the *Concertación*'s rhetorical commitment to "growth with equity" and the reality of pronounced social polarisation' (Taylor, 2004, p. 76). Nearly 36 per cent of Chile's labour force works today in the informal sector (Tokman, 2007). Low incentives for unionization and collective bargaining have also rendered effective collective representation a rarity. Union density as percentage of wage and salary earners in the private sector has declined from its post-dictatorship peak of 21 per cent in 1992, to 15 per cent in 2007 (Dirección del Trabajo, 2008a). In 2006, 68 per cent of workers worked in firms with no unions (Pulso, 2007). Likewise, the percentage of workers participating in collective bargaining each year declined from 10 per cent in 1991 to a mere 6 per cent in 2007 (Dirección del Trabajo, 2008b). Moreover, the outcomes of collective bargaining have worsened with wage improvements 'uncomfortably close to the level of inflation' (Frank, 2002b, p. 11).

Argentina

Neoliberal restructuring was also introduced in Argentina by a military dictatorship (1976–83).The military opened the economy to foreign capitals, reoriented the role of the state and promoted a series of financial reforms increasing the public debt and the dependence on international financial institutions (IFI). In contrast to Chile, however, Argentina's first democratic government (Alfonsín 1983–89) softened, and even questioned the neoliberal turn. Unions were able to obtain pro-labour reforms and secured rights that were enshrined in labour law.

Market reforms were only consolidated during the government of Peronist Carlos Menem (1989–99) elected under severe economic conditions, a hyperinflationary crisis and the pressure of IFI. Menem's 'Convertibility Plan' increased public debt to maintain an anti-inflationary peso–dollar parity, making Argentina even more dependent on IFI. The plan also involved a radical reform of the state including the privatization of state-owned utilities and enterprises, reduction of public spending, decentralization and tendering.

Menen's reforms certainly involved reversing its predecessor's short-lived labour protections. Individual labour rights and collective bargaining were reformed piecemeal to ease the introduction of flexible contracts and working practices, producing devastating effects on employment and having a profound impact on the employment relations system. The Peronist neoliberal offensive threw trade unions into disarray. Some powerful organizations supported the government, giving rise around the CGT to an 'entrepreneurial unionism' mainly focused on business opportunities to strength unions' financial resources, ultimately maintaining core interests linked to organizational survival and collective bargaining coverage. Other organizations contested neoliberal policies, resulting in the emergence of a rival confederation in 1992, the *Central de Trabajadores de la Argentina* (CTA), as well as of an oppositional faction within the CGT in 1994, the *Movimiento de Trabajadores Argentinos* (MTA).

Throughout the 1990s, flexibility became the leitmotif of employers and the government. Employers introduced flexibility in the newly privatized utilities and enterprises, in a largely piecemeal fashion. Their offensive at firm level impacted on four main areas: the legal nature of the employment relationship, wage determination, distribution of working hours and the definition and organization of the labour process.

The government sought flexibility by legal reform and collective bargaining. Although eventually successful, it was a highly contested process. Between 1992 and 1999, the CGT, the CTA and the MTA launched nine general strikes against governmental policies. During Menem's first term (1989–95), only eight out of 20 bills to reform labour laws were passed in Parliament. This was mainly the result of a number of Peronist MPs with union backgrounds who, despite the profound de-unionization of the PJ, were able to block legislative initiatives to flexibilize contracts. But after the government reached a corporative pact with the CGT in 1994, these MPs stopped blocking neoliberal legislation.

Indeed, during Menem's second term (1995–99), Argentina's traditional centralized system of national collective bargaining was reversed by favouring collective negotiations at plant level in a bid to facilitate the introduction of flexibility. This certainly debilitated trade unions' bargaining power, but in exchange for introducing reforms – and to co-opt the CGT – the government increased protection and financial support to the *obras sociales*, and allowed unions to invest in the new business opportunities brought about by the privatization and deregulation of the health, pensions and industrial accidents insurance systems.

During the 1990s, neoliberal restructuring had a highly negative impact on the labour market, particularly in terms of the growth of the informal sector. Whereas from 1992 to 1996 the rate of unregistered employees oscillated between 22 and 25 per cent, by the end of 2009, this figure stood at 36 per cent (TEL, 2009). Increasing informalization translated into relative union demobilization at local and industry level. But between 1997 and 2002, informalization was also responsible for activating an unprecedented process of mass mobilization led by the unemployed who began to organize in new territorial organizations. These organizations played an important role in the mass protests that overthrew the government in December 2001 in the midst of a severe economic crisis.

As the economy began to recover in 2003, traditional trade unions regained a prominent role. First, at 40 per cent, union density among unionizable workers remains very high for Latin American standards. Second, the number of collective agreements has increased from 348 in 2004 to 1231 in 2008, covering the great majority of workers employed in the formal sector. In 2005, for instance, although union density in formal sector enterprises stood at 37 per cent, 90 per cent of them signed some type of agreement with a trade union, covering 83 per cent of their workforce (Trajtemberg and Attorresi, 2005). Third, even though flexibility has not been reversed, some unions have been able to obtain important benefits in areas including working hours, pay, outsourcing and health. Last, while decentralization of collective bargaining remains high, the tendency is to favour national sector agreements and to coordinate these by linking wage increases in less dynamic sectors where unions have less bargaining power with those obtained by more powerful and representative unions.

NEOLIBERALISM, MOBILIZATION AND EVOLVING FORMS OF COLLECTIVE ACTION

Analyses like the above, based largely on traditional actors, national-level and formal regulations, run the risk of overlooking interesting developments occurring elsewhere, particularly in terms of the increasing diversity in struggles and evolving forms of collective action. These can be observed in Chile and Argentina, partly as a result of a constant tension between the rank and file and trade union confederations legitimizing (or weakly opposing) neoliberal restructuring. They suggest a renewed potential for contestation in both countries, but the nature of the most relevant of these experiences varies greatly.

In Chile, CUT engaged in social dialogue with the state and employers, and accepted the legitimacy of neoliberalism in exchange for meagre labour reforms. With the exception of some public and strategic sector unions, rank and file militancy was largely contained within the system or marginalized throughout the 1990s and early 2000s. However, increasing signs of discontent and significant pockets of resistance can be observed, particularly amongst workers in the 'rough end' of the labour market, particularly those working in outsourced employment relationships. Increasingly successful 'contract labour unions' have organized within the system but mobilized outside it, achieving remarkable gains.

In Argentina, the CGT showed an ambivalent attitude to Menem's neoliberal reforms, exchanging labour flexibility for protection for trade unions' organizational and financial structures. But this strategy produced growing tensions, the fragmentation of workers' organizations and hesitant tactics, which included bitter industrial action. Until 2002, all these contradictions caused workers' demobilization and the rise of alternative forms of collective action, mainly by organizations of unemployed workers outside trade unions' domain. Since 2003, however, the resurgence of industrial conflict has concentrated on, and been accompanied by radical grassroots experiences, which have questioned the top-down oligarchic control of most traditional trade unions.

Chile

No other group of workers has come closer to symbolizing the precarious state of the Chilean labour market than contract workers (*subcontratistas*).[3] Contract workers labour in outsourced employment relationships occupying the frontier between formality and informality.[4] This is because more often than not outsourcing is used to intentionally disguise the employment relationship that de facto exists between user enterprises and contract workers. User enterprises are not obliged to observe labour legislation with regard to workers legally employed by a third party and, in this way, reducing labour costs while remaining in control of the employment relationship (Durán-Palma and López, 2009). Contract workers earn significantly less than 'direct' workers performing work of equal value, labour in relatively unsafe working conditions and present low levels of unionization and collective bargaining (Echeverría, 2006). Unsurprisingly, outsourced employment has been generally characterized as precarious and contract workers are widely seen and see themselves as a second-class labour force.

Outsourcing in Chile has increased rapidly as large user enterprises have developed extensive networks based on the contracting out of labour and/ or services, provided by numerous small and medium enterprises. In 2007 over half of all companies outsourced at least one function and 35 per cent of all workers in the formal sector work under outsourced employment contracts (Dirección del Trabajo, 2007; Pulso, 2007).

Outsourcing remained poorly regulated until the presidential elections of December 2005 installed the 'contract labour question' on top of the political agenda. Unions representing contract workers labouring for state giant CODELCO (*Corporación del Cobre de Chile*), the world's largest copper producer, conducted massive mobilizations demanding better employment and working conditions. In early 2006, the incumbent Lagos government reintroduced a Bill on Outsourcing dormant in Congress since 2001. After a rocky legislative process, newly elected President Michelle Bachelet promulgated the Outsourcing and Supply of Labour Act on 16 October 2006, claiming that it represented 'a definite, decisive, and clear step in terminating with the division between first and second class workers' (Bachelet, 2006, p. 4).

Immediately after the Act came into force on 16 January 2007, the National Labour Bureau began a comprehensive plan of labour inspections. The Bureau detected numerous irregularities involving disguised employment relationships and, in a series of emblematic rulings, demanded user enterprises to internalize thousands of contract workers. Whereas some employers began to diligently employ these workers, many others successfully challenged in court the Bureau's competency to rule on such matters.

As the Bureau's position was undermined and employer opposition to the Act grew stronger, a sudden wave of labour discontent, mass mobilization and violent industrial conflict began to engulf the country. Hitherto a largely invisible majority, contract workers in flagship commodity export sectors began solid mass mobilizing drives in late 2005. Unions of contract workers particularly in the copper mining and forestry sectors did not confine themselves to demanding new legislation, or try to engage in firm-level negotiations, which they had painfully used to lose. Instead, they chose to organize contract workers across provider enterprises, and to mobilize outside formal institutional channels to put direct pressure on user enterprises. This ultimately allowed them to bargain from a position of strength and to achieve remarkable gains, setting a bargaining pattern throughout the forestry sector and forcing the state-owned copper mining sector to improve employment and working conditions. In 2009, top leaders of the now called 'contract labour movement' (*movimiento obrero subcontratista*) successfully bid for top positions in CUT.

Although it is still too early to assess the long-term significance of these events, it seems that a qualitatively different period in Chile's employment relations may be emerging. While the neoliberal establishment has been able to resist challenges from above by employing constitutional prerogatives and relying on the hegemony of the ruling elite, it has appeared far less prepared to contain the direct challenge represented by subordinate forces mobilizing outside institutional channels. Indeed, it is the first time since the return of democracy that rank and file labour mobilization appears to be the main driver for changes in Chilean employment relations.

Argentina

The main and long-lasting effect of the processes of privatization, downsizing and outsourcing of the 1990s in Argentina, has been the segregation of an important part of the population into a secondary labour market. In contrast to Chile, however, traditional union organizations have recovered their importance, particularly since 2003.

Certain analyses have explained the resilience of traditional unions employing the concept of 'segmented neo-corporatism'. Etchemendy and Collier (2007, p. 366) have described it as 'a pattern of peak-level negotiation in which monopolistic unions, business associations, and the government coordinate on inflation-targeted, sector wide wage agreements and minimum wage floors, which apply to a substantial minority of the labour force'. According to this logic, segmented corporatism has helped large portions of formal workers to recover wage levels and to strengthen the role of the CGT, but also to simultaneously reinforce the divide between formal and informal workers.

Even if analytically useful to explain the resilience and limits of traditional union power in Argentina, a focus on peak-level negotiation risks losing sight of important local and grassroots phenomena. Indeed, over the course of the last two decades there have been important changes in the level, type and composition of struggles, following the ups and downs of the economic cycle. Based on the decline in the number of strikes relative to the total of social protests until 2002, some scholars have argued the demise of trade unions as the main promoters of social protest (Farinetti, 2002). But disaggregated data shows that half of social protests recorded between 1989 and 2002 corresponded to union initiatives, although strikes represented only 24 per cent of them. Moreover, even between 1997 and 2002, when organizations of unemployed workers led the most radical struggles, unions showed a high level of unrest (Schuster et al., 2006). It should not be surprising that with the economy growing at an average of 8 per cent a year, unemployment diminishing and a friendlier political environment, private sector strikes have recovered significantly since 2003 (Atzeni and Ghigliani, 2007). But the state has tightened repression since the second half of 2005, with police suppressing labour protests, sit-in strikes and factory occupations.

Most importantly, the resurgence of labour activism in Argentina has featured a number of workplace structures across several economic sectors, including the Buenos Aires underground, hospitals, teachers, communications, airlines and workers from the textile, rubber and food processing industries. These organizations have taken industrial action mobilizing workers through grassroots democracy structures and maintained lengthy conflicts with significant media impact (ibid.).

They gained further momentum in 2009 when Buenos Aires underground and Kraft-food workers led a series of collective actions that questioned the oligarchic control and lack of democratic accountability of most traditional union leaderships, and opened a public debate on renewing the very model of Argentina's union organization dating back to the mid-1940s (Vocos, 2010). However much an important development, this cannot hide the significant decline in and uneven nature of workplace union representation. In 2004, only 12 per cent of formal sector enterprises had shop stewards, although in companies with more than 200 employees, this figure reaches 53 per cent (Trajtemberg and Attorresi, 2005).

CONCLUSION

As this chapter has suggested, a more systematic comparative analysis of Chile and Argentina may contribute to addressing a number of broader theoretical and empirical issues. First, the comparison illustrates how the breakdown and reconstruction of employment relations institutions results from changing patterns of accumulation and the contentious interaction of class actors (Howell, 2005). Chile and Argentina have undergone broadly similar trajectories in their patterns of economic development, from laissez-faire to ISI, and from ISI to neoliberal restructuring. However, the milieus of political, economic and social adjustments that have developed under these models have differed significantly between the two countries. While there have been strong common variables involved, concrete national realities have played a fundamental role in shaping the contours of change, continuity and struggle. This has been particularly evident in terms of different political systems, economic structure, the nature and timing of initial labour legislation, the pattern of relationship between labour and the state and political parties and the varying strength and organization of employment relations actors.

Second, the exclusionary nature of the current neoliberal pattern of accumulation has resulted in a trend towards the re-commodification of labour. As elsewhere, the most noticeable impact of neoliberal restructuring in individual employment relations in Chile and Argentina has been the significant increase in atypical forms of employment, precariousness, informality and inequality. This high level of informal work undermines the validity of analyses based exclusively on the role of institutions and actors in regulating the employment relations system and compels the rethinking of the prospects of extending protective employment legislation to the vast majority of the population and the potential role of trade unions in its promotion.

Third, organized labour has suffered a major setback in both countries as a result of the imposition of neoliberalism. In general, unions' capacity to affect the political and economic transformations on course, protect hard won rights and organize an increasingly heterogeneous working class has been limited, but their decline has been significantly more pronounced in Chile than in Argentina. Pinochet's brutal, radical and protracted authoritarian rule, as well as the unbroken sequence of neoliberal governments that succeeded it, have played a fundamental role in the near obliteration of worker resistance and the marginalization of traditional trade unions. In Argentina, workers have suffered job losses, salary reduction and precariousness but have always opposed resistance, not just building on their trade unions' relatively stronger institutional position but also renewing grassroots structures and experimenting with new forms of organizing in the informal sector. Recent experiences of renewed labour activism in Argentina and the rise of the 'contract labour movement' in Chile are further demonstration that a bottom-up process of workers' organizing might be as important as the institutional power of trade unions in the revitalization of the labour movement.

Finally, the overview presented in this chapter should also be read as the result of processes that workers have profoundly shaped – albeit in different forms, under different conditions and with uneven organizational strength – proving once more the everlasting dimension of labour unrest under capitalism.

NOTES

1. The citations included within this section are for illustrative purposes only and are not intended to provide an exhaustive overview of the literature in question.
2. However, the instability of the parliamentary system, the strong development of workplace organizations, and since 1980s the de-unionization of the political structures of the *Partido Justicialista* point to a less linear relationship between the state and the labour movement in Argentina.
3. This section draws liberally from Durán-Palma (2009) and Durán-Palma and López (2009).
4. Outsourcing (*subcontratación*) refers herein to triangular employment relationships where a worker ('contract worker') employed by an enterprise (the 'provider') performs work for a third party (the 'user') to whom their employer provides labour or services (ILO, 2006). It should not be confused with the supply of labour under commercial contracts.

REFERENCES

Abarzúa, E. (2008), 'Acción sindical de trabajadores contratistas', in A. Soto Roy (ed.), *Flexibilidad laboral y subjetividades: Hacia una comprensión psicosocial del empleo contemporáneo*, Santiago: Lom.
Agacino, R., González, C. and Rojas, J. (1998), *Capital transnacional y trabajo: El desarrollo minero en Chile*, Santiago: LOM.
Alexander, R. (1962), *Labor Relations in Argentina, Brazil and Chile*, New York: McGraw-Hill.
Angell, A. (1972), *Politics and the Chilean Labour Movement*, Oxford: Oxford University Press.
Arriagada, G. (2004), *Los empresarios y la política*, Santiago: LOM.
Atzeni, M. and Ghigliani, P. (2007), 'The resilience of traditional trade union practices in the revitalisation of the Argentine labour movement', in C.L. Phelan (ed.), *Trade Union Revitalisation: Trends and Prospects in 37 Nations*, Dusseldorf: Peter Lang.
Atzeni, M. and Ghigliani, P. (2009), 'Trade unionism in Argentina since 1945: The limits of reformism', in C.L. Phelan (ed.), *Trade Union Revitalisation: Trends and Prospects in 37 Nations*, Dusseldorf: Peter Lang.
Bachelet, M. (2006), 'Intervención de S.E. la Presidenta de la República, Michelle Bachelet, en acto de publicación de ley sobre subcontratación y trabajo transitorio', Santiago: Dirección de Prensa del Gobierno de Chile.
Barría, J. (1971), *El movimiento obrero en Chile. Síntesis histórico-social*, Santiago: Colección Trígono.
Bergquist, C. (1986), *Labor in Latin America: Comparative Essays on Chile, Argentina, Venezuela, and Colombia*, Stanford: Stanford University Press.
Campero, G. and Cortázar, R. (1985), 'Lógicas de Acción Sindical en Chile', *Estudios CIEPLAN*, **108**, 5–37.
Collier, R.B. and Collier, D. (1991), *Shaping the Political Arena, Critical Junctures, the Labor Movement and Regime Dynamics in Latin America*, New Jersey: Princeton University Press.
Collins, J. and Lear, J. (1995), *Chile's Free Market Miracle: A Second Look*, Oakland: Institute for Food and Development Policy.
Cook, M.L. (1998), 'Towards flexible industrial relations? Neoliberalism, democracy and labour reform in Latin America', *Industrial Relations*, **37**(3), 311–36.
Cook, M.L. (2002), 'Labor reform and dual transitions in Brazil and the Southern Cone', *Latin American Politics and Society*, **44**(1), 1–34.

Cook, M.L. (2007), *The Politics of Labor Reform in Latin America: Between Flexibility and Rights*, University Park: Pennsylvania State University Press.

Córdova, E. (1996), 'The challenge of flexibility in Latin America', *Comparative Labor Law Journal*, **17**(2), 314–37.

De Laire, F. (1999), 'El mundo del trabajo y su entorno: Una mirada retrospectiva. Algunas reflexiones a partir del análisis de la realidad minera en chilena', *Revista de Economía y Trabajo*, **9**, 85–98.

Di Tella, T., Brams, L., Reynaud, J.-D. and Touraine, A. (1966), *Huachipato et Lota. Etude sur la conscience ouvrière dans deux enterprises chiliennes*, Paris: CNRS.

Dinersein, A.C. (2001), 'Roadblocks in Argentina', *Capital and Class*, **74**, 1–7.

Dirección del Trabajo (2007), *Encuesta Laboral 2006: Relaciones de Trabajo y Empleo en Chile*, Santiago: Dirección del Trabajo.

Dirección del Trabajo (2008a), *Compendio de Series Estadísticas, Capítulo Sindicalismo*, available at: http://www.dt.gob.cl/documentacion/1612/article-62614.html; accessed 10 January 2011.

Dirección del Trabajo (2008b), *Compendio Series Estadísticas, Capítulo Negociación Colectiva*, available at http://www.dt.gob.cl/documentacion/1612/article-62612.html; accessed 10 January 2011.

Doyon, L. (2006), *Perón y los trabajadores. Los orígenes del sindicalismo peronista, 1943–1955*, Buenos Aires: Siglo 21.

Drake, P. (1996), *Labor Movements and Dictatorships: The Southern Cone in Comparative Perspective*, Baltimore: Johns Hopkins University Press.

Drake, P. and Jaksic, I. (eds) (1999), *El modelo chileno: Democracia y desarrollo en los noventa*, Santiago: Lom.

Durán-Palma, F. (2009), 'Chile's "contract labour movement": Prospects for union revitalisation?', Edinburgh: 27th International Labour Process Conference.

Durán-Palma, F. and López, D. (2009), 'Contract labour mobilisation in Chile's copper mining and forestry sectors', *Employee Relations*, **31**(3).

Durán-Palma, F., Wilkinson, A. and Korczynski, M. (2005), 'Labour reform in a neo-liberal "protected" democracy: Chile 1990–2001', *International Journal of Human Resource Management*, **16**(1), 65–89.

Echeverría, M. (1997), *Subcontratación de la producción y subcontratación del trabajo* (Temas Laborales No. 7), Santiago: Dirección del Trabajo.

Echeverría, M. (2006), 'Los riesgos laborales de la subcontratación', *Aportes al Debate Laboral*, **19**, Santiago: Dirección del Trabajo.

Etchemendy, S. (2004), 'Repression, exclusion, and inclusion: Government–union relations and patterns of labor reform in liberalizing economies', *Comparative Politics*, **36**(3), 273–90.

Etchemendy, S. and Collier, R.B. (2007), 'Down but not out: Union resurgence and segmented neocorporatism in Argentina (2003–2007)', *Politics & Society*, **35**(3), 363–401.

Falabella, G. (1989), 'Un nuevo sindicalismo? Argentina, Brasil y Chile bajo regímenes militares', *Proposiciones*, **17**.

Farinetti, M. (2002), 'La conflictividad social después del movimiento obrero', *Nueva Sociedad*, **182**.

Fernández, A. and Bisio, R. (1999), *Política y Relaciones Laborales en la Transición Democrática Argentina*, Buenos Aires: Humanitas.

Frank, V. (2002a), 'The elusive goal in democratic Chile: Reforming the Pinochet labor legislation', *Latin American Politics and Society*, **44**(1), 35–68.

Frank, V. (2002b), 'The labour movement in democratic Chile, 1990–2000', Working Paper No. 298, Helen Kellogg Institute for International Studies, University of Notre Dame.

Frank, V. (2004), 'Politics without policy: The failure of social concertation in democratic Chile, 1990–2000', in P. Winn (ed.), *Victims of the Chilean Miracle: Workers and Neoliberalism in the Pinochet Era, 1973–2002*, Durham and London: Duke University Press.

Frías, P. (1993), 'La afiliación sindical en Chile, 1932–1992', *Revista de Economía y Trabajo*, **1**(2), 261–89.

Ghigliani, P. (2010), *The Politics of Privatization and Trade Union Mobilisation: The Electricity Industry in the UK and Argentina*, Dusseldorf: Peter Lang.

González, C. (1998), 'La negociación colectiva en la transición chilena: Apuntes para una evaluación necesaria', *Economía y Trabajo en Chile Informe Anual*, **8**, 79–120.

Haagh, L. (2002), 'The emperor's new clothes: Labor reform and social democratization in Chile', *Studies in Comparative International Development*, **37**(1), 86–115.

Howell, C. (2005), *Trade Unions and the State: The Construction of Industrial Relations Institutions in Britain*, Princeton, NJ: Princeton University Press.

ILO (2006), *The Employment Relationship*, Report No. V, International Labour Conference, 95th Session, Geneva: ILO.

Iñigo Carrera, N. (2007), 'Strikes in Argentina', in S. van der Velden (ed.), *Strikes around the World, 1968–2005, Case Studies of 15 Countries*, Amsterdam: Aksant.

James, D. (1990), *Resistencia e integración. El peronismo y la clase trabajadora argentina*, Buenos Aires: Sudamericana.

Jobet, J.C. (1951), *Movimiento social obrero en Desarrollo de Chile en la primera mitad del siglo 20*, Santiago: Ediciones de la Universidad de Chile.

Krugman, P.R. and Obstfeld, M. (2003), *International Economics: Theory and Policy*, Boston: Pearson Education.

Lamadrid, A. and Orsatti, A. (1991), 'Una revisión de las medidas de la tasa de sindicalización en Argentina', *Estudios del Trabajo*, **2**.

Landsberger, H., Barrera, M. and Soto, A. (1964), 'The Chilean labor union leader. A preliminary report on his background and attitudes', *Industrial and Labor Relations Review*, **17**(3), 399–420.

Lenguita, P. and Montes Cató, J. (2008), *Resistencias laborales. Experiencias de repolitización del trabajo en Argentina*, Mexico: Picaso.

Levitsky, S. (2005), *La transformación del justicialismo. Del partido sindical al partido clientelista 1983–1989*, Buenos Aires: Siglo 21.

López, D. (2004), *Derechos, trabajo y empleo*, Santiago: LOM.

Lucena, H. and Covarrubias, A. (2006), 'Industrial relations in Latin America', in M.J. Morley, P. Gunnigle and D.G. Collings (eds), *Global Industrial Relations*, Abingdon: Routledge, pp. 53–70.

Marshall, A. (2006), 'Efectos de las regulaciones del trabajo sobre la afiliación sindical. Estudio comparativo de Argentina, Chile y México', *Cuadernos del Ides*, **8**.

Martínez, J. and Díaz, A. (1996), *Chile. The Great Transformation*, Washington, DC: The Brookings Institution.

Martínez, O. (1994), *Pensando la reconversión: Una visión crítica de la flexibilidad y la calidad total*, Buenos Aires: CIPES.

Mizala, A. and Romaguera, P. (2001), 'La legislación laboral y el mercado del trabajo: 1975–2000', in R. French-Davis and B. Stallings (eds), *Reformas, Crecimiento y Políticas en Chile desde 1973*, Santiago: LOM-CEPAL, pp. 201–31.

Monckeberg, M.O. (2001), *El Saqueo de los Grupos Económicos al Estado Chileno*, Santiago: Ediciones B.

Montero, C., Morris, P., De la Barrera, R., Guerra, R. and López, D. (2000), *Tendencias emergentes en la negociación colectiva: El tránsito del contrato al convenio*, available at: http://www.dt.gob.cl/documentacion/1612/article-62881.html; accessed 10 January 2011.

Morris, J.O. and Oyadener, R. (1967), *Afiliación y finanzas sindicales en Chile. 1932–1959*, Santiago: INSORA.

Munck, R. (1994), 'Workers, structural adjustment, and *concertación social* in Latin America', *Latin American Perspectives*, **21**(3), 90–13.

Murillo, M.V. (2001), *Labour Unions, Partisan Coalitions, and Market Reforms in Latin America*, Cambridge and New York: Cambridge University Press.

Novick, M. (2001), 'Nuevas reglas de juego en la Argentina: Competitividad y actores sindicales', in E. Garza Toledo (ed.), *Los sindicatos frente a los procesos de transición política*, Buenos Aires: CLACSO.

Petras, J. and Zeitlin, M. (1967), 'Miners and agrarian radicalism', *American Sociological Review*, **32**(4), 578–86.
Piñera, J. (1990), *La revolución laboral en Chile*, Santiago: Zig-Zag.
Pinto, J. and Salazar, G. (2002), *Historia contemporánea de Chile* (La economía: Mercados, empresarios y trabajadores), Santiago: Lom.
Piva, A. (2005), 'Acumulación de capital, desempleo y sobreocupación en Argentina', *Cuadernos del Sur*, **38/39**.
Pizarro, C. (1986), *La huelga obrera en Chile. 1890–1970*, Santiago: Sur.
Pulso (2007), *ENCLA 2006: Quinta Encuesta Laboral*, Santiago: Dirección del Trabajo.
Ramírez Necochea, H. (1956), *Historia del movimiento obrero. Antecedentes siglo XIX*, Santiago: Editorial Austral.
Roberts, K. (2002), 'Social inequalities without class cleavages in Latin America's neoliberal era', *Studies in Comparative International Development*, **36**(4), 3–33.
Roddick, J. (1989), 'Chile', in J. Carriere, N. Haworth and J. Roddick (eds), *The State, Industrial Relations and the Labour Movement in Latin America*, Vol. 1, Basingstoke: Macmillan, pp. 178–262.
Rojas, J. and Aravena, A. (1999), 'El mundo sindical y el trabajo asalariado en Chile', in P. Escobar (ed.), *Trabajadores y empleo en el Chile de los noventa*, Santiago: LOM Ediciones, pp. 137–222.
Ruiz-Tagle, J. (1989), 'Trade unionism and the state under the Chilean military regime', in E. Epstein (ed.), *Labor Autonomy and the State in Latin America*, London: Unwin Hyman.
Salazar, G. (2003), *Historia de la acumulación capitalista en Chile*, Santiago: Lom.
Schuster, F.L., Pérez, G.J., Pereyra, S., Armesto, M., Armelino, M., García, A., Natalucci, A., Vázquez, M. and Zipcioglu, P. (2006), 'Transformaciones de la protesta social en Argentina, 1989–2003', Grupo de Estudios sobre Protesta Social y Acción Colectiva (GEPSAC), Documento de Trabajo No. 48.
Segall, M. (1953), *Desarrollo del capitalismo en Chile. Cinco ensayos dialécticos*, Santiago Editorial del Pacífico.
Silva, E. (1996a), 'From dictatorship to democracy: The business–state nexus on Chile's economic transformation, 1975–1994', *Comparative Politics*, **28**(3), 299–320.
Silva, E. (1996b), *The State and Capital in Chile: Business Elites, Technocrats, and Market Economics*, Boulder, CO: Westview Press.
Silva, E. (2007), 'The import-substitution model: Chile in comparative perspective', *Latin American Perspectives*, **34**(3), 67–90.
Soto Roy, A. (ed.) (2008), *Flexibilidad laboral y subjetividades: Hacia una comprensión psico-social del empleo contemporáneo*, Santiago: Lom.
Streeck, W. (1987), 'The uncertainties of management in the management of uncertainty: Employers, labor relations and industrial adjustment in the 1980s', *Work, Employment & Society*, **1**(3), 281–308.
Taylor, M. (2004), 'Labour reform and the contradictions of the "Growth with Equity" strategy in postdictatorship Chile', *Latin American Perspectives*, **31**(4), 76–93.
TEL (2009), *Informe Trimestral de Estadisticas Laborales y Economicas*, Buenos Aires: Taller de Estudios Laborales.
Tokman, V. (2007), 'Modernizing the informal sector', *Economic and Social Affairs*, **42**.
Torre, J. (1988), *La vieja guardia sindical*, Buenos Aires: Sudamericana.
Trajtemberg, D. and Attorresi, P. (2005), 'Encuesta de Relaciones Laborales', *Congreso ASET*, **7**, Buenos Aires.
US Department of State (2000), *Hinchey Report: CIA Activities in Chile*, available at: http://www.foia.state.gov/Reports/HincheyReport.asp; accessed 10 January 2011.
US Senate (1975), *Church Report: Covert Action in Chile, 1963–1973*, available at: http://www.foia.state.gov/Reports/ChurchReport; accessed 10 January 2011.
Valenzuela, J.S. (1989), 'Labor movements in transitions to democracy: A framework for analysis', *Comparative Politics*, **21**(4), 445–72.
Villanueva, E. (ed.) (1997), *Empleo y globalización. La nueva cuestión social en la Argentina*, Buenos Aires: Universidad Nacional de Quilmes.

Vocos, F. (2010), 'Transformaciones y conflictos sindicales recientes. Apuntes para el debate sobre la situación actual del movimiento obrero', *II Encuentro Internacional. Teoría y Práctica Política en América Latina. Nuevas Derechas e Izquierdas en el Escenario Nacional*, Mar del Plata.

Walker, F. (2002), *Derecho de las Relaciones Laborales*, Santiago: Editorial Universitaria.

Winn, P. (ed.) (2004), *Victims of the Chilean Miracle: Workers and Neoliberalism in the Pinochet Era, 1973–2002*, Durham and London: Duke University Press.

7 Employment relations in Canada and the US

Sara Slinn and Richard W. Hurd

INTRODUCTION

Employment relations in Canada and the United States (US) share some common features, including founding their modern labour legislation on the model established by the Wagner Act passed in the US in 1935. However, in spite of many similarities, the employment relations systems and experiences of the two countries differ in many key respects. This chapter offers an overview of significant features of employment relations in these countries, highlighting the most significant points of similarity and difference. This is a large task, as these are large countries, with different labour regulations operating at several levels of government and between the public and private sectors. Therefore, this chapter is necessarily an overview that will omit many details, focusing on private sector labour relations regimes at the federal and provincial levels.

OVERVIEW

Canada and the US are both federal states. Canada, the younger of the two nations, achieved independence from Britain in 1867, and patriated a written Constitution including a Charter of Rights and Freedoms in 1982. Canada's federal government, ten provinces and three territories employ a multiparty, parliamentary system of government. Social democratic parties with formal and informal links to labour play a significant role in the nation's politics, regularly forming provincial governments and exercising substantial influence in minority or coalition governments.

The Canadian Constitution assigns primary responsibility for labour relations to the provinces, with the federal government having jurisdiction only over labour relations in specified industries, the government's own employees and employees of federal Crown corporations. Employment in all other industries is regulated by the provinces.[1] Consequently, the federal government regulates employment relations in a limited range of industries (aeronautics, air transport and airports, atomic energy, banking, customs, grain elevators, interprovincial transportation, most railways, postal services, shipping and navigation, telecommunications, television and radio broadcasting) accounting for about 10 percent of the country's workforce.

This constitutional division of authority has produced parallel sets of labour and employment legislation in each Canadian jurisdiction. Each has a basic collective bargaining statute covering the private sector and parts of the public sector. Some jurisdictions have numerous collective bargaining statutes specific to particular segments of the public sector; others include most parts of the public sector within the basic collective bargaining statute. Labour statutes are administered and applied by specialized labour relations boards or, in the case of the province of Québec, a labour court.

The US became independent of Britain in 1776 and adopted its written Constitution in 1788. The federal government and 50 states have a congressional system of government, involving a separately elected President, Congress and judiciary. In contrast to Canada, the US effectively has a two-party system of government and neither the Republican nor Democratic Party is social democratic nor has formal ties with labour. The US Constitution limits federal authority to certain enumerated powers. Most relevant to employment relations is federal jurisdiction over regulating interstate commerce. Unlike in Canada, federal laws and administrative action prevail over those of states where there is a conflict.

The US Constitution's commerce clause limits the federal government's authority to regulate labour relations to those enterprises with operations affecting interstate commerce (US National Labor Relations Board, 1997, p. 33). The federal government, of course, also has constitutional authority to regulate labour relations of its own employees. The constitutional preemption doctrine prohibits state or local regulation of matters that are covered by federal regulation. This has produced a complicated and, compared with Canada, more centralized regulation of labour relations as federal law plays a much larger role. This constitutional division of authority has produced a highly centralized labour relations system in the US.

The federal National Labor Relations Act (NLRA), administered and enforced by the National Labor Relations Board (NLRB), regulates labour relations for enterprises with operations affecting interstate commerce. The NLRA excludes certain categories of workers from the Act: agricultural workers, domestic workers, workers employed by a parent or spouse, government workers, independent contractors, supervisors and workers covered by the 1926 Railway Labor Act (RLA). The RLA, administered by the National Mediation Board, covers airline and railway employees. Moreover, the NLRB has exercised discretion to limit exercise of its authority to those enterprises with operations substantially affecting commerce, gauged by the annual business activity or sales and purchases of the enterprise. The NLRB has established specific standards for different types of enterprises (ibid.). Labour relations in the federal public sector, other than the postal service, are covered by the 1978 Federal Service Labor–Management Relations Act (FSMLRA), administered by the Federal Labor Relations Authority.

States' role in labour relations regulations is limited by the doctrine of preemption, prohibiting states from regulating activities that are already subject to federal regulation. Another preemption principle prohibits states from regulating matters that the federal government does not regulate, but has left to be determined 'by the free play of economic forces' (*Machinists* v. *Wisconsin Employment Relations Commission*, 1976). In general, states are free to regulate most labour relations that are not covered by the NLRA, FSMLRA or RLA. In practice, states may govern labour relations in most non-federal public sector labour relations and in smaller private sector enterprises that don't 'substantially' affect commerce. The preemption doctrines are criticized by some commentators as hindering modernization of labour relations law and as an impediment to achieving a more appropriate balance in labour–management power, while others urge states to realize the full extent of their labour relations jurisdiction to overcome the stagnation of federal labour law reform (see, e.g., Drummonds, 2009).

Though the countries are similar in area, Canada is only about one-tenth the size of the US in terms of population (33.8 million compared with 310.3 million), labour force (18.4 million and 154.2 million) and economy (1.3 trillion USD to 14.4 trillion USD) (CIA, 2010). Both nations are relatively wealthy with per capita GDP of $46 400 USD and $38 400 USD for US and Canada, respectively. Income inequality is higher in the US than in Canada, and is growing in both countries. The US, with a Gini index[2] of 45 (in 2007), is ranked the 42nd highest of 135 nations while Canada, with a Gini index of 32.1 (in 2007), is ranked 100th (CIA, 2010; see Lynk, 2009 regarding the link between this measure and labour standards). The two countries share a lengthy border, and have developed highly integrated economies. Each is the other's largest trading partner and there is a high level of US ownership in Canadian businesses. Forces of globalization, including international free trade agreements, also foster integration between the countries (Free Trade Agreement, 1989 and the North American Free Trade Agreement, 1993).

Labour relations systems in both Canada and the US reflect an industrial pluralist orientation. They provide for collective employee representation based on exclusive majoritarian representation of workers by a union formalized by certification of the bargaining rights by the governing labour relations board or, in Québec, a labour court. Representation is based on the concept of a 'community of interest' among a bargaining unit of workers. Representation is overwhelmingly at the individual workplace level in the private sector (although multi-employer and multi-unit representation and bargaining does occur). This has produced a highly decentralized system of collective labour relations commonly described as the 'Wagner Model', explained further below.

UNIONIZATION

The union structure in both countries is also highly fragmented and decentralized in the private sector and the US public sector, though more centralized in Canada's public sector. Union locals comprise one or more certified units and may be autonomous, holding no affiliation with a larger union structure. Most locals belong to national or international unions headquartered in another country, and most unions belong to central labour bodies. In turn, these central labour organizations are often affiliated to international labour organizations such as the International Trade Union Confederation.

In Canada, national, international and independent unions represent 67.1, 27.7 and 3.8 percent of union membership, respectively (HRSDC, 2009). Many unions are affiliated with central labour organizations, and some international unions in Canada are affiliated with both US and Canadian central labour organizations. Primary among these central bodies are the Canada Labour Congress, with 3.2 million members representing 70.7 percent of union membership, and the Confédération des Syndicats Nationaux, with over 300 000 members, representing 6.6 percent of union membership (ibid.).

The structure of the union movement is similar in the US. The country's 15.3 million union members are represented by 30 000 local unions. Of these about 1000 are independent locals, with the remainder affiliated with a national union. There are 96 national unions; among these most major private sector unions also operate in Canada and are therefore international. The two major central bodies are the American Federation of Labor and Congress of Industrial Organizations (AFL-CIO) established in 1955, and Change to Win (CTW) established in 2005. The AFL-CIO includes 57 affiliated national unions, and 50 percent of the country's union members. Although only four unions currently belong to CTW, three are among the nation's largest and this federation includes about 25 percent of US union members. There are also 35 independent national unions, including the National Education Association, which is the largest US union. These independent national unions combined with the unaffiliated local unions make up about 25 percent of represented workers (Masters et al., 2006, pp. 479, 491–2; Gifford, 2010).

Despite the many similarities and interdependence between Canada and the US, significant and in some cases growing, differences in labour relations exist that researchers struggle to explain adequately. For example: the workforce participation rate in Canada has been higher than that in the US since early 2002; employment growth in Canada has outpaced that in the US since 2002; and, since mid-2002 the Canadian employment rate has exceeded that of the US (Statistics Canada, 2009). One of the most puzzling disparities is union density.

Union density rates, and the pattern of changes in density, have long differed between the two countries. Growth of unionization followed a similar path in the two countries from the 1920s until the early 1950s, with union density exceeding 30 percent in both. Growth in Canadian union density lagged that of the US over this time. A period of slow decline followed in both countries. In the 1960s the trajectories of the two countries parted ways and have continued to diverge. US union membership rates began a steep decline, while they reversed and rose in Canada, reaching a zenith of about 40 percent, then stagnated and began a slow decline in the 1980s. While union membership continues to fall in the US, apart from a brief pause from 2006–08, after falling to about 30 percent in Canada in 2001 union density has remained relatively stable around that level (Kettler et al., 1990; Riddell, 1993; Statistics Canada, 2009).[3]

By 2008, both the rate of union membership and union coverage in Canada was more than double that in the US (29.4 percent compared with 12.4 percent, and 31.5 percent compared with 13.7 percent) (Table 7.1). While public sector union membership and coverage are much higher than that of private sector workers in each country, it is notable how much more unionized the Canadian public sector is compared with that of the US (74.5 percent compared with 40.7 percent union coverage), and how low US private sector unionization is (8.4 percent union coverage compared with 17.9 percent union coverage in Canada) (Table 7.1).

In both countries, union membership rates vary widely among states and provinces. In the US the average union membership rate among US states was 12.3 percent in 2009, but union density among states ranged from a low of 3.1 percent in North Carolina to a high of 25.2 percent in New York (US Bureau of Labor Statistics, 2010). Among Canadian provinces the average rate of union membership was 30.6 percent, with rates varying from 22.7 percent in Alberta to 36.8 percent in Newfoundland and Labrador in 2008 (Statistics Canada, 2009).

Table 7.1   Union membership and coverage, Canada and US

	Canada (2008)		US (2008)	
	Union membership (%)	Union coverage (%)	Union membership (%)	Union coverage (%)
All workforce	29.4	31.5	12.4	13.7
Male	28.7	31.1	13.4	14.5
Female	30.0	31.9	11.4	12.9
Public sector	71	74.5	36.8	40.7
Private sector	16.3	17.9	7.6	8.4

Note: Canada, as percentage of workforce age 15 and over. US, as percentage of workforce age 16 and over.

Sources: Statistics Canada, 2009; US Bureau of Labor Statistics, 2010.

DEVELOPMENT OF LABOUR RELATIONS REGULATION

Collective bargaining legislation is a relatively recent development in the US and Canada. It was not until well into the twentieth century that collective worker action or trade unions enjoyed legal protection. Until then, unions and their activities were regarded as illegal civil or criminal conspiracies interfering with trade and were frequently subject to court injunctions. By the mid-nineteenth century and early twentieth century common law and legislative changes in both countries repealed these laws or no longer applied them to unions.[4]

The first statute in the US granting positive rights for collective worker activity in the private sector was the 1926 Railway Labor Act, administered by the National Mediation Board (NMB) and introduced to address conflict in the railway industry. It established employee rights to engage in collective union action, but lacked a union recognition process, rendering it ineffective (Budd, 2002, p. 165). In 1934 amendments to the RLA restricted employer-dominated unions and introduced a secret ballot election union recognition process administered by the NMB (ibid.).

Broader labour legislation arose out of the economic and social crisis of the Great Depression, and President Roosevelt's 'New Deal' program. In 1933 the National Industrial Recovery Act (NIRA) was passed. Among its provisions was creation of industry-specific codes of conduct, including the requirement that each code contain a specific provision giving employees the right to organize and bargain collectively, through freely chosen representatives, and the right to be protected from employer interference with these activities. However, NIRA proved ineffective at establishing collective rights as the administering National Labor Board lacked specific enforcement authority (ibid., p. 163). In 1935 the US Supreme Court found NIRA unconstitutional as an overly broad regulation of economic activity (*Schecter Poultry Corp.* v. *United States*, 1935).

That same year, 1935, the National Labor Relations Act (NLRA, referred to as the 'Wagner Act' after Senator Wagner whose efforts produced this legislation) was passed. The NLRA's introductory section, entitled 'Finding and Policies', explicitly stated that the Act was an economic tool intended to increase purchasing power and, therefore, the deflationary effect of economic depression, by enabling unions to engage in collective bargaining. As James Gross notes though, '[T]his may have been a pragmatic choice to make passage of the highly contested Wagner Act possible, rather than reflecting the true intention of the Act's framers' (see Gross, 1974, pp. 144–7).

The Wagner Act provides workers with the right to bargain collectively with their freely chosen representative, prohibits employer interference with the organizing and administration of unions and provides remedies for violation of the Act; the Act is administered by the National Labor Relations Board. Notably, the Act provides for exclusive representation of a bargaining unit of employees, who share a community of interest, if the union establishes support of the majority of workers in that unit through a certification process. This is referred to as 'exclusive majoritarian representation'. The Act survived a number of constitutional challenges in its early years, and was finally confirmed as constitutional in 1937 with the Supreme Court's decision in *NLRB* v. *Jones and Laughlin Steel Corp.*

The Wagner Act was amended in 1947 by the Labor–Management Relations Act (referred to as the 'Taft-Hartley' Act). In an effort by conservative forces to reset the balance between union and management rights the amendments: introduced union unfair labour practices; prohibited closed shop agreements; increased individual rights; introduced express employer rights; and, amended the dispute resolution procedure (Budd, 2002, pp. 176–81). The Taft-Hartley amendments are widely regarded as tilting the balance in management's favour. In 1959 the Landrum-Griffin Act amendments to the Wagner Act focused on regulating internal union affairs to increase union democracy and combat corruption. These amendments grew out of concern ignited by the highly publicized problems with organized crime and the Teamsters and several other unions in the 1950s. This Act also limited the NLRB voting rights of permanently replaced striking workers to the first 12 months of a strike, increased restrictions on secondary boycotts, prohibited hot cargo agreements and prohibited union recognition picketing (ibid., pp. 181–4).

Other than expansion of the Act in 1974 to cover the healthcare industry, the Wagner Act has not been significantly revised since 1959, though several efforts have been made to introduce amendments.[5] It remains the key piece of US private sector labour legislation today and significantly influenced Canadian labour legislation. The key principles of this Act form a distinctive North American or Wagner Model of labour relations regulation.

Industrial strife and the federal government's determined economic vision for uniting Canada, rather than economic depression, catalyzed and shaped introduction of comprehensive labour legislation in this country (Kettler et al., 1990, p. 176; Webber, 1991). The roots of Canadian labour legislation, established in the early twentieth century, produced a distinctively Canadian approach to labour regulation, which continues to this day to include an ostensibly neutral role for the state coupled with regular state intervention in the name of the public interest, and compulsory conciliation and other mechanisms to discourage industrial disputes and promote compromise (Kettler et al., 1990, pp. 176–7; Webber, 1991, p. 57). The primary concern of Canadian labour law has been to secure industrial peace, not necessarily to promote unionization or workers' rights (Kettler et al., 1990, p. 176).

The defining pieces of labour legislation are commonly regarded as the federal Conciliation Act in 1900 and the 1907 Industrial Disputes Investigations Act (IDIA), which firmly established the Canadian policy of compulsory conciliation.[6] The Conciliation Act introduced a system of voluntary, government-assisted, conciliation. Though several provinces had experimented unsuccessfully with conciliation and arbitration legislation for industrial disputes in the late 1800s, it didn't influence the later federal legislation (Webber, 1991, pp. 20–21). Compulsory conciliation was the focus of these statutes; compulsory recognition was not legislated until after World War II.

The IDIA was passed in effort to secure industrial peace following strikes in several industries in the early 1900s. The IDIA made conciliation administered by a conciliation board a mandatory precondition to legal work stoppages. Conciliation boards investigated and reported on disputes, issuing recommendations for resolution and settlement. The IDIA was later extended to industries beyond the original mines and public utilities. In 1925, the IDIA was found to be unconstitutional as the federal government had exceeded its constitutional jurisdiction by regulating matters under provincial jurisdiction (*The Toronto Electric Commission* v. *Snider*, 1925). Many provinces then passed equivalent legislation.

Concern over threats to wartime production from a wave of strikes in 1943 impelled the federal government to exercise its wartime emergency powers to introduce the 1944 Wartime Labour Relations Regulations (referred to as 'PC 1003'), covering not only federal but also provincial industries. PC 1003 contained many elements of the Wagner Act and the IDIA, combining the Canadian preference for forcefully encouraging compromise and discouraging work stoppages, with elements of the Wagner Act such as compulsory union recognition, good faith bargaining requirements, unfair labour practices (ULPs) prohibitions and a labour tribunal to administer the legislation. PC 1003 and the Wagner Act were the models for the postwar labour statutes adopted in each Canadian jurisdiction. As Kettler et al. note:

> In contrast to the American Wagner Act experience, the Canadian move towards compulsory union recognition remained devoid of any stated intention to promote union growth either as a desirable democratic objective or as an economic recovery strategy. As in the past, the prime motivation remained the containment of industrial unrest. (1990, pp. 178–9)

They also note Canada's approach to regulating labour:

> 'Compulsion' has been the state's characteristic response to such conflicts, in the form of the compulsory conciliation and 'cooling off periods' of the Industrial Disputes Investigation Act (IDIA) in 1907, the compulsory union recognition and collective bargaining under P.C. 1003 in World War II or, more recently, compulsory back-to-work legislation in the 1970s and 1980s. (Ibid., pp. 176–7).

COMPARATIVE LABOUR RELATIONS

A large literature has developed addressing the divergent paths of union density rates between the countries, and trying to discern whether Canada is on its own trajectory or is simply lagging the downward path of US unionization (see, e.g., Troy, 1992, 2000, 2001; Riddell, 1993; Taras, 2001; Godard, 2003, 2009). Some explanations focus on 'demand' for unionization; others on the 'supply' of union representation.[7] The 'union density decline and convergence' thesis contends that union density is falling as a result of market forces and pressures for flexibilization, and that the US experience is not exceptional, but is simply leading an inevitable worldwide decline in unionization. Eventually union density in other countries will converge with that in the US. This transformation may be temporarily obscured in Canada because it has much higher union density in its public sector than does the US, and because Canada tends to lag the US. A key promoter of this view is Leo Troy (1992, 2000, 2001; see Godard, 2003 for a comprehensive response). Godard's (2003, pp. 485–6) study discerned little support for the density decline and convergence thesis, noting that though Canada has seen a decline in union density, it is concentrated in the private sector, has been much slower than in the US and this decline was concentrated in the late 1970s and early 1980s (a time of rapid economic change) and in two years (1992–93 and 1998–99), which Godard attributes to significant anti-union changes in law and policy in the largest province, Ontario, rather than market forces. If the density decline and convergence thesis is correct, then changes in labour law or other supply-side factors will not reverse or stay the decline.

Demand-side Explanations: Union Density

Demand-side explanations focus on structural changes to the economy and possible changes in workers' desire for unionization. Structural changes in employment including decline in highly unionized industries and occupations coupled with growth of industries associated with lows rates of unionization, and the growth of part-time employment, are forces at work in both countries.

Some studies also identify decreasing worker demand for unionization as an important cause of declining union density in the US (e.g., Farber and Western, 2001). However, this explanation is difficult to reconcile with the large body of survey evidence demonstrating that not only does a substantial proportion of US workers desire union representation, but that demand for unionization is about the same or higher than that found among workers in Canada (see Bowden, 1989; Freeman and Rogers, 1995, 1999, 2006; Lipset and Meltz, 1998; Gomez et al., 2001). Gomez et al. (2001, p. 8) also conclude, based on survey evidence, that while there is a degree of over-representation of workers in Canada, that this is relatively less crucial than the under-representation of workers in the US.

Some of the most powerful empirical support for supply-side arguments is provided by the work of Gomez et al. (2001), estimating that 67 percent of the difference in union density between the two countries in the 1990s was due to unsatisfied demand for union representation of US workers. Ninety percent of Canadians wanting representation are unionized, compared with 39 percent in the US. These authors calculated that a worker in Canada who wants union representation is 137 percent more likely to be unionized than a worker in the US who wants representation. Moreover, the authors predicted that if unsatisfied demand for union representation was satisfied in both countries, union density would be 4 percentage points higher in Canada, and 23 percentage points higher in the US than it was at the time the survey was conducted in 1996 (ibid., p. 8).

Supply-side Explanations: Union Density

A wide array of factors relating to the 'supply' of union representation has been proposed to explain the union density difference. These include legal, policy, political, governmental and administrative differences; different labour movement strategies; differences in managerial resistance to unions and historical differences.

Legal and policy environment: substantive law and administration
Differences in labour laws between the two countries are regarded by many as the leading explanation for decline in union density and the persistent Canada–US difference (see, e.g., Weiler, 1983, 1984; Bruce, 1989, 1990; Block, 1994; Taras, 1997; Sack, 2010).[8] Labour law and enforcement in the US is regarded as obstructing unionization, and not supportive or sufficiently protective of workers, even once union representation is obtained; also, Canadian labour standards are generally higher than those in the US (Block, 2003). John Godard's (2003, p. 486) comprehensive analysis of the issue concludes that labour law is the principal factor explaining the union density difference between US and Canada, and that Canadian-style labour law reforms may be essential to revitalizing US unionization. Kettler et al. (1990, pp. 167, 179) maintain that the explanation for union density difference lies not in the laws, per se, but in the different historical developments of labour laws in the two countries, which may have protected Canadian laws from being gutted in the 'postwar legislative backlash' suffered by US labour law and from which it has never recovered.

The labour law differences most commonly identified as crucially influencing unionization include differences in certification processes, access to unionization, ULPs regulation, first contract arbitration provisions, protection of successor rights, union security, the duty to bargain and regulation of work stoppages. A recent development, beginning in 2001 with the Supreme Court of Canada decision in *Dunmore* v. *Ontario (Attorney General)*, is that the Charter-protected freedom of association has undergone significant redefinition, providing more protection for labour relations. The Charter freedom of expression also protects some labour relations activities. The US Constitution and Bill of Rights provides little significant protection to unions or their activities.

Beginning in the early 2000s the Supreme Court of Canada has issued a series of decisions that have led to an express rejection by the Court of decades of jurisprudence holding that the freedom of association in the

Constitution's Charter of Rights and Freedoms did not extend to protection of collective bargaining. The Charter freedom of association is now expressly recognized as protecting the right to bargain collectively and to access collective representation. The Charter freedom of expression has also been explicitly applied to protect picketing and leafleting (Sack, 2010, p. 245).

Meanwhile, neither the US constitutional protection of freedom of association nor free speech has been applied to protect workers beyond protection of consumer leafleting and informational picketing. In fact, the protection of free speech has been used to support protection of employer anti-union speech, and to limit legislative protection from such anti-union employer action (see Story, 1995).

Certification   All federal US labour legislation requires unions to win a majority of ballots cast in a representation vote in order to be certified as the exclusive bargaining agent for a bargaining unit of employees, although some state legislation permits unionization without a vote. Representation elections are significantly more difficult for unions to win than card-check certification procedures, which permit unionization based on signed membership card evidence rather than an election (Johnson, 2002; Riddell, 2004; Slinn, 2004). At one time card-check certification was widespread in Canada and it was regarded as a distinctive feature of Canadian labour law. However, only four provinces and the federal jurisdiction now employ card-check certification. The remaining six provinces have adopted 'quick' mandatory representation votes. The expedited nature of Canadian 'quick' votes distinguishes it from US-style representation votes, which are associated with lengthy delays. The median time between petition (or application) for certification and representation vote under the NLRA, for example, declined from approximately 50 days to 37 days (US Dept. of Labor, 1994, p. 68; US National Labor Relations Board, 2009). 'Quick' votes are held within a short statutory time limit, generally falling within five to ten days from the date of application.[9] Research demonstrates that delay in the certification process, even under 'quick' vote systems, substantially reduces the certification win rate (Campolieti et al., 2007; Riddell, 2010).

Access to unionization   US labour legislation excludes supervisors from unionization. In contrast, Canadian labour laws take a flexible approach to permitting supervisors to unionize, either in separate or mixed units with non-supervisory employees. Labour boards enquire, on a case by case basis, into whether the supervisors in question actually perform managerial functions such that concerns over conflict of interest and loyalty to management make it necessary to exclude the supervisors from collective representation.

While both US and Canadian labour statutes explicitly exclude certain types of workers from unionization, recent Canadian court decisions have expanded the protection of the Charter freedom of association to include the right to access to collective representation (e.g., *Dunmore* v. *Ontario (Attorney-General)*, 2001; *Mounted Police Association of Ontario* v. *Canada (Attorney General)*, 2009). These decisions have struck down statutory exclusions from unionization, and prompted the federal and some provincial governments to pass statutes providing collective representation or bargaining to these formerly excluded workers (e.g., Ontario's Agricultural Employees Protection Act, 2002 and Colleges Collective Bargaining Act, 2008; and the proposed federal Royal Canadian Mounted Police Modernization Act, Bill C-43). The US Constitution does not protect access to collective representation or bargaining.

ULP regulation   Plenty of evidence exists of widespread and effective employer resistance and ULPs during union organizing in both the US and Canada under both representation election and 'quick' vote certification processes (see, e.g., Freeman, 1985; Riddell, 2001; Bentham, 2002). In the US, researchers attribute about 40 percent of the fall in unionization to increased employer anti-union activities (Freeman, 1985). What is not so clear is whether the prevalence or seriousness of the anti-union conduct is greater in the US than in Canada, though that is generally believed to be the case.

Although US managerial attitudes are often thought to be more negative towards unionization than those in Canada, the evidence is mixed. Some studies show Canadian employers can generally be described as adopting the 'union acceptance strategy' compared with most US companies, which take a 'union removal' approach, and that US companies operating in Canada do not generally bring US-style anti-union tactics with them (Thompson, 2009, p. 115). However, other research indicates that many Canadian employers hold anti-union preferences that they readily express, and that they adopt union avoidance strategies including, in a surprising proportion of instances, knowingly committing unfair labour practices (Saporta and Lincoln, 1995; Thompson, 1995; Bentham, 2002). One distinctly US feature of employer union avoidance is the development of a large and powerful union avoidance industry providing consulting services to help employers defeat or avoid union organizing (see Logan, 2002, 2006). So far, that industry has not apparently established a significant presence in Canada.

Canadian labour law does restrict employer anti-union conduct during union organizing more strictly than US law, especially employer communications with workers. Even though most Canadian labour legislation expressly protects employer speech, these provisions are limited by ULP prohibitions on coercive or intimidating conduct and employer speech remains quite restricted, compared with under the NLRA. Captive audience meetings and employer communications are strictly scrutinized and speech that, in other contexts, would not constitute a ULP, may be found to be illegal in these circumstances. As Taras (1997) notes, these limitations exist even where the statutory language is identical to the NLRB Taft-Hartley free speech protections. Challenges to these limitations as unconstitutional violations of employers' Charter-protected freedom of expression have failed, in contrast to the situation in the US, where limitations on employer speech have been foiled for decades on the basis of protection of employers' constitutional free speech rights (see Slinn, 2008a).

ULP complaint processing is also regarded as faster and fairer in Canada (see Bruce, 1990, p. 483; Block, 1993), including a reverse onus falling on employers in some circumstances to establish that their impugned conduct is not unlawful (Sack, 2010). At times some provinces have employed even faster 'expedited' ULP processing rules for alleged misconduct during union organizing, which have proved to significantly reduce the negative effects of employer ULP on the certification success (Campolieti et al., 2007).[10]

Labour relations boards in both the US and Canada are authorized to order a wide range of remedies to provide compensatory remedies for ULPs and other labour law violations, but cannot issue punitive remedies. Canadian labour law provides more remedial options than in the US and greater access to remedial certification and interim remedies, including interim reinstatement of terminated employees. However, remedies are criticized as inadequate and labour boards are criticized as failing to exercise their full remedial authority (Compa, 2002; Dannin, 2005; Slinn, 2008b). Moreover, Canadian labour legislation contains 'offence' provisions imposing substantial monetary penalties for refusing or neglecting to comply with a labour board order, or, in some jurisdictions, failing to comply with the legislation.[11] However, these penalty provisions are rarely invoked or applied (Slinn, 2008b, p. 708). Finally, Canadian labour board decisions may be filed in the superior courts, becoming a court order enforceable through contempt proceedings (Sack, 2010).

First contract arbitration   Many Canadian jurisdictions include first contract arbitration provisions in their general legislation. These provisions permit a union or employer to apply to have a first collective agreement imposed through interest arbitration. These provisions were first introduced in Canada in the early 1970s in an effort to reduce the conflict and disruption of especially bitter first negotiations occurring in the healthcare industry (Backhouse, 1980). Canadian studies of the outcomes of first contract arbitration find little support for fears that this process leads to unstable bargaining relationships (see, e.g., Sexton, 1987; Black and Hosea, 1994), and a recent study found that the presence of first contract arbitration provisions in a jurisdiction was associated with a significantly lower incidence of work stoppages (Johnson, 2008). First contract arbitration is not available in US labour legislation, although it is estimated that 30 to 50 percent of first negotiations in the US fail to reach agreement, and although it is strongly supported by some academics introduction of such provisions into the NLRA has been bitterly opposed by employers (see, e.g., Epstein, 2009; Fisk, 2009).

Successor rights   Unlike under US labour law, bargaining rights and collective agreements are protected in Canada where there is a sale or transfer of the business. In the US, successor employers are not required to respect a predecessor employer's collective agreements. Successors are only required to bargain with the union and even then only if the following conditions are met: a majority of the successor's workforce was employed by the predecessor; there is substantial continuity in the nature of the business; and the bargaining unit is still appropriate (see Sack, 2010, p. 249).

Union security provisions   Taras and Ponak (2001) contend that widespread existence of agency shop union security provisions as a statutory default in Canada is an important explanatory factor in US–Canada union density differences. Under agency shop provisions only dues payment, not union membership, is required of all employees in a bargaining unit. In the US, there is no statutory union security default and 'closed shop' provisions are prohibited. Twenty-two states have also passed 'Right-to-Work' legislation prohibiting any requirement that employees either join a union or pay union dues. Critics contend that Right-to-Work laws encourage free-ridership, weakening unions that are still obligated, under the duty of fair representation, to represent all employees in the bargaining unit whether or not they are members or pay dues (see Farber, 1984). In contrast, no Canadian jurisdiction prohibits parties from negotiating 'closed shop' security provisions, whereby only union members may be hired, or any other form of union security, and no jurisdiction has adopted Right-to-Work legislation.[12]

Duty to bargain   Employers and unions have a duty to bargain once the union has been certified for the bargaining unit, and one party has given notice to commence bargaining. US labour law categorizes topics of bargaining as either mandatory or permissive, and the duty applies only to the former category. This duty is much broader under Canadian law and has recently been recognized as protected under the Charter's freedom of association guarantee. Canadian law does not distinguish between different categories of bargaining topics and the duty applies to all matters the parties could include in an agreement (George Adams, 1993, para. 10.1470). However, a party may violate the duty by pressing to impasse a term that the other party could not reasonably be expected to accept, such as a demand that the union agrees to a clause immunizing employees who crossed the picket line from union sanctions, or to a clause prohibiting the union from filing a grievance to challenge the termination of striking workers (*Royal Oak Mines Inc.* v. *Canada (Labour Relations Board)*, 1996; George Adams, 1993, para. 10.1470). In 2007 the Supreme Court of Canada explicitly rejected two decades of its jurisprudence to redefine the Charter protection of freedom of association as encompassing the right to bargain collectively (*Health Services and Support – Facilities Subsector Bargaining Assn.* v. *British Columbia*, 2007). Collective bargaining receives no constitutional protection in the US.

Work stoppages   Canadian labour legislation imposes more restrictions on work stoppages than does the NLRA, prohibiting recognition strikes and work stoppages during the life of a collective agreement. Substantial procedural preconditions are imposed on parties before a strike or lockout is legal, including strike votes, notice, cooling-off periods and mediation, conciliation or interest arbitration processes. Echoing the compulsory conciliation policy established in the IDIA, these preconditions are intended to discourage work stoppages and encourage settlement. Union recognition strikes were made illegal in the US in 1947, but mid-term work stoppages are not prohibited in the US. However, collective agreements commonly include no strike clauses that prohibit such stoppages, and impose notice periods before any job actions; also, most union constitutions include strike vote procedures (Sack, 2010). In addition, unions in railroads and airlines are covered under separate legislation in the US, which imposes multiple hurdles before strikes are allowed.

Replacement workers   Unlike under US labor law, employers in Canada do not have an unrestricted ability to permanently replace striking workers. This prohibition is explicit in the statutes of two provinces (Manitoba and Prince Edward Island); elsewhere the effect of other rights and prohibitions is to prohibit permanent replacement workers. Many jurisdictions also include a statutory guarantee for striking employees of a right to return to work at the end of the work stoppage, with limited exceptions such as where the work is no longer being performed. Some provinces impose a time limit on this right, such as within six months (Ontario) or two years (Alberta) of a strike. In jurisdictions lacking express rights to return to work, length of use of replacement workers is limited by good faith requirements (Annis, 2009, p. 165).

The most restrictive approaches are found in legislation in Québec and British Columbia, which strictly limit use of temporary replacement workers. Although these provisions are often described as 'bans' this is not accurate, as neither jurisdiction provides for a complete ban on replacement workers. There is evidence that these strike replacement restrictions increases the incidence of strikes, but reduces strike length (Duffy and Johnson, 2009). The federal jurisdiction imposes a much more limited restriction on temporary replacement workers, prohibiting unit work being done by employees who were not unit employees on the date of notice to bargain was given 'for the demonstrated purpose of undermining a trade union's representational capacity rather than the pursuit of legitimate bargaining objectives'(*Canada Labour Code*, 1985, Section 94(2.1)).

Secondary picketing   Secondary picketing (picketing at a location other than at the primary employer's place of business) is dealt with in a variety of ways across Canada. Although labour legislation expressly addresses secondary picketing in some jurisdictions, in others it does not. In these situations the matters are regulated by the common law in courts, not by labour boards. For many years the common law treated secondary picketing as a tort and, therefore, illegal per se. This was expressly overruled in the 2002 Supreme Court of Canada *RWDSU, Local 558* v. *Pepsi-Cola Canada Beverages (West) Ltd* decision, which held that secondary picketing is legal per se, and that the common law includes the right to picket as part of the freedom of expression constitutionally protected by the Charter of Rights.[13] Labour statutes in other jurisdictions expressly regulate picketing and continue to do so even after the *Pepsi-Cola* decision. In these provinces secondary picketing is restricted with exceptions allowing picketing of allies and common sites. The 1947 amendments to the NLRA specifically forbid secondary strikes and boycotts in the US, but consumer boycotts are allowed. In both the US and Canada, leafleting and informational picketing are protected activities.

Government structure
A strong and continuing influence operating in opposite directions on labour law in the two countries has arisen from effect of the constitutional allocation of authority for labour relations and the structure of

government on the ease of legislative change. First, reform of federal legislation requires national consensus. Second, separation of executive and legislative branches of government under the US Congressional system of government makes it difficult to pass or amend legislation where special interest groups object, even where political consensus exists (Carter, 1992, pp. 4–5). Legislation must pass both Houses of Congress and be approved by the President to succeed. Situations where different parties control the Senate, House of Representatives and Presidency can lead to legislation being hampered or blocked for partisan reasons. Furthermore, in the Senate final votes on legislation are not allowed until debate has ended, and it takes 60 votes (out of 100) to stop debate. This practice allows the minority party to block unacceptable legislation, and has been used to block reform each time new labour legislation has been introduced since 1974. The net effect is that Canada has developed a diversity of frequently changing labour laws, while the US has highly centralized, stagnant labour statutes.

In a large country such as the US with substantial regional differences, but primarily federal control of labour relations and the hurdle of Congressional and Presidential approval, consensus is a difficult task and labour reform is hard to achieve and infrequent (Sack, 2010, p. 242). These features have acted as powerful brakes on legislative reform. A telling example is that the federal NLRA has been amended only three times since its inception in 1935, despite many more attempts.[14]

In Canada, primarily provincial authority over labour matters is a powerful decentralizing force and the absence of a need for national consensus and the Parliamentary system make legislative change more feasible. Commentators disagree about whether the legislative diversity it has fostered has benefited or hampered labour relations. Some view it as a positive feature, crediting it for more union- and worker-friendly laws, as a source of flexibility and innovation allowing each jurisdiction to operate as individual laboratories experimenting with different options, with successful innovations being adopted by other jurisdictions and failures being discarded, and producing solutions tailored to regional characteristics (Weiler, 1980, p. 11; 1986, p. 26; Carter, 1992, pp. 4–5; Sack, 2010, p. 242).

On the other hand, readily achievable legislative change can also produce regressive reforms, facilitating partisan and immoderate changes and encouraging pendulum swings in legislation in tandem with changes in government, instead of encouraging constructive innovation (Burkett, 1998; Lynk, 2009). Decentralized federalism may also be a restraining influence that has prevented development of national industrial relations policies that are necessary to effectively address the many inter-provincial disputes (Woods, 1977, p. 10), or to respond to global influences and challenges demanding coherent responses and national strategies, instead of simply producing 'a costly multiplication of nearly identical schemes' (Adams, 1984, p. 221). Decentralization also causes difficulty with Canada's role in international labour relations. While the federal government may ratify an international labour standards convention it cannot compel the provinces to adopt the convention or ensure that provincial legislation accords with those standards.

Tribunals: structure and functioning
Labour tribunals are composed differently in Canada and the US, affecting the boards' operation and their influence on labour law. Labour boards in several Canadian provinces are 'bipartite' or 'tripartite' boards: composed of equal numbers of decision-makers representing labour, management and, in the case of tripartite boards, neutrals representing the public. Board chairs are appointed by government. This is regarded as making it more likely that the concerns and interests of the parties will be properly considered, fosters acceptability of board decisions and creates 'commitment in the parties of interest to the workability of the system' (George W. Adams as quoted in Block, 1994, p. 256). Boards in other Canadian jurisdictions are non-partisan, or neutral, also with government-appointed chairs (George Adams, 1993). US labour boards have a very different composition. For example, the NLRB is made up of five political appointees appointed by the President with the advice and consent of Senate, and the NLRB's general counsel is also a political appointment. In contrast, as Block (1994, p. 255) notes, the NLRB is not charged with producing a workable labour relations system.

Some commentators charge that the NLRB board structure leads to politicized and partisan decision-making, such that true labour law change in the US tends to come about through wide swings in NLRB interpretation of the legislation rather than actual legislative change. This fosters instability in labour policy and lack of respect for the NLRB. It also obscures what should be separate roles for legislators, the NLRB and the courts in regulating labour, and allows Congress to cede its proper role in labour law and policy-making to the NLRB and courts (Gross, 1994, p. 49). A substantial body of empirical research has found bias and political influence in the NLRB's processing and decision-making in ULP cases (Moe, 1985; Cooke et al., 1995; Schmidt, 2002). No similar research has been done on Canadian labour boards, however; politicized appointments and terminations of labour board vice-chairs have attracted criticism and litigation (Burkett, 1998; Ellis, 1998; Ellis and Mackenzie, 2009).

A final important difference between Canadian and US labour boards is that Canadian labour board decisions are protected from judicial review by strong privative clauses; as a result Canadian labour board decisions are much less commonly appealed to or overturned by courts preserving boards' primacy in labour regulation (Bruce, 1990, pp. 503–5; Block, 2003).

Grievance arbitration

Canadian labour legislation requires that every collective agreement contain a provision for final and binding arbitration of disputes arising out of the collective agreement. Arbitration hearings are open to the public, subject to the arbitrator's discretion, and statutes require arbitrators to file awards so that they are publicly available. Jeffrey Sack notes, 'The situation in the US must surely work to the disadvantage of the development of arbitral jurisprudence . . . There is no question that Canadian arbitral jurisprudence has benefited greatly from the unfettered publication of arbitration awards' (2010, p. 252).[15] Arbitrators are expected to consider the public interest and not just parties' private interests. The Supreme Court of Canada has granted increasing judicial deference to arbitration and widened arbitral jurisdiction, including requiring arbitrators to consider and apply external statutes (Sack, 2010, pp. 251–6).

In contrast, US legislation doesn't require arbitration clauses in collective agreements (except under the RLA and some state public sector laws), hearings are private, decisions are not publicly accessible and many arbitrators take the position that external laws are simply interpretive aids, and should not influence their decisions unless the statute has been incorporated by reference into the agreement (ibid., pp. 253–5).

Labour movement strategies

Some commentators point to differing political characteristics of unions in the two countries as part of the explanation for higher union density in Canada. Canadian unions are described as more innovative, and more energetic at organizing than US unions (Rose and Chaison, 1990; Kettler et al., 1991, pp. 174–6; Kumar and Schenk, 2006). Other explanations credit Canadian unions' broader social agenda and greater effectiveness at attaining beneficial political and policy changes (Piore, 1983; Bruce, 1989), while others suggest that it is the more favourable Canadian public policy environment that allows unions to achieve such successes (Taras, 2001, p. 155).

What may be critical to more agreeable legislation and policy is that Canadian unions have historically enjoyed a close alliance with social democratic parties at both the provincial and federal level, sometimes including formal, constitutional links with the party (Carter, 1992, p. 5) – the federal and provincial New Democratic Party (NDP), founded in 1961 as an alliance between the Cooperative Commonwealth Federation and the Canada Labour Congress (CLC), and the Parti Québécois in the province of Québec. The resulting political leverage is credited for Canadian unions' greater success in obtaining a favourable legislative environment (e.g., Carter, 1992; Sack, 2010). However, some warn that the NDP, at least, has lost popular support and is no longer an effective source of political influence for unions (Taras, 2001, p. 155).

Such alliances can be a significant advantage for labour compared with countries such as the US, which lacks a viable social democratic party, and where no party has formal links with organized labour. In the US two-party system labour must look to the Democratic Party for support, though conservative elements in that party have repeatedly foiled labour's agendas (Carter, 1992, p. 6).

Apart from the question of the continuing political strength of Canadian social democratic parties, labour's influence over these parties is waning as ties with these parties unravel. Beginning in the mid-1990s increasing tensions and abrupt ruptures and repudiations of these alliances have occurred. Some labour groups have renounced their party allegiance; also, the NDP publicly has publicly rethought the necessity – or even desirability – of labour support. At the same time, many within organized labour regard the NDP as having betrayed workers and unions. This rift has expressed itself in unions' strategic voting campaigns supporting other parties,[16] public repudiation of leaders or the party and an attempt by one provincial NDP to reduce labour's formal role in the party.

US labour's traditional approach has been to focus on wages, benefits and other terms and conditions of employment, earning the label 'business unionism'. Indeed, historically and to some extent in the current era many labour leaders have eschewed political action, or at best viewed it as relatively unimportant. However, with rapid decline of union density in the 1980s there was a noticeable shift in union strategy with more emphasis placed on both political action and organizing/recruitment, though representation of current members remained the priority.

In 1995 the forces for change prevailed, and John Sweeney was elected as president of the AFL-CIO based on the promise to 'organize, organize, organize'. Under Sweeney's leadership the federation indeed promoted the organizing priority, and also increased the sophistication of its political operation. However, organizing stalled and political activism was not rewarded with any substantive shift in labour policy (Masters et al., 2006, pp. 481, 485; Hurd, 2009b). Labour's allies in the Democratic Party were thwarted not only by the Republican opposition, but also by lack of consensus in their own ranks.

In 2005, frustrated by labour's continuing decline, six unions left the

AFL-CIO, and, joined by a large independent union, formed CTW as an alternative. The presidents of the CTW unions expressed disdain for the lack of focus on organizing, and promised to lead the way to labour revitalization (Hurd, 2007, pp. 314–25; Chaison, 2007, p. 301). In spite of a positive shift in strategy and tactics within some of the key CTW unions, over the next five years the new federation was no more successful than the AFL-CIO in finding a path to growth.

Ultimately the two federations joined forces in 2008 in support of the Democratic Party, and especially its candidate for President Barrack Obama. His election victory inspired the optimistic assumption across organized labour that at last a political solution to labour's difficulty was at hand. Legislative reform to redress many of the perceived deficiencies in labour law was presumed to be high on Obama's agenda. The Employee Free Choice Act (EFCA), drafted by union allies in the US Congress, would borrow from Canadian law two key practices: card-check recognition in place of representation elections, and first contract arbitration (Slinn and Hurd, 2009; Hurd, 2009a). Two years into the Obama administration the mood has shifted. Once again the Democratic Party has failed to deliver, thwarted again by conservative forces in both major political parties. Although Obama himself still retains the allegiance of key unions, the hope for EFCA or any significant shift in labour policy has faded.

In a parallel development, the self-proclaimed optimism that CTW would solve the dilemma of union growth also has dissipated, and three of its seven national unions disaffiliated in 2009 and 2010, two returning to the AFL-CIO, the other becoming independent. In spite of energetic new leadership at both the AFL-CIO and CTW, and new initiatives to appeal to youth, immigrant workers and the LGBT (lesbian, gay, bisexual, transgendered) community, there seems to be little possibility of an imminent resurgence of unions in the US.

Non-union Representation[17]

The NLRA has broadly interpreted the s.8(a)(2) prohibition on employer-dominated organizations to include any representation plan in which employees participate, and which deals with management regarding conditions of work. However, disagreement exists over whether or not these prohibitions have actually hindered development of non-union representation in US workplaces as there is evidence that many US companies have employee participation programs (Rundle, 1994; Kaufman, 1999). US unions have resisted amending the s.8(a)(2) prohibition out of concern that doing so would deter unionization and there is evidence that workers' likelihood of unionizing is 14 to 20 percent lower if their employer has instituted an employee participation program (Freeman and Ostroff, 2000).

In contrast, in Canada, employer-dominated organizations are not eligible to be certified as trade unions under labour legislation to represent bargaining units of employees, but are not otherwise unlawful. These forms of representation are regulated by common law, non-labour statutes and the courts instead of labour legislation and tribunals (Taras, 2002, 2006). Survey evidence indicates that somewhere around 14 to 16 percent of Canadian employees have some form of non-union representation (Lipset and Meltz, 2000; Lowe and Schellenberg, 2001).[18]

Unionization Outside Statutory Labour Relations: Neutrality and Card-check Agreements and Representation Frameworks

Reflecting unions' frustration with the lengthy NLRB certification process and inadequate protection of employees from employer ULP and retaliation, many unions have turned to pressuring employers to enter into neutrality agreements or card-check agreements. With these, the unions secure the employer's agreement that it will not oppose union organizing or will agree to voluntarily recognize the union based on membership cards rather than requiring the union to seek recognition through the NLRA's statutory process (Hurd, 2008). This extra-statutory route to union recognition is now reportedly more often used than the statutory process (Brudney, 2005, p. 847). Though requiring employer participation, neutrality agreements do not violate the s.8(a)(2) NLRA (Malin, 2010, p. 58).

Neutrality and card-check agreements have not become a significant phenomenon in Canadian labour relations. However, in fall 2007 one of the largest Canadian unions, the Canadian Auto Workers (CAW) and Magna International, a major auto-parts producer with a long-standing non-union employee participation programme, crafted and agreed to a representation framework, the 'Framework of Fairness Agreement' (FFA). The FFA was introduced as a new, extra-statutory arrangement, better suited to the globalized economy. The FFA covered 45 facilities and 18 000 employees in Canada, and permits employees at each workplace to vote on whether to be represented by CAW for collective bargaining purposes and to come within the FFA. Under the FAA, CAW and Magna agreed not to strike but to use final offer arbitration to settle disputes, and an internal pre-grievance resolution process. The FFA, particularly its strike ban, was strongly opposed by many unions (Lewchuk and Wells, 2008).

Whether or not the FFA initiative proves to be a new, more flexible, approach to achieving union representation remains to be seen. To date, only three of the 43 facilities have voted to accept the FFA, but this may partly reflect the dire economic situation the automotive sector has experienced since shortly after the FFA was introduced. As unlikely as it seems that the FFA approach offers a new alternative for union representation for Canadian workers, it is not even an option for US workers or unions. Martin Malin (2010) concludes that this type of representation framework would be illegal in the US, violating both the s.8(a)(2) NLRA and Title IV of the Labor Management Reporting and Disclosure Act.

High-performance Work Practices

'High commitment', 'high involvement' and 'high performance' are the main labels used for a variety of relatively new work practices that tend to share the following elements: intensive recruitment and selection procedures, employee information-sharing; skills training; performance-based rewards; performance management; and opportunities for employee involvement in reformulating work and job roles (Blasi and Kruse, 2006, p. 553). This chapter uses the term 'high-performance practices' (HPPs) to describe such alternative work practices. Though much research exists on HPPs, it is difficult to gain an accurate view of incidence, diffusion or effects of these work practices from this research because of widely differing definitions, measures and sampling, among other difficulties (Godard, 2004, pp. 353–5; Blasi and Kruse, 2006, p. 547).

Although other US studies report higher incidence and diffusion of high-performance work practices (see, e.g., Ellwood et al., 2000; Osterman, 2000), perhaps the most comprehensive and representative study is that by Blasi and Kruse (2006), which found very low levels of HPP adoption among US firms. Using the 1994 and 1997 National Employer Survey, involving a US nationwide survey of a nationally representative sample of employers with 20 or more workers and an index of eight HPPs,[19] the researchers divided establishments into 'strong innovators' combining more than four of the eight practices measured; 'medium innovators' using three or four practices; and 'weak innovators' using none to two practices. Overall, for the 1997 data: the nationwide US sample showed 83.5, 15.4 and 1.1 percent of establishments were weak, medium and strong innovators, respectively. Among unionized establishments, 82.9 percent were weak, 15.4 medium and 1.7 percent strong innovators. Results were similar for non-union establishments: 83.1 percent, 15.8 percent and 1.1 percent, were weak, medium and strong innovators. Industries with the highest incidence of 'strong innovators' were utilities (4.1 percent), chemicals and petroleum (4.0 percent) and transportation and equipment (3.45 percent); while printing and publishing (0 percent), finance (0.1 percent) and textile and apparel (0.26 percent) had the lowest incidence of strong innovator establishments (Blasi and Kruse, 2006, Table 5).

There are no such detailed results for Canadian workplaces. However, using Statistics Canada Workplace and Employee Survey data from 1999 and 2001 for workplaces with ten or more employees, Verma and Taras (2009, pp. 143–5) found very limited HPP adoption among Canadian firms surveyed. Fewer than 5 percent of firms had implemented a combination of: teams, flexible job design and profit- or gain-sharing practices and only 2.1 percent of firms employed both this bundle of practices and formal teamwork-related training.

Though unions may be important to successful implementation of high-performance practices, they are often concerned that these initiatives are disguised anti-union efforts, which will weaken or prevent workplace unionization. In surveying the literature on the effects of HPPs on unionization, Godard (2004, pp. 360–63) notes that previous studies show that HPPs have often been used to avoid unions in the US, but he also notes that this may not be the only or primary objective of these practices. Godard concludes that most studies reveal no significant association between HPPs and union presence; US studies find that HPPs reduce the likelihood of unionization; and, in already-unionized establishments, studies seem to show worker support for unionization declines where HPPs exist.

CONCLUSION

Canadian and US labour laws have many surface similarities. However, the multiple differences described here clearly establish Canadian law as more supportive of both collective bargaining and labour unions. Union density is substantially higher in Canada, and for the past decade has been reasonably stable while the presence and influence of unions in the US continue to decline. Despite the difficulties that have emerged in the alliance between Canadian unions and social democratic parties, the political situation in the US is considerably bleaker. Efforts to borrow from Canadian law in proposed reforms to US labour statutes have been blocked, indicating that labour decline is likely to continue south of the Canadian border. Labour relations remains relatively strong and a viable part of the economic and social environment in Canada, but the close economic ties between the two countries may well create pressure that challenges the Canadian labour relations system in the future.

NOTES

1. The territorial governments have delegated power over employment relations, but have not yet passed their own employment relations legislation, instead adopting other jurisdictions' legislation.
2. The Gini index measures the degree of inequality of distribution of family income in a nation, from lowest inequality to highest, on a scale from zero to 100.
3. Differences in measuring union density between countries and over time make this type of comparison difficult. These challenges are explained in Godard (2003).
4. For instance: the 1914 Clayton Antitrust Act provided that unions would not be considered to be illegal combinations or conspiracies in restraint of trade; the 1932 Norris-LaGuardia Act prohibited federal courts from imposing injunctions in labour disputes; the 1872 Canadian Trade Union Act provided that trade unions were not conspiracies although their activities restrained trade.
5. Most recently this includes repeated, unsuccessful attempts beginning in 2003 to pass the Employee Free Choice Act in the US Congress.
6. In 1903 the Railway Labor Disputes Act was passed following a Canadian Pacific Railway strike, introducing conciliation process for disputes. This is not regarded as influencing broader Canadian labour legislation.
7. Lipset and Meltz (2000, pp. 230) use the 'supply' and 'demand' dichotomy to address the union divergence question.
8. See Sack (2010) for a comprehensive and current survey of US–Canada labour law differences. See Block (2003) for a recent comparative study of labour standards in the US and Canada, including assessment of enforcement. It concluded that standards are generally higher in Canada.
9. Unlike analogous legislation in other Canadian jurisdictions, private sector labour relations legislation in Alberta and Saskatchewan do not include election time limits and, therefore, do not use the 'quick vote' model.
10. Currently only the province of British Columbia offers expedited hearing of complaints that an employee has been unlawfully discharged, suspended, transferred or laid off from employment or otherwise disciplined, where no collective agreement is in place. The labour board must inquire forthwith into the matter, commencing a hearing within three days of filing, promptly proceed with the hearing and issue a decision within two days of the close of the hearing.
11. For instance, under the Ontario Labour Relations Act, the penalty is a maximum of $2000 for an individual and $25 000 for a corporation, trade union, or employers' organization, for each day the offence continues.
12. See Taras and Ponak (2001, pp. 554–7) for discussion of attempts to introduce Right-to-Work legislation in Canada.
13. This decision was also notable as 'the first time that the Court modified the common law in order to make it conform to Charter values' (Tucker, 2005, p. 133).
14. In 1977 an attempt to amend the Act failed in a Senate filibuster. The Employee Free Choice Act (US Bill H.R. 800, S. 1041, Employee Free Choice Act of 2007, 110th Cong., 2007, s. 4.) was introduced to Congress and Senate in 2003, 2005 and most recently in 2007, failing each time.
15. See Sack (2010, pp. 251–7) for extensive comparative treatment of grievance arbitration.
16. The rationale of strategic voting depends on the multi-party system of government in Canada, which allows a party to form the government with less than a majority of votes. The goal is to prevent a certain party from forming the government by ensuring votes are not split among the other parties. For instance, to prevent party A from winning, unions may urge members to vote strategically for party B instead of party C that the union traditionally supported. This makes it likely that B rather than A will win the election, and party C is not likely to win the election in any event.
17. The most comprehensive work on non-union representation in the US and Canada is Kaufman and Taras (2000).

18. See Taras (2002, p. 110; 2006, p. 324) for discussion of measurement issues in these studies.
19. Blasi and Kruse (2006, pp. 559–60) examined eight practices: (1) self-managed work teams; (2) work-related meetings; (3) training; (4) bench-marking; (5) job rotation; (6) organizational flatness; (7) recruitment resources; and (8) position on pay and benefits.

REFERENCES

Adams, George W. (1984), 'The impact of the Code beyond the province', in Joseph M. Weiler and Peter A. Gall (eds), *The Labour Code of British Columbia in the 1980s*, Calgary: Carswell, pp. 219–40.

Adams, George W. (1993), *Canadian Labour Law*, 2nd edition, Aurora, ON: Canada Law Book.

Annis, P. (2009), 'Work stoppages in the federal private sector: Innovative solutions', available at: http://www.hrsdc.gc.ca/eng/labour/labour_relations/wsfps/page00.shtml; accessed 12 January 2011.

Backhouse, C. (1980), 'The Fleck strike: A case study in the need for first contract arbitration', *Osgoode Hall Law Journal*, **18**(4), 495–553.

Bentham, K.J. (2002), 'Employer resistance to union certification: A study of eight Canadian jurisdictions', *Relations Industrielles*, **57**(1), 159–87.

Black, E. and Hosea, C. (1994), 'First contract legislation in Manitoba: A model for the United States?', *Labor Law Journal*, **45**(1), 33–40.

Blasi, J.R. and Kruse, D.L. (2006), 'U.S. high-performance work practices at century's end', *Industrial Relations*, **45**(4), 547–78.

Block, Richard N. (1993), 'Unionization, collective bargaining and legal institutions in the United States and Canada', *Queen's Papers in Industrial Relations (1993–94)*, Kingston, ON: Queen's University Industrial Relations Centre.

Block, Richard N. (1994), 'Reforming U.S. labor law and collective bargaining: Some proposals based on the Canadian system', in Sheldon Friedman, Richard W. Hurd, Rudolph A. Oswald and Ronald L. Seeber (eds), *Restoring the Promise of American Labor Law*, Ithaca, NY: Cornell University Press, pp. 250–59.

Block, Richard N. (2003), *Labor Standards in the United States and Canada*, Kalamazoo, MI: W.E. Upjohn Institute for Employment Research.

Bowden, G. (1989), 'Labour unions in the public mind: The Canadian case', *Canadian Review of Sociology and Anthropology*, **26**(5), 723–43.

Bruce, P. (1989), 'Political parties and labor legislation in Canada and the US', *A Journal of Economy and Society*, **28**(2), 115–41.

Bruce, P. (1990), 'The processing of unfair labor practice cases in the United States and Ontario Relations', *Relations Industrielles/Industrial Relations*, **45**(3), 481–511, available at http://id.erudit.org/iderudit/050605ar; accessed 11 January 2011.

Brudney, J. (2005), 'Neutrality agreements and card-check recognition: Prospects for changing paradigms', *Iowa Law Review*, **90**(3), 819–86.

Budd, John W. (2002), *Labour Relations: Striking a Balance*, 2nd edition, Boston, MA: McGraw-Hill Irwin.

Burkett, K.M. (1998), 'The politicization of the Ontario labour relations framework in the 1990s', *Canadian Labour & Employment Journal*, **6**, 161.

Campolieti, M., Riddell, C. and Slinn, S. (2007), 'Labor law reform and the role of delay in union organizing: Empirical evidence from Canada', *Industrial & Labor Relations Review*, **61**(1), 32–58.

Canada Labour Code (1985), R.S.C. 1985, v. L-2.

Carter, Donald D. (1992), 'Labour law reform: Radical departure of natural evolution?', *IRC Press Current Issues Series*, Kingston, ON: Queen's University Industrial Relations Centre.

180   *Research handbook of comparative employment relations*

Central Intelligence Agency (CIA) (2010), *The World Factbook: Field Listing: GDP (Official Exchange Rate)*, available at: https://www.cia.gov/library/publications/the-world-fact book/fields/2195.html; accessed 11 January 2011.

Chaison, G. (2007), 'The AFL-CIO split: Does it really matter?', *Journal of Labor Research*, **28**(2), 301–11.

Compa, Lance (2002), *Unfair Advantage: Workers' Freedom of Association in the United States Under International Human Rights Standards*, New York: Cornell University Press/ Human Rights Watch.

Cooke, W.N., Mishra, A.K., Spreitzer, G.M. and Tschirhart, M. (1995), 'The determinants of NLRB decision-making revisited', *Industrial and Labor Relations Review*, **48**(2), 237–57.

Dannin, E. (2005), 'Forum: At 70, should the National Labor Relations Act be retired? NLRA values, labor values, American values', *Berkeley Journal of Employment and Labour Law*, **26**(2), 223–74.

Drummonds, H.H. (2009), 'Reforming labor law by reforming labor law preemption doctrine to allow states to make more labor relations policy', *Louisiana Law Review*, **70**(1), 97–191.

Duffy, P. and Johnson, S. (2009), 'The impact of anti-temporary replacement legislation on work stoppages: Empirical evidence from Canada', *Canadian Public Policy*, **35**(1), 99–120.

Ellis, S.R. (1998), 'Appointments policies in the administrative justice system: Lessons from Ontario: four speeches', *Canadian Journal of Administrative Law & Practice*, **11**, 205–58.

Ellis, S.R. and McKenzie, M.E. (2009), 'Ocean port or the rule of law? The Saskatchewan Labour Relations Board', *Canadian Journal of Administrative Law & Practice*, **22**(3), 267–301.

Ellwood, D., Blank, R. Blasi, J. Kruse, D., Niskanen, W. and Lynn-Dyson, K. (2000), *A Working Nation*, New York: Russell Sage Foundation.

Epstein, Richard A. (2009), 'The case against the Employee Free Choice Act', University of Chicago Law & Economics, Olin Working Paper No. 452, available at: http://ssrn.com/ abstract=1337185; accessed 11 January 2011.

Farber, H.S. (1984), 'Right-to-Work laws and the extent of unionization', *Journal of Labor Economics*, **2**(2), 319–52.

Farber, H. and Western, B. (2001), 'Accounting for the decline of unions in the private sector', *Journal of Labor Research*, **22**(3), 459–85.

Fisk, Catherine (2009), 'Interest arbitration in the Employee Free Choice Act', in John Logan (ed.), *Academics on Employee Free Choice: Multidisciplinary Approaches to Labor Law Reform*, Berkeley, CA: University of California Center for Labor Research and Education.

Freeman, Richard B. (1985), 'Why are unions faring poorly in NLRB representation elections?', in Thomas A. Kochan (ed.), *Challenges and Choices Facing American Labor*, Cambridge, MA: MIT Press, pp. 45–64.

Freeman, Richard and Ostroff, Cheri (2000), 'The anatomy of employee involvement and its effects on firms and workers', National Bureau of Economic Research Working Paper No. 8059, Cambridge, MA: National Bureau of Economic Research Inc.

Freeman, Richard and Joel Rogers (1995), 'Worker representation and participation survey: First report of findings', in Paula Beth Vogel Voos (ed.), *Industrial Association Series, Proceedings of the Forty-Seventh Annual Meeting of the Industrial Relations Research Association: January 6–8, Washington, D.C.*, Madison, WI: Industrial Relations Research Association.

Freeman, Richard and Rogers, Joel (eds) (1999), *What Workers Want*, Ithaca, NY: Cornell University Press.

Freeman, Richard and Rogers, Joel (2006), *What Workers Want*, updated edition, Ithaca, NY and London: Cornell University Press.

Gifford, Court (2010), *Directory of U.S. Labor Organizations: 2010 Edition*, Arlington, VA: Bureau of National Affairs.

Godard, J. (2003), 'Do labor laws matter? The density decline and convergence thesis revisited', *Industrial Relations*, **42**(3), 458–92.

Godard, J. (2004), 'A critical assessment of the high-performance paradigm', *British Journal of Industrial Relations*, **42**(2), 349–78.

Godard, J. (2009), 'The exceptional decline of the American labor movement', *Industrial and Labor Relations Review*, **63**(1), 82–108.

Gomez, Rafael, Lipset, Seymour and Meltz, Noah (2001), 'Frustrated demand for unionisation: The case of the United States and Canada revisited', CEPD No. 492, London, UK: Centre for Economic Performance, London School of Economics and Political Science.

Gross, James (1974), *The Making of the National Labor Relations Board: A Study in Economics, Politics, and the Law, 1933–1937*, Albany, NY: State University of New York Press, pp. 144–7.

Gross, James A. (1994), 'The demise of the national labor policy: A question of social justice', in Sheldon Friedman, Richard W. Hurd, Rudolph A. Oswald and Ronald L. Seeber (eds), *Restoring the Promise of American Labor Law*, Ithaca, NY: ILR Press, pp. 45–58.

Human Resources and Skills Development Canada (HRSDC) (2010), *Union Membership in Canada–2009*, available at: http://www.hrsdc.gc.ca/eng/labour/labour_relations/info_analysis/union_membership/index2009.shtml; accessed 11 January 2011.

Hurd, Richard W. (2007), 'U.S. Labor 2006: Strategic developments across the divide', *Journal of Labor Research*, **28**(2), 313–25.

Hurd, R. (2008). 'Neutrality agreements: Innovative, controversial, and labor's hope for the future', *New Labor Forum*, **17**(1), 25–35.

Hurd, R. (2009a). 'Obama and the U.S. labour movement', *Transfer: European Review of Labour and Research*, **15**(3), 579–86.

Hurd, R. (2009b), 'Sweeney's legacy: Tempered ideals', *Labor and Working Class History Association Newsletter*, Fall, pp. 8–9.

Johnson, S. (2002), 'Card-check or mandatory representation vote? How the type of union recognition procedure affects union certification success', *The Economic Journal*, **112**(349), 344–61.

Johnson, S. (2008), *First Contract Arbitration: Effects on Bargaining and Work Stoppages*, Laurier Centre for Economic Research & Policy Analysis Economic Research Paper, Waterloo, ON: Wilfrid Laurier University.

Kaufman, B. (1999), 'Does the NLRA constrain employee involvement and participation programs in nonunion companies? A reassessment', *Yale Law & Policy Review*, **17**(2), 729–811.

Kaufman, B.E. and Taras, D.G. (eds) (2000), *Nonunion Employee Representation: History, Contemporary Practice, and Policy*, Armonk, NY and London: M.E. Sharpe.

Kettler, D., Struthers, J. and Huxley, C. (1990), 'Unionization and labour regimes in Canada and the United States: Considerations for comparative research', *Labour/Le Travail*, **25**, 161–87.

Kumar, Pradeep and Schenk, Christopher (eds) (2006), *Paths to Union Renewal: Canadian Experiences*, Peterborough, ON: Broadview Press.

Lewchuk, W. and Wells, D. (2008), 'Workplace cohesion and the fragmentation of society: The Magna model in Canada', in Robert O'Brien (ed.), *Solidarity First: Canadian Workers and Social Cohesion*, Vancouver, BC: UBC Press, pp. 63–85.

Lipset, S. and Meltz, N. (1998), 'Canadian and American attitudes toward work and institutions', *Perspectives on Work*, **1**(3), 14–19.

Lipset, S. and N. Meltz (2000), 'Estimates of non-union employee representation', in Bruce E. Kaufman and Daphne G. Taras (eds), *Nonunion Employee Representation: History, Contemporary Practice, and Policy*, Armonk, NY and London, UK: M.E. Sharpe, pp. 223–30.

Logan, J. (2002), 'Consultants, lawyers, and the "union free" movement in the United States since the 1970s', *Industrial Relations Journal*, **33**(3), 197–214.

Logan, J. (2006), 'The union avoidance industry in the United States', *British Journal of Industrial Relations*, **44**(4), 651–75.

Lowe, Graham and Schellenberg, G. (2001), *What's a Good Job? The Importance of Employment Relationships*, Changing Employment Relationships Project, CPRN Study No. W0/5, Ottawa, ON: Canadian Policy Research Network Inc.

Lynk, M. (2009), 'Labour law and the new inequality', *University of New Brunswick Law Journal*, **59**(1), 14–40.

Malin, M.H. (2010), 'The Canadian Auto Workers–Magna International, Inc. Framework of Fairness Agreement: A U.S. perspective', *Saint Louis University Law Journal*, **54**, 525.

Masters, M.F., Gibney, R. and Zagenczyk, T. (2006), 'The AFL-CIO v. CTW: The competing visions, strategies and structures', *Journal of Labor Research*, **27**(4), 473–504.

Moe, T.M. (1985), 'Control and feedback in economic regulation: The case of the NLR', *The American Political Science Review*, **79**(4), 1094–116.

Osterman, P. (2000), 'Work reorganization in an era of restructuring', *Industrial and Labor Relations Review*, **53**(2), 179–96.

Piore, M. (1983), 'Can the American labor movement survive re-gomperization', in B.D. Dennis (ed.), *Proceedings of the Thirty-Fifth Annual Meeting of the Industrial Relations Research Association*, Madison, WI: Industrial Relations Research Association, pp. 30–39.

Riddell, C.W. (1993), 'Unionization in Canada and the United States: A tale of two countries', in David Card and Richard Freeman (eds), *Small Differences that Matter*, Chicago, IL: University of Chicago Press, pp. 109–48.

Riddell, C. (2001), 'Union suppression and certification success', *Canadian Journal of Economics*, **34**(2), 396–410.

Riddell, C. (2004), 'Union certification success under voting versus card-check procedures: Evidence from British Columbia, 1978–98', *Industrial & Labor Relations Review*, **57**(4), 493–517.

Riddell, C. (2010), 'The causal effect of election delay on union win rates: Instrumental variable estimates from two natural experiments', *Industrial Relations*, **49**(3), 371–86.

Rose, J. and Chaison, G. (1990), 'New measures of union organizing effectiveness', *Industrial Relations: A Journal of Economy and Society*, **29**(3), 457–68.

Rundle, James (1994), 'The debate over the ban on employer-dominated labor organizations: What is the evidence?', in Sheldon Friedman, Richard W. Hurd, Rudolph A. Oswald, Ronald L. Seeber (eds), *Restoring the Promise of American Labor Law*, Ithaca, NY: ILR Press, pp. 161–76.

Sack, J. (2010), 'US and Canadian labor law: Significant distinctions', *ABA Journal of Labor and Employment Law*, **25**(2), 241–58.

Saporta, I. and Lincoln, B. (1995), 'Managers' and workers' attitudes toward unions in the U.S. and Canada', *Relations Industrielles/Industrial Relations*, **50**(3), 550–66.

Schmidt, D.E. (2002), 'Politicization and responsiveness in the regional offices of the NLRB', *American Review of Public Administration*, **32**(2), 188–215.

Sexton, J. (1987), 'First contract arbitration in Canada', *Labor Law Journal*, **38**(8), 508–14.

Slinn, S. (2004), 'An empirical analysis of the effects of the change from card-check to mandatory vote certification', *Canadian Labour & Employment Law Journal*, **11**, 259–301.

Slinn, S. (2008a), 'Captive audience meetings and forced listening: Lessons for Canada from the American experience', *Relations Industrielles*, **63**(4), 694–718.

Slinn, S. (2008b), 'No right (to organize) without a remedy: Evidence and consequences of failure to provide compensatory remedies for unfair labour practices in British Columbia', *McGill Law Journal*, **53**(4), 687–737.

Slinn, S. and Hurd, R.W. (2009), 'Fairness and opportunity for choice: The Employee Free Choice Act & The Canadian Model', *Just Labour*, **15**, 104–14.

Statistics Canada (August 2009), *Perspectives on Labour and Income*, **21**(1) (Catalogue no. 75-001-XPF), Ottawa, ON: Statistics Canada.

Story, A. (1995), 'Employer speech, union representation elections, and the First Amendment', *Berkeley Journal of Employment & Labor Law*, **16**, 356–457.

Taras, D. (1997), 'Collective bargaining regulation in Canada and the United States: Divergent cultures, divergent outcomes', in Bruce Kaufman (ed.), *Government in Regulation of the Employment Relationship*, Madison, WI: Industrial Relations Research Association, pp. 295–341.

Taras, D. (2001), 'Labor law, employer opposition, and the divergent development of U.S. and Canadian industrial relations', *IRRA 53rd Annual Proceedings*, pp. 153–62.

Taras, D.G. (2002), 'Alternative forms of employee representation and labour policy', *Canadian Public Policy/Analyse de Politiques*, **28**(1), 105–16.

Taras, D. (2006), 'Non-union representation and employer intent: How Canadian courts and labour boards determine the legal status of non-union plans', *Socio-Economic Review*, **4**(2), 321–36.

Taras, D. and A. Ponak (2001), 'Mandatory agency shop laws as an explanation of Canada–U.S. union density divergence', *Journal of Labor Research*, **22**(3)541–68.

Thompson, M. (1995), 'The management of industrial relations', in M. Gunderson and A. Ponak (eds), *Union–Management Relations in Canada*, 3rd edition, Don Mills, ON: Pearson Addison Wesley, pp. 105–30.

Thompson, M. (2009), 'The management of industrial relations', in M. Gunderson and D. Taras (eds), *Canadian Labour and Employment Relations*, 6th edition, Toronto, ON: Pearson Addison Wesley, pp. 106–24.

Troy, L. (1992), 'Convergence in international unionism, etc. The case of Canada and the U.S.A', *British Journal of Industrial Relations*, **30**(1), 1–43.

Troy, L. (2000), 'U.S. and Canadian industrial relations: Convergent or divergent?', *Industrial Relations*, **39**(4), 695–713.

Troy, L. (2001), 'Twilight for organized labor', *Journal of Labor Research*, **12**(2), 245–60.

Tucker, E. (2005), 'Great expectations defeated? The trajectory of collective bargaining regimes in Canada and the U.S. post-NAFTA', *Comparative Labor Law & Policy Journal*, **26**(1), 97–150.

United States Bureau of Labor Statistics (2010, 22 January), *Union Members Summary*, available at: http://www.bls.gov/news.release/union2.nr0.html; accessed 11 January 2011.

United States Dept. of Labor (1994), Commission on the Future of Worker–Management Relations, *Fact Finding Report on the Future of Worker–Management Relations*, by Mary Meagher, Washington DC, News: Department of Labor Office of Information.

United States National Labor Relations Board (1997), *Basic Guide to the National Labor Relations Act: General Principles of Law Under the Statute and Procedures of the National Labor Relations Board*, pp. 33–5, Washington, DC: US Government Printing Office, available at: http://www.nlrb.gov/nlrb/shared_files/brochures/basicguide.pdf; accessed 11 January 2011.

United States National Labor Relations Board (2009), General Counsel, *Summary of Operations: Fiscal Year 2009* (1 December), Memorandum GC 10-01available at: http://www.nlrb.gov/shared_files/GC%20Memo/2010/GC%2010-01%20Summary%20of%20Operations%20FY%2009%20.pdf; accessed 11 January 2011.

Verma, A. and Taras, D.G. (2009), 'Managing the high-involvement workplace', in M. Gunderson and D. Taras (eds), *Canadian Labour and Employment Relations*, 6th edition, Toronto, ON: Pearson Addison Wesley, pp. 125–63.

Webber, J. (1991), 'Compelling compromise: Canada chooses conciliation over arbitration 1900–1907', *Labour/Le Travail*, **28**, 17–57.

Weiler, P.C. (1980), *Reconcilable Differences: New Directions in Canadian Labour Law*, Toronto, ON: Carswell.

Weiler, P.C. (1983), 'Promises to keep: Securing workers' rights to self-organization under the NLRA', *Harvard Law Review*, **96**(8), 1769–827.

Weiler, P.C. (1984), 'Striking a new balance: Freedom of contract and the prospects for union representation', *Harvard Law Review*, **98**(2), 351–420.

Weiler, P.C. (1986), 'Milestone or tombstone: The Wagner Act at fifty', *Harvard Journal on Legislation*, **23**(1), 1–31.

Woods, H.D. (1977), 'The course of labour policy in Canada', in Frances Bairstow (ed.), Industrial Relations Centre 25th Annual Conference: The Direction of Labour Policy in Canada, Montreal, QC: McGill University.

8 Employment relations in China and India
Fang Lee Cooke

INTRODUCTION

There has been growing interest in comparative studies of China and India (e.g., Khanna, 2007; Sheth, 2008) since Jairam Ramesh, an Indian academic politician, coined the term 'Chindia' in his book *Making Sense of Chindia: Reflections of China and India* (2005). These studies have gone a long way in enlightening us of the similarities of and differences between the two countries in terms of their respective geo-political, economic and socio-cultural characteristics and their rising significance in the global politico-economic stage. However, few studies have been carried out to compare and contrast the labour markets and employment relations (ER) systems of the two countries. This is in spite of the fact that the characteristics displayed in these two important aspects of a nation's economy are important in understanding how they interact with other institutional forces and shape patterns of economic growth and competitive dynamics of each of the two countries.

Whilst a small number of comparative studies on the ER systems of Asian economies, including China and India, do exist, these pioneering and important studies have largely focused on the impact of industrialization strategy and globalization on the national ER systems of selected Asian countries in the 1990s (e.g., Kuruvilla, 1996; Kuruvilla and Venkata Ratnam, 1996; Frenkel and Peetz, 1998; Frenkel and Kuruvilla, 2002; Kuruvilla and Erickson, 2002). As Bhattacherjee (2001) pointed out, comparative studies on ER in Asian countries need to be cast on a longer historical horizon and based on a wider range of societal factors than just the impact of globalization and national economic strategy. They should also be conducted with countries that are of more comparable size (in terms of population and economy). This chapter is therefore a response to Bhattacherjee's (2001) suggestion to compare India and China as two more comparable nations, taking into account their respective historical and institutional specificities – an approach that Gall (1998) also argues for.

It must be noted at the outset, however, that a comparative study of two countries at the national level is inevitably an over-simplified exercise insensitive to norms, practices and characteristics displayed in different industries and institutional environments at the local level, as authors on comparative IR (industrial relations) have argued (e.g., Bean, 1994; Van Ruysseveldt, 1995; Bhattacherjee, 2001; Gospel, 2008). Moreover, for academic purposes, it is tempting to stylize the ER systems of the two countries, with or without reference to the Western-developed IR theories. However, conceptual modelling often comes with the inherent pitfalls of incompleteness, rigidity and outdatedness. IR theories developed primarily from Western industrialization and post-industrialization experience have been questioned for their utility in interpreting the experience of less developed countries (e.g., Siddique, 1989; Bhattacherjee and Ackers, 2010), particularly Asian economies based on a reciprocal relationship (Westwood et al., 2004). The objective of this chapter is therefore not concerned with identifying national models, but to highlight some of the historically prominent features and key issues in the ER system of the two countries as a result of their unique historical, cultural, economic and political circumstances and the dynamic interactions of institutional actors. In doing so, we will draw on examples from different ownership forms and sectors and in different historical periods as far as possible. In other words, we follow Poole's approach to comparative studies by exploring the environmental influences resulting from societal structures and processes from a multi-disciplinary perspective that incorporates both historical and contemporary data (cited in Bean, 1994, p. 4).

FEATURES

In this section, we examine a number of key features that together have shaped the ER systems of both countries against the backdrop of their national political, economic and socio-cultural characteristics (see Table 8.2). We investigate the role of traditional key actors, that is, the state/government, employers and trade unions/workers. We also examine aspects of the ER governance framework. These include: union recognition and strength, collective bargaining, workers' representation and participation, labour laws and labour disputes resolution mechanism, in order to assess their influence on employment outcomes (e.g., working conditions, wage level and employment security). The term 'industrial relations' (IR) is used when describing the Indian situation as IR is a more commonly used term in India than ER.

Background of the Two Countries

China and India are two fast-developing countries. China gained its liberation in 1949 after decades of civil wars and resistance battles against foreign invasions and colonizations. A socialist regime was subsequently established by the Chinese Communist Party (CCP), which has been the ruling party since 1949. A number of minority political parties are recognized by the CCP. They play a democratic political consultation role in determining the affairs of the country in principle, but in reality, their impact can hardly be felt. The country was developed under the socialist model of state-planned economy until 1978 when it adopted the 'Open Door' policy that marked the beginning of its economic transformation. By contrast, India gained its independence in 1947 after decades of British colonial rule and became the largest democratic country in the world. In the ensuing decades, India also largely followed a state-planned economy and welfare state model. India began its economic reform in 1991 officially with the introduction of the liberalization programme.

Since the 1990s, China and India have emerged as two major power houses in the development of Asian economy (Khanna, 2007). With their unique comparative advantages, China and India are also beginning to emerge in the global economy with growing competitiveness and impact. In certain sectors, they are major players, for example, China's low-cost manufacturing, and India's IT industry and its related offshore business process outsourcing (BPO) industry. Like its counterparts of Japan and South Korea, the Chinese government has pursued an export-oriented economic growth. By contrast, India's economic development in the last two decades has relied mainly on the increase of domestic demand.

With a population of 1.3 billion in China and 1.1 billion in India, the two countries make up over one-third of the world's population, although the majority of them live in the rural areas where a large proportion of those in poverty are concentrated. China's economic development has been accompanied by a substantial fertility decline as a result of the government's 'one child' policy enforced in the 1980s. By contrast, in spite of the government's policy encouragement to birth control, India's population has grown rapidly and is set to surpass that of China by 2050 (*BBC News*, 2004). In both countries, the education level has continued to rise (World Bank Group, 2006). However, there remains a gap between girls and boys, particularly in tertiary education, with the difference being more marked in India than in China. For instance, in 2004, 9 per cent of women in India, compared with 14 per cent men, were enrolled in tertiary education. In China, 17 per cent of men and 14 per cent of women were enrolled (ibid.).

Relatively speaking, China is a culturally fairly homogeneous country where Confucian values still prevail (e.g., Magoshi and Chang, 2009). In comparison, India is far more diverse in its religious and racial spread and influence. Family values remain strong in both societies and social hierarchy continues to play an important role in social and organizational life. A level of social equality, including gender equality, has been achieved in both countries, but the caste system remains a strong albeit weakening influence in the Indian society and workplaces. So do its religions (e.g., Budhwar, 2009; Cooke, 2010). Whilst China also has ethnic and religious diversities, these are mainly located in the northwest, western and south-west regions, notably the bordering provinces. In the central and eastern parts of the country where the economy is also relatively more developed, ethnicity and religion have largely not been issues in social and workplace relations.

Labour Market

In India, the labour market is divided into two sectors: the organized and unorganized. The proportion of employment in the organized (but not necessarily unionized) sector is low compared with that in the unor-ganized sector. It is estimated that only about 8 per cent of the Indian workers worked in the formal economy by 2000 (Venkata Ratnam, 2009). Women workers are concentrated in the informal sector, 'where wages and working conditions are inferior, largely unsecured and mostly devoid of social security benefits' (Venkata Ratnam and Jain, 2002, p. 279). The percentage of women in the total labour force in India has been in decline since the 1970s 'in both the organized and unorganized sectors' (Ghosh and Roy, 1997, p. 911). This is 'despite national efforts to increase the participation rate of women in the workforce' (ibid., p. 909). It should be noted, however, that this does not mean that those women who are not formally listed as employment active are not working. Rather, their work may be under- or unrecognized and inadequately remunerated. In 2004, the share of women in wage employment in the non-agricultural sector was 18 per cent in India, compared with 40 per cent in China (World Bank Group, 2006). Indian women made up only 20.5 per cent of the profes-sional and technical workforce in 2000. Nevertheless, the rapid develop-ment in the offshore BPO sector since the 2000s has led to an increasing proportion of women working in this sector. This is in part as a result of the amendment of the Factories Act to allow women to work on night shifts to combat skill shortages (Cooke, 2010).

The relatively low proportion of Indian women in formal employment and the way unions operate have led to the marginalization of women in unionism (e.g., Venkata Ratnam and Jain, 2002; Hill, 2008). And gender issues have not been given due attention in the mainstream Indian IR studies. It must be pointed out here that India has a long and strong tradition of organizing women in the informal sector, as observed by the

International Labour Organization (ILO) (cited in Venkata Ratnam and Jain, 2002). Empowerment groups, the Working Women Forum and Self-Employed Women's Association (SEWA) are amongst the major organizing bodies that have played an important role in organizing women and others in precarious employment and representing their needs (Venkata Ratnam and Jain, 2002; Hill, 2008).

The development of the labour market of the socialist China can be divided into three periods. The first period was a highly regulated, or more precisely controlled, labour market through administrative policy during the state-planned economy period (1949–78). Over 78 per cent of the urban workforce were employed in the state sector (*China Statistical Yearbook 2008*). They enjoyed employment security and extensive workplace welfare benefits such as medical health insurance, subsidized housing, subsidized canteen and free transport for work (Warner, 1996; Cooke, 2005; Hassard et al., 2007). Labour mobility was highly restricted, controlled by the *hukou* (residential registration) system in which individuals were registered with the local authority where they were born and live. The population was divided by two residential status categories: urban and rural residents. Rural residents were not allowed to enter urban areas for employment. This restriction was gradually relaxed during the deregulating/marketizing period that followed, between the 1980s and early 2000s, when millions of farmers migrated to urban areas for employment. In the same period, millions of state-owned enterprise (SOE) employees had been laid off and forced to seek re-employment in the labour market for the first time. The promulgation of three major employment-related laws in 2007 (see below) marked the beginning of the third period in which the government sought to re-regulate the labour market, through legislative intervention, in order to provide greater employment protection to workers, particularly those outside the state sector (Cooke, 2011). By 2007, less than 22 per cent of the urban workforce was employed in the state sector, and women made up 37.8 per cent of the urban full-time workforce (*China Labour Statistical Yearbook 2008*).

Labour Laws

As in other national ER systems, labour laws play an important role in the Chinese and Indian ER systems. The labour laws of India can be classified into four main categories: laws on working conditions, laws on labour relations, laws on wages and monetary benefits and laws on social security (Saini, 2009; also see Table 8.1). In all, over 60 major pieces of labour legislation have been enacted by the central legislature. This is in addition to over 150 labour regulations enacted by the state legislatures.[1]

Table 8.1   Major labour laws and regulations in India and China

India	China
Laws that regulate working conditions The Factories Act, 1948 The Mines Act, 1952 The Plantations Labour Act, 1951 The Contract Labour (Regulation & Abolition) Act, 1970 The Inter-State Migrant Workmen (Regulation of Employment & Conditions of Service) Act, 1979 Child Labour (Abolition and Regulation) Act 1985	*Laws* Trade Union Law (enacted 1950, 1992, amended 2001) The Labour Law (enacted 1995) The Labour Contract Law (enacted 2008) The Employment Promotion Law (enacted 2008) The Labour Disputes Mediation and Arbitration Law (enacted 2008)
Industrial relations laws The Trade Unions Act 1926 (TUA) The Industrial Employment (Standing Orders) Act 1946 The Industrial Disputes Act 1947 (IDA)	*Administrative regulations* Enterprise Minimum Wage Regulation (1993) Temporary Regulation for Labour Disputes Reconciliation in State-owned Enterprises (1987), which was superseded by:
Laws on wages and monetary benefits The Minimum Wages Act 1948 The Payment of Wages Act, 1936 (POWA) The Payment of Bonus Act, 1965 (POBA) The Equal Remuneration Act, 1976 (ERA)	Labour Disputes Reconciliation Regulation (1993) (which was later incorporated into the Labour Law) Special Regulation on Minimum Wage (2004), which superseded the 1993 regulation Regulations on Employment Services and Management (2008)
Social security laws Workmen's Compensation Act 1923 (WCA) Maternity Benefit Act 1961 (MBA) Payment of Gratuity Act 1972 (PGA) The Employees' State Insurance Act 1948 (ESIA) The Employees' Provident Fund (and Miscellaneous Provisions) Act 1952 (EPFA)	

Sources: Chandrashekar (1970); Sen Gupta and Sett (2000); Venkata Ratnam (2006); Cooke (2009); Saini (2009).

Each of these laws is specific to the needs of the state concerned (see Saini, 2009 for a detailed description of some of the laws). Some of these laws were introduced prior to India's independence. Over the decades, moderate amendments have been made to bring these laws up to date (Venkata Ratnam, 2006, 2009; Saini, 2009).

The labour laws of India are considered to be 'extremely protective of labour' (Kuruvilla, 1996, p. 650). They are also regarded to be 'among the most restrictive and complex in the world' and 'have constrained the growth of the formal manufacturing sector where these laws have their widest application' (World Bank, 2006, p. 3). Legislation that is aimed at providing an enhanced level of labour protection may actually prove to be counterproductive, especially when the laws are only applicable to certain sectors (e.g., the organized sector), industries and occupational groups. In particular, restrictions in lay-off and retrenchment have not only led to inefficiency, but also discourage employers from creating employment with a better job quality in the formal sector, forcing millions to continue to be trapped in poor jobs in the informal sector (see Sen Gupta and Sett, 2000 for an insightful overview of the Indian IR laws and the role of the key institutional actors).

However, this pro-labour government stance has not been equally applied across all groups of employees, notably those in the public sector providing public services (e.g., Mathur, 1966; Subramanian, 1973; Sen Gupta and Sett, 2000; Venkata Ratnam, 2009). Here, the tension caused by the multiple role of the Indian government as an employer, an economic manager and a legislator and policy-maker was borne out in full force. For example, strikes by certain groups of public employees (e.g., government employees and those providing public services) may be ruled by the government as unlawful, with some facing dismissal consequences (e.g., Subramanian, 1973; All India State Government Employees Federation, 2003). Public sector employees are considered to have a dual role as the master (as a citizen of the country) and servant (as a servant providing public services) (Mathur, 1966). In addition, the labour laws were enacted in a way that the state is the only arbiter of industrial conflicts (Sen Gupta and Sett, 2000; Venkata Ratnam, 2006, 2009).

Contrary to India's complex and detailed labour legislative framework, the regulation of the labour market and employment relations in socialist China has until recently relied primarily on administrative regulations and policy guidelines issued at the central, regional (provincial) and local (municipal and township) level. For example, the Enterprise Minimum Wage Regulation (enacted in 1993 and revised in 2004) was essentially a national administrative regulation that provides only a framework. It is up to the local governments to decide the level of minimum wage and coverage. The first major piece of labour legislation was only promulgated in 1994. This was followed by three major pieces of laws passed in 2007 (see Table 8.2). In general, all the laws are applicable to all employing organizations and groups of workers unless specified otherwise. Whilst laws are legislated by the central government to be enforced by the regional and local governments, the latter often develop local policy regulations and guidelines to dilute the impact of the laws in order to prioritize their economic development agenda (e.g., Taylor et al., 2003; Cooney, 2007; Cooke, 2009).

It has been argued that, with 'the major exception of freedom of association', the labour standards established by the series of labour laws and regulations of China 'are not markedly inferior to those of comparable countries and indeed many developed nations' (Cooney 2007, p. 674). What remains most problematic is the lack of effective enforcement (Taylor et al., 2003; Cooney, 2007). While implementation failures are characteristic of all regulatory systems (Cooney, 2007), the Chinese system is frustrated by the multiplicity of employment-related laws, directive regulations and administrative policies issued at the central, provincial and municipal government level, the ambiguous status of some of these regulative instruments and the confusing channels through which workers can seek to secure compliance of laws (Potter, 1999; Cooney, 2007). Scholars on labour disputes in China have also argued that regional institutional arrangements, managerial styles and characteristics of the workforce influence the level of labour disputes (e.g., Guthrie, 1999; Chan, 2001; Gallagher, 2005; Pun, 2005; Lee, 2007; Choi, 2008).

Both the Indian and Chinese labour disputes laws specify the procedures and processes of settling disputes – conciliation, arbitration and adjudication in India as specified in its Industrial Disputes Act (1947); and mediation, arbitration and litigation in China as specified in its recent Labour Disputes Mediation and Arbitration Law (2008). In both countries, a voluntary approach is emphasized, or at least encouraged, by the government as a cooperative way of resolving the conflicts. The inefficacy of the dispute resolution system appears to be a common characteristic of both countries (e.g., Chandrashekar, 1970; Taylor et al., 2003; Venkata Ratnam, 2006; Cooney, 2007; Saini, 2009; Cooke, 2011). In India, governments have been widely criticized for their discretionary power to overrule adjudication instead of accepting and implementing the rulings. In China, local governments have been found to force labour dispute cases back down to the workplace and request employers to resolve the dispute internally 'for the sake of building a harmonious society', although resource constraints to handle the rising number of cases may actually be the key reason for this (Cooke, 2009).

Trade Unions and Workers' Representation

Labour organizations such as the trade unions provide an additional potential source of labour protection. The strength and effectiveness of the trade unions, however, vary across industries and countries and over time. In India, trade unionism has a history of about 100 years, although less than 8 per cent of the workforce in India is unionized. There are five major trade unions, all of them affiliated to political parties (Venkata Ratnam, 2006). The All-Indian Trade Unions Congress (AITUC) was formed in 1920 mainly to meet the requirement of the ILO that workers' delegates should be representatives of the largest organization (see Pandey, 1967 for more detailed review). The legal incorporation of the Indian trade unions was established in 1926, much earlier than that in China (see Table 8.1).

The Indian trade unions are closely linked to political parties (Venkata Ratnam, 2006; Shyam Sundar, 2008), and some believe that the Indian trade unionism is more associated with political movement than labour movement (Dufty, 1965). As Dufty (ibid., p. 42) noted, in the early days of unionism, the Indian trade unions were to some extent 'an arm of liberalization movement'. Political parties allied with them because of 'their potential importance in the fight for independence' (ibid.). 'The Indian trade unions had considerable difficulty in gaining their legal positions' and had to form alliance with political parties and support pro-labour legislation to gain social and political recognition (ibid., p. 43). As such, 'their political strength has outweighed their industrial and economic strength' (ibid.). Inter-union rivalry began from the birth of the trade unions (Pandey, 1967). Union activists who have political ambition are more interested in positions at the industry or national level, whereas union representatives at the workplace level may find that their working class background presents a significant barrier to their ability to deal with elite managers in a caste-oriented society (Dufty, 1965). Whilst party loyalties may have been loosened since the late 1990s, this has been accompanied by the unions' weakening ability to organize nationally (Bhattacherjee, 2001; Candland, 2007; Beale and Noronha, 2009).

During the early stage of India's state-planned economy period, the Indian trade unions have been criticized for not being able to engage themselves with the wider goal of the national economic and social development beyond addressing the immediate needs and concerns of their members. The lack of strong and healthy trade unions was attributed to this problem (Srivastva, 1970). Cooperation of the trade unions was considered important by the state to support its agenda of the welfare state. This required them to carry out activities such as participating in the formation and implementation of five-year plans, productivity improvement, employee education and training, maintaining discipline and therefore peace and harmony of the industry (ibid.). The reluctance of the government to play its part as a model employer has also been attributed to the tension between the workers and the state employer, and the position the trade unions found themselves in (Mathur, 1966). Union movements exhibit strong regional/municipal distinctiveness in part due to the variations in the political stance, policy regulations and economic and social perform-ance of the state governments (e.g., Ramaswamy, 1988; Bhattacherjee, 2001; Kuruvilla and Erickson, 2002; Beale and Noronha, 2009).

Nevertheless, as Kuruvilla (1996, p. 651) observed, 'The political ori-entation of trade unions has provided the labor movement with political influence far greater than their union membership alone would warrant. Labor is the swing vote in at least 30% of all parliamentary constituen-cies', despite the relatively low level of unionization. Union power is particularly strong in the public sector. The power of the unions is believed to have been the cause of a swelling and inefficient public sector and the slow and difficult process of rationalization restructuring in the private sector (Venkata Ratnam, 1993). 'The protection from foreign competition afforded to Indian manufacturers, and a guaranteed inter-nal market, created huge and inefficient industries that were not able to compete internationally once the economy was liberalized' (Kuruvilla, 1996, p. 652).

Only one trade union – the All-China Federation of Trade Unions (ACFTU) – is recognized by the Chinese government (see Warner, 2008 for an overview). It is operated under the leadership of the CCP. The union–CCP tie dates back to the 1920s (the union was founded on 1 May 1925) when grassroots union organizations served as the Party member recruitment bases and provided vital support to the CCP by mobilizing workers. Although the relationship between the Party and the ACFTU has not always been smooth, attempts of the ACFTU to gain greater power and autonomy have been suppressed by the Party (Sheehan, 1999). Similarly, attempts to form autonomous workers' unions are crushed, as was the case during the Tiananmen Square event in 1989 (Cooke, 2010a).

The roles and responsibilities of the unions are set out by a number of laws, namely the Trade Union Law (1950, 1992, amended 2001), the Labour Law (1995) and the Labour Contract Law (2008). According to the Trade Union Law (2001), 'the basic function and duty of the trade unions is to safeguard the legal rights and interests of the employees. While upholding the overall rights and interests of the whole nation, trade unions shall, at the same time, represent and safeguard the rights and interests of employees' (Article 6). Article 7 further stipulates that the:

trade union shall mobilize and organize the employees to participate in the economic development actively, and to complete the production and work assignments conscientiously, educate the employees to improve their ideological thoughts and ethics, technological and professional, scientific and cultural qualities, and build an employee team with ideals, ethics, education and discipline.

Local branches of the ACFTU are partly funded by the fiscal budget of the local governments, which oversee the union activities. The legal and structural position of the ACFTU means that its primary responsibility is the state whose interests are not necessarily aligned with that of the workers. Under the socialist system in which the state employer and the workers are perceived to share the same interests, the trade union's main function is to organize social events, take care of workers' welfare, help management implement operational decisions, organize skill training, raise employees' morale and coordinate relations between management and workers (Verma and Yan, 1995). The way the ACFTU is set up and operationalized has led to the questioning by international trade union organizations, labour movement activists and scholars of the legitimacy of ACFTU as a trade union (e.g., Taylor and Li, 2007).

Since the mid-1990s when SOEs shed millions of their workers, skill training and assisting laid-off workers to regain employment have been two major functions of the unions. With the growth of new ownership forms outside the state sector and the concomitant social welfare reforms that were carried out in the state sector, the welfare role of the state has been diminishing. The once relatively harmonious management–labour relationship has been replaced with one that is characterized by conflicting interests and rising disputes. However, the role of the unions, or more specifically, the union officials' perception of their duties, has not changed in time to reflect the new reality. Union officials generally lack resources and power, skills and legal knowledge to fulfil their collective bargaining role and to defend their members' rights (Warner and Ng, 1999; Cooke, 2011). The union chair's role at the workplace level is often assumed by factory directors or CCP chairs. Union officials at the branch level are normally appointed by the local government and often rotate their positions in government departments as part of their political career. Where a union function is established membership level is high at over 90 per cent, notably in the state sector organizations (see *China Statistical Yearbook 2010*). However, trade unions are considered ineffective in representing workers' interests against management prerogatives and at times side with the management (O'Leary, 1998; Clarke, 2005).

Collective Bargaining

Collective bargaining in India takes a number of forms and occurs at different levels (see Venkata Ratnam, 2009 for a more detailed discussion). Interestingly, despite strong political ties, there is a striking absence in the Indian IR law of 'provisions on recognition of a trade union as a collective bargaining agent' (Sen Gupta and Sett, 2000, p. 145) at the national level; only a few states have legal provisions for it (Venkata Ratnam, 2009). The strong state intervention has inhibited the role of the trade union as an alternative and legitimate agent in collective bargaining and other IR issues (Sen Gupta and Sett, 2000). Nevertheless, Indian unions have had a longstanding involvement in collective bargaining. Through various means and forms, they have been able to achieve collective agreements often at the plant/enterprise level and sometimes at the industrial/national level (e.g., public sector firms). On some occasions, they did so through political ties and to preempt state intervention (Bhattacherjee, 1987). According to the ILO (1997/98) statistics, less than 2 per cent of the Indian workers are covered by collective bargaining agreements.

For most of the socialist Chinese history, the trade unions did not have any role in collective bargaining, as employment terms and conditions were set unilaterally by the state employer. The notion of 'collective bargaining' was not introduced in China until the early 1990s, after the Trade Union Law (1992) authorized unions at the enterprise level to conclude collective contracts with the employer. The term 'collective consultation' instead of 'collective bargaining' is preferred by the state. It is believed that consultation is a more constructive approach than 'bargaining', as it conforms to the Chinese culture of non-confrontation and conflict avoidance. In 1994, the Provisions on Collective Contracts was issued by the then Ministry of Labour, which provided detailed regulations to support the Collective Contract provision outlined in the Labour Law of China passed in 1994 (see Taylor et al., 2003 and Brown, 2006 for more detailed discussion). Trade unions have been given the official role of representing workers in consultation with employers. This position of the unions has been reinforced and expanded in subsequent labour laws. According to Article 20 of the Trade Union Law (2001), a trade union shall represent employees in equal negotiation and signing a collective contract. Matters that can be concluded in a collective contract may include labour remuneration, working time, rest and vacations, occupational safety and health, professional training and insurance and welfare.

This tripartite consultation system in China is promoted by the government as an important mechanism for the government, trade unions and enterprises to strengthen social dialogue and cooperation in coordinating labour relations in response to the new dynamics of ER during the period of economic transformation. However, limited achievements have been made after a decade's implementation of the system. According to the government statistics, the employment contract signing rate was less than 60 per cent in the mid-2000s; private enterprises had an even lower rate at 30 per cent (cited in Qiao, 2008). In spite of the legal requirement, many employers persistently refuse to sign contracts with their workers in order to avoid legal responsibility. Migrant workers in some areas also refuse to sign contracts with their employers in order to avoid paying into the social security insurance for which they must remain in the insuring city to benefit (Cooke, 2009).

Workers' Participation

India has a very long tradition of workers' participation in management, which dates back to 1918 (Mankidy, 1995). Various schemes of workers' participation have been introduced by the government since 1947 in an attempt to achieve industrial democracy. Important examples of these include works committees (1947), joint management councils (1957), worker-directors (1970) and shop and joint councils (1975). The works committees and joint management councils took the form of a legal approach, whereas the shop and joint councils were promoted as a voluntary scheme. The worker-directors scheme was only experimented with in the public sector (e.g., the banking industry) with the hope of rolling it out more widely. More schemes of workers participation were introduced in 1977, 1983 and 1985 (Venkata Ratnam, 2009). However, none of these schemes has taken root and enterprises generally have shown little interest in them (see Mankidy, 1995 and Venkata Ratnam, 2009 for more detailed overviews). This is perhaps not surprising given the fact that these initiatives have been government-led with the workers' interest at the heart of the schemes, at least in spirit. A common objection from the management of these schemes is that they represent sectional interests of the workers and not the enterprise as a whole (Venkata Ratnam, 2009).

However, it has been noted that the quality management type of management initiatives, such as quality circles (QCs), total quality management (TQM) and suggestion schemes, which require employee involvement (EI) have been widely adopted by firms since the 1980s. These schemes do not require the involvement of the trade unions and the changing attitude towards unionism and industrial relations is believed to have facilitated the propagation of the schemes (Mankidy, 1995). It needs to be noted that productivity and competitiveness enhancement remains the primary motive of these schemes and therefore employers' vested interests lies at the very heart of the popular uptake. As Cooke and Saini's (2010a) study on human resource management (HRM) and innovation in 54 Indian firms shows, EI is the second most widely used initiative by the companies studied. This is implemented mainly in the form of suggestion schemes. Quality initiatives, such as QCs, professional circles, problem-solving teams, lean initiatives, *kaizen*,[2] ISO 9000 series, TQM and total productivity management, are also commonly reported by firms that are innovation-oriented. These are essentially forms of EI requiring employees to participate actively and contribute their ideas for business improvement. Firms use reward mechanisms to incentivize their employees (e.g., financial reward, promotion and recognition when suggestions are adopted). Some even make it compulsory for professional employees to contribute ideas as part of their performance target.

In China, the formal 'representative function' of the unions, according to the Labour Law, is supplemented by the trade union-guided Workers' Representatives Congress (Workers' Congress hereafter). It is an official mechanism of workers' participation, through the workers' representative, in enterprise decision-making and management. Initially introduced in the late 1940s, the Workers' Congress has been given an enhanced role since the 1980s as a result of the economic reform. Again, in reality, the role of the Workers' Congress remains less than effective (Benson and Zhu, 2000; Cooke, 2005). Interestingly, an increasing number of private firms are setting up a Workers' Congress forum in recent years as evidence of law compliance, although they fall short of recognizing the trade union. These Workers' Congress forums serve as an extended HRM function in practice instead of playing an industrial democracy role on behalf of the workers.

Similar to Indian firms, quality management schemes have been adopted by Chinese firms since the 1980s for productivity enhancement. In fact, initiatives such as problem-solving teams, suggestion schemes and innovation task forces have long been deployed by SOEs during the state-planned economy period, often instructed by the state employer and organized by the unions at the plant level (Cooke, 2008). Suggestion schemes are also increasingly used as part of the performance management system in Chinese firms to institutionalize employees' participation.

Societal Cultures

IR scholars have argued that culture, tradition and custom play an important role in shaping the IR system in less developed countries (e.g., Siddique, 1989). It has been argued that paternalism is one of the most salient characteristics in the Asian national culture (Hofstede, 1984; Pye, 1986; Aycan, 2007). Aycan (2007, pp. 448–9) summarizes the paternalistic relationship at the workplace as such: superiors need to create a family atmosphere in the workplace, establish close and individual relationships with subordinates by getting involved with their non-work life, expect loyalty and maintain authority/status. In return, subordinates should treat the workplace as a family, be loyal and deferential, help the superior in their personal life if needed, and accept authority.

Paternalism has undoubtedly found its influence in the IR system of India and China. Both countries went through an initial period of state-planned economy that had resulted in a large and inefficient state-owned/public sector. Nevertheless, this had generated the much-needed employment in the formal/organized sector at the time when the living standard of both nations was low. The Indian traditional culture has been widely held to be responsible for a paternalistic IR system (e.g., Kennedy, 1982, cited in Siddique, 1989). Managers talk of the need to get to know their employees to understand and help them with their family problems as a precondition to establishing their managerial authority and winning commitment from the subordinates. Families of employees are invited to visit the company on its Open Days and participate in social events held by the firm to foster an emotional bond in the hope of enhancing employees' engagement with the firm. In addition, various forms of workplace welfare schemes may be introduced as evidence of being a good employer (Cooke and Saini, 2010b).

Similarly, in China, workplace welfare provisions such as subsidized canteen and entertainment programmes are expected. It is common for Chinese firms to have a range of employee-oriented activities sponsored and organized by the firm to enrich employees' social life and to embed societal and company values. These activities are paternalistic and patriotic. The interests of the state, the enterprise and the workforce are assumed to be unified (Cooke, 2008). In addition, unity, congruence and harmonization are seen to be the guiding principles of the Chinese enterprise culture. This reflects the Confucian philosophy, which places social harmony and cohesion in the central position of social relationships. Collectivism and self-sacrifice for the collective good are emphasized. As Chao (1995, p. 30) observes, 'Chinese cultural tradition fosters the internalization of self-discipline and self-restraint'. Moral obligation forms an important part of the enterprise's expectation of its employees and this expectation is institutionalized and reinforced through its cultural activities (Cooke, 2008).

Characteristics of ER

In view of the above, the ER systems of India and China display some similar as well as distinctive characteristics. The Indian IR system began to take shape after the Russian Revolution in 1917 and prior to its independence in 1947 (see Dufty, 1965 for an overview). This is evidenced by the fact that a number of labour laws had been introduced before 1947 (see Table 8.2). It is believed that the ILO 'has had a significant influence in the shaping of the Indian IR system' (Dufty, 1965, p. 41). The early years of post-Independence IR until the early 1960s were marked by 'the rise and dominance of state-sponsored unions', whose influence on terms and conditions was only exerted indirectly 'through their political links with ruling parties' (Bhattacherjee, 1987, p. 248). The ensuing two decades saw 'the phenomenal rise of strikes and lockouts due to rivalries between unions affiliated to different political parties' (ibid.). Inter-union competition in a given workplace also made it impossible to establish a stable partnership relationship between the union and management for collective bargaining (Venkata Ratnam, 1993). Union militancy in the 1960s and 1970s gave way to a gradual decline in the 1980s, when the unions realized the need to cooperate in the wake of the need to improve productivity and business performance of firms (Mankidy, 1995).

The 1980s and 1990s was characterized by incremental changes and adaptation of the Indian IR driven 'by endogenous forces of party politics, government policy, class segmentation, demography and geography' and not just 'by exogenous forces of globalization or by the functional requirements of a particular industrialization strategy' (Bhattacherjee, 2001, p. 261). The 1990s witnessed the growing power of the employers in IR and for the first time employers felt that the state was on their side (Venkata Ratnam, 1993). Still bounded by the rigid labour policy, employers launched a number of strategies to overcome legislative constraints on labour deployment to increase productivity and reduce cost. As Kuruvilla and Erickson (2002) noted, public sector firms introduced early retirement schemes and the private sector embraced numerical flexibility in order to cut labour cost. According to Sen Gupta and Sett (2000), enterprises had actually started to undertake reform sometime around the mid-1970s to increase labour flexibility and contain costs. This was in response to the economic crisis faced by the country in the mid-1960s after two wars and successive droughts. The 1980s witnessed 'a significant shift in employment from an organized to an unorganized sector' through the growing use of casual and contract employment and subcontracting (ibid., p. 148). In addition, union avoidance policies were increasingly adopted by employers, such as developing greenfield sites and promoting workers to above a certain rank so as to take them out of the legislative protection (e.g., Mathur, 1993; Venkata Ratnam, 1993; Kuruvilla and Erickson, 2002).

In both countries, political interest has tended to be the main concern of the unions at the national level rather than the pursuit of economic and labour movement, although the pursuit of any one of the three can rarely be achieved without the suppression or mobilization of the other two. It needs to be noted that, given the inter-union differences in their political stance, strategy and resources, it would be a gross simplification to classify Indian unionism as one national pattern. Both the Chinese and India governments have played a vital role in shaping the ER climate. For example, under the Industrial Dispute Act of India, 'the government enjoys the full discretionary power of whether or not, when, and how to intervene in an industrial dispute – actual or threatened' (Sen Gupta and Sett, 2000, p. 145). The government also has the power to refuse permission to the lay-off, retrenchment or closure of certain firms under the Industrial Disputes Act 1947 (Gopalakrishnan and Tortell, 2006; Saini, 2009). The state dominance in the Indian IR was attributed to its legacy of colonial past, which the post-independence Indian governments have failed to reform to be in line with its democratic political system and an industrializing economy (Sen Gupta and Sett, 2000; also see Bhattacherjee, 2001 for a comprehensive overview of the evolution of Indian IR from 1947 to 2000).

In China, state dominance as the policy-maker and employer spanned across the whole period of the state-planned economy and the first decade of the ensuing reform period. The strong state intervention is associated with its socialist ideology and the need felt by the government to keep a tight grip to maintain its authority. As such, there is no real 'partnership' between management and the trade union, or 'employee voice' in the management–labour relations. While unions may appear to be sympathetic to the plight of employees, their lack of autonomy from the state prevents any concerted action designed to influence the government (Frenkel and Peetz, 1998). The one-party system means that the CCP is able to hold down the ACFTU as its junior partner in the Party–union relationship. However, the dominance of state influence in the state-owned sector and the weakness of the trade unions in ER as a whole do not always guarantee a unilateral determination of employment practices by the (state) employers. During the state-planned economy period, conflict between management and workers as a result of the dominance of the Party within enterprises has been 'a far more common feature of industrial life in China than is generally recognized' (Sheehan, 1999, p. 2).

By the early 1990s, there were growing incidences of 'wildcat' strikes without any union presence or organization, especially in foreign-funded (including and especially in Hong Kong-, Macao- and Taiwan-funded)

Table 8.2   An overview of the ER systems of India and China

Key Features Influencing the ER System	India	China
Political system	Multi-party democracy	One-party reign since 1949, with other small parties in consultation role that does not challenge the leadership of the CCP
Role of the government	Labour laws Arbiter of labour conflicts Promoting initiatives to achieve peaceful ER and protect labour Economic development Holding tripartite meetings with social partners annually A large but shrinking state sector since the 1990s	Labour laws Suppression of non-ACFTU-led labour organization and movement Promoting initiatives to achieve harmonious ER Economic development A large but shrinking state sector since the 1980s
Current political ideology	Empowerment, inclusion and social development	Building a harmonious society through better social relationships and social development
Labour legislation	Extensive and complicated	Limited but growing coverage
Trade unions	Multiple unions, both independent and party-affiliated Inter-union rivalry exists Union strength once high but has been in decline since the 1980s Changing attitudes of unions in the wake of economic priority and global competition Unionism rivalled by professional associations and difficult to take roots in new industries (e.g., IT and BPO)	Single union, led by the CCP Union conventionally playing a welfare role with little impact on protecting workers' rights Widening role of the union since the 2000s in response to the growing private sector Union density is high in the state sector ACFTU facing formidable barriers to recognition in the private sector
Collective bargaining/ negotiation	No legal specification on the trade union's role in collective bargaining	The notion of collective bargaining/negotiation was introduced to the Chinese ER in the early 1990s

Table 8.2   (continued)

Key Features Influencing the ER System	India	China
	Scope of bargaining is constrained by law (Industrial Disputes Act 1947)	Recognized by laws and promoted by the government
		Wage level is the main issue of collective negotiation
	Collective bargaining and mutual consultation on a voluntary basis are encouraged by the government to resolve disputes	Bargaining mainly at workplace level but is encouraged by the government to take place at regional level (for multi-establishment firms)
	Bargaining at national and industrial level (e.g., public sector) and plant level (e.g., private firms)	
Workers' participation	Legal and voluntary initiatives historically promoted by the government, with limited uptake	Workers' Representative Congress, legal requirement but not effectively implemented
	Quality management schemes (e.g., suggestions schemes, problem-solving teams) promoted by employers since the 1980s, more widely adopted	Quality management schemes (e.g., suggestions schemes, problem-solving teams) promoted by employers since the 1980s
Labour dispute resolution mechanism	In place but not effective	In place but not effective
Labour market	Small organized sector	Urban workers v. rural migrant workers
	Large unorganized sector mostly unregulated	Formal v. informal employment
	Increasing level of workforce education	Increasing level of workforce education
	Worsening skill shortage alongside excessive labour surplus	Worsening skill shortage alongside excessive labour surplus
Gender issues	Relatively low proportion of women's participation, esp. in organized sector	High level of women's participation in full-time employment
	Low level of women unionization	

Table 8.2   (continued)

Key Features Influencing the ER System	India	China
	Gender organizing highly active in the informal sector	High level of union membership in unionized firms close to that of men
Societal culture	Collectivism, paternalism, strong social hierarchy influenced by the caste system	Collectivism, paternalism, egalitarianism influenced by Confucianism and socialism
Level of integration of the IR system	Decentralized due to variations in federal states' IR laws and other interventions, industrial and sectoral-based IR systems	Relatively centralized and homogeneous within industry, sector and ownership forms, but is diverging across ownership forms, industry and regions
Influence of HRM	Growing in the process of marketization and globalization and the isomorphic effect of MNCs	Growing in the process of marketization and globalization and the isomorphic effect of MNCs
Pressure for change	Economic and social development Global competition	Economic and social development Global competition

Source: The author.

enterprises (see Chan, 2001; Lee, 2007). These industrial actions by unorganized workers (or unrecognized unions) reflect both the ability of enterprises to prevent unionization and the failures of existing official unions (Frenkel and Peetz, 1998). In 1994, the number of officially recorded labour dispute cases brought before arbitration panels was 19 098; by the end of 2007, this number had risen to 350 182 (*China Statistical Yearbook 2008*). Major issues of disputes involve wage payment, labour contract, social insurance and welfare and work injury. This has led to the promulgation of the Labour Contract Law and the Labour Disputes Mediation and Arbitration Law in 2007, as noted earlier.

DISCUSSION

As already touched upon in the previous section, the ER systems of China and India have undergone some changes during their economic reform period. In this section, we recap how the changing institutional contexts and conditions are impinging upon the ER systems and the evolving role of the state in both countries. We also examine the impact of globalization and employers' strategy on ER at the firm level. And importantly, we explore the role of social policy and civil society as emerging institutional actors in shaping ER.

Changing Institutional Context and the Evolving Role of the State

Economic developments following the opening up of both countries' economy and the ensuing globalization of production and markets have been the major driving forces for the changes in the ER systems experienced by India and China. As a legislator, the two governments are expected to respond very differently. While the Chinese government has been subject to pressure to provide a more comprehensive regulatory framework to provide greater protection to the workers, the Indian government has been facing growing pressure to 'de-regulate' ER to allow employers more freedom to operate. However, numerous attempts to reform the labour laws in India since its independence have mostly ended up in inaction (e.g., Sen Gupta and Sett, 2000; Venkata Ratnam, 2009). Despite the rising competitive pressure, the Indian government has been considered slow in responding to the pressing need to relax the strong hold of the labour legislation, to entrust union recognition and to promote a labour disputes resolution system independent of the state executive (Sen Gupta and Sett, 2000; Kuruvilla and Erickson, 2002). Nevertheless, it should be noted that, since the 1980s, 'concomitant changes in the government's labour policy tended to become increasingly supportive' and even 'in favour of employers', as the government desperately needed private investments to stem its economic crises and revitalize the economy (Sen Gupta and Sett, 2000, p. 149). In addition to favouring employers, political parties in power also mobilized their affiliated trade unions to assist workplace restructuring (Sen Gupta and Sett, 2000).

As an economic manager, the two governments choose to play two rather different roles, although privatization has been a common strategy in the reform in both countries. As Khanna (2007) argued, the Chinese government is often the entrepreneur itself in its current vigorous economic growth. Governments at all levels continue to be heavily involved in businesses and the largest and best-performing firms tend to be state-owned/invested. Chinese-owned multinational corporations (MNCs) are also mostly state-owned or supported by the government. By contrast, entrepreneurship in India is driven mostly from the private sector and civil society, staying away from government interventions. It should be noted here that a countervailing view holds that the ever-present state intervention has been precisely the obstacle to the development of a strong private sector in China (e.g., Nolan, 2001; Huang, 2008), whereas the absence of government intervention has led to the growth of a number of highly internationally competitive Indian private firms. The presence or absence of government involvement, directly or indirectly, undoubtedly has implications for ER at the firm as well as sectoral level.

The Impact of Globalization and HRM Interventions on ER

Globalization and the economic policy pursued by the two govern-ments have had profound impact on the economic structure and ER in both countries, as has been the case in other Asian countries (see Lee and Eyraud, 2008). In other words, the new economy has brought new industries and new ways of managing ER at the firm level. Here, global integration has taken place at two levels: internationally and domestically (though the two are related and overlapped). Internationally, this has been achieved in part by the export-oriented industries that are largely privately owned, such as India's BPO industry, employing young English-speaking university graduates; and China's manufacturing industry, staffed by young but lowly educated rural migrant workers. Domestically, this has taken the form of attracting foreign direct investment (FDI) into the country through the establishment of MNC subsidiaries or joint ventures with local firms (also see Child and Rodrigues, 2005).

In India, the rise of the IT-enabled BPO industry (see Kuruvilla and Ranganathan, 2008 for an overview of the industry) presents opportuni-ties as well as constraints for unions to organize workers in this sector. Well-paid professionals in this industry largely fail to see the relevance of, and hardly identify themselves with, the trade union. Even when a union is established, the word 'association' instead of 'union' is used to avoid nega-tive connotation of the union's past and to gain acceptance of employers (Noronha and D'Cruz, 2009). A partnership approach and a combina-tion of union and professional association function, that is, a hybrid of the servicing and organizing model, are adopted to attract members and address IR problems (see Noronha and D'Cruz, 2009 for more detailed discussion). This development broadens the Indian IR system from the primarily manufacturing and public sector IR system in the organized sector to include the private and service sector that is knowledge-intensive, technology-driven and high value-adding. The new 'consumer capitalism' ethos also calls for the trade unions to embrace a wider social agenda than their conventional sectional interests (Bhattacherjee and Ackers, 2010). By contrast, the Chinese workers in the export-oriented manufacturing firms remain largely unorganized and unprotected, have little bargaining power and often work in sweatshop conditions (e.g., Chan, 2001; Lee, 2007; Pun and Smith, 2007). Labour disputes often erupt abruptly when the tolerance level of the workers reaches its limit. And resolution mechanisms commonly express themselves in radical forms of protests, walk-outs and violent struggles.

Another consequence of globalization has been the heightened differentiation in the labour market in both countries, with elite professionals whose skills are in great demand at the upper end and those unskilled and unprotected at the bottom end of the labour market. In order to attract, retain and motivate talented employees to enhance organizational competitiveness, Chinese and Indian firms have begun to show interest in Western-developed and MNC-imported HRM techniques. As discussed above, new management initiatives such as EI, TQM and suggestion schemes, performance management systems and learning organization are introduced. The growing awareness, or rather belief, of employers of the positive effects of HRM on organizational performance and the increasing level of professionalization of the management have fuelled the adoption of HRM techniques to solicit management–employee cooperation, with or without the union's participation. However, we should be careful not to overstate the impact of globalization and relatedly the influence of foreign MNCs in the changes in ER experienced by India and China. National ER systems are deeply embedded in their societal context, where interests of social groups are 'ambiguous and context dependent', and require multiple disciplinary perspectives to make sense of them (Williamson, 1985, cited in Bhattacherjee, 2001, p. 245; Zeitlin, 1987, p. 163). In the same spirit then, two emerging, albeit small, sources of influence must also be taken into account when assessing the changing dynamics of ER – the role of the social policy and civil society.

The Role of Social Policy and Civil Society in Shaping ER

Social policy has long played a role in the labour policy of both countries, as it has in most countries. What needs to be examined is how political ideologies have evolved as a result of the evolution of domestic institutions and international pressures/influences. For example, in view of the widening income gaps, rising levels of social unrests and international pressure to improve human rights, a top priority of the Chinese government now is to build a harmonious society. Its new social policy and interventions on ER very much reflect this agenda, although its ability to achieve this is contingent upon the local agenda (Cooke, 2009). In India, recognizing diversity and diverse social needs runs at the core of its social inclusion and empowerment policy initiatives, although the political motive has been questioned by some. An increasing number of organizations are developing HRM initiatives to demonstrate their commitment to this social agenda and to harness talent to enhance their competitiveness. The likely impact of these HRM interventions needs to be assessed, particularly from the employees' perspective (e.g., Cooke and Saini, 2010b).

In India, non-government organizations (NGOs) have had a long-standing presence in the informal sector and have been playing an active role in organizing and meeting some of the needs of the workers. By contrast, NGOs have only started to emerge in China in recent years due to the Chinese government's concern about alternative forms of political organizations outside the parameter of the state apparatus. Despite operating within immense political constraints and in limited locations and sectors, international NGOs and domestic ones under international patronage have been playing a role in monitoring the labour standards and legislative compliance of firms in China. They also provide financial, medical, legal, educational and emotional support to the workers in sweatshop plants through some forms of organizing primarily outside the workplaces. The promulgation of the new labour laws has undoubtedly provided the NGOs with more legal instruments to carry out their work. However, gaining a wider political recognition from the state and operational legitimacy from the local governments remains a formidable challenge in the foreseeable future. To some extent, the space created by the absence of the trade unions in the private and foreign-funded enterprises is filled by (international) NGOs, if in a somewhat temporary and discrete manner. The growing presence of NGOs may undermine the legitimacy of the unions and their ability to fulfil the range of functions prescribed to them by the state. That said, the institutional position of NGOs is far from being secure, as they rely heavily on external resource support on the one hand and the tolerance of the state on the other, and can easily be isolated through political discourse. The somewhat transient and precarious nature of NGOs in their labour standards monitoring role may regenerate sites that formal monitoring channels have not been able to reach (Cooke, 2009).

CONCLUSION

This chapter has provided a comparative, if somewhat over-simplified and over-generalized, account of the evolution of the ER context and characteristics of India and China since their independence/liberation in the late 1940s. It is one of the first attempts to provide a focused and comprehensive comparison of the two countries' ER systems at the national level. As we have seen, the historical IR system of India has unfolded itself with some shared characteristics to those found in the Western economies such as the UK (e.g., Chandrashekar, 1970). These include the rotating legal and voluntary approach to IR with various government-led workers' participation initiatives, the rising militancy of the union/labour in the 1960s and 1970s that had subsequently given way to management power. By contrast, China's ER was arguably more 'peaceful' under the grip of the state. However, marketization has weakened this grip and led to a more confrontational ER scenario.

In general, the governments of both countries have taken an interventionist approach to ER as they navigated through the industrialization process. Prior to the economic open-up era in both countries, the governments had adopted a labour protection-oriented approach to ER, at least for those in the formal/organized sector. The governments' main concern was 'industrial peace and employment-income protection' (Frenkel and Kuruvilla, 2002, p. 398). This was achieved primarily through strong legislation and unionism in India. In urban China, it was achieved through administrative regulations, job-for-life and extensive workplace welfare on the one hand, and the strong suppression of autonomous labour movement and labour unrest on the other. As a result, both countries had a large state-owned/public sector that was burdened by overstaffing, inefficiency and bureaucracy. As their process of economic reform deepens, the Indian government has been facing pressure to liberalize its legalistic IR framework, whereas the Chinese government has been urged to move from a directive to a more legalistic approach. In this sense, some convergence between the two ER systems appears inevitable.

In both countries, trade unions have played an important role as a political actor in assisting the political parties to gain power, which had led to the independence of India and the liberation of China. Whilst unions in both countries have close ties with the political parties, the ACFTU has little bargaining power as the subordinate partner to the only ruling party – the CCP. Its main function is to implement state decisions and to prevent and mediate conflicts between the employer and the workers, often in the name of national interest. By contrast, politically connected Indian unions are more able to influence regulations and policies in exchange for votes and party support. Party dependence of the ACFTU and party alliances of the Indian trade unions therefore characterize the development and functioning of the trade unions in the two countries.

Finally, different historical paths and political systems of the two countries have led to their rather different approaches to managing the economic transformation assumed by the Indian and Chinese government. As such, the ER systems of India and China are likely to retain their distinct and enduring features and co-evolve with other institutions and cultural values of the nations. One thing in common, to echo Gall's (1998) argument, is that the state will continue to play a dominant role and therefore remain an important focus for study, although the precise political process may differ. Given the scope of the chapter, it has not been possible to discuss the extent to which ER at the local level may be influenced by the vast variation in culture, language, history and level of economic development across the regions within the two countries, particularly India. As such, this study may have been trapped by the inherent problems associated with comparative IR studies at the national level as identified by a number of authors (e.g., Bean, 1994; Van Ruysseveldt, 1995; Gospel, 2008). Building on what we have learned so far, future studies on China and India should adopt an empirical approach to investigate IR issues at the micro-level based on the same industrial sectors and/or ownership forms. Particular attention should be paid on how the collectivist and reciprocation-oriented nature of social relations (Westwood et al., 2004) may shape the characteristics of ER in China and India and the extent to which these cultural characteristics may have been diluted or evolved as a result of recent economic development and growing global influence.

NOTES

1. In China, the word 'province' is used to refer to the level of administration below the central government level, whereas the word 'state' is used in India.
2. Japanese for 'improvement' or 'change for the better', a philosophy of focus on continuous improvement of processes in manufacturing, engineering, supporting business processes, and management and so on.

REFERENCES

All India State Government Employees Federation (2003), 'Public employees and workers cannot forego their right to strike', available at: http://www.tradeunionindia.org/miscellaneous/public_rights.htm; accessed 12 January 2011.
Aycan, Z. (2007), 'Paternalism: Towards conceptual refinement and operationalisation', in K.S. Yang, K.K. Hwang and U. Kim (eds), *Scientific Advances in Indigenous Psychologies: Empirical, Philosophical, and Cultural Contributions*, London: Cambridge University Press, pp. 445–66.
BBC News (2004), 'India population "to be biggest"', 18 August 2004, available at: http://news.bbc.co.uk/1/hi/3575994.stm; accessed 12 January 2011.
Beale, D. and Noronha, E. (2009), 'Indian public sector trade unionism in context: Gujarat and West Bengal compared', Unpublished working paper presented in the 'Fairness at Work Seminar Series' at Manchester Business School, University of Manchester, UK.

Bean, R. (1994), *Comparative Industrial Relations: An Introduction to Cross-National Perspectives*, London: Routledge.
Benson, J. and Zhu, Y. (2000), 'A case study analysis of human resource management in China's manufacturing industry', *China Industrial Economy*, **4**(1), 62–5.
Bhattacherjee, D. (1987), 'Union-type effects on bargaining outcomes in Indian manufacturing', *British Journal of Industrial Relations*, **25**(2), 247–66.
Bhattacherjee, D. (2001), 'The evolution of Indian industrial relations: A comparative perspective', *Industrial Relations Journal*, **32**(3), 244–63.
Bhattacherjee, D. and Ackers, P. (2010), 'Managing employment relations in India: Old narratives and new perspectives', *Industrial Relations Journal*, **41**(2), 104–21.
Brown, R. (2006), 'China's collective contract provisions: Can collective negotiations embody collective bargaining?', *Duke Journal of Comparative and International Law*, **16**(35), 35–77.
Budhwar, P. (2009), 'Managing human resources in India', in J. Storey, P. Wright and D. Ulrich (eds), *The Routledge Companion to Strategic Human Resource Management*, London: Routledge, pp. 435–46.
Candland, C. (2007), *Labour, Democratisation and Development in India and Pakistan*, London: Routledge.
Chan, A. (2001), *China's Workers under Assault: The Exploitation of Labor in a Globalizing Economy*, New York: M.E. Sharpe.
Chandrashekar, B.K. (1970), 'Labour relations in India: Report of the National Commission on Labour 1969', *British Journal of Industrial Relations*, **8**(3), 369–88.
Chao, Y.T. (1995), 'Culture and work organization: The Chinese case', in H. Kao, H. Sinha and S.H. Ng (eds), *Effective Organizations and Social Values*, London: Sage Publications, pp. 28–35.
Child, J. and Rodrigues, S. (2005), 'The internationalization of Chinese firms: A case for theoretical extension?', *Management and Organization Review*, **1**(3), 381–410.
China Statistical Yearbook 2008 and 2010, Beijing: China Statistics Publishing House.
Choi, Y.J. (2008), 'Aligning labour disputes with institutional, cultural and rational approach: Evidence from East Asian-invested enterprises in China', *The International Journal of Human Resource Management*, **19**(10), 1929–61.
Clarke, S. (2005), 'Post-socialist trade unions: China and Russia', *Industrial Relations Journal*, **36**(1), 2–18.
Cooke, F.L. (2005), *HRM, Work and Employment in China*, London: Routledge.
Cooke, F.L. (2008), 'Enterprise culture management in China: An "insiders'" perspective', *Management and Organization Review*, **4**(2), 291–314.
Cooke, F.L. (2009), 'The enactment of three new labour laws in China: Unintended consequences and emergence of "new" actors in employment relations', Paper presented at the Conference of the Regulating for Decent Work Network, 8–10 July, International Labour Office, Geneva, Switzerland.
Cooke, F.L. (2010), 'Women's participation in employment in Asia: A comparative analysis of China, India, Japan and South Korea', *International Journal of Human Resource Management*, **21**(12), 2249–70.
Cooke, F.L. (2011), 'Employment Relations in China', in Bamber, G., Lansbury, R. and Wailes, N. (eds), *International and Comparative Employment Relations*, 5th edition, London: Sage and New South Wales, Australia: Allen & Unwin Pty Ltd, pp. 307–29.
Cooke, F.L. and Saini, D.S. (2010a), '(How) does the HR strategy support an innovation-oriented business strategy? An investigation of institutional context and organizational practices in Indian firms', *Human Resource Management*, **49**(3), 377–400.
Cooke, F.L. and Saini, D.S. (2010b), 'Diversity management in India: A study of organizations in different ownership forms and industrial sectors', *Human Resource Management*, **49**(3).
Cooney, S. (2007), 'China's labour law, compliance and flaws in implementing institutions', *Journal of Industrial Relations*, **49**(5), 673–86.
Dufty, N.F. (1965), 'The evolution of the Indian industrial relations system', *Journal of Industrial Relations*, **7**(1), 40–49.

Frenkel, S. and Kuruvilla, S. (2002), 'Logics of action, globalization, and changing employment relations in China, India, Malaysia, and the Philippines', *Industrial and Labor Relations Review*, **55**(3), 387–412.

Frenkel, S. and Peetz, D. (1998), 'Globalization and industrial relations in East Asia: A three-country comparison', *Industrial Relations*, **37**(3), 282–310.

Gall, G. (1998), 'Kuruvilla: The political economy of industrialization and industrial relations: A comment', *Industrial Relations Journal*, **29**(1), 74–8.

Gallagher, M. (2005), *Contagious Capitalism: Globalization and the Politics of Labor in China*, Princeton: Princeton University Press.

Ghosh, R. and Roy, K. (1997), 'The changing status of women in India: Impact of urbanization and development', *International Journal of Social Economics*, **24**(7/8/9), 902–17.

Gopalakrishnan, R. and Tortell, L. (2006), 'Access to justice, trade union rights, and the Indian Industrial Disputes Act, 1947', *International Journal of Comparative Labour Law and Industrial Relations*, **22**(4), 529–62.

Gospel, H. (2008), 'Trade unions in theory and practice: Perspectives from advanced industrial countries', in J. Benson and Y. Zhu (eds), *Trade Unions in Asia: An Economic and Sociological Analysis*, pp. 11–23.

Guthrie, D. (1999), *Dragon in a Three-piece Suit*, Princeton, NJ: Princeton University Press.

Hassard, J., Sheehan, J., Zhou, M., Terpstra-Tong, J. and Morris, J. (2007), *China's State Enterprise Reform: From Marx to the Market*, London: Routledge.

Hill, E. (2008), 'India: The self-employed women's association and autonomous organizing', in K. Broadbent and M. Ford (eds), *Women and Labour Organizing in Asia: Diversity, Autonomy and Activism*, London: Routledge, pp. 115–35.

Hofstede, G. (1984), 'Cultural dimensions in management and planning', *Asia Pacific Journal of Management*, **1**(2), 81–99.

Huang, Y.S. (2008), *Capitalism with Chinese Characteristics: Entrepreneurship and the State*, Cambridge: Cambridge University Press.

International Labour Organization (ILO) (1997/98), *World Employment – National Policies in a Global Context*, Geneva: International Labour Office.

Khanna, T. (2007), *Billions of Entrepreneurs: How China and India Are Reshaping Their Futures and Yours*, Boston: Harvard Business School Press.

Kuruvilla, S. (1996), 'Linkages between industrialization strategies and industrial relations/ human resource policies: Singapore, Malaysia, the Philippines, and India', *Industrial and Labor Relations Review*, **49**(4), 635–57.

Kuruvilla, S. and Erickson, C. (2002), 'Change and transformation in Asian industrial relations', *Industrial Relations*, **41**(2), 171–227.

Kuruvilla, S. and Ranganathan, A. (2008), 'Economic development strategies and macro- and micro-level human resource policies: The case of India's "outsourcing" industry', *Industrial and Labor Relations Review*, **62**(1), 39–72.

Kuruvilla, S. and Venkata Ratnam, C.S. (1996), 'Economic development and industrial relations: The case of South and Southeast Asia', *Industrial Relations*, **27**(1), 9–23.

Lee, C.K. (2007), *Against the Law: Labor Protests in China's Rustbelt and Sunbelt*, Berkeley, CA: University of California.

Lee, S. and Eyraud, F. (2008), *Globalization, Flexibilisation and Working Conditions in Asia and the Pacific*, Oxford: Chandos Publishing.

Magoshi, E. and Chang, E. (2009), 'Diversity management and the effects on employees' organizational commitment: Evidence from Japan and Korea', *Journal of World Business*, **44**(1), 31–40.

Mankidy, J. (1995), 'Changing perspectives of worker participation in India with particular reference to the banking industry', *British Journal of Industrial Relations*, **33**(3), 443–58.

Mathur, J.S. (1966), 'India's labour policy', *Journal of Industrial Relations*, **8**(3), 283–97.

Mathur, A. (1993), 'The experience of consultation during structural adjustment in India (1990–1992)', *International Labour Review*, **132**(3), 331–45.

Nolan, P. (2001), *China and the Global Economy*, Basingstoke: Palgrave.
Noronha, E. and D'Cruz, P. (2009), 'Engaging the professional: Organising call centre agents in India', *Industrial Relations Journal*, **40**(3), 215–34.
O'Leary, G. (ed.) (1998), *Adjusting to Capitalism: Chinese Workers and the State*, New York: M.E. Sharpe.
Pandey, S.M. (1967), 'Inter-union rivalry in India: An analysis', *Journal of Industrial Relations*, **9**(2), 140–54.
Potter, P. (1999), 'The Chinese legal system: Continuing commitment to the primacy of state power', *The China Quarterly*, **159**, 673–83.
Pun, N. (2005), *Made in China: Women Factory Workers in a Global Workplace*, North Carolina: Duke University Press.
Pun, N. and Smith, C. (2007), 'Putting transnational labour process in its place: The dormitory labour regime in post-socialist China', *Work, Employment & Society*, **21**(1), 47–65.
Pye, L. (1986), 'The China trade: Making the deal', *Harvard Business Review*, **64**(4), 74–80.
Qiao, J. (2008), 'Labor contract law in China: Changes and implications', Paper presented in the International Conference 'Breaking down Chinese Walls: The Changing Faces of Labor and Employment in China', Cornell University, 26–28 September, Ithaca, New York.
Ramaswamy, E.A. (1988), *Worker Consciousness and Trade Union Response*, Delhi: Oxford University Press.
Ramesh, J. (2005), *Making Sense of Chindia: Reflections on China and India*, New Delhi: India Research Press.
Saini, D.S. (2009), 'Labour law in India: Structure and working', in P. Budhwar and J. Bhatnagar (eds), *The Changing Face of People Management in India*, London: Routledge, pp. 60–94.
Sen Gupta, A. and Sett, P. (2000), 'Industrial relations law, employment security and collective bargaining in India: Myths, realities and hopes', *Industrial Relations Journal*, **31**(2), 144–53.
Sheehan, J. (1999), *Chinese Workers: A New History*, London: Routledge.
Sheth, J. (2008), *Chindia Rising: How China and India Will Benefit Your Business*, New Delhi: McGraw-Hill Offices.
Shyam Sundar, K.R. (2008), 'Trade unions in India: From politics of fragmentation to politics of expansion and integration?', in J. Benson and Y. Zhu (eds), *Trade Unions in Asia: An Economic and Sociological Analysis*, pp. 157–76.
Siddique, S. (1989), 'Industrial relations in a third world setting: A possible model', *Industrial Relations Journal*, **31**(3), 385–401.
Srivastva, S.C. (1970), 'Trade unions' participation in the planned economy of India', *Journal of Industrial Relations*, **12**(2), 238–52.
Subramanian, S. (1973), 'The right to strike for public employees – a point of view', *Industrial Relations Journal*, **15**(2), 218–20.
Taylor, B. and Li, Q. (2007), 'Is the ACFTU a union and does it matter?', *Journal of Industrial Relations*, **49**(5), 701–15.
Taylor, B., Chang, K. and Li, Q. (2003), *Industrial Relations in China*, Cheltenham, UK and Northampton, MA, USA: Edward Elgar.
Venkata Ratnam, C.S. (1993), 'Impact of new economic policies on the role of trade unions', *Indian Journal of Industrial Relations*, **29**(1), 56–77.
Venkata Ratnam, C.S. (2006), *Industrial Relations*, Oxford: Oxford University Press.
Venkata Ratnam, C.S. (2009), 'Employment relations in India', in P. Budhwar and J. Bhatnagar (eds), *The Changing Face of People Management in India*, London: Routledge, pp. 23–59.
Venkata Ratnam, C.S. and Jain, H. (2002), 'Women in trade unions in India', *International Journal of Manpower*, **23**(3), 277–92.
Van Ruysseveldt, J. (1995), 'Growing cross-national diversity or diversity *tout court*? An introduction to comparative industrial and employment relations', in J. Van Ruysseveldt,

R. Huiskamp and J. Van Hoof (eds), *Comparative Industrial and Employment Relations*, London: Sage, pp. 1–15.

Verma, A. and Yan, Z.M. (1995), 'The changing face of human resource management in China: Opportunities, problems and strategies', in A. Verma, T. Kochan and R. Lansbury (eds), *Employment Relations in the Growing Asian Economies*, London: Routledge, pp. 315–35.

Warner, M. (1996), 'Human resources in the People's Republic of China: The "Three Systems" reforms', *Human Resource Management Journal*, **6**(2), 32–42.

Warner, M. (2008), 'Trade unions in China: In search of a new role in the "Harmonious Society"', in J. Benson and Y. Zhu (eds), *Trade Unions in Asia: An Economic and Sociological Analysis*, London: Routledge, pp. 140–56.

Warner, M. and Ng, S.H. (1999), 'Collective contracts in Chinese enterprises: A new brand of collective bargaining under "Market Socialism"?', *British Journal of Industrial Relations*, **37**(2), 295–314.

Westwood, R., Chan, A. and Linstead, S. (2004), 'Theorising Chinese employment relations comparatively: Exchange, reciprocity and the moral economy', *Asia Pacific Journal of Management*, **21**(3), 365–82.

World Bank (2006), *India Country Overview 2006*, the World Bank, available at: http://www.karmayog.org/worldbank/worldbank_1416.htm; accessed on 12 January 2011.

World Bank Group (2006), GenderStats Database of Gender Statistics, available at: http://web.worldbank.org/WBSITE/EXTERNAL/TOPICS/EXTGENDER/EXTANAT OOLS/EXTSTATINDDATA/EXTGENDERSTATS/0,,menuPK:3237391~pagePK:641 68427~piPK:64168435~theSitePK:3237336,00.html; accessed 12 January 2011.

9 Employment relations in the United Kingdom and Republic of Ireland

Tony Dundon and David G. Collings

INTRODUCTION

The United Kingdom (UK)[1] and Republic of Ireland (hereafter Ireland) share a number of broadly similar characteristics, in part owing to the close proximity of the two countries as well as the legacy of British imperialism and governance in the centuries before the formation of the Irish Free State in 1922. Both countries joined the European Union (EU) around the same time in the 1970s; English is the predominant language in both jurisdictions; and a considerable amount of commercial trade occurs between the two nations. Ireland is much smaller with a population of just over 4 million, compared with 61 million in the UK (Eurostat, 2009a). Ireland is the second most expensive country in which to live in the EU (after Denmark), with the UK ranked twelfth and marginally below the EU average (Eurostat, 2009b). Employees in the UK work on average 2.6 hours more per week than their counterparts in Ireland: 43.2 hours per week in the UK compared with an average of 40.6 in Ireland (Schäfer, 2006). Unemployment has risen in both countries in recent times, standing at 7.9 per cent in the UK and 12.5 per cent in Ireland (CSO Ireland, 2009; Labour Force Survey [UK], 2010). Labour market participation is higher in the UK than in Ireland: around 65 per cent of women are in employment in the UK compared with 56 per cent of women in Ireland (Schäfer, 2006).

It is against this descriptive backdrop that this chapter compares the 'institutions', 'actors', 'processes' and 'cultural legacies' that shape employment relations in both the UK and Ireland. As Jackson argues in Chapter 5 in this volume, comparative employment relations that focus too exclusively on cultural dimensions alone are likely to miss important geopolitical influences. The chapter commences with a brief overview of the post-war employment relations landscape in each country, illustrating the importance of political and cultural legacies between the paired countries. The next section assesses the role of the main actors to employment relations (e.g., employers, unions and the state), followed by a comparative review of some of the main employment relations institutions and

214

processes (e.g., collective bargaining and partnership, employee involvement, non-unionism). Finally, the conclusion comments on a number of current and likely future issues in each jurisdiction, arguing that against a similar heritage and cultural legacy, there remain important differences in approach, style and posture towards the regulation of employment between Ireland and the UK.

POST-WAR PATTERNS OF EMPLOYMENT RELATIONS: A BRIEF OVERVIEW

The post-war consensus in Ireland and the UK developed along broadly similar liberal pluralist lines with the main actors – such as government, employers and unions – occupying a central place in terms of consultation and bargaining, albeit from very different positions. In the UK, trade unions underpinned the war effort in terms of the supply of labour (including women) to factories and industry. Post-war full-employment in Britain accompanied the growth of trade unionism and saw the demise of a deferential society. The Protestant work ethic paved the way for increased demands for improved living standards amidst growing affluence and relatively rapid industrialization and modernization of large industry (Clegg, 1979). Above all, the war and post-war consensus effectively showed that trade unions were key agents that served a utilitarian interest for both worker and state (ibid.). Ireland, in contrast, was characterized by very different societal values after World War II. Ireland is a much smaller country, both geographically and by population, and the role and influence of Roman Catholicism penetrated virtually all aspects of public and private life. According to Von Prondzynski (1998, p. 58), Ireland emerged out of the 1940s in the grip of centralized coordination derived from Catholic teachings. Significantly, the agricultural sector was a key driver of industrial policy in Ireland in the first few decades after independence, accounting for 32 per cent of GDP and 54 per cent of all employment in 1926 (Haughton, 2000).

From quite different trajectories – early industrialization in the UK and a predominantly agrarian economy in Ireland – a broadly similar voluntarist system of employment relations developed in each jurisdiction. Pluralist traditions are engrained in the Irish Constitution with a formalized 'right of freedom of association'. In effect, Irish workers are free to join any trade union that they so choose. However, that right does not place any obligation on employers to recognize or negotiate with trade unions. In O'Mahony's (1964, p. 1) words, 'while the law recognizes collective bargaining as a right it does not normally impose it as a duty'.

In contrast, while the UK has no formal Constitution it does have statutory legislation that obliges employers to recognize a trade union of the workers' choosing.

After the formation of the Irish Free State in 1922, pluralist industrial relations machinery developed slowly, although the creation of the Labour Court in 1946 signalled a watershed in the institutionalization of industrial relations by establishing specific and permanent state machinery to regulate employment conditions and relations (Roche, 1997a). In 1948 Ireland withdrew from the British Commonwealth, with both countries joining the European Union in the early 1970s. In Ireland, Republican nationalism dominates the country's political and ideological landscape, with *Fianna Fáil* being the main governmental political party since late 1990s. In Britain, politics has been dominated by two main parties: Conservative and Labour. Ireland has experienced considerably higher growth (at least up to the 2009 recessionary period) and has developed a niche position as a knowledge-based economy with large inflows of foreign direct investment. Unlike the UK, around 80 per cent of production is devoted to exports in Ireland. Both countries have experienced a rise in service-based economic activity and employment in the last decade.

In employment relations terms the idea of voluntarism has remained a key foundational belief with the philosophy that the parties are best left to their own devices to resolve issues at workplace and industry levels. Government is seen as occupying a minimal role in terms of direct legal intervention in the regulation of employment relations, although this has recently been questioned. Ideally, trade unions and employers bargain over terms and conditions while the state provides institutional support to workers in relation to health and safety, minimum wages and individual employment rights protection. As in many other industrialized economies, union membership has declined dramatically and the structure and configuration of the labour market has changed from manufacturing/industry-based jobs to service-based employment. Non-unionism is the norm in both the UK and Ireland in the private sector, and the majority of workplaces are small to medium-sized enterprises (SMEs). The role of MNCs has been much more significant in Ireland compared with the UK (the role of multinationals in the global employment relations area is considered in greater detail in Chapter 17 in this volume by Collings, Lavelle and Gunnigle). For example, Ireland was the largest net recipient of FDI in the OECD over the period 1993–2003, recording a cumulative balance of inflows over outflows of $71 billion, making it the world's eleventh largest recipient of FDI (Collings et al., 2005). In Ireland, MNCs contribute approximately 80 per cent of industrial exports (O'Higgins, 2002). Further, over 49 per cent of employment in manufacturing is accounted

Table 9.1 FDI inflows 1970–2004 (millions of dollars)

	1970–79	%	1980–89	%	1990–99	%	2000–04	%
Ireland	1 370	0.76	2 210	0.31	39 225	1.41	100 419	3.24
Denmark	1 079	0.60	2 291	0.32	42 642	1.53	43 485	1.41
UK	32 572	18.06	103 919	14.37	324 769	11.65	294 114	9.49
Germany	14 364	7.96	15 140	2.09	124 615	4.57	263 915	8.51
Portugal	739	0.41	4 453	0.62	18 285	0.66	22 370	0.72
Italy	5 582	3.26	18 873	2.61	42 553	1.53	76 020	2.45

Source: Lavelle et al. (2009, p. 5).

for by those employed in affiliates under foreign control (OECD, 2005). Table 9.1 provides an illustration of the inflow of FDI in Ireland and the UK in comparative perspective.

There are further important structural factors affecting employment relations in the UK and Ireland. In both jurisdictions, the principle of voluntarism has become constrained owing to increasing regulation at both the national and European levels. Significantly, the prevalence of non-unionism in the multinational sector in Ireland has indirectly impacted on the nature of voluntarism (Gunnigle et al., 2005). In attempting to counterbalance the trend of non-unionism in this sector the trade union movement has been actively campaigning for statutory union recognition to bring to Ireland statutory rights similar to those in the UK and the US (Collings et al., 2008, pp. 255–6). Interestingly, Ireland and the UK have adopted different postures towards employment regulation in key areas, from what appear to be broadly similar European Directives. Ireland has developed a more corporatist regime with national-level partnerships seeking to promote a degree of social inclusion, while the UK faced an earlier (and some would argue alternative) neoliberal economic experience with the election of Thatcher and subsequent Conservative administrations between 1979 and 1997, essentially embarking on a concerted attempt to exclude and weaken trade unions. Post-1997 and the election of a Labour government in the UK, the direction has remained largely neoliberal with a social conscience and realignment towards a European social model. In the UK a Conservative–Liberal coalition government was elected in 2010. While Ireland has developed a much stronger corporatist regime, there also remains a neoliberal undercurrent in which political power favours capital and especially US multinational investment (Taylor, 2002). Arguably, the Irish state has engineered a European-style social model while appeasing the interests of large-scale capital investment. The result at the workplace has led to a less than positive picture for trade unions and employee voice. In 2009, faced with a growing budget deficit and the political desire to bail out a failing banking system, the Irish government sought to manage its way out of recession through fiscal restraint. One of the most draconian measures included public sector pay cuts of between 5 and 20 per cent. The once acclaimed model of national partnership between the state, unions and employers collapsed and public sector unions have responded with a national 'work-to-rule' programme of industrial action.

In summary then, a post-war pluralist consensus emerged in both countries, albeit from very different cultural contexts and social values. Amidst increasing European employment regulation in both Ireland and the UK, there remains a strong philosophical foundation in neoliberal market capitalism that has, arguably, favoured multinational capital at the expense of trade union membership and organization. These broad issues will be developed in greater detail in subsequent sections of the remainder of this chapter.

THE PARTIES TO EMPLOYMENT RELATIONS IN IRELAND AND THE UK

Unions

Trade unions in both Ireland and the UK share a common heritage, much of which developed as a result of early British industrialization with emerging economic, political and legal regimes that deemed union activities to be a form of criminal conspiracy until the repeal of the Combination Laws in 1825. Even then, collective action remained unlawful, as trade unions were seen as an interference with the idea of 'freedom of contract', which was at the time associated with progressive capitalism (O'Mahony, 1964, pp. 2–4). Trade unions were outlawed in Ireland in 1789, a move that predated the British legislation by some 20 years (Wallace et al., 2004). Consequently, unions developed slowly at first, often on a craft, localized or geographical basis, which resulted in a great deal of fragmentation.

At the beginning of the nineteenth century in Ireland trade unions were faced with moves to suppress them by government, largely because of the government's view that they were incompatible with the doctrine of 'freedom of contract' (O'Mahony, 1964). A quarter of a century later unions were at best tolerated, largely owing to the political and economic pressures to re-evaluate the principles of 'ownership, property and freedom' in the context of employees and labour power. Subsequently, within 50 years of the turn of the nineteenth century they were advanced to a position that afforded them legal protection. While it is important not to neglect the role of the state in altering the status of trade unions from one of criminal conspiracy to legitimate social and economic actors, significant is that 'organized labour consolidated its position and advanced the interest of its members largely through collective bargaining with employers' (Kelly and Roche, 1983, p. 224). Indeed, by the early 1900s trade unions were well established in many sectors of the Irish economy (Boyd, 1972). Thus, early in the twentieth century the state realized that it was necessary to redefine the rights and privileges accorded to organized labour and this was achieved through the 1906 Trade Disputes Act (O'Mahony, 1964).

Unlike other European countries, both the UK and Ireland have a single union federation: the Irish Congress of Trade Unions (ICTU) in the Republic and the Trades Union Congress (TUC) in the UK. These bodies are essentially umbrella federations to which separate trade unions affiliate, and they largely reflect the early development of trade unionism under British rule. The TUC was formed in 1868 and owing to the hostile political and legal environment towards trade unions at the time, it set up a parliamentary committee in 1871, which later became the Labour Party. In Ireland, early trade unions had been affiliated with the British Trades Union Congress. However, little time was devoted to Irish affairs at the TUC in the UK, leading to dissatisfaction among Irish members and the establishment of the Irish Trades Union Congress in 1894 (Hillary, 1989).

Largely because of the legacy of British colonial rule, organized labour in both Ireland and the UK developed an industrial base in advance of a countervailing political power (Kelly and Roche, 1983). Importantly, this stood in contrast to the experience in most other European countries at the time, which helps explain the distinctive nature of emerging voluntarist employment relations systems in both the UK and Ireland. It also stands in contrast to the experience in the US, where large industry gained legitimacy and power long before trade unions. In the formative years of economic development, the Anglo-Irish union movement sought to overcome a number of legal obstacles that retarded their path toward legitimacy. In contrast, in many other European countries, unions functioned in a subsidiary role to left wing or social democratic political parties, while in the Anglo-Irish system, political power was largely subservient to industrial power (Kelly and Roche, 1983; Von Prondzynski, 1998).

Trade union density rose consistently in both the both countries following World War II, peaking in both countries in 1980: 62 per cent in Ireland (Roche and Ashmore, 2002) and 54.5 per cent in the UK (Waddington, 2003). The significance of this upward trend in unionization since the War led leading scholars to focus almost exclusively on predicting 'when' non-union workers would organize. In the UK, Bain and Price (1983,

Table 9.2   Trade union membership and density in the UK and Ireland, selected dates, 1955–2008

Year	UK: Membership and Density (%)	Ireland: Membership and Density (%)
1955	9 460 000 (44.5)[a]	305 620 (45.7)[c]
1965	9 715 000 (43.0)[a]	358 050 (52.4)[c]
1975	11 561 000 (52.0)[a]	449 520 (60.0)[c]
1980	12 239 000 (54.5)[a]	527 960 (62.0)[c]
1985	10 282 000 (49.0)[a]	485 040 (61.3)[c]
1995	7 309 000 (32.1)[a]	504 450 (53.1)[c]
2000	7 120 000 (29.8)[b]	586 944 (43.2)[c]
2003	7 115 000 (29.3)[b]	641 633 (43.6)[c]
2008	6 883 000 (27.4)[b]	632 035 (36.0)[d]

Sources: For UK: a. 1955–95 Waddington (2003, p. 220); b. 2000–08 Barrett (2009, p. 8); for Ireland: c. 1955–2003 Wallace et al. (2004, p. 146); d. 2008, Dobbins (2009, p. 4).

p. 32) commented that 'The largest untapped potential for union growth in Britain is among the more than six million workers in private services', while in Ireland, Flood and Turner (1993, p. 54) went as far as to suggest that 'it appeared to commentators only a matter of time before all significant concentrations of employees became unionised'. However, the near demise of trade unions became apparent post-1980 with a steady and persistent decline in union density, summarized in Table 9.2. Several arguments have been advanced to explain this decline, although these differ between Ireland and the UK. Notably, as seen in Table 9.2, actual union membership has remained consistent in recent years in Ireland, but no so in the UK.

The comparative data in Table 9.2 show changes in union membership from 1955 to 2008, in both the UK and Ireland. The data show some remarkable similarity. In both the UK and Ireland, union density experienced a consistent rise up to 1980; thereafter, the proportion of the employed labour force in union membership declined in both countries, and at a different rate. The decline in density is considerably worse for the UK (from 54.5 per cent in 1980 to 27.4 per cent by 2008) than for Ireland (down from 62 per cent to 36 per cent over the same period).

Several explanations have been advanced to account for the decline in union density. First, in the UK, unions faced a political and legal assault from 1980 with the election of Thatcher and the desire to curb union power. Extensive legislation was enacted that actively sought to diminish the power of organized labour at the workplace. However, it remains debatable as to the precise impact of anti-union legislation in the UK on union density and membership (Disney et al., 1998). Waddington (2003) explains that the decline in unionization is closely related to other significant developments in the economy, particularly changes in the structure of industry and labour market composition of jobs with an increasing number of peripheral and atypical forms of employment. Second, economic changes in both Ireland and the UK at the time were extensive and consistent. For example, emigration was a key demographic trend in Ireland in the 1980s as unemployment rose from 5.5 per cent in the early 1970s to over 17 per cent in 1986 (Wallace et al., 2004). In short, union density declined because there were fewer people in employment. A third and related explanation concerns the changing structure of industry. Once the heartland of unionization, manufacturing employment declined and in its place emerged smaller service sector companies, many of which have proved notoriously difficult for trade unions to organize and represent workers. In Ireland the emergence of non-unionism in the multinational sector was also a key explanatory factor (we return to this below). Overall, declining union density is explained more by changes in the economy and labour market (in both Ireland and the UK) than anti-union laws per se (UK only). However, the effect of legislation cannot be dismissed entirely. It is feasible that the extent of legal privileges coupled with economic power afforded to employers supported an increasingly more assertive and aggressive managerial style towards unions and collective forms of employment relations.

Arguably, the most striking feature of Table 9.2 is that union membership, in absolute numbers, shows a general and consistent rise in the Ireland but a significant decline in the UK. Unionization has remained comparatively resilient and relatively stronger in Ireland than in the UK, and two reasons can be offered to account for this difference. In Ireland the government has developed a more sophisticated corporatist model of employment relations. In effect, a national partnership regime since the late 1980s has strengthened and legitimized the role of trade unions in terms of macroeconomic and employment policy with the state. Until 2009 the Irish model of social partnership gave trade unions (and employers) a voice within government that resulted in national wage and taxation agreements (Rittau and Dundon, 2010). Second, since 1990 the Irish economy experienced an unprecedented boom (the Celtic Tiger) with economic growth outperforming all other European countries. As a result there has been employment growth in the public sector with a strong union tradition compared with the private sector. Indeed, expansion of the newer sectors of the economy (such as services and high-tech) has been at such a fast pace unions found it difficult to keep pace.

Employers

In both the UK and Ireland there are several separate and independent employer associations; 146 in the UK and 65 in Ireland (Registrar Friendly Societies, 2007; Certification Officer, 2008). Similar to trade unions that affiliate to the TUC and ICTU in each jurisdiction, employer groups also affiliate to a peak employer confederation. In the UK the main employer confederation is the Confederation of British Industry (CBI), founded in 1965, and in Ireland the Irish Business and Employers Confederation (IBEC), which was founded from a merger of the Federation of Irish Employers (FIE) and the Confederation of Irish Industry in 1993 (Wallace et al., 2004). The history of employer organizations can be traced to the late 1930s with the formation of the Federated Employers Ltd, the forerunner of the FIE in 1937.

Historically, employer associations have been key actors shaping the direction of the voluntarist model of employment relations found in both countries. Employer groups of one sort or another existed as commercial and craft guilds as far back as the eighteenth century. However, the emergence of coordinated employer associations as significant employment relations actors developed in response to the growth in unionism during the nineteenth century. Notwithstanding oversimplification, the localized and sporadic nature of employer groups developed into more formalized and coordinated industry-wide bargaining, especially after World War II. In the UK this approach was legitimized more formally as a result of a government commission on the system of industrial relations and multi-employer and industry-wide collective bargaining, the Donovan Report (1968).

There are other employer or managerial groups who, while not officially registered as employer associations (e.g., with a negotiating licence), have a degree of influence over employment relations. For example, the Chartered Institute of Personnel and Development (CIPD) has over 130 000 individual members across both the UK and Ireland. The CIPD seeks to promote an agenda in support of human resource managers, often through advice on good practice and lobbying government on key employment relations issues. In Ireland, the Irish Small and Medium-sized Enterprise Association (ISME) provides a political voice on behalf of small firm owners and owner-managers. A more recent body that has lent its weight to political and ideological lobbying in favour of multinational corporations is the American Chamber of Commerce Ireland (AMCHAM); for example, lobbying the government on the transposition of European employment regulations such as the Information and Consultation Directive (Collings et al., 2008). In the UK there has also been a rise in management consultancy firms, many of US origin, with expertise in assisting employers who seek to avoid union recognition (Heery, 2000; Logan, 2006).

In both countries the range and spread of such employer bodies may help explain a general shift in managerial attitudes towards a more unitarist ideology (Gunnigle, 1995; Poole et al., 2005). However, such trends are not uniform or identical across both countries. The UK tended to experience a more assertive macho-management attitude than Ireland, perhaps owing to the stronger neoliberal agenda in the UK inspired by Thatcher's legacy of union exclusion. In contrast, Ireland opted for a national partnership model that moderated excessive union demands while facilitating a degree of inclusion at the highest levels of government policy-making, even though managers at enterprise level espoused a distinct preference for non-unionism based on unitarist values (Gunnigle, 1995).

The 1980s marks a departure in some of the key roles and functions of employers' associations between Ireland and the UK. During the 1980s the UK essentially shifted from patterns of industry-wide and multi-employer bargaining to enterprise-specific negotiation (Brown et al., 2003). Consequently, the role of employers' associations diminished considerably in terms of bargaining with trade unions, and many now focus on political lobbying and providing task-specific advice to members consistent with other European decentralized regimes (Traxler, 1999). In contrast, Ireland resembles a more corporatist and centralized model, in which the peak employer federation, IBEC, occupies a central bargaining role at a national level under the rubric of national partnership (with unions and government), negotiating and influencing social welfare, and taxation policy as well as wages.

The State

Although employment relations in both the UK and Ireland are often defined as voluntarist, in recent years the system is relatively more centralized in Ireland than in the UK, due in no small measure to the juridification by the state (Von Prondzynski, 1998). Indeed, it has been argued elsewhere that it is almost impossible to assess collective bargaining or pay determination in Ireland without acknowledging the role of the state (Roche, 1997b). For example, the Irish government has intervened through statutory pay measures between 1941 and 1946; between 1970 to 1980 through tripartite negotiations; and from 1987 to 2009 via a corporatist social partnership model at national level (ibid.). In the UK, government influence has been less direct and at a distance, with public policy support for collective bargaining or periods of incomes policy formation in the 1970s.

In both countries, there are comparable government institutions that affect the nature and contours of employment relations, although as noted above, the divergent history and cycle of industrialization has meant a different focus and emphasis by state institutions to employment regulation. For example, in the UK the Advisory, Conciliation and Arbitration Service (ACAS) and the Central Arbitration Committee (CAC) have powers to deal with matters pertaining to mediation, dispute resolution, conciliation and union recognition. In Ireland the Labour Relations Commission (LRC) has similar functional roles, although in Ireland the government stopped short of statutory union recognition legislation comparable to that in other countries, such as the UK or US (Logan, 2001). In Ireland, statutory union recognition was resisted by government (with considerable employer pressure) as it was felt it may put foreign direct investment at risk, particularly from the US (Gunnigle et al., 2002). Ireland and the UK also have similar judicial mechanisms to deal with individual and collective employment rights: the Labour Court in Ireland and Employment Tribunals in the UK.

The 1980s mark fundamental divergence concerning the role of the state between the two countries, both in structures and ideologies. In the UK the Thatcher-Major governments of 1979–97 embarked on a radical (right-wing) monetarist experiment in which trade unions were seen as the enemy within, or what economists call supply constraints to the free and efficient operation of the labour market. In Thatcher's famous words the 'frontiers of the state had to be rolled back' (Wedderburn, 1986). What were deemed restrictive (inefficient/protective) labour practices were believed to be caused by trade unions and, consequently, union powers were diminished. An ideological belief in individualism rather than collectivism prevailed and on average a law every two years was passed to curb union power and influence.

While unions in Britain were under pressure from a government intent on implementing laissez-faire economic doctrines, in Ireland unions appeared to hold their ground. As Roche and Turner (1994) note, the long-established legitimacy of trade unions in Irish economic and political life had yet to be trenchantly challenged by a strong political party or coherent anti-union employer body. Gunnigle et al. (2002) posit that an Irish 'exceptionalism' existed, which can be explained in terms of a particular socio-political environment that was conducive to a collectivist tradition. Traditionally, employment relations at the level of the firm were the preserve of personnel professionals and issues rarely concerned strategic decision-makers (Roche, 1990; Gunnigle, 1995). However, when faced with growing economic uncertainty and large-scale emigration of the population, the Irish state decided to embark on a corporatist employment relations model by including unions, employers, voluntary and community bodies in broad macroeconomic management. As will be considered more fully in the next section, the model resulted in national pay agreements for the country as a whole, which further reinforced a strong collectivist orientation in Irish employment relations. Although the precise causal effect can never be established with certainty, the model of national partnership in Ireland has been attributable to the Celtic Tiger boom during the 1990s (Donaghey and Teague, 2007). This embeddedness of a collective spirit in Ireland stands in stark contrast to the ideological and practical wave of individualism present in British social and political life at the time.

If the 1980s marked a divergence in the approach of the respective governments, the latter part of the 1990s may be seen more as a convergence, largely as a result of European regulations applicable in each member state. More recently, it can be observed that in both jurisdictions the state has had to review its approach to employment regulation: in the UK the *Gibbons Report* (2007) on the future of employment relations and individual dispute resolution, and in Ireland a review of employment rights institutions and dispute procedures (Teague and Thomas, 2008). Such recent developments have been on the crest of a European wave of employment regulation – such as working time, works councils and information and consultation, along with an increased trend for individual minimum labour standards. Contemporary debates now question the scope and extent of the so-called 'voluntarist' tradition of employment relations in both countries. For example, Roche (2007) questions the efficacy of voluntarism amidst continuing adversarial employment regimes underpinned by essential dispute resolution bodies, national-level partnership and increased legal intervention in minimum standards. In short, there appears to be a moderated pluralist canvas to employment relations regulation in both jurisdictions. Significantly, the Europeanization of extended individual worker protections and increased employment regulations for business helps to explain the convergence towards a neoliberal employment relations trajectory across both countries.

Parallel to a review of extant state institutions is a deeper socio-political dynamic concerning government roles and ideologies towards employment relations. In Ireland, Republican Party politics has remained dominant since the formation of the Free State in 1922, apart from occasional coalition governments with the Labour Party. Interestingly, Irish politics has developed a close affinity to neoliberal economics and a desire to appease multinational (typically US) capital, despite a rhetoric to social values (Allen, 2000; Taylor, 2002). Employment relations scholars have debated the juxtaposition of Ireland between Boston and Berlin, questioning the linkage to the EU social model in favour of free market US capitalism to appease foreign direct investment (Donaghey, 2004; Gunnigle et al., 2005; Collings et al., 2008). In the UK also, the Labour government under Blair and later Brown remained steadfast in propping-up a neoliberal economic agenda; for example, continuing with privatization initiatives while maintaining the same Thatcherite governments' prohibitive trade union laws on secondary picketing and the closed shop (Smith, 2009). The middle ground in the UK, referred to as 'Third Way' politics (Giddens, 2000; Ackers, 2002), has to some extent lubricated a more decentralized employment relations regime focused on enterprise-based bargaining and non-unionism, while Ireland has maintained a centralized system through what have been termed 'middle ground institutions' (e.g., LRC) favouring coordination with unions while allowing parallel non-union workplaces to flourish through encouraged multinational investment (Gunnigle, 1995; Roche and Geary, 1996).

EMPLOYMENT RELATIONS PRACTICES AND PROCESSES

The practices and processes that shape the rules of the game for employment relations can be determined in numerous ways: through union negotiation, by consulting and involving employees directly, through legal intervention or by unilateral managerial action. In assessing the extent and impact of employment relations processes, a number of selected practices will be compared: collective bargaining and partnership, employee involvement, dispute resolution and non-union employment relations.

Collective Bargaining and Partnership

Collective bargaining has had a long and deep history in both the UK and Ireland, often with qualified support from the state. Historically, collective bargaining between employers and unions existed at different levels in both countries. In the UK, industry-wide bargaining was the norm after World War II as the preferred mechanism to agree wages and ensure predicable industrial relations behaviour. In Ireland a similar preference for centralization was also deemed the most efficient way to regulate wage increases, although in practice industry-wide bargaining was rare in the Republic. Local workplace bargaining in Ireland tended to supplement or ring-fence 'special' issues, such as productivity improvements or changes in local work practices (Von Prondzynski, 1998). Several attempts in the 1940s and 1960s to establish a national (countrywide) pay bargaining agreement in Ireland failed. In response to proposed government-imposed controls over prices and wages (the Prices and Incomes Bill, 1970), the first national wage agreement between employers and unions was negotiated in 1971 for all workers in all sectors, with subsequent agreements every two years throughout the 1970s (Wallace et al., 2004).

Even though centralized bargaining was also a preferred approach by the UK government around the same time, in practice collective bargaining was moving in the opposite direction. In the UK in the 1960s, workplace shop stewards increased in both number and influence (Farnham and Pimlott, 1995). The result was a growth in workplace bargaining between plant managers and shop stewards that supplemented and amended industry-wide agreements that had been previously negotiated between union officials and employer bodies. The power and influence of shop stewards was seen as a major 'industrial relations problem' in Britain, and a Royal Commission was established to report on the matter. The Donovan Commission (1968) recommended that workplace collective bargaining be formalized, largely to control shop stewards and also because centralized agreements were unable to specify the detail of changes required at enterprise level. This signified a shift from centralized multi-employer/industry-wide bargaining, to single-employer negotiated agreements.

With economic recession in Ireland in the 1970s and 1980s, various government attempts to control macroeconomic policy through newly constituted National Wage Agreements (NWAs) met with variable success and failure. Despite attempts by government, NWAs were consistently rejected by local union activists. In response the government issued 'pay guidelines', which were mostly ignored in the private sector and seen by public sector workers as an opening point for negotiation (Von Prondzynski, 1998). With growing economic uncertainty, unemployment and widespread emigration, a 'new' model of centralization regulation was considered in 1987, named the Programme for National Recovery (PNR). The key difference from NWAs was that the PNR included government, employers and unions, as well as other interest groups (e.g., farmers and community groups). It also considered in addition to wages other matters, such as taxation and social welfare provision. Crucially, the PNR set guideline targets rather than a binding agreement, which allowed room for local bargaining and adjustment over a three-year period. This effectively set in motion a national corporatist regime that has lasted ever since, with six subsequent national partnership agreements based on the principle of stakeholder involvement, competitiveness and mutual interest, with the most recent agreement, entitled 'Towards 2016'. However, national partnership in Ireland is not without its critics. Allen (2000) argues that during the 1990s, when national partnership and economic growth was at its height, there has been a corresponding rise in the spread of low-quality jobs and atypical forms of employment. Furthermore, despite the Irish government's attempt to diffuse partnership to local level, there appears to have been little progress, with only 4 per cent of private sector employers reporting a formal partnership arrangement at enterprise level (O'Connell et al., 2004). But for the most part, national partnership has been accompanied by unprecedented economic growth and prosperity in the Republic, which has made it easier for the social partners to reach agreement, at least up until the economic crisis in 2009.

In the UK there have been government attempts to encourage partnership since the election of a Labour government in 1997, although on a wholly voluntary basis. Recent research suggests that there exist 248 partnership agreements, covering around 10 per cent of the workforce, with one-third of public sector employees covered by partnership (Bacon and Samuels, 2009). Whether via partnership or direct negotiation with unions, the scope of collective bargaining has diminished in both countries. In Ireland union membership has declined with minimal coverage of collective bargaining at enterprise level, especially in the private sector. In 2009–10 agreement on public sector reforms could not be reached between the social partners and the corporatist model collapsed. In the UK also, collective bargaining has been relegated to consultation, and joint consultation downgraded to communication (Marchington and Parker, 1990; Kersley et al., 2006). In short, around 39 per cent of the British workforce is covered by bargaining agreements (Kersley et al., 2006, p. 187), and little prospect of formal partnership given Conservative–Liberal coalition government elected in 2010.

Employee Involvement

Employee involvement has increased in recent years and has a long pedigree in both countries. Evidence suggests that managers in both Ireland and the UK prefer to engage with employees directly through employee involvement methods (O'Connell et al., 2004; Kersley et al., 2006). In the UK, less than half of all establishments use any form of collective participation, and in Ireland around one-fifth of private sector establishments have a collective partnership arrangement. Two broad underlying principles have shaped the approaches to involvement practices in both countries. The first is the notion of industrial democracy, as defined in the Irish Constitution or in Britain through public policy interventions such as the Bullock Committee on worker-directors in industry (Bullock, 1977). The democracy argument received greater attention in both jurisdictions during the 1970s. Public policy articulated that employee involvement practices, such as work committees or communication channels, are part of the democratic rights of workers to have a say over matters that affect them. The second idea concerns employee involvement as an economic efficiency argument. In this view it makes sense for companies to encourage greater employee involvement as a way of tapping into ideas for quality and improvement, resulting in improved organizational effectiveness. In the UK during the 1980s, the political climate was much more sympathetic to the efficiency principle of employee involvement as it had a resonance with government objectives to reduce union power and promote a more individualistic employment relations climate. In Ireland too the economic efficiency idea suited the prevailing political mood, not as a tool to weaken union power, but as a way to engender foreign direct investment by allowing multinational enterprises choice over union recognition or preferring to avoid collective bargaining and worker participation (Gunnigle, 1995; Gunnigle et al., 2005).

However, the new millennium signified yet another twist in the development of employee involvement, with both Ireland and the UK being the only two European member states not to have a statutory and permanent system of employee involvement (Sisson, 2002). The twenty-first century has witnessed a significant proliferation of employment regulations and laws affecting employee involvement practices, particularly those originating from the European Commission. According to Ackers et al. (2005), the significance of this has resulted in a complicated policy dialectic that shapes management choice for employee involvement on the one hand, and state regulations ensuring workers have the right to receive information and be consulted on the other. Arguably, the twenty-first century has ushered in a period of legal re-regulation, which can be divided between those policies that directly affect employee involvement (European Directives, for example) and those that indirectly alter the environment in which employee participation operates (the competitive environment and pressures from multinational corporations).

The most significant development in this area affecting Ireland and the UK has been the EU Directive for Employee Information and Consultation (2002). It has been argued that this single initiative has altered the basis of the long-held voluntarist employment relations tradition in both jurisdictions (Sisson, 2002). The UK has transposed the EU Directive into domestic legislation through the Information and Consultation of Employees (ICE) Regulations (2004). In Ireland the same EU Directive has been transposed into national law through the Provision of Employee Information and Consultation Act (2006). Interestingly, the respective national regulations have taken slightly different interpretations of the EU Directive. Both have allowed for a direct approach to employee information and consultation if this is agreeable to the parties (e.g., team briefings, quality circles, etc.). Both also have inserted a trigger mechanism to the regulation, which means that the right for workers to receive information and be consulted is not universal or automatic but has to be requested by a proportion of the workforce. They differ, however, in small though not insignificant ways. In Ireland, for example, there is an explicit reference to trade union involvement in any ICE arrangement in enterprises where unions are already recognized. This is not evident in the ICE Regulations in the UK. Moreover, in Ireland the Act stipulates a statutory fall-back mechanism that is much closer to works council arrangements that might be found more commonly in countries such as Germany. No such statutory consultation forum exists in the UK regulations.

The impact and broader implications of a move from voluntarism to mandated employee involvement is as yet unclear (Geary and Roche, 2005). What is evident, however, is that managers in both the UK and Ireland find the language of collectivist-type consultation arrangements pioneered at an EU-level somewhat unpalatable and alien (Wilkinson et al., 2004; Dundon et al., 2006). It is arguable that this tension in the discourse of meaning translates into an uncertainty of practice when managers interpret external regulations and implement new internal arrangements for information-sharing and employee involvement. Moreover, evidence seems to suggest that unless pushed by the trigger mechanism to invoke the new rights to be involved, employers remain cautious of setting up new structures and prefer to 'stick' with what they already know (Wilkinson et al., 2007). To this end workers may view the regulatory approach as falling short in terms of meeting their expectations and interests, especially as the economies in the UK and Ireland move further into economic recession on the back of a banking and financial market sector crisis.

Dispute Resolution

While the principle of voluntarism may appear under threat from increasing European employment regulations, the institutions of dispute resolution in both the UK and Ireland remain anchored in a voluntarist approach, albeit in different ways (Teague and Thomas, 2008). In Ireland state bodies such as the Labour Court and Labour Relations Commission (LRC) rely on the goodwill of the parties to accept recommendations made with regard to disputes. In contrast, in the UK the functions of ACAS and the CAC can mandate employers in certain areas, such as union recognition. In Ireland it has been reported that around 75 per cent of all disputes concerning pay and terms and conditions of employment before the Labour Court resulted in employers accepting the court's judgement (IRN, 2004, p. 22). The situation is somewhat different, however, with regard to recommendations on union recognition. Gunnigle et al. (2002) found that of 81 recommendations on union recognition cases during the period 1990 to 1999, only 30 per cent of organizations actually recognized a union after being recommended to do so.

In recent years there has been some emerging evidence concerning the impact of alternative dispute resolution (ADR) services, defined as alternatives to progressing disputes through the legislature in preference for the intervention of a neutral and objective third party. In Britain, a government commission, the *Gibbons Report* (2007), found that disputes were more rapidly resolved through informal dialogue and interaction at the workplace level with the assistance of facilitators from state bodies such as ACAS. In the Irish context, Collings et al. (2008) argue that ADRs take on a different dimension with important implications for the tradition of voluntarist industrial relations. They argue ADRs represent a further shift away from an institutionalized heritage with two potential implications. First, ADR avoids the prospect of state institutions making determinations against the management of a firm that might otherwise appear in a detrimental light in the public arena. Second, ADR effectively keeps issues of workplace disagreement 'in-house' and helps satisfy managerial demands for choice rather than constantly having to revert to state-imposed solutions to what can be minor as well as major employment relations matters. In short, there appears a move towards more detailed and informally driven dispute resolution practices based at the workplace level in both jurisdictions.

Non-unionism

Without doubt the emergence of non-unionism has been a key shift in employment relations in recent decades in both jurisdictions. This is significant as while the UK government promoted an active non-union employment agenda in the 1980s (Dundon and Rollinson, 2004), Ireland arguably did not. Thus, the significant prevalence of non-unionism has emerged in both countries but from very different political and industrial positions. In Ireland the most pertinent manifestation of non-unionism is the tendency for MNCs establishing a base in the state to do so without union recognition. Trade union recognition has recently become an area of very significant debate in Ireland, largely due to the fall in density and emergence of the non-union firm, particularly among the MNC sector. While the decline in union density reflects the impact of a confluence of factors, it is clear that the FDI sector has played a significant contributory role. In discerning the impact of the FDI sector on union density, an important issue is the pattern of union recognition itself. A study of firms in the manufacturing and internationally traded services sectors, which were established at greenfield sites over a ten-year period in 1987–97, found a particularly high incidence of union avoidance: 65 per cent of firms were non-union (Gunnigle et al., 2002). Non-unionism was most prevalent amongst US MNC subsidiaries in the ICT sector, a factor commonly attributed to both the prevalence of a unitarist managerial ideology among US-owned companies and also to the competitive nature of the technology sector and consequent managerial preference for maintaining high levels of numerical and functional flexibility.

However, the idea that MNCs automatically undermine pluralist traditions is questionable. For example, Enderwick (1986) found no evidence that MNCs operating in Ireland were eager to dismiss any pluralist tradition by refusing to recognize or deal with trade unions. Significantly, this related to the role played by Ireland's industrial promotions agencies, which, since the 1960s, had assumed responsibility for attracting FDI to Ireland. In the 1960s and 1970s these agencies recommended union recognition among new inward-investing firms, specifically by arranging introductions to trade union officials and encouraging MNCs to conclude recognition agreements with trade unions prior to start-up. These studies formed the basis for what was termed the 'convergence thesis': namely that the employment policies and practices of MNC subsidiaries, including those from the US, would be largely similar to host country practices, which in Ireland (and to lesser extent the UK) were characterized then by widespread trade union recognition and the utilization of collective bargaining (Kelly and Brannick, 1985).

This 'convergence' thesis has recently come under challenge as a result of the emergence of data pointing to the predominance of 'country of origin' effects (Ferner, 1997). This school argues that MNCs, most especially US MNCs, are now less likely to adjust their employment practices to suit local (host country) norms and are more likely to impose practices and policies similar to those in the parent company (Roche and Geary, 1995; Turner et al., 1997). The most significant evidence in this regard concerns the growing pattern of trade union avoidance among MNCs, especially US subsidiaries, in 'high-tech' sectors (Gunnigle, 1995; Gunnigle et al., 2002). A change in the pro-union recognition stance of Ireland's industrial promotions agencies undoubtedly contributed to increased union avoidance among inward-investing firms. Since the 1980s these agencies have adopted a more neutral position, indicating to inward-investing firms that they have the freedom to recognize or avoid trade unions (McGovern, 1989; Gunnigle et al., 1998). A variety of factors contributed to this important change, most significantly increased international competition for FDI and Ireland's increasing focus on the ICT area, specifically US MNCs in the electronics and software areas. These sectors of the US economy are widely seen as hotbeds of opposition to union recognition (Foulkes, 1980; Kochan et al., 1986).

In summary, non-unionism in both countries has been shaped considerably by the role of the state. In the UK this was to a large degree witnessed in the government's own anti-union approach to employment relations by fostering an individualistic and non-union employment relations climate. For example de-recognizing trade unions at the government's communications headquarters, GCHQ, also sent an important signal to private sector employers that this was a preferred way to manage workers and unions (Dundon and Rollinson, 2004). In Ireland, while the government incorporated trade unions through national partnership, at the same time state agencies concerned with FDI presented to would-be employers the option of union recognition or non-unionism. Evidently, many MNCs opted for the latter.

CONCLUSION

While allowing for their common heritage, more recently Irish and British employment relations trajectories have taken radically different paths. While Thatcher's Conservative government in the UK introduced a number of initiatives designed to reduce union power and influence during the 1980s, unions in Ireland were ensured continued influence at a macro-level through centralized national agreements (Gunnigle et al., 2002). Indeed, the trend of union marginalization has not abated under 'New' Labour in Britain either (Smith, 2009) and the so-called 'Third Way' has failed to materialize to any great extent. Ewing (2003, p. 149) posits: 'what we have [in the UK] is a system of labour law [and an employment relations system more generally] which is a synthesis of competing values: a labour law which accepts a great deal of Thatcher inheritance . . . but which is shaped to accommodate new values'. Thus, while unions in the UK have seen their influence decline in the closing decades of the twentieth century, they have been granted statutory union recognition procedures that Ackers and Wilkinson (2003, p. 13) argue may help to 'staunch the decline of collective-bargaining'.

In contrast, it appears that trade unions have remained to the fore in the Irish context through their involvement in national pay agreements. Thus, while the voluntarist tradition has been considerably diluted in Ireland in recent years owing to European developments (Gunnigle, 1995), in contrast to the UK experience, there remains a resilient corporatist-style model based on national agreements. However, it is important to note that the issue of statutory union recognition has emerged as a key issue in the re-negotiation of Ireland's corporatist regime, so much so that it is possible that this issue could de-stabilize the system as unions press for comparable rights to those found in the UK (and the US). Above all, the longevity of Irish partnership is under considerable strain owing to economic recession as employers and the state search for ways to make redundancies and impose decisions on a weakened workforce. The controversy is likely to intensify as the courts have found in favour of one of Ireland's most notoriously anti-union employers (Ryanair) concerning management's rights not to bargain with unions (Hardiman, 2000; Dobbins, 2002).

This chapter has summarized the key employment relations systems, institutions and practices between Ireland and the UK. While there is a similar heritage to the development and emergence of the system, there remains important policy divergence. This provides a number of important lessons that paired country comparisons tell us about comparative employment relations systems. First is the relevance of unique contextual and cultural settings (see Jackson, Chapter 5 this volume). In this regard both Ireland and the UK followed a similarly unique voluntarist employment relations path compared with the rest of mainland Europe. The legacy of British colonial rule left a blueprint for such matters as union structure, representation and legal regulation prior to the formation of the Irish state in 1922. Second, and parallel to this cultural legacy explanation, is the explanatory power of an institutional approach. Ireland and the UK show that state institutions and public policy options are significant comparative dimensions that help explain the patterns of employment relations. In the UK the laissez-faire economic doctrines of Thatcherism accelerated a unitarist shift in managerial attitudes that espoused individualistic values based on state support for non-unionism. In contrast, Ireland opted for a more institutionalized collectivist system by incorporating unions at a national level through corporatist social partnership. Yet at the same time, institutionalized collectivism did not negate or prevent the preference for non-unionism among (mostly) MNCs. Arguably, the government's approach allowed for such variation and divergence through low corporate taxation and state support for foreign direct investment. Finally, the Europeanization of employment relations explains some individual worker protections in each country. In part this signals a legal convergence of employment relations that would be difficult to imagine without European coordination and centralization based on an agenda of worker and human rights, organizational flexibility and efficiency. Thus, the comparative analysis of the UK and Ireland reveals both similarity, but also significant differences, in culture, tradition and institutional arrangements for employment relations regulation.

NOTE

1. Strictly speaking, the United Kingdom (UK) is different from Great Britain (GB). The UK includes England, Wales, Scotland and Northern Ireland, whereas GB tends to exclude Northern Ireland. Nonetheless, it is common to use the terms UK and GB interchangeably. In some areas employment laws are slightly different in Northern Ireland and Scotland from those in England and Wales. Definitions can also be slightly more complicated because some of the larger unions (and some employer bodies) in Britain have members in Northern Ireland. Similarly, some trade unions representing workers in the Irish Republic have their head offices in the UK (e.g., UNITE).

REFERENCES

Ackers, P. (2002), 'Reframing employment relations: The case for neo-pluralism', *Industrial Relations Journal*, **33**(1), 32–47.

Ackers, P. and Wilkinson, A. (eds) (2003), *Understanding Work and Employment: Industrial Relations in Transition*, Oxford: Oxford University Press.

Ackers, P., Marchington, M., Wilkinson, A. and Dundon, T. (2005), 'Partnership and voice, with or without trade unions: Changing UK management approaches to organizational participation', in M. Stuart and M. Martinez Lucio (eds), *Partnership and Modernization in Employment Relations*, London: Routledge.

Allen, K. (2000), *The Celtic Tiger: The Myth of Social Partnership*, Manchester: Manchester University Press.

Bacon, N. and Samuels, P. (2009), 'Partnership agreement adoption and survival in the British private and public sectors', *Work, Employment & Society*, **23**(2), 231–48.

Bain, G.S. and R. Price (1983), 'Union growth: Dimensions, determinants and destiny', in G.S. Bain (ed.), *Industrial Relations in Britain*, Oxford: Blackwell.

Barrett, C. (2009), *Trade Union Membership 2008*, London: Department for Business, Enterprise and Regulatory Reform.

Boyd, A. (1972), *The Rise of Irish Trade Unions: 1729–1970*, Anvil: Tralee.

Brown, W., Marginson, P. and Walsh, J. (2003), 'The management of pay as the influence of collective bargaining diminishes', in P.K. Edwards (ed.), *Industrial Relations: Theory and Practice*, 2nd edition, Oxford: Blackwell.

Bullock, A. (Lord) (1977), *Report of the Committee of Inquiry on Industrial Democracy*, Cmnd. 6706, London: HMSO.

Certification Officer (2008), *Annual Reports 2007–2008*, London, available at: http://www.certoffice.org; accessed 13 January 2011.

Clegg, H.A. (1979), *The Changing System of Industrial Relations in Great Britain*, Oxford: Blackwell.

Collings, D.G., Gunnigle, P. and Morley, M.J. (2005), 'American multinational subsidiaries in Ireland: Changing the nature of employment relations?', in G. Boucher and G. Collins (eds), *The New World of Work: Labour Markets in Contemporary Ireland*, Dublin: Liffey Press, pp. 125–44.

Collings, D.G., Gunnigle, P. and Morley, M.J. (2008) 'Boston or Berlin: American MNCs and the shifting contours of industrial relations in Ireland', *International Journal of Human Resource Management*, **19**(2), 240–61.

CSO Ireland (2009), 'Labour market principal statistics', Cork: Central Statistics Office Ireland, available at: www.cso.ie; accessed 13 January 2011.

Disney, R., Gosling, A., Machin, S and McCrea, J. (1998), *The Dynamics of Union Membership in Britain*, Research Report No. 3, London: Department of Trade and Industry.

Dobbins, T. (2002), 'SIPTU broadly positive on PPF outcomes, internal consultation begins', *Industrial Relations News*, 17, 2 May.

Dobbins, T. (2009), 'Ireland: EIRO annual update 2008 on trade union membership', Dublin: European Foundation for the Improvement of Living and Working Conditions, available at: http://www.eurofound.europa.eu/eiro/2009/country/ireland.htm; accessed 13 January 2011.

Donaghey, J.M. (2004), 'Social partnership and labour market governance in the Republic of Ireland', Unpublished PhD Thesis, Belfast: School of Management and Economics, Queens University.

Donaghey, J. and Teague, P. (2007), 'The mixed fortunes of Irish unions: Living with the paradoxes of social partnership', *Journal of Labor Research*, **28**(1), 19–41.

Donovan (Lord) (chairperson) (1968), *Royal Commission on Trade Unions and Employers Associations Report*, Cmnd. 3623, London: HMSO.

Dundon, T. and Rollinson, D. (2004), *Employment Relations in Non-union Firms*, London: Routledge.

Dundon, T., Curran, D., Maloney, M. and Ryan, P. (2006), 'Conceptualising the dynamics of employee voice: Evidence from the Republic of Ireland', *Industrial Relations Journal*, **37**(5), 492–512.

Enderwick, P. (1986), 'Multinationals and labour relations: The case of Ireland', *Journal of Irish Business and Administrative Research*, **8**(2), 1–12.

Eurostat (2009a), 'EU Population Statistics' (at 1 January 2009), available at: http://epp.eurostat.ec.europa.eu/tgm/table.do?tab=tableandlanguage=enandpcode=tps00001andtab leSelection=1andfootnotes=yesandlabeling=labelsandplugin=1; accessed 13 January 2011.

Eurostat (2009b), 'Consumer Price Levels in 2008. Report 104/2009', 16 July 2009, available at http://epp.eurostat.ec.europa.eu/cache/ITY_PUBLIC/2-16072009-AP/EN/2-16072009-AP-EN.PDF; accessed 13 January 2011.

Ewing, K. (2003), 'Industrial relations and law', in P. Ackers and A. Wilkinson (eds), *Understanding Work and Employment: Industrial Relations in Transition*, Oxford: Oxford University Press.

Farnham, D. and Pimlott, J. (1995), *Understanding Industrial Relations*, 2nd edition, London: Thomson Learning.

Ferner, A. (1997), 'Country of origin effects and human resource management in multinational companies', *Human Resource Management Journal*, **7**(1), 19–36.

Flood, P. and Turner, T. (1993), 'Human resource strategy and the non-union phenomenon', *Employee Relations*, **15**(6), 54–65.

Foulkes, F. (1980), *Personnel Policies in Large Non-union Companies*, New York: Prentice Hall.

Geary, J. and Roche, W. (2005), 'The future of employee information and consultation in Ireland', in J. Storey (ed.), *Adding Value Through Information and Consultation*, Palgrave Macmillan.

Gibbons, M. (2007), *Better Dispute Resolution: A Review of Dispute Resolution in Britain*, London: Department of Trade and Industry.

Giddens, A. (2000), *The Third Way and Its Critics*, Cambridge: Polity Press.

Gunnigle, P. (1995), 'Collectivism and the management of industrial relations in greenfield sites', *Human Resource Management Journal*, **5**(3), 24–40.

Gunnigle, P., Collings, D.G. and Morley, M. (2005), 'Exploring the dynamics of industrial relations in US multinationals: Evidence from the Republic of Ireland', *Industrial Relations Journal*, **36**(3), 241–56.

Gunnigle, P., O'Sullivan, M. and Kinsella, M. (2002), 'Organized labour in the new economy', in D. D'Art and T. Turner (eds), *Irish Employment Relations in the New Economy*, Dublin: Blackhall.

Gunnigle, P., Turner, T. and D'Art, D. (1998), 'Counterpoising collectivism: Performance-related pay and industrial relations in greenfield sites', *British Journal of Industrial Relations*, **36**(4), 565–79.
Hardiman, N. (2000), 'Social partnership, wage bargaining and growth', in B. Nolan, P.J. O'Connell and C.T. Whelan (eds), *Bust to Boom: The Irish Experience of Growth and Inequality*, Dublin: IPA.
Haughton, J. (2000), 'The historical background', in J.W. O'Hagan (ed.), *The Economy of Ireland: Policy and Performance of a European Region*, Dublin: Gill and Macmillan.
Heery, E. (2000), *Research Bulletin No. 8: New Unionism Research Project*, Cardiff University.
Hillary, B. (1989), 'The Irish Congress of Trade Unions', in Department of Industrial Relations UCD (eds), *Industrial Relations in Ireland, Contemporary Issues and Developments*, Dublin: UCD.
Industrial Relations News (IRN) (2004), 'Unions being pushed out of multinational sector', *Industrial Relations News*, **9**, 26 February, 22–6.
Kelly, A. and Brannick, T. (1985), 'Industrial relations practices in multinational companies in Ireland', *Journal of Irish Business and Administrative Research*, **7**, 98–111.
Kelly, A. and Roche, W.K. (1983), 'Institutional reform in Irish industrial relations', *Studies: An Irish Quarterly Review*, **72**, 221–30.
Kersley, B., Alpin, C., Forth, J., Bryson, A., Bewley, H., Dix, J. and Oxenbridge, S. (2006), *Inside the Workplace: Findings from the 2004 Workplace Employment Relations Survey*, London: Routledge.
Kochan, T., Katz, H. and McKersie, R. (1986), *The Transformation of American Industrial Relations*, New York: Basic Books.
Labour Force Survey (2010), Office for National Statistics (January), available at: www.statistics.gov.uk; accessed 13 January 2011.
Lavelle, J., McDonnell, A. and Gunnigle, P. (eds) (2009), *Human Resource Practices in Multinational Companies in Ireland: A Comparative Analysis*, Dublin: Government Publications Office.
Logan, J. (2001), 'Is statutory recognition bad news for British unions? Evidence from the history of North American industrial relations', *Historical Studies in Industrial Relations*, **11**(Spring), 63–108.
Logan, J. (2006), 'The union avoidance industry in the United States', *British Journal of Industrial Relations*, **44**(4), 651–75.
Marchington, M. and Parker, P. (1990), *Changing Patterns of Employee Relations*, Hemel Hempstead: Harvester Wheatsheaf.
McGovern, P. (1989), 'Union recognition and union avoidance in the 1980s', UCD Department of Industrial Relations, *Industrial Relations in Ireland: Contemporary Issues and Developments*, Dublin: UCD.
O'Connell, L., Russell, H., Williams, J. and Blackwell, S. (2004), *The Changing Workplace: A Survey of Employees' Views and Experiences*, Dublin: Economic and Social Research Institute (ESRI) and National Centre for Partnership and Performance (NCPP).
OECD (2005), *Country Statistical Profiles 2005: Ireland*, Paris: OECD.
O'Higgins, E.R. (2002), 'Government and the creation of the Celtic Tiger: Can management maintain the momentum?', *Academy of Management Executive*, **16**(3), 104–20.
O'Mahony, D. (1964), 'Industrial relations in Ireland: The background', Research Paper No. 9, Dublin: The Economic Research Institute.
Poole, M., Mansfield, R., Gould-Williams, J. and Mendes, P. (2005), 'British managers' attitudes and behaviour in industrial relations: A twenty-year study', *British Journal of Industrial Relations*, **43**(1), 117–34.
Registrar Friendly Societies (2007), *Annual Report 2006–2007*, Dublin: Office of the Registrar Friendly Societies.
Rittau, Y. and Dundon, T. (2010), 'The roles and functions of shop stewards in workplace partnership: Evidence from the Republic of Ireland', *Employee Relations*, **32**(1).
Roche, W.K. (1990), 'Industrial relations research in Ireland and the trade union interest',

Dublin: Paper presented to the Irish Congress of Trade Unions conference on Joint Research Between Trade Unions, Universities, Third Level Colleges and Research Institutes.

Roche, W.K. (1997a), 'Industrialization and the development of industrial relations', in T.V. Murphy and W.K. Roche (eds), *Irish Industrial Relations in Practice* (revised edition), Dublin: Oak Tree Press.

Roche, W.K. (1997b), 'Pay determination, the state and the politics of industrial relations', in T.V. Murphy and W.K. Roche (eds), *Irish Industrial Relations in Practice* (revised edition), Dublin: Oak Tree Press.

Roche, W.K. (2007), 'Social partnership in Ireland and new social pacts', *Industrial Relations*, **46**(3), 395–425.

Roche, W.K. and Ashmore, J. (2002), 'Irish unions in the 1990s: Testing the limits of social partnership', in P. Fairbrother and G. Griffin (eds), *Changing Prospects for Trade Unionism: Comparisons between Six Countries*, London/New York: Continuum, 137–76.

Roche, W.K. and Geary, J. (1995), 'The attenuation of "host-country effects"? Multinationals, industrial relations and collective bargaining in Ireland', Working Paper IR-HRM No. 94-95, Dublin: Business Research Programme, Graduate School of Business, University College Dublin.

Roche, W.K. and Geary, J. (1996), 'Multinational corporations in Ireland: Adapting to or diverging from national industrial relations practices and traditions?', *Journal of Irish Business and Administrative Research*, **17**, 14–31.

Roche, W.K. and Turner, T. (1994), 'Testing alternative models of human resource policy effects on trade union recognition in the Republic of Ireland', *International Journal of Human Resource Management*, **5**(2), 721–53.

Schäfer, G. (ed.) (2006), *Key Figures on Europe: Statistical Pocketbook: 2006 Edition*, Luxemburg: Office for Official Publications of European Communities.

Sisson, K. (2002), 'The Information and Consultation Directive: Unnecessary "regulation" or an opportunity to promote "partnership"?', *Warwick Papers in Industrial Relations*, No: 67, Coventry: Industrial Relations Research Unit (IRRU), Warwick University.

Smith, P. (2009), 'New Labour and the commonsense of neoliberalism: Trade unionism, collective bargaining and workers' rights', *Industrial Relations Journal*, **40**(4), 337–55.

Taylor, G. (2002), 'Hailing with an invisible hand: A cosy political dispute amid the rise of neoliberal politics in modern Ireland', *Government and Opposition*, **37**(4), 501–24.

Teague, P. and Thomas, D. (2008), *Employment Dispute Resolution and Standard Setting*, Dublin: Oak Tree Press.

Traxler, F. (1999), 'Employers and employer organizations: The case of governability', *Industrial Relations Journal*, **30**(4), 345–56.

Turner, T., D'Art, D. and Gunnigle, P. (1997), 'US multinationals: Changing the framework of Irish industrial relations?', *Industrial Relations Journal*, **28**(2), 92–102.

Von Prondzynski, F. (1998), 'Ireland: Corporatism revived', in A. Ferner and R. Hyman (eds), *Changing Industrial Relations in Europe*, 2nd edition, Oxford: Blackwell.

Waddington, J. (2003), 'Trade union organization', in P.K. Edwards (ed.), *Industrial Relations: Theory and Practice*, 2nd edition, Oxford: Blackwell.

Wallace, J., Gunnigle, P. and McMahon, G. (2004), *Industrial Relations in Ireland*, 3rd edition, Dublin: Gill and Macmillan.

Wedderburn, Lord (1986), *The Worker and the Law*, 3rd edition, Harmondsworth: Penguin.

Wilkinson, A., Dundon, T. and Grugulis, I. (2007), 'Information but not consultation: Exploring employee involvement in SMEs', *International Journal of Human Resource Management*, **18**(7), 1279–97.

Wilkinson, A., Dundon, T., Marchington, M. and Ackers, P. (2004), 'The changing patterns of employee voice: Case studies from the UK and Republic of Ireland', *Journal of Industrial Relations*, **46**(3), 298–323.

10 Employment relations in Japan and Korea

EeHwan Jung

INTRODUCTION

It has been generally believed that employment relations in Japan and Korea are quite different. Until the 1980s, comparing Japan's and Korea's employment relations was regarded almost as nonsense, as Korea's industrial relations under successive authoritarian regimes were not fully developed, while Japan had well-developed industrial relations. Korea's employment relations were compared more often with those of other developing countries such as East Asian NICs (newly industrialized countries) that failed to build democratic industrial relations (Deyo, 1989, 1997). In particular, Korea was often compared with Taiwan, as the two countries belonged to the same phase of economic development (Bamber and Ross, 2000; Kong, 2005).

Even after political democratization and the growth of the labor movement in Korea, differences rather than similarities have been stressed in comparing employment relations in Japan and Korea. More than anything, industrial relations in Korea have been much more adversarial than in Japan. Whitley (1999, p. 202) anticipated that the Japanese level of employer–employee interdependence and commitment was unlikely to become institutionalized in Korea in the near future. Indeed, it does not seem to make sense to argue that Korea's employment relations system is a variant of the Japanese model.

It is also true, however, that employment relations in Japan and Korea share many similarities. If we agree to the common view that lifetime employment, seniority pay and enterprise unionism are three pillars of employment relations in Japan (OECD, 1973), Korea also has at least two of these pillars. Unions are enterprise-based and the payment system in large corporations is strongly seniority-based in Korea. Although employers' commitment to the norm of lifetime employment is weak, labor mobility is quite low in large corporations. From the 'internal labor market' point of view, both Japan and Korea have developed strong, firm internal labor markets in large corporations. Some maintained that Korea's employment relations system should be categorized as the same as the Japanese (Kim, 2000). There are also some who said that Korea had all three pillars of Japanese employment relations, including lifetime employment (Yoon, 1998; Kim et al., 2000). It is beyond doubt that the country that shares the most similarities in employment relations with Japan is Korea. Recently, another similarity in employment relations in the two countries has received attention. It is the increase of non-regular workers, including part-time, temporary, daily and dispatched workers. Japan and Korea belong to the group of OECD countries with the highest rate of non-regular workers. The issue of non-regular work is regarded as the most serious labor problem in both Japan and Korea.

INDUSTRIAL RELATIONS: VARIETIES OF ENTERPRISE UNIONISM

Similarity

The most conspicuous similarity in industrial relations between Japan and Korea is enterprise unionism (Jeong, 1995). Unions are generally organized by firms. Although the majority of enterprise unions in the two countries are affiliated with federations outside the enterprise, sovereignty is retained almost exclusively at the enterprise union level.

Enterprise unionism has a long history in both countries. In Japan, enterprise unions were formed as early as the 1920s among workers in large firms. Although most of them were forced to dissolve before World War II, they revived quickly as enterprise unions after the war (Shirai, 1983, p. 124). The political and economic situations after the war contributed to the formation of enterprise unionism. The US Occupation that ruled Japan strongly encouraged free union movement to promote democracy. Economic hardship also pushed both blue-collar and white-collar workers to form unions to protect their interests (Takahashi, 1970, pp. 28–9). In these situations, the Japanese found that the easiest and fastest way to form unions was to organize workers at the enterprise level.

In Korea, the free labor union movement in the true sense started as late as 1987 with political democratization. A rush of union organization followed political democratization. However, a number of unions, mostly enterprise unions, were present before democratization, and these enterprise unions became the model for forming new unions. Also, organizing unions by enterprise was faster and easier than organizing at the industrial or occupational level. There were even some legal obstacles to organizing industrial and occupational unions (Lee and Lee, 2004). Recently, almost half of enterprise unions have converted into branches of industrial unions in Korea. However, enterprise unionism still prevails in that branches of industrial unions in large corporations behave like enterprise unions. Collective bargaining still takes place predominantly at the enterprise level even after enterprise unions have been transformed into branches of an industrial union (Lee and Lee, 2004; Jeong, 2007).

Difference 1: Cooperative or Confrontational

It is well known that industrial relations are peaceful in Japan. Japanese unions rarely strike, and the strikes that do occur are usually of short duration (Shirai, 1983, p. 135). Unions share many of the management's values. In particular, unions agree with management that employees' welfare is dependent on the viability of the company and workers need to actively participate in enhancing productivity and competitiveness. It is even said that the enterprise union is 'the second personnel affairs division'. Indeed, it is not unusual for staff members of the personnel affairs division to become union officials (Suzuki, 2004, p. 121).

Peaceful industrial relations are reinforced by union participation in management in Japan. Unions usually have close consultation with management concerning business, sometimes strategic, issues (Nakamura, 1997). According to the Labor Management Communication Survey conducted by the Ministry of Labor, 80.5 percent of unionized firms had joint consultation bodies in 2004. Strategic management issues such as overall management policy or basic plans of production and marketing were discussed in about 70 percent of these bodies. Although the most common way of discussing strategic issues was 'reporting and explaining', some employers had to have prior consultation with unions or even get the consent of unions. Union participation in management is especially active on workshop issues such as the transfer of employees within and between establishments (ibid., p. 286).

Korea's industrial relations are much more confrontational than Japan's. Unions generally do not trust management in Korea. They would rather rely on the power of collective action to improve working conditions than cooperate with management to improve productivity and competitiveness. There is a strong sense of 'them and us' between unions and management.

Good indicators of labor–management confrontation in Korea are the number of strikes and workdays lost. As is shown in Table 10.1, Korea has more strikes and lockouts than Japan. Korea also has a larger number of workers involved in strikes and lockouts than Japan. The most striking difference is the number of workdays lost due to strikes and lockouts per

Table 10.1　Number of strikes and workdays lost in Japan and Korea

	Number of Strikes and Lockouts	Workers Involved in Strikes and Lockouts (1000 persons)	Workdays Lost Due to Strikes and Lockouts per 1000 Employees
Japan			
2000	118	15	0.7
2003	47	4	0.1
2006	26	2	–
Korea			
2000	250	178	114
2003	320	137	90
2006	138	131	77

Source:　Korea Labor Institute, *KLI Foreign Labor Statistics 2008.*

1000 employees in the two countries. While Japan lost less than a workday per 1000 employees in the 2000s, Korea lost more than 70 workdays. Assuming that the number of workdays lost per 1000 employees is the best indicator of peace in industrial relations, Korea's industrial relations are more than 100 times more confrontational than Japan's.

This confrontation comes partly from unions' ideological orientation. A part of the Korean union movement has a strong orientation toward social and political reform. Many enterprise unions regard cooperation with management almost as a taboo for unions as it could weaken the class consciousness of the rank and file members. Employers' attitude towards unions, however, is generally said to be more responsible for labor–management confrontation. Employers are reluctant to accept unions as genuine partners in their businesses.

Formally, union participation in management is institutionalized by the law in Korea. The Act on the Promotion of Worker Participation and Cooperation stipulates that all firms with more than 30 employees form a council and hold regular meetings every quarter. A variety of issues including plans for productivity enhancement, plans for hiring and deployment, guidelines for employment adjustment, changes in work schedules, the revision of work rules and the introduction of new technology should be discussed at this council (Lee, 2003, p. 209). The councils, however, have failed to promote labor–management cooperation. Union representatives do not think employers genuinely intend to build partnerships with unions.

The Korean case shows that enterprise unionism does not necessarily promote labor–management cooperation. It is commonly believed that enterprise unions tend to cooperate with management because their very existence is dependent on the survival of the company, but the Korean situation defies this belief.

Difference 2: Coordinated or Uncoordinated

Wage negotiation in Japan is called *shunto*, the spring offensive. It is called the spring offensive because most enterprise unions negotiate with respective employers for wage increases in the spring. Although the final amount of wage increase is determined between the management and the union within a company, the process of the spring offensive reveals strong coordination among employers as well as among unions (Sako, 1997b, p. 236). Recent OECD indicators (OECD, 2006, p. 81) showed that Japan, in spite of the lowest bargaining centralization score, was among the countries with the highest bargaining coordination scores. Japan's coordination score for the period of 1995–2000 was 4, while those of the US and the UK were only 1 (ibid.).

The inter-union coordination of *shunto* bargaining takes place mainly at the industry level. Under the leadership of industry-level federations, member unions make uniform wage demands during a synchronized schedule of negotiations. Federations not only suggest uniform wage demands, but monitor the process of negotiations at the enterprise level (to equalize wage increases). In response to coordination on the union side, employers also closely coordinate their standpoints about the wage increase (Lee, 2000, p. 37).

Shunto wage negotiation has been a typical example of pattern bargaining. Once the amount of wage increase is determined in the 'top batter' industry, it becomes the standard, the '*shunto* rate', for other industries. Even companies without labor unions take this standard very seriously.

Since the break of the 'bubble' in 1990, however, the coordination of wage bargaining has been weakened. Nikkeiren, the national organization of employers, stressed that wage determination should be based strictly on productivity growth and 'the capacity of each company to pay' (Suzuki, 2004). Surveys by the government show that the *shunto* rate is becoming less important in determining the amount of wage increase.

In contrast to Japan, collective bargaining in Korea is decentralized and uncoordinated. According to OECD, Korea scored only 1 in both bargaining centralization and coordination scores during the period 1995–2000. This is not to say that umbrella organizations of employers and unions have no role at all in collective bargaining. They suggest nationwide standards of wage increases every year (Lee, 2003, p. 208).

Some industrial unions intervene deeply in wage negotiations at the enterprise level. Overall collective bargaining, however, is decentralized. The guidelines for wage increases suggested by the umbrella organizations of unions and of employers seldom have binding force for unions or management at the enterprise level. As a result, wage increase rates settled at the wage negotiations are diverse across firms in a sector, unlike in Japan where wage increase rates are more or less uniform across unionized firms in a sector. The bargaining schedule is also more fragmented in Korea than in Japan. While most wage negotiations start and settle in April and May every year in Japan, those in Korea are spread throughout the year.

HUMAN RESOURCE MANAGEMENT: VARIETIES OF FIRM INTERNAL LABOR MARKETS

Similarities

Japan and Korea share similarities that are distinct from the Western countries in human resource management practices. The fundamental similarity is that both Japan and Korea have developed internal labor markets in large corporations. Although firm internal labor markets are also found in Western countries like the US, those in Japan and Korea are stronger because working conditions in firm internal labor markers are far superior to those in external labor markets. Employers are expected to take care of regular employees' well-being in the firm. Workers in firm internal labor markets are provided with a variety of fringe benefits including housing and tuition subsidies. In this respect, human resource management practiced in firm internal labor markets has a paternalistic character in both countries (Lee and Rhee, 2004).

Firm internal labor markets are, to some extent, the products of enterprise unionism in both countries. Enterprise unions, mainly organized in large companies by regular workers, demanded employment security and wage increases within a company. As a result, working conditions in union-organized sectors became superior to small and medium companies, in which unionization was low.

Another similarity is seniority pay applied in firm internal labor markets. Workers' length of service is an important factor in determining wages. Statistical analyses show strong correlations between workers' wages and the length of service in both Japan and Korea (Ono, 1989; Cheon and Chong, 1998).

Difference in Employment Security

It is well known that lifetime employment is one of the key features of employment practices in Japan. Nomura said that lifetime employment is the strongest norm out of three pillars of employment relations (Nomura, 2007, p. 109).

Literally, lifetime employment means that workers employed by a company immediately after graduation work for the company until their retirement age. However, it is not true that the majority of Japanese workers work for just one company throughout their career (Takanashi, 1999, p. 7). Mid-career resignations and changes of employment often occur even within large companies. Government statistics show that less than 20 percent of all employees work for one company throughout their career until retirement. But it cannot be denied that there is a social consensus that employers should not dismiss their employees. Companies that conduct lay-offs are regarded as bad companies and their stock prices tend to fall (Nomura, 2007, p. 107).

Even during the economic crisis caused by the oil shock in the early 1970s, employers refrained from dismissing employees. Instead, they resorted to such practices as the reduction of overtime and reassigning workers to affiliated companies (*shukko*). During the long economic recession in the 1990s and 2000s, many have become skeptical about the viability of lifetime employment (Chuma, 2002). However, the majority of researchers agree that lifetime employment has been maintained as far as regular workers are concerned (Watanabe, 2000; Nitta, 2003; Rebick, 2005; Vogel, 2006).

In contrast to Japan, Korea does not have the norm of lifetime employment. Until the mid-1980s, workers' employment was very insecure in Korea. Employers were free to dismiss workers as labor laws were not respected and workers had almost no voice in the workplace (Lee and Rhee, 2004).

This situation changed drastically after the rise of the labor movement in 1987, mainly in large companies. The most noticeable change was the enhancement of workers' employment stability within a company. As it became very difficult for employers to dismiss workers deliberately, turnover rates began to decline, particularly in large companies. The enhancement of employment stability was most striking among blue-collar workers. The enhancement of employment stability led some academics like Kim et al. to argue that lifetime employment had become the norm in Korean management practices (Kim et al., 2000, p. 141). Other researchers are, however, skeptical about this view. There is little evidence that employers came to commit themselves to the norm of lifetime employment. Although employers refrained from dismissing workers, this was rather a pragmatic adaptation to union power than the expression of commitment to the norm of lifetime employment.

Survey results show that the norm of lifetime employment is weaker in Korea than in Japan. While 56.9 percent of Japanese employers who answered a survey said that they would stick to the principle of lifetime employment, only 11.6 percent of respondents favored the principle in a similar survey conducted in Korea in 1998. The majority of Korean employers preferred 'flexible long-term employment' to lifetime employment (Park, 1999).

Korea's employment practices, however, remain distinct from the Western model. Unlike US employers who lay off workers in a recession, Korean employers use honorary retirement as a principal tool for downsizing. Although honorary retirement is not purely voluntary, it is true that Korean employers do not have as many options in reducing their workforce as their US counterparts.

Difference in Pay Systems

Japan's pay system is well known as seniority-based pay. Seniority-based pay means that a worker's wages increase according to his or her age and/ or length of service. Without a doubt, seniority has been a major factor in determining wages in Japan. Nonetheless, it does not mean that wages rise directly in proportion to workers' age or the length of service. The most common pay system is the 'composite pay system' in which various factors such as ability, skill, attitude, education, age and seniority determine wages. Moreover, seniority becomes an important factor in wage determination because workers' ability is expected to grow with the length of service through training and experience within a company.

A typical pay system in large companies since the 1980s has been the combination of pay for living cost (*seikatsu-kyu*) and merit-based pay (*shokuno-kyu*). Pay for living cost is largely determined by workers' age and/or seniority. Merit-based pay is determined by workers' skill qualifications (*shokuno shikaku*). The Japanese companies have a qualification system in which employees are placed along the hierarchy of grades according to skill qualifications (Sako, 1997a, pp. 6–7). It is also to be noted that merit-based pay is not entirely independent from seniority. It was common until recently that workers with a certain length of service were promoted automatically along the skill grades.

Japan's pay system has continuously changed and the role of seniority has decreased. The age–wage profile has been flattening since the 1980s. The most remarkable development since the 1990s is the introduction of performance-based pay. Many firms claimed that they will attach greater importance to manifest performance than latent ability in wage determination. At the same time, firms are eliminating wage components determined by workers' age. It is not clear, however, whether the introduction of performance-based pay is a departure from traditional merit-based pay. There are divergent views on this issue. Regardless of the views on this issue, there are few who expect that Japan will have a Western-style pay system in the near future.

Seniority has been a factor in determining pay in Korea as well as in Japan. Korea's large companies, following Japan's, have applied the practice of periodic step promotion of wages to white-collar workers since the 1970s. As a result, white-collar workers' wages increased according to the length of service within a company. But this practice was seldom applied to blue-collar workers, even in large companies. The rise of the labor movement in 1987 changed this situation. The practice of periodic step promotion of wages began to be applied to blue-collar workers, too. Since then, seniority pay has become an important feature of employment relations in Korea.

Pay systems are more seniority-based in Korea than in Japan. Statistical analyses (Ono, 1989; Cheon and Chong, 1998) show that the tenure–wage profile is steeper in Korea than in Japan. Case studies at the corporate level (Oh, 2001) also show that, unlike Japan where ability as well as seniority is an important factor in determining wages, seniority is the most important factor for wage determination in Korea, especially in large companies. In many Korean companies, workers' wages increase almost automatically according to the length of service regardless of their performance. During the period of labor uprising, unions demanded that management abolish the practice of differentiated wage increases based on individual evaluations on the grounds that the evaluations were not fair. Employers reluctantly accepted this demand for industrial peace.

Employers have tried to introduce flexible wage systems with some success in Korea. A number of companies have introduced the Western-style 'annual salary system'. However, Korean pay systems are still focused on seniority. According to a survey conducted by the Korea Labor Institute, an institute sponsored by the government, more than 50 percent of the companies chose seniority-based pay as their main pay system, among different pay systems including seniority-based, job-based, ability-based and performance-based pay.

LABOR MARKET STRUCTURE: CORE AND PERIPHERY

Similarities

The increase of non-regular, or non-standard, workers, including part-time, temporary, daily and dispatched workers, is the most serious labor issue in both Japan and Korea. The proportion of non-regular workers out of total employees increased from 19.1 percent to 33.5 percent between 1989 and 2007 in Japan and from 26.8 percent to 35.9 percent between 2001 and 2007 in Korea.

Although non-regular workers have increased in virtually all of the advanced countries since the 1990s (Houseman and Osawa, 2003a), this becomes a particularly serious issue in Japan and Korea, where working conditions are significantly unequal between regular and non-regular workers. The employment practices of firm internal labor markets, such as long-term employment and seniority pay, are applied only to regular workers, who constitute the 'core' workforce. Non-regular workers, in contrast, are subject to market-driven competition.

Non-regular workers face disadvantages in many respects in both countries (Houseman and Osawa, 2003b; Kim, 2004). First, they are paid lower wages than regular workers. The lack of occupational wage rates in both countries further enlarges wage inequality between regular and non-regular workers, even when they do the same job. Second, their employment is unstable. The majority of non-regular workers are employed on fixed-term contracts. It is usual for a troubled company to dismiss non-regular workers while preserving regular workers. Non-regular workers are used as a buffer for economic fluctuations. Third, many of them are excluded not only from fringe benefits provided by employers but also from social security programs. Non-regular workers are far less likely than regular workers to be covered by social security programs in both countries. Fourth, they are not provided with proper opportunities for skill development. In Japan and Korea where workers develop their skills mainly through on-the-job training and change of tasks within a company, non-regular workers with short tenure have difficulty in improving their skills.

The growth of non-regular workers is among the most important factors in the increase of income inequality in Japan and Korea. Until the 1980s, both countries had boasted income equalities, with Gini coefficients smaller than in Anglo-Saxon countries, albeit larger than in Nordic countries. Japan regarded itself as the 'hundred million people middle-class society', and Korea became a role model for developing countries as it succeeded in achieving both economic growth and income equality. With the fast increase of non-regular and low-waged workers since the 1990s, however, the concern for social division has been widespread in both countries. 'The differentiated society' and 'the polarization' have become key phrases in social and political debates in Japan and Korea respectively.

Differences in the Characteristics of Non-regular Workers

In Japan, the majority of non-regular workers are part-timers, who work shorter hours than regular workers. According to the Labor Force Survey conducted by the Statistics Bureau of the Ministry of Internal Affairs and Communication, the percentage of workers called *paato* (part-timer) or *arubaito* (from the German word *arbeit*) in the workplace out of total non-regular workers was 67.2 percent in 2007. Although many of these types of workers work as long hours as regular workers, it is also true that the vast majority of these types of workers are genuine part-timers.

The majority of *paatos* in Japan are married female workers who want to work short hours to take care of their families. They voluntarily choose to be part-timers as this type of employment enables them to reconcile paid work and housework. Young workers called *arubaito*, mostly students, also tend to prefer this type of employment. Involuntary non-regular workers, who are forced into their present mode of employment by the lack of opportunity to be regular workers, are a minority within total non-regular workers (Sato, 2001).

Unlike in Japan, the vast majority of non-regular workers in Korea are temporaries, whose working hours are as long as those of regular workers. Only a minority of non-regular workers are part-timers who work less than 35 hours a week. At the same time, the majority of non-regular workers took their jobs involuntarily due to the lack of regular jobs. An analysis of surveys conducted by the Korea Labor Institute shows that non-regular workers are much less satisfied with their jobs than regular workers (Jung, 2007).

Non-regular workers have featured prominently in recent labor disputes in Korea. Labor disputes caused by non-regular workers tend to be violent and long-lasting. Having little resources to cope with employers, non-regular workers often resort to radical measures such as hunger strikes and workplace occupation to get social attention. This often leads to dismissal, arrest and imprisonment.

It is also to be noted that the characteristics of non-regular workers are changing these days in Japan. First, the types of non-regular workers other than part-timers are increasing. The most important category is dispatched workers. The number of these employees, which stood at about 430,000 in 2002, has grown to over 1.3 million in 2007. Many of the dispatched workers are sent to jobs for a very short period. Second, more young workers, both male and female, are getting non-regular jobs after graduating from school. Many of them are called *freeter* – a coined term combining 'free' and the German word *'arbeiter'*. This term is used mainly in discussion of young school graduates under the age of 30 who are not bound up in long-term employment (Rebick, 2005, p. 153). Third, the percentage of involuntary workers, who got their present job because they were unable to find a regular job, is increasing. Fourth, non-regular workers are becoming less satisfied with their jobs. In these respects, the characteristics of non-regular workers in Japan are becoming similar to those in Korea.

DISCUSSION

Summarizing Similarities and Differences

It has been demonstrated that employment relations in Japan and Korea have both similarities and differences. It is noticeable that Japan and Korea share many similarities in employment relations. Both countries have enterprise unionism, seniority wages, paternalistic management, strong firm internal labor markets and labor market segmentation into core and periphery. These similarities enable us to categorize Japan's and Korea's employment relations as a type of employment system. It could labeled the 'strong firm internal labor market type' employment system.

At the same time, employment relations in Japan and Korea reveal numerous differences, which make it impossible to classify the Korean employment system as a variant of the Japanese model. More than anything else, Korea does not have the practice of lifetime employment. It reflects the fact that the idea of the firm as a community is much weaker in Korea than in Japan. It is generally agreed that the uniqueness of Japanese employment relations is not so much in its practices such as lifetime employment, seniority wages and enterprise unionism as in the social conceptions and norms that regard the enterprise as a community (OECD, 1973; Inagami, 1999). These norms failed to take root in Korea. In particular, Korean employers are at once more authoritarian and market-driven than their Japanese counterparts. This is why Korea's industrial relations are much more confrontational than in Japan. In this sense, Korea's employment system could be categorized as a mixture of the US model and the Japanese model.

Explaining Similarities and Differences

To explain these similarities and differences, we will initially consider the causes of similarities. First, Japan and Korea share some cultural backgrounds. More than anything else, both countries have Confucian culture, which stresses harmony and order (Michio, 1988; Janelli and Yim, 1997). This could be a reason why paternalism is relatively strong in both countries. Employers are expected to be benevolent to workers. Employment relations are regarded as something more than just an economic contract. The explanatory power of Confucian culture, however, is limited in that the idea of a firm as a community and the norm of lifetime employment are weak in Korea.

Second, the process of economic development in Korea has been heavily influenced by Japan. Korea was colonized by Japan for 36 years until 1945. Even after gaining independence, Korea relied much on Japan's technology and experience in economic development. Korean firms introduced much of Japan's human resource management practices. It is also true, however, that Korea was selective in emulating Japan. Korean employers were influenced by not only the Japanese employment system but also Anglo-Saxon employment practices. With the increase of managers trained in the US, the influence of US-style management became stronger in Korea. Indeed, the push toward the liberal economic order has been stronger in Korea than in Japan (Lee, 2006).

Third, there is a similarity in the timing of the rise of free and democratic labor union movements. In both countries, free and democratic labor movements started after the growth of large and monopolistic corporations. In this situation, it was natural that collective bargaining took place at the enterprise level (Aoki, 1988, p. 187). Lack of the tradition of occupational labor movements furthered this trend (Nimura, 1997). Labor unions, mainly organized in large corporations in the form of enterprise unions, pursued employment security and seniority wages through negotiations within a company. This resulted in the development of firm internal labor markets.

Similarities aside, the causes of differences between the two countries will now be considered. We will concentrate on the reasons why Korea failed to develop cooperative employment relations, including lifetime employment, like those found in Japan.

Prior studies mentioned three causes. The first is cultural differences. Although Japan and Korea share Confucian culture, the characteristics of the Confucian tradition were different in the two countries. Yoon (1998) argued that the organization principle of traditional society was different between Korea and Japan. In traditional Japan, the basic unit of the society was *ie* (house), the membership of which was not confined to blood relations. Members of an *ie* were expected to devote limitless loyalty to the *ie*, which looked after members throughout their lives. Today, the company is regarded as *ie*, which looks after members, including the management and workers, until their retirement. The management and workers are devoted to their company in return. In traditional Korea, the basic unit of the society was family, whose membership was confined to blood relations. Filial piety to parents and ancestors was the most valued virtue of family members. Those not related by blood were not accepted as family members even if they were living and working together with family members. They were regarded as servants. Today, a company is regarded as the property of the family who owns it, while workers are regarded as servants of the family. Kim (1999) also argued that differences in the culture of collectivism are the major causes of divergences in industrial relations in Korea and Japan.

It goes without saying that Japan's and Korea's cultural traditions are different, and the differences must have affected the behavior of employers and workers. However, cultural differences cannot explain the fact that Japan also had a period of severe conflict between labor and management. The perspective that finds the source of the Japanese employment system in the traditional *ie* relationship has been widely criticized in Japan (Koike, 1988; Ogoshi, 2006; Nomura, 2007).

The second cause of differences is the difference between business systems. The issue is whether the business conglomerates (the *zaibatsu* in Japan and the *chaebol* in Korea) dominate the economy. In Japan, *zaibatsus* were dissolved by the US Occupation after World War II. Although the companies of a dissolved *zaibatsu* formed *keiretsu*, the alliance, after the 1950s, the autonomy of individual companies was maintained. This company structure, together with the practice of internal promotion, reinforced the idea that managers are senior employees who have been internally promoted, not agents who act on behalf of shareholders or families of founding fathers. In contrast, Korea still has the *chaebol* system, in which major companies are owned and managed by several families. Companies that belong to *chaebols* are completely in the hands of the 'owners', the sons or grandsons of the founding fathers, of the *chaebols*. The 'owners' tend to think that companies that belong to *chaebols* are their belongings rather than social institutions. As a result, they are generally reluctant to share decision-making with labor unions. Samsung, the No.1 *chaebol* in Korea, still holds the 'no union' strategy and never hesitates to commit unfair labor practices. As the 'owner' has absolute power within a *chaebol*, line managers do not have enough discretion to develop collaboration with unions. In this situation, workers tend to have 'them and us' feelings towards managers.

This explanation reveals an important aspect of industrial relations in Japan and Korea. However, the idea that family-owned conglomerates hinder cooperation between labor and management cannot explain the fact that the Wallenberg family is a forerunner in developing labor–management cooperation in Sweden.

The third difference is in union structure. While white-collar workers and lower-ranking managers join enterprise unions with blue-collar workers in Japan, enterprise unions in Korea mainly represent blue-collar workers. This difference in the scope of membership affects union behavior (Jeong, 1995, p. 267; Suzuki, 2004, p. 120). The presence of white-collar workers and lower-ranking managers contributes to unions' cooperative stance toward the management in Japan. Blue-collar domination, on the other hand, contributes to more militant union behaviors in Korea.

This explanation, while insightful, cannot explain the fact that enterprise unions mainly composed of white-collar workers are often as militant as unions representing blue-collar workers in Korea.

I would like to mention two additional causes of differences. The first is the economic environment. Unlike Japan, which enjoyed an economic boom long enough to develop cooperative and efficient employment relations, Korea faced an economic crisis and pressure of globalization not long after the development of its independent labor movement. In Japan, there were serious labor disputes over lay-offs after the World War II. Realizing the cost of disputes, employers accepted the norm of lifetime employment. This practice, together with seniority-based wages, might have damaged the competitiveness of firms. But high economic growth in the 1950s and 1960s enabled Japanese firms to maintain lifetime employment. During this period, Japanese firms introduced skill formation and qualification systems, which laid the basis of efficiency of firms. As Aoki noted (Aoki, 1988), cooperative relations were shaped and evolved only gradually in Japan. Korea faced an economic crisis ten years after the rise of labor movement in 1987. Although employers had tried to build cooperative and efficient employment relations with labor unions after 1987, ten years was too short for cooperative employment relations to take root. Since 1997, the central concern of actors, especially employers and the government, has become flexibility and competitiveness rather than labor peace and stability (Kuruvilla and Erickson, 2002). This concern hampered the development of cooperative employment relations as workers and unions resisted the introduction of flexibility measures.

The second difference is the power relations at the time of the rise of the labor movement. Major employers in post-war Japan were regarded as responsible for World War II. They found themselves in a position to welcome democracy and compromise with labor unions. This is why

Japanese employers accepted unions' demand for employment security. Unlike in Japan, Korean employers, those of *chaebols* in particular, retained their class power against labor. Although many of them were indicted and often found guilty of illegally supporting authoritarian governments, they succeeded in appearing to be the leaders of economic growth. The role of the state was crucial in this respect. In Japan, the US Occupation encouraged the free labor movement. Subsequent governments also respected labor rights. In contrast, the Korean government from 1987 to 1997 did not fully permit free labor movements. Strikes were often suppressed by the police. In this situation, employers would rely on the police rather than compromise with unions.

CURRENT CHANGES AND PROSPECTS

Employment relations in Japan and Korea have been under strong pressure for change since the economic crises in the 1990s. Continued recession and globalization forced employers to aggressively pursue cost reduction measures. Aging of the working population increased the burden of seniority pay. Technological change and the growth of the service sector seem to make both lifetime employment and seniority wage inappropriate. Some argue that the traditional Japanese employment system can survive only under conditions of high economic growth (Yashiro, 2008). Indeed, there have been considerable changes in the direction of greater flexibility in both countries.

However, changes have been path-dependent and contingent on the social context. In Japan, lifetime employment is maintained as far as regular workers are concerned. Although seniority has become less important in wage determination, it is generally agreed that the pay system in Japan will remain distinct from Western models (Nakamura, 2007; Miyamoto, 2009). In Korea, employment stability of regular workers has become considerably weakened as employers pursue flexibility and cost reduction. There are not a few who argue that Korea's labor market was transformed into a neoliberal one after the economic crisis of 1997 (Lee, 2007; Yang, 2007). Nevertheless, US-style lay-offs are not widely used for restructuring. During the recent economic downturn caused by the US financial crisis in 2008, most Korean companies did not lay off workers. Seniority pay is, in spite of some changes, still maintained in large companies.

We expect that there will be more changes in employment relations in Japan and Korea as pressures to change still exist. But further changes, like previous ones, will be path-dependent. Even when small changes add up to a qualitative change, employment relations in the two countries will remain something distinct from the Western, especially the US model. The US financial crisis in 2008 strengthened the view that the US labor market is not the model to follow.

It is to be mentioned that there are differences as well as similarities in changes of employment relations in Japan and Korea. The most striking difference is that, while lifetime employment is maintained in Japan, employment security of regular workers has substantially weakened in Korea. The threat of losing jobs was an important reason why many Korean workers chose to transform their unions from enterprise unions to industrial unions. With these changes, employment relations of regular workers in Japan and Korea have become less similar after the economic crisis in the 1990s than before (Jung and Cheon, 2006).

The prospect of employment relations is also different in Japan and Korea. More changes are expected in Korea than in Japan. The reason is that the economic efficiency of existing employment relations is lower in Korea than in Japan (ibid.). This is why Korean employers, unlike their Japanese counterparts, often express their strong desire to change employment relations. Although this desire has not been fulfilled due to the opposition of labor unions, the shift in the balance of power relations between management and labor could bring about profound changes.

The most serious challenge to existing employment relations in Japan and Korea is the increase of non-regular workers. As mentioned above, the percentage of non-regular workers out of the total labor force is more than 30 percent in both countries. Non-regular workers are generally excluded from collective bargaining, internal labor markets and many types of social insurance. How to incorporate non-regular workers into the existing system of employment relations and social safety net is an impending task for employers, unions and the government. This task, however, is not an easy one at all. Employment security and higher wages of regular workers in the firm internal labor market has been dependent on the very existence of non-regular workers in both countries. Equal treatment of regular and non-regular workers may lead to drastic changes in the working conditions of regular workers. Indeed, there are many who argue that genuine equality between regular and non-regular workers is only possible when the firm internal labor market is abolished (Kinoshita, 1999; Mori, 2005). This means that the practice of lifetime employment and seniority pay should be drastically weakened, if not abolished. This is, however, no easy task. Moreover, it could jeopardize labor peace and the skill formation system, which have been important conditions of economic competitiveness, especially in Japan.

CONCLUSION

The Japan–Korea comparison has numerous implications for theories of employment relations. Four points deserve special attention.

First, it may be useful to establish the East Asian model of employment relations as a sub-type of employment relations in the world. Prior studies focused on the Japanese employment system as a model distinct from the Western model of employment relations. However, Japan's and Korea's employment relations could be categorized as the East Asian model as they share many similarities. In this case, essential features of the East Asian model of employment relations are strong firm internal labor markets and labor market segmentation, rather than lifetime employment or the idea of the firm as a community. This model could be labeled the 'strong firm internal labor market type' employment system. There might be more countries that can be included in this model.

Second, it is necessary to distinguish formal institutions from their actual functions and social consequences. Although Japan and Korea share many institutional features, their effects on employment relations are different. While enterprise unionism is the basis of labor–management cooperation in Japan, the same institution fails to foster labor peace in Korea. While decentralized negotiations have been coordinated in Japan, they have been fragmented in Korea. The actual function of seniority wages is also different between Japan and Korea. These differences suggest that we need to understand institutions in the social and historical context.

Third, a comprehensive viewpoint is needed in the study of comparative employment relations. As we have shown above, various factors such as culture, the state, business systems, economic environment, power relations between labor and management, and the timing of the rise of the labor movement all played their roles in forming the similarities and differences of employment relations in Japan and Korea. It is impossible to determine the single, most important factor.

The last point is the relevance of path dependency. In spite of the strong pressures to change after the economic crises in the 1990s, basic traits of employment relations have been maintained in both Japan and Korea. It is beyond doubt that there have been considerable changes in employment relations in the two countries. Changes, however, were path-dependent, and did not lead to a paradigm shift.

REFERENCES

Aoki, Masahiko (1988), *Information, Incentives, and Bargaining in the Japanese Economy*, Cambridge: Cambridge University Press.
Bamber, Greg J. and Ross, Peter K. (2000), 'Industrialization, democratization and employment relations in the Asia-Pacific', in G.J. Bamber et al. (eds), *Employment Relations in the Asia-Pacific*, St Leonards: Allen and Unwin, pp. 3–19.
Cheon, Byung-You and Chong, Kyun-Sung (1998), 'Seniority pay, turnover and job training in Korea', *Hankook Gyeongje Nonjip (The Korean Economic Review)*, **14**(2), 59–78.
Chuma, A. Hiroyuki (2002), 'Employment adjustment in Japanese firms during the current crisis', *Industrial Relations*, **41**(4), 653–82.
Deyo, Frederic C. (1989), *Beneath the Miracle: Labor Subordination in the New Asian Industrialism*, Berkeley, CA: University of California Press.
Deyo, Frederic C. (1997), 'Labor and post-Fordist industrial restructuring in East and Southeast Asia', *Work and Occupations*, **24**(1), 97–118.
Houseman, Susan and Osawa, Machiko (2003a), 'Introduction', in S. Houseman and M. Osawa (eds), *Nonstandard Work in Developed Economies*, Kalamazoo, MI: W.E. Upjohn Institute for Employment Research, pp. 1–14.
Houseman, Susan and Osawa, Machiko (2003b), 'The growth of nonstandard employment in Japan and the United States', in S. Houseman and M. Osawa (eds), *Nonstandard Work in Developed Economies*, Kalamazoo, MI: W.E. Upjohn Institute for Employment Research, pp. 175–214.
Inagami, Takeshi (1999), 'Nihon no Sangyoshakai to Roudou (Japan's industrial society and labor)', in T. Inagami and T. Kawakita (eds), *Kouza Shakaigaku 6: Roudou (Lecture in Sociology 6: Labor)*, Tokyo: University of Tokyo Press (in Japanese), pp. 1–31.
Janelli, Roger L. and Yim, Dawnhee (1997), 'The mutual constitution of Confucianism and capitalism', in T. Brook and H. Luong (eds), *Culture and Economy: The Shaping of Capitalism in Eastern Asia*, Ann Arbor, MI: The University of Michigan Press, pp. 107–24.
Jeong, Jooyeon (1995), 'Enterprise unionism from a Korean perspective', *Economic and Industrial Democracy*, **16**(2), 253–73.
Jeong, Jooyeon (2007), *Industrial Relations in Korea*, London: Routledge.
Jung, EeHwan (2007), 'Bijeonggyu Nodong Shijang ui Teukseong e gwanhan Han-il Bigyo Yeongyu (A comparative study of the characteristics of non-standard labor markets in Korea and Japan)', *Saneop Nodong Yeongyu (Korean Journal of Labor Studies)*, **13**(1), 1–32 (in Korean).
Jung, EeHwan and Cheon, Byung-You (2006), 'Economic crisis and changes in employment relations in Japan and Korea', *Asian Survey*, **46**(3), 457–76.
Kim, Dong-Won, Bae, Johngseok and Lee, Changwon (2000), 'Globalization and labour rights: The case of Korea', in C. Rowley and J. Benson (eds), *Globalization and Labour in the Asia Pacific Region*, London: Frank Cass, pp. 133–53.
Kim, Jong-Han (1999), 'Hanil Nosagwangye Seongkyuk ui Bigyosajeok Yeongyu (A comparative historical study of industrial relations in Korea and Japan)', *Bigyo Gyeongje Yeongu (Journal of Comparative Economic Studies)*, **7**(1), 159–96 (in Korean).
Kim, Sam-Soo (2000), 'Nosa Gwangye ui Hanil Bigyo (Korea–Japan comparison in industrial relations)', in Y. Park and S. Nojoem (eds), *Dong Asia Gyeongje Hyeoplyeok ui Hyeonsang gwa Ganungseong (The Phenomena and Possibilities of Economic Cooperation in East Asia)*, Seoul: Asiatic Research Center, Korea University, pp. 219–72 (in Korean).
Kim, Yoo-Sun (2004), *Nodong Shijang Youyeonhwa wa Bijeonggyujik Goyong (Labor Market Flexibility and Non-regular Employment)*, Seoul: Korea Labour and Society Institute (in Korean).
Kinoshita, Takeo (1999), *Nihonjin no Chinkin (Wages of the Japanese)*, Tokyo: Heibonsha (in Japanese).
Koike, Kazuo (1988), *Understanding Industrial Relations in Modern Japan*, London: Macmillan Press.

Kong, Tat Yan (2005), 'Labour and neo-liberal globalization in South Korea and Taiwan', *Modern Asian Studies*, **39**(1), 155–88.
Korea Labor Institute (2008), *KLI Foreign Labor Statistics 2008*, Seoul: Korea Labor Institute.
Kuruvilla, Saroshi and Erickson, Christopher L. (2002), 'Change and transformation in Asian industrial relations', *Industrial Relations*, **41**(2), 171–27.
Lee, Byeong-Cheon (2007), 'Yanggeukhwa Shidae ui Kaejin Yaksok (Broken promises in the era of polarization)', in B. Lee (ed.), *Segyehwa Shidae ui Kankuk Jabonjuui (The Korean Capitalism in the Globalized Era)*, Seoul: Hanul, pp. 21–99 (in Korean).
Lee, Byoung-Hoon (2003), 'Industrial relations system', in J. Kim (ed.), *Employment and Industrial Relations in Korea*, Seoul: Korea International Labour Foundation, pp. 171–213.
Lee, Chung H. (2006), 'Institutional reform in Japan and Korea: Why the difference?', in M. Blomström and S. La Croix (eds), *Institutional Change in Japan*, London: Routledge, pp. 71–93.
Lee, Hyo-Soo and Rhee, Jaehooni (2004), 'PDR systems theory perspective on employment relations in a globalizing Asia: A Korean case', in R. Blanpain (ed.), *Labour Relations in the Asia-Pacific Countries*, The Hague: Kluwer Law International, pp. 89–106.
Lee, Minjin (2000), *Chinkin Kettei Seido no Kan-Nichi Hikaku (A Comparison of Wage Determination Institutions in Korea and Japan)*, Tokyo: Azusashupansha (in Japanese).
Lee, Wonduck and Lee, Joohee (2004), 'Will the model of uncoordinated decentralization persist?', in H. Katz, W. Lee and J. Lee (eds), *The New Structure of Labor Relations*, Ithaca, NY: ILR Press, pp. 145–65.
Michio, Morishima (1988), 'Confucianism as a basis for capitalism', in D. Okimito and T. Rohlen (eds), *Inside the Japanese System*, Stanford, CA: Stanford University Press, pp. 36–8.
Miyamoto, Mitsuharu (2009), 'Naze Nihonkata Seikashugi wa Umaretanoka? (Why was the Japanese-style performancism born?)', *Nihon Roudou Kenkyu Zatsi (Japan Labor Review)*, **585**, 30–33 (in Japanese).
Mori, Masumi (2005), *Nihon no Seisabetsu Chinkin (Gender Discrimination in Wages in Japan)*, Tokyo: Yuhikaku (in Japanese).
Nakamura, Keisuke (1997), 'Worker participation', in M. Sako and H. Sato (eds), *Japanese Labour and Management in Transition*, London: Routledge, pp. 280–95.
Nakamura, Keisuke (2007), 'Seikashugi to Jinjikaigaku (Performancism and personnel management reform)', *Nihon Roudou Kenkyu Zatsi (Japan Labor Review)*, **560**, 43–7 (in Japanese).
Nimura, Kazuo (1997), 'Nitkan Roshikanke no Hikakushiteki Kento (A comparative historical consideration of Japan's and Korea's industrial relations)', *Ohara Shakai Mondai Zatsi (Ohara Journal of Social Issues)*, **460** (in Japanese).
Nitta, Michio (2003), *Henka no Naka no Kouyou Sisutemu (Employment Systems in Transformation)*, Tokyo: Tokyo University Press (in Japanese).
Nomura, Masami (2007), *Nihonteki Koyoukankou (Japanese Employment Practices)*, Tokyo: Minerva Shobou (in Japanese).
OECD (Organisation for Economic Co-operation and Development) (1973), *Manpower Policy in Japan*, Paris: OECD.
OECD (Organisation for Economic Co-operation and Development) (2006), *OECD Employment Outlook*, Paris: OECD.
Ogoshi, Yonosuke (2006), *Shushin Koyou to Nenkou Chinkin no Tenkan (The Transformation of Lifetime Employment and Seniority Pay)*, Tokyo: Mineruva Shobou (in Japanese).
Oh, Hak-Soo (2001), 'Koyoukankou to Roshikanke no Nit-Kan Hikaku (Japan–Korea comparison of employment practices and industrial relations)', PhD dissertation, Tokyo: Tokyo University (in Japanese).
Ono, Akira (1989), *Nihonteki Koyoukankou to Roudoushijou (Japanese Employment Practices and Labor Market)*, Tokyo: Toyoukeizaishinbunsha (in Japanese).
Park, Joon Sung (1999), 'Goyong-gwanli ui Byeonhwa: Han-il Bigyo (Changes in human

resource management: Korea–Japan comparison)', *Gyeongyeong Nonjip (The Korea Business Journal)*, **33**(4), 244–76 (in Korean).

Rebick, Marcus (2005), *The Japanese Employment Systems: Adapting to a New Economic Environment*, Oxford: Oxford University Press.

Sako, Mari (1997a), 'Introduction: Forces for homogeneity and diversity in the Japanese industrial relations system', in M. Sako and H. Sato (eds), *Japanese Labour and Management in Transition*, London: Routledge, pp. 1–24.

Sako, Mari (1997b), '*Shunto*: The role of employer and union coordination at the industry and inter-sectional levels', in M. Sako and H. Sato (eds), *Japanese Labour and Management in Transition*, London: Routledge, pp. 236–64.

Sato, Hiroki (2001), 'Atypical employment: A source of flexible work opportunities?', *Social Science Japan Journal*, **4**(2), 161–81.

Shirai, Thaishiro (1983), 'A theory of enterprise unionism', in T. Shirai (ed.), *Contemporary Industrial Relations in Japan*, Madison, WI: The University of Wisconsin Press, pp. 117–43.

Suzuki, Akira (2004), 'The rise and fall of interunion wage coordination and tripartite dialogue in Japan', in H. Katz, W. Lee and J. Lee (eds), *The New Structure of Labor Relations*, Ithaca, NY: ILR Press, pp. 119–42.

Takahashi, Takeshi (1970), *Nihonteki Roshikanke no Kenkyu (A Study of Japanese Industrial Relations)*, Tokyo: Miraisha (in Japanese).

Takanashi, Takeshi et al. (1999), *Japanese Employment Practices*, Tokyo: The Japan Institute of Labour.

Vogel, Steven K. (2006), *Japan Remodeled*, Ithaca, NY: Cornell University Press.

Watanabe, Susumu (2000), 'The Japan model and the future of employment and wage systems', *International Labour Review*, **139**(3), 307–33.

Whitley, Richard (1999), *Divergent Capitalisms: The Social Structuring and Change of Business Systems*, Oxford: Oxford University Press.

Yang, Jun-Ho (2007), 'Goyong mit Imgum Jojeong ui Yuyeonseong gwa Geoshi Gyeongjejeok Bulanjeongseong (The flexibility of employment and of wage adjustment and macroeconomic instability)', in H. Kim (ed.), *Hyeondai Jabonjuui Bunseok (An Analysis of Contemporary Capitalism)*, Seoul: Hanul, pp. 190–226 (in Korean).

Yashiro, Naohiro (2008), 'Roudoushijou no Kaikaku (The labor market reform)', RIETI Discussion Paper Series No. 08-J-040 (in Japanese).

Yoon, Sook-Hyun (1998), 'Nikkan niokeru Roshikanke no Genryu Hikaku (Origins of industrial relations in Japan and Korea)', *Higashi Asia Kenkyu (East Asian Studies)*, **22**, 91–102 (in Japanese).

11 Employment relations in Belgium and the Netherlands

Hester Houwing, Maarten Keune,
*Philippe Pochet and Kurt Vandaele**

INTRODUCTION

Inspired by the welfare states in the northern part of Europe, 'activation' of the welfare state became a dominant policy idea in Western Europe in the 1990s, the assumption being that such activation was required, in the first instance, to cope with so-called 'new social risks' and, ultimately, for the long-term sustainability of social and welfare arrangements (Bonoli, 2006).[1] This new approach is widely believed, especially among policy-makers, to have significantly contributed to the success of the Nordic welfare states over the last decade, during which they have achieved a combination of high standards of social protection, high employment participation rates and low unemployment rates (De Beer and Schils, 2009a, p. 1). Most of all, the so-called 'flexicurity model' of Denmark has, in recent years, been perceived as an influential role model. The Danish trajectory towards 'flexicurity' – a neologism for gluing together, in a positive manner, flexibility with security in the labour market – combines high external-numerical flexibility resulting from a low level of protection against dismissal with high levels of income security deriving from, among other things, generous and long-lasting unemployment benefits and a strong emphasis on early and obligatory activation of job-seekers through active labour market policies – often described as the 'golden triangle' (Madsen, 2006). Additionally, the role of the so-called 'social partners', that is, trade unions and employers' organizations, is considered important for developing and legitimizing flexicurity policies in Denmark.

Apart from Denmark, the Netherlands is also singled out as a model of flexicurity although it combines flexibility and security in a different way, emphasizing the use of flexible contracts (temporary contracts and temporary agency work), and the extension of social security rights to these contracts.[2] The existence of more than one model indicates that flexicurity is less a scientific than a loose multidimensional concept. Indeed, while one variant of this approach focuses on the positive linkage between labour market, welfare state and training policies, a second focuses on equality between those inside and those outside the labour market and a third on the role of 'learning' enterprises and trust within companies (Keune and Pochet, 2009). Nor is flexicurity a purely political concept, though it is employed for political purposes. The different relevant dimensions of flexicurity are indeed hard to pin down and to measure, in terms of their failure or success (Bertozzi and Bonoli, 2010). The concept emerged in an academic context, as a result of the need to explain the widely differing labour market performances observed in Europe, and was also associated with the political goal of achieving a positive combination between flexibility and security, in other words, catering simultaneously to the needs of both employers and workers (the so-called 'third way' approach).

This chapter conducts a country comparison between flexicurity policies pursued in Belgium and the Netherlands, insofar as both these countries provide prima facie cases when regarded from a 'most similar design' perspective (Lijphart, 1975). First of all, both countries are small but densely populated members of the European Union (EU), sharing a largely common history up to the late sixteenth century and having much in common in the economic and political spheres (Huyse and Berting, 1983). Both Belgium and the Netherlands are also small in the economic sense: given their narrow domestic markets, they are economically dependent upon access to world markets but unable to influence world market prices (Jones, 2008). Due to their relative size and position in the world economy, economic vulnerability is a widespread assumption among the political and economic elites, so that competitiveness of companies is a major concern. Both countries have promoted social partnership by establishing corporatist institutions, with the sectoral level as the dominant level for collective bargaining; the employers' organizations and trade unions have also been involved in the administration and management of the welfare system. Finally, liberal, religious and socialist political parties dominated the party system in both countries until the 1960s, with Christian-democratic parties often playing a pivotal role. As new political parties broke through and the electorate became increasingly volatile, electoral loyalty to the traditional parties dropped rapidly in recent decades.

Yet dissimilar developments are also to be observed. First of all, Belgium has a more heterogeneous population than the Netherlands since it is located on the cultural boundary of Germanic and Latin Europe. As an institutional answer to uneven economic development in conjunction with 'territorialization' of the language conflict, the piecemeal constitutional change of Belgium officially turned the country into a federal state in 1993 (for details, see Swenden and Jans, 2006). Its centrifugal federalism (accompanied by ongoing economic differences) has not, however, guaranteed enduring overall stability and sustainability of the political system.

Furthermore, the industrial structure of the two countries has displayed differences from the outset. Belgium is the oldest industrial nation in continental Europe and enjoyed a strong position in the production of coal, steel and related industrial products until the 1960s, while the Netherlands industrialized later. Industry largely accounts for Belgium's exports, particularly to the neighbouring countries, with intermediate goods still constituting the major portion of exports and Flanders the principal region of export. The Dutch economy is mainly based on transportation and logistics, international finance, business services and agro-industry. Finally, compared with other countries of Bismarckian tradition, the Netherlands seems to have moved in the last two decades away from the continental cluster and toward the Scandinavian group of countries, a path-breaking development that has been described by some commentators as the 'Dutch miracle' (Visser and Hemerijck, 1997). Belgium's unemployment and growth performances have arguably been less good, and this country is never cited in the international or European literature as an example (see Appendix at the end of the chapter for the data). Many in Belgium (especially the Flemish policy-makers) see the Dutch labour market as the model to be copied (Sels and Van Hootegem, 2001, p. 328; Houwing and Vandaele, 2011). In short, what we have here are two countries that have in the past shared many institutional traits but that, over the past 20 or 30 years, have gone down different roads.

The chapter is structured as follows. The next section briefly presents the flexicurity concept and its definition at EU level. The third section underlines the differences between Belgium and the Netherlands. The fourth and fifth sections shed light on the different paths chosen, addressing the question of external-numerical flexibility and dismissal regulation, on the one hand, and of internal-numerical flexibility and temporary unemployment on the other. The sixth explains the differences between the two countries; then we conclude.

FLEXICURITY: A PROMINENT BUT CONTESTED CONCEPT AT EUROPEAN LEVEL

In the first few years of the new millennium, flexicurity, after its development in Dutch academic circles in the late 1990s, rapidly became a very prominent concept in Europe. One reason for this growing interest in flexicurity is that it constitutes a possible alternative to the (largely bankrupt) neoliberal view of the labour market that dominated the debate during much of the 1980s and 1990s (Keune, 2008a). The main reason, however, has been that the European Commission adopted flexicurity and placed it at the core of the European Employment Strategy (EES) as of 2006. The EES is one of the main examples of soft regulation in the EU (as opposed to hard, legal regulation) and is based on common objectives, EU guidelines and recommendations, a set of indicators for monitoring, as well as policy learning and policy transfer through the Open Method of Coordination (OMC) (e.g., Zeitlin and Pochet, 2005). The fact that flexicurity was at the centre of the EES and was advocated by the Commission in many other forums too led to its entering the national debates around Europe in subsequent years.

It is no coincidence that the Commission adopted the flexicurity concept and included it in the EES. Indeed, flexicurity is compatible in a number of ways with the Commission's role and discourse in the area of economic and social policy in general and employment policy in particular. This compatibility concerns, in particular, three aspects (Keune and Jepsen, 2007). The first is the Commission's role as disseminator of knowledge and 'best practices', key to the EES. In recent years, the two member states with the highest employment rates, the key EES indicator, were also the two main national cases associated with the flexicurity concept, that is, the Netherlands and Denmark. This strong performance is often argued to be, to an important extent, an outcome of the two countries' flexicurity approaches. The European Commission shares this conclusion and has consequently identified flexicurity as a best practice that it should disseminate.

Second is the Commission's role as a broker between interests, both between economic interests and between (national) political interests. Where economic interests are concerned, the Commission calls for a balance between flexibility (largely in the interest of employers, although some types of flexibility are in the interest of workers as well) and security (in the interest of workers, although some types of security are in the interest of employers as well). Where national interests are concerned, the flexicurity discourse is open and vague enough for all member states to find it compatible with their national policy agenda and not too threatening since, as part of the EES, it does not require them to adopt any policies in particular.

Third, because of its dual character (flexibility and security), as well as its close links to social dialogue through its insistence on win–win solutions, the flexicurity concept also fits neatly into the broader Commission discourse concerning the European Social Model, which starts out from the idea that competitiveness and social cohesion should be reconciled and that the two sides of the labour market, that is, trade unions and employers' organizations, should participate in the policy-making process (e.g., Jepsen and Serrano Pascual, 2005). Flexicurity expresses in one single word this interlinkage between the economic and the social, between markets and social protection, while the Commission continuously stresses the importance of the 'social partners' in designing and implementing flexicurity policies. This threefold compatibility makes flexicurity a useful and powerful discursive tool in strengthening the Commission's (soft) regulatory capacity towards the member states.

This does not mean, however, that there is a consensus on the implications of flexicurity for policy-making. On the contrary, flexicurity has become a widely accepted but at the same time deeply contested phenomenon (Keune, 2008a). For this there are two main reasons.

One reason is that flexicurity is, by design, an ambiguous concept (Keune, 2008b). In the eyes of the Commission, as well as for the main proponents of flexicurity in the literature (e.g., Wilthagen and Tros, 2004; Bekker and Wilthagen, 2008), a variety of combinations of different types of flexibility and security can produce flexicurity policies and outcomes. There is no one best way or single model to be followed, but rather a range of possibilities or pathways. And this ambiguity is deliberate. For example, Rogowski (2008, p. 86) argues that 'for the success of flexicurity policies it seems crucial that the definition of the term flexicurity remain vague so that it can be used to address a range of sometimes contradictory policy goals'. However, this also means that diametrically opposed views of labour market problems and solutions can be plausibly argued to fit the flexicurity philosophy (Keune and Jepsen, 2007). For example, it can be argued that a model combining strong dismissal protection and high flexibility of workers within the firm follows the flexicurity idea, while at the same time it is possible to argue that a model combining low dismissal protection with high income protection through social benefits exemplifies flexicurity.

Moreover, in politics, this ambiguity has, at least at the European level, led to a situation in which almost all European-level actors (Commission, Council, European Parliament, European Trade Union Confederation, BusinessEurope, etc.) endorse the importance of flexicurity for addressing Europe's labour market problems, while entertaining very different views on how to translate the abstract concept into policy; indeed, their respective positions are largely their traditional ones now presented under the heading of flexicurity (Keune, 2008a). This leads to a situation in which the flexicurity concept has become widely accepted but where, at the same time, a struggle takes place in which different actors try to impose upon the others their favourite interpretation of it (ibid.).

A second reason for the contested character, intimately linked to the first, is that the European Commission, in spite of the fact that it subscribes to the open and ambiguous notion of flexicurity, in its more detailed policy proposals and recommendations places much more emphasis on increasing flexibility than on improving security (ibid.). Indeed, it seems most inspired by the Danish flexicurity model, which builds on (1) flexible standard employment, resulting from low dismissal protection; (2) extensive unemployment benefits providing income security to the unemployed; and (3) active labour market policies aimed at skill upgrading and activation of the unemployed (Madsen, 2006). The Commission, however, in its policy recommendations places the emphasis on increasing flexibility and active labour market policies, while largely ignoring the requirement of extensive unemployment benefits. We will now turn to the two case studies, Belgium and the Netherlands.

A DIFFERENT 'GESTALT' OF FLEXICURITY IN BELGIUM AND THE NETHERLANDS

As already indicated, the Netherlands, alongside the Danish model, has often been praised as an archetypal model of flexicurity that has largely contributed to a similarly high employment rate (European Commission, 2007a). Yet it looks like that in the Netherlands, in contrast to Denmark, less emphasis is placed on activation strategies for helping the unemployed back into work (Viebrock and Clasen, 2009, p. 315). The Danish expenditures for such strategies are higher per participant than in the Netherlands (De Beer and Schils, 2009b, p. 211). In the Dutch approach to flexicurity, as emphasized by the European Commission, the focus is rather on regulating flexible types of employment and enhancing rights for flexible workers (Houwing, 2010, pp. 253–4). Therefore, to gain a better understanding of the flexicurity model of the Netherlands (and Belgium), the focus should not be restricted to the interaction between the unemployment benefit system, employment protection legislation and Active Labour Market Policies (ALMP) (as in Denmark). Moreover, for the country comparison, income security and ALMP would seem to be of less importance for examining and comparing the flexicurity model in Belgium and the Netherlands.[3] Although the unemployment risk is much higher and the unemployment benefit system is more generous in Belgium, particularly due to its (theoretically) unlimited duration, the country differs only little from the Netherlands in terms of income security (De Beer and Schils, 2009b, p. 215).[4] Furthermore, both countries have shifted away from passive income-protection measures and have embarked on more supply-side activation programmes on the labour market and made the eligibility conditions for unemployment benefits stricter (Vielle et al., 2005; CRB, 2008, pp. 91–2; De Deken, 2009, pp. 162–4; Schils, 2009).[5]

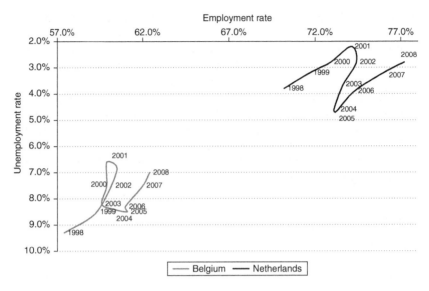

Source: Eurostat.

*Figure 11.1   Unemployment and employment rate in the 'Low Countries',
1998–2008*

Nevertheless, looking at the unemployment and employment rates, Figure 11.1 shows significant differences between Belgian and Dutch labour market developments. The unemployment rate is significantly higher in Belgium than in its northern neighbour.[6] Although the trends in the unemployment rate are similar in all three economic regions of Belgium, persistent regional differences still exist. Flanders has a rather low unemployment rate, while there is a high rate in Wallonia, particularly due to long-term unemployment, and especially in Brussels with its high rate of youth unemployment (CRB, 2008, pp. 138–40; De Deken, 2009, pp. 164–6). These regional differences are long term in nature and thus cannot be explained by the fact that Flanders started the activation of job-seekers just a bit earlier than the other regions. In the Netherlands the unemployment rate stood at a remarkably low level from the 1990s until the economic downturn of 2008, and its rate is still the lowest in the EU today (second quarter of 2009).

The employment rate, measured as the share of the population aged 15–64 in employment, is consistently more than ten percentage points higher in the Netherlands than in Belgium. The most recent figures (of 2008) show an employment rate of 62.4 per cent in Belgium compared with 77.2 per cent in the Netherlands. This difference is above all pronounced in the employment rate of women: while the Belgian rate stands at 43 per cent, the employment rate of women in the Netherlands is 58 per cent. Furthermore, Belgium's employment rate is territorially diverse, with a low rate among young people in the Brussels region, a low rate among elderly people in the Flanders region and Wallonia somewhere in the middle of the other regions (CRB, 2008, p. 63). While the Belgian employment rate is clearly lagging behind the employment guideline of the European Employment Strategy goal of 70 per cent, the level of the Dutch employment rate is similar to that of the Scandinavian countries and close to the top in the EU-27 comparison.

Yet when employment rates are expressed in full-time equivalents (FTEs), a different picture emerges, placing the Dutch job miracle in a different perspective. First of all, the Dutch employment rate in FTEs is considerably lower than the Scandinavian countries. Second, Belgium's employment rate in FTEs was higher than the Dutch rate before 1997 (Van Rie, 2008, p. 9). Today, with an employment rate in FTEs of 58.0 per cent, Belgium still nearly equals the Netherlands where the rate is 59.6 per cent (CRB, 2009, p. 50, figures for 2008; cf. Salverda, 2005, pp. 44–5; Tielens and Herremans, 2007, pp. 7–9). In other words, the FTE rates indicate that both economies have approximately the same number of working hours per adult person. So, despite, for instance, the fact that different legislative frameworks on job security promote alternative policy routes to flexicurity (with different effects on workers' precariousness), the 'gestalts' of the Belgian and Dutch models of flexicurity can most likely be regarded as 'functional equivalents' of each other. The two countries have similar outcomes, even though different (flexible) work arrangements are in place on the Belgian and Dutch labour markets.

One of these functional equivalents relates to exit routes from the labour market: whereas early retirement is an important scheme for mitigating mass lay-offs of older workers in Belgium, disability insurance has taken on this function in the Netherlands. But while the Dutch government has been able to introduce a far more drastic change in its disability policy by diminishing the role of the social partners in the social security system since the late 1990s, Belgium, due to the stronger veto powers of the social partners in the social security system, has been able to do no more than adopt more incremental adjustments of its unemployment policy (Kuipers, 2006). Attempts to change its unemployment policy in 1993 (the 'Global Pact') and 2005 (the so-called 'Solidarity Pact between the Generations') could pretty much be regarded as failures, mainly because of the trade unions' ability to mobilize to demonstrate their disagreement with the government proposals. Yet the difference between the employment rate and its full-time equivalent is caused mainly by the large share of part-time work in the Netherlands, which is more than double the share in Belgium (47.3 per cent against 22.6 per cent in 2008) and plainly above the EU-15 average of 20.4 per cent (see Table 11A.1 in the Appendix).[7] The fact that part-time workers in Belgium are working more hours per week than their Dutch colleagues also plays a role, albeit a much lesser one.

One of the more apparent dissimilarities between Belgium and the Netherlands is the use of temporary employment that 'absorbs most of the flexibility of the Dutch labour market' (De Beer and Schils, 2009b, p. 216). Temporary employment can be subdivided into fixed-term employment and – in those cases where a worker is hired out by an agency to work in another firm – temporary agency work. Both types of temporary work are more widespread in the Netherlands than in Belgium. On the one hand, the regulation on temporary agency work in both countries has been liberalized (Sels and Van Hootegem, 2001, p. 333) and temporary agency work has increased in both countries but is still modest: 2.1 per cent in Belgium and 2.9 per cent in the Netherlands in 2008, while the EU-15 average stands at 1.8 per cent (www.ciett.org). On the other hand, the share of fixed-term contracts shows a very different trajectory of development. In Belgium the incidence of fixed-term contracts has declined over roughly the last decade from 9.1 per cent in 2000 to 8.3 per cent in 2008, well below the EU-15 average of 14.4 per cent.[8] In the Netherlands, meanwhile, this type of employment is much more widespread and has increased from 13.7 per cent in 2000 to 18.2 per cent in 2008. A clear divergence between the 'Low Countries' is thus very much in evidence here. The next sections map the different combinations of flexibility and security in the Belgian and Dutch labour markets.

EXTERNAL-NUMERICAL FLEXIBILITY AND DISMISSAL REGULATION

When explaining country differences in the incidence and development of temporary employment, the strictness of dismissal regulation for regular contracts, on the one hand, and for temporary contracts, on the other, is often considered of importance. In a relaxed dismissal regime employers are likely to have fewer incentives to avoid dismissal regulation by deploying temporary employees, while a 'stricter' dismissal regime often empirically goes hand in hand with a higher share of temporary (agency) employment (Deelen et al., 2006). A comparison between Belgium and the Netherlands based on the OECD measure for strictness of employment protection legislation (EPL) in Table 11.1 makes it clear that overall EPL has been only slightly stricter in Belgium and that the difference

Table 11.1   *OECD measure for strictness of EPL (broken down into differing components), 1995–2008*

	1995	2000	2005	2008
Overall strictness				
Belgium	3.15	2.18	2.18	2.18
Netherlands	2.73	2.12	2.12	1.95
Regular employment				
Belgium	1.68	1.73	1.73	1.73
Netherlands	3.08	3.05	3.05	2.72
Temporary employment				
Belgium	4.63	2.63	2.63	2.63
Netherlands	2.38	1.19	1.19	1.19
Collective dismissals				
Belgium	n.a.	4.13	4.13	4.13
Netherlands	n.a.	3.0	3.0	3.0

Source: OECD stats.

from the Netherlands has become narrower over time, although it was again slightly wider in 2008.[9] Looking at the EPL for various employment categories, the EPL in relation to collective dismissals is stricter in Belgium.[10] However, the main difference between the two countries can be seen in relation to protection for regular and temporary employees. Regular employees are more protected from dismissal in the Netherlands, especially due to the two-tiered structure of the dismissal procedure with either notification periods or monetary compensation. In addition, protection for temporary employees is much lower in the Netherlands than in Belgium. These differences in protection for regular and temporary employees are an important factor explaining why temporary employment is much more widespread in the Netherlands.

Because regular workers have a relatively large degree of security, Dutch employers seek to achieve external-numerical flexibility by means of temporary work, which is facilitated by low dismissal protection for these workers. In Belgium, an employer can unilaterally terminate an employment contract for regular workers at any time, provided that the statutory provisions have been complied with. Furthermore, the difference in dismissal regulation between blue-collar and white-collar workers is striking, with the period of notice being the most important aspect of the regulation. Viewed in a European perspective, the statutory period of notice for blue-collar workers can be regarded as very short (and the compensation as low in the case of failure to observe the period of notice), while for white-collar workers it is much longer (Sels and Van Hootegem, 2001, pp. 337–40; De Deken, 2009, pp. 156–8).[11] This disparity in the period of notice forms part of the broader distinction between blue-collar and white-collar employment status under Belgian employment law, which has increasingly come under pressure from politicians and the employers' organizations since the economic downturn of 2008. But the debate seems to be in a gridlock: while trade unions favour an equalization or harmonization of statuses, employers' organizations support an explicit deregulation of the dismissal protection, which is especially feared by the trade unions organizing white-collar workers since it would set in a downward levelling of the white-collar status.

In the Netherlands the debate on labour market flexibility has centred on dismissal regulation since the 1960s (Houwing and Vandaele, 2011). The system, introduced under the German Occupation in 1940–45, is regarded as restrictive as it has a dual system of, on the one hand, preventive dismissal tests based on a permit system and, on the other, the possibility of dissolving a contract through lower district courts. In 85–90 per cent of all cases, employers receive a permit when they can demonstrate the economic necessity of the dismissal, although special clauses for older workers and in case of sickness may create considerable delays. During the 1990s, the permit system was increasingly criticized, and circumvented by going through a legal route via the lower district court.[12] When an employment relationship is dissolved by a court, monetary compensation is required. Because of these pressures on the permit system, the Minister of Social Affairs and Employment issued a memorandum in 1995 entitled 'Flexibility and Security', calling for a new balance between flexible and regular employment. After negotiations and a unanimous statement by the Dutch social partners, the Flexibility and Security Law (F&S law) was implemented in 1999.

The F&S law was a package deal: the permit system for dismissals of regular contracts was maintained with slight modifications in exchange for greater flexibility in fixed-term contracts. The law is clearly reflected in the EPL figures given above: after 1999 EPL for temporary workers plummeted from 2.38 to 1.19. On the other hand, security increased for people on small, flexible, on-call contracts, such as temporary agency workers. In short, security was largely maintained for regular employees, while it was increased for only a very small group of workers, that is, temporary agency workers and those employed on small or zero-hours contracts that structurally work a higher number of hours than stated in their contract. Flexibility was increased mainly by extending the possibilities for use of consecutive fixed-term contracts, that is, for a section that makes up more than 15 per cent of the workforce (Knegt et al., 2007). The 'flexicurity balance' was achieved by increasing external-numerical flexibility with an increase in rights for (very) flexible workers. The protection of regular workers remained largely unchanged. Despite the 'flexicurity reform', discussions on reform of the dismissal system are today as topical as ever. After a near collapse of the Dutch government over the issue in the autumn of 2007, a commission was set up to give advice on the issue. The innovative recommendations issued by the commission were, however, set aside by the social partners in the autumn of 2008 since the issue remained too controversial, mainly for the trade unions. Subsequently this issue made its return to the agenda in the context of the reforms required to mitigate the effects of the economic crisis.

Finally, the number of own-account workers, that is, employers without employees, could also be considered an indicator of external-numerical flexibility. In Belgium the percentage of own-account workers has been steadily declining over the last ten years, while the contrary is the case in the Netherlands (see Table 11A.1 in the Appendix). In the 'Entrepreneurship Survey' report, it is stated that 21 per cent of respondents in the Netherlands find it desirable to become self-employed and 73 per cent of respondents consider it an opportunity to set up their own business (European Commission, 2007b, pp. 44 and 73). In Belgium the entrepreneurial spirit or culture is weaker and the corresponding percentages are 18 per cent and 64 per cent. According to Statistics Netherlands (CBS), the share of own-account workers in the working population has increased in the last decade (1996–2009) from 6.4 to 8.6 per cent, this increase having taken place mainly after 1999 (CBS Statline).[13] Though the share of own-account workers has increased in the Netherlands, it still lags behind both that in Belgium and the EU average. Indeed, the increase is quite moderate, especially when measured as the share-out of total working population. In spite of media focus on the developments in own-account workers, the data actually show no striking increase and the moderate rise can be understood as part of a more general development towards increasing flexibilization, individualization and a demand for autonomy on the supply side of the labour market (Bourgonje, 2008).

INTERNAL-NUMERICAL FLEXIBILITY AND TEMPORARY UNEMPLOYMENT

While temporary (agency) work often compensates for a 'restrictive' dismissal regime, dismissal regulation may not, in every respect, be decisive for explaining differences in temporary employment between Belgium and the Netherlands (cf. Sels and Van Hootegem, 2001, pp. 340–43).

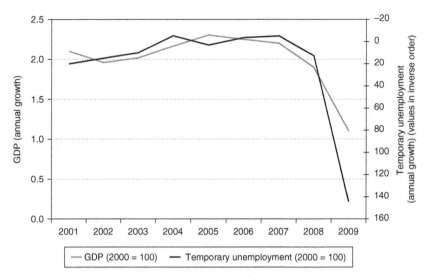

Source: GDP: OECD; temporary unemployment: RVA/ONEM (measured in terms of expenditures).

Figure 11.2   Growth in GDP and temporary unemployment in Belgium, 2001–09

Job security might be affected not only by dismissal regulation but also by other labour market institutions. In Belgium, the substantial use of a flexible system of temporary unemployment, which reduces the need for temporary (agency) work, might be considered at least equally as important as dismissal regulation for influencing job security (at least for blue-collar workers).[14] Under the scheme, blue-collar workers are entitled to unemployment benefit for a certain period of time during which the employment contract (and thus the payment of wages) is not terminated but partly or wholly suspended on a temporary basis.[15] In practice, the scheme is especially applied in the case of blue-collar workers performing relatively easy tasks, that is, with low human asset specificity and limited performance ambiguity (Gryp, 2004). While, from the workers' perspective, temporary unemployment can be regarded as providing job security, for employers it means a flexible tool for coping with short-term economic difficulties that can save costs (for application procedures and vocational training) pending economic recovery. Figure 11.2 shows the very close relationship between the temporary unemployment scheme (measured in terms of expenditures) and GDP development.

In fact, it is understood that employers in Belgium regard 'in-depth company loyalty as more important than flexicurity' (Sels and Van

Hootegem, 2001, p. 337), an orientation quintessentially expressed in the temporary unemployment scheme introduced in 1978. However, one of the detrimental effects of the system of temporary unemployment is that it enables multinational companies to roll off production losses on their Belgian plants so that plants outside Belgium are less affected – or unaffected – by those losses. Moreover, as a reaction to the economic downturn since 2008, the scope of the system of temporary unemployment has been extended to agency workers and workers on fixed-term employment contracts, that is, providing them with more job security; a related, albeit temporary, arrangement has also been put in place for white-collar workers since 2009 (Vandaele, 2009, pp. 589–92).

In the Netherlands, a similar system was abolished in 2006: it was far less popular than in Belgium and mainly used in construction and agricultural sectors. However, under pressure of rising unemployment, a temporary crisis-related scheme was introduced in the Netherlands in 2009. Just like the temporary unemployment scheme for white-collar workers, but unlike the scheme for blue-collar workers in Belgium, the Dutch scheme has a limited duration and is set to expire in June of 2010. It might be concluded that job security is provided by stricter dismissal regulation for Dutch workers on a standard employment contract with compensation for this aspect in the form of a flexible use of temporary employment. While in Belgium dismissal regulation for workers on a standard employment contract has been more relaxed, especially for blue-collar workers, their job security is guaranteed by the flexible use of the system of temporary unemployment, which explains why temporary employment has been fairly stable in Belgium.

Turning to other indicators of internal-numerical flexibility, Table 11A.1 in the Appendix shows that in Belgium Saturday and Sunday work has increased compared with the mid-1990s, while night work has been fairly stable and shift work shows a declining trend. As such, whereas at the end of the 1990s Belgium was still making significantly more use of shift work and overtime work than the Netherlands (Sels and Van Hootegem, 2001, p. 332; Vander Steene et al., 2002a, 2002b), this situation has now altered. Apart from the temporary unemployment scheme and shift work, all other indicators of internal-numerical flexibility in Table 11A.1 demonstrate that the Netherlands is today placing more emphasis on working time flexibility than is Belgium. Indeed, recent discussions on the reform of the Dutch labour market are focusing increasingly on working time issues, in addition to the above-mentioned discussions on reform of dismissal protection arrangements. Two relatively recent measures, in particular, have increased the internal flexibility of the Dutch labour market in terms of working time. The first is the 2000 Adjustment of Hours Law, according to which an employee is entitled to file a request to work less or more hours a week, a request that should, in most cases, be honoured by the employer. Second, as of April 2007, a new Law on Working Hours increased flexibility for employers by extending time frames and enabling longer working hours. This last flexibility measure is closely related to labour costs, as the extension of working time means that employers have to pay fewer overtime premiums. Nevertheless, flexible working time arrangements have also been promoted in Belgium since 2004 by cutting the cost of overtime work and since 2007 by reducing the employers' payroll taxes if they make use of shifts and night work (CRB, 2008, p. 153). To date, however, there has been no introduction, as an individualized system favoured by the employers' organizations, of a time-saving arrangement that would enable workers to save up overtime and holidays or a part of their wage to take time off at later date in their career.[16]

Part-time work offers another form of internal-numerical flexibility. Unlike the growth of temporary work, which was stimulated by legal reforms, the substantial increase in part-time employment in the Netherlands was largely the result of an autonomous development, namely, the rising labour market participation of women. This development on the supply side of the labour market was stimulated by the decreasing number of children, the increasing number of divorces and higher female participation in education. This led to a change in attitudes and behaviour such that female labour market participation became increasingly common. At the same time, childcare facilities have been extended and this increasing supply was met by a shift in the demand for labour as a result of the rise of the service economy (Visser, 2002). Since the 1990s, part-time work has also been rising in Belgium, especially among women (Meulders and O'Dorchai, 2009). Apart from demographic differences, the timing of governmental incentives for promoting part-time work may also help to explain the lower incidence of part-time work in Belgium: not only did the Belgian government encourage part-time work a decade later than in the Netherlands but it did so in a far more inconsistent manner since cost-saving measures actually caused a decline in the number of workers using the schemes at the end of the 1980s (Vander Steene et al., 2002b, p. 21).

In the 1990s financial incentives together with career-break schemes (for parental, medical care or palliative care) were introduced and the replacement obligation was liberalized in Belgium. In 2000 several 'thematic' career-break schemes were replaced by the time-credit scheme, which was aimed at providing incentives for workers to work more and remain longer on the labour market in order to raise the employment rate, as well as at facilitating the combination of work and family/private life. The deregulation of the earlier career break system indicates a shift from the redistribution of labour within the full employment framework to the improvement of the work–life balance in combination with an employment-enhancing tool (Vanderweyden, 2002). The social partners were not only involved in the decision-making process but are also in a position to fill in details of the time-credit scheme by means of collective labour agreements negotiated at the sectoral – or sometimes the firm – level. The time-credit scheme has become the most important career break scheme (Debacker et al., 2004). Its success seems to be attributable, in particular, to the promotion of supplementary benefits, either by the Flemish government (called 'care credit' or 'study credit') or by the federal government, in addition to the benefit paid out by the unemployment insurance. As another internal adjustment measure for firms, the time-credit system, for which the admission requirements have been temporarily relaxed, is increasingly being used (in addition to the temporary unemployment system) to cushion the effects of the economic downturn.

EXPLAINING DIFFERENCES BETWEEN BELGIAN AND DUTCH FLEXICURITY

From the two previous sections it is possible to conclude that each of the two 'Low Countries' seem to follow, in a more or less incremental manner, its own policy route towards more (or less) flexicurity. Particularly from distinctions in the dismissal regime and resulting differences in the use of temporary employment and unemployment, it may be seen that the labour market policy routes towards flexicurity are of a different nature in Belgium and the Netherlands. The Belgian route, what is more, is characterized by a greater degree of path dependency, given the stability of its labour market institutions and even their periodic reinforcement or – temporary – extension. The Dutch trajectory, by contrast, has shown more path-breaking tendencies. While the strictness of EPL for both regular and temporary employment became manifestly more relaxed, the Netherlands has made increasing use of flexible working hours and a system of temporary unemployment has been temporarily reintroduced. Insofar as the two countries have similar labour market participation in terms of FTE rates, the labour market regimes may, however, be regarded as functional equivalents.

Dutch and Belgian 'Flexicurity Institutions' and Institutional Complementarities

Labour market performance is not, however, solely the result of domestic policies and arrangements. Its performance is also affected by exogenous factors. Yet the 'national' models are commonly studied without taking into account the country's position within the international division of labour. But from an open-system perspective, while the success of a national model's success can be attributed to its use of the international environment, the model might 'leave little or no room for its successful adoption and application by other countries at the same time' (Salverda, 2005, p. 60).

Furthermore, insofar as flexible working arrangements at the national level are often channelled via lower levels, there may well be a gap between formal rules and the actual implementation of labour market flexicurity. As such, in any study of flexicurity, attention should also be paid to socially embedded, informal institutions, especially those existing at the firm level, such as 'shared values related to factory performance, trust and informal agreements' (Kahancová, 2007, p. 72).[17] In other words, flexicurity cannot always be examined exclusively on the basis of quantitative indicators as measured at the national level.

A more important ingredient of a successful labour market policy would seem to be the existence of institutional complementarities (De Beer and Schils, 2009a, pp. 8ff), while the interests and preferences of the state, employers and trade unions are also influenced by the institutional divergence of the Belgian and Dutch labour markets.

Particularly typified by its increasing regional governance, pronounced intra-regional competitiveness, and hollowing out of the national state, Belgium can be considered a quintessential 'post-Fordist' state. Yet this 'post-Fordist' character does not exclude 'Fordist' labour market policies. In order to explain, for instance, differences in working time arrangements, the specific economic configuration at the sectoral level also needs to be taken into account (European Foundation for the Improvement of Living and Working Conditions, 2007, pp. 25–7). Working time policies at the federal level, but also at the Flemish level, are to a large extent geared towards preserving jobs in the 'Fordist' industry, particularly in the automobile sector, which is mainly based in Flanders. So not only Belgium's temporary unemployment scheme but also the flexible working hours and shift arrangements have been embedded in a policy strategy to cope with production shocks experienced by its industry, which is particularly exposed to the world markets. As a result, although there is a declining trend in employment in industry, deindustrialization in Belgium slowed down in the 1990s in comparison with its northern neighbour (Houwing and Vandaele, 2011). The larger weight of industry in Belgium's economy has been, to a large extent, the result of a deliberate policy at the regional and federal levels, both influenced by powerful employers' organizations and trade unions in industry. In the Netherlands, part-time and temporary employment has gone hand in hand with the growing service economy and long-term wage moderation. As a result, the Netherlands remained on the track of moving further towards a service economy with a large role for financial services.

Moreover, an accurate alignment and coordination between various labour market measures is something that is particularly challenging in a federal country like Belgium. As a result of a devolutionary process, labour market responsibilities between the federal and regional levels are split (cf. De Deken, 2009, pp. 146–8). Employment policy is the responsibility of both levels. The evaluation of job search efforts (together with employment regulation, social security and taxation) takes place almost exclusively at the federal level. Job search assistance, re-employment, activation and training are the responsibility of the regional authorities. This distribution of responsibilities is time and again perceived as suboptimal, particularly by Flemish nationalists[18] who argue, among other things, that the federal level is often damaging to the labour market policy devised at the regional levels to cope with the diverse labour markets in the regions. Yet recent cooperation agreements between the regional employment offices, which have substantial autonomy, have strengthened coordination of the regional labour market policies. Nevertheless, Flemish nationalists continue to demand further devolution of labour market policies, even though progress in this direction might further impede inter-regional mobility.

Economic Fortune, Labour–Capital Relations and Sectoral and Firm-level Flexibility

Although the concept of 'functional equivalence' is, to a certain extent, useful for transcending institutional differences, its explanatory value might be rather limited due to its teleological tendencies and post hoc reasoning. Often what is considered an optimal flexicurity route is actually not the outcome of a proactive, consciously designed labour market policy, but rather the historical result of a mixture of traditions, economic fortune, experimentation and political struggles and compromises (Streeck, 2001). We have already pointed to the industrial tradition of Belgium and to the fact that the Netherlands has never been an industrial nation. The persistence of a different economic and employment structure partly explains why the flexicurity trajectories in the 'Low Countries' continue to show divergence. Furthermore, lucky economic circumstances have been at least as important as deliberate flexicurity policy efforts for explaining the Dutch labour market performance. Hence, apart from the socio-demographic developments such as the late but strong female employment participation and the ageing of the working population, wage differentiation and the strong domestic consumption growth stemming from house price and mortgage bubbles also played a prominent role (Salverda, 2005, pp. 58–61). In this respect, it remains to be seen whether the costly active labour market programmes, which have been the subject of study in times of economic prosperity, will continue, given the current economic downturn in both countries. Finally, stressing the open-ended character of flexicurity is in line with the prevailing literature that considers well-established traditions of 'social dialogue' between social partners and public authorities to be a precondition of flexicurity (Viebrock and Clasen, 2009, p. 320).

Although historically the so-called 'social dialogue' in Belgium has rather evolved from an 'institutionalization of conflict', while in the Netherlands it could be rather defined as an 'institutionalization of cooperation' (cf. Therborn, 1992), both countries share this tradition of a so-called 'social partnership'. Of particular importance for the Belgian case is that collective bargaining between the employers' organizations and trade unions at the sectoral level is more likely to take into account employment measures (including flexible work arrangements) if, in that particular sector, the organization rate of the employers *and* trade union density is relatively high and if collective bargaining is more dominant at the sectoral level than at the company level (Van Ruysseveldt, 2000, p. 278). While, in relation to the inclusion of more employment measures in the collective labour agreements, there is almost no difference between the industry and services sector, sheltered sectors and sectors dominated by large firms are significantly inclined to include more employment measures (ibid., pp. 282–7).

In the Netherlands, social partners also play a crucial role in the implementation of legislation, such as the majority of provisions of the Dutch flexicurity law. This is because these provisions are 'three-quarters mandatory', which means that social partners can negotiate deviating provisions within collective labour agreements. Analyses show that, in relation to provisions on temporary (agency) work, social partners have agreed to a larger degree of flexibility than is stated in the law, to some extent at the expense of security for temporary workers. This might be partly explained by the fact that temporary workers do not constitute the main constituency of trade unions (Vandaele and Leschke, 2010). More importantly, trade union membership in the Netherlands is quite low, much lower than in Belgium, and this especially influences the outcomes of collective bargaining as the balance of power at that decentralized level skews towards the employers' side of the bargain. This is in contrast to the national level, where the Dutch social partners have a strong institutionalized role in the corporatist institutions (Houwing, 2010).

Furthermore, the union involvement in social security management, particularly the 'de facto Ghent system', that is, de facto union dominance in the unemployment insurance through unions' involvement in the benefit administration, not only explains to a certain degree Belgium's relatively high union density but also the unions' sustained interest in the temporary unemployment scheme (Vandaele, 2009, pp. 592–3). In fact, while Dutch trade unions have lost members since the 1980s, union density in Belgium has remained fairly stable. Additionally, Belgian unions have a significant strong presence on the work floor, especially in large firms, via union-dominated works councils or union representatives in particular, or both, whereas Dutch unions rely on a rather weak single system of workers' representation via works councils (Mok, 1985). Thus, in addition to the collective labour agreement at the sectoral level, the strong union presence on the work floor provides the Belgian workplace management with an opportunity structure. It enables them to negotiate with the unions over implementation of various flexible working arrangements, which are laid down in collective labour agreements at the firm level or introduction of tailor-made arrangements concluded in informal agreements. Accordingly, in Belgium about 18 per cent of companies have at least 20 per cent of their employees regularly exposed to changing working hours, while this is the case in only 10 per cent of companies in the Netherlands (European Foundation for the Improvement of Living and Working Conditions, 2007, p. 14, figures for 2004). Furthermore, the notice of changes in working hours is more flexible as well: whereas 71 per cent of companies in Belgium give notice of changes in working hours less than two weeks in advance, this applies to only 54 per cent of companies in the Netherlands (ibid., pp. 34–5). Thus, despite the prescriptive law, it is said that 'anything goes regarding the introduction of flexible hours, as long as it is regulated in an agreement between the social partners' (Sels and Van Hootegem, 2001, p. 347). Such a workplace management–union interaction is likely to take place even where management could legally act unilaterally to increase flexible working arrangements or where economic advantages are not obvious (Kahancová, 2007, pp. 80–81). It may be assumed that the incidence of workplace management–union interaction and informal agreements on flexicurity is likely to be lower in the Netherlands, given the weaker workers' representation. Furthermore, such agreements might tend to be reflected to only a lesser extent in aggregate quantitative indicators on flexicurity.

CONCLUSION

Rather than summarize in conclusion the substantive content of the arguments developed in the earlier sections, we would like to focus here on what this exercise has enabled us to learn about the conduct of international comparisons. We have compared in this chapter two countries that, though for a long period presented similar features, have, over the last 30 years, followed different paths. Measured in terms of flexicurity (and with awareness of the considerably ambiguity attaching to this term, as indicated in the second section), the two come to appear highly dissimilar. Our analysis of the situation in the two countries enables us to stress the extent to which changes have taken place and the need to understand the underlying dynamic processes. The changes would seem to have been much more path-breaking in the Netherlands than in Belgium, which has remained more path-dependent. And yet such a reading – presenting one country that succeeds in redefining its institutions to cope with a changing world alongside another that proves unable to do so – would be, as we have shown, simplistic. There is a need to examine what each of the two countries has achieved, and in relation to employment rates the results achieved by the Netherlands are not so different from those of Belgium if measured by the 'full-time equivalent' indicator.

This prompts us to remember the importance, in any theoretical discussion, of establishing comparisons based on appropriate aspects and, in particular, of choosing the most appropriate indicators. What is more, in the Netherlands the balance between flexibility and security is less impressive than frequently claimed, particularly when assessed in relation to the terms of employment of temporary workers. By the same token, negotiated flexibility is stronger in Belgium than mere perusal of the legislation in force would seem to suggest. As such, this comparison reminds us once again of the pitfalls of an excessively stylized comparison that fails to seek understanding of the dynamic processes that underlie change. In order to understand these basic dynamics, we have referred to functional equivalents and examined the way in which each of the two countries has chosen a different path – on the one hand, that of external numerical flexibility and, on the other, that of internal flexibility – accompanied by differing forms of institutional flexibility. In this way, different institutional set-ups and measures may be seen to give rise to similar results. In the context of the 'varieties of capitalism' debate, therefore, it is interesting to stress that whereas the Netherlands, considered in terms of institutions, appears close to the Scandinavian countries, when considered in terms of outcome, the reality is not so far removed from the situation prevailing in Belgium.

Another facet of the awareness gained through this exercise in country comparison would be to argue for the inclusion in international comparisons of little studied countries such as Belgium, Spain, Portugal, or Finland, a shift that would entail the possibility of revising certain approaches based on a limited number of countries (and frequently the same ones).

NOTES

*   We would like to thank Janine Leschke for her comments and suggestions.
1.   The new social risks have arisen from socio-demographical challenges, for example, the entry of women into the labour market and the demise of the traditional breadwinner model, as well as socioeconomic changes like the tertiarization of employment with its diverse career profiles (which differ from the male-dominated, full-time and continuous career patterns of the past), deindustrialization and structural unemployment.
2.   More generally, the flexicurity discourse argues that labour market can be conceived as a field where a number of different types of flexibility (external-numerical flexibility; internal-numerical flexibility; functional flexibility; wage flexibility) and security (job security, employment security, income security and combination security) interact. However, it also argues that multiple combinations of these types can produce flexicurity.
3.   In particular, early and obligatory activation is not a feature of the Belgian unemployment system.
4.   In Belgium unemployment benefits are, in principle, unlimited in duration but this particular feature has gradually been hollowed out since the 1980s.
5.   On the flexicurity strategies of firms on older workers, see Bredgaard and Tros (2008).
6.   This counts also for long-term and youth unemployment.
7.   The definition in the European Labour Force Survey of full-time and part-time work differs between Belgium and the Netherlands. Whereas in Belgium it is self-defined by the respondents, in the Netherlands work is deemed to be part-time if usual hours are fewer than 35 hours and full-time if they are 35 hours or more.
8.   It seems that fixed-term contracts have been used more since the economic downturn (CRB, 2009, p. 44). Eurostat data make no distinction between fixed-term contracts and temporary agency work.
9.   The EPL indicator of the OECD is not immune to criticism.
10.   Following the closure of the Renault plant in Vilvoorde in 1997, the Belgian legal framework for collective dismissals and restructuring procedures was strengthened in 1998 (cf. Naedenoen, 2008 for details). Since 2007 employers have become obliged to arrange outplacement for all dismissed workers aged over 45 with at least one year of employment.
11.   In early 2010 the federal government unilaterally decided to introduce a crisis premium of 1666 euros, one-third to be paid by the employer, for increasing the compensation of blue-collar workers in the case of individual dismissal. This is a temporary measure that will expire in the second half of 2011.
12.   In that case the contract will be dissolved with wage compensation or severance payment.
13.   The figures reported in 'Employment in Europe 2008' diverge quite substantially from these figures. The reason for this is likely to be a matter of definition, a recurring issue in the debate on self-employment.
14.   The system of temporary unemployment in Belgium displays similarities with the German *Kurzarbeit* system.
15.   Blue-collar workers can be on temporary unemployment for a maximum of four successive weeks when their contract is fully suspended. The duration is longer or even unlimited in the case of partial suspensions of the employment contract.
16.   In the auto-assembly industry, however, an agreement on working time flexibility was reached in 2006, under which workers' working hours may be varied over a six-year reference period.

17. On possible differences in civic attitudes towards implementing flexicurity policies, see Algan and Cahuc (2006).
18. This is especially the case since 2009 when the Flemish government adopted a more proactive stance against labour market measures taken at the federal policy level.

REFERENCES

Algan, Y. and Cahuc, P. (2006), 'Civic attitudes and the design of labour market institutions. Which countries can implement the Danish flexicurity model?', Discussion Paper No. 1928, Bonn: IZA.
Bekker, S. and Wilthagen, T. (2008), 'Europe's pathways to flexicurity. Lessons presented from and to the Netherlands', *Intereconomics*, **43**(2), 68–73.
Bertozzi, F. and Bonoli, G. (2009), *Measuring Flexicurity at the Macro Level – Conceptual and Data Availability Challenges*, Edinburgh: RECWOWE.
Bonoli, G. (2006), 'New social risks and politics of post-industrial social policies', in K. Armingeon and G. Bonoli (eds), *The Politics of Post-industrial Welfare States. Adapting Post-war Social Policies to New Social Risks*, London: Routledge, pp. 3–26.
Bourgonje, A. (2008), *Flexibilitijden: Naar een flexibele arbeidsmarkt in 2020*, Hilversum: Hiteq.
Bredgaard, T. and Tros, F. (2008), 'Flexicurity and human resources management for older workers in the Netherlands, Denmark, Germany and Belgium', in R. Blanpain and L. Dickens (eds), *Challenges in European Employment Relations. Employment Regulations Trade Union Organization, Equality, Flexicurity, Training and New Approaches to Pay*, The Hague: Kluwer Law International, pp. 73–100.
CRB (2008), *Technisch verslag van het secretariaat over de maximale beschikbare marges voor de loonkostontwikkeling, Volledig verslag*, 4 November 2008, Brussels: CRB.
CRB (2009), *Technisch verslag van het secretariaat over de maximale beschikbare marges voor de loonkostontwikkeling*, 12 November 2009, Brussels: CRB.
Debacker, M., de Lathouwer, L. and Bogaerts, K. (2004), 'Time credit and leave schemes in the Belgian welfare state', Paper presented at TLM.net conference, Antwerpen: CSB.
De Beer, P. and Schils, T. (2009a), 'Introduction: Achieving an optimal social policy mix', in P. De Beer and T. Schils (eds), *The Labour Market Triangle. Employment Protection, Unemployment Compensation and Activation in Europe*, Cheltenham, UK and Northampton, MA, USA: Edward Elgar, pp. 1–25.
De Beer, P. and Schils, T. (2009b), 'Conclusion: Is there a golden triangle?', in P. De Beer and T. Schils (eds), *The Labour Market Triangle. Employment Protection, Unemployment Compensation and Activation in Europe*, Cheltenham, UK and Northampton, MA, USA: Edward Elgar, pp. 198–220.
De Deken, J. (2009), 'Belgium', in P. De Beer and T. Schils (eds), *The Labour Market Triangle. Employment Protection, Unemployment Compensation and Activation in Europe*, Cheltenham, UK and Northampton, MA, USA: Edward Elgar, pp. 145–73.
Deelen, A., Jongen, E. and Visser, S. (2006), *Employment Protection Legislation: Lessons from Theoretical and Empirical Studies for the Dutch Case?*, The Hague: CPB.
European Commission (2007a), *Towards Common Principles of Flexicurity: More and Better Jobs through Flexibility and Security*, Luxembourg: Office of the Official Publications of the European Community.
European Commission (2007b), 'Entrepreneur survey of the EU (25 member states), United States, Iceland and Norway: Analytical report', *Eurobarometer*, 192, The Gallup Organization.
European Foundation for the Improvement of Living and Working Conditions (2007), *Extended and Unusual Working Hours in European Companies. Establishment Survey on Working Time 2004–2005*, Luxembourg: Office for Official Publications of the European Communities.

Gryp, S. (2004), 'Jobstructuren en flexible arbeid in Vlaamse organisaties: Aanbevelingen voor een uitgebalanceerd flexibliteitsbeleid', in G. Van Hootegem and B. Cambré (eds), *Over werk(t) in de actieve welvaartstaat*, Leuven: Acco, pp. 158–70.

Houwing, H. (2010), 'A Dutch approach to flexicurity? Negotiated change in the organization of temporary work', Doctoral dissertation, Amsterdam: Universiteit van Amsterdam.

Houwing, H. and Vandaele, K. (2011), 'Liberal convergence, growing outcome divergence? Institutional continuity and changing trajectories in the "Low Countries"', in U. Becker (ed.), *The changing political economies of small West European countries*, Amsterdam: Amsterdam University Press.

Huyse, L. and Berting, J. (1983), *Als in een spiegel? Een sociologische kaart van België en Nederland*, Leuven: Kritak.

Jepsen, M. and Serrano Pascual, A. (2005), 'The European social model: An exercise in deconstruction', *Journal of European Social Policy*, **15**(3), 231–45.

Jones, E. (2008), *Economic Adjustment and Political Tranformation in Small States*, Oxford: Oxford University Press.

Kahancová, M. (2007), 'One company, four factories. Coordinating employment flexibility practices with local trade unions', *European Journal of Industrial Relations*, **13**(1), 67–88.

Keune, M. (2008a), 'Flexicurity: A contested concept at the core of the European labour market debate', *Intereconomics*, **43**(2), 92–8.

Keune, M. (2008b), 'Between innovation and ambiguity: The role of flexicurity in labour market analysis and policy making', in F. Hendrickx (ed.), *Flexicurity and the Lisbon Agenda: A Cross-disciplinary Reflection*, International Studies on Social Security Series, Antwerp: Intersentia, pp. 49–63.

Keune, M. and Jepsen, M (2007), 'Not balanced and hardly new: The European Commission's quest for flexicurity', in H. Jørgensen and P.K. Madsen (eds), *Flexicurity and Beyond*, Copenhagen: DJOF Publishing, pp. 189–211.

Keune, M. and Pochet, P. (2009), 'Flexicurité en Europe: Une approche critique', *Revue de l'IRES*, **63**(4), 75–96.

Knegt, R., Klein Hesselink, D.J., Houwing, H. and Brouwer, P. (2007), *Tweede evaluatie Wet Flexibiliteit en Zekerheid*, Amsterdam: TNO/HSI.

Kuipers, S. (2006), *The Crisis Imperative. Crisis Rhetoric and Welfare State Reform in Belgium and the Netherlands in the Early 1990s*, Amsterdam: Amsterdam University Press.

Lijphart, A. (1975), 'The comparable-cases strategy in comparative research', *Comparative Political Studies*, **8**(2), 158–77.

Madsen, P.K. (2006), 'How can it possibly fly? The paradox of a dynamic labour market in a Scandinavian welfare state', in J. Campbell, J. Hall and O. Pedersen (eds), *National Identity and the Varieties of Capitalism: The Danish Experience*, Montreal: McGill-Queen's University Press.

Meulders, D. and O'Dorchai, S. (2009), 'Gender and flexibility in working time in Belgium', Working Paper No. 09.08.RS, Brussels: Dulbea.

Mok, A.L. (1985), 'Arbeidsverhoudingen in Nederland en België. Een oefening in differentiële sociologie', *Tijdschrift voor Arbeidsverhoudingen*, **1**(1), 4–17.

Naedenoen, F. (2008), 'Belgium: A corporatist regime', in B. Gazier and F. Bruggeman (eds), *Restructuring Work and Employment in Europe. Managing Change in an Era of Globalization*, Cheltenham, UK and Northampton, MA, USA: Edward Elgar, pp. 78–100.

Rogowski, R. (2008), 'Governance of the European social model: The case of flexicurity', *Intereconomics*, **43**(2), 82–91

Salverda, W. (2005), 'The Dutch model: Magic in a flat landscape?', in U. Becker and H. Schwartz (eds), *Employment 'Miracles'. A Critical Comparison of the Dutch, Scandinavian, Swiss, Australian and Irish Cases Versus Germany and the US*, Amsterdam: Amsterdam University Press, pp. 39–63.

Schils, T. (2009), 'The Netherlands', in P. De Beer and T. Schils (eds), *The Labour Market Triangle. Employment Protection, Unemployment Compensation and Activation in Europe*, Cheltenham, UK and Northampton, MA, USA: Edward Elgar, pp. 96–118.

Sels, L. and Van Hootegem, G. (2001), 'Seeking the balance between flexibility and security. A rising issue in the Low Countries', *Work, Employment & Society*, **15**(2), 327–52.

Streeck, W. (2001), 'Introduction: Explorations into the origins of nonliberal capitalism in Germany and Japan', in W. Streeck and K. Yamamura (eds), *The Origins of Nonliberal Capitalism. Germany and Japan in Comparison*, Ithaca, NY and London: Cornell University Press, pp. 1–38.

Swenden, W. and Theo Jans, M. (2006), '"Will it stay or will it go?" Federalism and the sustainability of Belgium', *West European Politics*, **29**(5), 877–94.

Therborn, G. (1992), 'Lessons from "corporatism" theorizations', in J. Pekkarinen, M. Pohjola and B. Rowthorn (eds), *Social Corporatism. A Superior Economic System?*, Oxford: Clarendon Press, pp. 24–43.

Tielens, M. and Herremans, W. (2007), *Over arbeidsvolume en arbeidsduur in Vlaanderen en Europa*, Leuven: Steunpunt WSE.

Vandaele, K. (2009), 'The Ghent system, temporary unemployment and the Belgian trade unions since the economic downturn', *Transfer*, **16**(3–4), 589–96.

Vandaele, K. and Leschke, J. (2010), *Following the 'Organizing Model' of British Unions? Organizing Non-standard Workers in Germany and the Netherlands*, Brussels: ETUI.

Vander Steene, T. et al. (2002a), *Cahier 1: Feiten en cijfers van flexibiliteit. Definities van flexibiliteit en een caleidoscopisch flexibiliteitsoverzicht*, Leuven: Katholieke Universiteit Leuven – Steunpunt Werkgelegenheid, Arbeid en Vorming.

Vander Steene, T. et al. (2002b), *De impact van het institutionele kader op de politiek van flexibiliteit. Een vergelijking België-Nederland*, Leuven: Katholieke Universiteit Leuven – Steunpunt Werkgelegenheid, Arbeid en Vorming.

Vanderweyden K. (2002), 'Van loopbaanonderbreking naar tijdskrediet. Een verhaal van een wijzigend maatschappelijk discours', PSW-Paper No. 2002/6, Antwerpen: Universiteit Antwerpen.

Van Rie, T. (2008), *Sociaaleconomische uitkomsten in Nederland, België en zijn gewesten*, Antwerpen: CRB.

Van Ruysseveldt, J. (2000), *Het belang van overleg. CAO-onderhandelingen in België*, Leuven: Acco.

Viebrock, E. and Clasen, J. (2009), 'Flexicurity and welfare reform: A review' *Socio-Economic Review*, **7**(2), 305–31.

Vielle, P., Pochet, P. and Cassiers, I. (eds) (2005), *L'état social actif. Vers un changement de paradigme?*, Bern: Peter Lang.

Visser, J. (2002), 'The first part-time economy in the world: A model to be followed?', *Journal of European Social Policy*, **12**(1), 23–42.

Visser, J. and Hemerijck, A. (1997), *'A Dutch Miracle': Job Growth, Welfare Reform and Corporatism in the Netherlands*, Amsterdam: Amsterdam University Press.

Wilthagen, T. and Tros, F. (2004), 'The concept of "flexicurity": A new approach regulating employment and labour markets', *Transfer*, **10**(2), 166–86.

Zeitlin, J. and Pochet, P. (eds), with Lars Magnusson (2005), *The Open Method of Coordination in Action. The European Employment and Social Inclusion Strategies*, Brussels: P.I.E. Peter Lang.

APPENDIX: LABOUR MARKET REGIMES IN BELGIUM AND THE NETHERLANDS

Table 11A.1   Labour market regimes in Belgium and the Netherlands, 1998–2008 (in per cent)

	1998	1999	2000	2001	2002	2003	2004	2005	2006	2007	2008
External-numerical labour market flexibility											
1. Temporary agency work											
Belgium	1.6	1.6	1.7	1.7	1.6	1.6	1.8	1.9	2.1	2.2	2.1
Netherlands	2.4	2.5	2.3	2.2	2.1	1.9	1.9	2.2	2.5	2.8	2.9
2. Temporary workers[c]											
Belgium	8.2	9.9	9.1	8.8	8.1	8.4	8.7	8.9	8.7	8.6	8.3
Netherlands	13.0	12.3	13.7	14.3	14.4	14.5	14.8	15.5	16.6	18.1	18.2
3. Self-employment[a]											
Belgium	n.a.	9.0	9.3	8.4	8.5	8.5	7.9	8.3	8.4	8.6	8.7
Netherlands	n.a.	7.0	7.2	7.2	7.1	7.1	7.4	7.6	8.0	8.2	8.5
Internal-numerical labour market flexibility											
4. Part-time work											
Belgium	16.5	18.4	18.9	18.5	19.1	20.5	21.4	22.0	22.2	22.1	22.6
Netherlands	38.9	39.7	41.5	42.2	43.9	45.0	45.5	46.1	46.2	46.8	47.3
5. Shift-time work											
Belgium	16.6	8.8	9.0	10.3	9.6	9.6	10.0	8.8	8.7	10.1[b]	8.3
Netherlands	9.0	8.5	[b]	[b]	[b]	[b]	[b]	[b]	8.1	8.4	8.2
6. Night-work[c]											
Belgium	5.2	2.4	4.4	4.2	3.9	3.8	4.1	4.3	4.6	4.4	4.3
Netherlands	2.2	2.2	[b]	[b]	[b]	[b]	[b]	[b]	9.8	9.5	9.2
7. Working on Saturday[c]											
Belgium	12.0	5.0	11.6	12.3	12.0	11.6	12.5	13.8	14.2	14.9	14.6
Netherlands	24.4	23.4	[b]	[b]	[b]	[b]	[b]	[b]	26.4	26.3	26.0
8. Working on Sunday[c]											
Belgium	6.5	2.1	6.4	6.8	6.3	6.6	6.9	7.6	7.8	8.2	8.2
Netherlands	13.8	13.6[b]	[b]	[b]	[b]	[b]	[b]	[b]	16.6	16.4	16.1

Note: 15–64 years; a. Excluding employers. Own calculation. b. Unreliable data. c. Including temporary agency workers.

Source: 1: www.ciett.org; 2–8: Eurostat, Labour Force Survey.

12 Employment relations in Australia and New Zealand
Nick Wailes

INTRODUCTION

Australia and New Zealand are almost perfect real world examples of very similar cases. The two countries are former British colonies and developed at similar times and in similar ways. The two share a common heritage of a unique form of labour market regulation, known as compulsory concili-ation and arbitration, which played a significant role in shaping industrial relations outcomes in the two countries for much of the twentieth century. However, during the 1980s and early 1990s, significant differences emerged in the labour market policies adopted by governments in these two similar cases. In New Zealand, first under a Labour government and then under a conservative National government, the search for increased labour market flexibility resulted in a dramatic move away from arbitration. This process culminated with the introduction of the Employment Contracts Act (ECA) 1991, a radical piece of legislation that swept away all remain-ing vestiges of the arbitration system and replaced it with a regime based largely on individual employment contracts. In Australia, during the same period, the Australian Labor government sought to achieve greater labour market flexibility through the existing institutions of arbitration and in cooperation with the labour movement.

This apparent divergence in these two very similar countries sparked intense comparative interest. Scholars from both countries exploited the similarities between the two to help them identify the sources of policy divergence. The resulting literature highlighted the causal significance of organizational and institutional factors. Specifically this literature highlighted the role that differences in the organization of unions and employers and in the relative autonomy of the state played in produc-ing differences across similar cases. In doing so, the Australia–New Zealand comparative literature gave strong empirical support to the new institutionalist arguments that have come to dominate debates about globalization and industrial relations.

More recently, however, the stark differences between the two coun-tries that developed in the early 1990s have diminished. In Australia the conservative Liberal National Coalition government, which was elected in 1995, introduced legislation that sought to drastically limit the role of arbitration and encourage the growth of individual statutory employment contracts, bringing Australia much closer to New Zealand under the ECA. In 1999 Labour was re-elected in New Zealand with a mandate to repeal the ECA and through the Employment Relations Act 2000 sought to reintroduce collective elements into employment relations. In late 2008 a Labor government was elected in Australia with a similar mandate and has tried to re-collectivize aspects of Australian employment relations with its Fair Work legislation.

This chapter critically reviews the comparative literature on employment relations in Australia and New Zealand that emerged in the 1980s and early 1990s in light of these more recent developments. It argues that while institutional arrangements are important, the Australia–New Zealand comparison also highlights the significance that underlying differences in material interests, often masked by institutional similarities, played in shaping industrial relations policies and outcomes. The chapter is structured as follows. The next section provides a brief historical background on the development of the arbitration systems in the two countries and the dominant pattern of employment relations that characterized them for much of the twentieth century. The third section reviews the comparative literature on the two countries that emerged during the late 1980s and early 1990s. The fourth section outlines developments in both since the early 1990s. The fifth briefly reconsiders the comparative literature in light of these developments. The chapter concludes by assessing the implications of the Australia–New Zealand comparison for contemporary debates about the impact of globalization on employment relations.

HISTORICAL BACKGROUND

Social sciences like industrial relations are often criticized for being overly descriptive and being unable to establish causal inferences. A number of authors have suggested that, because they make it possible to control many potential sources of variation, comparison of very similar cases can help overcome the limitations of small-*n*, qualitative studies and provide the context within which to establish causal inferences (Prezworski and Teune, 1970; Skopcol and Somers, 1980; Strauss, 1998).

In many respects, Australia and New Zealand represent almost perfect real world examples of very similar countries. While there are a number of grounds for treating Australia and New Zealand as very similar cases, this section focuses on four areas of particular significance to the study of industrial relations in the two countries: similarities in the timing and nature of economic development; a shared heritage of labour market regulation; strong similarities in the broader pattern of public policy; and similarities in the problems both economies faced during the 1970s and 1980s.

While the colonies of Australia and New Zealand were originally settled for different reasons, during the nineteenth century the two neighbouring territories experienced a similar pattern of economic development and integration into the international economy. Denoon (1983) calls this pattern 'settler capitalism'. He argues that rapid industrialization in Britain created demand for raw materials and also made large amounts of capital available for export. This created the conditions for the economic development of areas of recent European settlement, like the colonies of Australia and New Zealand. The Australasian colonies received significant inflows of capital and labour from Britain during the nineteenth century that were used to open up agricultural land to produce raw materials (predominantly wool) for export to Britain. In both territories, the development of a strong export sector created the conditions for relatively high wages, employment growth and the development of domestic manufacturing and the services sector.

Because of their heavy reliance on commodity exports both countries were affected by the falls in commodity prices associated with the Long Depression of the 1880s. In both Australia and New Zealand declining economic performance led to deteriorating wages and working conditions and the emergence of 'sweated labour' particularly in the domestic manufacturing sector. It also created the conditions for industrial conflict, particularly in the export-oriented agricultural sector, between newly formed occupational unions and employers. One of the major industrial disputes, the 1890 Maritime Dispute, took place simultaneously on both sides of the Tasman (the body of water that separates Australia from New Zealand). In both Australia and New Zealand the state intervened to crush industrial militancy in the export economy (Denoon, 1983; Schwartz, 1989).

One of the major policy responses to sweated labour and widespread industrial conflict in the 1890s was the introduction of a novel form of labour market regulation, known as compulsory conciliation and arbitration, which was heavily influenced by British social liberalism (Macintyre, 1989). Arbitration was seen by its proponents as a means of replacing the brutality of the market with 'a new province of law and order'. The first bill proposing compulsory conciliation and arbitration was introduced by Charles Kingston in South Australia in 1890. This was followed by the successful introduction of the Industrial Conciliation and Arbitration

Act in New Zealand in 1894 and the Conciliation and Arbitration Act in New South Wales in 1901. In 1904 the newly formed parliament of Commonwealth of Australia passed the Commonwealth Conciliation and Arbitration Act (Holt, 1986; Patmore, 1991).

Despite some minor differences, the arbitration systems in both countries operated on a similar basis. Under arbitration, both countries established mechanisms for the registration of trade unions and of groups of employers. Once registered, either party had the right to refer an industrial dispute to a permanent independent tribunal for arbitration. If the dispute could not be resolved through conciliation between the parties, this independent tribunal was given the authority to resolve the dispute in the public interest and its decision (known as an award) was binding on all parties. The establishment of industrial tribunals with the power to arbitrate was designed to replace the need for industrial action and in both countries legal sanctions were introduced to prevent the parties from taking industrial action (Woods, 1963; Mitchell, 1989)

Many of the distinctive features of Australian and New Zealand industrial relations in the twentieth century have been attributed to the impact of arbitration. While originally designed to prevent major widespread industrial conflict, as Mitchell and Wilson (1993, p. 42) note, in both Australia and New Zealand arbitration quickly became:

> a formal centralised process whereby the settlement of major national or industry cases provided the standard . . . for the wages and conditions settled in other awards and agreements. The process of flow of wages and conditions helped to maintain a uniform level of minimum employment guarantees throughout both Australia and New Zealand.

In both Australia and New Zealand, arbitration tribunals quickly developed quasi-legal principles for the determination of award wages. The Australian tribunal established a basic wage principle in 1907 and also developed a series of 'margins for skill' (Hancock [1979]1984). The New Zealand tribunal initially set 'fair wages' based on the wage rates paid by good employers and later supplemented this with 'standard wage pronouncements' with minimum basic pay rates for unskilled, semi-skilled and skilled workers to be included in all awards (Woods, 1963). Importantly, in both countries award wages were set with reference not just to the capacity of industry to pay but also with regard to the costs of living. In both countries awards functioned as extension mechanisms, with the wages and conditions set in relation to a particular dispute applying to all employees and employers in the relevant industry or occupation. This is functionally similar to the role that extension agreements played in wage bargaining in many European countries (see Traxler et al., 2001).

In both countries it has been argued that these wage-setting principles had a pervasive influence on the structure of relative wages. For much of the twentieth century, wages were more evenly dispersed in Australia and New Zealand than in other countries and arbitration had the effect of compressing both inter-industry and skill differentials in the wage structure (Martin, 1974; Norris, 1986). Arbitration also played a role in sustaining gender inequality in the wage structure of the two countries. In setting the 'basic wage', H.B. Higgins, the first president of the Commonwealth arbitration tribunal in Australia, explicitly noted that it was a family wage. He later set the basic wage for women at 54 per cent of the male basic wage. Similar differentials were adopted by the New Zealand tribunal. As has been noted this decision was closely linked to widespread concerns amongst social liberals about slow population growth (Kirkby, 1989; Robertson, 1991). In both countries there were significant differentials in male and female award rates until the early 1970s.

It has also been argued that arbitration had a dramatic impact on the nature of trade unionism in the two countries. In comparative perspective there are two distinctive features of trade unionism in Australia and New Zealand before the early 1980s: the large number of unions and the relatively high percentage of workers who were members of trade unions. Howard argues that arbitration allowed unions to overcome two problems. First, because it provided a system of registration, it allowed weak trade unions to gain recognition from strong employers. Second, because award provisions applied to all workers in an industry, arbitration allowed unions to overcome the threat of non-union labour. However, it has also been argued that the dependency of Australasian trade unions on arbitration also had negative consequences. In particular it has been suggested that under arbitration unions focused on advocacy and the industrial tribunals and failed to develop organizational capacity and effective workplace structures (Howard, 1983; Hince, 1993).

Castles (1988) argues that in both Australia and New Zealand arbitration was part of a broader pattern of public policy, which he calls 'domestic defence'. According to Castles the four main elements of this domestic defence pattern of public policy were reliance on tariff protection; legal wage regulation through compulsory arbitration; limitations and control on the pattern of immigration and an early but minimalist welfare state. He argues that domestic defence meant that:

> almost every section of early twentieth century Australia [and New Zealand] society was protected in some way; the exporters and the pastoralists by the very profitability of the export trade in staple commodities; the manufacturers by the tariff; and the working class by a minimum wage and a mechanism for controlling labour supply. (Castles, 1988, p. 93).

In part because of the domestic defence policy, Australia and New Zealand faced similar economic problems from the late 1960s on. In the immediate post-World War II period, comparative advantage in primary product production, economic growth in their major trading partners, limited competition and preferential access to markets produced favourable terms of trade for Australia and New Zealand and allowed for the continued development and expansion of the sheltered domestic manufacturing sector. However, in the late 1960s both countries experienced a dramatic decline in the terms of trade for their main export commodities. These problems were exacerbated during the 1970s by the impact of the oil shocks and instability of the international monetary system. In both countries, slowing economic growth, increased unemployment and inflation and increased industrial conflict called into question the sustainability of the domestic defence policy pattern (Easton and Gerritsen, 1996).

In the early 1980s, newly elected Labour governments in the two countries set about introducing widespread market-oriented economic reform and dismantling many traditional features of the domestic defence policy pattern in an effort to improve economic performance. These reforms included floating the currency, deregulating the banking sector, establishing an independent central bank and corporatizing and privatizing much of the public sector (Castles et al., 1996).

DIVERGENCE IN INDUSTRIAL RELATIONS POLICY IN AUSTRALIA AND NEW ZEALAND

Despite the similarities in the industrial relations heritage, the economic problems facing Australia and New Zealand and the market-based reform agendas of the Labour governments therein, in the late 1980s and early 1990s there was a marked divergence in industrial relations policy in these two countries. Immediately before the 1983 election the Australia Labor Party (ALP) and the peak union body, the Australia Council of Trade Unions (ACTU), entered into a social pact, known as the Price and Incomes Accord (hereinafter, the Accord). From 1983 until 1996, when the ALP lost power, the Accord was the primary vehicle for industrial relations reform in Australia.

For the first two years of its operation the Accord functioned as an incomes policy, with the ACTU pledging no extra wage claims by its affiliates in return for indexation of award wages to the consumer price index. In doing so it exploited the centralizing tendencies of the arbitration system. From 1986 on the Accord was renegotiated and efforts were made to use the traditional arbitration system to decentralize bargaining and wage determination in Australia. Between 1986 and 1989, increases in award wages above certain minima were tied to productivity-related changes in industry-based awards. From 1990 on there was shift from industry towards enterprise-based bargaining in Australia. The shift to enterprise-based bargaining was further cemented by the introduction of the 1993 Industrial Relations Reform Act, which amongst other things recast industry awards as a safety net of minimum conditions, placed limits on the ability of the federal industrial tribunal, the Australian Industrial Relations Commission (AIRC), to intervene in enterprise bargaining and made provision for a stream of non-union collective bargaining for the first time in the federal industrial relations system (Lansbury and Wailes, 2010).

In New Zealand, the Lange Labour government, elected in 1984, quickly rejected the option of a formal incomes policy and abandoned compulsory arbitration. While preserving some of the protections of the traditional system, the 1987 Labour Relations Act attempted to create the conditions for enterprise-level collective bargaining, by amongst other things, forcing unions to amalgamate and removing consideration of wage relativities from the determination of wages. The State Sector Act 1988 extended private sector bargaining arrangements to all public sector employees (Walsh, 1991; Haworth, 1993).

Election of a conservative National government in New Zealand in 1990 set the stage for much more dramatic labour market reform. The 1991 Employment Contracts Act (ECA) removed all vestiges of the traditional institutions of industrial relations in New Zealand and replaced them with an individual contractual order that provided only minimal regulation of the employment relationship (Anderson, 1991). As an indication of just how radical the ECA was, the word 'union' was not mentioned at all in the legislation and there were no special provisions for the registration of trade unions, something that had been a feature of New Zealand employment relations for almost a century.

As Bray and Neilson (1996, p. 70) put it, by the early 1990s 'industrial relations policy in Australia and New Zealand diverged more than at any other time since the turn of the century'. This apparent divergence of industrial relations policy in these two very similar cases sparked considerable comparative interest from industrial relations scholars in both countries and produced a significant body of comparative analysis. Broadly speaking, this literature highlighted the importance of institutional variables in producing this policy divergence and focused on three sets of institutional differences between the countries: differences in the organization of the labour movement, differences in the organization of employer opinion and differences in the autonomy and capacity of the state (for a review see Wailes, 2003, ch. 5).

A number of comparative scholars, seeking to explain differences in industrial relations policy in the two countries, focused on the impact that differences in the organization of the Australian and New Zealand labour movements had on policy development (see, for example, Sandlant, 1989; Bray and Walsh, 1993, 1998; Gardner, 1995). First, there were noticeable differences in the unity of the labour movements in the two countries and the power and authority of the peak union bodies. By the early 1980s the Australian labour movement had achieved a high degree of organizational unity, with all major unions affiliated to a single peak union body, the ACTU. On the eve of the election of the Labor government, the ACTU was in a position to exert a substantial degree of control over its affiliates and was therefore able to provide the incoming government with credible commitments to wage control. By contrast in the early 1980s, the New Zealand union movement remained organizationally divided. There were two trade union peak bodies in New Zealand, the Federation of Labor and the Combined State Unions. These two bodies merged in 1987 to form the New Zealand Council of Trade Unions (NZCTU); however, a number of important private sector trade unions remained outside the structure. Lacking the national authority and the cohesiveness of its Australian counterpart, the New Zealand trade union movement was unable to convince the Lange Labour government that it could effectively restrain the wage demands of its affiliates.

There were also important differences in the relationship between the trade union movement and the Labour Party governments in the two countries. In Australia many of the senior cabinet ministers in the ALP government came from a union background, including the Prime Minister Bob Hawke, a former ACTU secretary. In New Zealand, however, only one of the Lange government's ministers had a union background. Furthermore, while unions continued to play a formal role in policy formation in the ALP, reforms in the mid-1970s had eroded the formal role of unions in New Zealand Labour Party (NZLP) policy development. These differences it was argued not only made the ALP more open to considering the use of an incomes policy, than was the case in the NZLP, but also allowed the Australian union movement to contest free-market-oriented policy advice from Treasury.

A second notable difference between the two cases, which for comparative scholars helped explain industrial relations policy divergence in the late 1980s and early 1990s, related to the organization of employer opinion. In New Zealand during the 1980s there was growing unity of employer opinion around the need for radical labour market reform, whereas Australian employer opinion about the nature and extent of labour market reform was more divided. Plowman and Street (1993, p. 94) argue that this difference in employer opinion had little to do with differences in the economic imperatives facing employers in the two countries but rather reflected 'differences in the respective patterns of employer organization which mediated the policy debate among employers'.

During the 1970s the New Zealand Employers Federation (NZEF) undertook a series of reforms, which increasingly centralized the formation of employer opinion (Wanna, 1989). In the late 1970s a new organization, the New Zealand Business Roundtable (BRT), representing the CEOs of the 50 largest companies in the country, was formed with the explicit aim of influencing government economic policy. In the wake of the introduction of the Labour Relations Act in 1987, the BRT began an active campaign for more radical labour market deregulation in New Zealand. By 1990 the NZEF had shifted its policy position on labour market reform to closely resemble that of the BRT (Walsh and Ryan, 1993). As a result the conservative National government, elected in 1990, was faced with unified employer opinion about the need for radical labour market reform. In Australia, however, the organization of employer opinion remained fragmented. Australian employer organizations have historically been organized around industry sectors and on a state-by-state basis (reflecting Australia's federal political system). Attempts during the 1970s to create a single, effective national employer federation, the Confederation of Australian Industry, largely failed. Not only did fragmentation of employer organizations prevent employers playing a formal role in the Accord social pact; it also limited their influence on the formation of industrial relations policy during the 1980s (Mathews, 1991). O'Brien (1994) argues that fragmentation of employer opinion meant that the Business Council of Australia, an organization that was very similar to the BRT in New Zealand, was less successful than its New Zealand counterpart in advocating radical labour market reform.

A third difference between Australia and New Zealand that comparative scholars focused on to explain divergence in industrial relations policy related to the ability of the national government to introduce reforms (see Mitchell and Wilson, 1993; Boston and Uhr, 1996; Bray and Neilson, 1996). While both Australia and New Zealand follow the Westminster system of government, reflecting their shared origin as British colonies, there are notable differences in the organization of government power. Australia is a federation with a written Constitution that specifies, and therefore places limits on, the power of the Commonwealth government to legislate. The Australian Commonwealth government is bicameral. The upper house, the Senate, acts as a house of review and has the ability to slow and even moderate reform initiatives. New Zealand, on the other hand, is a unitary state with an unwritten Constitution and a unicameral parliament. Comparative scholars argued that differences in the institutionalization of state power produced differences in the relative autonomy of the state, making it easier for governments in New Zealand to introduce radical market-oriented reforms while at the same time limiting the scope for the Australian government to pursue dramatic changes in employment relations.

The focus of the Australia–New Zealand comparative literature on the importance of organizational and institutional variables was consistent with the arguments of the 'new institutionalism'. The new institutionalism argued that globalization was unlikely to produce convergence in economic and social policy in developed market economies because of the important role that national-level institutional arrangements played in mediating the impact of common external economic pressures (see Thelen and Steinmo, 1992). The new institutionalism has become increasingly influential in comparative employment relations (for a review see Wailes et al., 2003). The Australia–New Zealand comparative literature that developed in the late 1980s and early 1990s not only demonstrated the causal significance of institutional arrangements but also suggested that relatively small differences in these factors can have a significant impact on policy outcomes.

RECENT DEVELOPMENTS IN AUSTRALIAN AND NEW ZEALAND INDUSTRIAL RELATIONS

While Australian and New Zealand industrial relations diverged significantly in the later 1980s and early 1990s, since the mid-1990s the differences between the two countries have diminished significantly. This re-convergence of industrial relations policy in both countries since the mid-1990s calls into question the overwhelming emphasis placed on the role of organizational and institutional factors in the comparative literature and suggests that the relationship between international economic change and national patterns of industrial relations is more complex than the new institutionalism suggests.

In late 1995 the ALP lost the national election to a conservative Liberal National Coalition government. In 1996 the Howard government introduced new legislation, the Workplace Relations Act, which was informed by the same free-market ideologies that had resulted in the introduction of the ECA in New Zealand. Lacking a majority in the Senate, the Howard government was forced to compromise on the more radical elements of its reform agenda and to preserve some aspects of the traditional arbitration system. Nonetheless, the Workplace Relations Act (WR Act) introduced some major changes into Australia industrial relations. While the WR Act retained the AIRC and its awards, it severely limited the scope of arbitration by restricting awards to 20 allowable matters. Second, the WR Act made the negotiation of collective agreements easier and reduced the power of the Commission to vet the outcomes of these agreements. Third, the WR Act introduced legally sanctioned non-union individual agreements, called Australian Workplace Agreements (AWAs), in the federal jurisdiction for the first time. Finally, the WR Act introduced a series of provisions designed to constrain the actions of trade unions, including restrictions on union access to the workplace and legal sanctions against unlawful industrial action (McCallum, 1997; Naughton, 1997).

In the aftermath of the 2004 federal election, in which the Liberal and National Coalition won a majority in both the lower and upper houses of the Federal Parliament, the Howard government introduced further, far-reaching changes to Australian industrial relations with its 2005 Workplace Relations Amendment (Work Choices) Legislation (hereafter Work Choices). Work Choices removed many of the restrictions and the oversight that had been placed on individual contracts (AWAs – Australian Workplace Agreements) and made it much easier for employers to force employees into individual contracts. It also severely limited the scope of industrial awards, to five allowable matters, placed a range of restrictions on union-based activity and substantially eroded existing protections against unjustified dismissal (Lansbury and Wailes, 2010). While the two pieces of legislation differed in their approach, Work Choices set out to achieve similar aims to the ECA in New Zealand and had a number of similar effects. These included declining union density and collective bargaining coverage, and increased wage dispersion. Both the ECA and Work Choices had particularly negative effects on the wages and conditions of low-paid, part-time workers in the services sector, many of whom are women (Peetz, 2007).

In New Zealand the election of a Labour Alliance Coalition government in 1999 produced further change in employment relations policy. During the election campaign Labour promised to repeal the ECA and replace it with a fairer and more equitable system of employment relations. Analysts suggest that concern about the impact of the ECA on wages and working conditions played a significant part in determining the election outcome. The Employment Relations Act (ERA) 2000 repealed the ECA and sought to shift the emphasis of employment relations away from individual contracts in the ECA and towards collective bargaining. One of the most significant changes introduced by the act was the obligation on employees and employers to bargain in 'good faith', a concept that has its origins in North American labour law. To facilitate the development of collective bargaining the ERA also included a number of provisions designed to improve union access to workplaces and to give unions exclusive rights to represent workers in collective bargaining arrangements. Finally, the ERA significantly increased the floor of minimum standards for all employees in New Zealand (see Walsh and Harbridge, 2001).

There have been similar developments in Australia recently. As in New Zealand, employment relations issues played an important role in the 2007 federal election in Australia and the ALP, who won the election, promised to repeal Work Choices and to reintroduce balance and fairness into employment relations. While not a direct copy of the New Zealand legislation, the Fair Work Act 2009 has a number of similar elements including an emphasis on good faith bargaining, greater access and bargaining rights for unions and a strengthened floor of minimum individual employment provisions and rights (Lansbury and Wailes, 2010).

While both the Employment Relations Act and the Fair Work Act seek to strike more balance in employment relations and to promote collective bargaining, as many commentators have noted, neither constitute an attempt to return to the traditional arbitration systems of the two countries (Boxall, 2001; Peetz, 2007). In both cases there is only limited scope for the intervention of government agencies into the bargaining process. The ERA has no provisions for arbitration, while Work Choices restricts arbitration to a very limited set of circumstances. Rather, both pieces of legislation are designed to foster and encourage enterprise-based, as opposed to industry-wide, collective bargaining as the primary means of determining wages and employment conditions. Therefore, since the mid-1990s employment relations in the two countries have once again converged on a new form of post-arbitral labour market regulation.

REASSESSING THE AUSTRALIA–NEW ZEALAND COMPARATIVE LITERATURE

As was noted in the previous section, the significant divergence in employment relations policy that developed in Australia and New Zealand in the late 1980s and early 1990s has diminished since the mid-1990s. By early 2010, when the Australian Fair Work Act came into operation, the employment relations systems in the two countries had once again converged on a similar model, albeit one that differs significantly from the arbitration systems that had operated in the two countries for much of the twentieth century. These recent developments suggest the need to reassess the comparative literature on the two countries that developed in the late 1980s and early 1990s. In particular these recent developments raise questions about the overwhelming emphasis that this literature placed on organizational and institutional factors.

In recent years there has been a growing body of literature that criticizes aspects of the new institutionalism and its application to employment relations (see Wailes et al., 2003). Briefly, this critique argues that while institutions are important, the new institutionalism tends to exaggerate the role that institutions play and at the same time downplays or ignores the impact of material interests on social action (Pontusson, 1995). These criticisms provide a useful starting point for reassessing the Australia–New Zealand comparison.

As has been noted in the comparative literature, New Zealand abandoned arbitration much more quickly and dramatically than was the case in Australia. A focus on underlying material interests suggests a number of reasons why this may be the case. First, while the two countries adopted very similar arbitration systems, historical analysis suggests that arbitration was not the only factor that shaped the development of employment relations in each (Barry and Wailes, 2005). Importantly the economic context within which arbitration operated in the two countries differed significantly. Despite the similarities in their policy frameworks, in the aftermath of the Long Depression of the 1880s, Australia and New Zealand pursued quite different economic development strategies. In New Zealand renewed economic growth was based on a shift of production away from wool towards meat and dairy production based on intensive farming techniques. In Australia, however, the development of a domestic manufacturing sector played a much more significant role in economic growth during the twentieth century. As a consequence, arbitration played different roles in the two countries (Macintyre, 1987; Schwartz, 1989; Wailes, 2003).

As Barry and Wailes (2004) argue these economic differences, which shaped the attitudes of employers and employees to arbitration, produced an earlier policy divergence in Australia and New Zealand in the late 1960s. While falls in commodity prices led to collapse of arbitration in New Zealand in 1967 and ushered in a prolonged period of statutory incomes policies, in Australia by the mid-1970s arbitration was re-established with the support of employers interested in controlling wages growth.

Wailes et al. (2003) argue that the policy divergence that developed in the late 1980s and early 1990s in Australia and New Zealand was not only a function of institutional and organizational differences between the two countries, but also reflected important differences in the economic situation facing each one. While both countries faced similar economic pressures, the economic crisis facing New Zealand during the 1980s was much more serious than that which faced Australian governments. The differences in external economic imperatives shaped the extent to which employers and governments regarded the existing institutional arrangements as sustainable. By the mid-1990s, however, continued economic restructuring eroded many of the benefits that employers gained from arbitration and produced new calls for further labour market deregulation.

It is also worth noting that, despite differences in the paths of reform taken in the two countries, there are strong similarities in the labour market outcomes associated with these changes. During the 1990s both countries have experienced dramatic declines in trade union density, collective bargaining coverage and significant increases in individual contracting. For example, union density fell from 41.5 per cent to 17.0 per cent in New Zealand between 1990 and 1999 (Walsh and Harbridge, 2001). In Australia union density fell from 47 per cent in June 1991 to 22.7 per cent by the end of 2005. Under Work Choices this fall in density accelerated, falling to 18.9 per cent by early 2008 (Cooper and Ellem, 2008). Furthermore, both countries have witnessed significant increases in wage inequality. While many of these features are shared with other developed countries, in international comparative terms Australia and New Zealand represent extreme cases. The original comparative literature's focus on institutions and policy outcomes, rather than the consequences of those policies, may therefore exaggerate the differences between the cases.

CONCLUSION

Australia and New Zealand represent almost perfect real world examples of very similar cases. The two countries had similar patterns of economic development and share a unique form of labour market regulation, known as arbitration, which influenced industrial relations in each country for most of the twentieth century. Despite these similarities, during the late 1980s and early 1990s divergences in industrial relations policy in the two countries sparked the development of an interesting comparative literature that sought to exploit the similarities between them in order to identify the sources of this policy divergence. This literature focused in particular on the significance of institutional and organizational differences between the two countries. However, since the mid-1990s industrial relations policy in Australia and New Zealand began to follow a similar path. By the end of the first decade of the twenty-first century the two countries had again converged on a similar pattern of labour market regulation that differs significantly from the traditions of arbitration in the two countries. Policy developments in the two countries since the mid-1990s suggest that the earlier comparative literature placed too much emphasis on the role in institutions and ignored the potential significance of underlying material interests in shaping industrial relations policies and outcomes.

The Australia–New Zealand comparison has implications for the broader comparative industrial relations literature. The notion that national institutional differences play a significant role in shaping the impact of globalization on national patterns of employment relations is highly influential in the comparative industrial relations literature (see Wailes et al., 2010). The Australia–New Zealand comparison suggests that there is a need for industrial relations scholars to go beyond a focus on institutional arrangements and to examine a broader range of factors that shape the relationship between international economic change and national patterns of employment relations. That is, the Australia–New Zealand comparison suggests that while institutions matter, they are not the only thing that matters.

REFERENCES

Anderson, G. (1991), 'The Employment Contracts Act: An employers' charter?', *New Zealand Journal of Industrial Relations*, **16**(2), 127–42.
Barry, M. and Wailes, N. (2004), 'Contrasting systems? 100 years of arbitration in Australia and New Zealand', *Journal of Industrial Relations*, **46**(4), 430–47.
Barry, M. and Wailes, N. (2005), 'Revisiting the Australia–New Zealand comparison', *New Zealand Journal of Employment Relations*, **30**(3), 4–20.
Boston, J. and Uhr, J. (1996), 'Reshaping the mechanics of government', in F. Castles, R. Gerritsen and J. Vowles (eds), *The Great Experiment: Labour Parties and Public Policy Transformation in Australia and New Zealand*, Sydney: Allen and Unwin.
Boxall, P. (2001), 'Evaluating continuity and change in the Employment Relations Act 2000', *New Zealand Journal of Industrial Relations*, **26**(1), 27–44.
Bray, M. and Neilson, D. (1996), 'Industrial relations reform and the relative autonomy of the state', in F. Castles, R. Gerritsen and J. Vowles (eds), *The Great Experiment: Labour Parties and Public Policy Transformation in Australia and New Zealand*, Sydney: Allen and Unwin.
Bray, M. and Walsh, P. (1993), 'Unions and economic restructuring in Australia and New Zealand', in M. Bray and N. Haworth (eds), *Economic Restructuring and Industrial Relations in Australia and New Zealand: A Comparative Analysis*, Sydney: Australian Centre of Industrial Relations Research and Training.
Bray, M. and Walsh, P. (1998), 'Different paths to neo-liberalism? Comparing Australia and New Zealand', *Industrial Relations*, **37**(3), 358–87.
Castles, F. (1988), *Australian Public Policy and Economic Vulnerability: A Comparative and Historical Perspective*, Sydney: Allen and Unwin.
Castles, F., Gerritsen, R. and Vowles, J. (1996), *The Great Experiment: Labour Parties and Public Policy Transformation in Australia and New Zealand*, St Leonards: Allen and Unwin.
Cooper, R. and Ellem, B. (2008), 'The neoliberal state, trade unions and collective bargaining in Australia', *British Journal of Industrial Relations*, **46**(3), 532–54.
Denoon, D. (1983), *Settler Capitalism: The Dynamics of Dependent Development in the Southern Hemisphere*, Oxford: Clarendon Press.
Easton, B. and Gerritsen, R. (1996), 'Economic reform: Parallels and divergences', in F.

Castles, R. Gerritsen and J. Vowles (eds), *The Great Experiment: Labour Parties and Public Policy Transformation in Australia and New Zealand*, St Leonards: Allen and Unwin.

Gardner, M. (1995), 'Labour movements and industrial restructuring: Australia, New Zealand and the United States', in L. Turner and K. Wever (eds), *The Comparative Political Economy of Industrial Relations*, Madison, WI: IRRA.

Hancock, K. ([1979]1984), 'The first half century of wage policy', in B. Chapman, J. Isaac and J. Niland (eds), *Australian Labour Economics: Readings*, Melbourne; Macmillan Australia.

Haworth, H. (1993), 'Deregulation and reform of the New Zealand Union Movement', in S. Frenkel (ed.), *Organized Labor in the Asia Pacific Region: A Comparative Study of Trade Unionism in Nine Countries*, Ithaca, NY: Cornell University Press.

Hince, K. (1993), 'Is Euro-American union theory universally applicable? An Australasian perspective', in R. Adams and N. Meltz (eds), *Industrial Relations Theory: Its Nature, Scope and Pedagogy*, Metuchen, NJ: IMLR Press/ Rutgers University.

Holt, J. (1986), *Compulsory Arbitration in New Zealand: The First Forty Years*, Auckland: Auckland University Press.

Howard, W. (1983), 'Trade unions and the arbitration system', in B. Head (eds), *State and Economy in Australia*, Melbourne: OUP.

Kirkby, D. (1989), 'Arbitration and the fight for economic justice', in S. Macintyre and R. Mitchell (eds), *Foundations of Arbitration: The Origins and Effects of State Compulsory Arbitration, 1890–1914*, Melbourne: Oxford University Press.

Lansbury, R. and Wailes, N. (2010), 'Employment relations in Australia', in G. Bamber, R. Lansbury and N. Wailes (eds), *International and Comparative Employment Relations*, 5th edition, Sydney: Sage.

Macintyre, S. (1987), 'Holt and the establishment of arbitration: An Australian perspective', *New Zealand Journal of Industrial Relations*, **12**(3), 151–9.

Macintyre, S. (1989), 'Neither labour nor capital: The politics of the establishment of arbitration', in S. Macintyre and R. Mitchell (eds), *Foundations of Arbitration: The Origins and Effects of State Compulsory Arbitration, 1890–1914*, Melbourne: Oxford University Press.

Martin, D. (1974), 'A discussion of wage structure in New Zealand', in J. Howells et al. (eds), *Labour and Industrial Relations in New Zealand*, Melbourne: Pitman.

Mathews, T. (1991), 'Interest group politics: Corporatism without business?', in F. Castles (ed.), *Australia Compared: People, Policies and Politics*, Sydney: Allen and Unwin.

McCallum, R. (1997), 'Australian workplace agreements – an analysis', *Australian Journal of Labour Law*, **10**(1), 50–61.

Mitchell, R. (1989), 'State systems of conciliation and arbitration: The legal origins of the Australasian model', in S. Macintyre and R. Mitchell (eds), *Foundations of Arbitration: The Origins and Effects of State Compulsory Arbitration, 1890–1914*, Melbourne: Oxford University Press.

Mitchell, R. and Wilson, M. (1993), 'Legislative change in industrial relations: Australia and New Zealand in the 1980s', in M. Bray and N. Haworth (eds), *Economic Restructuring and Industrial Relations in Australia and New Zealand: A Comparative Analysis*, Sydney: Australian Centre of Industrial Relations Research and Training.

Naughton, R. (1997), 'Sailing into uncharted seas: The role of unions under the Workplace Relations Act 1996 (Cth)', *Australian Journal of Labour Law*, **10**(1), 112–32.

Norris, K. (1986), 'The wages structure: Does arbitration make a difference?', in J. Niland (ed.), *Wage Fixation in Australia*, Sydney: Allen and Unwin.

O'Brien, J. (1994), 'McKinsey, Hilmer and the BCA: The new management model of labour market reform', *Journal of Industrial Relations*, **36**(4), 468–90.

Patmore, G. (1991), *Australian Labour History*, Melbourne: Longman Cheshire.

Peetz, D. (2007), *Assessing the Impact of Work Choices: One Year On*, Victoria: Report to Department of Innovation, Industry and Regional Development.

Plowman, D. and Street, M. (1993), 'Industrial relations and economic restructuring in Australia and New Zealand: Employers' agendas', in M. Bray and N. Haworth (eds), *Economic Restructuring and Industrial Relations in Australia and New Zealand: A*

Comparative Analysis, Sydney: Australian Centre of Industrial Relations Research and Training, Sydney.
Pontusson, J. (1995), 'From comparative public policy to political economy: Putting political institutions in their place and taking interests seriously', *Comparative Political Studies*, **28**(1), 117–48.
Prezworski, A. and Teune, H. (1970), *The Logic of Comparative Social Inquiry*, New York: Wiley.
Robertson, S. (1991), 'Women workers and the New Zealand Arbitration Court, 1894–1920', in R. Frances and B. Scates (eds), *Women, Work and the Labour Movement in Australia and Aotearoa/New Zealand*, Sydney: Australian Society for the Study of Labour History.
Sandlant, R. (1989), *The Political Economy of Wage Restraint: The Australian Accord and Trade Union Strategy in New Zealand*, Auckland: The University of Auckland.
Schwartz, H. (1989), *In the Dominions of Debt: Historical Perspectives on Dependent Development*, Ithaca, NY: Cornell University Press.
Skopcol, T. and Somers, M. (1980), 'The uses of comparative history in macrosocial inquiry', *Comparative Studies in History and Society*, **228**(2), 174–92.
Strauss, G. (1998), 'Comparative international industrial relations', in K. Whitfield and G. Strauss (eds), *Researching the World of Work: Strategies and Methods in Studying Industrial Relations*, Ithaca, NY: ILR Press/Cornell University Press.
Thelen, K. and Steinmo, S. (1992), 'Historical institutionalism in comparative politics', in K. Thelen, S. Steinmo and F. Longstreth (eds), *Structuring Politics: Historical Institutionalism in Comparative Perspective*, New York: Cambridge University Press, pp. 1–32.
Traxler, F., Blanske, S. and Kittel, B. (2001), *National Labour Relations in Industrialised Countries: A Comparative Study of Institutions, Change and Performance*, Oxford: Oxford University Press.
Wailes, N. (2003), 'The importance of small differences: Globalization and employment relations in Australia and New Zealand', Unpublished PhD thesis, Sydney: The University of Sydney.
Wailes, N., Bamber, G. and Lansbury, R. (2010), 'An introduction to international and comparative employment relations', in G. Bamber, R. Lansbury and N. Wailes (eds), *International and Comparative Employment Relations*, 5th edition, Sydney: Sage.
Wailes, N., Lansbury, R. and Ramia, G. (2003), 'Interests, institutions and industrial relations', *British Journal of Industrial Relations*, **41**(4), 617–37.
Walsh, P. (1991), 'The State Sector Act 1988', in J. Boston, J. Martin, J. Pallot and P. Walsh (eds), *Reshaping the State: New Zealand's Bureaucratic Revolution*, Auckland: Oxford University Press.
Walsh, P. and Harbridge, R. (2001), 'Re-regulation of bargaining in New Zealand: The Employment Relations Act 2000', *Australian Bulletin of Labour*, **27**(1), 43–60.
Walsh, P. and Ryan, R. (1993), 'The making of the Employment Contracts Act', in R. Harbridge (ed.), *Employment Contracts: New Zealand Experiences*, Wellington: Victoria University Press, pp. 13–29.
Wanna, J. (1989), 'Centralisation without corporatisation: The politics of New Zealand employers in the recession', *New Zealand Journal of Industrial Relations*, **14**(1), 1–15.
Woods, N. (1963), *Industrial Conciliation and Arbitration in New Zealand*, Wellington: R.E. Owen, Government Printer.

13 Employment relations in South Africa and Mozambique
Geoffrey Wood

INTRODUCTION

This chapter compares and contrasts the practice of employment relations in South Africa and Mozambique from a broadly historical perspective. Whilst geographically in close proximity, the two countries have had very different colonial legacies, and this has been reflected in great differences in the scale and scope of industrialization and general development. In common, both countries have very high unemployment rates and large informal sectors; however, the relative strength of unions also varies greatly between the two countries. The latter reflects both objective circumstances, and key differences in strategic choices made by the unions.

UNDERSTANDING EMPLOYMENT RELATIONS IN SOUTH AFRICA AND MOZAMBIQUE

There is an extensive body of literature on employment relations in South Africa. First, there is the rich literature on South African labour history, locating it within the broader political economy. Second, there is literature on unionization and union renewal. Related to this is a third body of literature that focuses on changes in regulation and firm practices. The first body of literature focuses on South Africa's experience of industrialization and how this process was associated with the refinement of a system of racial repression to ensure cheap and controllable labour supplies from South Africa's black majority (Simons and Simons, 1969; Webster, 1987). Key debates here centre on the extent to which institutionalized racial discrimination was, in practice, really functional to business (Simons and Simons, 1969; Karis and Carter, 1977). The second body of literature concerns itself with the nature of unionization, why early attempts to organize black workers generally failed, the nature of racially exclusive unionism, the rise of black-dominated unions from the 1970s onwards, and present challenges facing organized labour in South Africa (Lewis, 1984; Maree, 1986, 1987; Wood and Psoulis, 2001;

Donnelly and Dunn, 2006). The third stream explores changes in labour law and firm practices following on the gradual deracialization of South African employment relations from the late 1970s onwards, ongoing reforms to South African labour relations legislation and changes in work organization at firm level (Webster, 1986; Wood and Mahabir, 2001; Von Holdt, 2003).

In contrast, the literature on contemporary Mozambican employment relations is rather more limited (Gumende, 1998; Webster and Wood, 2005; Webster et al., 2006a and 2006b). There is a body of historical studies on slavery and forced labour in colonial Mozambique (cf. Newitt, 1995). More recently, work by authors such as Hanlon (1991, 1996), Haines and Wood (1995), Wood (1999) and Pitcher (2002), explores changes in the political economy that took place following the winning of independence, focusing on the effects of the short-lived experiment with state socialism and later neoliberal reforms. Whilst this might suggest radical changes in employment relations, several authors point to many continuities, with forced labour extending well into the post-colonial period, and, more recently, the persistence of patriarchal workplace relations, and a widespread flouting of employment relations legislation (Hanlon, 1991; Pitcher, 2002; Webster and Wood, 2005; Webster et al., 2006a).

Despite their geographical proximity, there has been little comparative work done on similarities and differences in employment relations between the two countries. In part, this reflects differences between the two that make drawing direct comparisons more difficult. First, the legal systems are different: Mozambique is a civil law country and South Africa a common law one. Second, whilst South Africa is Anglophone, Mozambique is Lusophone, with legislation and much primary documentation being in Portuguese; moreover, knowledge of English is very limited in that country. This makes it difficult for scholars to systematically research both countries from a comparative starting point, unless they are conversant in both languages, which relatively few industrial relations scholars are. Nonetheless, a small, but emerging body of literature has attempted to make some comparisons, highlighting differences, as well as shared issues such as the relatively high importance of the informal sector, and the challenges this poses for both unions and regulatory authorities (Webster et al., 2006a and 2006b).

KEY FEATURES OF MOZAMBICAN AND SOUTH AFRICAN EMPLOYMENT RELATIONS: HISTORICAL LEGACIES AND CURRENT ISSUES

The central concerns of the literature on South African labour history are about the role of state and industry in attempting to ensure supplies of cheap and disciplined labour up until the demise of apartheid, and the process of resistance to this, including periodic attempts at unionization (Simons and Simons, 1969; Lewis, 1984; Webster, 1986). Up until the late nineteenth century, South Africa was a poor backwater, with the local economy centring on agriculture. In the Western Cape, higher and more regular rainfall and a temperate Mediterranean climate made intensive wheat and fruit farming possible. However, this remained on a relatively small scale until the construction of solid roads over the mountain passes, and the development of irrigation technology so that crop farming could expand beyond a narrow coastal and immediate interior belt. Large areas of the rest of South Africa are semi-desert; in the remainder of the country, climatic variations, and great fluctuations in rainfall patterns have always made agriculture more tenuous. Hence, South Africa remained an unattractive option to immigrants, and of only passing interest to colonial authorities, other than its role as a supply centre and base on the sea route to the East (cf. Karis and Carter, 1977).

The discovery of diamonds in 1867, and, above all, the massive gold reserves of the Witwatersrand in 1886, dramatically changed the situation (Wilson, 1972). Not only did this bring about the forced political unification of South Africa under British rule by means of the 1899–1902 Boer War, but it also raised serious issues regarding the utilization of labour (Simons and Simons, 1969). The Witwatersrand gold reserves may have been plentiful, but the ore was of low grade, requiring large amounts of cheap labour to make its extraction commercially viable (Simons and Simons, 1969; Wilson, 1972; cf. Karis and Carter, 1977).

Trade unions first emerged in South Africa in the nineteenth century, being founded by immigrants from Europe and Australia (Simons and Simons, 1969). These unions were organized on the lines of craft, and were, in practice, generally racially exclusive. Skills shortages meant that their members were able to extract a wage premium. The great mining houses that emerged faced the challenge of maintaining profits in the face of high-technology, equipment (as a result of the need for ever deeper mining) and labour costs, and had to contend with a further disruption of their labour supplies as a result of the Boer War (ibid.). After an experiment with indentured Chinese labour over the years 1903–08 (which had to be abandoned as a result of a political backlash) attention was turned to the utilization of black labour (Richardson, 1977). This led to the promulgation of a series of laws designed to force the black peasantry off the land and into wage labour, an example being the Natives Land Act (No. 27 of 1913), which limited black land ownership to a small portion of the country.

Increasing mechanization both in the mines and in the rapidly expanding industrial sector undercut the skilled position of white workers at the same time as large numbers of African workers were entering the workforce. This led to a series of backlashes, culminating in the 1922 Rand Rebellion, when white miners seized central Johannesburg, a rebellion founded on a mix of socialist ideals and a desire to protect the white workers over blacks, typified by the slogan, 'Workers of the World Unite for a White South Africa' (Wilson and Thompson, 1971). The authorities responded through aerial bombing and using artillery against white working class suburbs of Johannesburg (cf. Karis and Carter, 1977). This, in turn, led to a political backlash, with the then government being voted out; the incoming PACT government entered into a historic compromise with white workers embodied in the 1924 Industrial Conciliation Act and the expansion of racial job reservation. Effectively, white workers traded off militancy and compromised on job reservation on skill lines, in turn for a privileged position on racial lines. The Industrial Conciliation Act allowed for collective bargaining on industrial lines, but excluded Africans from the definition of employee (see Webster, 1978); in practice, white-dominated unions became increasingly bureaucratic, increasingly relying on their protected position and political clout to protect members, rather than militancy and skill. Ever-expanding pass laws restricted African mobility in urban areas, enhancing labour discipline (ibid.).

However, it would be incorrect to conclude that the formative years of South African employment relations were about white resistance and black compliance. Whilst white mine owners and farmers became increasingly reliant on cheap black labour, the latter regularly engaged in acts of collective resistance (Simons and Simons, 1969). In 1924, the first attempt was made to organize African workers under the Industrial and Commercial Workers Union (ICU) (Bradford, 1987). The ICU expanded rapidly, indiscriminatingly signing up not only industrial and service workers, but also peasants. The ICU soon faced bitter leadership disputes, and was never able to build a significant grassroots organization (Bonner, 1978). In the 1930s, communist activists established a number of small industrial unions, under the Federation of Non-European Trade Unions (FNETU), later replaced by the Council of Non-European Trade Unions (CNETU) (Simons and Simons, 1969; Lewis, 1984). However, they remained reliant on a small number of activists, and never expanded beyond a handful of workplaces (see Lewis, 1984). The accession to power of the National Party in 1948 resulted in the expansion of racial discrimination under the apartheid system, which combined petty racism with ever-more rigid job reservation, and a tightening up of the pass laws.

An attempt to unite both black and white workers under the South African Trades and Labour Council (SATLC) failed; in the aftermath, a number of black trade unions united under the umbrella of the South African Congress of Trade Unions (SACTU) in the mid-1950s (Lambert, 1988). SACTU played a prominent role in the African National Congress's campaigns of the later 1950s. However, SACTU faced the same problems of an over-reliance on a few key activists, and an inability to expand beyond a few key employers. By the early 1960s, SACTU was forced into exile, following the banning of the African National Congress.

The years 1972 to 1973 saw a resurgence in efforts to organize black workers, coordinated by a small number of white students and lecturers, and former union activists (Maree, 1986, 1987). Initially, worker advice bureaus were founded, but these soon transformed themselves into unions. However, two strands emerged as a result of differences in tactics: those formerly involved in the white-dominated union movement wished to expand unionism to Africans without necessarily competing with the former, whilst those who had fewer links to the white-dominated unions were united in a principle of non-racism. This led to the establishment of not one, but two 'independent' union federations, the Federation of South African Trade Unions (FOSATU), and the (blacks only) Council of Unions of South Africa (CUSA) (ibid.). Both federations decided to concentrate on building a strong shop floor organization inspired by both the strength of the British labour movement at the time, and the failure of previous efforts at organizing blacks to move beyond a reliance on a small coterie of leaders to building a sustainable shop floor organization (ibid.). As workplace issues were prioritized over political campaigning in the community, this strand of unionism soon became known as 'workerism' (Friedman, 1987).

Meanwhile, African students involved in the black consciousness movement founded the Black Allied Workers Union (BAWU). BAWU soon split, with most members going on to form the South African Allied Workers Union (SAAWU). However, like BAWU, SAAWU remained committed to community organizing, and campaigning around political issues beyond the workplace, a policy that became known as 'populism' (Morris, 1982). By the early 1980s, the independent unions had expanded rapidly. At the same time, the limitations of both workerism and populism became clear. Belonging to a workerist union did not exempt activists from arbitrary arrests or worse, whilst increasingly membership urged leaders to become more politically outspoken, following the start of the mass insurrection of the 1980s (Friedman, 1987). Meanwhile, shop floor weaknesses made the populist unions more vulnerable to state repression (ibid.). This made both strands of unionism more willing to compromise, leading to the formation of the Congress of South African Trade Unions (COSATU) in 1985 (Baskin, 1991). However, a minority of unions continued to be committed to black only membership, and went on to form the National Council of Trade Unions.

The apartheid regime's response to the resurgence of union activity from the 1970s onwards was mixed. A 1973 legislative reform allowed black workers the option of some representation on a consultative basis under specific circumstances. Many unions took advantage of this opportunity to get their workplace activists elected onto the committees, indirectly forcing managers to deal with unions. After the 1976 Soweto uprising, the banning (a form of house arrest) of a number of union activists nearly brought about the collapse of the independent unions in their entirety (Maree, 1986; Friedman, 1987). In 1979, the apartheid government took, under the 'Wiehahn reforms', the step of deracializing the Industrial Council system; black unions could now participate in centralized bargaining (ibid.). There is little doubt that the government hoped that broadening the system would have the same effect on the independent unions as it had on the old white ones: promoting compliance (ibid.). For the same reason, many independent unions were initially reluctant to participate in the system; however, increasing numbers chose to do so, with no discernable ill effects, whilst being able to reap all the benefits of centralized bargaining (ibid., cf. Baskin, 1991). Nor did the Wiehahn reforms stop at deracializing collective bargaining: an Industrial Court was set up to arbitrate in industrial disputes (Friedman, 1987). A series of progressive decisions extended worker rights in a range of areas, from collective bargaining to industrial action. Parallel to this process was the gradual movement of African workers into semi-skilled and skilled jobs as a result of skills shortages; racial job reservation proved increasingly unworkable (ibid.).

Increasing militancy in the factories and in the mines – reforms notwithstanding – and growing civil unrest in the communities prompted the apartheid government to declare two successive states of emergency, in 1985 and 1986. In addition to outright repression, the apartheid government attempted to roll back some of the more progressive Industrial Court decisions through the 1987 Labour Relations Act Amendments (Baskin, 1991). Three major trials of strength took place in the same year, on the mines, and, in two parastatals, the railways and the post office. In the end, the unions won valuable concessions as a result of the latter two disputes, although the heavy violence on both sides during the railway strike meant that at times the unions lost the moral high ground (cf. Markham and Mothibeli, 1987; Baskin, 1991). In contrast, the strike in the mines set back union organization for many years in that sector (cf. Baskin, 1991). Finally, by the late 1980s, the unions began to expand into the public sector.

The close of the 1980s saw the deracialization of key aspects of the employment relations system, the skilling of a sizable component of the African labour force and increasing levels of unionization. It also saw the persistence of high levels of strike action, state repression notwithstanding. In summary, employment relations under late apartheid remained confrontational, despite increasing union rights. The underlying reason for this was the continued political exclusion of blacks, mirrored by petty and systematic workplace racism; effectively, the state was unable to 'politically incorporate the unions' (Webster, 1987).

The 1990 De Klerk reforms started South Africa's political transformation. The accession to power of the formerly banned African National Congress (ANC) in 1994 resulted in the COSATU unions gaining unprecedented political influence, as a result of the Alliance they had entered into with that organization in the early 1990s (Wood and Psoulis, 2001). This Alliance gave the COSATU unions a voice on ANC policy forums, and the right to nominate a proportion of the ANC's party list (political reforms included the introduction of a modified proportional representation electoral system with universal adult franchise) (Wood, 2002). At the same time, the ANC introduced a wide range of neoliberal reforms that opened up South African industry to increased global competition and led to large-scale job losses. The following section explores the implications of these changes for South African employment relations.

Even more than South Africa, the history of employment relations in Mozambique is that of forced labour. Mozambique has been part of global trading networks for very much longer than South Africa. In ancient times, Shirazi Persians traded with East Africa, establishing city states that were later subsumed under rule by Arab traders from about AD 800 onwards, Mozambique being a major supplier of gold, ivory and slaves. The arrival on the scene of the Portuguese in the late fifteenth century shattered the Swahili city state system, with the Portuguese soon establishing trading entrepôts along the coast and up the Zambezi valley. A central feature of Portuguese role was the use of slavery, replaced with indentured labour in the nineteenth century. Moreover, little attention was accorded to the development of Mozambique up until the late 1800s (Newitt, 1995). For most of the twentieth century, the Mozambican economy centred on trade with South Africa, and through supplying labour to the South

African mines, for which the Portuguese colonial authorities were paid in gold (Newitt, 1995; Pitcher, 2002).

Under fascist rule from the 1930s onwards, the Portuguese government made attempts to promote the large-scale settlement of Portuguese peasants, and industrial diversification (BIP, n.d.; Newitt, 1995; Pitcher, 2002). The latter led to the emergence of industries in inter alia, automobile components, food, beverages and textiles; however, the economy continued to centre on providing labour supplies to South Africa, trade (the port of Maputo providing a natural outlet for exports from the greater Johannesburg region, and Beira for the then Rhodesia), with the rapid growth of a tourism sector. The distinguishing feature of forced labour persisted, with peasants in areas of the north of the country being forced to grow cotton. In the closing years of colonial rule, the official Portuguese colonial policy of Lusotropie[1] sought to provide a safety valve for the grievances of the indigenous majority by allowing for blacks to attain equal status with whites on meeting educational and economic criteria of 'civilization'. In Mozambique, this policy was even less successful than in the Portuguese West African colonies of Cape Verde, Sao Tome et Principe, Guinea-Bissau and Angola; the country's close proximity to South Africa and the movement of labour between the two proved infectious in making for a very much more racist society (mirrored in a racist division of labour in most workplaces), than the distinctly creole societies that emerged in Lusophone West Africa.

From the early 1960s onwards, the Portuguese had to contend with an armed insurrection under the leadership of FRELIMO (the Revolutionary Front for the Liberation of Mozambique). Weary with escalating guerrilla war in three of its African colonies, young Portuguese officers mounted a coup in Portugal; this led to the rapid decolonization of all Portugal's African colonies, with Mozambique gaining full independence in 1974, under FRELIMO. Officially following Marxist Leninism, FRELIMO had to contend with both the immediate flight of most white settlers and a wave of spontaneous strikes and worker takeovers (Pitcher, 2002, p. 47). Those owners that stayed continued to operate their private enterprises much as before, albeit that many faced challenges to their authority by workers (Hanlon, 1996, p. 10). Clusters of workers and community activists founded the Dynamizing Groups that sought to force worker control of the means of production. FRELIMO soon reined these groups in, ostensibly in the interests of order and more effective coordination of the national economy: the groups were reformed as party cells, and subject to party discipline (Pitcher, 2000, p. 70). The state then turned its attention to reviving the large industrial enterprises and plantations (Hanlon, 1996, pp. 12–16).

Neglected by all this were the peasantry. The flight of Portuguese small traders from the rural areas deprived them of easy access to manufactured goods and buyers of their produce (Hanlon, 1991; Newitt, 1995). The abolition of the system of chiefs (*regulos*) on the basis of the latter's collaboration with the colonial authorities worsened relations, making it easy for the then Rhodesian authorities to establish, and the South African apartheid regime to sponsor RENAMO (the Mozambican National Resistance) (ibid.). The latter successfully mounted a growing insurgency in the rural areas, greatly fuelled by the ill-advised decision of FRELIMO to resume the forced cultivation of cotton.

What did all this mean for employment relations? In practical terms, independence saw the spontaneous emergence of grassroots attempts at worker democracy that were soon reined in by the authorities. Whilst undoubtedly less racist, post-colonial work and employment relations in the industrial and service sector reassumed the authoritarian form that they had followed under colonialism (Webster and Wood, 2005). At the same time, the early years of the socialist experiment were characterized by attempts to expand education and health care: this meant that job-seekers often had a bigger range of skills than before, whilst there were extensions of worker rights in the areas of health and safety, and security of tenure. Surviving small and medium firms often remained under the direction of managers that had served prior to independence; a reluctant and uneven compliance with the law was matched by a persistence of patriarchal ways of doing things. In the rural areas, the return of coerced labour was another symptom of a reversion to the past.

What then are the key post-1945 patterns of employment relations in South Africa and Mozambique? Both countries have a long history of widespread labour coercion, which only ended in the 1990s. This made in both cases for a great deal of inefficiency: there was a tendency for firms to solve productivity problems simply by throwing more cheap labour at them (Smith and Wood, 1998). A general lack of competitiveness was solved through heavy state intervention, including protective tariffs and developmental and other incentives. Since then, both countries have gone through protracted – and often painful – neoliberal reforms. In the case of South Africa, this has led to the development of a higher productivity, higher labour cost model, but with reduced employment. In Mozambique, this has led to the persistence of a cheap labour model, but with structural changes in the composition of the Mozambican economy (including a decline in the role of industry). In South Africa, employment relations up until the end of apartheid were adversarial, with rises in strikes being coterminous with the rise of the independent unions from the 1970s onwards. In common with many other common law countries, South African employment relations moreover tended to be fairly litigatious. In contrast, whilst there is no evidence to suggest that Mozambican employment relations were any more cooperative, the weaker relative position of employees in that country (above all, a very much narrower range of employment alternatives) made for a greater degree of labour compliance than was associated with South Africa from the early 1970s onwards (Webster et al., 2006a and 2006b). As a civil law country, Mozambican employment relations was generally less litigatious (see Chapter 4 by Cooney et al. in this volume), whilst there is considerable evidence to suggest that labour laws have, for many years, been more honoured in the breach (Webster and Wood, 2005; Webster et al., 2006a and 2006b).

THE REMAKING OF EMPLOYMENT RELATIONS IN SOUTH AFRICA AND MOZAMBIQUE

Both South Africa and Mozambique underwent far-reaching political changes in the 1990s, in a large part impelled by economic exigencies. Parallel to the political negotiations between the ANC and the then ruling National Party from 1990 to 1994, negotiations took place between representatives of political parties, the state and employers to discuss reforms to labour legislation in South Africa (Wood and Mahabir, 2001; Wood and Psoulis, 2001). Employers had gradually come to the conclusion that, rather than strengthening their hands, the 1987 Labour Relations Act amendments had destabilized workplace relations. These amendments were generally scrapped. Second, a high strike rate, and the success of independent mediation bodies (such as the Independent Mediation Service of South Africa) prompted the establishment of a Commission for Conciliation, Arbitration and Mediation (CCMA) with the brief of seeking to resolve disputes at an early stage (Wood and Psoulis, 2001; Donnelly and Dunn, 2006). Third, the Industrial Councils had enjoyed wide legitimacy: they were now renamed Bargaining Councils and their role expanded. However, the presence of a Council in a particular industry remained contingent on the agreement of employers and the relevant unions; in this sense, the system retained an element of voluntarism (ibid.). Fourth, the Industrial Court was replaced by a Labour Court and a Labour Appeal Court. On the one hand, the new Labour Court was formally defined as a court of law (which the old Industrial Court had not been), giving a greater weight to its decisions (cf. COSATU, 2007). On the other hand, this meant that the South African system retained a strong element of litigatiousness. Fifth, the bargaining rights enjoyed by private sector workers were extended to the public sector. All these reforms were embodied in the 1995 Labour Relations Act (Wood and Psoulis, 2001). Other legislative reforms expanded South Africa's body of health and safety legislation, and required organizations to devise policies to advance members of formerly disadvantaged groupings (Southall, 2007).

How did the unions respond to these new challenges and opportunities? First, the political reforms – and the greatly weakened bargaining position of union members as a result of job losses – greatly reduced the incidence of industrial action (Wood, 2002). Instead, unions entered into increasingly complex cooperative deals with managers, aimed at securing jobs and organizational competitiveness. Not surprisingly, this process was a contentious one, with period outbreaks of wildcat action by groups of workers who accused union officials of selling out to management (Rachleff, 2001). Second, black majority rule and pressures on business to be seen to be advancing Africans drained the unions of experienced activists and leaders at plant, regional and national levels (ibid.; Wood and Psoulis, 2001). Third, political reforms opened up new opportunities for unionization in the public sector: whilst union membership (but not densities) began to decline in many areas of the private sector, it expanded in the public sector (Baskin, 1991; Buhlungu et al., 2008). Finally, the unions have battled to define their relationship with the ANC (Buhlungu et al., 2006, 2008). On the one hand, the Alliance has brought about progressive legislative reforms. On the other hand, the ANC has not been diverted from its essentially neoliberal orientation, although the unions have been able to halt planned privatizations. Whether the Alliance has emasculated the unions, or allowed them to consolidate their rights remains the subject of bitter debate within and without the union movement (ibid.).

The war brought the Mozambican economy to the brink of collapse by the early 1980s. Declining Soviet aid forced the Mozambican government to turn to the tender mercies of the IMF and the World Bank. Support for the latter was, in turn, contingent on neoliberal shock therapy. By the early 1990s, this had led to massive cutbacks in health and education spending, the cutting back of protective tariffs and cutting back of basic labour standards (Hanlon, 1996). In turn, increased overseas competition led to massive job losses: many of the rights and benefits workers had gained in the early years of independence were simply shed, whilst high levels of unemployment gave the remaining workers few options other than to simply comply with managerial authority, no matter how arbitrary.

The end of a protracted drought, which resulted in the wholesale desertion of peasant soldiers from both warring armies, and their return to peasant agricultural production, and the start of national-level negotiations towards democratization in South Africa, paved the way for a peace settlement in 1992, and democratic elections in 1994; RENAMO's continued support of the settlement was secured through the effective bribery of its leaders (Haines and Wood, 1995).

The benefits end of the war and the good rains were, however, marred by the adverse consequences of structural adjustment. From 1987 to 1999, large numbers of jobs were lost, and much of industry, education and health care devastated (Hanlon, 1996). However, by the end of the 1990s, the transport and service sectors revived, albeit that the lopsided nature of investment resulted in development being skewed towards the capital, on an even greater scale than had been the case in the past (Wood, 1999). Meanwhile, over-hasty privatizations and poor wages in the public sector contributed to a climate of worsening corruption (Hanlon, 1996).

But, what was the state of the Mozambican unions through all these adjustments? Following on independence, production councils were established in all Mozambican workplaces, drawing on the Dynamizing Groups. In 1983, these were grouped together into unions under the OTM, the Organization of Mozambican Workers. The OTM and individual unions were under the control of the ruling party, on the lines of the East European transmission belt model but remaining firmly under control of the ruling party (Hanlon, 1996, p. 78). In the early 1990s, OTM shed its links with FRELIMO, and became a sharp critic of the latter's conversion to neoliberalism (ibid.). By 2006, the OTM had 18 affiliates, and approximately 90 000 members (Webster et al., 2006b). In 1998, the breakaway Confederation of Free and Independent Trade Unions of Mozambique (CONSILMO) was launched by three former OTM affiliates that represented employees in the construction, hotel and transport industries.

As Webster and Wood (2005, p. 380) note, 'Mozambican labour law centres on the 1998 Labour Law, which accords workers a degree of job security and collective bargaining rights; however, casual workers are not included under its provisions'. In turn, this has meant that many firms have simply designated their employees as casuals to avoid falling under the law (Levy, 2003). A tripartite forum, the Consultative Labour Commission was established in 1994: its main activity has been setting a minimum wage, which is, in practice generally honoured in the breach (Webster and Wood, 2006a and 2006b).

CHANGES IN THE BALANCE OF POWER

How has the balance of power shifted between employers and employees in South Africa? On the one hand, employers are now very much more reluctant to underpin workplace practices with crudely racist measures. Rather, they are under considerable pressure to advance blacks into positions of management, which has, as we have seen, has had the effect of weakening shop floor organization. Whilst unions enjoy more legal rights (recent amendments to the law have, for example, strengthened the rights of subcontracted labour), high unemployment (up to 50 per cent) has weakened the relative bargaining power of unions (Wood and Glaister, 2008, Buhlungu et al., 2008). Hardly surprisingly, this has led to a decline in the incidence of strike action (ibid.). Finally, divisions in the unions opened up by far-reaching compromises with management (but also reflecting divisions dating back to debates within the unions in the 1980s), have led to the rise of a number of breakaway splinter unions, which, in turn, have forged links with local community organizations (Desai, 2002). However, splinter unions have, in most instances, made only limited headway. The most effective unions remain the COSATU ones, and the ANC remains the dominant political party.

Democratization has also resulted in white-dominated unions redefining themselves. In some cases – most notably in the public sector – they have engaged in joint industrial action with their COSATU counterparts. Whilst global competition has resulted in job losses, a large proportion of South African manufacturing (particularly European-owned firms, but also US firms such as General Motors) has opted for high wage–high productivity participative strategies, more on continental European than Third World sweatshop lines (Wood and Glaister, 2008). High levels of union penetration and centralized bargaining are often married with other participative bodies (e.g., quality circles) aimed at enhancing productivity (ibid.). This has allowed South Africa to become a leading exporter of high value-added goods such as automotive components. However, the high efficiencies have been associated with minimal job creation. South Africa also has a secondary industrial sector – largely in peripheral areas – that relies on very low wages and labour repression, discipline being enforced by the 'iron whip of hunger'. However, such enterprises are often only marginally profitable, with high entrance and exit rates.

High unemployment, and his denialist policies regarding AIDS, contributed to the fall of President Thabo Mbeki in 2008, and the rise of his long-term rival, Jacob Zuma. However, Zuma represents a broad coalition of interests, and it is not clear what he will bring to the table in terms of new policy options (Buhlungu et al., 2008). Where does all this leave unions? Union penetration rates in South Africa remain high, they enjoy a wide range of organizational rights backed up by the law, there are new signs of inter-union cooperation across racial divides and the fall of President Mbeki was partially the result of sustained union campaigning, lessons that his successors are sure to bear in mind. However, unions have battled to sustain organizational effectiveness in the face of all the problems reviewed above – the brain drain to management, periodic breakaways and the problems of formulating coherent policy alternatives to the broadly neoliberal policy direction of government. And, wholesale job losses have greatly weakened the position of employees vis-à-vis employers. South African employment relations remains bifurcated between sectors where employee rights – and responsibilities – are deeply entrenched, and areas where they are fragile and subject to endemic downward renegotiation (Buhlungu et al., 2008).

Neoliberal reforms in Mozambique have had, as we have seen, even more devastating effects. There has been little move towards high value-added manufacturing, with many firms closing or radically downsizing, seeking to secure competitiveness through low wages. Does this make Mozambique an archetype of bleak house employment relations? An extensive survey of Mozambican employers and employees by Webster and Wood (2005) revealed that most Mozambican employers relied on traditional approaches to people management, characterized by authoritarian patriarchalism, mitigated by informal personal relations with employees. For example, many employers prefer to make use of relatives of existing staff in recruiting (ibid.; Webster and Wood, 2006a). Again, low wages may be mitigated by the extension of informal credit (ibid.). Whilst formal structures for employee representation are generally absent, informal briefings and general meetings are commonly used to keep communications open (ibid.). South African multinationals have made some inroads into Mozambique, most notably in the retail sector, but, in general have exhibited a preference for low-wage models, rather than importing more pluralist South African practices. Whilst there have been some changes to Mozambican labour law regarding employee rights (e.g., strengthening minimum wages) these have been widely ignored by employers (ibid.).

Given their historical role in the state socialist era, as a transmission belt for the disseminating policies of the ruling party, and mobilizing its supporters, unions retain a residual role in many Mozambican workplaces, in the public and what remains of the manufacturing sectors (Webster et al., 2006b). However, their position is a weak one, with serious limitations in shop floor organization. A sizeable proportion of employers engaging in collective bargaining openly admit to regularly breaking collective agreements (Gumende, 1999; Webster et al., 2006a and 2006b). This has led Webster et al. (2006b) to conclude that Mozambican unionism may best be referred to as 'residual unionism', union membership reflecting a historical legacy, rather than a real expression of union strength.

What Mozambique and South Africa have in common is the prominence of the informal sector. Reduced job opportunities in the formal sector in both countries have made the informal sector a major employer. Most informal enterprises remain very small and undercapitalized, and with high exit rates (Webster et al., 2006a and 2006b). Employment relations are characterized by high levels of job insecurity, the widespread flouting of health and safety legislation, and generally poor terms and conditions of service (ibid.). Attempts by the unions to organize informal sector workers have had poor results. There is little sign that the unemployment rate will significantly drop in either country in the foreseeable future.

This leads us on to the issue as to the underlying forces impelling the changes. In both cases, reforms were impelled by serious underlying economic difficulties that in return, reflected both specific policy choices, and structural changes in the relative position of primary product producers in global markets. In the case of South Africa under high apartheid, minerals exports provided the basis for prosperity. Racial Fordism – that is, a combination of Fordist methods and racism both within and beyond the workplace as a mechanism for ensuring labour compliance – provided the dominant paradigm for work organization in mining and manufacturing. However, stagnant and declining prices for key minerals, and chronic skills shortages, forced the political and economic reforms reviewed above. In the case of Mozambique, the end of Soviet sponsorship, drought and protracted civil war led to radical changes in government policy, culminating in the neoliberal reforms of the 1990s.

FUTURE TRENDS AND ISSUES

South African labour legislation is highly progressive in world terms, entrenching a wide range of union rights, and positive measures to eradicate discrimination on the lines of gender, race and sexual orientation. At the same time, the bargaining position of unions has been undercut by very high unemployment. Whilst the country has a vibrant civil society that can provide a check against government power, the site of most meaningful political competition is within the ruling party. Despite internal divisions in the ANC, South Africa remains a dominant party system. Moreover, legislation remains common law based, with corporate governance practices being in line with the Anglo-American model. All these realities are unlikely to shift significantly in the foreseeable future. Hence, South African employee relations practices are likely to remain segmented, between cooperative pluralism in the high value-added export sector, and more repressive practices in smaller businesses and the informal sector. There is no evidence that the unions will be any more successful in organizing the latter areas than in the past. In the case of Mozambique, a civil law tradition is combined with a tradition of weak enforcement of the law. Politics has returned to a dominant party model, largely thanks to the incompetence of the opposition. There is no evidence that unions have devised viable new strategies to overcome their structural weaknesses. As is the case in South Africa, the informal sector is likely to grow in importance.

Does this mean that South Africa and Mozambique are becoming more alike? Both have governments that have followed broadly neo-liberal macroeconomic policies, have dominant party political systems, high unemployment and large informal sectors. In reality, there are many differences. First, South African civil society is relatively strong, whilst Mozambique's is weak. This means that there are fewer checks and balances on abuses of power by state and employers in the latter. Second, South Africa retains a large and highly competitive high wage–high productivity-based manufacturing sector, which provides both a bedrock of union power, and an example of best practice in terms of pluralist employment relations. Third, and, related to the second point, South Africa is a relatively wealthy country with a first-rate physical infrastructure, and Mozambique a poor one. South Africa is far better and more equitably integrated into global patterns of trade. This means that, whilst the relative position of each country may be subject to some adjustment, the gross disparities between the two are likely to persist for the foreseeable future: in employment relations terms, the key divide will be between 'sector-specific pluralism' in South Africa, and more general 'autocratic paternalism' in Mozambique.

CONCLUSION

Despite their geographic proximity, very different historical experiences have made for fundamental differences in employment relations between South Africa and Mozambique. In the case of South Africa, a long struggle for democratization was mirrored by challenges within the workplace to the racial Fordist status quo. This led to both the end of apartheid and the redefinition of work and employment relations. Within the export-orientated sector pluralist employment relations have been married with high value-added participative production paradigms. However, South Africa's relatively robust economic performance in the early 2000s has been a 'growth without jobs', with most South Africans being forced to seek work within the informal sector, or secondary, lower value-added firms servicing the domestic market.

Within Mozambique, democratization and neoliberal reforms brought wide-scale job losses. However, unions were in a very much weaker position than in South Africa, in part due to their historic role as a transmission belt for the ruling party. This has made for an employment relations model that is generally characterized by autocratic paternalism, with very few islands of genuine pluralism. Nor is it likely that the two countries are likely to become more alike. Very different legal traditions – and traditions of law enforcement – are matched by great disparities in the relative strength of unions and civil society, and in physical infrastructure. Whilst South African employment relations is likely to remain bifurcated, in Mozambique, there appears to be little prospect for the dissemination of more pluralist alternatives on a significant scale.

There are a number of broader theoretical implications and comparative lessons flowing from these cases. First, within a tropical African context, a comparative focus on formal institutional frameworks and laws can at best only provide an incomplete analysis. A full critique of comparative approaches to legal origins is provided in Chapter 4 in this volume by Cooney et al. However, there are specific limitations of such approaches that become immediately apparent through the Mozambican case study. Within Mozambique – and, indeed, much of tropical Africa – the capacity of the state to enforce laws is at best uneven, a capacity that has been further hollowed out through cutbacks in government spending imposed through the imposition of structural adjustment policies. Whilst formal regulation in South Africa is very much more effective, the large informal sector is still poorly regulated. Nonetheless, an analysis of formal institutions and regulations in South Africa will reveal far more about the practice of industrial relations in that country than would a comparable study in Mozambique. Second, the changing nature of employment relations in Africa needs to be understood in terms of broader changes in the global economy, and the volatile nature of terms of trade for primary commodities. South Africa has a very more developed – and resilient – manufacturing sector, making that country better equipped to withstand fluctuations in primary commodity prices, making for a larger and more durable formal jobs base.

Finally, union experiences of coping with adversity, successes and setbacks reflect the effects of specific sets of social circumstances, highlighting limitations on the transferability of models of union renewal between contexts. This does not preclude theorizing on the conditions for union renewal, but rather on the limits of best practice models that seek to identify ideal strategies and practices. Within South Africa, the specific historical experience of increasingly crisis-ridden authoritarian rule followed on by democratization provided both a basis for mobilization and a growing

political space for organization; the challenge for unions there is in securing and consolidating earlier gains. In contrast, within Mozambique,
the transmission belt role played by the unions in the state socialist era
ill-equipped them for the challenges of remobilization under structural
adjustment.

NOTE

1. The policy of seeking to integrate the colonies closely with the metropole; in practice this
   centred around encouraging the mass migration of unskilled peasants from Portugal and
   limited possibilities for advancement for educated blacks.

REFERENCES

Baskin, J. (1991), *Striking Back: A History of COSATU*, Johannesburg: Ravan.
BIP (n.d.), 'Industry in Mozambique', Maputo.
Bonner, P. (1978), 'The decline and fall of the ICU: A case in self-destruction', in E. Webster
   (ed.), *Essays in South African Labour History*, Johannesburg: Ravan.
Bradford, H. (1987), *A Taste of Freedom: The ICU in Rural South Africa, 1924–1930*, New
   Haven, CT: Yale University Press.
Buhlungu, S., Southall, R. and Webster, E. (2006), 'Conclusion: COSATU and the demo-
   cratic transformation of South Africa', in S. Buhlungu (ed.), *Trade Unions and Democracy:
   COSATU Workers' Political Attitudes in South Africa*, Pretoria: HSRC Press.
Buhlungu, S., Wood, G. and Brookes, M. (2008), 'Trade unions and democracy in South
   Africa: Union organizational challenges and solidarities in a time of transformation',
   British Journal of Industrial Relations, **46**(3), 439–68.
COSATU (2007), *About COSATU*, Johannesburg: COSATU.
Desai, A. (2002), *We are the Poors: Community Struggles in Post-Apartheid South Africa*,
   New York: Monthly Review Press.
Donnelly, E. and Dunn, S. (2006), 'Ten years after: South African employment relations
   since the negotiated revolution', *British Journal of Industrial Relations*, **44**(1), 1–29.
Friedman, S. (1987), *Building Tomorrow Today*, Johannesburg: Ravan.
Gumende, A. (1999), 'Industrial relations in a restructuring economy: Implications for cor-
   porate strategy and human resource management in Mozambique', Unpublished MBA
   dissertation, Nottingham: Nottingham Trent University.
Haines, R. and Wood, G. (1995), 'The 1994 election and Mozambique's democratic transi-
   tion', *Democratization*, **2**(3), 362–76.
Hanlon, J. (1991), *Mozambique: Who Calls the Shots?*, London: James Currey.
Hanlon, J. (1996), *Peace without Profit: How the IMF Blocks Rebuilding in Mozambique*,
   Oxford: James Currey.
Karis, T. and Carter, G. (1977), 'Overviews', in T. Karis and G. Carter (eds), *From Protest
   to Challenge: A Documentary History of African Politics in South Africa*, Vol. 3, Stanford:
   Hoover.
Lambert, R. (1988), 'Political unionism in South Africa: SACTU 1955–1965', Unpublished
   PhD thesis, Johannesburg: University of Witwatersrand.
Levy, S. (2003), 'The legal and administrative framework for labor relations in
   Mozambique', draft report, Maputo: SAL Consultoria e Investimentos.
Lewis, J. (1984), *Industrialization and Trade Union Organization in South Africa*, Cambridge:
   Cambridge University Press.

Maree, J. (1986), 'An analysis of the independent trade unions in South Africa in the 1970s', Unpublished PhD thesis, Cape Town: UCT.

Maree, J. (1987), 'Overview: The emergence of the independent trade union movement', in J. Maree (ed.), *The Independent Trade Unions*, Johannesburg: Ravan.

Markham, C. and Mothibeli, M. (1987), 'The 1987 mineworkers strike', *South African Labour Bulletin*, **13**(1), 58–95.

Morris, M. (1982), 'Wilson Rowntree: A history of SAAWU's organization', *South African Labour Bulletin*, **7**(4), 18–27.

Newitt, M. (1995), *A History of Mozambique*, London: C. Hurst.

Pitcher, A. (2002), *Transforming Mozambique: The Politics of Privatization*, Cambridge: Cambridge University Press.

Rachleff, P. (2001), 'The current crisis of the South African labour movement', *Labour/Le Travail*, **47**, 151–70.

Richardson, P. (1977), 'The recruitment of indentured Chinese labour for the South African gold mines 1903 to 1908', *Journal of African History*, **18**(1), 85–108.

Simons, H. and Simons, R. (1969), *Class and Colour in South Africa 1850–1950*, Harmondsworth: Penguin.

Smith, M. and Wood, G. (1998), 'The end of apartheid and the organization of work in South Africa's Eastern Cape Province', *Work, Employment & Society*, **12**(3), 479–95.

Southall, R. (2007), 'The ANC, black economic empowerment and state-owned enterprises', in S. Buhlungu, J. Daniel, R. Southall and J. Lutchman (eds), *State of the Nation: South Africa 2007*, Pretoria: HSRC Press.

Von Holdt, K. (2003), *Transitions from Below: Forging Trade Unions and Workplace Change in South Africa*, Durban: University of Natal Press.

Webster, E. (ed.) (1978), *Essays in South African Labour History*, Johannesburg: Ravan.

Webster, E. (1986), *Cast in a Racial Mould*, Johannesburg: Ravan.

Webster, E. (1987), 'Introduction to labour section', in G. Moss and I. Obery (eds), *SA Review*, **4**, Johannesburg: SARS/Ravan.

Webster, E. and Wood, G. (2005), 'Human resource management practice and institutional constraints: The case of Mozambique', *Employee Relations*, **27**(4), 369–85.

Webster, E., Wood, G. and Brookes, M. (2006a), 'International homogenization or the persistence of national practices?: The remaking of industrial relations in Mozambique', *Relations Industrielles/Industrial Relations*, **61**(2), 247–70.

Webster, E., Wood, G., Mtyingizana, M. and Brookes, M. (2006b), 'Residual unionism and renewal: Organized labour in Mozambique', *Journal of Industrial Relations*, **48**(2), 257–78.

Wilson, F. (1972), *Labour in the South African Gold Mines*, Cambridge: Cambridge University Press.

Wilson, M. and Thompson, L. (1971), *Oxford History of South Africa*, Vol. 2, Oxford: Oxford University Press.

Wood, G. (1999), 'Democratization in Mozambique: Trends and practices', *Democratization*, **6**(2), 156–70.

Wood, G. (2002), 'Organizing unionism and the possibilities for reconstituting a social movement role', *Labor Studies Journal*, **26**(4), 29–50.

Wood, G. and Glaister, K. (2008), 'Union power and new managerial strategies', *Employee Relations*, **30**(4), 436–51.

Wood, G. and Mahabir, P. (2001), 'South Africa's workplace forum system: A failed experiment in the democratization of work?', *Industrial Relations Journal*, **32**(3), 231–44.

Wood, G. and Psoulis, C. (2001), 'Globalization, democratization, and organized labor in transitional economies', *Work and Occupations*, **28**(3), 293–314.

14 Employment relations in France and Germany
Stefan Zagelmeyer

INTRODUCTION

France and Germany are two of the largest economies in Europe and are among the main driving forces of the European integration process. Despite their geographical proximity, marked differences in their historical, economic, political and social developments – associated with quite distinct institutional and cultural characteristics – have contributed to the development of two specific and different employment relations systems.

Since the mid-1970s, the two countries feature prominently in cross-national comparative research related to employment relations, broadly defined. Many projects can be linked to the convergence-versus-divergence debate as well as to the discussion of employment relations models (Hyman, 1994; Freeman, 1998).

In brief, the 'convergence hypothesis' claims that economic and/or technological pressures lead to a general trend towards the adoption of 'best practices' or global standards in management. This implies a trend towards convergence, which occurs irrespective of cultural and institutional factors; it is caused by such external contingencies as industry, size, technology and competitive imperatives. By contrast, the 'divergence hypothesis' suggests that management practices are embedded in cultures and institutions that are largely confined to geographical entities, such as regions and nation states, and that prohibit a rapid diffusion of 'best practice' across geographical and organizational boundaries.

There is an abundance of research on different employment relations models. In an analysis of work structure and work relations in relation to education, business organization and industrial relations, Maurice et al. (1980, 1986) – and likewise Silvestre (1974), Maurice and Sellier (1979), Sorge and Maurice (1990) and Marsden (1999) – find little evidence of convergence between the two countries, and conclude that differences between the two countries derive from significant societal effects.

In the varieties of capitalism and the comparative political economy literature, Germany features as the reference model for a coordinated market economy (Hall and Soskice, 2001), and Schmidt (2003) proposes the addition of French state capitalism as an additional category. In Esping-Andersen's (1990) typology of welfare capitalisms, both Germany and France are classified as conservative welfare regimes.

In addition, much comparative employment relations research has been undertaken on the two countries, focusing, for example, on shop stewards (Marsden, 1980), management and labour (Lane, 1989), communication and consultation (Kessler et al., 2004), workplace representation (Gumbrell-McCormick and Hyman, 2006), restructuring and collective bargaining (Boni, 2009), and the establishment of works councils (Rigby et al., 2009).

While it is impossible to summarize and discuss the existing research on France and Germany in a single chapter, the objective of this contribution is to introduce the reader to the similarities and differences concerning the industrial relations actors and processes in the two countries and to summarize and discuss recent developments in the light of the convergence-versus-divergence debate. After a short sketch of the historical development of employment relations in the two countries, this chapter first introduces the core features of the current employment relations systems. It then outlines the prevailing pattern of employment relations and recent developments, focusing first on employment relations actors and then on employment relations processes. The chapter concludes with a comparative analysis and discussion of the two employment relations systems.

The chapter has a number of limitations. To begin with, as far as Germany is concerned, it focuses mainly on the West German institutions and organizations established after World War II. Employment relations in East Germany between 1945 and 1990 are discussed elsewhere (e.g., Gill, 1991; Lumley, 1995; Maydell, 1996; Schwarzer, 1996). In addition, it cannot do justice to the research literature on the implications of reunification for employment relations and the East German transition (Koch, 1982; Jürgens et al., 1993; Schmidt, 1995; Upchurch, 1995; Hyman 1996; Schwarzer, 1996; Kädtler et al.,1997; Streeck, 1997; Frege, 1998a, 1998b, 1999a, 1999b; Turner, 1998; Fay, 2000; French, 2000; Schröder, 2000). Both topics would merit separate treatment. Also, we largely ignore employment relations in the public sector. For information on public sector employment relations, see Mosse and Tchobanian (1999) for France, Keller (1999) for Germany, and for recent developments in both countries see Bordogna (2007), Vincent (2008) and Dribbusch (2008b). A further shortcoming is the focus on traditional employment relations actors and institutions, while the literature on human resource management is not integrated. Again, if readers are interested in comparative HRM, they may wish to consult Rojot (1990), Cerdin and Peretti (2001) and Buyens et al. (2004) for France, and Conrad and Pieper (1990), Wächter and Müller-Carmen (2002) and Dietz et al. (2004) for Germany.

CORE FEATURES OF EMPLOYMENT RELATIONS IN FRANCE AND GERMANY

Both France and Germany industrialized later than Britain, during the mid-nineteenth century. In both countries, the unions came into existence in the second quarter of the nineteenth century, and became legal in 1869 in Prussia/Germany, and in 1884 in France. The first collective agreements occurred in the 1830s–40s in France and in 1873 in Germany (Goetschy and Jobert, 2010; Keller and Kirsch, 2010).

In France, while most of the current employment relations institutions and organizations were established in the immediate post-World War II period, and with an important turning point in the establishment of the Fifth Republic in 1958, they have their roots in development prior to World War II (Goetschy and Rozenblatt, 1992; Jefferys, 2000; Jenkins 2000; Capron, 2001; Goetschy and Jobert, 2010). In Germany, employment relations institutions were established both during and immediately after the foundation of the Federal Republic of Germany in 1949, with many institutions building on the pre-World War II experiences, especially those concerning employment relations during the 1919–33 Weimar Republic (Beal, 1955, 1956; Wachenheim, 1956; Fichter, 1990; Fürstenberg, 1993; Jacobi et al., 1998).

West Germany, the Federal Republic of Germany (FRG), recovered relatively quickly after World War II, while the eastern part (the German Democratic Republic, or GDR) joined the eastern block of satellite states of the Soviet Union (Gregory and Stuart, 1980, 1998). With German reunification in 1990 after the end of the Cold War, Germany became a unique kind of transition country, which integrated the socialist planned economy of the former GDR into the Western capitalist market-based economic system, and transferred its Western employment relations institutions to Eastern Germany.

Today, France and Germany are among the largest economies in the world. France is a leading European economy in the areas of transport equipment, retail and business services and in 2008 produced a gross domestic product (at market prices) of €1950 billion (estimated), had a population of 64 million, had an unemployment rate of 7.8 per cent and had an employment rate of 64.9 per cent (females: 58.3 per cent) (Eurostat 2009a, 2009b). In the same year, Germany had a GDP of €2495 billion, a population of 82 million, an unemployment rate of 7.3 per cent and an employment rate of 70.7 per cent (females: 59.2 per cent). Within the European Union, Germany is a leading economy for the manufacture of machinery, equipment and motor vehicles (ibid.).

Both countries are characterized by specific configurations of employment relations that are embedded in respective specific forms of political economies. France is famous for its *dirigiste* type of political economy (or state-managed capitalism), economic planning and industrial policy (Mitchell, 1972; Gregory and Stuart, 1980, 1998; Schmidt ,1996, 1997). The French economy, and thus also French employment relations, have always been strongly influenced by the state and the government in power at the time, be it in terms of public industrial policies, legislation or public ownership.

With respect to employees and employee representation, French trade unionism represents a patchwork rug of many competing trade unions, which are organized along political and/or religious lines, dominated by five major union confederations. Compared with other industrialized countries, union density in France is very low by international standards. The French employers, by and large, have a reputation for being either paternalistic or reactionary. Weak unions, unitarist employers – with the resulting lack of mutual recognition of social partners – paired with the continuous and discretionary intervention of the state in the economy and employment relations, led to a fragmented and complex employment relations system, operating under the auspices of a strong and determined state. Yet, despite the complexity of the institutional arrangements and the low levels of union density, collective bargaining coverage in France has traditionally been very high. So one may ask from the perspective of employee representation and voice, whether a high degree of collective bargaining coverage renders low levels of unionization and union density irrelevant.

Jenkins (2000, p. 3) argues that there are four core elements of the French model of employment relations, namely: 'powerful and dense bureaucracy in the administration of organizations, omnipresence of the state in the process of economic life (*dirigisme*), profound respect for hierarchy and tenacious status ascription in management, low-trust union-management relations liable to periodic explosive conflicts'.

The German system of employment relations, which was established in the Federal Republic of Germany after 1949 and extended after reunification to the new German states (*Länder*) in 1990, is closely associated with the principles of a social market economy, which are enshrined in the German Constitution. This form of political economy is characterized by a general preference for market coordination as organizing principle of economic activities, within a strong legislative framework, which on the one hand seeks to minimize market failures, and on the other hand ensures the implementation of democratic and ethical norms. This is supplemented by social policy and welfare state policies, which also includes the works constitution and co-determination (Gregory and Stuart, 1980, 1998; Ebner, 2006).

The 'German model' of employment relations has a number of core characteristics (Jacobi et al., 1992, 1998; Müller-Jentsch, 1995). The most important feature of the German model is the dual system of interest representation, which stipulates that unions and employers – or their respective associations – are responsible for collective bargaining, while works councils are the main bodies of collective interest representation outside collective bargaining. This dual system is based on a comprehensive set of statutory regulations. The Collective Agreement Act (*Tarifvertragsgesetz*, TVG) of 1949 stipulates that only trade unions have the right to conclude collective agreements, while the Works Constitution Act (*Betriebsverfassungsgesetz*, BetrVG) of 1952, as amended in 2001, regulates collective employee representation in private sector workplaces. Industrial action is lawful only if connected to collective bargaining, and strikes need to be officially recognized by a trade union. During the period covered by a collective agreement, both parties are obliged to maintain industrial peace (*Friedenspflicht*). Further characteristics of the traditional 'German model' are the high degree of legal regulation (or juridification), the relative centralization of collective bargaining, usually at industry level and the representative character of the organizations of collective interest representation, that is, trade unions, works councils and employers' associations (Jacobi et al., 1992)

EMPLOYMENT RELATIONS ACTORS

Trade Unions

Trade unions represent the interests of workers within the labour market, the political system and wider society. Union membership, organization, structure and power differ markedly between the two countries. Both countries have experienced a significant decline in overall union membership since the 1970s. In France, union membership declined from approximately 22 per cent of the workforce in 1975 to 14 per cent in 1985, to 9.1 per cent in 1995, and to less than 8 per cent (1.8 million members) in 2007 (OECD, 2010), with union membership concentrated in the public sector. France thus has the lowest union density of any of the OECD countries.

Trade union density in Germany moved from 35 per cent in 1975 and 1985 to 29 per cent in 1995, and to less than 20 per cent in 2007 (ibid.).

Immediately after reunification in 1990, when the Western employment relations structures were transferred to the new German states, union membership numbers soared from 8 to 12 million. Since then, union membership almost halved to 6.6 million in 2007 (ibid.).

The French union system can be characterized by pluralism, competition, fragmentation as well as lack of resources (Goetschy and Jobert, 2010). There are five national multi-industry trade union confederations, which are organized along political and religious lines, and have been competing throughout most of the post-war period (for details, see Goetschy and Rozenblatt, 1992; Freyssinet, 1993; Goetschy, 1998, 2010; Van Ruysseveldt and Visser, 1996):

- the *Confédération Générale du Travail* (CGT – General Confederation of Labour), established in 1895, with anarcho-revolutionary and communist origins and traditionally strong links to the French communist party;
- the *Confédération Française Démocratique du Travail* (CFDT – French Democratic Confederation of Labour), established in 1919, with Christian-democratic origins;
- the *Force Ouvrière* (FO – Workers' Power), established in 1948 via a split from the CGT, with a reformist but radicalized approach;
- the *Confédération Française des Travailleurs Chrétiens* (CFTC – French Christian Workers Confederation), established in 1964 via a split from the CFDT after the latter abandoned its Christian roots; and
- the *Confédération Française de l'Encadrement-Confédération Générale des Cadres* (CFE-CGC – General Confederation of Professional and Managerial Staff), which was established as a white-collar union in 1944.

These five unions have the status of 'representative' unions, which permits them to negotiate collective agreements, to nominate candidates for different bodies of employee representation, to get involved in the formulation of labour law, to be represented in governmental bodies and to have seats on social security bodies (N.N., 2007). In addition to these five unions, there are several additional autonomous union confederations, for example the UNSA (*Union Nationale des Syndicats Autonomes*), and the USS (*Union Syndicale Solidaire*), and autonomous sector-specific or occupational unions, which play a role in French employment relations, but are not 'representative' (Goetschy and Jobert, 2010).

The status of 'representative unions' was granted by public authorities in 1966, but has been challenged and became the most important topic in French employment relations in recent years. The regulations previously in force were amended by the 'Aubry Law' of 1998. In order to get state support, a trade union needs to obtain a majority of votes in the works council elections. Alternatively, it needs to be ratified by employees through a referendum. Collective agreements could no longer be valid if only signed by a 'representative' union, despite representing a minority of the workforce. Furthermore, the 1998 legislation then introduced the use of 'mandating' in collective bargaining, which allows a union without representative status to mandate an employee to negotiate a collective agreement in its name (Vincent, 1998).

In 2004 and 2008, statutory reform of collective bargaining aimed to increase dynamism in French collective bargaining. The 2004 law stipulated that for a collective agreement to be valid, it must have the support of a majority of representative unions or of trade unions with a majority of votes in workplace elections. In addition, lower-level collective agreements were allowed to deviate from higher-level agreements unless this would be explicitly forbidden by higher-level agreements, thus providing greater flexibility in collective bargaining. Finally, the reform allowed for negotiations at regional and local levels, permitting elected or mandated employees to negotiate where there were no union representatives at the company (N.N., 2000; Dufour, 2002, 2004).

In 2008, law fundamentally changed the rules in relation to both the validation of agreements and union representativeness (Pernot, 2009). It stipulates that unions seeking representativeness and wishing to bargain at company level (sectoral and national level) need to win 10 per cent (8 per cent) of the votes in the first round of workplace elections. 'Collective agreements will be valid only if they have been concluded by one or several trade unions that have obtained at least 30 per cent of the votes at workplace elections and without objection from trade unions that have obtained a majority of the votes' (Robin, 2008). Furthermore, where there are no union representatives in companies with fewer than 200 employees, employers will be permitted to negotiate with non-union workforce representatives (ibid.).

Despite Germany's reputation for its encompassing industry unions, the structure of the German trade union movement is more complex and merits careful attention. Keller and Kirsch (2010) argue that the structure of the trade union system established after World War II was organized according to the principles of industrial unionism (*Industriegewerkschaft*) and unitary unionism (*Einheitsgewerkschaft*). Accordingly, workers join the union that covers the company's industry, irrespective of occupation, religious or political orientation, or white-collar vs. blue-collar status. In addition, unions would not be affiliated to political parties, and there would be no competition or demarcation disputes between unions in one organization, because of a clear-cut sectoral division of labour between the industry unions. As far as the vertical division of labour between different unions is concerned, the (industry) unions are engaged in collective bargaining, while the peak federations engage in political lobbying activities.

At the national level, there are three trade union confederations. The most important one is the Confederation of German Trade Unions (*Deutscher Gewerkschaftsbund*, DGB), which organized 6.3 million members, 32.4 per cent of whom were women, in 2009 (DGB, 2010). The DGB is the umbrella organization of eight industry-related trade unions, the most important of which are the German Metalworkers' Union (*Industriegewerkschaft Metall*, IG Metall) with 2.3 million members in 2009, 17.7 per cent of whom were women, and the United Services Union (*Vereinte Dienstleistungsgewerkschaft*, ver.di) with 2.1 million members, 50.4 per cent of whom were women (DGB, 2010).

In addition to the DGB, there are two other union confederations. The German Civil Service Association (*Deutscher Beamtenbund und Tarifunion*, dbb) has 40 affiliated unions operating in the public and private service sectors, but focuses predominantly on the terms and conditions of civil servants. In 2009, DBB membership stood at 1.3 million members. The Christian Confederation of Trade Unions in Germany (*Christlicher Gewerkschaftsbund Deutschlands*, CGB) organizes 16 affiliated unions, with about 280 000 members in 2009.

There are a number of additional trade unions that are not affiliated to either of the three confederations but that are involved in collective bargaining. These cover, for example, occupations such as airline pilots, doctors, or engine-drivers, and are characterized by high levels of organizational density and the resulting collective bargaining power.

Recent years have seen a number of challenges for trade unions in Germany (Hassel, 2007). As one of the consequences of the precipitous falls in membership starting in the 1990s, the unions have reacted with a number of organizational changes, and union mergers in particular. In Germany in 1997, the miners' union (*IG Bergbau und Energie*), the chemical workers' union (*IG Chemie-Papier-Keramik*), and the leather workers' union (*Gewerkschaft Leder*) merged into the mining, chemicals and energy union (*Industriegewerkschaft Bergbau, Chemie, Energie*, IG BCE). The textiles and clothing industry workers' union (*Gewerkschaft Textil-Bekleidung*) and the union for employees in the wood and plastics industries (*Gewerkschaft Holz und Kunststoff*) merged with the metalworkers' union, IG Metall (Schulten and Zagelmeyer, 1997).

The year 2001 saw another major reorganization of the German trade union structures, when the German White-Collar Workers'

Union (*Deutsche Angestellten-Gewerkschaft*, DAG), the Public Services, Transport and Traffic Union (*Gewerkschaft Öffentliche Dienste, Transport und Verkehr*, OTV), the Media Union (*IG Medien*), the Commerce, Banking and Insurance Union (*Gewerkschaft Handel Banken und Versicherungen*, HBV), and the Postal Workers' Union (*Deutsche Postgewerkschaft*, DPG) merged to create the Unified Service Sector Union (*Vereinte Dienstleistungsgewerkschaft*, ver.di), representing almost 3 million workers in some 1000 different occupations (Behrens et al., 2002).

Employers and their Associations

The development and activities of employers and their associations have not yet attracted as much academic attention as the trade unions have done. For comprehensive introductions to business interest associations in the two countries, see Bunel and Saglio (1984) and Saurugger (2007) for France, and Bunn (1984) and Grote et al. (2007) for Germany.

In France, employers' associations emerged from the 1840s, first in order to oppose free trade, and later to oppose trade unions (Goetschy, 1998). At the national level, employer interests are mainly represented by MEDEF (*Mouvement des Entreprises de France*), which was established in 1999 as the successor organization of the CNPF (*Conseil National du Patronat Français*). MEDEF organizes 87 federations with over 600 associations and 165 regional organizations (Woll, 2005). There is no direct company membership at the confederation level (Van Ruysseveldt and Visser, 1996).

The CNPF, established in 1945, started to become involved in multi-sectoral negotiations in the late 1960s. However, there are other national-level employer organizations. Small and medium-sized enterprises are organized by the CGPME (*Confédération Générale des Petites et Moyennes Entreprises*), self-employed artisans by the UPA (*Union Professionnelle Artisanale*), and companies in the non-profit sector by USGERE (*Union des Syndicats et Groupements d'Employeurs Représentatifs de l'Economie Sociale*). Furthermore, there are the union of liberal professions *Union Nationale des Professions Libérales* (UNAPL) and the agricultural confederation *Fédération Nationale des Syndicats d'Exploitants Agricoles* (FNSEA). Finally, in contrast to these voluntary associations, there are the Chambers of Commerce and Industry (CCI), that is, the *Assemblée des Chambres Françaises de Commerce et d'Industrie* (ACFCI) and the *Assemblée Permanente des Chambres des Métiers* (APCM). Membership in these organizations is mandatory (Van Ruysseveldt and Visser, 1996; Woll, 2005).

In Germany, employers' interests are represented by a three-tier system.

The chamber system, with its peak association *Deutscher Industrie- und Handelstag* (German Association of Industry and Commerce, DIHT), represents the general economic interest of member companies and performs semi-governmental tasks, for example, within the training system. Membership is compulsory. The trade associations, with their umbrella association *Bundesverband der Deutschen Industrie* (Federation of German Industries, BDI), represent their members in the field of economic policy, mainly to the general public and government institutions. The original employers' associations, with their umbrella association *Bundesvereinigung der Deutschen Arbeitgeberverbände* (Confederation of German Employers' Associations, BDA), represent employers' interests in the field of social policy, and they negotiate collective agreements above company level. The employers coordinate their activities in the *Gemeinschaftsausschuss der Deutschen Gewerblichen Wirtschaft* (Joint Committee of German Business) and there are interconnections, especially between the BDI and the BDA, both in terms of individual delegates and in terms of national single-industry associations affiliated to both umbrella associations. This structure allows the employers to choose different strategies in different policy areas (Jacobi et al., 1992, 1998; Keller and Kirsch, 2010).

The employers' associations are organized as follows. The BDA represents the multi-industry and inter-regional interests of its members to government institutions, to the public and to international organizations, but it is not directly involved in collective bargaining. It amalgamates national single-industry employers' associations and regional multi-industry employers' associations. Companies are voluntary members of single-industry employers' associations, which exist at local, regional and national level. All members are also affiliated to multi-industry associations, which exist at local and regional but not national level. The employers' associations carry out a number of authorized functions under public law in delegated legislation, administration and jurisdiction, as well as collaborating in the enactment of regulations and ensuring the participation of their representatives in the administrative committees of self-governing institutions. Furthermore, they have the right to propose candidates for the labour courts and to represent their members in labour trials.

Membership statistics for the German employers' associations are not publicly available. For the united Germany, Jacobi et al. (1992) report a representation of 80 per cent of the workforce. Since the 1990s, both German trade unions and employers' associations have had growing membership problems. In Eastern German manufacturing, for example, membership fell from 36 per cent of companies (with 74 per cent of the workforce) in 1993–94 to below 10 per cent (with less than 30 per cent of the workforce) in 2003 (Zagelmeyer, 1997; Behrens et al., 2002; Brenke, 2004).

Silvia and Schroeder (2007) and Streeck (2009) report that the organizational density of the umbrella association of the regional employers' associations in the German metal and electrical industry (*Gesamtmetall*) in Western Germany had declined from 54.6 per cent of companies (with 73.8 per cent of the workforce) in 1985 to 25.5 per cent of companies (with 58.5 per cent of the workforce) in 2003. In Eastern Germany, organizational density declined from 35.7 per cent of companies (with 60.0 per cent of the workforce) in 1993 to 7.6 per cent of companies (with 21.5 per cent of the workforce) in 2003.

The employer associations reacted to these challenges in various ways. Some regional associations, for example in the engineering sector, have founded new parallel organizations that will not participate in industry-level bargaining. First reports of this phenomenon occurred in the early 1990s. This trend accelerated after the conclusion of the 1999 metalworking agreements. Some employers' associations have started to offer a so-called 'OT membership' status (OT stands for *ohne Tarifbindung*: 'not bound by collective agreement'), under which companies are full members of the association but are not covered by their association's industry-wide collective agreements (Behrens and Schulten, 2003; Silvia and Schroeder, 2007).

The State

Historically, the role of the state has been of great significance for employment relations in France and Germany, albeit in different ways. In France, three aspects of the relationship between the state and employment relations are of specific relevance. First, at historic turning points, when the left was becoming more powerful, the unions have pressed for new legislation. Second, beginning in the 1960s, the government has enacted laws based either on previous multi-sectoral agreements or on discussions between the social partners and the state. And third, more than in other countries, the French government influences wage-setting in the private sector through adjusting the national minimum wage (SMIC – *Salarie Minimum Interprofessional de Croissance*) (Goetschy and Jobert, 2010).

Thus, in France the state defines employment relations more closely than is the case in other Western European countries. As employer, the state not only sets the terms and conditions for the civil service but it also influences working conditions in the relatively strong public-sector enterprises. A related issue is the frequent attempt to modify terms and conditions in the public sector and thus to set an example for the private sector. In addition, the government frequently engages in revising the Labour Code (*Code du Travail*) and in extending collective agreements, and in this way it is often directly involved in shaping collective bargaining structures (Van Ruysseveldt and Visser, 1996).

There are several national tripartite bodies where the social partners are consulted in public policy-making. The Economic and Social Council (ESC) and the Planning Commissions involve employer and union representatives, as well as representatives of other interest groups. It appears, then, that the French government pursues its policies with respect to large-scale reforms, for example, through both the ESC and the Planning Commissions rather than by seeking consensus through a fully-fledged consultation process. In addition, the social partners are involved in bodies managing specific social security provisions (e.g., public health insurance and unemployment benefits), vocational training, as well as in the supplementary private health insurance system (*mutuelles*) and pension plans (N.N., 2007).

In Germany, too, the role of the state is also very strong, but the state defines the legal framework for economic transactions; it does not intervene directly in the markets. Thus, in the area of employment relations, there is a tight web of regulation that defines the rules of the game. There are a number of legal rules and principles that constitute the statutory framework of employment relations, ranging from the freedom of association enshrined in the Constitution (*Grundgesetz*) of 1949 to free collective bargaining as outlined in the Collective Agreements Act (*Tarifvertragsgesetz*) of 1949 and in the Co-Determination Act (*Betriebsverfassungsgesetz*) of 1952. Collective labour disputes, however, are based on case law.

In addition to defining the legal framework for employment relations, there have been several instances when the state has attempted to exert influence on the social partners through neo-corporatist policy arrangements, with major initiatives occurring and failing in the 1970s as well as in the 1990s (for details see below).

The importance of the state and the legal system in both countries justifies a closer look at the development of their political systems, which have been more volatile in France than in Germany, especially during the Fourth Republic from 1946 to 1958. After several successive conservative presidents since 1958, in 1981 the Socialists took over the presidency until 1995. Since then, centre-right presidents have been in office. Currently, the main actors in France are the *Union pour un Movement Populaire* (UMP), two small centrist parties, the Communist Party, the Socialist Party and the Greens. While the extreme right has recently declined in importance, especially after its defeat in the 2002 presidential election, the extreme left has gained political ground (Van Ruysseveldt and Visser, 1996; Goetschy and Jobert, 2010).

In Germany, with the exception of the reunification process, the political situation has been relatively stable since World War II. Governments of changing orientation and composition usually have considerable staying power, with only seven changes of government over the past six decades (Keller and Kirsch, 2010). However, the German party system has recently made a transition from a three-party system with two main conglomerates, the Social Democratic Party (SPD) and the Christian Democratic/Social Parties (CDU/CSU) with one small Liberal Party (FDP), to a more complex five-party system, which also includes the Green Party and the left wing DIE LINKE. The latter is the successor of the party (the SED) formerly ruling the German Democratic Republic, which merged with a Western left-wing election platform to extend its operations to West Germany. This change is particularly noteworthy, since the fragmentation occurred at the left of the political spectrum and thus may have important repercussions within the trade union movement.

EMPLOYMENT RELATIONS PROCESSES

This chapter distinguishes four different types of employment relations processes, namely workplace-level employee representation, board-level employee representation, collective bargaining and union involvement in national-level public policy-making.

Workplace-level Employee Representation

The picture of employee representation at the workplace and enterprise levels in France is quite complex, owing to the coexistence of several bodies with diverse composition, functions and legal bases. The different types of employee representation body are the result of government policies and/or legislation. Goetschy and Jobert (2010) report that these bodies were established in the context of particular social events. For example, workplace delegates (*délégués du personnel*), which deal with individual employee grievances, were set up by the Popular Front in 1936. The works councils (*comités d'entreprise*), dealing with workplace consultation, were established in 1945 following the end of World War II. And the workplace union branches (*sections syndicales*), which are involved in collective bargaining, came into existence after May 1968.

The two most important structures are the employee delegates and the works councils. The employee delegates (*délégués du personnel*) are elected by all workers in all establishments with ten or more employees, with additional specific regulations for smaller organizations. They are not union representatives, but they are often union members. The delegates are responsible for the implementation of collective agreements and legislation, and they pass on individual and collective grievances to management, which must see delegates collectively every month (Van Ruysseveldt and Visser, 1996; Goetschy and Jobert, 2010).

Works councils exist in private-sector organizations with more than 50 employees at company level (*comité d'entreprise*) or at plant level (*comité d'établissement*). They consist of an employer representative and elected workforce representatives. Representative unions can choose a union observer. In multi-establishment organizations, works councils also form a central works council (*comité central d'entreprise*) or a group-level works council (*comité de groupe*). Works councils have information rights in areas such as the economic and social situation and new technologies. Employers need to inform the works council every three months on the state of the company, and the employment structure and situation. Every year the works council receives a fairly comprehensive annual report covering all aspects of business management. The works council needs to be informed and consulted on an ad hoc basis on issues related to the economic and legal organization of the company, including redundancies, mergers and acquisitions, social plans, employment conditions and vocational training; they have a budget to manage social and cultural activities. Works councils are obliged to discuss profit-sharing arrangements and working hours policies, the implementation of which requires mutual agreement (Van Ruysseveldt and Visser, 1996; Capron, 2001; Goetschy and Jobert, 2010).

While employee delegates and the works council are normally separate, the same people can be elected to both institutions, and since 1993 both institutions may form – under certain conditions, for example, in establishments between 50 and 200 employees – a single entity, the *délégation unique*. A third type of committee is responsible for health and safety issues (Van Ruysseveldt and Visser, 1996; Goetschy and Jobert, 2010).

While the committees mentioned above include employee representatives elected by the entire workforce, local union branches have the right since 1968 to appoint delegates (*délégués syndicaux*) from among the workforce, their total numbers varying with the size of the company. These delegates are responsible for collective bargaining at company level.

As far as an assessment of the different structures is concerned, Goetschy and Jobert (2010) argue that the French institutions of employee representation did not grow in a carefully designed and systematic way, thus leading to a high degree of complexity, a lack of role clarity and some overlap of responsibility.

Apart from collective employee representation, French employees have the right to individual representation with respect to working conditions. The specific form of this, for example, regular meetings between worker and supervisor, needs to be regulated by company-level collective agreement.

In Germany, private-sector workplace-level employee representation is governed by the Works Constitution Act (*Betriebsverfassungsgesetz*, BetrVG), which was passed in 1952 and amended in 1972, 1988 and 2001. In establishments with five or more employees, employees have the right to elect a works council, should they so wish. Works councillors are formally independent of the trade unions but are often union members. Works councils have certain information, consultation and co-determination rights, but they are not allowed to bargain on issues that are subject to collective agreements except in cases where such agreements explicitly delegate bargaining authority to the works council. Works council rights relate, among other things, to compensation, staffing, overtime, transfers and dismissals, and economic or financial issues. In contrast to the trade unions, works councils cannot resort to any form of industrial action. Management and works councils negotiate – by law, in a spirit of mutual trust – works agreements (*Betriebsvereinbarungen*), regulating issues that fall into the domain of works council competence. Where works councils have co-determination (or veto) rights, they restrict the prerogative of management. Public-sector employees are covered by several Staff Representation Acts (*Personalvertretungsgesetze*) (Jacobi et al., 1992, 1998; Keller and Kirsch, 2010).

In addition to the formal structures of employee representation via works councils, there is also a system of union workplace representatives (*gewerkschaftliche Vertrauensleute*), who represent the link between the trade union and the union members concerning collective bargaining or any other issues. Yet, the relationship between the two elements of workplace employee representation is an intricate one, as the works council has traditionally been dominated by union members, and the unions have over certain periods of time used the works council as bargaining agent (Miller, 1978; Marsden, 1980; Streeck, 1981; Klikauer, 2004).

In 2001, the new Works Constitution Act (*Betriebsverfassungsgesetz*, BetrVG) adjusted several provisions of the old Act to the altered business environment. The new Act included stipulations concerning the simplification of the election procedures, reform of organizational structures, and the extension of the councils' participation rights. It also included a 'gender equality quota' to boost women's representation in works councils (Behrens, 2001; Behrens and Schulten, 2003; Addison et al., 2004b).

The relationship between collective bargaining and co-determination is a separate and additional issue. In 1999, the Federal Labour Court (*Bundesarbeitsgericht*, BAG) ruled that a union can take the employer to court if it feels that a works agreement between employer and works council violates a valid collective agreement. This judgement needs to be seen against the background of a growing number of so-called 'employment pacts' (*Bündnisse für Arbeit*), in which employer and works council agree on employee concessions in exchange for employment-related guarantees, for example to reduce job losses or to maintain jobs. In some cases, there have been discussions as to whether these agreements contravene collective agreements (Behrens et al., 2002).

The IAB Establishment Panel (*IAB Betriebspanel*) provides for information on the coverage rate of works councils and of other forms of employee representation. Of all the establishments that are eligible for a works council (five or more employees), only 10 per cent had a works council in 2009, covering 45 per cent of the workforce in West Germany and 38 per cent of the workforce in Eastern Germany. However, works council coverage is strongly related to establishment size, as 90 per cent of German establishments with more than 500 employees have a works council. While there is no significant change in works council coverage in comparison to 1996, workforce coverage has declined by 6 per cent in West Germany and 5 per cent in Eastern Germany (Ellguth and Kohaut, 2010).

Board-level Employee Representation

In France as well as in Germany, corporate governance regulations and policies involve employee representatives, albeit in quite different forms and configurations (Charkham, 1994, 2005). In France, based on the French Declaration of Human Rights, Article 31 of the Constitution of the 5th Republic of 1958 states the following: 'Every worker, through his/her delegates, has the right to participate in the collective determination of working conditions and the management of companies'. A 1946 decree provides that two or four members of the works council may participate on the board of directors or the supervisory board. In 1993, the Socialist government extended the presence of elected workforce representatives to the boards of all publicly controlled companies (Rehfeldt, 1998).

While in theory the French system of board-level representation is monistic – with the board being authorized to manage and monitor the management of the company – in practice, however, the company is managed by a group of top executives, and the role of the board of directors is limited to establishing the company's overall strategy and monitoring its implementation. Usually, the managing director is both president of the board of directors and head of the company. In very rare cases, the board of directors has been replaced by a supervisory board, which then includes workforce representatives. The number of the employee representatives on the board depends on the status of ownership (public versus private), legal status and on whether or not there is a works council. If representatives are appointed by the works council, they will be members of the works council and thus employees of the company, and they will have a consultative vote only (Rehfeldt, 1998).

Complexity and a high level of juridification are the key characteristics of the German system of board-level employee representation. In practice, Germany witnesses a growing diversity in the way that co-determination is implemented and also in the growing importance of informal additions to and modifications of formal co-determination legislation (Schulten and Zagelmeyer, 1998b). In Germany it is legislation rather than collective bargaining that plays the key role in the regulation of board-level employee representation.

Traditionally, German corporate governance knows the institutional and functional separation of management and direction on the one side and supervision on the other, a so-called 'dualistic' or 'two-tier structure'. The legal framework for the German company constitution (*Unternehmensverfassung*) observes a distinction between the management board (*Vorstand*), which is responsible for managing the business, the shareholder's meeting (*Hauptversammlung*), within which the shareholders exercise their powers by voting on resolutions, and the supervisory board (*Aufsichtsrat*), which is obligatory for some companies, depending on the legal status. Its essential function is to supervise the way in which the business is managed. It monitors the management board and has the authority to appoint and to remove members of that board.

The German system of board-level employee representation is mainly based in co-determination law plus, in a relatively small number of cases, company-level agreements. Three statutes for different sectors of the economy as well as sizes and types of company regulate board-level co-determination.

Co-determination in the coal, iron and steel industry is governed by the 1951 Coal, Iron and Steel Industry Co-Determination Act (*Montan-Mitbestimmungsgesetz*) as amended on 19 December 1985, and by the Co-Determination Amendment Act of 7 August 1956 as amended on 20 December 1988. Its sector-specific operation applies to companies in these industries that regularly employ over 1000 workers. The law also applies to corporations in other sectors of economic activity but with subsidiaries within the coal, iron and steel industry if those subsidiaries produce at least 20 per cent of the group's output or employ more than 2000 workers. Half of the members on the supervisory board represent the employees and half represent the shareholders ('parity co-determination'). And there is also one additional member, who has a casting vote and who must be elected by the shareholders' meeting on the proposal of the majority of both factions on the supervisory board. The company's management board must include a labour director, a member who is responsible for personnel management and whose nomination requires the approval of the employees' representatives on the supervisory board.

The 1952 Works Constitution Act (*Betriebsverfassungsgesetz*) covers companies with 500 or more employees, and was superseded by the One-Third Participation Act (*Drittelbeteiligungsgesetz*) in 2004. Under this law, employee representatives occupy one-third of seats on the supervisory board. Representatives are elected by the entire workforce in a secret ballot. Candidates for election may be nominated either by the works council or by at least 10 per cent of the workforce.

Last, the 1976 Co-Determination Act (*Mitbestimmungsgesetz*) covers all standard forms of company normally employing more than 2000 workers. This provides for equal numbers of representatives from the employee and company sides on the supervisory board. The seats allocated to workers' representatives are divided between company employees and candidates proposed by trade unions represented in the company. In principle, representatives in companies employing fewer than 8000 employees are directly elected by the workforce, while those in larger companies are elected through a delegate-based electoral college system. Candidates for election as trade union representatives on the board must be nominated by trade unions represented in the company. However, the procedure for electing the chair of the supervisory board stipulates that, if a second ballot is necessary, the chair is elected by the shareholders' representatives while the employee representatives may elect only the vice-chair. In the event of a tie, the chair has two votes in the second ballot and hence can give the casting vote in favour of the shareholders' side. The shareholders' representatives are elected by the appropriate shareholders' meeting or the company general meeting.

Collective Bargaining

Collective bargaining is the core process of traditional industrial or employment relations, which may occur in a multiplicity of configurations (Zagelmeyer, 2004). In France, collective bargaining can theoretically take place at all levels in the economy, as long as recognized actors are involved. Agreements are usually concluded at national level, multi-industry level, branch level and company level (Goetschy and Rozenblatt, 1992; Van Ruysseveldt and Visser, 1996; Goetschy, 1998; Goetschy and Jobert, 2010). There are few cases of local or regional collective bargaining.

The relationship between the different bargaining levels was traditionally based on the principle of favourability (*principe de faveur*), which allowed lower-level deviations from higher-level regulation if the local regulation was more favourable from the perspective of the employee. This principle has been abandoned in favour of the principle of the legality of the agreement (*plancher legal*), according to the 2004 Fillon Law, which permits derogation agreements and allows for decentralized collective bargaining with greater autonomy and flexibility (N.N., 2007).

While several government-initiated reforms have increased the importance of decentralized collective bargaining, for example the 1982 Auroux Laws (Caire, 1984; Eyraud and Tchobanian, 1985; Howell, 1992), collective agreements at industry level remain important. Industry-level agreements establish the basic terms and conditions of employment for the industry and can be extended by the Minister of Labour (Van Ruysseveldt and Visser, 1996). The extension of collective agreements partly explains the high level of collective bargaining coverage in France. As far as bargaining issues are concerned, labour laws stipulate that collective bargaining on wages, job qualifications, equal opportunities and lifelong learning are to be conducted on a regular basis. Companies with 300 or more employees are legally required to bargain on working conditions, human resource planning and qualifications (Goetschy and Jobert, 2010).

After two decades of decline, the 1990s saw the resurgence of multi-industry bargaining, often initiated by the government to support and stabilize social partnership in employment relations and social policy (ibid.). A number of national inter-sectoral agreements were reached, for example on pension reform, unemployment benefit and lifelong access to training in 2003 (Dufour, 2004), on teleworking, temporary employment workers and on the employment of older workers in 2005 (Broughton, 2007), or on the development of training throughout the working life, professionalization and securing career paths in 2009 (Alleki, 2009). Some of the negotiations took several years before an agreement was reached. Thus, over the years, multi-industry bargaining has embarked on national-level political change in the areas of social as well as European policy.

In Germany, collective bargaining is relatively centralized and takes place mainly in the form of regional industry-level bargaining. In order to be able to participate in multi-employer collective bargaining, a company has to be member of a *Tarifträgerverband*, an employer association meeting the legal conditions for being a collective bargaining partner according to the Collective Bargaining Agreements Act. Collective agreements are binding for all members of the negotiating groups. At the request of one of the social partners, the Federal Minister for Labour and Social Affairs can declare the general binding validity of a collective agreement that covers not less than 50 per cent of the employees to all employees within that region and industry (*Allgemeinverbindlicherklärung*, Section 5 TVG), if the trade union and/or employer organization signing the agreement have applied for such an extension, if the extension is deemed to be 'in the public interest' and if a parity committee consisting of six union and employer representatives (from other industries) approve the request by a majority of at least four votes. Since 1999, the Federal Ministry of Labour is allowed to declare a collective agreement to be generally binding by a ministerial directive under certain circumstances, without consulting the committee.

Trade unions may conclude collective agreements with employers' associations (*Verbandstarifverträge* – multi-employer collective agreements), or individual employers (*Firmentarifverträge* – single-employer collective agreements). There are three main types of collective agreements: (1) wage agreements, (2) wage classification framework agreements and (3) umbrella agreements about working conditions. In addition, hybrid forms and agreements concerning special issues, for example, work organization, exist. Decisions about issues, duration and level of negotiation are left to the social partners.

Collective bargaining is mainly conducted at industry level, but is – in certain industries – also quite frequent at national or company level. Theoretically, collective bargaining is even possible at the level of the umbrella organization. Coordination of the negotiations takes place within the national single-industry associations across regions and within the BDA across industries. Every year the BDA sets up recommendations that create a framework for the conduct of collective bargaining. Since 1965 they have been brought together periodically in the strictly confidential 'catalogue of questions concerning the coordination of wage and collective bargaining'.

Compared with many other industrialized Western countries, collective bargaining coverage is still relatively high in France and Germany. In France, collective agreements determine the terms and conditions of employment for about 90 per cent of the workforce, largely as a result of the widespread extension of collective agreements to entire sectors, other geographical regions or other economic sectors.

Despite a substantial increase in the total number of collective agreements since the mid-1990s, there has been a controversial debate about the erosion of centralized collective bargaining in Germany. In 2007, about 70 000 valid collective agreements were registered at the Federal Ministry of Labour and Social Affairs (*Bundesministerium für Arbeit und Soziales*, BMAS), 53 per cent of which were multi-employer agreements and 47 per cent of which were company agreements (Dribbusch, 2008a). This compares with 38 000 agreements in 1991 (71.1 per cent of which were multi-employer agreements and 28.9 per cent of which were company agreements) and 51 600 in 1999 (62.2 per cent of which were multi-employer agreements and 37.8 per cent of which were company agreements) (Müller-Jentsch and Ittermann, 2000), implying an increase of 84 per cent in 16 years.

While the total number of collective agreements has increased, there has been a steady decline of collective bargaining coverage since the early 1990s. According to information from the IAB Establishment Panel, 39 per cent of all establishments in Western Germany (with 65 per cent of employees) and 23 per cent of all those in Eastern Germany (with 51 per cent of employees) were covered by collective bargaining agreements in 2009 (Ellguth and Kohaut, 2010). However, about 40 per cent of companies with no collective agreement used sectoral agreements as a point of reference for determining pay and working conditions. In 1995, collective bargaining coverage stood at 62 per cent of workplaces (with 83 per cent of the workforce) in Western Germany. The earliest data available for Eastern Germany is 43 per cent of workplaces (with 73 per cent of the workforce) in 1996 (Müller-Jentsch and Ittermann, 2000).

In 2009, 36 per cent (1995: 54 per cent) of West German and 19 per cent (1996: 28 per cent) of Eastern German workplaces were covered by a sectoral collective agreement. The proportion of the workforce covered by a sectoral agreement was 56 per cent (1995: 73 per cent) in West Germany and 38 per cent (1996: 56 per cent) in Eastern Germany. As far as company-level bargaining is concerned, in 2009, 3 per cent (1995: 8 per cent) of West German and 4 per cent (1996: 15 per cent) of Eastern German workplaces were covered. The percentages of the workforce covered by these agreements were 9 per cent (1995: 10 per cent) in West Germany and 13 per cent (1996: 17 per cent) in Eastern Germany (Ellguth and Kohaut, 2010; Müller-Jentsch and Ittermann, 2000).

The debate about the erosion of collective bargaining in Germany is controversial (Hassel, 1999, 2002; Klikauer, 2002). On the one hand, there is evidence of the decentralization of various collective bargaining issues and a continued creeping erosion of branch-level bargaining coverage, with increasing numbers of private-sector companies bargaining at the company level. In addition, there are reports of breaches of collective agreements (Schulten and Zagelmeyer, 1998a; Ellguth and Kohaut, 2010).

On the other hand, there have been reports of new collective agreements in emerging sectors such as industry-related services or new telecommunications operations, which previously had no agreements

(Schulten and Zagelmeyer, 1998a). In particular, employers are demanding more company-specific regulations on working conditions, leading to the increasing importance of opening clauses in branch-level agreements, which allow companies to a certain extent to diverge from collectively agreed standards (Schnabel and Kohaut, 2007).

Involvement of the Social Partners in Public Policy-making

While the extent to which the French employment relations system includes corporatist elements remains controversial, recent years have seen an increase in the number of tripartite conferences organized by the French government. The government's intention in organizing these conferences is often to encourage the social partners to reach an inter-sectoral agreement on a particular issue. Occasionally, the government threatens to pass a law based on its own proposals if the social partners are unable to reach an agreement. Examples of such events include conferences on working conditions and occupational health in 2008 (Lecomte, 2008), and on working conditions and gender equality, employment, purchasing power and working conditions at small companies in 2007 (Rehfeldt, 2008).

Sometimes these national tripartite conferences fail, as the conference on employment, pay and working time failed in 1997, when government proposals to establish a statutory 35-hour working week led the CNPF to pull out of the negotiations and the president of the CNPF to step down from his position (Bilous, 1997).

The year 2007 saw the emergence of a new law on social dialogue (*Loi de Modernisation Sociale*), which obliges the French government to consult with trade unions and employers' associations before proposing labour law reforms in the areas of labour relations, employment and vocational training. Based on background information provided by the government, consultations with social partners could lead to a cross-sectoral collective agreement, which could then be considered by the government when drafting new legislation. In 'emergency' situations, the government can act unilaterally but needs to justify its position, which can be challenged by the social partners. The consultation process takes place in the National Collective Bargaining Commission (*Commission Nationale de la Négociation Collective*, CNNC); the Higher Employment Committee (*Comité Supérieur de l'Emploi*); and the National Council for Lifelong Vocational Training (*Conseil National de la Formation Professionnelle Tout au Long de la Vie*, CNFPTLV). In return, the law requires the social partners to provide a progress report on cross-sector collective bargaining and an annual programme, while the government reports on consultation developments (Rehfeldt, 2007).

Discussion of a draft bill had taken place in 2003. It was intended – subject to certain conditions – to give decentralized collective bargaining priority and to permit deviations vis-à-vis sectoral, inter-sectoral and national-level collective bargaining, thus changing the previous 'favourability' principle that stipulated that lower-level regulations (such as company-level or sector-level negotiations) may only improve terms and conditions stipulated at higher level(s). In addition the law stipulates that, in order to be valid, collective agreements must have the support of (or not be opposed by) the majority of representative trade unions or of unions representing a majority of employees (Dufour, 2004). The law is based on a 'common position' of the social partners adopted in 2001 and needs to be seen in the broader context of discussions of comprehensive employment relations and collective bargaining reform (N.N., 2000; Dufour, 2002). Topics in this controversial debate range from social policy issues (e.g., sickness insurance) to employment policy issues (e.g., vocational training) and the representativeness of unions, as well as the general structure of employment relations, especially as far as the demarcation between social partners and the government is concerned (Dufour, 2000, 2002). Arguing that the state would not leave sufficient discretion for the social partners, MEDEF and CGPME withdrew their involvement in the joint management of social security funds (Dufour, 2002). While MEDEF hoped for increased employer flexibility in autonomous collective bargaining, the unions feared that employees in weaker companies might be disadvantaged (Dufour, 2000).

An illustration of the link between the social partners' involvement in public policy-making and collective bargaining is provided by developments concerning the statutory introduction of the 35-hour working week, which represents the most controversial and most important issue in French employment relations during the past two decades. The debate on mandatory reductions in weekly working hours started to become serious in 1997, with the tripartite conference. Criticism of CNPF of the government plans led CNPF to withdraw its involvement in national inter-sectoral negotiations (Freyssinet, 1998).

In 1998, a guidelines and incentives law on the reduction of working time (*loi d'orientation et d'incitation relative à la réduction du temps de travail*) – the first Aubry Law – became effective, leading to an unexpected dynamism of sectoral bargaining (Freyssinet, 1998) and an expansion of collective bargaining activities in the following years. The first Aubry Law was in force until the end of 1999; to encourage bargaining on reduced working time before the adoption of definitive legislation, the second Aubry Law was passed in 1999 (Jefferys, 2000).

In 2002, the new French government allowed small businesses with fewer than 20 employees to raise their overtime quotas (Dufour, 2003), and in 2005 it permitted additional overtime as well as collective or even individual bargaining on increased working hours to all companies (Dufour, 2005).

Eventually, the 2008 law on 'renewing social democracy and working time reform' permitted the renegotiation of those agreements, ten years after the passage of the Aubry Law. Among other strategies for employers to increase flexibility, companies are now allowed to negotiate the amount of overtime previously set at sectoral level (Robin, 2008).

The developments in Germany have been quite different. In the mid-1990s, initiatives involving the social partners and the federal as well as the regional governments spread to establish employment alliances and pacts at all levels (except at the national level) in order to avoid redundancies and sometimes even to create new jobs. These have ranged from regional or sectoral tripartite or bipartite employment alliances or pacts to company-level agreements between management and works councils or trade unions. Some agreements took the form of declarations of intent, others of legally binding collective or works agreements (Schulten and Zagelmeyer, 1997). The first national pact was the 'Employment Alliance' for Eastern Germany established by the social partners and the CDU–CSU–FDP government, which was abandoned by the DGB in May 1998, arguing that employers and government would not have kept their part of the bargain, while unions had delivered a moderate wage policy (Schulten and Zagelmeyer, 1998a).

In December 1998, following the election of a SPD–Green government, the government and representatives of the social partners agreed to establish a new national 'Alliance for Jobs, Training and Competitiveness' (*Bündnis für Arbeit, Ausbildung und Wettbewerbsfähigkeit*) in a 'Joint Declaration of the Alliance for Jobs, Vocational Training and Competitiveness' (*Gemeinsame Erklärung des Bündnisses für Arbeit, Ausbildung und Wettbewerbsfähigkeit*). This declaration described the parties' common goals and set out the organizational structures of the permanent tripartite body (ibid.). The tripartite forum led to several initiatives aimed at creating and safeguarding employment (Behrens et al., 2002). Among other things, the alliance adopted a joint statement on an 'employment-oriented bargaining policy' in January 2000, which for the first time in German history implied that a tripartite institution had issued recommendations, albeit not legally binding ones, before the beginning of a collective bargaining round. The statement included demands that (1) the available 'distributive margin' (*Verteilungsspielraum*) should be based on productivity and used primarily to create new jobs for job-creating agreements, and that (2) early retirement schemes should be extended

(Behrens et al., 2000). However, criticism of the alliance over time gradually increased among employers and trade unions, leading to the opting out of two DGB-affiliated unions of the alliance (ibid.). In 2001, the alliance promulgated a joint statement recommending that the social partners should conclude new collective agreements to secure and improve further training at the company level (Behrens et al., 2002). Following increasing tensions between employers and unions on the issue of pay policy in a top-level meeting in January 2002, no further top-level meetings took place in 2002, and ceased to occur in February 2003, when the unions withdrew their support as a consequence of a conflict with the employers' side over wage policy (Dribbusch, 2005)

Industrial Action

While the right to strike is guaranteed by the French Constitution, there is little regulation of strike activities for the private sector. Since 1963, public-sector unions have been required to give five days notice before a strike. According to the French courts, a strike is lawful if it is related to employment relations issues. A sophisticated system for dispute settlement, which includes conciliation, mediation and arbitration, is not very frequently used (N.N., 2007). While industrial action in France is rather spontaneous, and escalation is unpredictable, the duration of strike activity is usually fairly short. Reasons for this may be the lack of financial resources of the trade unions and the absence of strike pay (Goetschy and Jobert, 2010). The fragmented and uncoordinated union system as well as the rather adversarial orientation of unions and employers leads to frequent industrial action activities in France.

In Germany, strikes and lockouts are lawful instruments of industrial action, but they need to be connected to terms and conditions of new collective agreements, which are bargained over (Keller and Kirsch, 2010). Strike activity is usually related to collective bargaining processes at industry or company level. Industry-level industrial action is usually coordinated centrally by the trade unions and employer associations. The overall level of strike activity in Germany is relatively low by international standards, stemming possibly from the degree of centralization, the separation of collective bargaining at industry level from workplace/ employment relations, and a sophisticated grievance, arbitration and mediation system (ibid.). While statutory mediation and arbitration procedures are absent, trade unions and employers' associations have concluded joint dispute resolution procedures (*Schlichtungsvereinbarungen*) in many industries.

DISCUSSION: FRENCH AND GERMAN EMPLOYMENT RELATIONS BETWEEN CONTINUITY AND CHANGE

The previous sections have summarized the main trends concerning the employment relations actors and processes since the 1990s, while largely ignoring employment relations policies, outcomes and performance implications (for reviews of recent work on Germany, see Frege, 2002; Addison et al., 2004a; Behrens and Jacoby, 2004).

Employment relations in France and Germany have gone though a number of changes over time. The changes concern almost all areas and levels of employment relations and the crucial question is about the extent to which they can have a significant impact on the structures and principles upon which employment relations in both countries are based as well as on the day-to-day operations. Both France and Germany have witnessed a decline in union membership and coverage, albeit from different baselines. The jury is still out about the impact of the new regulations on representativeness on union structures in France. Germany has experienced a wave of union mergers, and has recently become aware of the challenges of occupational unions. On the employers' side, there is (still) relatively little information available on the developments of the French employers' associations. German employers' associations have seen a serious decline in membership figures, and – as a reaction – dissociation of associational membership from collective bargaining by establishing new associations or introducing a differentiated membership status.

The picture concerning collective bargaining is somewhat mixed. Both countries have experienced an increase in overall collective bargaining activities, measured in terms of the total number of agreements. In France, this has certainly been triggered by the legislative reforms supporting decentralized bargaining. The causes of this phenomenon are less obvious for Germany, especially considering the declining collective bargaining coverage. In France, collective bargaining coverage has remained fairly stable, at a very high level. Both countries have witnessed the growing importance of decentralized collective bargaining.

Concerning employee representation, coverage rates concerning works councils in both countries (and other bodies in France) seem to be fairly stable, and in recent years these institutions have taken on additional tasks and functions in areas related to collective bargaining. In France, this was largely the result of state intervention and legislation, while the driving forces in Germany were the respective actors, management and works councils.

Beyond the somewhat simplifying description of actors, institutions, processes and the respective developments, two questions arise. First, what factors act as drivers of stability, ensuring continuity in the respective employment relations systems, and which factors act as drivers of change? And second, moving to a comparative analysis, to what extent can we identify trends of convergence and divergence between France and Germany?

Concerning the issue of drivers of stability and change, commentators (Howell, 1992; Streeck, 1997; Schmidt, 2003) argue that the economic imperative of competitiveness – no matter whether contextually associated with internationalization, globalization or Europeanization – pushes both countries towards deregulation, privatization, more flexible arrangements and decentralized institutional configurations. In both countries, there are reports that this trend has shifted the balance of power in employment relations in favour of the employer side. Schmidt (1993), Hancké (2002) and Streeck (2009) argue that companies have been given increased liberties in the respective employment relations systems and that business subsequently used and instrumentalized the institutional structures available to them for pressing for institutional changes in order to increase competitiveness. Streeck (2009) for Germany and Jenkins (2000) for France, argue that the existing and traditional employment relations institutions are no longer capable of performing their functions effectively vis-à-vis the current challenges. Streeck (1997, 2009) goes even further by claiming that the existing institutions would suffer from exhaustion and would have difficulties reproducing effectively.

For France, Howell (1992), Schmidt (1993) and Parsons (2005) to varying extents argue that the state has retreated and passed on the initiative in running the economy to business, as a result of, among other things, deregulation, privatization, Europeanization and regional integration. Hancké (2002) maintains that large firms have become the drivers of economic adjustment. Yet, several authors (Schmidt, 1993; Amadieu, 1995; Jefferys, 2000) emphasize the continuing importance of the state for shaping employment relations, yet with different agendas, priorities and programmes. In the words of Parsons (2005), state-centred labour regulation has given way to micro-corporatism, where the state forces management and workforce representatives to cooperate and to negotiate. Amadieu (1995) claims that this results from traditionally weak and ineffective industrial relations organizations and institutions.

As far as Germany is concerned, while there is by and large agreement that the traditional employment relations system is changing, commentators disagree about the magnitude and implications of the changes. Hassel (1999, p. 484) argues – and reinforces and supports her argument with new empirical information in Hassel (2002) – that 'two parallel developments undermine the stability of the German model' and would lead to a gradual erosion of the German model of employment relations with its specific and exclusive characteristics and properties. First, the traditional industrial relations institutions would struggle to cope with new forms of organizational structures of companies and to extend their impacts beyond the traditional (manufacturing) base into the new growth sectors, thus losing the capacity to regulate labour markets effectively. Second, collective bargaining decentralization and the changing employment structures would lead to a redefinition of the relationship between employee representation in the workplace and (industry-level) collective bargaining. As a consequence, the capacity for macroeconomic fine-tuning and for ensuring cooperative workplace employment relations, both prerequisites for successful cooperative modernization, would suffer.

In contrast, Klikauer (2002) maintains that while the basic characteristics of the German system of employment relations, that is, the works council system, union representatives in the workplace, regional multi-employer collective bargaining and tripartite arrangements, would be still intact and quite stable, Hassel's (1999) erosion thesis would just relate to unification and continuing differences in employment relations between Eastern and Western Germany, and to the public sector.

Tüselmann and Heise (2000, p. 174) argue that there are trends of continuity as well as of change in current German industrial relations, and that because of the vested interests of the employment relations actors as well as because of path dependency of institutional change, the German system would rather follow the 'trajectory of centrally coordinated decentralization by striking a subtle balance between stability and change'.

CONCLUSION

Are employment relations in France and Germany converging or diverging? While the challenges and pressure on the two systems, for example, internationalization, European integration, structural change in the economy and the labour market, liberalization, deregulation and the imperative of competitiveness have been rather similar – with German reunification being a unique and singular external influence – these pressures have been accommodated in different ways in the two countries, due to institutional and cultural differences. Thus, both employment relations systems have so far retained their distinct features and characteristics. Yet, in both countries the employment relations actors were not just institution-takers, but actively trying to shape institutions to serve their interests, for example, as far as the role of workplace representation in both countries is concerned.

With respect to the extent and direction of change processes, Streeck

(2009) criticizes the proposition of the varieties of capitalism approach (Hall and Soskice, 2001) that institutional complementarities in political economies would push for moving in the direction of the initial equilibrium (a political economy following either the liberal market economy type or the coordinated market economy type) after, for example, external shocks. Looking at the relationship between convergence and divergence, Streeck's (2009, p. 10) account of institutional change claims that this issue is multidimensional, resulting from an interplay of economic and political pressures, and that the consideration of time and history can lead to situations where: 'long-lasting divergence between two systems may go hand in hand with parallel change in the same direction, and growing convergence in the course of such change may be hidden by one system having started its transformation earlier than the other'.

General developments in France and Germany point to the continuing role of the state and government as innovator, driver and stabilizer in employment relations, albeit in different ways. Despite all the changes and challenges, with the demise of unionism and the growing importance of employers in the restructuring of the French political economy (Hancké, 2002), the interventionist French government still has an omnipresent role in French employment relations. And in Germany, despite all continuing signs of erosion, employment relations are still largely driven by the initiatives of the social partners, within the robust legal framework of the social market economy and social partnership as enshrined in the German Constitution.

From the material presented on both countries, in line with Hancké (2002, p. 199), I conclude that: 'while the pressures. . .to adjust appear very similar, the different national institutional frameworks refract these pressures in quite different ways, and offer quite different adjustment paths to the central actors'.

REFERENCES

Addison, J.T., Schnabel, C. and Wagner, J. (2004a), 'The course of research into the economic consequences of German works councils', *British Journal of Industrial Relations*, **42**(1), 255–81.
Addison, J.T., Bellmann, L., Schnabel, C. and Wagner, J. (2004b) 'The reform of the German Works Constitution Act: A critical assessment', *Industrial Relations*, **43**(2), 392–420.
Alleki, N. (2009), 'Inter-sectoral agreement lays basis for training system reform', *EIROnline*, 19 August.
Amadieu, J.-F. (1995), 'Industrial relations: Is France a special case?', *British Journal of Industrial Relations*, **33**(3), 345–51.
Beal, E.F. (1955), 'Origins of co-determination', *Industrial and Labor Relations Review*, **8**(4), 483–98.

Beal, E.F. (1956), 'Communications – origins of co-determination – reply', *Industrial and Labor Relations Review*, **10**(10), 126–9.

Behrens, M. (2001), 'Works Constitution Act reform adopted', *EIROnline* 28 July.

Behrens, M. and Jacoby, W. (2004), 'The rise of experimentalism in German collective bargaining', *British Journal of Industrial Relations*, **42**(1), 95–123.

Behrens, M. and Schulten, T. (2003), '2002 annual review for Germany', *EIROnline*, 24 March.

Behrens, M., Scheele, A. and Schulten, T. (2000), '2000 annual review for Germany', *EIROnline*, 28 December.

Behrens, M., Scheele, A. and Schulten, T. (2002), '2001 annual review for Germany', *EIROnline*, 25 March.

Bilous, A. (1997), '1997 annual review for France', *EIROnline*, 28 December.

Boni, G. (2009), 'Towards socially sensitive corporate restructuring? Comparative remarks on collective bargaining developments in Germany, France and Italy', *International Labour Review*, **148**(1–2), 69–91.

Bordogna, L. (2007), *Industrial Relations in the Public Sector*, Dublin: European Foundation for the Improvement of Living and Working Conditions.

Brenke, K. (2004), 'East German manufacturing – many firms moving away from collective wage bargaining', *Economic Bulletin*, **41**(4), 119–26.

Broughton, A. (2007), 'Comparative overview of industrial relations in 2005', *EIROnline*, 29 January.

Bunel, J. and Saglio, J. (1984), 'Employers associations in France', in J.P. Windmuller and A. Gladstone (eds), *Employers Associations and Industrial Relations – A Comparative Study*, Oxford: Clarendon Press, pp. 232–63.

Bunn, R.F. (1984), 'Employers associations in the Federal Republic of Germany', in J.P. Windmuller and A. Gladstone (eds), *Employers Associations and Industrial Relations – A Comparative Study*, Oxford: Clarendon Press, pp. 169–210.

Buyens, D., Dany, F., Dewettinck, K. and Quinodon, B. (2004), 'France and Belgium: Language, culture and differences in human resource practices', in C. Brewster, W. Mayrhofer and Morley, M. (eds), *Human Resource Management in Europe: Evidence of Convergence?*, Amsterdam: Elsevier Butterworth Heinemann, pp. 123–60.

Caire, G. (1984), 'Recent trends in collective bargaining in France', *International Labour Review*, **123**, 723.

Capron, M. (2001), 'Accounting and management in the social dialogue: The experience of fifty years of works councils in France', *Accounting, Business and Financial History*, **11**(1), 29–42.

Cerdin, J.-L. and Peretti, J.-M. (2001), 'Trends and emerging values in human resource management in France', *International Journal of Manpower*, **22**(3), 216.

Charkham, J. (1994), *Keeping Good Company: A Study of Corporate Governance in Five Countries*, Oxford: Clarendon Press.

Charkham, J. (2005), *Keeping Better Company: Corporate Governance Ten Years On*, Oxford: Oxford University Press.

Conrad, P. and Pieper, R. (1990), 'Human resource management in the Federal Republic of Germany', in R. Pieper (ed.), *Human Resource Management: An International Comparison*, Berlin: de Gruyter, pp. 109–42.

DGB (2010), *DGB Mitgliederstatistik*.

Dietz, B., Hoogendoorn, J., Kabst, R. and Schmelter, A. (2004), 'The Netherlands and Germany: Flexibility or rigidity?', in C. Brewster, W. Mayrhofer and M. Morley (eds), *Human Resource Management in Europe: Evidence of Convergence?*, Amsterdam: Elsevier Butterworth Heinemann, pp. 73–94.

Dribbusch, H. (2005), '2004 annual review for Germany', *EIROnline*, 14 July.

Dribbusch, H. (2008a), 'Germany: Industrial relations developments in Europe 2007', *EIROnline*, 23 September.

Dribbusch, H. (2008b), 'Industrial relations in the public sector – Germany', *EIROnline*, 11 December.

Dufour, C. (2000), '2000 annual review for France', *EIROnline*, 28 December.
Dufour, C. (2002), '2001 annual review for France', *EIROnline*, 25 March.
Dufour, C. (2003), '2002 annual review for France', *EIROnline*, 26 March.
Dufour, C. (2004), '2003 annual review for France' *EIROnline*, 18 June.
Dufour, C. (2005), '2004 annual review for France', *EIROnline*, 20 July.
Ebner, A. (2006), 'The intellectual foundations of the social market economy', *Journal of Economic Studies*, **33**(3), 206–23.
Ellguth, P. and Kohaut, S. (2010), 'Tarifbindung und betriebliche Interessenvertretung: Aktuelle Ergebnisse aus dem IAB-Betriebspanel 2009', *WSI-Mitteilungen*, **62**, 1–7.
Esping-Andersen, G. (1990), *The Three Worlds of Welfare Capitalism*, Cambridge: Polity Press.
Eurostat (2009a), *Europe in Figures: Eurostat Yearbook 2008*, Luxembourg: Office for Official Publications of the European Communities.
Eurostat (2009b), *European Economic Statistics: 2009 Edition*, Luxembourg: Office for Official Publications of the European Communities.
Eyraud, F. and Tchobanian, R. (1985), 'The Auroux Reforms and company-level industrial relations in France', *British Journal of Industrial Relations*, **23**(2), 241–59.
Fay, D. (2000), 'Working in East German socialism in 1980 and in capitalism 15 years later: A trend analysis of a transitional economy's working conditions', *Applied Psychology: An International Review*, **49**(4), 636.
Fichter, M. (1990), *Einheit und Organisation: Der Deutsche Gewerkschaftsbund im Aufbau 1945 bis 1949*, Köln: Bund-Verlag.
Freeman, R.B. (1998), 'War of the models: Which labour market institutions for the 21st century?', *Labour Economics*, **5**(1), 1–24.
Frege, C.M. (1998a), 'Institutional transfer and effectiveness of employee representation: Comparing works councils in East and West Germany', *Economic and Industrial Democracy*, **19**(3), 475–504.
Frege, C.M. (1998b), 'Workers' commitment to new labour institutions: Comparing union members in East and West Germany', *European Journal of Industrial Relations*, **4**(1), 81–101.
Frege, C.M. (1999a), *Social Partnership at Work: Workplace Relations in Post-unification Germany*, London: Routledge.
Frege, C.M. (1999b), 'Transferring labor institutions to emerging economies: The case of East Germany', *Industrial Relations*, **38**(4), 459.
Frege, C.M. (2002), 'A critical assessment of the theoretical and empirical research on German works councils', *British Journal of Industrial Relations*, **40**(2), 221.
French, S. (2000), 'The impact of unification on German industrial relations', *German Politics*, **9**(2), 195–216.
Freyssinet, J. (1993), 'France: Towards flexibility', in J. Hartog and J. Theeuwes (eds), *Labour Market Contracts and Institutions: A Cross-national Comparison*, Amsterdam: North-Holland, pp. 267–97.
Freyssinet, J. (1998), '1998 annual review for France', *EIROnline*, 28 December.
Fürstenberg, F. (1993), 'Industrial relations in Germany', in G.J. Bamber, R.D. Lansbury and N. Wailes (eds), *International and Comparative Industrial Relations*, 5th edition, London: Sage, pp. 175–96.
Gill, U. (1991), *FDGB: Die DDR-Gewerkschaft von 1945 bis zu ihrer Auflösung 1990*, 13th edition, Köln: Bund-Verlag.
Goetschy, J. (1998), 'France: The limits of reform', in A. Ferner and R. Hyman (eds), *Changing Industrial Relations in Europe*, Oxford: Blackwell, pp. 357–94.
Goetschy, J. and Jobert, A. (2010), 'Employment relations in France', in G.J. Bamber, R.D. Lansbury and N. Wailes (eds), *International and Comparative Employment Relations*, 5th edition, London: Sage, pp. 169–95.
Goetschy, J. and Rozenblatt, P. (1992), 'France: The industrial system at a turning point', in A. Ferner and R. Hyman (eds), *Industrial Relations in the New Europe*, Oxford: Blackwell, pp. 404–44.

Gregory, P.R. and Stuart, R.C. (1980), *Comparative Economic Systems*, Boston: Houghton Mifflin.

Gregory, P.R. and Stuart, R.C. (1998), *Comparative Economic Systems*, 5th edition, Boston: Houghton Mifflin.

Grote, J.R., Lang, A. and Traxler, F. (2007), 'Germany', in F. Traxler and G. Huemer, (eds), *Handbook of Business Interest Associations, Firm Size and Governance: A Comparative Analytical Approach*, London: Routledge, pp. 141–76.

Gumbrell-McCormick, R. and Hyman, R. (2006), 'Embedded collectivism? Workplace representation in France and Germany', *Industrial Relations Journal*, **37**(5), 473–91.

Hall, P.A. and Soskice, D. (2001), 'An introduction to the varieties of capitalism', in P.A. Hall and D. Soskice (eds), *Varieties of Capitalism: The Institutional Foundations of Comparative Advantage*, Oxford: Oxford University Press, pp. 1–70.

Hancké, B. (2002), *Large Firms and Institutional Change: Industrial Renewal and Economic Restructuring in France*, Oxford: Oxford University Press.

Hassel, A. (1999), 'The erosion of the German system of industrial relations', *British Journal of Industrial Relations*, **37**(3), 483–505.

Hassel, A. (2002), 'The erosion continues: Reply', *British Journal of Industrial Relations*, **40**(2), 309.

Hassel, A. (2007), 'Die Nachteile institutioneller Stabilität: Die Erosion der deutschen Gewerkschaften', *Industrielle Beziehungen*, **14**(2), 176–91.

Howell, C. (1992), 'The dilemmas of post-Fordism: Socialists, flexibility, and labor market deregulation in France', *Politics & Society*, **20**(1), 71–99.

Hyman, R. (1994), 'Industrial relations in Western Europe: An era of ambiguity?', *Industrial Relations*, **33**(1), 1.

Hyman, R. (1996), 'Institutional transfer: Industrial relations in Eastern Germany', *Work, Employment & Society*, **10**(4), 601–39.

Jacobi, O., Keller, B. and Müller-Jentsch, W. (1992), 'Germany: Codetermining the future', in A. Ferner and R. Hyman (eds), *Industrial Relations in the New Europe*, Oxford: Blackwell, pp. 218–69.

Jacobi, O., Keller, B. and Müller-Jentsch, W. (1998), 'Germany: Facing new challenges', in A. Ferner and R. Hyman (eds), *Changing Industrial Relations in Europe*, Oxford: Blackwell, pp. 190–238.

Jefferys, S. (2000), 'A "Copernican revolution" in French industrial relations: Are the times a' changing?', *British Journal of Industrial Relations*, **38**(2), 241–60.

Jenkins, A. (2000), *Employment Relations in France: Evolution and Innovation*, New York: Kluwer Academic/Plenum Publications.

Jürgens, U., Klinzing, L. and Turner, L. (1993), 'The transformation of industrial relations in Eastern Germany', *Industrial and Labor Relations Review*, **46**(2), 229.

Kädtler, J., Kottwitz, G. and Weinert, R. (1997), *Betriebsräte in Ostdeutschland: Institutionenbildung und Handlungskonstellationen, 1989–1994*, Opladen: Westdeutscher Verlag.

Keller, B.K. (1999), 'Germany: Negotiated change, modernization and the challenge of unification', in S. Bach, L. Bordogna, G. Della Rocca and D. Winchester (eds), *Public Service Employment Relations in Europe: Transformation, Modernization or Inertia?*, London: Routledge, pp. 45–75.

Keller, B.K. and Kirsch, A. (2010), 'Employment relations in Germany', in G.J. Bamber, R.D. Lansbury and N. Wailes (eds), *International and Comparative Employment Relations*, 5th edition, London: Sage, pp. 196–223.

Kessler, I., Undy, R. and Heron, P. (2004), 'Employee perspectives on communication and consultation: Findings from a cross-national survey', *International Journal of Human Resource Management*, **15**(3), 512–32.

Klikauer, T. (2002), 'Stability in Germany's industrial relations: A critique on Hassel's erosion thesis', *British Journal of Industrial Relations*, **40**(2), 295.

Klikauer, T. (2004), 'Trade union shopfloor representation in Germany', *Industrial Relations Journal*, **35**(1), 2–18.

354 *Research handbook of comparative employment relations*

Koch, K. (1982), 'The false promise of co-determination (book review)', *Journal of Common Market Studies*, **20**(4), 392.
Lane, C. (1989), *Management and Labour in Europe: The Industrial Enterprise in Germany. Britain and France*, Aldershot, UK and Brookfield, VT: Edward Elgar.
Lecomte, E. (2008), 'Tripartite conference issues proposals for occupational risk prevention', *EIROnline*, 7 October.
Lumley, R. (1995), 'Labour market and employment relations in transition: The case of German unification', *Employee Relations*, **17**(1), 24–37.
Marsden, D. (1980), 'Shop stewards in Great Britain, West Germany and France', *Employee Relations*, **2**, 2–5.
Marsden, D. (1999), *A Theory of Employment Systems: Micro-foundations of Societal Diversity*, Oxford: Oxford University Press.
Maurice, M. and Sellier, F. (1979), 'Societal differences in organizing manufacturing units: A comparison of France, West Germany, and Great Britain', *British Journal of Industrial Relations*, **17**(3), 322–36.
Maurice, M., Sellier, F. and Silvestre, J.-J. (1986), *The Social Foundation of Industrial Power: A Comparison of France and Germany*, Cambridge, MA: MIT Press.
Maurice, M., Sorge, A. and Warner, M. (1980), 'Societal differences in organizing manufacturing units: A comparison of France, West Germany, and Great Britain', *Organization Studies*, **1**(1), 59–86.
Maydell, B. von (1996), *Die Umwandlung der Arbeits- und Sozialordnung*, Opladen: Leske and Budrich.
Miller, D. (1978), 'Trade union workplace representation in the Federal Republic of Germany: An analysis of the post-war Vertrauensleute policy of the German Metalworkers' Union (1952–77)', *British Journal of Industrial Relations*, **16**(3), 335–54.
Mitchell, D.J.B. (1972), 'Incomes policy and the labour market in France', *Industrial and Labor Relations Review*, **25**(3), 315–35.
Mosse, P. and Tchobanian, R. (1999), 'France: The restructuring of employment relations in the public services', in S. Bach, L. Bordogna, G. Della Rocca and D. Winchester (eds), *Public Service Employment Relations in Europe: Transformation, Modernization or Inertia?*, London: Routledge, pp. 106–32.
Müller-Jentsch, W. (1995), 'Auf dem Prüfstand: Das deutsche Modell der Industriellen Beziehungen', *Industrielle Beziehungen*, **2**(1), 11–24.
Müller-Jentsch, W. and Ittermann, P. (2000), *Industrielle Beziehungen: Daten, Zeitreihen, Trends 1950–1999*, Frankfurt: Campus-Verlag.
N.N. (2000), '1999 annual review for France', *EIROnline*, 28 December 1999.
N.N. (2007), 'France: Industrial Relations Profile', EIROnline database, available at: http://www.eurofound.europa.eu/eiro/country/france.htm; accessed 2 February 2011.
OECD (2010), 'OECD.StatExtracts' OECD online database, available at: http://stats.oecd.org/Index.aspx?DatasetCode=U_D_D; accessed 2 February 2011.
Parsons, N. (2005), *French Industrial Relations in the New World Economy*, London: Routledge.
Pernot, J.-M. (2009), 'Workplace elections test new system of representation', *EIROnline*, 11 May.
Rehfeldt, U. (1998), 'Board-level employee representation – France', EIROnline database, available at: http://www.eurofound.europa.eu/eiro/1998/09/word/fr9809128s.doc; accessed 2 February 2011.
Rehfeldt, U. (2007), 'New law obliges government to consult with social partners prior to labour reforms', *EIROnline*, 4 June.
Rehfeldt, U. (2008), 'Government launches tripartite conferences and consultations on social reforms', *EIROnline*, 4 February.
Rigby, M., Contrepois, S. and Smith, F.O.B. (2009), 'The establishment of enterprise works councils: Process and problems', *European Journal of Industrial Relations*, **15**(1), 71–90.
Robin, B. (2008), 'New rules for union representativeness and working time', *EIROnline*, 20 October.

Rojot, J. (1990), 'Human resource management in France', in R. Pieper (ed.), *Human Resource Management: An International Comparison*, Berlin: de Gruyter, pp. 87–100.

Saurugger, S. (2007), 'France', in F. Traxler and G. Huemer (eds), *Handbook of Business Interest Associations, Firm Size and Governance: A Comparative Analytical Approach*, London: Routledge, pp. 122–40.

Schmidt, R. (1995), 'Rationalization and social differentiation at East German industrial workplaces', *International Journal of Political Economy*, **25**(4), 91–107.

Schmidt, V.A. (1993), 'An end to French economic exceptionalism? The transformation of business under Mitterrand', *California Management Review*, **36**(1), 75–98.

Schmidt, V.A. (1996), 'The decline of traditional state "dirigisme" in France: The transformation of political economic policies and policymaking processes', *Governance*, **9**(4), 375–405.

Schmidt, V.A. (1997), 'Running on empty: The end of "dirigisme" in French economic leadership', *Modern and Contemporary France*, **5**(2), 229–41.

Schmidt, V.A. (2003), 'French capitalism transformed, yet still a third variety of capitalism', *Economy and Society*, **32**(4), 526–54.

Schnabel, C. and Kohaut, S. (2007), 'Tarifliche Offnungsklauseln – Verbreitung, Inanspruchnahme und Bedeutung', *Sozialer Fortschritt*, **56**, 33–40.

Schröder, W. (2000), *Das Modell Deutschland auf dem Prüfstand: Zur Entwicklung der industriellen Beziehungen in Ostdeutschland (1990–2000)*, Wiesbaden: Westdeutscher Verlag.

Schulten, T. and Zagelmeyer, S. (1997), '1997 annual review for Germany', *EIROnline*, 28 December.

Schulten, T. and Zagelmeyer, S. (1998a), '1998 annual review for Germany', *EIROnline*, 28 December.

Schulten, T. and Zagelmeyer, S. (1998b), 'Board-level employee representation – Germany', available at: EIROnline database, http://www.eurofound.europa.eu/eiro/1998/09/word/de9809172s.doc; accessed 2 February 2011.

Schwarzer, D. (1996), *Arbeitsbeziehungen im Umbruch gesellschaftlicher Strukturen: Bundesrepublik Deutschland, DDR und neue Bundesländer im Vergleich*, Stuttgart: Steiner.

Silvestre, J.J. (1974), 'Industrial wage differentials: A two-country comparison', *International Labour Review*, **110**, 495.

Silvia, S.J. and Schroeder, W. (2007), 'Why are German employers associations declining?: Arguments and evidence', *Comparative Political Studies*, **40**(12), 1433–59.

Sorge, A. and Maurice, M. (1990), 'The societal effect in strategies and competitiveness of machine-tool manufacturers in France and West Germany', *International Journal of Human Resource Management*, **1**(2), 141–72.

Streeck, W. (1981), 'Qualitative demands and the neo-corporatist manageability of industrial relations', *British Journal of Industrial Relations*, **19**(2), 149–69.

Streeck, W. (1997), 'German capitalism: Does it exist? Can it survive?', *New Political Economy*, **2**(2), 237.

Streeck, W. (2009), *Re-forming Capitalism: Institutional Change in the German Political Economy*, Oxford: Oxford University Press.

Turner, L. (1998), *Fighting for Partnership: Labor and Politics in Unified Germany*, Ithaca, NY: Cornell University Press.

Tüselmann, H. and Heise, A. (2000), 'The German model of industrial relations at the crossroads: Past, present and future', *Industrial Relations Journal*, **31**(3), 162.

Upchurch, M. (1995), 'After unification: Trade unions and industrial relations in Eastern Germany', *Industrial Relations Journal*, **26**(4), 280.

Van Ruysseveldt, J. and Visser, J. (1996), 'Contestation and state intervention forever? Industrial relations in France', in J. Van Ruysseveldt and J. Visser (eds), *Industrial Relations in Europe*, London: Sage, pp. 42–81.

Vincent, C. (1998), 'Debate over mandating employees to conclude collective agreements', *EIROnline*, 28 July.

Vincent, C. (2008), 'Industrial relations in the public sector – France', *EIROnline*, 11 December.

Wachenheim, H. (1956), 'Communications – origins of co-determination', *Industrial and Labor Relations Review*, **10**(1), 118–26.
Wächter, H. and Müller-Camen, M. (2002), 'Co-determination and strategic integration in German firms', *Human Resource Management Journal*, **12**(3), 76–87.
Woll, C. (2005), 'The difficult organization of business interests: MEDEF and the political representation of French firms', MPIfG Discussion Paper No. 05/12, Cologne: Max-Planck-Institute for the Study of Societies.
Zagelmeyer, S. (1997), 'The erosion of employers' associations and industry-level bargaining in Eastern Germany', *EIROnline*, 28 August.
Zagelmeyer, S. (2004), *Governance Structures and the Employment Relationship: Determinants of Employer Demand for Collective Bargaining in Britain*, Oxford: Peter Lang.

15 Employment relations in oil-rich Gulf countries
Kamel Mellahi and Ingo Forstenlechner

INTRODUCTION

Labour markets of emerging Gulf economies – the Kingdom of Saudi Arabia, Bahrain, Kuwait, Qatar, the United Arab Emirates and Sultanate of Oman – share a wide range of communalities. They are defined by a strong dependence on expatriates, low levels of national workforce participation, uncertainties in the applicability and practicability of the labour law and a lack of understanding of the need to professionally manage people. All of these factors have strong implications for employee relations. For example, investment in human capital has only very recently started to receive attention in most organizations, as it simply wasn't necessary. Most positions were filled by expatriates who were on one-year visas and discouraged from becoming permanent residents. High turnover numbers were seen as perfectly normal. As Al Ali (2008) notes, this has resulted in a lack of focus on a commitment-oriented corporate culture aimed towards supporting long-term employees with training or career paths. It has not only had implications for expatriates, but also for citizens who joined organizations not used to longer-term employment relations.

The low levels of workforce participation in many of the Gulf countries represent an increasingly urgent challenge to governments (Al Qudsi, 2006; *Economist*, 2007; Abdalla et al., 2008; De Boer and Turner, 2008) and to both local and multinational businesses operating in the region (Al Lamki, 2005; Budhwar and Mellahi, 2006, 2007; Mellahi, 2007; Barhem et al., 2008). This challenge is at the centre of our contribution to this handbook, as it is one major issue really differentiating employee relations in the Gulf from many other countries. While organizations enjoy high levels of liberty with regards to their management of expatriate employees, it is workforce localization that really challenges traditional approaches to employee relations. As noted by Alserhan et al. (2010), citizens in the United Arab Emirates not only have significantly higher expectations towards pay, but are also more difficult to dismiss, except under the most extreme circumstances.

The traditional employment relations topics of employee voice or employee representation are largely absent in the countries of the Gulf

Cooperation Council (GCC). Trade unions exist in GCC countries, though their role is heavily restricted (see Table 15.1). The outlook for employment relations remains uncertain across the GCC; however, signs of reform are somewhat visible at, for example, the level of collective bargaining, for example, a concept previously unthinkable in the context of Gulf countries (see Table 15.1). This can – according to Davidson (2009) – be largely traced back to the Gulf countries having joined a number of international economic organizations, among them the World Trade Organization (for example, UAE in 1996, Oman in 2000) and, by extension, the International Labour Organization. This has resulted in blue-collar workers' associations not being dissolved, and members of such associations not facing deportation for organizing themselves and their colleagues. Such rights, as Davidson (ibid.) notes, would have been inconceivable for earlier generations of expatriate workers.

Localization, however, and the amount of compliance or resistance to it, is a topic dominating the agenda of many organizations whether they are serious about it or are looking for ways around it (Forstenlechner, 2008). Harry (2007, p. 141) goes as far as considering workforce nationalization a question of survival for the countries themselves: 'The ability to develop effective solutions will be a major factor in the survival of the governments and maybe even for the continued existence of the GCC countries in their present form'.

This chapter is organized as follows. First, we discuss the characteristics of GCC labour markets before addressing issues related to legitimacy, explaining the context of organizations operating within the region. We then explore hiring practices in the context of institutional theory before identifying some of the key issues currently hindering localization. We conclude with an outlook on the medium-term future of employment relations in the GCC.

CHARACTERISTICS OF GCC LABOUR MARKETS

All GCC states have, over the past decades, started labour nationalization agendas and policies that initially sought to replace expatriate workers with nationals. This has been done by limiting employer choice of employees for certain job categories that must be exclusively staffed by nationals, and by imposing top-down quotas on private sector entities (Oxford Business Group, 2008a, 2008b, 2008c). Nevertheless, the number of expatriate workers in the GCC states increased fivefold between 1970 and 2000 (Fasano and Goyal, 2004). Even during previous periods of economic stagnation, 1985 and 1999, the number of foreign workers coming into

Table 15.1   Trade unions and employee relations in Gulf State countries

Country	Employee Relations
United Arab Emirates	
Bahrain	The General Federation of Workers Trade Unions in Bahrain (GFWTUB) was established in 2002 as the national umbrella for unions in Bahrain. It is governed by Workers' Trade Union Law, which grants workers the right to organize collectively. The GFWTUB is very active and the only trade union from the GCC countries to become a member of the International Confederation of Free Trade Unions (ICFTU). Strikes and collective bargaining are allowed but heavily circumscribed. Workers engaged in union activities are protected by law
Kuwait	The Kuwait Trade Union Federation (KTFU) is the only legal union allowed by the government. Local unions and occupational unions also exist. Kuwait has the most active unions in the GCC region. Strikes are allowed but heavily restricted. All workers are allowed to join with the exception of domestic workers
Oman	The General Federation of the Sultanate of Oman (GFSO) is the single trade union federation representing workers in Oman. Union activities are protected by law. Workers in a number of vital public sectors are not allowed to form unions. Collective bargaining and peaceful strike actions are allowed but heavily restricted
Saudi Arabia	Trade unions are not allowed. Workers' committees are allowed in organizations employing more than 100 workers. The role of workers' committees is restricted to workplace issues such as work environment and health and safety standards and training
Qatar	The 2005 Labour Code allows free trade unions for Qatari nationals only. The only trade union – the General Union of Workers of Qatar – is made up of General Committees for workers in different trades or industries. Each committee must have a minimum of 100 members. Foreign workers are not allowed to join the trade union. Government workers are not allowed to organize. The main role of the union is collective bargaining. Other roles are heavily curtailed by the government. Private sector workers are allowed to strike after the Labour Department of the Ministry of Civil Services rules on the dispute. Workers in critical public sectors such as health, public utility and security are not allowed to strike. Recent labour reforms banned employment of youth under the age 16 years, provided equal labour rights for women and legislated for a maximum of an eight hour working day

Source: Compiled by authors.

Table 15.2   Demographics as reported by Kapiszewski (2006)

	Nationals (%)	Expatriates (%)	Total Population
Bahrain	62	38	707 160
Kuwait	35.6	64.4	2 992 000
Oman	80.1	19.9	3 102 000
Qatar	30	70	855 000
Saudi Arabia	72.9	27.1	27 020 000
UAE	19	81	4 700 000
GCC	62.9	37.1	39 376 160

Source: Kapiszewski (2006).

the region grew by almost 2 million (Winckler, 2005, p. 99; Niblock, 2007, p. 139). This was despite well-publicized and supposedly serious nation-alization drives in most GCC countries. Even during Saudi Arabia's Fifth Development Plan (1991–95), which actively sought to reduce the number of foreign workers, their number grew in some years by as much as 10 per cent (Cordesman, 2003, p. 273). While there are, of course, differences across the GCC with regards to the share of expatriates in the population, the last somewhat reliable figures across the GCC countries are provided by Kapiszewski (2006) in Table 15.2.

While there are more recent figures for single countries, their reliability is uncertain, as there are serious difficulties in getting reliable empirical information or statistical data for the region (see also Cordesman, 2002; Harry, 2007) . However, in principle these figures underline the very spe-cific situation in the GCC countries. These labour markets exhibit a high degree of segmentation, a public sector staffed predominantly by nation-als and a private sector dominated by expatriates (Rutledge, 2009), and accompanied by distortionary employment and wage policies (Ruppert, 1999). According to the Oxford Business Group (2008b) the UAE's 2008 federal budget was the largest ever. A major reason for this is the necessity to set aside the 70 per cent increase in salaries for public sector workers that were granted in 2008.

Many scholars have argued that the way to make the public sector less desirable for nationals would be to reduce the generous remuneration packages, as such acts of generosity make nationals all the more deter-mined to hold out for public sector employment, and as a consequence stay unemployed in the interim (Al Shamsi et al., 2009).

Graduated Emiratis can expect to receive more than double the salary of a better qualified and experienced employee from South or East Asia (Quilliam, 2003, p. 56). Newly graduated secondary school educated

Kuwaitis cost 135 per cent of the cost of a secondary school educated expatriate worker aged between 20 and 29, despite the latter having, on average, eight more years of experience (Al Qudsi, 2006), while in Saudi Arabia, nationals earned between two and three times as much as expatriates on average (Wilson et al., 2004; Niblock, 2007).

Cordesman (2003, p. 272) argues that 'It is obvious that the Saudi economy cannot afford to replace the non-Saudi jobs at twice the present cost, much less three times the present cost'. In Bahrain, a study cited by the Oxford Business Group (2008c) revealed that the average Bahraini earns $15 000 annually and the average expatriate worker earns just a third of this ($5240); almost two-thirds of private sector jobs pay only $3180 per year.

A key underlying reason for such issues of productivity is the so-called social contract, where ruling elites distribute oil wealth by providing citizens with well-paid public sector employment (Dyer and Yousef, 2007). This has understandably led to a strong preference amongst nationals for such jobs and has resulted in 'a low elasticity of substitution' between national and foreign workers (Fasano and Goyal, 2004). This has led to most GCC countries 'struggling for decades to come to terms with dealing efficiently with the existence and demand for foreign workers on one side and employing their young nationals in productive and decent jobs in the growing private sectors' (Dito, 2006, p. 109).

A good example to illustrate this preference for public over private sector employment is provided by Niblock (2007, p. 222), who cites a 2006 media story that reported '10,000 Saudi men sought to submit applications for 500 jobs advertised by the passports department. Police had to be called in to control the demonstration which ensued'. The Oxford Business Group (2008d) point out that in Kuwait there are a whole range of jobs 'at the bottom end of the spectrum' that nationals would not do.

The longer-term consequence of the GCC countries' dual-labour market mechanism is likely to be a steady increase in national unemployment, as citizens are too expensive for the private sector to afford and too many in number for the public sector to absorb (Winckler, 2005).

Underlying these various labour market distortions is the issue of productivity. According to Niblock (2007, p. 223), many of those employed in the public sector 'would be more gainfully employed elsewhere, but it is not in their interest' and adds, 'nor is it in the interests of private sector employers to seek to attract them'. As Wilson et al. (2004, p. 94) point out, jobs should 'enhance the supply capacity of the economy and contribute to sustainable higher living standards', and creating ever more positions in an already overstaffed public sector does not achieve this. According to the Oxford Business Group (2008d), 87 per cent of Kuwaitis are employed in the administration of government or state-controlled business where productivity rates are infamously low and the few statistics available for other GCC countries suggest similarly high levels for some of them.

EXTERNAL LEGITIMACY AND EMPLOYMENT OF LOCALS IN THE MIDDLE EAST

Employment of nationals in GCC countries is also closely connected to deliberation made by multinational enterprises in the context of legitimacy. Multinational enterprises (MNEs) require legitimacy to succeed in foreign markets as much as they require economic efficiency (Kostova and Zaheer, 1999; Kostova and Roth, 2002; Chan and Makino, 2007). Over the years, there has been considerable debate in the Middle East over the costs and benefits of localization. Though there is general agreement over its importance, there is also contention regarding the impact of localization on organizational efficiency. Recent research cautions that localization is not necessarily advantageous for firms operating in the region, and its effectiveness depends on a number of contingent factors (Mellahi, 2007).

External legitimacy – possibly obtainable via means of employing nationals – may provide MNEs with greater ability to overcome the liability of foreignness and achieve social acceptance in host markets (Suchman, 1995). Baum and Oliver (1991, p. 187) argued that, 'External legitimacy elevates the organization's status in the community, facilitates resource acquisition, and deflects questions about an organization's rights and competence to provide specific products or services'. Current thinking points towards a near consensus that MNEs need to obtain external legitimacy in order to operate (Zimmerman and Zeitz, 2002) and prosper in foreign markets (Dowling and Pfeffer, 1975; Human and Provan, 2000).

MNEs operating in the Middle East are vulnerable to external risks from a wide variety of informal organizations and movements, ranging from negative publicity to calls for boycott by consumers. Although these groups do not control access to critical resources, they hold the power to confer or withhold legitimacy to foreign firms. Recent wars and other conflicts in the Middle East have created considerable challenges for MNEs operating in the region. Among the notable challenges is animosity towards products made in Western countries or by Western MNEs. As put by Knudsen et al. (2008, pp. 17–18):

> The turmoil in the Palestinian territories, the war in Iraq, US support for Israel, the Danish cartoons that were considered blasphemous in the Muslim

world because of their depiction of Muhammad in a derogatory manner, and the Dutch anti-Islam film (*Fitna*) have fuelled anti-Western sentiments in the Middle East, obliging Western multinationals to battle boycotts and public relations nightmares.

Thus, MNEs have a strong incentive to adopt practices that are considered desirable, and appropriate within the norms and values of the larger society in the Middle East.

Given the high level of unemployment in all Gulf countries, people expect MNEs to create job opportunities for locals. Further, given the intensifying pressure on governments in Gulf countries to create jobs for locals, governments expect local firms and MNEs alike to adopt certain HRM practices that ease the problem of high unemployment among the indigenous population and exert significant pressure on them to do so. In particular, governments in the Middle East display a positive bias for employment of locals and favour firms that employ local workers to those that fill jobs with predominantly foreign workers. Indeed, employment of locals in many Middle Eastern countries, such as Egypt and Saudi Arabia, has become an important requirement for firms operating in the region. The concept of localization of employment goes well beyond considering it inappropriate to employ foreign workers when locals are available and willing to take the job. It includes both investing in, and supporting locals to build their skills, thus enhancing their chances in the job market. Therefore, it seems plausible that MNEs that employ and invest in local employees are more likely to attain external legitimacy and subsequently increase their chances to access critical resources, thereby reducing their vulnerability to external uncertainties and risk.

INSTITUTIONAL THEORY AS AN EXPLANATION FOR HIRING PRACTICES

According to institutional theory (DiMaggio and Powell, 1983; Scott and Meyer, 1983), MNEs adapt to the local institutional environment as a result of three types of pressures: (1) mimetic isomorphism, which comes from imitating other firms in host countries; (2) coercive isomorphism, which rises from the explicit demands of the government and its agents, or other societal demands such as pressure by the media; (3) normative legitimacy, as a result of professionally imposed standards. Chan and Makino (2007, p. 623) argued that, 'Firms in uncertain situations often opt to conform to institutional pressure by mimicking the prevalent organizational practices and structures of their successful competitors to gain legitimacy in their institutional environment'.

Similarly, Zaheer (1995, p. 345) argued that mimetic isomorphism 'Is likely to be particularly important in the area of free and unregulated economic competition'. Given the uncertain environment and lack of regulation in the UAE (Rattab et al., 2008), one would expect that the pressure of mimetic isomorphism would push MNEs to adopt similar practices to that of local firms as a way of attending to the pressures of the local environment. As far as the employment of locals is concerned, it is well documented that, generally, local firms tend to defy laws governing the employment of locals and engage in mere window dressing practices: employing the minimum quota required by law and often employing locals in non-strategic jobs (Budhwar and Mellahi, 2007).

Alternatively, MNEs may not mimic local firms' approach to the employment of locals for two reasons. First, although local firms benefit from preferential treatment, they are not the best-performing exemplars in the UAE and, therefore, MNEs may not mimic their practices blindly in their bid to cultivate legitimacy. Second, simply mimicking local firms might not suffice, given the advantage local firms have over MNEs because of local personal connections.

As a result, MNEs may have to go beyond simple mimicking of local firms to obtain legitimacy and compete in the host market. Thus, given the acute problem of employment of locals in the UAE, employment of nationals beyond what is required by law – coercive isomorphism – becomes an option for MNEs seeking to legitimize themselves and gain acceptance in their new environment by promoting themselves as contributors to the country's development. Furthermore, rules and regulation in relations-based economies, such as the Middle East, are rarely systematically enforced and/or implemented equitably. Rather, firms may be rewarded with preferential treatment or unfairly disadvantaged based on their perceived legitimacy by legitimating actors. Budhwar and Mellahi (2007) noted that political and social actors in the Middle East tend to interfere and intervene extensively in firms' affairs. This is because, as pointed out by Hoskisson et al. (2002), the rules of the game in most emerging and developing economies are less predictable, as legal infrastructures are still evolving.

Given the inherent uncertainty associated with arbitrariness of law enforcement and lack of transparency governing economic transaction in the Middle East, MNEs may access unmerited resources and be offered contracts and protection from external risks. They may also extract favourable terms and opportunities as an exchange for legitimating efforts (Ring et al., 1990; Boddewyn and Brewer, 1994; Boddewyn, 1998; Frynas et al., 2006).

While the government is one of the strongest legitimating actors in the

UAE, MNEs must deal with other powerful actors such as local business partners (see Zaheer, 1995; Kostova and Zaheer, 1999 for an extensive discussion of the multiple isomorphic pulls on MNEs' subsidiaries in host markets). We expect firms that successfully balance these conflicting demands would be more successful in obtaining legitimacy from legitimating actors. Mellahi's (2007) study of the impact of legal frameworks in Saudi Arabia on employment of locals found that, while firms were reluctant to engage in outright defiance of laws requiring firms to employ locals, they tried to bypass the law through window dressing practices. Extant research (Oliver, 1991) posits that the degree of adaptability to coercive isomorphism depends on the level of consistency between what is required of firms and their internal strategies, structures and processes. The higher the consistency between the required practices and firms' internal logics, the more likely it is that firms will accede to local legal pressures and so comply without resistance (ibid.).

The third institutional pressure for employing locals is normative isomorphism. Normative isomorphism relates to pressures emanating from the development of rules and regulations governing certain professions. We believe that – given the lack of professionalism in the UAE – normative isomorphism probably does not play a strong role in pressuring MNEs to employ locals. Nonetheless, it is reasonable to expect that normative isomorphism varies according to sectors of activities. In sectors where firms interact with each other extensively because of, for example, belonging to professional associations, they may learn more about proper conduct in the sector than firms that operate in isolation.

LOCALIZATION IN THE GULF STATES

One of the more extreme examples of the necessity for localization is the United Arab Emirates (UAE). A unique characteristic of the UAE, even among fellow GCC countries, is the demographic setting. Depending on the source consulted (Toledo, 2006; Government of the UAE, 2007; Grant et al., 2007), citizens are estimated to account only for 15 to 20 per cent of the total population. The remainder consists of expatriates on residence visas attained mostly through sponsorship from an employer, sponsorship from a business partner, or ownership of a freehold property. This expatriate majority can be seen as a direct result of ambitious development plans to transform the country into a regional economic power (Mohamed, 2002), which required a large number of qualified or able expatriates owing to a national population that was not only lacking in the necessary skills, but also too small in number to physically staff the infrastructure required.

The share of foreign nationals in the overall workforce is estimated to be around 90 per cent (Harry, 2007), while the share of citizens in the 3 million-strong private sector workforce is currently at only 13 000 or 0.34 per cent (Hafez, 2009). A further defining detail is the age distribution among the nationals, where, according to the 2005 census, 51 per cent are below the age of 20 (Grant et al., 2007) while government statistics (Government of the UAE, 2007) put the number of new graduate entrants into the job market at 16 187 for 2006, a number that could not be absorbed by the already saturated public sector and one that is projected to rise to almost 20 000 by 2010 and 40 000 by 2020. This has created what the World Bank (2004) describes as an unprecedented job creation challenge across all GCC states, with approximately 100 million new jobs needed by 2020 to employ new entrants and reduce unemployment to sustainable levels.

The business incentives for organizations to comply are limited as several factors harm the prospects of nationals in the labour market and often make them the last choice of private employers:

1. A cheap pool of skilled labour puts downward pressure on wages and consequently reduces the incentives of nationals to compete in many sectors of the economy (Bremmer, 2004).
2. A strong preference of nationals for employment in the public sector, which usually offers higher salaries (De Boer and Turner, 2008), significantly more job security and a less demanding environment compared with the private sector (Kuntze and Hormann, 2006; Mellahi, 2007).
3. The educational system in the Gulf countries has so far failed to provide sufficient education and preparation for the rigor of working in the private sector (De Boer and Turner, 2008).
4. The widespread perception that local workers are less disciplined and more difficult to control (Mellahi and Wood, 2002).

The International Monetary Fund (IMF, 2004) has suggested that the private sector should be made equally attractive to nationals by lowering benefits in the government sector. On the employers' side, failed localization initiatives in the past have also contributed to an emerging negative stereotype of nationals. Rees et al. (2007) found that these stereotypes significantly lowered the desire of the private sector to employ locals. Thus, while localization would clearly result in external legitimacy, it is also associated with high cost and even inefficiency, which may deter MNEs from fully committing to Emiratization.

OTHER PARTICULARITIES OF THE NATIONAL WORKFORCE

Compensation

The labour market context described above has strong implications for the employability of citizens. It is generally the case that employment conditions and packages for nationals are significantly above market rate and above what a readily available pool of expatriate labour is willing to accept. This – in combination with the expectation that positions will be handed down to citizens almost as a welfare entitlement – has led to a strong preference amongst citizens for jobs in the public sector (Mellahi, 2007) and has resulted in highly segmented labour markets and 'a low elasticity of substitution between national and foreign workers' (Fasano and Goyal, 2004, p. 3). Among the reasons for the preference of UAE citizens to work in the government sector are higher salaries, better employment conditions, greater job security and often shorter working hours (Godwin, 2006; Kuntze and Hormann, 2006; Mellahi, 2007).

Legal Situation

Another problematic issue is the legal framework that gives employers more powers and control mechanisms over expatriate workers than over citizens (Mellahi, 2007). Residence permits tie expatriates to one specific employer, tipping the balance in labour turnover unfavourably against citizens, who are not tied in this way (Mellahi and Wood, 2002) and are free to change jobs as they please.

While this was certainly not meant to discourage the employment of nationals, but to protect them, in reality it discourages their employment. Harry (2007, p. 138) explains this by stating that 'the formal or informal "rights" of the citizens compared to alternative candidates cause employers to avoid recruiting them' and indeed this goes well beyond the aforementioned motivational or discipline issues (Mellahi, 2007). While in the case of expatriates it is easier to dismiss an employee and hire another one (Harry, 2007) there is a certain degree of uncertainty regarding dismissals of citizens. This is – among other factors – due to a lack of predictability. Hoskisson et al. (2002) suggest that the rules of the game in most emerging and developing economies are less predictable and uncertain as legal infrastructures are still evolving. While we are not suggesting the laws are being applied arbitrarily, both quotas and restrictions on expatriate visas have in the past been signed into law with very limited effect. It remains unknown though whether this has been the case for the lack of uptake, application or, as Harry (2007) suggests, due to powerful business owners finding ways to circumvent these quotas and restrictions. We therefore posit that yet another factor could be the coercive 'touch' in the very basic approach to Emiratization itself and the major difference in rights that employees enjoy.

Cultural Disposition

Cultural limitations are relevant as they lower the suitability of citizens for traditional white-collar jobs, mainly in terms of the compatibility of local graduates to a mostly Western-style business environment. Jones (2008) – in a study of conflict coping strategies in a group of local graduate bank trainees – argues that Western-style management styles are mediated by national cultural context influencing perceptions of how they should react.

In her study, a strong predisposition towards compromising or avoiding conflict was identified as one of the key problems of local trainees. Jones (2008) argues that such a preference suggests a tendency towards convention and avoiding conflict at all cost and 'implies a reluctance to take responsibility' (ibid., p. 57). This may well be the case due to a lack of recognition of the value or appropriateness of admitting to being wrong or learning from mistakes.

A further difficulty for organizations employing particularly female locals stems from the dominant cultural limitations on women, such as the resentment against women working far from home or mixing with non-family (Harry, 2007). There is, however, previous evidence of GCC countries overcoming such cultural dispositions, for example in the Sultanate of Oman, where just over a decade ago Al Lamki (1998) found similar issues. Oman today is a country of female Omani shop assistants and female Omani hotel employees.

CONCLUSION

In the context of white-collar work, we know slightly more about working conditions from scholarly literature and studies on the globalization of higher education. While as recently as 2003, Mazawi – in commenting on the more autocratic nature of the decision-making processes in Gulf universities – noted that 'The broader social and political culture seems to have pervaded the university space and affected administrative and governance styles' (p. 236), there is anecdotal evidence suggesting more rights are being given to professors at both public and private higher education institutions than before in terms of institutional governance and academic freedom. With the opening of New York University's Abu Dhabi campus in 2010, the institution professes that the full academic freedoms and tenure positions that are enjoyed by faculty at its Washington Square campus will be enjoyed by faculty in Abu Dhabi (New York University, 2009). Although not a public UAE institution, NYU Abu Dhabi is heavily financed by the local government, which may signify a positive change with regards to academic freedom and tenure. In the case of another GCC county, Rupp (2009) cites the example of a new university in Saudi Arabia (KAUST) where faculty coming in from Stanford have been guaranteed equal rights like they enjoy in the US. However, this so far only concerns those travelling into the country on an infrequent basis, not independent expatriates on longer-term contracts.

While the most substantial changes in terms of the sheer number of people concerned can certainly be found in the blue-collar sector, localization initiatives – which were discussed at length in this chapter – are unlikely to have a major effect on this sector as GCC nationals are unlikely to compete against expatriates in this sector.

The effect of localization initiatives on employee relations in white-collar jobs remains to be seen. Thus far, the influence of a permanent workforce on employee relations has been largely positive insofar as the introduction of professional development and career planning – to name only two examples – has not entirely been limited to the national workforce, but has also benefitted the expatriate workforce. Until a decade ago, a line manager's organizational exit would have almost certainly led to recruiting a replacement from abroad; these days it is more likely to trigger an internal promotion where suitable candidates are available and expatriates don't necessarily leave the country in the same position they arrived in the country, something that was a commonplace situation until recently.

Nevertheless, the arrival of a national workforce in organizations has also led to understandable fears and tensions in the expatriate workforce, who often feel left behind or are afraid of being replaced by national staff.

REFERENCES

Abdalla, I., Al Waqfi, M., Harb, N., Hijazi, R. and Zoubeidi, T. (2008), 'Study of Dubai labor market: Summary of main results', Paper presented at the 9th Annual Research Conference of the UAEU.

Al Ali, J. (2008), 'Emiratisation: Drawing UAE nationals into their surging economy', *International Journal of Sociology and Social Policy*, **28**(9/10), 365–79.

Al Lamki, S.M. (1998), 'Barriers to Omanization in the private sector: The perceptions of Omani graduates', *International Journal of Human Resource Management*, **9**(2), 377–400.

Al Lamki, S.M. (2005), 'The role of the private sector in Omanization: The case of the banking industry in the Sultanate of Oman', *International Journal of Management*, **22**(2), 176–89.

Al Qudsi, S.S. (2006), *Unemployment Evolution in the GCC Economies: Its Nature and Relationship to Output Gaps, Labor Market Study No.22*, Abu Dhabi: Center for Market Research and Information (CLMRI).

Alserhan, B.A., Forstenlechner, I. and Al-Nakeeb, A. (2010), 'Employees' attitudes toward diversity in a non-Western context', *Employee Relations*, **32**(1), 42–55.

Al Shamsi, F., Rutledge, E., Sheikh, H. and Bassioni, Y. (2009), *Implications of GCC Nationalisation Policies for Indigenous Female Jobseekers*, Gender Economic Research and Policy Analysis.

Barhem, B., Salih, A.H. and Yousef, D.A. (2008), 'The business curriculum and the future employment market: UAE business leaders' views', *Education, Business and Society: Contemporary Middle Eastern Issues*, **1**(2), 124–37.

Baum, J.A.C. and Oliver, C. (1991), 'Institutional linkages and organizational mortality', *Administrative Science Quarterly*, **36**(2), 187–218.

Boddewyn, J.J. (1998), 'Political aspects of MNE theory', *Journal of International Business Studies*, **19**(3), 341–63.

Boddewyn, J.J. and Brewer, L.T. (1994), 'International-business political behavior: New theoretical directions', *Academy of Management Review*, **19**(1), 119–43.

Bremmer, I. (2004), 'The Saudi paradox', *World Policy Journal*, **21**(3), 23–30.

Budhwar, P. and Mellahi, K. (2006), *Managing Human Resources in the Middle East*, London: Routledge.

Budhwar, P. and Mellahi, K. (2007), 'Introduction: Human resources management in the Middle East', *International Journal of Human Resource Management*, **18**(1), 2–10.

Chan, C.M. and Makino, S. (2007), 'Legitimacy and multi-level institutional environments: Implications for foreign subsidiary ownership structure', *Journal of International Business Studies*, **38**(4), 621–38.

Cordesman, A.H. (2002), *Saudi Arabia Enters the 21st Century: Economic, Demographic and Social Challenges*, Washington, DC: Center for Strategic and International Studies.

Cordesman, A.H. (2003), *Saudi Arabia Enters the Twenty-first Century: The Political, Foreign Policy, Economic, and Energy Dimensions*, Washington DC: Greenwood Publishing Group.

Davidson, C.M. (2009), 'The United Arab Emirates: Prospects for political reform', *The Brown Journal of World Affairs*, **15**(2), 117–27.

De Boer, K. and Turner, J. (2008), 'Beyond oil: Reappraising the Gulf States', *McKinsey Quarterly*, 13 March, 7–17.

DiMaggio, P. and Powell, W. (1983), 'The iron cage revisited: Institutional isomorphism and collective rationality in organizational fields', *American Sociological Review*, **48**(2), 147–60.

Dito, M. (2006) 'What can we learn from Bahrain's labour market reform?', in C. Kuptsch (ed.), *Merchants of Labour*, Switzerland: International Labour Organization, International Institute for Labour Studies.

Dowling, J. and Pfeffer, J. (1975), 'Organizational legitimacy: Social values and organizational behaviour', *Pacific Sociological Review*, **18**(1), 122–36.

Dyer, P. and Yousef, T. (2007), *Will the Current Oil Boom Solve the Employment Crisis in the Middle East?*, World Economic Forum.

Economist (2007), *UAE: Country Risk Summary. EIU Viewswire*, New York: Economist Intelligence Unit.

Fasano, U. and Goyal, R. (2004), *Emerging Strains in GCC Labour Markets*, Washington, DC: International Monetary Fund.

Forstenlechner, I. (2008), 'Workforce nationalization in the UAE: Image versus integration', *Education, Business and Society: Contemporary Middle Eastern Issues*, **1**(2), 82–91.

Frynas, J.G., Mellahi, K. and Pigman, A.G. (2006), 'First mover advantage in international business and firm-specific political resources', *Strategic Management Journal*, **27**(4), 321–45.

Godwin, S. (2006), 'Education and Emiratization: A case study of the United Arab Emirates', *The Electronic Journal of Information Systems in Developing Countries*, **27**(1), 1–14.

Government of the UAE (2007), The official website of the United Arab Emirates, available at: http://www.uaeinteract.com; accessed 20 January 2011.

Grant, J., Golawala, F. and McKechnie, D. (2007), 'The United Arab Emirates: The twenty-first century beckons', *Thunderbird International Business Review*, **49**(4), 507–33.

Hafez, S. (2009), 'Ministry confirms ban on sacking of Emirati workers', *The National*, 17 February, Abu Dhabi.

Harry, W. (2007), 'Employment creation and localization: The crucial human resource issues for the GCC', *International Journal of Human Resource Management*, **18**(1), 132–46.

Hoskisson, R.E., Hitt, M.A., Johnson, R.A. and Grossman, W. (2002), 'Conflicting voices: The effects of institutional ownership heterogeneity and internal governance on corporate innovation strategies', *Academy of Management Journal*, **45**(4), 697–716.

Human, S.E. and Provan, K.G. (2000), 'Legitimacy building in the evolution of small firm multilateral networks: A comparative study of success and demise', *Administrative Science Quarterly*, **45**(2), 327–69.

IMF (2004), *Staff Report for 2004 Article IV Consultation. IMF Country Report No. 04/174 and 175*, Washington DC: International Monetary Fund Publication Services.

Jones, S. (2008), 'Training and cultural context in the Arab Emirates: Fighting a losing battle?', *Employee Relations*, **30**(1), 48–62.

Kapiszewski, A. (2006), *Arab Versus Migrant Workers in the GCC Countries*, Beirut: United Nations Secretariat.

Knudsen, K., Aggarwal, P. and Maamoun, A. (2008), 'The burden of identity: Responding to product boycotts in the Middle East', *Journal of Business & Economics Research*, **6**(11), 17–26.

Kostova, T. and Roth, K. (2002), 'Adoption of an organizational practice by subsidiaries of multinational corporations: Institutional and relational effects', *Academy of Management Journal*, **45**(1), 215–33.

Kostova, T. and Zaheer, S. (1999), 'Organizational legitimacy under conditions of complexity: The case of the multinational enterprise', *The Academy of Management Review*, **24**(1), 64–81.

Kuntze, J. and Hormann, M. (2006), 'Migrating to skills-based nationalisation', *Pipeline Magazine*, April, Dubai.

Mazawi, A.E. (2003), 'The academic workplace in public Arab gulf universities', in P.G. Altbach (ed.), *The Decline of the Guru*, New York: Palgrave Macmillan.

Mellahi, K. (2007), 'The effect of regulations on HRM: Private sector firms in Saudi Arabia', *International Journal of Human Resource Management*, **18**(1), 85–99.

Mellahi, K. and Wood, G. (2002), 'Desperately seeking stability: The making and remaking of the Saudi Arabian petroleum growth regime', *Competition and Change*, **6**(4), 345–62.

Mohamed, A. (2002), 'Assessing determinants of departmental innovation: An exploratory multi-level approach', *Personnel Review*, **31**(5/6), 620–41.

New York University (2009), NYU-Abu Dhabi: Frequently Asked Questions, available at: http://nyuad.nyu.edu/about/faq.html; accessed 20 January 2011.

Niblock, T. (2007), *The Political Economy of Saudi Arabia*, London: Routledge.

Oliver, C. (1991), 'Strategic responses to institutional processes', *Academy of Management Review*, **16**(1), 145–79.

Oxford Business Group (2008a), *The Report: Qatar 2008*.

Oxford Business Group (2008b), *The Report: Dubai 2008*.

Oxford Business Group (2008c), *The Report: Bahrain 2008*.

Oxford Business Group (2008d), *The Report: Kuwait 2008*.

Quilliam, N. (2003), 'The states of the Gulf Cooperation Council', in T.P. Najem and M. Hetherington (ed.), *Good Governance in the Middle East Oil Monarchies*, London: Routledge.

Rattab, B., Anis, B. and Mellahi, K. (2008), 'A study of the relationship between CSR and business performance in fast developing economies', AIB Annual Conference.

Rees, C., Mamman, A. and Bin Braik, A. (2007), 'Emiratization as a strategic HRM change initiative: Case study evidence from a UAE petroleum company', *International Journal of Human Resource Management*, **18**(1), 33–53.

Ring, P.S., Lenway, S. and Govekar, M. (1990), 'Management of the political imperative in international business', *Strategic Management Journal*, **11**(2), 141–51.

Rupp, R. (2009), 'Higher education in the Middle East: Opportunities and challenges for U.S. universities and Middle East partners', *Global Media Journal*, **8**(14).

Ruppert, E. (1999), *Managing Foreign Labour in Singapore and Malaysia: Are there Lessons for GCC Countries?*, Washington DC: World Bank.

Rutledge, E.J. (2009), *Monetary Union in the Gulf – Prospects for a Single Currency in the Arabian Peninsula*, London: Routledge.

Scott, R. and Meyer, J. (1983), 'The organization of societal sectors', in J. Meyer and R. Scott (eds), *Organizational Environments: Ritual and Rationality*, Newbury Park, CA: Sage.

Suchman, M.C. (1995), 'Managing legitimacy: Strategic and institutional approaches', *Academy of Management Review*, **20**(3), 571–610.

Toledo, H. (2006), *The Problems and Prospects of Emiratization: Immigration in an Imperfect Labor Market*, Dubai: Dubai Economic Research Awards.

Wilson, R., Al-Salamah, A., Malik, M. and Al-Rajhi, A. (2004), *Economic Development in Saudi Arabia*, London: Routledge.

Winckler, O. (2005), *Arab Political Demography: Population Growth and Nationalist Policies*, Sussex: Sussex Academic Press.

World Bank (2004), *Unlocking the Employment Potential in the Middle East and North Africa: Toward a New Social Contract*, Washington, DC: World Bank.

Zaheer, S. (1995), 'Overcoming the liability of foreignness', *The Academy of Management Journal*, **38**(2), 341–63.

Zimmerman, M. and Zeitz, G. (2002), 'Beyond survival: Achieving new venture growth by building legitimacy', *Academy of Management Review*, **27**(3), 414–32.

PART 4

BROADER
COMPARATIVE
INFLUENCES

16 Corporatism meets neoliberalism: the Irish and Italian cases in comparative perspective
Lucio Baccaro

INTRODUCTION

Until a few years ago the consensus among comparative political economists and industrial relations scholars was that corporatism was, if not dead, at least seriously ill, and that it would not be able to survive the blows of (depending on the observer's angle) globalization, European integration, technological change and a generalized employer offensive (Schmitter, 1989; Streeck and Schmitter, 1991; Gobeyn, 1993; Streeck, 1993; Thelen, 1994; Locke, 1995; Iversen, 1999; Iversen et al., 2000; Hall and Soskice, 2001a).

This chapter begins by arguing, based on a new measure of corporatist policy-making, that the analyses predicting a demise of corporatist bargaining are unduly extrapolated from a limited number of highly symbolic events like the demise of centralized bargaining in Sweden (Swenson, 1991; Iversen, 1996; Swenson and Pontusson, 2000). In fact there is no sign of systematic decline in corporatism as institutional structure, as also witnessed by the recent literature on the emergence of social pacts in numerous countries and regions (Regini, 1997; Wallerstein et al., 1997; Perez, 2000; Compston, 2002; Culpepper, 2002, 2008; Molina and Rhodes, 2002; Baccaro, 2003; Traxler, 2004; Hassel, 2006; Hamann and Kelly, 2007; Baccaro and Simoni, 2008; Hassel, 2009; Avdagic, 2010).

However, the political-economic function of the new corporatism is pointedly different from that of golden age corporatism. The latter was an alternative to liberal capitalism, namely to a political-economic regime in which the market is the main mechanism of economic coordination, and conscious, political intervention in the economy is kept to a minimum. It was dubbed a 'superior economic system' exactly for its ability to reconcile good economic performance with a large and activist public sector, a capillary social protection system and an egalitarian income and wage distribution (Pekkarinen et al., 1992; Pontusson, 2005). The new corporatism is instead a process by which governments, which are for various reasons (e.g., parliamentary weakness or fear of electoral retribution) unable or unwilling to proceed unilaterally, implement essentially neoliberal policies.

Internally, the new corporatist institutions are much more participatory and democratic than in the old days. Unions, in particular, take great pain to democratically legitimate the outcomes of national bargaining through debates and referenda. This coexistence between market-conforming policy outcomes and democratic organizational features is not a coincidence, the chapter argues, but a causal relationship. In the new political-economic regime, trade unions are no longer rewarded for bargaining moderation through more generous social protection programs as they once were. The search for procedural legitimacy compensates for declining (or even absent) output legitimacy (Scharpf, 1999).

The remainder of the chapter develops the argument sketched above as follows: it begins with an overview of recent trends in corporatist policy-making. It goes on to discuss the new corporatism as adaptation to a neoliberal political-economic regime. It illustrates the argument by analyzing developments in Ireland and Italy, the two countries in which the corporatist renaissance has been both most evident and most surprising. It concludes by pondering the implications of the argument for institutional change in advanced countries.

MEASURING CORPORATIST POLICY-MAKING

Neo-corporatist policy-making was originally conceived of as the combination of two elements (Schmitter, 1982): (1) a structure of the interest group system characterized by singular, monopolistic and internally hierarchical interest groups (Schmitter, 1974); and (2) a process of public policy formation in which the above groups were systematically involved (Pizzorno, 1978b; Lehmbruch, 1979; Streeck and Kenworthy, 2005). The label adopted, '(neo)-corporatism', was meant to simultaneously draw attention to the structural similarities between the interest group systems of some modern democracies and those of the old (i.e., fascist) corporatist systems (Crouch, 1983), and to underscore that typical of the policy regime in question was the 'incorporation' of interest groups into the machinery of government (Martin, 1983).

Structure and process were thought to be strictly connected, if not logically at least empirically (Cawson, 1986). A corporatist organization of the interest group system was deemed to provide the most hospitable institutional environment for the emergence and reproduction over time of corporatist (a.k.a. 'concertative') policy-making. This was because the types of policies negotiated in corporatist forums required interest groups to have (or develop) a capacity to sacrifice the short-term interests of their constituents in exchange for gains that furthered the long-term interests of the organization, which in turn largely coincided with the general interest of the national economy as whole. Only interest groups that were both monopolistic in their domain, that is, insulated from competition from similar groups, and internally hierarchical, that is, with leaders that could ignore the members' dissent, would be reliable partners in corporatist deals.

The early indicators of corporatism consisted of rankings of countries based on rather impressionistic assessments of interest group participation in policy-making, associational centralization, organizational density (capturing the extent of organizational *encompassingness* [Olson, 1982]), and collective bargaining structure (centralized or coordinated) (Schmitter, 1981; Cameron, 1984; Bruno and Sachs, 1985; Tarantelli, 1986a; Lehner, 1987; Calmfors and Driffill, 1988; Soskice, 1990; Dell'Aringa and Samek Lodovici, 1992). In addition, these indexes were snapshots taken at a particular point in time. As such, they made it very difficult to analyze change.

Recently, however, a number of time-series cross-country databases have become available, thus permitting a detailed evaluation of the various dimensions implicated in the corporatist construct (Kenworthy, 2003; Golden et al., 2006; Visser, 2009). Here I rely on these data, as well as others I collected myself, to elaborate a time-changing measure of corporatist policy-making, which I then use to address the question of whether corporatism is in crisis or not.

The measure of corporatist policy-making presented here focuses on the process dimension of corporatism, that is, concertation. It centers on the degree of coordination of collective bargaining on the one hand – which is what particularly the early scholarship on corporatism focused upon (Cameron, 1984; Bruno and Sachs, 1985; Tarantelli, 1986b; Calmfors and Driffill, 1988; Rowthorn, 1992) – and on a new index measuring the extent of tripartite involvement in macroeconomic, social and labor market policy on the other hand. These two components are weighted equally in the composite index.

For data on collective bargaining structure, I rely on the well-known index elaborated by Lane Kenworthy, updated to 2005. For the measure of tripartite policy-making, I use data that I jointly collected with John-Paul Ferguson of Stanford University. They are based on the monthly coding of articles from the *European Industrial Relations Review*, a practitioners' publication, supplemented with yearly data from Visser's database (2009) for three non-European countries: Australia, Canada and the US.[1] The data record if and when a negotiated agreement was signed; the policy

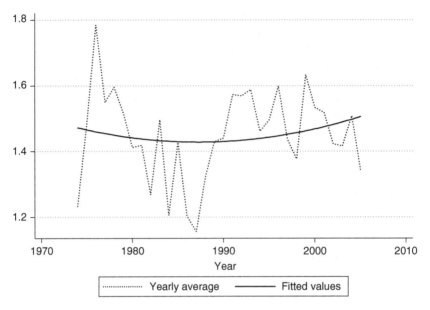

Sources: Kenworthy (2003), Visser (2009) and *European Industrial Relations Review*.

*Figure 16.1   Mean yearly index of corporatist policy-making
             (16 countries)*

issues covered by such agreement (centralized wage regulation, labor
market policy, welfare policy); the actors that signed it; and its duration.
The data are recorded monthly and then aggregated in yearly averages.

The two components of the indicator complement each other. While
the first component focuses on the degree of collective bargaining coordination, which may be the result of purely bipartite interaction, the
second component focuses on negotiated public policy-making and does
not record purely bipartite centralized agreements (rather common in
Scandinavian and other Northern European countries), which should
be captured by the first term. In addition, because not all agreements are
perfectly tripartite, the scores of tripartite policy-making are weighted by
the extent to which unions and employer organizations buy into them. A
country scores high on the corporatist policy-making index not just when
its bargaining structure is highly coordinated, but also when its policy-
making process involves the social partners on macroeconomic, labor and
social policies.

Figure 16.1 displays yearly averages of the index for 16 advanced countries (Australia, Austria, Belgium, Canada, Denmark, Finland, France,

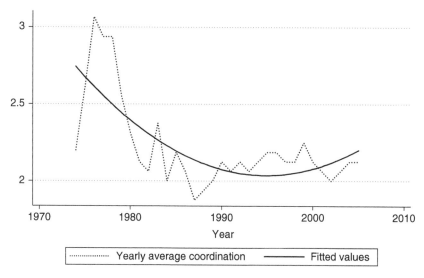

Source: Kenworthy (2003).

Figure 16.2 Mean yearly index of collective bargaining coordination

Germany, Ireland, Italy, Netherlands, Norway, Spain, Sweden, UK and US) between 1974 and 2005. The graph suggests that there was indeed a decline of corporatist policy-making from the late 1970s to the late 1980s, but also a renaissance in the 1990s. This is clearly evident in Finland, Ireland, Italy and Spain. Australia, Denmark, Sweden and the UK are cases of decline.

Figures 16.2 and 16.3 plot the two components of the index, collective bargaining coordination and tripartite policy-making, separately. The structure of collective bargaining became less coordinated between the late 1970s and the early 1980s, thus confirming the insights of the literature on collective bargaining decentralization (Locke, 1992; Katz, 1993; Locke et al., 1995; Katz and Darbishire, 2000), but then remained stable (Figure 16.2). Instead, tripartite involvement in policy-making grew continuously throughout the 1980s and 1990s, albeit at a declining rate. This suggests that the corporatism that re-emerged in the 1990s was of a particular kind: it combined a less coordinated organization of industrial relations with deeper involvement of the social partners in the political sphere (Katz et al., 2004).

Table 16.1 displays rankings of countries based on the corporatist policy-making index described above. The index for 1974–89 is similar to the various indexes produced in the 1980s as it places Belgium, Sweden, Austria and other Scandinavian countries towards the top, US, Canada,

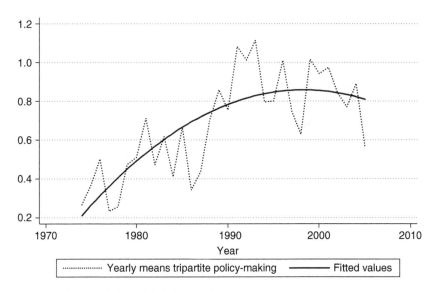

Yearly means tripartite policy-making .... ———— Fitted values

Source: *European Industrial Relations Review.*

Figure 16.3   Mean yearly index of tripartite policy-making

Table 16.1   Corporatism index: country scores and rankings

	1974–1989		1990–2005		Change in Ranking		Change in Score
Belgium	2.56	Ireland	3.76	Ireland	10	Ireland	2.44
Sweden	2.04	Belgium	2.89	Italy	7	Italy	0.85
Norway	2.03	Norway	2.82	Germany	2	Norway	0.79
Austria	2.00	Finland	2.70	France	2	Finland	0.72
Finland	1.98	Italy	1.90	Finland	1	Belgium	0.32
Spain	1.90	Austria	1.84	Netherlands	1	Netherlands	0.26
Denmark	1.56	Netherlands	1.79	Canada	1	Germany	0.19
Netherlands	1.53	Germany	1.69	Norway	0	France	0.01
Australia	1.52	Denmark	1.22	US	0	US	0.00
Germany	1.50	Spain	1.13	Belgium	−1	Austria	−0.16
Ireland	1.32	Sweden	1.13	Austria	−2	Denmark	−0.34
Italy	1.05	France	0.56	Denmark	−2	Canada	−0.38
UK	0.68	Australia	0.48	UK	−2	UK	−0.68
France	0.55	Canada	0.00	Spain	−4	Spain	−0.78
Canada	0.38	UK	0.00	Australia	−4	Sweden	−0.92
US	0.00	US	0.00	Sweden	−9	Australia	−1.03

Source: Kenworthy (2003), Visser (2009) and *European Industrial Relations Review.*

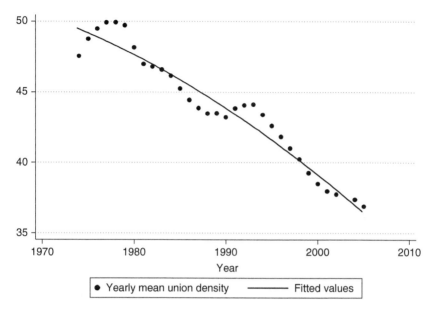

Source: Visser (2009).

Figure 16.4   Mean yearly union density in 16 OECD countries

France, UK and Italy towards the bottom and Germany somewhere in the middle (see Schmitter, 1981). Germany has never been a poster case for national-level macro-corporatism (Martin and Thelen, 2007).

The ranking for 1990–2005 is considerably different, with two countries, Italy and Ireland, with much greater corporatist scores than in the previous period, and two other countries, Australia and Sweden, falling to the bottom of the table as a result of the dismantling of the Accord in Australia and the demise of centralized bargaining in Sweden.

A peculiarity of the new corporatism relative to the old is that it took place in a context of generalized decline in union strength (see Figure 16.4). This phenomenon did not just affect a handful of Anglo-Saxon countries in which institutional protections are traditionally less extensive than in Continental European countries, but was equally significant in comparatively union-friendly countries such as Austria, Germany and the Netherlands. Even the Ghent countries (Belgium, Denmark, Finland and Sweden) were affected by it, although to a lesser extent than other countries.

In brief, the evidence suggests that there has been no crisis of corporatist policy-making: there has been a decline in the 1980s, but it has been followed by a re-emergence in the 1990s. Compared with the old, however, the new corporatism has been characterized by a less coordinated bargaining structure and a more explicit involvement of the social partners in national policy-making. Also, it has emerged against the backdrop of generalized labor decline. Interestingly, the countries that have been at the forefront of the corporatist renaissance have been Ireland and Italy, that is, two countries that previous scholarship had qualified as particularly inhospitable for this kind of policy-making.

The next section examines whether continuity in institutional structure also implies continuity in institutional function, that is, whether the new corporatism plays the same role in current European political economies as its golden age progenitor.

THE CORPORATIST RENAISSANCE AS ADAPTATION TO THE NEOLIBERAL REGIME

When scholars wrote about the 'crisis' or 'demise' of corporatism, their arguments rested on two elements: the problems encountered by corporatist policy-making in symbol countries like Sweden, and the realization that the international macroeconomic context had become much less conducive to a system based on the institutionalized involvement of trade unions in policy-making than had previously been the case. As is appropriate for Hegel's 'owl of Minerva', which spreads its wings only at the coming of dusk, scholarship reflected real-world developments with a temporal gap: the literature on crisis reached its peak of popularity in the 1990s, when (as we now know with the benefit of hindsight) there were already considerable signs of regeneration.

For many political economists, corporatist policy-making was essentially an institutional arrangement specialized in the delivery of wage moderation (Flanagan et al., 1983; Bruno and Sachs, 1985; Tarantelli, 1986a). Centralized control over wage dynamics was deemed indispensable in a Keynesian political economy committed to full employment (Kalecki, 1943), but superfluous in a new regime in which the commitment to full employment was relaxed and independent central banks could assure wage moderation by threatening to deflate the economy (Scharpf, 1991; Notermans, 2000).

For other scholars, corporatism had broader significance than just centralized wage restraint, and represented nothing less than a systemic alternative to liberal capitalism. In a corporatist economy, trade unions had much more institutionalized power than under liberal capitalism. However, rather than using this power disruptively in the economic sphere, they learned to use it in the political sphere to expand public consumption, decommodify public services and bring about greater levels of economic equality than in other capitalist economies at comparable levels of development (Pizzorno, 1978b; Korpi and Shalev, 1979; Stephens, 1979; Korpi, 1983; Glyn and Rowthorn, 1988; Esping-Andersen, 1990; Streeck, 2006).

To be sure, some scholars criticized labor incorporation as a sell-out, perpetrated by union leaders behind the back and at the expense of the working class (Jessop, 1977; Panitch, 1979). For most scholars, however, particularly those of social-democratic leaning, corporatist institutions provided unions with opportunities to gain access and influence in areas that had traditionally been beyond their reach. The result was a *negotiated economy* in which the sphere of production remained solidly capitalist, because property rights were protected and management discretion at the workplace level guaranteed, but the sphere of distribution was largely politically managed, both through collective bargaining and through the redistributive policies of an activist welfare state.

With the collapse of the Bretton Woods regime and with the policy of high interest rates of the US Reagan government (which, combined with the progressive dismantling of capital controls, made it costly for governments to engage in expansionary fiscal policies), the room for maneuver for any kind of economically interventionist government, including one that negotiated policy decisions with the unions, shrank dramatically. The widespread transition to a 'hard currency' regime took care of inflation with no need for costly involvement of trade unions in policy-making (Notermans, 2000). By the end of the 1980s, the problem of inflation was largely under control in advanced countries, albeit at the cost of a large increase in unemployment (see Figure 16.5).

Incomes policies run into problems of their own: more often than not, centralized negotiations ended up being undone by wage drift at the workplace level, even in countries, like Sweden, in which unions supposedly had the ability to discipline their members. It soon became clear that the government's policy of full employment created perverse incentives for unions to renege on their commitments to deliver wage moderation (Scharpf, 1991), and that the goal of wage moderation was more effectively pursued when bargaining actors heeded the signals launched by inflation-conscious independent central banks (Hall and Franzese, 1998; Soskice and Iversen, 2000; Franzese, 2002).

In brief, it looked as if corporatism – an important institution in the now forgone era of national control over the economy, Keynesian demand management and 'embedded liberalism' (Ruggie, 1982) – no longer had a clear role to play in the new political-economic context.

Consistent with this view, employers no longer began to regard union involvement in national collective bargaining and public policy as the

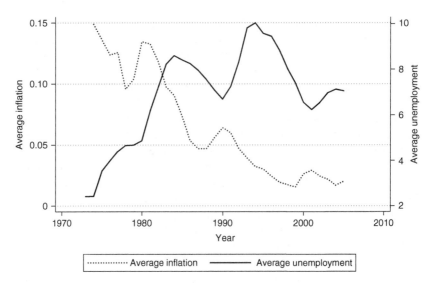

Source: OECD.

Figure 16.5   Inflation and unemployment in 16 countries

inevitable price to pay for social peace and economic stability, but increasingly as a costly and inefficient rigidity that was no longer necessary and that could be safely disposed of (Streeck, 1984; Gobeyn, 1993; Soskice, 1999; Swenson and Pontusson, 2000).

For some time it was hoped that the process of European integration would reconstitute state sovereignty at the supra-national level, and provide a new ground for the corporatist exchange to prosper. It soon became clear, however, that the European project relied on 'negative' (i.e., market) integration much more than on 'positive' (i.e., political) integration (Scharpf, 1999), and that by allowing for mutual recognition of national regulatory regimes, it did not include a significant social dimension.

In the light of these premises, the scholars writing about the demise of corporatism in the 1990s could be forgiven for thinking that the institutions of the corporatist era had outlived their function and had been dispatched to the dustbin of history. However, this view overlooked the fact that the transition to the new (neoliberal) regime was not going to be automatic but needed to be politically managed. The structural reforms European economies arguably needed to withstand the competition of the more dynamic Anglo-Saxon economies (Alesina and Giavazzi, 2006) were tough and potentially electorally damaging for the governments that sought to implement them. They included not just wage moderation as in the old days, but also fiscal rectitude (implying a 'rationalization' of the public sector), labor market flexibility and welfare state reform.

These reforms reduced benefits, tightened eligibility conditions and shifted risks from the state (or the employers) to workers and citizens. Not all governments had the institutional resources or political will needed to drive them through. Those governments that due to limited parliamentary strength or volatile electoral competition were unable or unwilling to impose unilaterally a series of measures that were more or less imposed on them by international economic constraints found that corporatist pacts were an expedient way to increase the legitimacy of their policies (Hamann and Kelly, 2007; Baccaro and Simoni, 2008). Thus, corporatist policy-making became one of the channels by which neoliberal policies made their way into the institutionally dense political economies of some European countries (Rhodes, 1996, 2001; Streeck, 2000, 2006).

To see what exactly is meant by neoliberal policy, it is helpful to make reference to what is often considered one of its clearest statements: John Williamson's (in)famous 'Washington Consensus' paper: 'What Washington means by policy reform' (Williamson, 1989). The document was meant to summarize the policy approach shared by Washington institutions such as the IMF, the World Bank and the US Treasury when dealing with developing countries applying for international loans. It took a strong stance in favor of fiscal discipline: balanced budgets were to be achieved not through tax increases, but rather through expenditure cuts (see also Alesina and Perotti, 1997a, 1997b; Alesina and Ardagna, 1998). Indeed, marginal tax rates should be reduced and the tax base broadened. Interest rates should be determined by the market, which ruled out bureaucratic allocation of credit, and the exchange rate should also be market-determined, but kept 'competitive' (that is, undervalued) to favor export-led growth. Trade should be liberalized, policies should be put in place to attract foreign direct investment and to ensure full repatriation of foreign profits, state-owned enterprises should be privatized and industries should be deregulated.

While some of the points discussed in the document – for example, about the importance of ensuring adequate protection of property rights, or about the need to shift public expenditures from subsidies to education and health care – were not especially relevant for European and advanced countries, most other points were absolutely pertinent. In fact I would argue that they expressed the consensus shared not just by the IMF and the World Bank but by other international organizations as well, such as the OECD and the European Commission.

In addition to those listed in the Williamson (1989) paper, another policy reform figured prominently in the European debate of the 1990s: the reform of the welfare state, particularly pensions and labor market shock absorbers. In the case of pension reform the emphasis was on adapting European pension systems to changing demographic and economic conditions by increasing the retirement age, shifting from defined benefit systems (in which financial risks are borne by the provider) to defined contribution systems (in which pension benefits are strictly proportional to contributions accumulated and risks are shifted onto the pensioners' shoulders) and introducing supplementary fully funded private pension funds (Bonoli, 2001; Myles and Pierson, 2001; Pierson, 2001; Immergut and Anderson, 2007).

In the case of labor market reform, the consensus was that generous unemployment benefits were counterproductive as they sapped incentives to actively search for jobs, encouraged long-term unemployment and caused real wages to rise beyond productivity increases. The emphasis was therefore on reform initiatives that reduced both the level and duration of benefits, and that made benefit payment contingent on active search and willingness to accept available jobs. Employment protection legislation was also targeted for reform. It was argued that by discouraging firms' ability to hire and fire at will it limited labor market mobility and strengthened the divide between labor market insiders and outsiders (Lindbeck and Snower, 1988; Bertola, 1990; OECD, 1994; Nickell, 1997; Siebert, 1997; Blanchard and Wolfers, 2000; Saint-Paul, 2002; Layard et al., 2005; Rueda, 2005; Blanchard, 2006).

The corporatist agreements of the 1990s frequently dealt with issues of welfare state and labor market reform. The form that these agreements took was often that of a deal between government and unions. The employers could afford to sit on the sidelines and, if the opportunity arose, ask for more. Not all governments sought out union cooperation on these matters, and not all unions agreed to provide it. Also, even within the same country, not all policy reforms were negotiated; some were passed unilaterally (Regini, 2000). When a corporatist pact was struck, the unions often managed to soften the sharpest edges of policy reform, but not to reverse its main thrust, which remained neoliberal.

Centralized control of wage dynamics was solidly at the core of the new corporatist pacts, just as it had been at the center of the old corporatist pacts. In this period, however, the key goal was no longer disinflation but real wage containment. In an environment of fixed exchanges rates, and later on a single European currency, real wage moderation, that is, wages growing less than productivity, was tantamount to real exchange rate devaluation. Like real exchange rate devaluation, it bolstered the cost competitiveness of the national economy (Baccaro and Simoni, 2010). All of this was premised on a growth model in which domestic demand grew sluggishly and exports were the most dynamic component of aggregate demand.

The model worked remarkably well in small open economies, such as Ireland or the Netherlands, where cost competitiveness spurred profit accumulation, which in turn led to employment and growth, but it did not work for countries characterized by larger domestic markets, where wage moderation ultimately depressed aggregate demand (Carlin and Soskice, 2009).

Given the type of policies the new corporatism dealt with, it is not surprising that its outcomes were much less egalitarian than those of the old one (Baccaro, 2009). Worse, corporatism began to be perceived in some quarters as positively anti-egalitarian, that is, as an institutional device that served the interests and further entrenched the privileges of labor market insiders – middle-aged union members – at the expense of outsiders, that is, younger workers and women (AAVV, 2002; Rueda, 2005; Alesina and Giavazzi, 2006; Boeri and Galasso, 2007).

Unions have generally brandished the 'sword of justice' and this has greatly contributed to their legitimacy in the eyes of the public at large (Flanders, 1970). This time, however, the sword of justice was turned against them. They were often accused of preventing reforms that would have been not only efficiency-enhancing but also more equitable than the status quo. Union-negotiated pension reforms were often criticized for overly generous grandfathering rules (aimed at protecting aging workers, the unions' main constituency), which shifted most of the costs of reforms onto the younger generations (Aprile, 1996; Castellino, 1996; Schludi, 2003; Ferrera and Jessoula, 2007; OECD, 2007). Labor market reforms were also perceived as inadequate: they left levels of job protection virtually unchanged for workers on unlimited duration contracts, while they liberalized other forms of contingent work, thus contributing to labor market dualism (Ichino, 1996; OECD, 1999; Baccaro and Simoni, 2004).

In most circumstances, the new corporatist pacts presented unions with the unpleasant alternative of having to choose between consenting to macro-concessionary bargaining or refusing to do so. Political exchange as quid pro quo between wage moderation and more generous social protection (Glyn and Rowthorn, 1988; Mares, 2006) virtually disappeared as most governments' public budgets became too constrained to allow for significant side payments. Where political exchange continued to be practiced (e.g., in Ireland and Finland), it traded wage moderation for tax reductions, that is, it sought to increase private, not public, consumption.

Why did unions accept the new corporatist deals? Here a difference needs to be made between leaders and followers. The explanation for why union leaders accepted the new corporatist game is overdetermined by considerations of leaders' self-interest: union leaders may have a direct interest in peak-level bargaining as this strengthens their role and visibility (Pizzorno, 1978b; Sabel, 1981); organizational characteristics: encompassing organizations spontaneously embrace policies serving the general interest, as for them group interests approximately coincide with general interests (Olson, 1982; Lange, 1984); and rational consideration of alternatives: although not particularly attractive, the terms offered by corporatist pacts were still better than if government had proceeded unilaterally.

As for followers, a plausible answer to the question of why rank-and-file workers went along with the leaders' decisions is that what members want does not matter much: when organizational leaders are equipped with appropriate institutional resources, for example, a highly centralized organizational structure, compulsory membership, public recognition, they can silence or ignore internal dissent. This is the classic corporatist answer to the problem of 'compliance' (Schmitter, 1974; Crouch, 1983; Wolfe, 1985; Cawson, 1988; Streeck, 1988).

The problem with this explanation is that it does not find a lot of support in the data. It is simply not the case that the new corporatist pacts succeeded in countries with corporatist interest groups (e.g., Austria, Belgium and Sweden), and failed elsewhere. On the contrary, pacts mushroomed in countries like Italy, Ireland, Portugal, Spain and others, which had traditionally been seen as lacking corporatist preconditions (Baccaro, 2003).

The changes in the terms of political exchange help to make sense of the changes in organizational structures. It is conceivable that when union concessions are compensated with side payments there is no particular need for trade union leaders to pay a lot of attention to the internal process; when instead exchange resources are scant or absent, and union virtue is largely a prize to itself, it becomes much more important for leaders to make sure that their decisions are perceived as procedurally legitimate. Procedural legitimacy substitutes for faltering output legitimacy (Scharpf, 1999).

As illustrated below, the leaders of unions engaged in new corporatist pacts relied heavily on organizational processes based on democracy and discussion. This allowed them to activate two mechanisms of consensus mobilization, one purely aggregative (that is, not implying the shaping or transformation of preferences), the other with a transformative effect on preferences. The adoption of formal voting procedures (aggregative mechanism) altered the internal political game between moderate and radical factions within trade unions as a 'logic of mobilization' (one in which the faction prevails that is better able to mobilize workers in strikes)

(Pizzorno, 1978a) was replaced by an electoral 'logic of representation' (in which the faction prevails that is better able to mobilize the largest number of votes). Because the principle 'one head, one vote' abstracts from consideration of preference intensity, workers with very intense preferences, that is, ready to mobilize in support of their claims, found themselves having exactly the same impact on collective choices as other, more apathetic, but more numerous, workers (Dahl, 1956).

Additionally, the vote was preceded by workplace assemblies in which leaders used various arguments, mostly pragmatic, but also ethical and moral, to explain why particular decisions were worth taking, and then debated with workers the appropriateness of the particular solutions proposed. This process of discursive democracy contributed to shape the preferences of a non-negligible portion of the unions' membership, and favored the emergence of consensus for unpalatable reforms.

To summarize, this section has argued that unlike the old, the new corporatism is perfectly compatible with neoliberal policy-making. Indeed, it is an institutional arrangement by which governments unable or unwilling to proceed unilaterally render their policy reforms more palatable. The transition from organizational centralization to internal democracy allows union leaders to increase the legitimacy of the changes introduced. The next section illustrates the argument through case studies of Ireland and Italy.

THE TRAJECTORY OF CORPORATISM IN IRELAND AND ITALY

For many years, Ireland and Italy were both considered problem cases in respect to corporatist policy-making. In Ireland, collective bargaining had been conducted at the national level in the 1970s in an effort to control inflation (Roche, 1997). Yet employers had been dissatisfied with it, as centrally negotiated wage rates had often been supplemented by 'above the norm' wage increases negotiated at the enterprise level. Consequently they had promoted the return to decentralized bargaining in the 1980s. In Italy, too, several attempts had been made in the late 1970s and early 1980s to introduce national-level corporatism, but these attempts had been torpedoed by grassroots mobilizations promoted particularly by the metalworkers and their unions (Lange and Vannicelli, 1982; Golden, 1988).

Yet in both countries corporatist policy-making emerged in the 1990s. As shown in Table 16.1, Ireland and Italy are the two countries in which the index of corporatism increased the most. In addition, Ireland topped the corporatist ranking in 1990–2005. The emergence of corporatist institutions in these two countries occurred despite apparently inhospitable institutional and organizational environments, at least according to prevailing scholarly views. In 1988, an Irish scholar wrote that:

> the organizational and political conditions which would tend to be conducive to sustaining neo-corporatist agreements were not well developed in Ireland, therefore concertative wage bargaining could not develop very far. In particular, the trade union movement's authoritative centralization was limited, and it was constrained in its ability to devise a central strategy and secure the compliance of all affiliates. (Hardiman, 1988, p. 3)

Similar judgments were often expressed about Italy, which was constantly ranked at or near the bottom of the various indexes of corporatism.

In both countries the choice to engage in corporatist policy-making was made by electorally weak governments faced with deep economic crises. The most important allies of government were unions that were willing to make sacrifices to strengthen national competitiveness. In both cases the union movement was rather organizationally fragmented and not particularly centralized; it relied on democratic decision-making procedures to silence the internal opposition and rally consensus within their own ranks. Also, in both countries centralized wage regulation led to wages that systematically trailed productivity increases, thus producing a decline in the wage share. However, only in Ireland the gains in competitiveness translated into lower unemployment and faster growth, at least for some time. Italy's economic performance remained instead lackluster: unemployment continued to rise and growth stagnated (see Figure 16.6).

When the first of eight three-year 'social partnership' agreements was signed in Ireland in 1987, the country was in the midst of perhaps the most serious economic crisis of its post-war history. Public debt and deficit were skyrocketing, investments were stagnant, and, undeterred by migration of Irish workers to other countries (particularly the UK), unemployment was on the rise (NESC, 1986; Government of Ireland, 1987). The government that initiated social partnership was a minority government of the *Fianna Fáil*, which held 48.8 per cent of seats in the Irish lower chamber (*Dáil*). Additionally, the weakness of the *Fianna Fáil* government was compounded by the party's own interclass nature, which made it difficult for the leadership to pass policy decisions that penalized the party's labor constituency (Hardiman, 1988, pp. 200–204).

In Italy, too, the government was pushed to engage in corporatist negotiations by a highly volatile political-economic environment in the early 1990s, characterized by the simultaneous occurrence of a serious financial crisis, which eventually pushed the Italian currency out of the

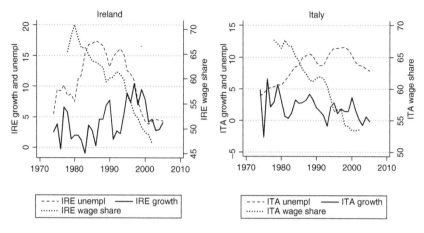

Source: OECD.

Figure 16.6 *Growth, unemployment (left axis), and wage share (right axis) in Ireland and Italy*

European Monetary System (Vaciago, 1993), and popular outrage at what the unfolding *clean hands* judicial investigation was divulging about corruption practices within all major political parties, particularly the Christian Democratic and Socialist ones. The 1992 government that initi-ated the season of Italian corporatism (by negotiating the 1992 abolition of national wage indexation) was remarkably weak, even by national standards: it was supported by a coalition of four parties, among which the most important were the Christian Democrats and the Socialists, both overwhelmed by scandals. This government had a majority of only one seat in the Senate (Ginsborg, 1998, p. 481). Moreover, seven cabinet members had to resign between 1992 and 1993 because they became impli-cated in judicial investigations (ibid., p. 515). The government that fol-lowed in 1993 was a 'technical' government, composed by experts in their fields, and did not have a clear parliamentary majority.

These electorally weak governments were faced by organizationally weakened unions: union density declined from 64 to 56 per cent between 1983 and 1987 in Ireland, and from 45 to 39 per cent between 1984 and 1992 in Italy. The unions' capacity to mobilize workers in strikes remained, however, considerable. Sharing policy-making responsibility with the organizations representing those that were most likely to bear the brunt of policy changes, namely workers, protected these weak gov-ernments from the popular discontent that they may have been unable to handle otherwise.

Collaboration with the employers was instead more inconsistent, but also probably less essential than collaboration with the unions. The Irish organized employers were relatively happy with the decentralized collective bargaining, which they had been keen to promote (Hardiman, 1988, pp. 200, 221, 236). In December 1986 and then again in June 1987, the General Council of the major employer association 'asserted that negotiations with the trade unions on pay and related matters should continue to take place at local level' (ibid., p. 236; 1992, p. 350). Government had to work hard to persuade them to stay at the bargaining table (Roche, 1997, p. 200; Gunnigle et al., 1999, p. 206). It was only after social partnership became a clear success (that is, from the mid-1990s on) that the employers became clear supporters. The attitude of Italian employers was similarly ambiguous: they agreed on the abolition of wage indexation in 1992 and the centralization of collective bargaining in 1993, but then withdrew from negotiations over pension reform in 1995 (Mascini, 2000).

Getting the unions to collaborate with government was not without problems. Within the unions there were powerful forces that for ideological or interest-related reasons did not agree with the corporatist strategy adopted by the confederations. In Ireland, the craft unions believed that decentralized bargaining would be more advantageous for them (Teague, 1995). In Italy, particularly the metalworking unions, which had blocked previous attempts at institutionalizing centralized wage regulation through spectacular grassroots mobilization (Lange and Vannicelli, 1982; Golden, 1988), regarded the strategic shift towards centralization as illegitimate (Baccaro, 2000).

In both countries, the way union confederations went about overcoming the internal opposition was by relying on the legitimating power of democracy. Workers were given binding power to decide through their vote whether or not they accepted the agreements. Worker referenda were organized. They were preceded by workplace assemblies. Because the majority of voters approved, the union leaders could then sign the agreements with full legitimacy (see Baccaro, 2003 for more on this). In Italy, the practice of balloting on major national agreements was introduced for the first time in 1993 and applied to all the most controversial national agreements, like those on pension reform in 1995 and 2007. In Ireland this practice already existed, but it was strengthened and generalized after the onset of social partnership.

In both the Irish and Italian cases, corporatist policy-making centered on a solid core of centralized wage bargaining. One important difference between the two cases was in the scope and breadth of the agreements: in Ireland social pacts covered all major policy-making issues simultaneously; in Italy there was instead a succession of single-issue deals: on the abolition of wage indexation, on collective bargaining structure, on pension reform, on labor market flexibility, on the reform on employment protection, and so on. Another important difference was in the type of exchange involved: while in Ireland there was a quid pro quo between wage moderation and lower personal income tax rates, in Italy (where the government was more fiscally constrained) no such exchange was present. The only reward for the unions was participation itself (Molina and Rhodes, 2002).

In both countries corporatism and wage moderation came with none of the compensations usually associated with them in the golden age of corporatism: no statutory gains or special recognition procedures for unions were introduced; no attempts were made centrally to reduce wage differentials and thus reduce wage inequality; public expenditures were kept well under control and social programs were careful not to sap work incentives. However, the consequences for the two national economies were dramatically different.

In Ireland centralized wage regulation became the lynchpin of a very different regulatory model from the social corporatism model of the past (Pekkarinen et al., 1992), but remarkably economically successful nonetheless. This new model focused on making the country attractive for mobile international capital and on strengthening the cost competitiveness of exports by systematically reducing unit labor costs, that is, decreasing the labor share of output. Beginning from the mid-1990s, this model began to pay off, as it led to increased investments, economic growth and lower unemployment.

In Italy, instead, despite substantial wage restraint and repeated reforms of both the welfare state and labor market regulation, economic performance lagged behind other advanced countries, including European. Riccardo Faini and André Sapir (2005) have offered an interesting analysis of Italy's economic predicament focusing on comparative advantage and sectoral specialization. Italy – goes their argument – has been hit in the face by globalization, which implies greater economic integration with developing countries, particularly China. Unlike other European countries, Italy is specialized in labor-intensive sectors, and thus competes head-to-head with China and other developing countries. Also, while other European countries have upgraded their productive structure in the 1990s and moved towards higher value-added markets, Italy is the only country to have become even more specialized in traditional sectors.

Clearly not all Italian problems stemmed from the industrial relations sphere. The above remarks point to some historic weaknesses of the Italian economy: for example, low investments in R&D, prevalence of small firms, inefficient public services. However, they also hint at a role that the collective bargaining system could have played and did not play: that of acting as a 'beneficial constraint' (Streeck, 1997). If unit labor costs fall dramatically, if the low road is not sealed off, managers and entrepreneurs probably have fewer incentives to upgrade.

The diverging economic fortunes of Ireland and Italy in the 1990s suggest that the economic success of the new corporatism may depend on the country's growth model: in an economy like the Irish, in which foreign demand is much more important than domestic demand, the gains in competitiveness associated with centralized wage regulation may be an unequivocal boon. Instead, in an economy like the Italian, just as in every large country, the export-benefiting effects of cost competitiveness may be dominated by the recessionary effects of shrinking domestic demand (Carlin and Soskice, 2009).[2]

CONCLUSION

In a nutshell, the argument of this chapter has been one of *institutional conversion* (Streeck and Thelen, 2005): corporatist policy-making did not disappear as widely anticipated in the late 1980s, but experienced an unexpected resurgence in the 1990s. However, while corporatism managed to survive *qua* institutional structure, it began to operate in ways that were rather different from the past: while it was still able to soften the sharpest edges of mainstream neoliberal policy, it no longer provided a fundamental alternative to it. Specifically, it helped national economies to adapt to the hard constraints of the new international economic regime (requiring fiscal rectitude, welfare state reform and labor market liberalization), but lost the redistributive and decommodifying features of the corporatist golden age, which defined it as a systemic alternative to liberal corporatism.

Internally, the new corporatist institutions developed different, and probably more attractive, organizational features than their predecessors. They became more participatory and democratic than in the old days. Unions, in particular, began to go to great lengths to democratically legitimate the outcomes of national bargaining through debates and referenda. These organizational transformations were linked to the changing terms of the political exchange between governments and unions. In the new international economic regime, side payments were much less available than in the past. Consequently, trade unions felt the need to invest in democratic mechanisms of decision-making much more heavily. These were necessary to persuade the unions' constituents that the choices leaders make were acceptable and legitimate. Procedural legitimacy became necessary to compensate for declining (or absent) output legitimacy.

This story of resilience and transformation suggests a reconsideration of the effects of economic integration on the institutional structures of advanced countries. A large and influential literature emphasizes the resilience of national institutions in the face of broad transformative trends such as globalization and European integration (see, for example, Berger and Dore, 1996; Garrett, 1998; Hall and Soskice, 2001b; Campbell, 2004). The empirical material presented in this chapter suggests that a more nuanced interpretation is probably in order: it is true that the labor market institutions of several European countries did not converge on the Anglo-Saxon model of decentralized bargaining and arm's length relationship between government and interest groups, and that corporatism even experienced a surprising renaissance. Continuity in institutional structure masks, however, discontinuity in institutional function. The way these same institutions now work is profoundly different from the past. Corporatism was once the lynchpin of a *negotiated economy*. It has now become one of the channels – not the only one – by which neoliberal policy makes its way in institutionally dense European political economies.

NOTES

1. The coding of these countries is straightforward because, with the exception of Australia in the age of the Accord (1983–92), they have no experience with corporatist policy-making.
2. In 2009, the Irish situation changed dramatically as a result of the international financial crisis. The government was forced to drastically cut public expenditures. This would have implied the acceptance of nominal wage cuts by public sector unions. The unions refused and the government unceremoniously jettisoned social partnership and decided to proceed unilaterally.

REFERENCES

AAVV (ed.) (2002), *Non Basta Dire No*, Milan: Mondadori.
Alesina, A. and Ardagna, S. (1998), 'Tales of fiscal adjustments', *Economic Policy*, **13**(27), 489–545.
Alesina, A. and Giavazzi, F. (2006), *The Future of Europe: Reform or Decline*, Cambridge, MA: MIT Press.
Alesina, A. and Perotti, R. (1997a), 'Fiscal adjustment in OECD countries: Composition and macroeconomic effects', *International Monetary Fund Staff Papers*, **44**(2), 210–48.
Alesina, A. and Perotti, R. (1997b), 'The welfare state and competitiveness', *American Economic Review*, **87**(5), 921–39.
Aprile, R. (1996), 'La Riforma Del Sistema Pensionistico. Le Critiche Che Non Si Merita', *L'Assistenza Sociale*, **50**, 163–87.
Avdagic, S. (2010), 'When are concerted reforms feasible? Explaining the emergence of social pacts in Western Europe', *Comparative Political Studies*, **43**(7), 628–57.
Baccaro, L. (2000), 'Centralized collective bargaining and the problem of "compliance":

Lessons from the Italian experience', *Industrial and Labor Relations Review*, **53**(4), 579–601.

Baccaro, L. (2003), 'What is dead and what is alive in the theory of corporatism', *British Journal of Industrial Relations*, **41**(4), 683–706.

Baccaro, L. (2009), 'Similar structures, different outcomes: The surprising resilience of corporatist policy-making in Europe', Paper presented at the 21st SASE Conference, Paris.

Baccaro, L. and Simoni, M. (2004), 'The referendum on Article 18 and labour market flexibility', in S. Fabbrini and V. Della Sala (eds), *Italian Politics*, New York/Oxford: Berghahn Books, pp. 166–83.

Baccaro, L. and Simoni, M. (2008), 'Policy-concertation in Europe: Explaining government choice', *Comparative Political Studies*, **41**(10), 1323–48.

Baccaro, L. and Simoni, M. (2010), 'Organizational determinants of wage moderation', *World Politics*, **62**(4), 594–635.

Berger, S. and Dore, R. (1996), *National Diversity and Global Capitalism*, Ithaca, NY: Cornell University Press.

Bertola, G. (1990), 'Job security, employment and wages', *European Economic Review*, **34**(4), 851–86.

Blanchard, O. (2006), 'European unemployment: The evolution of facts and ideas', *Economic Policy*, **21**(45), 5–59.

Blanchard, O. and Wolfers, J. (2000), 'The role of shocks and institutions in the rise of European unemployment: The aggregate evidence', *The Economic Journal*, **110**(462), 1–33.

Boeri, T. and Galasso, V. (2007), *Contro I Giovani. Come L'italia Sta Tradendo Le Nuove Generazioni*, Milan: Mondadori.

Bonoli, G. (2001), 'Political institutions, veto points, and the process of welfare state adaptation', in P. Pierson (ed.), *The New Politics of the Welfare State*, Oxford: Oxford University Press, pp. 238–64.

Bruno, M. and Sachs, J. (1985), *The Economics of Worldwide Stagflation*, Cambridge, MA: Harvard University Press.

Calmfors, L. and Driffill, J. (1988), 'Bargaining structure, corporatism, and macroeconomic performance', *Economic Policy*, **3**(6), 13–61.

Cameron, D. (1984), 'Social democracy, corporatism, labour quiescence, and the representation of economic interest in advanced capitalist society', in J.H. Goldthorpe (ed.), *Order and Conflict in Contemporary Capitalism*, Oxford: Clarendon, pp. 143–78.

Campbell, J.L. (2004), *Institutional Change and Globalization*, Princeton, NJ: Princeton University Press.

Carlin, W. and Soskice, D. (2009), 'German economic performance: Disentangling the role of supply-side reforms, macroeconomic policy and coordinated economy institutions', *Socioeconomic Review*, **7**(1), 67–99.

Castellino, O. (1996), 'La Riforma Delle Pensioni: Forse Non Sarà L'ultima', in M. Caciagli and D.I. Kertzer (eds), *Politica in Italia. I Fatti Dell'anno E Le Interpretazioni*, Bologna: Il Mulino, pp. 179–96.

Cawson, A. (1986), *Corporatism and Political Theory*, Oxford: Blackwell.

Cawson, A. (1988), 'Reply to Leo Panitch's review article "Corporatism: A growth industry reaches the monopoly stage"', *Canadian Journal of Political Science*, **21**(4), 819–22.

Compston, H. (2002), 'The strange persistence of policy concertation', in S. Berger and H. Compston (eds), *Policy Concertation and Social Partnership in Western Europe: Lessons for the 21st Century*, New York/Oxford: Berghahn Books, pp. 1–16.

Crouch, C. (1983), 'Pluralism and the new corporatism: A rejoinder', *Political Studies*, **31**(3), 452–60.

Culpepper, P. (2002) 'Powering, puzzling and "pacting": The informational logic of negotiated reforms', *Journal of European Public Policy*, **9**(5), 774–90.

Culpepper, P.D. (2008), 'The politics of common knowledge: Ideas and institutional change in wage bargaining', *International Organization*, **62**(1), 1–33.

Dahl, R. (1956), *A Preface to Democratic Theory*, Chicago: University of Chicago Press.

Dell'Aringa, C. and Samek Lodovici, M. (1992), 'Industrial relations and economic performance', in T. Treu (ed.), *Participation in Public Policy-making: The Role of Trade Unions and Employers' Associations*, Berlin: De Gruyter, pp. 26–58.

Esping-Andersen, G. (1990), *The Three Worlds of Welfare Capitalism*, Cambridge: Polity.

Faini, R. and Sapir, A. (2005), 'Un Modello Obsoleto? Crescita E Specializzazione Dell'economia Italiana', in T. Boeri, R. Faini, A. Ichino, G. Pisauro and C. Scarpa (eds), *Oltre Il Declino*, Bologna: Il Mulino, pp. 19–65.

Ferrera, M. and Jessoula, M. (2007), 'Italy: A narrow gate for path-shift', in E.M. Immergut, K.M. Anderson and I. Schulze (eds), *The Handbook of West European Pension Politics*, Oxford: Oxford University Press, pp. 396–453.

Flanagan, R.J., Soskice, D.W. and Ulman, L. (1983), *Unionism, Economic Stabilization, and Incomes Policies: European Experience*, Washington, DC: Brookings Institution.

Flanders, A. (1970), *Management and Unions*, London: Faber.

Franzese, R.J. (2002), *Macroeconomic Policies of Developed Democracies*, Cambridge, UK/ New York: Cambridge University Press.

Garrett, G. (1998), *Partisan Politics in the Global Economy*, Cambridge: Cambridge University Press.

Ginsborg, P. (1998), *L'Italia Del Tempo Presente. Famiglia, Società Civile, Stato*, Torino: Einaudi.

Glyn, A. and Rowthorn, B. (1988), 'West European unemployment: Corporatism and structural change', *The American Economic Review*, **78**(2), 194–9.

Gobeyn, M.J. (1993), 'Explaining the decline of macro-corporatist political bargaining structures in advanced capitalist societies', *Governance*, **6**(1), 3–22.

Golden, M. (1988), *Labor Divided: Austerity and Working-class Politics in Contemporary Italy*, Ithaca, NY: Cornell University Press.

Golden, M., Lange, P. and Wallerstein, M. (2006), 'Union centralization among advanced industrial societies: An empirical study', Dataset available at: http://www.shelley.polisci. ucla.edu/; version dated 16 June 2006.

Government of Ireland (1987), *Programme for National Recovery*, Dublin: The Stationery Office.

Gunnigle, P., McMahon, G. and Fitzgerald, G. (1999), *Industrial Relations in Ireland: Theory and Practice*, Dublin: Gill and Macmillan.

Hall, P.A. and Franzese, R.J. (1998), 'Mixed signals: Central bank independence, coordinated wage bargaining, and European Monetary Union', *International Organization*, **52**(3), 505–35.

Hall, P.A. and Soskice, D. (2001a), 'An introduction to varieties of capitalism', in P.A. Hall and D. Soskice (eds), *Varieties of Capitalism*, New York: Oxford University Press, pp. 1–68.

Hall, P.A. and Soskice, D. (eds) (2001b), *Varieties of Capitalism: The Institutional Foundations of Comparative Advantage*, New York: Oxford University Press.

Hamann, K. and Kelly, J. (2007), 'Party politics and the reemergence of social pacts in Western Europe', *Comparative Political Studies*, **40**(8), 971–94.

Hardiman, N. (1988), *Pay, Politics, and Economic Performance in Ireland 1970–1987*, Oxford: Clarendon Press.

Hardiman, N. (1992), 'The state and economic interests: Ireland in comparative perspective', in J.H. Goldthorpe and C.T. Whelan (eds), *The State and Economic Interests: Ireland in Comparative Perspective*, Oxford: Oxford University Press.

Hassel, A. (2006), *Wage Setting, Social Pacts and the Euro: A New Role for the State*, Amsterdam: Amsterdam University Press.

Hassel, A. (2009), 'Policies and politics in social pacts in Europe', *European Journal of Industrial Relations*, **15**(1), 7–26.

Ichino, P. (1996), *Il Lavoro E Il Mercato. Per Un Diritto Del Lavoro Maggiorenne*, Milan: Mondadori.

Immergut, E.M. and Anderson, K.M. (2007), 'Editors' introduction: The dynamics of pension politics', in E.M. Immergut, K.M. Anderson and I. Schulze (eds), *The Handbook of West European Pension Politics*, Oxford: Oxford University Press, pp. 1–45.

Iversen, T. (1996), 'Power, flexibility, and the breakdown of centralized wage bargaining: Denmark and Sweden in comparative perspective', *Comparative Politics*, **28**(4), 399–436.

Iversen, T. (1999), *Contested Economic Institutions: The Politics of Macroeconomics and Wage Bargaining in Advanced Democracies*, Cambridge: Cambridge University Press.

Iversen, T., Pontusson, J. and Soskice, D.W. (2000), *Unions, Employers, and Central Banks: Macroeconomic Coordination and Institutional Change in Social Market Economies*, Cambridge/New York: Cambridge University Press.

Jessop, B. (1977), 'Corporatism, parliamentarism and social democracy', in P. Schmitter and G. Lehmbruch (eds), *Trends Toward Corporatist Intermediation*, London: Sage, pp. 185–212.

Kalecki, M. (1943),'Political aspects of full employment', *Political Quarterly*, **14**(4), 322–31.

Katz, H.C. (1993), 'The decentralization of collective bargaining: A literature review and comparative analysis', *Industrial and Labor Relations Review*, **47**(1), 3–22.

Katz, H.C. and Darbishire, O. (2000), *Converging Divergences: Worldwide Changes in Employment Systems*, Ithaca, NY: Cornell University Press.

Katz, H.C., Lee, W. and Lee, J. (2004), *The New Structure of Labor Relations: Tripartism and Decentralization*, Ithaca, NY: ILR Press, an imprint of Cornell University Press.

Kenworthy, L. (2003), 'Quantitative indicators of corporatism', *International Journal of Sociology*, **33**(3), 10–44.

Korpi, W. (1983), *The Democratic Class Struggle*, London: Routledge.

Korpi, W. and Shalev, M. (1979), 'Strikes, industrial relations and class conflict in capitalist societies', *British Journal of Sociology*, **30**(2), 164–87.

Lange, P. (1984), 'Unions, workers, and wage regulation: The rational bases of consent', in J. Goldthorpe (ed.), *Order and Conflict in Contemporary Capitalism*, Oxford: Clarendon Press, pp. 98–123.

Lange, P. and Vannicelli, M. (1982), 'Strategy under stress: The Italian union movement and the Italian crisis in developmental perspective', in P. Lange, G. Ross and M. Vannicelli (eds), *Unions, Change, and Crisis*, Boston: George Allen and Unwin, pp. 95–206.

Layard, P., Nickell, S.J. and Jackman, R. (2005), *Unemployment: Macroeconomic Performance and the Labour Market*, Reissue with a new introduction, Oxford/New York: Oxford University Press.

Lehmbruch, G. (1979), 'Liberal corporatism and party government', in P.C. Schmitter and G. Lehmbruch (eds), *Trends Toward Corporatist Intermediation*, London: Sage Publications, pp. 147–83.

Lehner, F. (1987), 'Interest intermediation, institutional structure and public policy', in H. Keman, H. Paloheimo and P.F. Whiteley (eds), *Coping with the Economic Crisis*, London: Sage, pp. 54–82.

Lindbeck, A. and Snower, D. (1988), *The Insider–Outsider Theory of Employment and Unemployment*, Cambridge, MA: MIT Press.

Locke, R.M. (1992), 'The decline of the national union in Italy: Lessons for comparative industrial relations', *Industrial and Labor Relations Review*, **45**(2), 229–49.

Locke, R.M. (1995), *Remaking the Italian Economy*, Ithaca, NY: Cornell University Press.

Locke, R.M., Kochan, T. and Piore, M. (eds) (1995), *Employment Relations in a Changing World Economy*, Cambridge, MA: MIT Press.

Mares, I. (2006), *Taxation, Wage Bargaining, and Unemployment*, Cambridge: Cambridge University Press.

Martin, C.J. and Thelen, K. (2007), 'The state and coordinated capitalism: Contributions of the public sector to social solidarity in postindustrial societies', *World Politics*, **60**(1), 1–36.

Martin, R.M. (1983) 'Pluralism and the new corporatism', *Political Studies*, **31**(1), 86–102.

Mascini, M. (2000) *Profitti E Salari*, Bologna: Il Mulino.

Molina, O. and Rhodes, M. (2002), 'Corporatism: The past, present and future of a concept', *Annual Review of Political Science*, **5**(1), 305–31.

Myles, J. and Pierson, P. (2001), 'The comparative political economy of pension reform', in P. Pierson (ed.), *The New Politics of the Welfare State*, Oxford: Oxford University Press, pp. 305–33.

NESC (1986), *A Strategy for Development. 1986–90*, Dublin: National Economic and Social Council.

Nickell, S. (1997), 'Unemployment and labor market rigidities: Europe vs North America', *Journal of Economic Perspectives*, **11**(3), 55–74.

Notermans, T. (2000), *Money, Markets, and the State. Social Democratic Economic Policies since 1918*, Cambridge: Cambridge University Press.

OECD (1994), *The OECD Jobs Study. Facts, Analysis, Strategies*, Paris: OECD.

OECD (1999), 'Employment protection and labour market performance', in *Employment Outlook*, Paris: OECD.

OECD (2007), *Pensions at a Glance*, Paris: OECD.

Olson, M. (1982), *The Rise and Decline of Nations: Economic Growth, Stagflation, and Social Rigidities*, New Haven/London: Yale University Press.

Panitch, L. (1979), 'The development of corporatism in liberal democracies', in P.S. Lehmbruch (ed.), *Trends Towards Corporatist Intermediation*, London: Sage, pp. 119–48.

Pekkarinen, J., Pohjola, M. and Rowthorn, B. (eds) (1992), *Social Corporatism: A Superior Economic System?*, Oxford: Clarendon Press.

Perez, S. (2000) 'From decentralization to reorganization: Explaining the return to national bargaining in Italy and Spain', *Comparative Politics*, **32**(4), 437–58.

Pierson, P. (2001), 'Post-industrial pressures on mature welfare states', in P. Pierson (ed.), *The New Politics of the Welfare State*, New York: Cambridge University Press, pp. 80–104.

Pizzorno, A. (1978a), 'Le Due Logiche Dell'azione Di Classe', in A. Pizzorno (ed.), *Lotte Operaie E Sindacato: Il Ciclo 1968–72 in Italia*, Bologna: Il Mulino, pp. 7–45.

Pizzorno, A. (1978b), 'Political exchange and collective identity in industrial conflict', in C. Crouch and A. Pizzorno (eds), *The Resurgence of Class Conflict in Western Europe since 1968*, London: Macmillan.

Pontusson, J. (2005), *Inequality and Prosperity: Social Europe vs. Liberal America*, Ithaca, NY: Cornell University Press.

Regini, M. (1997), 'Still engaging in corporatism? Recent Italian experience in comparative perspective', *European Journal of Industrial Relations*, **3**(3), 259–78.

Regini, M. (2000), 'Between deregulation and social pacts: The responses of European economies to globalization', *Politics & Society*, **28**(1), 5–33.

Rhodes, M. (1996), *Globalisation, Labour Markets and Welfare States: A Future of Competitive Corporatism?*, Florence: European University Institute.

Rhodes, M. (2001), 'The political economy of social pacts: "Competitive Corporatism" and "European Welfare Reform"', in P. Pierson (ed.), *The New Politics of the Welfare State*, Oxford: Oxford University Press, pp. 165–94.

Roche, W.K. (1997), 'Pay determination, the state and the politics of industrial relations', in T. Murphy and W.K. Roche (eds), *Irish Industrial Relations in Practice*, Dublin: Oak Tree Press, pp. 145–226.

Rowthorn, B. (1992), 'Corporatism and labour market performance', in J. Pekkarinen, M. Pohjola and B. Rowthorn (eds), *Social Corporatism: A Superior Economic System?*, Oxford: Clarendon Press, pp. 82–131.

Rueda, D. (2005), 'Insider–outsider politics in industrialized democracies: The challenge to Social Democratic parties', *American Political Science Review*, **99**(1), 61–74.

Ruggie, J.G. (1982), 'International regimes, transactions, and change: Embedded liberalism in the postwar economic order', *International Organization*, **36**(2), 379–415.

Sabel, C.F. (1981), 'The internal politics of trade unions', in S. Berger (ed.), *Organizing Interest in Western Europe*, New York: Cambridge University Press, pp. 209–44.

Saint-Paul, G. (2002), 'The political economy of employment protection', *Journal of Political Economy*, **110**(3), 672–704.

Scharpf, F.W. (1991), *Crisis and Choice in European Social Democracy*, Ithaca, NY: Cornell University Press.

Scharpf, F.W. (1999), *Governing in Europe: Effective and Democratic?*, Oxford: Oxford University Press.

Schludi, M. (2003), 'The reform of Bismarckian pension systems. A comparison of pension politics in Austria, France, Germany, Italy, and Sweden', PhD thesis, Humboldt University, Berlin.

Schmitter, P. (1974), 'Still the century of corporatism?', *Review of Politics*, **36**(1), 85–131.

Schmitter, P. (1981), 'Interest intermediation and regime governability in contemporary Western Europe and North America', in S. Berger (ed.), *Organizing Interest in Western Europe*, New York: Cambridge University Press, pp. 287–330.

Schmitter, P. (1982), 'Reflections on where the theory of corporatism has gone and where the praxis of neo-corporatism may be going', in G. Lehmbruch and P. Schmitter (eds), *Patterns of Corporatist Policy-making*, London: Sage, pp. 259–90.

Schmitter, P.C. (1989), 'Corporatism is dead! Long live corporatism!', *Government and Opposition*, **24**(1), 54–73.

Siebert, H. (1997), 'Labor market rigidities: At the root of unemployment in Europe', *Journal of Economic Perspectives*, **11**(3), 37–54.

Soskice, D. (1990), 'Wage determination: The changing role of institutions in advanced industrialised countries', *Oxford Review of Economic Policy*, **6**(4), 36–61.

Soskice, D. (1999), 'Divergent production regimes: Coordinated and uncoordinated market economies in the 1980s and 1990s', in H. Kitschelt, P. Lange, G. Marks and J.D. Stephens (eds), *Continuity and Change in Contemporary Capitalism*, New York: Cambridge University Press, pp. 101–34.

Soskice, D. and Iversen, T. (2000), 'The nonneutrality of monetary policy with large price or wage setters', *Quarterly Journal of Economics*, **115**(1), 265–84.

Stephens, J.D. (1979), *The Transition from Capitalism to Socialism*, London: Macmillan.

Streeck, W. (1984), 'Neo-corporatist industrial relations and the economic crisis in West Germany', in J. Goldthorpe (ed.), *Order and Conflict in Contemporary Capitalism*, Oxford: Clarendon Press, pp. 291–314.

Streeck, W. (1988), 'Editorial introduction to special issue on organizational democracy in trade unions', *Economic and Industrial Democracy*, **9**(3), 307–18.

Streeck, W. (1993), 'The rise and decline of neocorporatism', in L. Ulman, B. Eichengreen and W.T. Dickens (eds), *Labor and an Integrated Europe*, Washington, DC: The Brookings Institution.

Streeck, W. (1997), 'Beneficial constraints: On the economic limits of rational voluntarism', in J.R. Hollingsworth and R. Boyer (eds), *Contemporary Capitalism: The Embeddedness of Institutions*, Cambridge: Cambridge University Press, pp. 197–219.

Streeck, W. (2000), 'Competitive solidarity: Rethinking the "European Social Model"', in K. Hinrichs, H. Kitschelt and H. Wiesenthal (eds), *Kontingenz und Krise: Institutionenpolitik in kapitalistischen und postsozialistischen Gesellschaften*, Frankfurt: Campus Verlag, pp. 245–62.

Streeck, W. (2006), 'The study of organized interests: Before the "century" and after', in C. Crouch and W. Streeck (eds), *The Diversity of Democracy: Corporatism, Social Order and Political Conflict*, Cheltenham, UK and Northampton, MA, USA: Edward Elgar Publishing, pp. 3–45.

Streeck, W. and Kenworthy, L. (2005), 'Theories and practices of neocorporatism', in T. Janoski, R.R. Alford, A.M. Hicks and M.A. Schwartz (eds), *The Handbook of Political Sociology*, Cambridge: Cambridge University Press, pp. 441–60.

Streeck, W. and Schmitter, P. (1991) 'From national corporatism to transnational pluralism', *Politics & Society*, **19**(2), 133–64.

Streeck, W. and Thelen, K.A. (2005), 'Introduction: Institutional change in advanced political economies', in W. Streeck and K.A. Thelen (eds), *Beyond Continuity*, Oxford: Oxford University Press, pp. 1–39.

Swenson, P. (1991) 'Bringing capital back in, or social democracy reconsidered', *World Politics*, **43**(4), 513–44.

Swenson, P. and Pontusson, J. (2000), 'The Swedish employer offensive against centralized bargaining', in T. Iversen, J. Pontusson and D. Soskice (eds), *Unions, Employers, and Central Banks: Macroeconomic Coordination and Institutional Change in Social Market Economies*, New York: Cambridge University Press, pp. 77–106.

Tarantelli, E. (1986a), *Economia Politica Del Lavoro*, Turin, Italy: UTET.
Tarantelli, E. (1986b), 'The regulation of inflation and unemployment', *Industrial Relations*, **25**(1), 1–15.
Teague, P. (1995), 'Pay determination in the Republic of Ireland: Towards social corporatism?', *British Journal of Industrial Relations*, **33**(2), 253–73.
Thelen, K. (1994) 'Beyond corporatism: Toward a new framework for the study of labor in advanced capitalism', *Comparative Politics*, **27**(1), 107–24.
Traxler, F. (2004), 'The metamorphoses of corporatism: From classical to lean patterns', *European Journal of Political Research*, **43**(4), 571–98.
Vaciago, G. (1993), 'Exchange rate stability and market expectations: The crisis of the EMS', *Review of Economic Conditions in Italy*, **1**, 11–29.
Visser, J. (2009), The ICTWSS Database: Database on Institutional Characteristics of Trade Unions, Wage Setting, State Intervention and Social Pacts in 34 Countries Between1960 and 2007, Amsterdam: Amsterdam Institute for Advanced Labour Studies AIAS, University of Amsterdam.
Wallerstein, M., Golden, M. and Lange, P. (1997), 'Unions, employers' associations, and wage-setting institutions in Northern and Central Europe, 1950–1992', *Industrial and Labor Relations Review*, **50**(3), 379–401.
Williamson, J. (1989), 'What Washington means by policy reform', in J. Williamson (ed.), *Latin American Readjustment: How Much Has Happened?*, Washington, DC: Institute for International Economics, pp. 5–20.
Wolfe, J.D. (1985), 'Corporatism and union democracy: The British miners and incomes policies, 1973–74', *Comparative Politics*, **17**(4), 421–36.

17 The role of MNEs
David G. Collings, Jonathan Lavelle and Patrick Gunnigle

INTRODUCTION

Multinational enterprises (MNEs) have become dominant players in the global economy. Despite the recent economic downturn, UNCTAD data indicate that there are some 82 000 multinational enterprises with some 810 000 subsidiaries operating in the global economy (UNCTAD, 2009). The largest MNEs are comparable to large countries in terms of their economic worth. Of the largest 150 global economic entities, 74 are nation states and the remaining 76 are MNEs (Butler, 2007). The significance of MNEs in the world economy is highlighted by the fact that they employ some 77 million employees (UNCTAD, 2009). It is therefore evident that employment practices and employment relations in MNEs affect the work experiences of an ever-growing number of employees on a global scale.

Rather than taking a comparative focus and examining differences between employment relations issues in different countries (see Part 3 of this volume), this chapter adopts an international focus. Following Collings (2008, p. 175) we define international employment relations[1] as 'the IR [industrial relations] issues and problems, for both capital and labour, arising from the internationalization of business, and the IR strategies, policies and practices which firms, employees and their representatives pursue in response to the internationalization of business'. In this chapter, we adopt a pluralist frame of reference that recognizes the existence of a conflict of interest between capital and labour and the key role of power in the interaction between the parties in employment relations. Drawing on the institutional literature our review also recognizes that MNEs 'are embedded in larger and wider societal collectivities' (Sorge, 2004, p. 118). Thus, they do not operate in isolation from the environment around them but rather must organize their activities in the context of the multiple institutional environments in which they operate. Indeed, they may also play a part in shaping these environments (cf. Boyer et al., 1998; Streeck and Thelen, 2005; Gunnigle et al., 2006), which may further impact on the experiences of employees in host countries. In considering these issues we recognize that much of the extant literature in the area has concentrated on MNEs emanating from Western economies (for notable exceptions see Bae and Rowley, 2003; Glover and Wilkinson, 2007; Chang et al., 2009). Indeed, Clarke et al. (1999) in a review of studies conducted between 1977 and 1997 found that the UK, US, Japan, France and Germany accounted for some 48 per cent of all studies in the area of international human resource management. While our knowledge base has expanded in recent years, Ferner (2010) argues that significant gaps in our knowledge remain. He identifies our knowledge of MNEs operating in India as a particular gap. Thus, studies in these emerging economies should represent a key focus of research moving forward.

Our review commences with a consideration of the impact of MNEs on the various host countries in which they operate. We then consider the extent to which MNEs' actions can effectively be regulated and consider the actors who can potentially engage in this regulation process, with a focus on the role of trade unions, and international institutions.

MNEs AND SUBSIDIARY-LEVEL INNOVATION

The impact of MNEs on the employment relations (ER) systems of the various host countries in which they operate has long represented a key research agenda among ER scholars. In this regard, Gennard and Steuer (1971, p. 144) have argued that it is 'the foreignness of subsidiary behaviour which matters to industrial relations'. The key influence of MNEs on host country ER is the fact that they 'act as agents of change by introducing innovations into their subsidiaries and thence into the host business system' (Ferner and Quintanilla, 2002, p. 245). Thus, the MNE acts as 'a powerful element of change that challenges existing interests and structures in the labour market and at the bargaining table' (Weber, 1974, p. 249). Indeed, because of their global standing it has been argued that MNEs are generally in a position to promote new structures and practices rather than respond to pressures to adopt them in the global context, pointing to the potential for these firms to manage differently from local firms in various host countries (Kostova et al., 2008). The study of the introduction of these new departures in ER policies and practices thus represents an important stream in the ER literature.

While MNEs are not the only means through which HRM and ER innovation may be introduced into a foreign business system (other examples include management consultancies and business associations – Smith and Meiskins, 1995), they are the single most important conduit through which these are diffused from one business system to another (Ferner, 2003). Indeed they have been described as the 'foremost "innovators" – for good and ill – within national business systems' (Ferner and Varul, 2000, p. 115), a description that highlights MNEs' potential for positive and negative consequences for the countries that host their subsidiaries. Just as innovation can have varied outcomes, innovations have a number of antecedents that include ideas (ideologies, management fads etc.), actors (managers, MNEs, governments, trade unions, consultants etc.), structure (firm structures, industry structures, supply chains etc.), institutions, (EU, WTO etc.) contexts (organizational contexts, global economic environment, local labour markets, etc.) and process (knowledge management systems, reporting systems, etc.) (see Wolfe, 1995 for a discussion).

In exploring the nature of innovation in MNE subsidiaries and on host ER systems, a number of terms require clarification and definition. First, the concept of innovation itself is a complex one that lacks clear definition in the extant literature. In the international ER literature it is generally presented as an alternative to adaptation, whereby practices are modified to fit the host environment (Gennard 1974; Marginson, 1992; Ferner, 2003). Rogers (1995, p. 11) defines an innovation as: 'an idea, practice or object that is perceived as new by an individual or other unit of adoption'. In terms of the unit of adoption (which has implications of the level of analysis in empirically studying the concept) innovation can occur at a number of levels. At an individual level, innovation can be defined as an idea that seems new to the individual (ibid., p. 11). At an organizational level, an HR/ER innovation has been defined as 'an idea, programme or practice, or system which is related to the HRM function and is new to the adopting organization' (Wolfe, 1995, p. 314). In the context of this chapter, we suggest that the 'adopting organization' can be conceptualized as the subsidiary operation, or more specifically, a specific site within the subsidiary operation. While at a societal or business system level, innovation can be defined as the introduction of an organizational practice or policy that is alien to the host context. Thus, it is not necessarily conceptualized as 'good' or 'bad' but simply different from the tradition within the host environment. For example, it may involve the introduction of individualized performance-related pay to a country that has a tradition of jointly determined pay and conditions through collective bargaining.

Further, the very notion of innovation is fraught. 'In the minds of policymakers it has tended to carry positive connotations of progress, higher productivity and more "harmonious" employment relations. Yet the positive nature of innovations is often a matter of debate' (Ferner, 2003, p. 88). In contrast to the work of Gennard (1974) and Ferner (2003) amongst others who differentiate between innovative and disruptive developments[2] in MNE subsidiaries, we introduce a schema that differentiates between adaptive and disruptive innovation. Thus, innovation is not a value-laden concept and can refer to either positive or negative departures in ER policy and practice in MNE subsidiaries. The distinction is between whether the innovations are adaptive or disruptive in the context of the host ER system. Adaptive innovation can be defined as where MNEs display a healthy regard for local established traditions and institutions and seek only to build on such traditions through congruent and workable innovations. In other words they work 'with the grain' of the host ER system, for example, the preference for single union bargaining agreements favoured by US MNEs in Ireland in the 1980s (Gunnigle, 1995).

In contrast, disruptive innovation is defined as where the MNEs might be seen to display a marked preference for jettisoning local established practice in favour of practices that are at odds with host traditions. In other words they attempt to buck the system and work 'against the grain' of the established host ER system. A clear example of this would be McDonald's attempts to circumvent key aspects of the German ER system through, for example, its refusal to negotiate a collective agreement with trade unions in the 1980s (Royle, 2002). While it did ultimately acquiesce to union recognition in the 1989, McDonald's continues to resist any attempt to establish statutory works councils in the German context. Similar disruptive trends are evident across other Western European countries (Royle, 2002, 2004, 2006). The retailing giant Walmart has also attempted to introduce such disruptive innovations in countries such as Canada; it vehemently resisted trade union organizing drives and ultimately shut down stores to resist recognizing trade unions (Adams, 2005).

MNEs, INNOVATION AND HOST COUNTRY EMPLOYMENT RELATIONS

In addition to exploring the nature of ER innovation at subsidiary level, it seems a natural development to consider the impact of these and other innovations on the institutions and operation of broader ER systems. In this regard, the aim should be to explore the transformative effect of these innovations on national institutional frameworks. For example, a key question could focus on the extent to which these innovations, in the context of flexible, de-regulated ER systems, result in convergence on a 'lowest common denominator "Bleak House"' model of ER where 'companies fail to invest either in collective relationships or effective individual bases of employee relationships' (Ferner, 2003, p. 100). In other words how do governments balance the trade off between the financial efficiency outcomes of courting further FDI investment (through, for example, a weakly regulated institutional context) while at the same time balancing the social equity outcomes for employees (Kleiner and Ham, 2003)? In exploring these debates an institutional lens seems appropriate. Drawing in particular on European institutional traditions, and utilizing the example of Hall and Soskice's *Varieties of Capitalism* approach (Hall and Soskice, 2001a), we recognize the theoretical challenge that institutions tend to be defined by their relative durability. However, following Hall and Soskice (2001b, p. 54) 'we expect the corporate strategies, policies, and institutions of each nation to evolve in response to the challenges they face'. Previous work on comparative capitalism has been criticized for failing to adequately conceptualize how national systems change (cf. Hall and Soskice, 2001b). For example, Lane (2003) critiques Hall and Soskice and Whitley's contributions for predominantly focusing on institutional reproduction and persistence. However, in recent years contributions such as those in Streeck and Thelan (2005) and Mahoney and Thelan (2010) have moved the debate forward with regard to change in business systems. Such contributions remain the exception rather than the rule, however. Thus, an exposition of the impact of MNEs of the host institutional employment system will be a useful addition to the literature in this regard. For example, in the Irish context where multinational investment is hugely significant there has been a significant degree of study of the extent to which foreign-owned MNEs conform to or diverge with host ER traditions (see, for example, Gunnigle, 1995; Geary and Roche, 2001; Gunnigle et al., 2005; Lavelle, 2008; Turner et al., 2001). However, the impact of these MNEs on the Irish ER system has received far less attention (for an initial exploration of this issue based on case evidence of US MNEs see Collings et al., 2008).

In contrast to the pessimistic 'race to the bottom' advanced by institutional theorists, which predicts convergence around a number of key areas of management practice, many of which are based around Taylorist principles, due in large measure to their US origin (Kerr et al., 1960), the European institutional approach recognizes differences between firms of different national origin. It also rejects the notion of whole-scale 'social dumping' whereby firms will always transfer operations to the lowest labour cost environment in an attempt to reduce costs. Rather, the localization decision of MNC production facilities is a far more complex decision-making process, which is endowed with political significance.

However, a clear implication of this line of argument is that in contrast to convergence of institutional arrangements across nations, the impact of institutional arbitrage (Hall and Soskice, 2001b, p. 57) whereby firms shift operations to other nations in an attempt to secure advantages offered by the particular institutional frameworks, will reinforce differences between nation states. This is because, in this instance, the very reason firms have moved their operations is to take advantage of the different institutions offered in the new host environment. In Porter's (1998, p. 155) words: 'in a world of increasingly global competition, nations have become more, not less, important'. The key question for policy-makers and government is to decide where to best position their respective country to take advantage of the possibilities offered by institutional arbitrage. This is, of course, easier in those countries that can be classified as 'late industrializers' as they have little in terms of institutional heritage or baggage to jettison in attempting to position themselves in this regard. In contrast, more developed economies, such as the UK, Germany, Australia and the like, must operate within the broad constraints of the legacy of the institutional heritage of the nation state. Nonetheless, governments do make decisions as to how best position themselves in terms of attracting FDI and the prevailing institutions can be altered. These modifications are not solely driven by national governments but may also be driven by external agencies or even MNEs themselves. The following section will consider the drivers of change in European institutional theories.

Having considered the extent to which MNEs can act as potentially powerful agents of change in business systems, we now explore the extent to which their actions can effectively be regulated and consider the actors who can potentially engage in this regulation process. In this regard we consider the role of trade unions and international institutions.

INTERNATIONAL REGULATION OF MNEs

As noted earlier in the chapter, the significance and power of MNEs in the global business environment is without question. One school of thought is that the scale and mobility of capital is undermining labour organization, labour standards and working conditions (Bronfenbrenner, 2000; Babson, 2003; Huxley, 2003). A critical question therefore arises – how can the actions of MNEs with regard to labour relations be regulated at a global level? A key limitation in answering this question is that the very term regulation is open to question. Authors such as Julia Black question whether traditional analyses of regulation are still appropriate. Black (2002) offers a view of regulation that is no longer 'centred' on the state, but rather is 'decentred' or diffused throughout society, recognizing the key role of non-state actors in the regulatory process. While acknowledging the complexities of the nature of regulation, we focus in particular on two key actors, beyond the nation state, with the potential to counterbalance the power of MNEs – international trade unions and international organizations.

International Trade Unions

As companies became progressively more global it was anticipated that the natural progression for organized labour was to follow suit (Rojot, 2006). As individual MNEs have numerous subsidiary operations in a number of different countries it is likely that a number of different trade unions could be negotiating with the same employer across these countries. Thus, it would seem logical for these trade unions to join forces, pool resources and share information at an international level so as to better position themselves as a more powerful and legitimate counterweight to MNEs. However, there are many characteristics of MNEs that hamper trade unions in acting as viable countervailing forces to the power of these MNEs. These characteristics include the significant financial resources MNEs have access to; alternative sources of supply, through, for example, switching production globally; their footloose nature whereby MNEs have the ability to move from one country to the next or threaten to do so; a remote locus of authority and consequent difficulty in accessing decision-makers at corporate HQ; subsidiary operations in many industries and the potential to compare performance across sites and potentially play countries off each other; and superior knowledge and expertise in employment relations, particularly at the international level (Kennedy, 1980; Collings, 2008).

Arguably, in order for trade unions to have any success in regulating MNEs, there is a strong requirement for higher levels of international coordination (Collings, 2008). Outlining international trends in this regard, Cooke (2006, p. 339) surmises, 'in response to the growing power of MNEs, national unions and global union federations have stepped up their broader social, political, legal and grassroots movement agendas designed to enhance union countervailing power'. A number of different international structures have been created by trade unions in order to establish a global presence with the intention of acting as a countervailing power to MNEs at global, regional and sectoral levels. We now consider some examples in this regard.

The International Trade Union Confederation (ITUC) brings together national confederations with the aim of representing the trade union movement at the international level through formulating policies and engaging with intergovernmental organizations such as the European Trade Union Confederation, Global Union Federations, the Trade Union Advisory Committee to the OECD (TUAC), the International Labour Organization and other UN agencies. An amalgamation of the affiliated trade union organizations of the International Confederation of Free Trade Unions (ICFTU), the World Confederation of Labour (WCL) along with eight other national trade union organizations, the ITUC represents 170 million workers in 157 countries and territories and has 312 national affiliates, making it the largest trade union federation in the world. Its primary mission is the promotion and defence of workers' rights and interests, through international cooperation between trade unions, global campaigning and advocacy within the major global institutions. Whilst the size of the Confederation is considerable (and is expected to increase) its success will arguably depend on its ability to lobby international organizations. It is in its relations with these types of organizations that ICTU will need to create a platform for organized labour to grow at the international level.

The European Trade Union Confederation (ETUC) is argued to be the most influential international trade union organization within Europe (Leat, 2007). Better known as a political lobby group as opposed to an 'orthodox' trade union (Abbott, 1998; Bartolini, 2005), the ETUC modus operandi is to promote the interests of working people at European level and to represent them in the European Union institutions. At present, ETUC membership includes 82 national trade union confederations from 36 European countries, and 12 European industry federations, bringing its representation to a total of 60 million members. Significantly the ETUC acts as one of the European social partners and is recognized as the only representative cross-sectoral trade union organization by the European Union, by the Council of Europe and by the European Free Trade Association (EFTA), thereby the ETUC with some other international organizations in the EU has the power to make and enforce employment laws, which renders the lobbying role of the ETUC at the European level all the more significant. Gennard (2009a) notes the ETUC, in conjunction with the other social partners in Europe (Business Europe, European Centre of Employers and Enterprises [CEEP], and European Association of Craft, Small and Medium-sized Enterprises [UAEPME]), has negotiated 'framework agreements', which in turn have been transposed into European Directives and thus implemented in member states.[3] Because of its ability to lobby the EU and potential to shape and influence employment legislation, the role of the ETUC is arguably much more important in the regulation of MNE behaviour than any other international organization representing labour. Indeed, O'Hagan et al. (2005) argue that developments within the EU may actually provide models of regulation for employees globally in the future.

Global Union Federations (GUFs), previously known as International Trade Secretariats (ITSs), have been in existence since the early nineteenth century (Dowling et al., 2008). These GUFs essentially act as international trade union organizations by affiliating trade unions from a particular trade or industry. Each GUF is autonomous and governed by their affiliated trade unions. At present there are 11 such GUFs[4] with the largest GUF, the Union Network International (UNI), reportedly having 15 million members in 900 unions covering each continent. These bodies are the vehicle through which workers across the world can join together in solidarity and target particular MNEs. The overriding objective of these organizations is to engage with MNEs in transnational bargaining, and a demonstrable step in this direction is the negotiation of International Framework Agreements (IFAs) (see Papadakis, 2008 for more detail). These IFAs are essentially documents whereby the MNE and the GUF agree broad principles of regulation covering issues such as the right to minimum standards with respect to trade union membership and recognition and to commit the MNE to pay fair wages and benefits according to the good industry standards of the country concerned (Gennard, 2009b, p. 6). Although the specific contents of IFAs vary, a key component of the majority of agreements is the reference to the ILO Core Labour Standards.[5] Latest figures show that GUFs have negotiated over 60 IFAs with MNEs – for example, UNI has established IFAs with a range of organizations including Adecco, Allianz, Barclays, Carrefour, Danske Bank, Telefonica and G4S to name but a few.

On the positive side, this development is clearly more significant than the simple sharing of information across unions in relation to particular MNEs. It demonstrates that GUFs have successfully engaged with MNEs, are building relations with MNEs and securing agreement on how the MNE should behave, particularly in locations where employees have little protection. It is a clear demonstration of international dialogue between MNEs and representatives of organized labour. Indeed, Müller and Rüb (2004) posit that it demonstrates a degree of legitimacy on the part of GUFs as management acknowledge their role in representing workers. Furthermore, Telljohann et al. (2009, p. 6) note that these IFAs are distinguishable from voluntary codes of conduct that many MNEs have produced (e.g., commitment to corporate social responsibility), as IFAs can be seen as the start of a bargaining procedure at transnational level.

Whilst these IFAs are seen as a broadly positive move by organized labour in dealing with MNEs at an international level, there are a number of limitations. For example, GUFs lack the authority to enforce their instructions against affiliated unions. Thus, when a dispute arises in relation to an MNE's offshoring or outsourcing of operations to lower-cost countries, it is very difficult to put international solidarity before nationalistic feelings (Gennard, 2009b). Another important issue for GUFs is the complexity of the organization and governance structure of some MNEs (Leat, 2007). Many MNEs operate across industries and thus it is highly likely that more than one GUF will seek to engage with that MNE. This clearly favours the MNE, as it has the opportunity and capacity to take advantage of possible competing agendas pursued by the different GUFs.[6] Finally, an external determinant of their success, and possibly the most important, is the willingness of MNEs to engage with GUFs in the first instance, given that such engagement is voluntary. Indeed, the ability to get MNEs to the negotiation table is not through any compulsion or demonstration of significant bargaining power by GUFs, but rather goodwill on the part of MNEs (Rojot, 2006). In summary, as noted by Telljohann et al. (2009, p. 3), 'because of their limited spread, not to mention their relatively short existence, the contribution of IFAs to the internationalisation of industrial relations has so far been slight'.

It has been argued that if international labour organizations are to be effective as a counter-balance to the power of MNEs, then the merger of individual trade unions across national boundaries is required (Gennard, 2009b). And as noted in the literature, there are many difficulties to be overcome in achieving cross-border trade union mergers such as declining union membership, employee apathy and cynicism and legal problems (Collings, 2008; Gennard, 2009b). Notwithstanding these, there appears to be significant determination and willingness on the part of trade unions to advance cross-border mergers and one can anticipate that the number of such mergers will continue to increase in the future. A significant development in this regard in recent years has been the establishment of the Workers Uniting trade union. In July 2008 Unite the Union (2.5 million members), the UK's largest union and the North American private sector union, the United Steelworkers (850 000 members) announced the establishment of the world's first global trade union. The major motivation for this merger was to develop more effective coordination of collective bargaining with MNEs and to increase their power base in their political campaigns (Gennard, 2009b). The significance, and more importantly the success of such a venture, is of enormous interest to all actors in the global environment. Whilst it is too early to reasonably assess the success of such a project, it is undoubtedly an area for future research. Thus far, the literature suggests that global trade union organizations and collaboration have had relatively limited success in acting as a counterbalance to the power of MNEs (see Collings, 2008 for detailed analysis of the failure of international collective bargaining). In line with some of the more recent developments identified above, there remains a great deal of scope for further study on the role and influence of global unions in acting as a countervailing force to the power of the MNE sector globally.

We now turn to the role of international organizations and consider the role of two key international organizations in regulating the

412   *Research handbook of comparative employment relations*

actions of MNEs – the International Labour Organization (ILO) and the Organisation for Economic Co-operation and Development (OECD).

International Organizations

The two most significant institutions that are involved in the regulation of MNEs are the International Labour Organization and the Organisation for Economic Co-operation and Development. (Chapter 18 by Royle in this volume considers the issue of international labour standards and corporate voluntary initiatives in regulating global capital and provides additional insights in this regard.)

The ILO (established 1919) has been one of the most significant institutions responsible for standard-setting in relation to the area of human and labour rights, primarily through the development of conventions and recommendations (currently there are 185 conventions and 195 recommendations). Conventions are the most important mechanism of standard-setting due to their legal status; they become legally binding once ratified at a national level. Whilst all conventions are important in their own right, some, such as those dealing with freedom of association and freedom from forced labour, child labour and discrimination, are more significant than others (Ewing, 2006). The importance of the conventions is evidenced by the fact that many international organizations use the ILO standards as a reference point in developing standards. For example, the OECD Guidelines on MNEs makes explicit reference to the ILO, and as seen earlier, the ILO conventions represent a significant component of the IFAs between GUFs and MNEs and also the ILO conventions have significantly influenced the EU's Charter of Fundamental Rights.

However, these international labour standards suffer from two particular problems – ratification and compliance (ibid.). In relation to the former, there are no obligations on the part of any ILO member to ratify a convention, even though its government representative may have supported it. In a review of the ILO conventions, Ewing (ibid.) estimates that of 32 040 potential ratifications only 22 per cent have been ratified. For example, both the US and China have relatively low levels of ratification, whilst 24 conventions have failed to secure even ten ratifications (ibid.). Thus, governments are clearly quite selective about which conventions they ratify (Kim, 2010). Second is the problem of compliance with standards. The ILO does not have the power to sanction any member that does not comply with the convention. Indeed, the only available recourse is publicity and encouragement for compliance. A further problem is that these ILO standards are ill-equipped to deal with MNEs as they are addressed to governments and not to MNEs (Ewing, 2006). Ewing (ibid.,

p. 246) notes that 'although there is an ILO Declaration of 1977 on MNEs, international law has not yet found an effective way of holding transnational companies accountable to the obligations it imposes on states'.

The OECD is another important international institution involved in the regulation of MNEs. Specifically we refer here to the OECD Guidelines for Multinational Enterprises (the guidelines), approved in 1976, which are a set of voluntary recommendations to MNEs in all major areas of business and employment. Blanpain (2006, p. 312) describes how these guidelines address issues such as freedom of association, child labour, forced labour, discrimination, collective bargaining, provision of information and consultation, health and safety, observance of employment standards, skills and training, reasonable notice and cooperation in case of major changes and access to decision-makers. The OECD's aim is to create a good relationship between the MNE and the society in which it operates, by ensuring that it abides by government policies, improves the foreign investment climate and contributes to sustainable development. Member governments have committed to promoting the guidelines among MNEs operating in or from their respective countries. There is a committee on International Investment and Multinational Enterprises (IME), which consists of representatives of the governments of the OECD member countries that hear complaints about non-compliance with the guidelines.

Dowling et al. (2008) draw attention to a key section of the guidelines, the 'umbrella' or '*chapeau*' clause that precedes the guidelines themselves. This clause states that MNCs should adhere to the guidelines 'within the framework of law, regulations and prevailing labour relations and employment practices in each of the countries in which they operate'. However, as Campbell and Rowan (1983) observe, this has been the cause of much contention. For example, MNEs have understood this clause as relating to the observance of local laws, which supersede the guidelines, whereas labour unions argue that the guidelines should act as a supplement to national law (ibid.). This confusion or contention over the meaning of the *chapeau* clause, coupled with the fact that the OECD guidelines are voluntary, suggests that rather than regulating MNE behaviour, the guidelines will act as an area of controversy (Dowling et al., 2008). The effectiveness of these guidelines has received some attention in the literature and is indeed the subject of much debate. This debate is exemplified by the Badger case, which was the first test of the guidelines. Rojot (2006) notes that along with some other cases, the Badger case[7] (Blanpain, 1977) illustrates the effectiveness of the guidelines, as the MNE was forced to adopt its behaviour in line with the guidelines . In this regard, Rojot (ibid.) points to the influential role played by the Trade Union Advisory Committee (TUAC) in changing MNE behaviour by raising or threatening to raise unwelcome adverse publicity. However, others suggest this case demonstrates the weakness of the guidelines as deeper analysis reveals that only the 'social forces of each separate country must apply pressure on their respective governments if they want the guidelines applied' (Liebhaberg, 1980, p. 85). Indeed, in this particular case, significant pressure by both the US and Belgian government were critical in altering the behaviour of the MNE.

In summary, we have illustrated the role that key actors can play in regulating the behaviour of MNEs at the international level. It appears that whilst both international trade unions and international organizations have made some progress in acting as a countervailing power to MNEs, there remains some way to go. Two particular barriers inhibit effective regulation of MNEs. First, the codes aimed at regulating MNEs, established by the ILO and OECD, have had relatively little impact on MNE behaviour, largely because there are no sanctions attached and adherence is purely voluntary. Until such time as this situation changes, it is unlikely that they will have a significant impact. Second, there is significant reluctance on the part of both national governments and trade unions to accord power to international representative organizations (De Nijs, 1995). While there have been some instances (e.g., Workers Uniting), these have been the exception rather than the rule. It is widely acknowledged that for effective regulation of MNEs to occur, national organizations must transfer essential elements of their jurisdiction to international organizations but this is also unlikely to happen any time soon (ibid.).

CONCLUSION

The significance of multinational enterprises to the global economy is without question. Given that employment in these MNEs is in the region of 77 million worldwide their actions as employers and their influence on employment practice is of great interest. Given the size and the power they wield in the global economy they have the potential to introduce innovative employment relations practices into the diverse host economies in which they operate. While clearly some of these innovations are adoptive and build on extant host employment practices, others are more disruptive and can challenge the extant framework of employment relations in the host economies. This creates a significant challenge for government and policy-makers who attempt to trade off the financial efficiency outcomes of courting further FDI investment (through, for example, weakly regulated institutional context supportive of these innovations) with the social equity outcomes for employees (Kleiner and Ham, 2003). This balance is in many developed and developing economies increasingly biased towards capital. In this regard, O'Brien (2000) points to the three faces of industrial relations that the international union movement faces in the global environment, namely social democracy, neoliberal and authoritarian. While a detailed discussion of each type is beyond the scope of this chapter it is increasingly apparent that labour's favoured form of regulation, social democracy, is being replaced by neoliberal and authoritarian regimes in many developed economies (ibid.).

Thus, organized labour faces a number of significant challenges in countervailing the power of MNEs. In this regard, it appears that global trade union arrangements have as of yet had limited success in engaging with the multinational sector. Empirical research moving forward should focus on unearthing examples of successes of global trade unions in engaging with multinationals on a global scale and providing insights on how these relationships can be structured to most effectively act as a countervailing force to MNE power. Additionally, the impact of different international institutions and organization on MNE regulation also represents and important avenue for future study.

Furthermore, the impact of the innovations that MNEs introduce in various host countries could provide a useful lens through which to explore the nature of change in business systems. This is something that has been relatively under-theorized thus far and that has great potential for future development. In this regard, Lane (2003) identifies a number of key theoretical questions that must be considered in attempting to explore the nature of change in business systems. First, one must consider how one type of change differs from another. How can we determine whether institutional innovation is bounded and within the system versus fundamental system change and the adoption of a new path? In this regard she postulates: 'system change has occurred when a new logic has replaced the old one', i.e. when it is accepted by most influential actors in the political economy (ibid., p. 84). Second, she questions how system change differs from hybridization, whereby the latter implies the concurrent adoption of different logics within a business system. She notes that in hybrid situations there is generally no complementarity within the system and thus different parts of the system are dominated by different logics. An important point to note is that if a cumulative change in a key institution has resulted in fundamental changes in the logic that underscores the system combined with support from powerful actors then the longevity of hybridization is likely to be short-lived as the new logic will become dominant and institutionalized. For example, Collings et al. (2008) point to some evidence of the emergence of a complementary approach to ER in US multinational operating in Ireland.

Although there are a number of drivers of systems change identified in the literature including cross-national coordination and control, internationalization of capital markets, and so on, the impact of foreign-owned MNEs on the host system is particularly apposite. A key concern in the context of this discussion is how and when incremental changes to the business system alter the ER institutions of a host environment. While acknowledging that the potential for system-wide change to occur is mediated by the strength and cohesion of institutions in the host business system, we point to a number of key characteristics of the business system that may facilitate systems change. Whitley (1999, pp. 127–9) identifies a number of further factors that mediate the impact of inward FDI on the host business system. These include, inter alia: the overall weight and relative significance of FDI in the host economy; the concentration of such FDI from a particular type of business system; the dependence of foreign firms on domestic organizations and agencies; the strength of the sector and its centrality to the economy.

NOTES

1. While Collings uses the term international industrial relations, we use employment relations for consistency with the remainder of the chapter.
2. Gennard (1974) conceptualized innovative practices in a positive light suggesting that these practices aided industry in minimizing underutilization of labour. He contrasted these innovative practices with what he termed disruptive practices, which involved foreign firms departing radically from the values and structures of the host business system
3. Latest evidence shows that three such framework agreements have been negotiated covering parental leave, part-time work and fixed-term employment (Gennard, 2009a).
4. The 11 GUFs are the Building and Wood Workers' International, Education International, International Federation of Chemical, Energy, Mine and General Workers' Unions, International Federation of Journalists, International Metalworkers' Federation, International Transport Workers' Federation, International Textile, Garment and Leather Workers' Federation, International Union of Food, Agricultural, Hotel, Restaurant, Catering, Tobacco and Allied Workers' Associations, Public Service International, Union Network International and the International Arts and Entertainment Alliance.
5. ILO Core Labour Standards include freedom of association, abolition of forced labour and child labour, and freedom from discrimination.
6. Some exceptions do exist, for example the International Federation of Chemical, Energy, Mine and General Workers' Unions and Public Service International both negotiated an IFA with *Electricité de France*.
7. The Belgian company, Badger Belgium Naamloze Vennootschap (BBNV), a subsidiary of Raytheon, a US MNE, went out of business in 1976 and a dispute arose over termination payments under Belgian law. The Belgian trade unions argued that the parent company should honour BBNV's financial obligations, which Raytheon refused. After intense pressure from Belgian and US trade unions, and the Belgian government, a case was brought before the OECD. The Committee on International Investments and MNEs (CIIME), using the OECD Guidelines for MNEs, found that the parent company did

have some shared responsibility with the subsidiary and a settlement was eventually agreed.

REFERENCES

Abbott, K. (1998), 'The ETUC and its role in advancing the cause of European worker participation rights', *Economic and Industrial Democracy*, **19**(4), 605–31.
Adams, R.J. (2005), 'Organizing Wal-Mart: The Canadian campaign', *Just Labour*, **6/7**, 1–11.
Babson, S. (2003), 'Dual sourcing at Ford in the United States and Mexico: Implications for labor relations and union strategies', in W.N. Cooke (ed.), *Multinational Companies and Global Human Resource Strategies*, Westport, CT: Quorum Books.
Bae, J. and Rowley, M. (2003), 'Changes and continuities in South Korean HRM', *Asia Pacific Business Review*, **9**(4), 76–105.
Bartolini, S. (2005), *Restructuring Europe: Centre Formation, System Building, and Political Structuring Between the Nation State and the European Union*, Oxford: Oxford University Press.
Black. J. (2002), 'Critical reflections on regulation', *Australian Journal of Legal Philosophy*, **27**(1), 1–37.
Blanpain, R. (1977), *The Badger Case and the OECD Guidelines for Multinational Enterprises*, Deventer, the Netherlands: Kluwer.
Blanpain, R. (2006), 'The juridification of industrial relations: The role of labour law in a globalised economy', in M.J. Morley, P. Gunnigle and D.G. Collings (eds), *Global Industrial Relations*, London: Routledge.
Boyer, R., Charron, E., Jürgens, U. and Tolliday, S. (eds) (1998), *Between Imitation and Innovation: The Transfer and Hybridisation of Productive Models in the International Automobile Industry*, Oxford: Oxford University Press.
Bronfenbrenner, K. (2000), 'Uneasy terrain: The impact of capital mobility on workers, wages, and union organizing', available at: http://works.bepress.com/kate_bronfenbrenner/5/; accessed 31 January 2011?
Butler, R.A. (2007) 'Corporations agree to cut carbon emissions', available at: http://news.mongabay.com/2007/0220-roundtable.html; accessed 23 January 2011.
Campbell, D.C. and Rowan, R.L. (1983), *Multinational Enterprises and the OECD Industrial Relations Guidelines*, Pennsylvania, Industrial Research Unit: University of Pennsylvania.
Chang, Y.Y., Mellahi, K. and Wilkinson, A. (2009), 'Control of subsidiaries of MNCs from emerging economies in developing economies', *International Journal of Human Resource Management*, **20**(1), 75–95.
Clark, T., Gospel, H. and Montgomery, J. (1999), 'Running on the spot? A review of twenty years of research on the management of human resources in comparative and international perspective', *International Journal of Human Resource Management*, **10**(3), 520–44.
Collings, D.G. (2008) 'Multinational corporations and industrial relations research: A road less travelled', *International Journal of Management Reviews*, **10**(2), 173–93.
Collings, D.G., Gunnigle, P. and Morley, M.J. (2008), 'Boston or Berlin: American MNCs and the shifting contours of industrial relations in Ireland', *International Journal of Human Resource Management*, **19**(2), 240–61.
Cooke, W.N. (2006), 'Industrial relations in MNCs', in M.J. Morley, P. Gunnigle and D.G. Collings (eds), *Global Industrial Relations*, London: Routledge.
De Nijs, W. (1995), 'International human resource management and industrial relations', in A.W. Harzing and J. Van Ruysseveldt (eds), *International Human Resource Management*, London: Sage.
Dowling, P.J., Festing, M. and Engle, A.D. (2008), *International Human Resource Management: Managing People in a Multinational Context*, 5th edition, London: Cengage Learning.

Ewing, K.D. (2006), 'International labour standards', in M.J. Morley, P. Gunnigle and D.G. Collings (eds), *Global Industrial Relations*, London: Routledge.

Ferner, A. (2003), 'Foreign multinational and industrial relations innovation in Britain', in P.K. Edwards (ed.), *Industrial Relations: Theory and Practice*, 2nd edition, Oxford: Blackwell.

Ferner, A. (2010), 'HRM in multinational companies', in A. Wilkinson, N. Bacon, T. Redman and S. Snell (eds), *The Sage Handbook of Human Resource Management*, London: Sage.

Ferner, A. and Quintanilla, J. (2002), 'Between globalisation and capitalist variety: Multinationals and the international diffusion of employment relations', *European Journal of Industrial Relations*, **8**(3), 243–5.

Ferner, A. and Varul, M.Z. (2000), 'Country-of-origin effects, host-country effects, and the management of HR in multinationals: German companies in Britain and Spain', *Journal of World Business*, **36**(2), 107–28.

Geary, J. and Roche W.K. (2001), 'Multinationals and human resource practices in Ireland: A rejection of the "new conformance thesis"', *International Journal of Human Resource Management*, **12**(1), 109–27.

Gennard, J. (1974), 'The impact of foreign-owned subsidiaries on host country labour relations: The case of the United Kingdom', in A.W. Weber (ed.), *Bargaining Without Boundaries*, Chicago: University of Chicago Press.

Gennard, J. (2009a), 'Development of transnational collective bargaining in Europe', *Employee Relations*, **31**(4), 341–6.

Gennard, J. (2009b), 'A new emerging trend? Cross-border trade union mergers', *Employee Relations*, **31**(1), 5–8.

Gennard, J. and Steuer, M.D. (1971), 'The industrial relations of foreign owned subsidiaries in the United Kingdom', *British Journal of Industrial Relations*, **9**(2), 143–59.

Glover, L. and Wilkinson, A. (2007), 'Worlds colliding: The translation of modern management practices within a UK based subsidiary of a Korean-owned MNC', *International Journal of Human Resource Management*, **18**(8), 1437–55.

Gunnigle, P. (1995), 'Collectivism and the management of industrial relations in Greenfield sites', *Human Resource Management Journal*, **5**(3), 24–40.

Gunnigle, P., Collings, D.G. and Morley, M. (2005), 'Exploring the dynamics of industrial relations in US multinationals: Evidence from the Republic of Ireland', *Industrial Relations Journal*, **36**(3), 241–56.

Gunnigle, P., Collings, D.G. and Morley, M.J. (2006), 'Accommodating global capitalism? State policy and industrial relations in American MNCs in Ireland', in A. Ferner, J. Quintanilla and C. Sanchez-Runde (eds), *Multinationals and the Construction of Transnational Practices: Convergence and Diversity in the Global Economy*, Basingstoke, Hampshire and New York: Palgrave Macmillan.

Hall, P.A. and Soskice, D. (eds) (2001a), *Varieties of Capitalism: The Institutional Foundations of Comparative Advantage*, Oxford: Oxford University Press.

Hall, P.A. and Soskice, D. (2001b), 'An introduction to varieties of capitalism', in P.A. Hall and D. Soskice (eds), *Varieties of Capitalism: The Institutional Foundations of Comparative Advantage*, Oxford: Oxford University Press.

Huxley, C. (2003), 'Local union responses to continental standardization of production and work in GM's North American truck assembly plants', in W.N. Cooke (ed.), *Multinational Companies and Global Human Resource Strategies*, Westport, CT: Quorum Books.

Kennedy, T. (1980), *European Labour Relations*, Lexington, MA: Lexington Books.

Kerr, C., Dunlop, J.T., Harbison, F.H. and Myers, C.A. (1960), *Industrialism and Industrial Man: The Problems of Labour and Management in Economic Growth*, London: Penguin.

Kim, W. (2010), 'The ratification of ILO conventions and the provision of unemployment benefits: An empirical analysis', *International Social Security Review*, **63**(1), 37–55.

Kleiner, M. and Ham, H. (2003), 'The effects of different industrial relations systems in the United States and Europe on foreign direct investment flows', in W.N. Cooke (ed.), *Multinational Companies and Global Human Resource Strategies*, Westport, CA: Quorum.

Kostova, T., Roth, K. and Dacin, M.T. (2008), 'Institutional theory in the study of multinational corporations: A critique and new directions', *Academy of Management Review*, **33**(4), 994–1006.

Lane, C. (2003), 'Changes in corporate governance of German corporations: Convergence to the Anglo-American model?', *Competition and Change*, **7**(2–3), 79–100.

Lavelle, J. (2008), 'The contours of union recognition in foreign-owned MNCs: Survey evidence from the Republic of Ireland', *Irish Journal of Management*, **29**(1), 45–64.

Leat, M. (2007), *Exploring Employee Relations*, 2nd edition, Oxford: Butterworth-Heinemann.

Liebhaberg, B. (1980), *Industrial Relations and Multinational Corporations in Europe*, London: Cower.

Mahoney, J. and Thelen, K. (2010), *Explaining Institutional Change: Ambiguity, Agency, and Power*, Cambridge: Cambridge University Press.

Marginson, P. (1992), 'European integration and transnational management–union relations in the enterprise', *British Journal of Industrial Relations*, **30**(4), 529–46.

Müller, T. and Rüb, S. (2004), 'Towards internationalisation of labour relations? Global union networks and International Framework Agreements – status quo and prospects', Unpublished paper.

O'Brien, R. (2000), 'Workers and world order: The tentative transformation of the international union movement', *Review of International Studies*, **26**(4), 533–55.

O'Hagan, E., Gunnigle, P. and Morley, M.J. (2005), 'Issues in the management of industrial relations in international firms', in H. Scullion and M. Linehan (eds), *International Human Resource Management: A Critical Text*, Basingstoke: Palgrave Macmillan.

Papadakis, K. (2008), 'Research on transnational social dialogue and International Framework Agreements (IFAs)', *International Labour Review*, **147**(1), 100–104.

Porter, M.E. (1998), 'The competitive advantage of nations', in M.E. Porter (ed.), *On Competition*, Boston, MA: Harvard Business School Press.

Rogers, E. (1995), *Diffusion of Innovations*, New York: Free Press.

Rojot, J. (2006), 'International collective bargaining', in M.J. Morley, P. Gunnigle and D.G. Collings (eds), *Global Industrial Relations*, London: Routledge.

Royle, T. (2002), 'Undermining the system? Labour relations in the German fast-food industry', in T. Royle and B. Towers (eds), *Labour Relations in the Global Fast-Food Industry*, London: Routledge.

Royle, T. (2004), 'Employment practices of multinationals in the Spanish and German quick-food sectors: Low road convergence', *European Journal of Industrial Relations*, **10**(1), 51–71.

Royle, T. (2006), 'The dominance effect? Multinational corporations in the Italian quick-food service sector', *British Journal of Industrial Relations*, **44**(4), 757–79.

Smith, C. and Meiskins, P. (1995), 'System, society and dominance effects in cross-national organisational analysis', *Work, Employment & Society*, **9**(2), 241–68.

Sorge, A. (2004) 'Cross-national differences in human resources and organisation', in A.W. Harzing and J. Van Ruysseveldt (eds), *International Human Resource Management*, London: Sage.

Streeck, W. and Thelen, K. (2005), *Beyond Continuity: Institutional Change in Advanced Political Economies*, Oxford: Oxford University Press.

Telljohann, V., da Costa, I., Müller, T., Rehfeldt, U. and Zimmer, R. (2009), *European and International Framework Agreements: Practical Experiences and Strategic Approaches*, Dublin: European Foundation for the Improvement of Living and Working Conditions.

Turner, T., D'Art, D. and Gunnigle, P. (2001), 'Multinationals and human resource practices in Ireland: A rejection of the "new conformance thesis": A reply', *International Journal of Human Resource Management*, **12**(1), 128–33.

United Nations Conference on Trade and Development (UNCTAD) (2009), *World Investment Report. Transnational Corporations, Agricultural Production and Development*, New York and Geneva: United Nations.

Weber, A.W. (1974), 'Bargaining without boundaries: Industrial relations in the multinational firm', in A.W. Weber and R.J. Flanagan (eds), *Bargaining Without boundaries: The Multinational Corporation and International Labor Relations*, Chicago: University of Chicago Press.
Whitley, R. (1999), *Divergent Capitalisms: The Social Structuring and Change of Business Systems*, Oxford: Oxford University Press.
Wolfe, R.A. (1995), 'Human resource management innovations: Determinants of their adoption and implementation', *Human Resource Management*, **34**(2), 313–27.

18 Regulating global capital through public and private codes: an analysis of international labour standards and corporate voluntary initiatives
Tony Royle

INTRODUCTION

An increasingly important influence on the way in which employment relations are played out in different countries is the impact of global capital
and the activities of multinational corporations (MNCs). No national
economy is completely insulated from global capital flows and this has
become increasingly the case since the deregulation of the stock market
and opening up of the global economy since the late 1980s. However, this
is not a new phenomenon; as early as the eighteenth century it was recognized that countries with higher labour standards may be at a disadvantage to those countries with lower standards and this could put pressure on
states to lower their labour standards accordingly (Hepple, 2005). Existing
variations in national labour standards reflect different stages of development, differing industrial relations systems and welfare systems, which are
subject to varying historical trajectories and different structural, political,
economic and cultural factors. Part of the solution to this problem would
be to try to achieve the same minimum levels of pay and conditions of
work for all workers across the globe through a set of internationally recognized and effectively enforced international labour standards. However,
this proposition is extremely difficult in practice; developing countries'
main competitive advantage in attracting foreign investment may be based
on having relatively low standards and nation states are often averse to
giving up any sovereignty to international institutions and, especially in
the sphere of employment, which is usually strongly embedded within
national societal arrangements (Ferner and Hyman, 1998).

Nevertheless, in the last three decades or so global (inward) foreign
direct investment increased almost threefold (from $693 billion in 1980, to
$15 210 billion in 2007), the numbers of MNCs increased almost eightfold
to 79 000 in 2007, employing an estimated 82 million workers (UNCTAD,
2008) and, the emergence of other forms of global capital (such as hedge

funds, private equity firms and real estate investment trusts), have increased the pressure on *national* labour standards, arguably making a stronger case for international labour standards.

This chapter therefore examines the current state and development of international labour standards and the extent to which these standards are effective in practice in the face of such challenges. We begin by briefly reviewing some of the problems that global capital creates for workers' rights and conditions of work. We then examine the role played by the International Labour Organization in developing the existing system of international labour standards and its shift away from a broad set of conventions towards a core set of 'principles' from the late 1990s. We also examine how this shift in emphasis can be understood in the context of the developments in the voluntary private initiatives of MNCs.

THE CHALLENGE FOR LABOUR

Some commentators are fairly optimistic about MNC activity, suggesting that MNCs are subject to the constraints of the global competitive economy (Gray, 1992) and are mostly interested in promoting the common good, being a benign source of investment, technology transfer and a means of upgrading labour forces and national infrastructures (Dunning, 1993; UNCTAD, 2008). However, for all the positives that may be claimed for MNC activity there are also many negatives, particularly those relating to labour and human rights violations. Global capital flows present the labour movement with considerable problems, not only because investment can be moved from one country to another, but also because those acting on the behalf of global capital appear to have the ability to behave in qualitatively different ways from national capitals, having a greater degree of power vis-à-vis labour as well as having a greater ability to influence national governments (Ramsay, 1999). The expansion of global capital and its various forms as well as the numbers and size of MNCs have played a considerable part in driving the trend towards 'financialization', changing the incentives of top managers to place more emphasis on short-term stock market price movements and align top managers and shareholder interests through the increasing use of stock options. This has arguably resulted in the drive for profit through the elimination of productive capacity and employment, leading to less job security, more job losses and degradation of working conditions through outsourcing, casualization, production transfers and plant closures, with non-financial MNCs acting more like financial market players and being rewarded for the reduction of their payrolls (Crotty, 2005). Overall this has given increasing credence to the claims that global capital has become too big, too powerful and too unaccountable.

It has been suggested that the day to day exploitation of workers in the global supply chains of MNCs has almost become routine and unnoticed (Bakan, 2004; Lewis, 2009). In the more than 5000 Export Processing Zones (EPZs) worldwide (which are estimated to employ over 40 million people, 70–90 per cent of whom are probably women) workers have to endure low wages and poor working conditions. In addition, freedom of association and collective bargaining are constrained often due to the non-enforcement of national labour laws (Gordon, 2000; ILO, 2004; Gunawardana, 2006). Many of the scandals that have made it into the mainstream media have involved the suppliers of well-known brands or the brands themselves, such as Coca-Cola, Rio-Tinto, McDonald's, Nike, Nestlé and Walmart (Klein, 2001; Royle, 2010). In 1999, in one of Walmart's Chinese supplier factories, 900 workers were locked up in a walled compound, working 14-hour days, seven days a week, 30 days a month, for an average wage of three (US) cents per hour, and were beaten, fined and fired if they complained about it (Roberts and Bernstein, 2000). Despite Walmart's promises to improve conditions, in 2004 it was shown that Chinese workers in Walmart's supplier firms were still experiencing terrible working conditions, unauthorized wage deductions and forced overtime (Goodman and Pan, 2004; NLC, 2005). In 2005 the International Labour Forum confirmed many similar problems in Walmart's suppliers in Africa, China, Bangladesh, Indonesia and Nicaragua, where labour standards were routinely violated (ILRF, 2009). Other large MNCs in the fast-fashion industry such as Gap, Primark, Tesco and Walmart/Asda have also been repeatedly involved in allegations of child labour, bad working conditions and poverty wages in some of their suppliers in the last five years, with no improvement in sight (McDougall, 2007; *Panorama*, 2008; Taylor, 2009).

Whilst the most extreme forms of labour rights abuses tend to be found in developing countries MNCs also pose problems for workers in the developed countries. One of the most common problems is the issue off-shoring. IBM, for example, one of the most profitable companies in its sector, recently announced huge job cuts in the US, Germany, Ireland and the UK, with jobs going to Eastern Europe, China, India and South America, whilst existing Indian workers at IBM earn a tenth or less of their US counterparts (Doran, 2009). Other management tactics associated with MNCs (but not exclusively MNCs) such as 'whipsawing'[1] and union suppression are used to keep labour costs low and workers quiet (Royle, 2000, 2001, 2005a, 2005b, 2010; Taylor and Bain, 2003; Hepple, 2005; Pulignano, 2006; McDougall, 2009; Royle and Ortiz, 2009). There is also evidence in some low-paid service sectors such as fast-food, that MNCs not only depress wages and abuse core labour standards on a global level, but often influence their local competitors to follow suit (Royle, 2004, 2006). These trends all add to the growing concern that an increasing number of workers in both developed and developing countries are outside effective legal protection (Voss, 2002; Stone, 2006; Pollert, 2007).

However, laying the blame entirely on the MNC and mobile capital is too simplistic; governments continue to play an important part in promoting or adhering to neoliberal ideology that sustains a framework in which international free trade takes priority over other issues, suggesting that it is also national governments that are part of the problem (Gordon, 2000; McCallum, 2006; Smith and Morton, 2006; Wedderburn, 2007). MNCs are part of a global system in which governments largely dictate the rules of the game; it is governments that have steadily removed barriers and conditions to trade, investment and outsourcing and they appear to be more concerned with trade than workers' rights. If MNCs and/or their suppliers continue to commit labour violations it seems that this is because there is nothing in our international trading rules to stop them doing so. To what extent then do existing international labour standards and private voluntary initiatives of MNCs protect workers from human and labour rights abuses? How have such mechanisms developed and changed and how effective are they in practice?

THE DEVELOPMENT OF INTERNATIONAL LABOUR STANDARDS

Before the International Labour Organization (ILO) was created in 1919 existing worker protections were predominantly based on a variety of national laws. The idea of creating international labour standards (or international public codes of conduct) that could in theory question the authority of nation states was therefore unique and significant. The growth of radical and reformist social movements that developed in the late nineteenth to early twentieth centuries provided the impetus for the establishment of the ILO. Those on the left had originally proposed an International Parliament of Labour, which would have produced international statutes, having the same effect as national laws. Instead, the ILO that emerged fell well short of this ideal, providing only for *conventions* and *recommendations* that require the approval of two-thirds of delegates at the ILO annual conference. Furthermore, ILO conventions or recommendations do not have automatic effects, but must be submitted to member governments to consider whether to accept them or not. They only become binding on member states when they are ratified by the member state and when they have passed through the relevant national constitution (such as an Act of Parliament in the UK). The ILO provides for one union delegate, one employer delegate and two government delegates from each country. ILO member countries have a duty to consider all ILO conventions and report on how they intend to implement the conventions they ratify or alternatively explain why they chose not to ratify.

There is a weak form of supervision and complaints (for example, regarding non-enforcement) can be made to the International Labour Office (the permanent secretariat of the ILO). However, this relies on publicity, encouragement and tripartism (the active involvement of employer, government and union representatives); there are no sanctions for non-compliance. In effect the ILO that was created left the decision-making power with nation states, allowing them to interpret, select, ratify or simply ignore conventions (Standing, 2008). Despite the relative weakness of the ILO system, from the late 1940s until the early 1970s, the ILO was in the ascendency, operating in a context of rising trade unionism, standardized employment relations and considerable state involvement in a wide range of economic activities and various forms of social corporatism that emphasized the importance of collective and substantive rights over individual and procedural rights. However, from the early 1970s the ILO faced a number of challenges.

The first challenge was decolonization, which gradually increased the number of member states in the ILO from a group of 52 mainly Western countries in 1946 to 180 members by 2007; new members from the developing countries were demanding better representation for their interests and for more flexible standard-setting within the ILO (Hepple, 2005). The second challenge was the increasingly difficult relationship with successive US administrations; from 1953 to 1988, for example, the US refused to ratify any ILO convention. The ILO stood for a model of national welfare capitalism that did not match the US's world view, which the US saw as a threat to free enterprise and an attempt to impose socialism on the US (Alston, 2004; Hepple, 2005). After delaying subscriptions to the ILO over preceding years, in 1970 the US government (which contributed a quarter of the ILO's budget) finally stopped its contributions altogether and then suspended its membership in 1975 causing huge financial difficulties for the ILO. Although the ILO survived the US's five-year absence, it never fully recovered from this action. The US rejoined the ILO in 1980 but only on the basis that US nationals would take a number of senior positions (Standing, 2008).

Third, after the election of neoliberal governments of Thatcher (UK) and Reagan (US) in the early 1980s the whole emphasis of the world trading system and its institutions, the World Bank and the International Monetary Fund (IMF) shifted towards neoliberalism. From the 1980s the IMF began to see governments as the problem and free markets as the solution, commercial interests and values now predominated, while concern for the environment, democracy, human rights and social justice were often to be ignored, undermined or seen as obstacles to be overcome (Stiglitz, 2002). The US's influence was central to this shift in policy, the US had always had the biggest influence on IMF policy through the 'Washington Consensus' (i.e., the IMF, the World Bank and the US Treasury) and this was particularly evident in the 1980s. The neoliberal agenda was also at its height when the World Trade Organization was established in 1995, arguably further marginalizing the ILO in international trade (Hepple, 2005; Standing, 2008).

A fourth factor that boosted the neoliberal agenda and undermined the attempt to develop a comprehensive code to regulate labour issues in the ILO was the fall of the Soviet bloc. Alston (2004) suggests that whilst the reformist nature of international labour standards had always been an ally against communist regimes, now that communism appeared to have failed, it removed the pressure that had long prompted Western politicians to pay attention to labour standards, arguably unleashing latent hostility against the trade union movement.

UK Conservative government policy from 1979 until 1997 was symptomatic of this hostility; the UK government at that time refused to ratify 25 new ILO conventions and denounced a number of ILO conventions it had already ratified. The UK was also on the receiving end of a number of complaints during this period relating to labour standards violations, including freedom of association and the right to organize. The UK's position has not changed significantly since that time, there has been no change in the strike laws instigated by the previous Conservative regimes, which remain inconsistent with ILO conventions (Hepple, 2005; Standing, 2008).

In 2008 there were some 188 ILO conventions, but production and ratification of conventions has slowed, with only eight conventions having been produced since 2000. Only three-fifths of ILO member states had ratified less than one-quarter of ILO conventions and more than one-fifth had ratified less than 20 conventions. In addition many countries that do ratify conventions do not implement or enforce them. Hepple (2005) argues that this trend can be partly explained by 'bogus' or 'empty' ratification. Although governments are often required to ratify ILO conventions in order to get assistance from the World Bank and the IMF, this does not mean that such conventions are applied in practice. Many states have model labour codes, but do not enforce them, either due to lack of resources, incompetence or corruption. The result is huge disparity between developed countries complying with a relatively high number of ratifications and a large number of developing countries with few ratifications and a high level of non-compliance. Many major violations of standards continue with ILO procedures having little effect, largely because the ILO's supervisory system relies on voluntary action by member states and strong and independent trade union movements and employer organizations at the national level. The system cannot function if these are weak or non-existent. This is exacerbated in developed countries by the decline in trade union strength in some sectors and where the main spokespersons for the workers are NGOs. NGOs are not classed as representative organizations at the ILO even though the ILO draws some of its technical experts from NGOs. By the mid-1990s the increasing internationalization of trade, the ILO's inability to produce conventions, the concessions made to neoliberalism, the shift away from collective rights, the unwillingness or refusal of governments to implement and ratify conventions and the increasing marginalization of the ILO by other international bodies took its toll. In addition, employer groups and countries favouring a more deregulated approach increasingly took the opportunity to question the ILO's relevance in the globalized economy (Alston, 2004).

THE 1998 DECLARATION ON FUNDAMENTAL PRINCIPLES AND RIGHTS AT WORK

The ILO's response to these difficulties was a major overhaul of its approach to labour standards. It would now prioritize a 'core' of conventions over others and adopt a different approach to their implementation. The new initiative was based on four core labour standards that covered eight core labour conventions in what became the 1998 Declaration on Fundamental Principles and Rights at Work. The eight core conventions are freedom of association (C. 87) and collective bargaining (C. 98), forced labour (C. 29 and C. 105), non-discrimination (C. 100 and C. 111), minimum employment age (C. 138) and elimination of child labour (C. 182). However, these conventions were now to be subsumed under four 'principles' and 'rights': freedom of association and the effective recognition of the right to collective bargaining; the elimination of all forms of forced and compulsory labour; the effective abolition of child labour; and the elimination of discrimination in respect of employment and occupation. The principles would be pursued not by sanctions, but through technical assistance and development policies. In addition they apply to all

ILO members whether they have ratified the conventions or not (Hepple, 2005).

The focus on these eight particular conventions arguably came out of an OECD report in 1994, which suggested that improved enforcement of non-discrimination standards, the elimination of child and forced labour might raise economic efficiency and that the concerns of developing countries that freedom of association and the right to collective bargaining would negatively affect their performance was unfounded. However, the thinking behind this approach reflected the difficult situation that the ILO found itself in by the 1990s. Before the Declaration was drafted, for example, various employer groups at the ILO made it clear that they wanted a focus on principles not rights, no new legal obligations, no new reporting obligations, no obligations on countries arising from existing conventions, no legal or technical matters included, no new complaints-based bodies and no questions of links with trade (Alston, 2004).

A number of commentators, often those associated with the ILO itself, have argued that the Declaration is a positive step forward, providing the ILO with a new tool for promoting the ratification and enforcement of core conventions through its follow-up reporting mechanism (Langille, 2005; Maupain, 2005). The US administration and employer groups were also strong supporters of the Declaration. Others, however, have been much less positive about these developments. Alston (2004), for example, argues that first, the Declaration has arguably weakened the ILO by making (even the limited number of) core labour standards subject to monitoring only by promotional means and moves away from the idea of sanctions. Second, the selection of a core suggests that other conventions become sidelined and neglected. Third, the more decentralized system significantly reduces governmental responsibilities and encourages others (such as consumers and MNCs) to take the lead in enforcing standards through corporate voluntary initiatives. For example, the United Nation's Global Compact, which followed in 1999, typifies this voluntaristic approach and has been criticized for allowing MNCs to 'blue wash' themselves with the UN flag without having to make any serious commitment to abide by such principles (TRAC, 2000). Fourth, the more flexible form of the Declaration could divorce existing conventions from their legal context, undermining the existing system. Finally, although superficially it looks as though the ILO is responding appropriately to the changing global trade regime, it raises serious questions about the ILO's effectiveness (Alston, 2004; Alston and Heenan, 2004).

Standing (2008) suggests that the 1998 Declaration glossed over a crisis in the role of labour standards and took the focus away from the possibility of including social clauses in the WTO. It also gave the ILO a more legitimate role in global forums and brought millions of dollars into the ILO from the US administration, which was very influential in shifting the ILO's orientation towards promotional principles rather than legally binding conventions. The US government made it clear that the ILO would in effect have to align itself with US economic policy if it was to enjoy US support and the Chair of the Declaration Drafting Committee was a US employer's delegate. It is interesting to note that by the time of the 1998 Declaration, the US had ratified only one of the eight core ILO conventions and by 2004 had only ratified two (No. 105 on forced labour and No. 182 on the worst forms of child labour). Despite the US's claims to be the champion of internationally recognized workers' rights, the US has still not ratified the core conventions dealing with freedom of association, the right to collective bargaining, non-discrimination and child labour in general. Of the 177 member states of the ILO, the US has the fifth worst record on ratification of fundamental conventions, equalling Burma and Oman. The US's interpretation of the 1998 Declaration seems to suggest that member states no longer have to ratify conventions to be in compliance with the Principles of the Declaration, suggesting that conventions can now be ignored; governments can decide what the ILO standards mean. The core standards arguably represent what was acceptable to the US government at the time, in effect resulting in less pressure for the US to comply with ILO conventions and as a result less pressure to change its existing labour law in accordance with such conventions (Alston, 2004; Blanpain et al., 2007). In 1999 the ILO closed its industrial relations department and replaced it with the 'social dialogue' department, moving away from traditional collective bargaining and the idea of equalizing bargaining power and collective social rights, to a focus on encouraging dialogue. The new director of this department (who had no previous experience of the ILO) came from the US White House. The ILO also now formally embraced the 'soft' law of private voluntary initiatives being promoted by MNCs (Standing, 2008).

The ILO has to some extent tried to respond to some of these criticisms by promoting new platforms for action such as 'Decent Work' in 1999. This was supposed to shift the ILO's attention towards people on the periphery of formal systems of employment, the unwaged and those in the informal economy. On the surface it appeared to be an important shift in attempts to create more effective international labour standards for marginalized workers in the context of the voluntary private codes drawn up by MNCs. It was also supposed to broaden representation at the ILO to include NGOs, but both employer and union groups have opposed this (Voss, 2002; Hepple, 2005). However, ILO initiatives like 'Decent Work' appear to represent an acceptance that 'rights' have been downgraded to the more vague notion of 'goals'. Standing (2008) suggests that the ILO has discouraged attempts to 'measure' what 'Decent Work' really means in practice and can be seen as an attempt to reassert the ILO's relevance and connect with other debates at the United Nations on poverty and globalization, while at the same time portraying 'Decent Work' as non-ideological and with neoliberalism as the only game in town. In effect the ILO appears to be sidelining equality whilst espousing the vagueness of 'decency', 'fairness' and 'social dialogue'. It can be argued that the combination of the existing ILO conventions and the newer soft law mechanisms such as the 1998 Declaration, the 1976 OECD Guidelines for Multinational Enterprises, the ILO's 1977 Tripartite Declaration of Principles Concerning Multinational Enterprises (revised in 2000 and 2006) and the United Nation's 1999 Global Compact is creating confusion and a reluctance to cite conventions in case the reference to conventions will complicate the promotion of the newer soft law principles.

It is hard to avoid the conclusion that the overall result of the ILO's shift in policy since the 1998 Declaration has been more complexity in competing and conflicting standards, principles and platforms, fewer ratifications and lower respect for international labour standards, a lower capacity to monitor, no capacity to enforce and a marked shift to less confrontational policies in the context of neoliberalism. The ILO's relevance as a standard setter has not been revived since the Declaration. Furthermore, its position in the system of economic global governance has been increasingly marginalized. The WTO has made it clear that it will not accept any formal linkage between labour standards and trade and that it is the ILO (not the WTO itself) which is the proper body for improving labour standards; the ILO still does not even have observer status at the WTO.

PRIVATE CORPORATE INITIATIVES

It is probably no coincidence that at the same time we see the ILO entering a period of crisis we also see the private voluntary initiatives of global capital gaining in influence, with corporate codes, social labelling and corporate social responsibility (CSR) all being pushed forward by MNCs and national governments as the free market solution to labour rights abuses. By the 1990s interest in corporate codes of conduct has risen significantly, with clothing manufacturers and retailers leading the way. MNCs were increasingly drafting their own non-binding private corporate codes and principles, espousing high ethical standards not only in their own operations, but also in their supplier companies. The variety and range of these private sector initiatives has multiplied dramatically since the early 1990s, and probably reflects the explosion in capital flows and increase in offshoring since the collapse of the Soviet bloc, the opening up of China and more liberal trade policies in other developing countries (Jenkins, 2001).

However, by the mid- to late 1990s as the early corporate codes failed to reduce the growing criticism of MNCs, MNCs began to develop more advanced forms of code that were more substantial than statements of good intentions. Sometimes these were drafted with human rights groups or ethical investment specialists, some applying to individual factories or particular countries and some allowing for outside monitoring. In a reflection of what was going on in the ILO, MNCs also renewed their lobbying activity with governments arguing that voluntary measures are a better approach than legally binding measures (Diller, 1999; Klein, 2001; Hepple, 2005). By the end of the 1990s the situation was further confused by a number of MNCs (including those with very questionable track records such as Rio Tinto, Dow Chemicals, Unocal and Nestlé) rushing into partnership with human rights groups or signing up to the United Nations Global Compact, promising better communication and cooperation with humanitarian organizations (TRAC, 2000; Hepple, 2005). Some academics were also enthusiastic, declaring the dawn of a new age in which brand-based activism was so successful that it had created a 'spotlight phenomenon' in which there was no need for outside regulation, as it was now in the MNCs' own interests to comply with labour standards (Klein, 2001). By 2004 no less than 85 per cent of FTSE 100 companies referred to corporate social responsibility in their annual reports and all of the companies in the US Fortune 500 now have private codes of conduct.

Those more positive about private codes and monitoring suggest that in some circumstances they can be an appropriate and a flexible way to improve rights and conditions in global production networks especially in developing countries, which may be less able or less willing to enforce their own labour laws or raise their standards (O'Rourke, 2003; Rodriguez-Garavito, 2005), whilst others argue that codes of conduct can be seen as one useful component in a larger integrated system for managing, regulating and enforcing labour standards and improving conditions (Locke et al., 2007). However, the more positive analyses of corporate codes may be overly optimistic and are often based on case studies of well-known brands. The problem is that the private voluntary initiatives of MNCs are based on the assumption that accurate information will be collected in factory audits and this will be used by NGOs or other third parties to put pressure on MNCs to reform their suppliers. However, who will monitor the codes through all the layers of subcontracting? Who will enforce them? What are the sanctions and penalties for non-compliance? When abuses are found do MNCs work with their suppliers to improve conditions or cut and run?

Critics argue that private codes fail to produce generally accepted principles for their content or their implementation, have unreliable verification methods, are not enforceable, are not drafted in response to the needs and demands of employees, may discriminate against producers in developing countries, are actually designed not to protect labour rights or improve conditions, but instead limit the legal liability of global brands while improving their public reputation and displace government regulation and trade union intervention (Diller, 1999; Klein, 2001; Esbenschade, 2004). For example, several large MNCs such as Primark, Asda and Tesco have all signed up to the Ethical Trading Initiative (ETI), which is a voluntary organization funded by the UK government that has a voluntary code of conduct setting out basic rights for employees. However, all three of these MNCs have been in violation of the ETI code and their own private codes on more than one occasion in recent years (McDougal, 2007; McVeigh, 2007; *Panorama*, 2008; Taylor, 2009).

Frank (2008) suggests that after a number of high-profile scandals (including child labour), Nike's compliance and monitoring system is now one of the best and it is seen as a leader in the field, pre-screening supplier factories, disclosing the names and addresses of all its suppliers and making much of its monitoring public. In their analysis of Nike's operations, Locke et al. (2007) also state that Nike has gone a lot further than many other MNCs in putting considerable resources into monitoring compliance within its own suppliers, for example employing some 80 corporate social responsibility and compliance managers operating under a distinct department. However, despite all this they found that based on Nike's own auditing system, there was considerable variation in the working conditions of Nike's supplier plants, with a considerable number providing poor conditions; furthermore, 80 per cent of suppliers had either remained the same or had worsened over time. They conclude that even if companies put resources into compliance and monitoring, without the effective enforcement of national law and the existence of independent trade unions or other means for workers to express their voice in an effective manner, corporate codes will be of questionable value. Another study commissioned by Nike in 2005 covered 569 Chinese supplier factories employing more than 300 000 workers. It found labour code violations in every single one; factories were hiding their real work practices by maintaining two or even three sets of books and by subcontracting part of the work to unauthorized contractors (Roberts et al., 2006).

Reporting his experience as a factory inspector, Frank (2008) points out that corporate codes are only as good as the intentions of those who wrote them, many MNCs are happy to be 'tricked' by their suppliers into 'believing' that good standards are being applied when in practice they are not. False time cards, payroll records and employees trained to give false answers to questions are common problems. Inspectors themselves also make mistakes. In other cases some monitoring firms are not reliable and have a cosy relationship with supplier firm and client MNC that benefits everyone except workers. MNCs often only have short-term relationships with suppliers, which means the abuses are repeated elsewhere, or supplier firms simply get better at concealing abuses. When labour rights abuses were discovered by BBC journalists in Primark's supplier firms, Primark's response was 'cut and run', cancelling its contract with those suppliers. This action was criticized by the ETI and NGOs as the only real solution would be to work with suppliers and improve pay and conditions. Primark will simply take out new contracts with new suppliers, but this provides no guarantee that abuses will be avoided and the closure of the original suppliers also means unemployment for others (Roberts et al., 2006; McDougal, 2007; McVeigh, 2007; *Panorama*, 2008; Taylor, 2009).

Klein (2001) points out that many commentators and existing studies on private codes have tended to focus on well-known branded MNCs with whom the public are well acquainted. If Nike is as good as it gets then what does that say about the effectiveness of corporate codes elsewhere? When the 'spotlight' of brand activism on MNCs is both 'roving and random', when one big name is targeted, other MNCs may be getting off the hook. Furthermore, the lesser-known brands and MNCs with no brand image often receive little or no attention in the media, as Klein (2001) argues that the public and media only appear to be interested in 'designer injustices' in what is an 'image obsessed' world. For example, whilst most MNCs were withdrawing from Burma in the 1990s in the wake of its appalling use of forced and child labour and other human rights abuses, the 'non-branded' oil company Unocal (and source of one of the largest foreign investments in Burma) was apparently quite indifferent to protests. In 1997 it stated that the only way it would leave the country would be if forced to do so by law (Klein, 2001). Unocal has since been taken over by Chevron/Texaco in April 2005, but despite continuing criticism of its Burmese operations, Chevron again made it clear it had no intention of withdrawing from Burma (*Democracy for Burma*, 2009).

In some cases activists have tried to get around the problem of the 'low-profile' MNC by secondary boycotts where branded MNCs are targeted to put pressure on the unbranded MNC supplier. For example, British supermarkets were successfully targeted with the 'Frankenfoods' campaign, which largely stopped the sale of Monsanto's genetically modi- fied products in supermarkets. However, this suggests that labour rights are increasingly defined in terms of consumer choices and the market. Klein (2001) argues that this represents a privatization of employees' and citizens' political rights. Whether private voluntary initiatives are an effective mechanism for improving working conditions or not, they represent a power struggle to decide who will place controls on MNCs: citizens through their democratically elected representatives or MNCs themselves. The proliferation and acceptance of such codes and the failure to introduce legally binding instruments on MNCs suggests that it is global capital that is winning this struggle, having persuaded policy-makers and citizens to share the same goals as MNCs when it comes to deciding how to regulate against labour and human rights abuses. The danger is that branded activism becomes a means for stopping any serious discussion of binding labour regulation, with governments and MNCs both capturing the agenda for another round of voluntary non-binding measures.

Despite all this some commentators still argue that MNCs in their role as the drivers of globalization are crucial to a ratcheting-up of labour standards, setting in train a process of continuous improvement in the treatment of labour (Sabel et al., 2000). However, after more than two decades of MNCs claiming that labour abuses can be resolved by private codes of conduct or other voluntary initiatives, the evidence suggests otherwise. We argue that voluntary approaches will not fundamentally change the nature of work and conditions in supplier firms, nor for that matter, improve job security and conditions of work for those in developed countries. The continuous pressure for lower production costs is only likely to lead in one direction; a further erosion of labour standards.

CONCLUSION

It seems difficult to avoid the conclusion that human and labour rights are still much lower down the pecking order than interests of shareholders, global capital and trade. The persistent and high levels of human and labour rights abuses look set to continue, with ordinary workers suffering the most. In the developed countries this will probably continue to focus around union-busting, health and safety violations, more work intensification, stress, job losses, more job insecurity and pay cuts (Human Rights Watch, 2000; Compa, 2004; NACAAB, 2007; Inman and Kollewe, 2009; Webb and Wearden, 2009). In the developing world, the problems of poverty wages, bad or dangerous working conditions, forced labour, child labour and harassment and intimidation for those seeking to claim their labour rights look set to continue (see, for example, Gordon, 2000; Bakan, 2004; ILO, 2004; Gunawardana, 2006; McDougall, 2007; *Panorama*, 2008; ILRF, 2009; Taylor, 2009). In this scenario how can labour and human rights abuses be effectively addressed?

Our analysis suggests first that private codes or other voluntary initiatives are unlikely to do more than scratch the surface of the problem and will not substantially improve labour standards for workers. MNCs and other forms of global capital are the dominant players in the new global economy and far too much of the voluntary corporate social responsibility agenda reflects their interests rather than that of employees or local communities. These corporate initiatives are much more about improving public relations and winning the battle to stop binding regulation, rather than improving the situation for workers. Although the ILO still plays a useful role in promoting labour standards, the shift towards the vaguer notion of 'principles' in the 1998 Declaration arguably represents a victory for global capital and its voluntarist orientation and shifts the emphasis away from more the more binding mechanism of the conventions. It can also been seen as a pragmatic response to the ILO's declining influence in the system of global economic governance and the dominance of the economic and foreign policy of the US. The focus on the 'core' eight conventions also arguably undermines many other important conventions, not least those on health and safety, protection against abuse in the workplace and adequate rest periods. The proliferation of various guidelines from the ILO, the OECD, the UN's Global Compact, the 1998 Declaration as well as the conventions and private voluntary corporate initiatives have also led to complexity and confusion from which it could be argued global capital has also benefited. These changes have neither significantly improved ratification of conventions nor improved the enforcement of conventions and have left us with a situation in which half of the world's workers still do not enjoy protection under Convention 87 (freedom of association) and Convention 98 (collective bargaining), as Brazil, China, India, Mexico and the US have still not ratified these conventions (Alston, 2004; Hepple, 2005). It seems that neoliberal ideology appears to be difficult to dislodge in the minds of policy-makers. The marginalization of the ILO and the failure to achieve more effective international labour standards also suggests that global capital is winning the debate about how its activities should be regulated. It is global capital that is increasingly deciding which rights will be upheld or whether rights will be upheld at all, not citizens through their governments (Klein, 2001). The weakness of international standards means we still rely on national governments to protect workers' rights at a time when they are either unable or unwilling to respond. This suggests that it is trade unions, community groups, consumers and NGOs that will have to try to bring MNCs to account by whatever means at their disposal (Bronfenbrenner, 2006). However, it seems unlikely that without more binding international labour standards, or stronger collective national laws and stronger trade unions such new alliances will not be enough by themselves to significantly change the status quo. This analysis illustrates how broader developments in the system of global economic governance have implications for employment relations at both the national and transnational level and also helps to explain the choices and constraints facing employers, trade unions, workers and their governments in the employment sphere.

NOTE

1. A term for the corporate tactic of pitting employees at one plant against workers at another plant of the same company. Workers who produce similar components find themselves in competition to get new work into their plant. When one group of workers agrees, under intense pressure, to certain concessions, the second group will often agree to give up even more to hold on to their jobs.

REFERENCES

Alston, P. (2004), 'Core labour standards and the transformation of the international labour rights regime', *European Journal of International Law*, **15**(3), 457–521.
Alston, P. and Heenan, J. (2004), 'Shrinking the International Labour Code', *International Law and Politics*, **36**(2/3), 221–64.
Bakan, J. (2004), *The Corporation: The Pathological Pursuit of Profit and Power*, London: Constable and Robinson.
Blanpain, R., Bisom-Rapp, S., Corbett, W.R. and Josephs, H.K. (2007), *The Global Workplace: International and Comparative Employment Law*, Cambridge: Cambridge University Press.
Bronfenbrenner, K. (2006), 'Conclusion', in K. Bronfenbrenner (ed.), *Global Unions: Challenging Transnational Capital through Cross-border Campaigns*, Ithaca, NY: Cornell University Press.
Compa, L. (2004), *Blood, Sweat, and Fear: Workers' Rights in U.S. Meat and Poultry Plants*, London: Human Rights Watch.
Crotty, J. (2005), 'The neoliberal paradox: The impact of destructive product market competition and modern financial markets on non-financial corporation performance in the neoliberal era', in G. Epstein (ed.), *Financialization and the World Economy*, Cheltenham, UK and Northampton, MA, USA: Edward Elgar.
Democracy for Burma (2009), 'Chevron determined to retain investments in Burma', 29 May, available at: http://democracyforburma.wordpress.com/2009/; accessed 25 January 2011.
Diller, D. (1999), 'A social conscience in the global marketplace? Labour dimensions of codes of conduct, social labelling and investor initiatives', *International Labour Review*, **138**(2), 99–129.
Doran, J. (2009), 'IBM set to axe thousands in move to cheap labour abroad', *The Observer*, 12 April, 38.
Dunning, J. (1993), *Multi-national Enterprises in a Global Economy*, Wokingham: Addison-Wesley.
Esbenschade, J. (2004), *Monitoring Sweatshops: Workers, Consumers and the Global Apparel Industry*, Philadelphia, PA: Temple University Press.
Ferner, A. and Hyman, R. (1998), 'Introduction: Towards European industrial relations',

Regulating global capital through public and private codes 437

in A. Ferner and R. Hyman (eds), *Changing Industrial Relations in Europe*, Oxford: Blackwell.
Frank, T.A. (2008), 'Confessions of a sweatshop inspector', *Washington Monthly*, April, available at: http://www.washingtonmonthly.com/features/2008/0804.frank.html; accessed 24 January 2011.
Goodman, P. and Pan, P. (2004), 'Chinese workers pay for Wal-Mart's low prices', *The Washington Post*, 8 February.
Gordon, M.E. (2000), 'Export processing zones', in L. Turner and M.E. Gordon (eds), *Transnational Cooperation among Labor Unions*, Ithaca, NY: Cornell University Press.
Gray, J. (1992), *The Moral Foundations of Market Institutions*, London: Integra.
Gunawardana, S. (2006), 'Struggle, perseverance, and organization in Sri Lanka's Export Processing Zones', in K. Bronfenbrenner (ed.), *Global Unions: Challenging Transnational Capital through Cross-border Campaigns*, Ithaca, NY: Cornell University Press.
Hepple, B. (2005), *Labour Laws and Global Trade*, Oxford and Portland: Hart Publishing.
Human Rights Watch (2000), *Unfair Advantage: Workers' Freedom of Association in the United States under International Human Rights Standards*, London: Human Rights Watch.
ILO (2004), 'Export Processing Zones', available at: www.ilo.org/public/english/dialogue/sector/themes/epz.htm; accessed 24 January 2011.
ILRF (2009), 'Wal-Mart campaign, international labour rights forum', available at: http://www.laborrights.org/creating-a-sweatfree-world/wal-mart-campaign; accessed 24 January 2011.
Inman, P. and Kollewe, J. (2009), 'RBS cuts 9,000 jobs – days after boss denies staff are at risk', *The Guardian*, 8 April, 18.
Jenkins, R. (2001), 'Corporate codes of conduct: Self-regulation in a global economy', Geneva: United Nations Research Institute for Social Development, available at: http://www.eldis.org/assets/Docs/29520.html; accessed 24 January 2011.
Klein, N. (2001), *No Logo*, London: Harper Collins.
Langille, B. (2005), 'Core labour rights – the true story', *European Journal of International Law*, 16(3), 411–39.
Lewis, P. (2009), 'Too high, too fast: The party's over for Dubai', *The Guardian*, 14 February, 6–7.
Locke, R., Kochan, T., Romis, M., Qin, F. (2007), 'Beyond corporate codes of conduct: Work organisation and labour standards at Nike's suppliers', *International Labour Review*, 146(1–2), 21–37.
Maupain, F. (2005), 'Revitalization not retreat. The real potential of the 1998 ILO Declaration for the Universal Protection of Workers' Rights', *European Journal of International Law*, 16(3), 440–66.
McCallum, R. (2006), 'The new work choice laws: Once again Australia borrows foreign labour law concepts', *Australian Journal of Labour Law*, 19(2), 98–104.
McDougall, D. (2007), 'Child sweatshop shame threatens Gap's ethical image', *The Observer*, 28 October, 36–7.
McDougall, D. (2009), 'Primark faces ethical storm over conditions at UK suppliers', *The Observer*, 11 January, 1, 5.
McVeigh, K. (2007), 'Asda, Primark and Tesco accused over clothing factories', *The Guardian*, 16 July, 1, 8–9.
NACAAB (2007), 'Rooting out the rogues: Why vulnerable workers and good employers need a fair employment commission', London: National Association of Citizens' Advice Bureaux, available at: http://www.citizensadvice.org.uk/index/campaigns/policy_campaign_publications/evidence_reports/er_employment/rooting_out_the_rogues; accessed 24 January 2011.
NLC (2005), 'Blood and exhaustion: Behind bargain toys made in China for Wal-Mart and Dollar General', *The National Labor Committee*, available at: http://www.nlcnet.org/reports?id=0102; accessed 24 January 2011.
O'Rourke, D. (2003), 'Outsourcing regulation: Analyzing nongovernmental systems of labor standards and monitoring', *Policy Studies Journal*, 31(1) 1–30.

Panorama (2008), 'Primark: On the rack', London: BBC, 23 June, available at: http://news. bbc.co.uk/1/hi/programmes/panorama/7468781.stm; accessed 24 January 2011.
Pollert, A. (2007), *The Unorganized Vulnerable Worker: The Case for Union Organizing*, Liverpool: Institute for Employment Rights.
Pulignano, V. (2006), 'Going national or European?', in K. Bronfenbrenner (ed.), *Global Unions: Challenging Transnational Capital through Cross-border Campaigns*, Ithaca, NY: Cornell University Press.
Ramsay, H. (1999), 'In search of international union theory', in J. Waddington (ed.), *Globalization and Patterns of Labour Resistance*, London: Mansell.
Roberts, D. and Bernstein, A. (2000), 'Inside a Chinese sweatshop: A life of fines and beating', 2 October, *Business Week*, available at: www.businessweek.com/2000/00_40/ b3701119.htm; accessed 24 January 2011.
Roberts, D., Engardio, P., Bernstein, A., Holmes, S. and Ji, X. (2006), 'Secrets, lies and sweatshops', *Business Week*, 27 November, available at: http://www.businessweek.com/ magazine/content/06_48/b4011001.htm; accessed 24 January 2011.
Rodriguez-Garavito, C. (2005), 'Global governance and labour rights: Codes of conduct and anti-sweatshop struggles in global apparel factories in Mexico and Guatemala', *Politics & Society*, **33**(2), 203–333.
Royle, T. (2000), *Working for McDonald's in Europe: The Unequal Struggle?*, London: Routledge.
Royle, T. (2001), 'Worker representation under threat? The McDonald's Corporation and the effectiveness of statutory works councils in seven European Union countries', *Comparative Labor Law and Policy Journal*, **22**(2/3), 395–431.
Royle, T. (2004), 'Employment practices of multinationals in the Spanish and German quick food service sectors: Low road convergence?', *European Journal of Industrial Relations*, **10**(1), 51–71.
Royle, T. (2005a), 'Realism or idealism? Corporate social responsibility and the employee stakeholder in the global fast-food industry, *Business Ethics: A European Review*, **14**(1), 42–55.
Royle, T. (2005b), 'The union-recognition dispute at McDonald's Moscow food-processing factory', *Industrial Relations Journal*, **36**(4), 318–32.
Royle, T. (2006), 'The dominance effect? Multinational corporations in the Italian quick food service sector', *British Journal of Industrial Relations*, December, **44**(4), 757–9.
Royle, T. (2010), 'McDonald's and the global "McJob": A longitudinal study of work, pay and unionisation in the international fast-food industry', *Labor History*, **51**(2), 249–69.
Royle, T. and Ortiz, L. (2009), 'Dominance effects from local competitors: Setting the institutional parameters for employment relations in multinational subsidiaries: A case from the Spanish supermarket sector', *British Journal of Industrial Relations*, **47**(4), 653–75.
Sabel, C., O'Rourke, D. and Fung, A. (2000), 'Ratcheting labour standards: Regulation for continuous improvement in the global workplace', available at: http://www2.law.colum bia.edu/sabel/papers/ratchPO.html; accessed 24 January 2011.
Smith, P. and Morton, G. (2006), 'Nine years of New Labour: Neoliberalism and workers' rights', *British Journal of Industrial Relations*, **44**(3), 401–20.
Standing, G. (2008), 'The ILO: An agency for globalization?', *Development and Change*, **39**(3), 355–84.
Stiglitz, J. (2002), *Globalization and its Discontents*, London: Penguin.
Stone, K.M.V. (2006), 'Legal protections for atypical employees: Employment law for workers without workplaces and employees without employers', *Berkeley Journal of Employment and Labour Law*, **27**(2), 251–86.
Taylor, M. (2009), 'Retailers accused of ignoring Bangladeshi workers' plight', *The Guardian*, 5 December, 22.
Taylor, P. and Bain, P. (2003), 'Call centre organizing in adversity: From Excell to Vertex', in G. Gall (ed.), *Union Organizing: Campaigning for Trade Union Recognition*, London: Routledge.
TRAC (2000), *Tangled up in Blue: Corporate Partnerships at the United Nations*, Transnational

Resource and Action Centre, available at http://www.corporate-accountability.org/eng/documents/2000/sept_2000_tangled_up_in_the_blue_corporate_partnerships_at_the_united_nations_by_transnational_resource__action_center_pdf_818_kb.pdf; accessed 24 January 2011.

UNCTAD (2008), *World Investment Report 2008: Transnational Corporations and the Infrastructure Challenge*, United Nations Conference on Trade and Development, New York and Geneva: United Nations.

Voss, L.F. (2002), 'Decent work: The shifting role of the ILO and the struggle for global justice', *Global Social Policy*, **2**(1), 19–46.

Webb, T. and Wearden, G. (2009), 'Honda workers back 3 per cent wage cut to protect jobs', *The Guardian*, 23 May, 39.

Wedderburn, Lord (2007), 'Labour Law 2008: 40 years on', *Industrial Law Journal*, **36**(4), 397–424.

Index

and institutionalism 33–4
see also industrial disputes; strikes;
    union militancy
Collective Agreements Act 1949
    (Germany) 326, 333, 340–41
collective bargaining/agreements
    and comparative employment
        relations 27
    and corporatist/neo-corporatist
        policy-making 377–8, 382, 383,
        386, 391–3
    employment relations in Australia
        and New Zealand 289–90,
        291–2, 296–7, 299
    employment relations in Canada
        and the US 154, 158, 159, 161,
        167–8, 175–5, 429
    employment relations in Chile and
        Argentina 132, 133, 134, 135–6,
        137, 138, 139, 140, 141, 142,
        145
    employment relations in China and
        India 195–6, 199, 201–202
    employment relations in France
        and Germany 59, 63, 67, 324,
        325, 326, 327, 328, 331, 332–3,
        334–5, 336–7, 339–43, 344, 345,
        346, 347, 349, 405
    employment relations in Italy
        391–3
    employment relations in Japan and
        Korea 241, 243–4, 251, 256
    employment relations in oil-rich
        Gulf countries 358, 359
    employment relations in South
        Africa and Mozambique 306,
        308, 315, 316
    employment relations in the UK
        and Republic of Ireland 60, 67,
        68–9, 70, 215, 216, 222, 223,
        224–5, 226–8, 233, 389, 391–3
    flexicurity in Belgium and the
        Netherlands 261, 278, 279
    historical aspects 56
    industrial relations system 36
    international labour standards 413,
        427, 428, 429, 435
    international trade unions 409
    and MNEs 405, 423
    and neoliberalism 382–3

    and political economy of
        comparative employment
        relations 59, 60, 68–9, 70
    varieties of capitalism (VoC) 48, 49,
        65, 66, 67
collective dismissals 269
collective employee representation
    155–6
collectivism
    and comparative employment
        relations 27, 40–41
    cultural values 101, 107, 108, 109,
        110, 111, 113, 115–16
    employment relations in Chile and
        Argentina 132
    employment relations in China and
        India 198, 203, 209
    employment relations in Japan and
        Korea 252
    employment relations in Republic of
        Ireland 224, 225, 234–5
    and varieties of capitalism (VoC)
        48
Collings, D.G. 13, 18, 69, 216, 217,
    222, 226, 231, 402, 406, 408, 411,
    415, 416
colonization
    and cultural values 99, 121–2
    and employment relations in
        Australia and New Zealand 288,
        294
    and employment relations in Japan
        and Korea 251
    and employment relations in South
        Africa and Mozambique 304,
        305, 309–10
    and legal origins theory 77, 79, 82,
        88
    see also British Commonwealth; neo-
        colonialism; post-colonialism
commodity exports 288, 290, 291, 298,
    319
commodity theory of labour 35, 38
common law
    employment relations in Canada and
        the US 158, 169, 175
    and legal origins theory 77, 78–9,
        80, 81, 83, 84, 85, 86, 88, 89, 90,
        91–2
    South Africa 304, 311–12, 317

and Marxist comparative
employment relations theories
32
and neoclassical employment
relations/industrial relations
theories 31–2
theories 322, 350
convergence of trade union density
161–2
Cook, M.L. 131, 133, 137, 138
Cooke, F.L. 12–13, 187, 188, 189, 191,
193, 194, 196, 197, 198, 206, 207
Cooney, S. 8–9, 83, 86, 89, 93, 191, 312,
319
cooperation
employment relations in Japan 241,
251–2, 253–4, 256
and employment relations in South
Africa 313, 315, 317–18
neo-corporatist employment systems
40, 41
and varieties of capitalism (VoC)
50
coordination 40, 41, 42, 243, 256, 377,
378, 379, 380
Core Labour Standards (ILO) 410,
424, 427–30, 435
corporate governance 46–7, 48, 66,
337–9, 415
corporate social responsibility 410,
430, 431, 432
corporatism/neo-corporatism
adapting to neoliberalism 382–9
employment relations in Germany
333
employment relations/industrial
relations theories 40, 41, 42, 43
and flexicurity in Belgium and the
Netherlands 261, 278
Ireland 217, 223, 224–5, 227, 228,
233, 379, 380, 381, 382, 387,
388–90, 391, 392–3, 394
Italy 379, 380, 381, 382, 388, 389,
390–91, 392–4
measuring corporatist policy-making
376–82
corruption 79, 132, 133, 159, 314, 391,
427
COSATU (Congress of South African
Trade Unions) 308, 309, 315

cost minimization 36–7, 49, 50
see also labour cost minimization
'country of origin' effects 232–3
courts 77, 270
see also Industrial Court (South
Africa); judiciary; labour
courts; Supreme Court of
Canada
craft unions 36, 218, 222, 305, 392, 409
cross-cultural studies
conclusions 122–4
GLOBE cultural constructs 108,
115–16
interfaces and the cultural-
institutional debate 120–22,
123–4
transferability and appropriateness:
critique of cross-cultural studies
116–20
see also cultural values
crossvergence of cultural values
119–20, 124
Crouch, C. 27, 28, 40–41, 42, 45, 48,
66, 67, 376, 388
cultural identity 120, 122, 124
cultural values
and employment relations in China
and India 197–8, 203, 209
and employment relations in Japan
and Korea 251–2
and employment relations in the UK
and Republic of Ireland 234–5
Hofstede's theories 99, 101, 107, 109,
110, 111–14, 115, 116, 117, 120,
121, 122–3, 124
overview 99–100
Schwartz's value dimensions 99,
100–104, 107, 109, 110, 111,
115, 116
Smith's reinterpretation of
Trompenaars' work 106, 107,
108–10
World Values Survey 100–104, 105,
107–108
culture
and comparative employment
relations theories 25–6, 41
definitions 120–21
employment relations in China and
India 186–7, 197–8, 203, 209

white-dominated unions 306, 307, 308,
    315
white workers 306, 307
Whitley, R. 47, 239, 406, 416
Williamson, J. 385–6
Wilson, M. 289, 294
women workers
    employment relations in Australia
        and New Zealand 290, 296
    employment relations in China and
        India 187, 202–203
    employment relations in oil-rich
        Gulf countries 359, 368
    flexible labour in Japan and Korea
        249, 250
    flexicurity in Belgium and the
        Netherlands 267, 274, 277–8
    and MNEs 423
Wood, G. 15, 303, 304, 309, 311, 312,
    313, 314, 315, 316, 366, 367
Work Choices Amendment 2005
    (Australia) 296, 297, 299
work stoppages 160, 161, 163, 167,
    168, 206
    see also strikes
workerist unions, South Africa
    307–308
Workers' Congress (China) 197, 202
workers' participation 196–7, 202, 206,
    208, 228–30, 241, 242, 278–9
working/employment conditions
    employment relations in Australia
        and New Zealand 288, 289, 296
    employment relations in Chile and
        Argentina 143–4, 145
    employment relations in China and
        India 189, 206
    employment relations in France and
        Germany 332, 335–6, 340, 341,
        343
    employment relations in Japan and
        Korea 244, 248, 255
    employment relations in oil-rich
        Gulf countries 359, 367
    employment relations in the UK and
        Republic of Ireland 230–31

and markets 59, 60
and MNEs 422, 423, 432, 433, 434
and strategic choice 63
working hours 32, 59, 66, 86, 214, 343,
    344–5, 359, 367
    see also flexible labour/working
        conditions; night working;
        overtime; part-time workers;
        Saturday working; shift work;
        Sunday working; temporary
        workers; time-credit schemes
workplace-level employee
    representation 334–7, 349
Workplace Relations Act 1996
    (Australia) 295–6
workplace structures 135, 136, 137
workplace welfare benefits 188, 194,
    198, 201, 208, 244, 248
Works Constitution Acts 1952 and
    2001 (Germany) 326, 336, 339
works councils
    employment relations in Europe 417
    employment relations in France and
        Germany 59, 63, 326, 328, 334,
        335, 336–7, 338, 347, 349
    flexicurity in Belgium and the
        Netherlands 279
    historical aspects 56
    and MNEs 405
World Bank 75–6, 84, 86–7, 88, 186,
    187, 190, 313, 366, 385, 426
World Values Survey 100–104, 105
WTO (World Trade Organization) 358,
    404, 426, 428, 430

Yoon, S.-H. 240, 251–2
young workers 60, 174, 205, 249, 250,
    267, 359, 361, 366, 387
youth unemployment 84, 266, 267

Zagelmeyer, S. 15–16, 329, 331, 338,
    339, 342, 343, 345
zero-sum game 38, 40, 41
Zuma government (South Africa)
    315–16
Zweigert, K. 77, 79